READING AND WRITING

WITH

MULTICULTURAL

LITERATURE

In search of reconciliation and peace

by

Abdul Jabbar, Ph.D.

Published by Montezuma Publishing.

Please direct comments regarding this product to:

Montezuma Publishing
Aztec Shops Ltd.
San Diego State University
San Diego, California 92182-1701
619-594-7552

or email: *orders@montezumapublishing.com*

website: www.montezumapublishing.com

Production Credits
    Production mastering by: Gianna Punzalan
    Quality control by: Scott Leyland

ISBN-10:   0-7442-9784-2
ISBN-13: 978-0-7442-9784-3

This anthology contains copyrighted material requiring payment of royalties to the publisher of $110.45.

CONTENTS

Details of contents follow this brief table of contents.

PART ONE: ELEMENTS OF LITERATURE

PART TWO: READING AND WRITING ADVICE
applicable to all genres

PART THREE: STUDY BY GENRE

Detailed Table of Contents

Contents

Contents

Contents

Contents

Contents

Contents

Preface to the Third Edition

Benefiting from suggestions by professors and students who used the first and second editions of my book, I have added 33 new poems, ten new short stories, four new essays, and one new play. I have also added a new chapter on the essay form of literature. These new works add to the existing diversity of selections in that they are drawn from South Asia, Southeast Asia, the Middle East, Europe, and North and Latin America.

Among the poems new to this edition, two especially important ones are Michael Lassell's stunning "How to Watch Your Brother Die" and Muhammad Iqbal's "The Story of Adam." Lassell's poem can be used as a crash course to underscore the necessity of pluralism and acceptance of diversity. Iqbal's poem emphasizes humanity's ability to transform potential tragedy into triumph and the collective human responsibility for the state of the world. Both poems have special relevance to this book's thematic emphasis on reconciliation and peace.

Added to the drama chapter is the British playwright Caryl Churchill's very short play *Seven Jewish Children: A Play for Gaza.* Through historical allusions, this play traces the sources of the tragic conflict between Israel and Palestine and even hints at possible solutions.

As for the new Chapter Nine on the essay, the following brief list of works will give you an idea:

1. Albert Camus' essay "Between Hell and Reason: Thoughts on the Defining Moment of the Twentieth Century." He wrote this essay when the U.S. dropped the atomic bomb on Hiroshima. For world peace, this essay is even more relevant today than it was when he wrote it. Equally important are his "Letters to a German Friend" that he wrote clandestinely during the Nazis' occupation of France in the Second World War. Camus' "Letters" are discussed in that context.

2. Albert Camus' essay "The Myth of Sisyphus" with its theme of ways to overcome seemingly impossible odds in the worst of circumstances and retain one's dignity and humanity.

3. Discussion of Bertrand Russell's essay "A Free Man's Worship." Russell's famous essay is a wise and deeply felt meditation on human crises and ways to cope with them.

4. Discussion of Edward Said's book *Orientalism* – one of the most important books of the twentieth century – is now added to his essay "Reflections on Exile." Said's work has the potential to promote acceptance of differences and diversity to achieve personal as well as global peace.

New to this edition is the book's subtitle: "In search of reconciliation and peace." It clarifies the nature of most of this book's literary selections. It, moreover, reveals my personal emphasis to make this book much more than just another textbook. The subtitle is also meant to point out that this book is not limited to students' use; it is equally relevant to the general reader who is interested in outstanding world literature with themes of reconciliation and peace.

Readers who have adequate mastery of the elements of literature, such as topics and themes, characters, plot, and style, covered in Part One, can use those chapters on an as-needed basis and go directly to the outstanding literary works and insightful essays on them. Regretfully, several literary works had to be left out because of their excessive permissions cost, but links are provided for easy access to them.

I am confident the readers of this new edition will find in it a life-long companion in their search for enjoyment of literature that emphasizes reconciliation, peace, and equity.

Preface for Students

I have been collecting my students' outstanding essays over the past thirty years. They are a valued treasure because they have helped me in my teaching and my students in their learning process. To those students whose writing appears in this book or on the website related to this book, I offer warm thanks for becoming allies in this worthy cause by sharing the fruits of your labor with fellow students. For me there is an added satisfaction: whenever I come across your writing, I will have the pleasure of remembering our time together when we tried to rescue and cherish a few moments from the blur of the stream of hours – something that great literature enables us to do. The literature and movie selections that you contributed to the book strengthen the view that ultimately and ideally, reading and writing courses are just an attractive excuse to sharpen our intellect and nurture our hunger for empathy, thereby making us better human beings.

Regretfully, space constraints permit inclusion of only a limited number of students' essays in the book. However, those essays that could not be included in the book appear on the website that is linked to this book. All students can benefit from seeing how your peers have crafted outstanding papers. After reading a student's essay on a literary work or a movie, you may wish to offer your own interpretation of the work and thus build on your peers' work in a unique way. In writing essays, finding a decent topic is quite often the problem. It can be solved by the numerous sample essays of your peers.

Besides the student authors featured in this book, I will remember others for your articulate participation in class discussions. Still others I will remember for your exemplary classroom conduct and a caring attitude in making this learning and teaching enterprise a rewarding experience for all participants. Such students more than make up for the inevitable rigors and challenges inherent in the teaching profession.

There are very few relationships that are as enduring and special as the one between teachers and students. Invoking here the help of Shakespeare, let me assure you that

> When to the sessions of sweet silent thought
> I summon up remembrance of things past,

you will figure prominently among them.

Abdul Jabbar
San Francisco
July, 2013

Acknowledgements

It is a pleasure to acknowledge my gratitude to several colleagues at City College of San Francisco, specifically, in alphabetical order, Donald Beilke, Loren Bell, Jessica Brown, Jim Cagnacci, Margaret Cruikshank, Marc Dulman, Beth Ericson, Francine Foltz, Carol Fregly, Tia Greenfield, Kinneret Israel, Shehla Khan, Mary La Mattery, Steve Levinson, Steven Mayers, H. Brown Miller, Lauren Muller, Louise Nayer, H. W. Prewett, Javaid Sayed, Leslie Simon, Glen Simpson, Lesley Tannahill, Ellen Wall, and Joan Wilson for their guidance and valuable feedback on my manuscript. Special thanks to Jennifer Brych, Marc Dulman, Brown Miller, Louise Nayer, and Ellen Wall for their suggestions after using my book in their teaching. Thanks to Lesley Tannahill for her ideas to reduce the cost of copyright permissions; thanks also to my colleagues Vic Fascio for teaching me formatting and other computer-related mysteries, to Carol Reitan for help with my City College website, and to Joao Barretto for looking over the "Appendix on Information on Research and Citation" and making helpful suggestions. Very special thanks to my daughter Huriya Jabbar for setting up my website for this book. Doris Smith has earned my gratitude for reading my book from start to finish, formatting every single page with the care of an outstanding editorial assistant, and proofreading it with a passion for perfection.

I would also like to thank my students who have written many of the book's sample essays. Their names appear throughout the book. Here they are listed in alphabetical order: Caroline Alcantara, Talib Ali, Katherine Allen, Adrienne Anderson, Arienne Aramchikova, Jovi Bondoc, Paul Brandt, Nancy Brill, Victoria Candau, Stella Carey, John Coetzee, Cody Corbett, Larry Devich, Andrea Deyzel, Eithne Doorly, Julie Doyle, Lisa Embry, Allan Fisher, Davina Fok, Laura Franklin, Samantha Gibson, Nick Glasser, Margaret Ghuman, Dana Gong, Phil Haggerty, Greg Hamaguchi, Jennifer Hammer, Katherine Hijar, Serena Hoe, Dennis Johnson, Navneet Kaur, Erin Kehoe, Andrew Keller, Vincent Largo, Thom Lee, Maxwell Lynch, Mariana Maguire, Ron Matestic, Mara McCain, Sydney McIver, Jack Murray, Carolyn Nash, Aaron Nathan, Jeff Neilson, Nicky Newton, Joseph Nugent, Lisa Palmer, Veena Parekh, Ineca Quiteno, Noah Reinhertz, Laurian Rhodes, Jarrod Roland, Scott Roland, Hiromi Ortega Roque, Renee Rose-Perry, Joanne Rotella, Arjuna Sayyed, Kirstin Schneider, Janey Skinner, Serrana Smith-Kassamali, Martin Spence, John Starks, Ayana Summers, Melanie Talienian, Jeffery Tarbell, Kyle Taylor, Victor Rivas Umana, Kristen Vandling, Devin White, Indigo Wilmann, and Kathleen Wong. To keep the cost affordable, some of the students' essays are placed on my website.

I also acknowledge my indebtedness to several other people who have helped me in the completion of this book:

My late, beloved younger brother Abdul Khaliq for his unfailing moral support and for his cost-cutting suggestions.

My wife Talat Jabbar for her patience and encouragement during the long composition period of this book.

My daughter Huriya Jabbar, and Joshua Roebke for suggesting inclusion of feminist theories in the study of fiction and for their help with proofreading. Thanks to Huriya also for helping me with the index.

My son Talib and my daughter Iram for looking at the book from students' perspectives to give me valuable feedback. Thanks to Iram also for helping me with the index.

To Lisa Moore and Lisa Pinto, editors, McGraw Hill, I am thankful for their valuable suggestions and for obtaining various professors' reviews of my book.

For their gentle coercion to make me send my manuscript out for publication, thanks are due, in alphabetical order, to Javed Akhtar, Ilyas Anwar, Julia Bergman, Tariq Bukhari, Dr. Don Griffin, Prof. Hamid Iqbal Butt, Javed Iqbal Butt, Prof. Zafar Iqbal Butt, Prof. Thalia Dorwick, Mukhtar Hai, Mrs. M. B. Hassan, Rubena Ilyas, Fahad Javed, Hina Javed, Nadia Javed, Nighat Javed, Dr. Rizwan Khan, M.D., Shahram Khan, Farooq Malik, Dr. Tariq Mahmood Malik, M.D., George McCown, Karen McCown, Greg Mortenson, co-founder of Central Asia Institute, Munaf Sattar, Prof. Javaid Sayed, and Willie Thompson.

For the many ways in which they pushed me to complete the book, specifically, when they started asking about the health of my book rather than my own health and well-being, I am indebted to my sisters Azra Bashir, Safoora Iqbal, Ghania Isad, Atika Yusuf, Khalida Sajid, Prof. Zakia Isad, and many other members of my immediate and extended family and friends.

Thanks to:

Naeem Mazhar for recording for YouTube the review videos of the third edition of my book.

My niece Riffat Shahid for introducing me to some beautiful Urdu poems.

Farid Warraich and Aisha Subedar for help in typing my manuscript.

Victoria Candau, and Veena Parekh for help with typing and proofreading the first draft.

Lynn Klopfer for a helpful critical review of my entire book.

Rose Twyman of City College Book Store for putting me in touch with Montezuma Publishing and for decades of painstaking service with a smile to the College community.

Special thanks, moreover, are due to Kim Mazyck, Pablo Agrio, Ryan Dee, Alyce Foshee, Esperanza Montiel, and the entire wonderful team of Montezuma Publishing, San Diego, for their help with copyright permissions and designing the book cover and printing the book.

For granting permission to reproduce copyrighted material, I am indebted to Waseem Barelvi, who allowed me to translate into English and include in my book his poem "'The Artist."' Thanks are also due to the publishers/copyright holders listed at the end of this book.

All who have helped me in various ways to make this book possible have earned my gratitude. In these acknowledgements, if I unintentionally left out any name, my apologies.

Reviews

Excerpts from pre-publication reviews of Abdul Jabbar's book obtained anonymously by McGraw Hill Publishers

1. "This text would be perfect for our English Comp. II classes. I love the idea of having step-by-step instructions about how to interpret literature and the clear instruction about how to structure a literary analysis or explication (p. 3 of the proposal). Also I love the idea of the text's inclusion of literature from non-Western writers and the inclusion of a section on film. This text follows the exact structure of our Comp. II classes, so our students could read the text from start to finish and be able to enter literature courses with confidence."

"The first few paragraphs of the introduction are wonderful for our students because they need a quick justification for their reading or they won't continue the reading assignment. The second paragraph of the introduction offers them a wonderful justification by listing the three enrichments that the text should provide them. I particularly like #1 -- 'showing ways to cope with dilemmas of human existence.' Also, I think that the preview of the book's contents will aid the students in seeing a quick summary of what the text includes."

"I love the explanation that the chapter provides about theme. The statement that "all other features, including style, become incidental to theme" is wonderful. Often, texts refer to theme as just another literary element. Also, the various sections relating to the numerous ways one can understand and write about literature are helpful. This chapter covers all of the methods that I normally teach my students plus methods that I sometimes forget to explain to them. I particularly love the section on explicit *versus* implied themes."

"The sample essays are great. They are much better than the sample essays that I have seen in most introduction to literature texts."

"This is a text that can replace our stacks of notes and supplementary materials that we add to our current literature anthology text. Our students can read this text cover to cover in one semester and be well-prepared for any discussion of literature or any situation where writing about literature is required."

"I would love to have this text in class because it contains instructions that are well-stated, clear, and insightful. This author's explanations seem effortless, yet they convey the exact idea about interpreting and writing about literature that I attempt to provide to my students. This text is much better than my current text."

2. "The author gives many examples of literary interpretation and then does provide a very careful and detailed listing and explanation of the steps necessary to write an effective interpretation. Students will feel confident in their ability to write an interpretive essay because they have the steps readily available to them."

"The sample essays are a great tool for students to use. It is particularly helpful for them to know that these are student written."

3. "I am most impressed by the promise of meeting students' needs in their struggle to move from summarizing to discussing style and technique."

"The step-by-step explanation is the basis for the success of this text. Students can profit from such instruction."

"The author not only gives clear instructions, but he does so in a manner that will encourage students to express their own ideas. Students often fear that their ideas about literature are not valid. This author removes that fear by showing them papers written by students like themselves and by leading them through the thinking and analyzing process."

"The guidelines throughout the book, replete with students' essays, are quite clear and helpful and will, I think, encourage students to investigate the various types of literature and come to their own conclusions."

"The tone is quite down-to-earth and engaging. I believe students will appreciate that. There are a few learned words that they won't know; however, that will simply serve to stretch their vocabularies a bit."

"I find the student essays quite interesting. Some demonstrate a level of abstract thinking that will be most beneficial to my students."

"The selections in this section are extremely well chosen for college freshmen. I believe these selections will capture their interest, expand their vocabulary and jump-start their imagination."

"I particularly like the discussion concerning character analysis. Students need to know what questions to ask. They need to know why they like or dislike a character -- not just that they do. I particularly like the discussion on page 200 that show students how to become involved in a piece of literature. In the first section, I like that you have an example of a plot summary side by side with analytic and interpretive comments."

4. "I currently use two texts in my introduction to literature course. . . . I considered the following texts . . . (I was also serving on a textbook selection committee at that time, which exposed me to many offerings.)

> *Literature: Reading, Writing, and Reacting* (Kirszner/Mandel)
> *Bedford Introduction to Literature (*Meyer)
> *Literature: An Introduction to Reading and Writing* (Roberts/Jacobs)
> *Understanding Literature* (Kalaidjian)
> *Literature* (XJ Kennedy/Gioia)

[Reading and Writing with Multicultural Literature] is the most original and creative literature textbook I have ever seen. For years I have supplemented anthologies with works like Griffith's *Writing Essays About Literature,* which proves a cumbersome and expensive practice. Now, with [*Reading and Writing with Multicultural Literature*] I can teach literature with one comprehensive, pedagogically sound text."

A. [*Reading and Writing with Multicultural Literature*] "literally walks students through the process of thinking and writing about literature."

B. "Moreover, it is full of wonderful student writing samples: my students will literally be able to see that thinking and writing about literature is within their grasp."

C. "Additionally, the readings are highly original for an introduction to literature text and I think that my students will enjoy them. Demographically, Arabs comprise part of my ethnically diverse classroom and they will appreciate the inclusion of Middle Eastern authors."

D. "[This text] would work well at a two-year or four-year institution because it is general enough for the former but comprehensive enough for the latter."

"[*Reading and Writing with Multicultural Literature*] is in almost every way superior to *Making Literature Matter* [the text that I am now using]. *Reading and Writing* , through its methodical, theme-based approach, should demonstrate textual relevancy for students because they will discover facets of a given work through/by writing about it. As the author notes, they will learn 'how to treat literature as an enjoyable mind-expanding experience rather than an unpleasant hurdle to cross,' I, like the author, see writing as a discovery tool integral to thinking. This is why I am especially excited about the material on journaling in *Reading and Writing with Multicultural Literature.*"

"The section entitled "Structured and In-Depth Journal Entries" is wonderful -- very direct, informative language used, and section provides practical advice like the need for returning to the text being analyzed and finding supporting assertions. . . . The integration of readings with journal responses strikes me as a highly original strategy."

"The material on timed/self-testing responses (158) is very useful -- many anthologies give but a perfunctory – or no – attention to this critical aspect of responding to literature."

"The chapter contains a wonderful diversity of readings."

"Under "Structure and Organization" a wonderful statement asserted on how 'support for the thesis comes primarily from relevant details from the work itself' (254)."

"Material on revision is practical and rooted in solid tenets of composition." (261)

"Step by step instructions" are by far the best rubric I have ever seen for writing a critical essay -- brilliant, succinct, essential, and clear. The cost of the text is worth [this]Chapter alone."

"I would describe [*Reading and Writing With Multicultural literature*] as a brilliant, innovative work that truly makes a textual apparatus an all-in-one pedagogical asset. The text's focus on writing as a discovery tool is its greatest quality, followed by the diversity and quantity of readings. Clearly the text deserves a grade of 'A'. My current text [*Making Literature Matter*] would, relative to [*Reading and Writing*], earn a 'C.'"

"I will wholeheartedly adopt [*Reading and Writing with Multicultural Literature*] because I believe it can, through writing, help students see the relevance of literature to their lives. Our department just selected Kirszner and Mandell's intro to lit. text but when the review committee -- of which I am a member -- meets again I will most certainly lobby for *Reading and Writing.* I would adopt the text as it is, regardless of whether you add the suggested readings in section III or not."

5. "After reading the proposal and the first five chapters, . . . I am, in general, impressed. It is very clear that the author is an experienced teacher who understands writing students and the challenges they face when they write about literature. The book's strengths are obvious:

- The clear explanation of the differences between topic, theme, and thesis. (Excellent!)
- The flexibility of choice in the literature.
- The diversity of the pieces.
- The student sample essays.
- The author's sample essays.
- The careful, step-by-step instruction on writing the literary analysis. (Excellent)."
- "I would consider adopting [*Reading and Writing With Multicultural Literature*] because of the explanation of the differences between topic, theme, and thesis; the discussion on generating and supporting topic and thesis statements; the instructions on writing a literary analysis; and the text's multi-cultural focus."
- "I have never seen this level of instructional specificity in an introductory text before."

Reviews by professors who have used this book

As Chair of the English Department I am very involved with curriculum choices for our courses. Most of the texts used in our literature course English I B are limited to the literary canon, but Dr. Abdul Jabbar's book brings in multiple perspectives for a more diverse literature for students. His textbook framework is very solid. The book has a wonderful variety of student writings that he has collected over the years. Those essays can be used as examples for students to learn from in their reading and writing development. I highly recommend the book and if I were teaching English I B I would certainly use it. It is the kind of textbook that should be showing up on bookshelves in colleges all over the country.

Jessica Brown
Chair, English Department
City College of San Francisco

* * *

I have used Reading and Writing with Multicultural Literature for several semesters and have always been pleased with the way students are able to apply Dr. Jabbar's guidelines and suggestions. It puts them in touch very quickly with the essence of literature and with the key methods of literary analysis and criticism.

This excellent textbook gives students clear step-by-step directions to guide them in reading, interpreting, explicating, and analyzing literary texts. It has separate chapters on formal and informal modes of writing about literature and film, both clearly explained and amply illustrated with sample papers by students. I am especially happy that the discovery and expression of theme receive special attention and in-depth treatment, concepts which are reinforced throughout the book.

There is also a surprising chapter covering playful approaches to writing about literature. This chapter helps students realize that sometimes the best way to gain a deeper understanding of a serious work is to have fun with it.

Equally important are Dr. Jabbar's instructions aimed at helping students improve their own writing style, going beyond the bare basics of composition and into the use of more sophisticated devices such as isocolon, anaphora, and chiasmus—devices that most students have never heard of. When students are introduced to these devices, I have found that they are often eager to try them in their writing, which in turn sparks their enthusiasm for developing their thinking and feeling about what they have read.

Most important of all, perhaps, is the book's emphasis on multicultural literature, giving students a vital awareness of the diversity of subject and approach across many cultures, while simultaneously showing that all literary works share a common commitment to rendering human experience in all its conflicts and contrasts, exploring universal emotions, such as anger, fear, defeat, and despair, balanced by courage, hope, reconciliation, joy, love, and celebration.

I agree with the McGraw-Hill reviewers who praised Dr. Jabbar's step-by-step instructions as the "best rubric" they had seen for writing a critical essay, adding that the book's "down-to-earth tone" will certainly appeal to students and engage their interest.

H. Brown Miller
Professor of English
City College of San Francisco

* * *

I have been using Prof. Abdul Jabbar's book *Reading and Writing with Multicultural Literature* in my university-level reading and writing class. The book is comprehensive in its scope, introducing students to all forms of literature in a clear and inviting style. Students love the short fiction segment, the stories and the essay discussions on them. The discussion of Albert Camus' *The Stranger* is very helpful to introduce students to challenging modern forms of fiction.

For example, inspired by Chapter Eleven of Dr. Jabbar's book, I assigned "Apotheosis" as an essay topic on the two novels, that is, *The Stranger* and my own just published novel *Soul on the Run*. From the outcome of this assignment, I can say that the book helps shape the course without intruding.

I fully agree with the McGraw Hill reviewer's following comment on the quality and variety of literary selections: "The selections . . . are extremely well chosen for college freshmen. I believe these selections will capture their interest, expand their vocabulary and jump-start their imaginations."

Marc Dulman
Professor of English
City College of San Francisco

9

5.0 out of 5 stars   **Posted on Amazon website**

Excellent choice for literature classes, July 22, 2010
By Louise Nayer (San Francisco, CA)

This review is from: *Reading and Writing with Multicultural Literature Vol. I & II* (Perfect Paperback)

I used Reading and Writing with Multicultural Literature in my English 1B (transfer level literature class) at City College of San Francisco. The amazing variety of works (Chitra Divakaruni, Maya Angelou, Albert Camus, Sherman Alexie, Elizabeth Bishop, Sylvia Plath, F. Scott Fitzgerald, Rabindranath Tagore, Leslie Silko, Saadat Manto, Li-Po, E. M. Forster, Ernest Gaines, Kyalo Mativo, Waseem Barelvi, Faiz Ahmed Faiz, Alifa Rifaat, Lu Hsun, Langston Hughes), to name a few, illustrate the breadth of the multicultural literature that is used--not just one or two works thrown in--but works from a multiplicity of cultures.

But it is not just the choice of stories/poems/plays which creates such an astounding book, but the way students are led, step by step, to understand how to read and love literature. From distinguishing topic from theme, learning how to write an interpretive essay and later a research-based essay, students are calmly led through the process. Excellent exercises and ideas for journal entries help students understand literature in terms of structure and content. Students learn to clearly organize their papers and retain a passion for literature. Creative and even humorous ways of looking at these works keep the classroom lively and interesting. Other media is included (movies, on line sites) which enrich the classroom experience. Most importantly, students who are exposed to literature from many cultures become more empathetic citizens of the world.

Louise Nayer
Professor of English
City College of San Francisco, CA 94112
E-mail: lnayer@ccsf.edu

* * *

Abdul Jabbar's new text, *Reading and Writing with Multicultural Literature*, is an outstanding contribution to the study of literature in college classes. First, it contains a wide variety of readings by authors that have not traditionally been part of the literary canon, such as Saadat Hansan Manto and Rabindranath Tagore. Yet it also contains the full range of authors with whom we are familiar, such as William Faulkner, E.M. Forster, and Kate Chopin. The text is rich in student writing which Dr. Jabbar has collected in his years of teaching literature at City College of San Francisco. Using student examples, plus his own essays on the various elements of literature, Dr. Jabbar leads students to write excellent literary analyses of the works they are reading. I highly recommend this text for college literature classes.

Ellen Wall
Professor of English
City College of San Francisco
E-mail ewall@ccsf.edu

Introduction

Not just another textbook

It is important to understand the kind of book it is because there are many books in the market that sound like my book but are very different. My book is not a typical anthology of literature, even though it has many selections from world literature. It is primarily a companion and guide that uses literary selections to elucidate relevant principles and teach the crafts of reading and writing. Moreover, as the book's subtitle indicates, its literary selections were made with an eye on their potential to promote reconciliation and peace. To keep the book's cost affordable for students, only outstanding literary works are included, supplemented by links to other great works that could not become a part of my book.

This book is the result of my nearly forty years' experience of teaching literary studies and writing at the college level. It is designed for use in literature, composition, and humanities courses from freshman through senior years. It is meant for both English majors and the general reader and makes writing and literary studies an enjoyable, uplifting experience rather than an unpleasant hurdle to cross.

Teaching philosophy

The book reflects my teaching philosophy that students' college years should be a memorable time during which they pick up life-long learning skills of critical thinking, reasoning, analysis, and enjoyment of literature. In the process, they should acquire a reasonable mastery of language resources to make their own expression of ideas engaging, thus transforming themselves from mere admirers to practitioners of good writing.

Students need not experience fear and confusion in their introduction to literary studies. Inadequate grasp of necessary skills causes this problem. A large number of students are fearful of taking composition and literature classes because they are often unsure of what is expected of them, especially when they write about literary works. In situations when they know what is expected of them, they do not feel they have the necessary skills to complete their assignments. When asked to write an analysis or interpretation, many of them write little more than a summary or paraphrase. Often they have a very vague understanding of the concept of style and how it shapes literary creations and their own writing.

Solutions to typical problems

To solve these problems, I have provided step-by-step instructions that guide students systematically through the process of reading and writing. Sample essays, many of them written by students, demonstrate how relevant assignments are to be completed. Using this book, students can also learn from their peers' accomplishments. I have addressed the very basic as well as the more sophisticated needs of students. With these guidelines, students can respond to great works with confidence, depth, and self-enrichment.

Professors who teach literature and composition classes invariably notice a wide divergence in the levels of preparation among their students. Some students need repetition of instruction in certain areas, whereas those with a higher level of preparation tend to be bored with that repetition. In addressing the needs of those at the bottom, we sometimes end up neglecting those who are looking for more challenging assignments. While accommodating all levels, this book allows relatively advanced students to skip over the information that they do not need. At the same time, help with basic skills is also included for less advanced students. Thus the book frees professors of the onerous and uninspiring burden of repetition of basic concepts without overlooking the needs of less advanced students. Moreover, since well-known works have been chosen to illustrate essential principles of reading and writing, professors may appreciate this putting together of a practical and interesting instructional resource, which they can supplement with choices of their own. The assignments of this book honor that independence of choice.

Three enrichments

This book is guided by the belief that study of literature should bring about at least three enrichments:

- A wealth of enduring ideas and fresh insights celebrating life and showing ways to cope with dilemmas of human existence.

- Participation in the pains and pleasures of humanity to develop empathy and openness.

- Continuous improvement in reading and writing skills.

To achieve these goals, the book's literary selections are drawn from outstanding international literary works. Both the works and their interpretations have a humanistic emphasis. They affirm the hope that study of literature can enhance our pleasures, mitigate our suffering, raise our consciousness, and develop our ability to empathize, in short, make us better human beings. Those points of emphasis make my book unusual.

Teaching methodology

The book's teaching approach consists of five components:

1. Necessary background information to explain various literary forms
2. Clearly worded assignments
3. Step-by-step instructions on how to complete the assignments
4. Sample essays (some of them by students), showing how the assignments are actually completed
5. Exercises to determine mastery of covered material and to suggest topics for further study.

The book's organization

The book is divided into three parts:

1. Part One introduces the elements of literature – topics, themes, character, plot, and style.

2. Part Two offers general reading and writing advice (with instructions and samples) that apply to all major forms of literature. Knowledge of concepts learned in Part One is here applied to informal as well as formal literary interpretation.

3. Part Three consists of study by genre, with chapters on the essay form of nonfiction, short story, novel, drama, poetry, and film, with a concluding chapter on "Playful Responses to Literature." A few works for further study are included at the end of the poetry and short story chapters.

Multi-purpose usefulness of the book

1. As a writing text

To meet its major goal as a writing text, the book offers detailed instructions, explanations of key concepts and principles, clearly worded assignments, and their sample completions. It should be noted that the book's usefulness as a writing text extends beyond purely literature-based writing. Even though most of the sample essays of this book are based on imaginative literature and film, they can serve as samples for all forms of expository writing, since the principles of organization, creating a thesis, and crafting effective topic sentences always remain the same. The only notable difference between literature-based and other expository writing is that in the former, the support for the essay's thesis comes from the literary work itself. In the latter, the source of support is the writer's knowledge and experiences. Interpretation is literature-based; argumentation, ordinarily, is experience-based.

2. As a reading text

This book can also be used with equal benefit in a reading course. Since we must first understand literary works before we can write about them, the act of interpretation is an ideal synthesis of reading and writing. To use this book as a reading text, simply change the word "'write'" to "'discuss'" in all of the writing assignments. Selected poems and short stories as well as expository and critical essays written on them make this book a rich reading anthology as well.

3. As a film appreciation tool

The practice of interpretation taught in this book will also enhance the ability of film appreciation. To interpret movies, we need to be aware of their surface *versus* suggested meanings. The book provides ample guidance to teach that skill.

4. As a means to enhance speech communication

A bonus aspect of this book is its potential for speech improvement. Like good writing, good speeches also make optimum use of language resources. The concluding part of the chapter on style introduces a method whereby students can broaden their range of written expression and make it engaging. The same strategy may be used to make speech communication vibrant.

Reviews of the book

The pre-publication reviews by McGraw Hill's professional reviewers as well as reviews by professors who have used my book have been extremely positive. Here are just a few excerpts from McGraw Hill's reviewers. Keep in mind that these reviewers don't know the author's identity, and the author doesn't know who they are other than the fact that they are professional reviewers engaged by the publisher to gauge the value of a book to make their publishing decision. Publishers often withhold the reviewers' identity even after the publication of a book.

Excerpts from McGraw Hill's professional reviewers

"The most original and creative literature textbook I have ever seen"

"I am most impressed by the promise of meeting students' needs in their struggle to move from summarizing to discussing style and technique."

"The tone is down-to-earth and engaging. I believe students will appreciate that."

"Step by step instructions are by far the best rubric I have ever seen for writing a critical essay – brilliant, succinct, essential, and clear."

"The selections in this section are extremely well chosen for college freshmen. I believe these selections will capture their interest, expand their vocabulary and jump-start their imagination."

". . . a brilliant, innovative work that truly makes a textual apparatus an all-in-one pedagogical asset. The text's focus on writing as a discovery tool is its greatest quality, followed by the diversity and quantity of readings."

"I have never seen this level of instructional specificity in an introductory text before."

In the end, I am very happy to announce that Barnes and Noble have selected my book for digitizing. It is an exciting development, and I can hardly wait for that to happen. I hope that readers will accept my book as a passport to the fascinating world of literary studies and to becoming better readers, better writers, and a better human beings.

Preview of the Book's Contents

Ideally the chapters of this book should be read sequentially. However, various parts of the book can also be read on an as-needed basis. The following preview of the book would help students focus on areas in which they need more guidance.

Learning to distinguish between topic and theme, between summarizing and theme formulation, between mere re-telling versus analyzing (Chapter One).

Understanding and analyzing conventions relating to character (Chapter Two).

Understanding and analyzing conventions relating to plot (Chapter Three).

Understanding definitions and conventions relating to style, assessing an author's style and connecting it with themes in a literary work, and transferring some of the graces and power of literary style to their own writing (Chapter Four).

Reading and writing advice applicable to all genres (Chapter Five).

Distinctive features of various literary genres and informal, journal-like responses to them (Chapter Six).

Formal interpretation (Chapter Seven).

Revising (Chapter Eight).

Study by specific genre: essays, short stories, novels, drama, poetry, and film (Chapters Nine through Fourteen).

Humorous Literature and Playful Responses to Serious Literature (Chapter Fifteen).

Part One

Elements of Literature

C H A P T E R   O N E

TOPICS AND THEMES:
BASIC COMPONENTS OF INTERPRETATION
AND TOOLS TO SHARPEN CRITICAL THINKING

An understanding of topics and themes is central to interpretation. Together with characters, plot, and style (covered in the next three chapters), they make up the essential elements of literature. Part One of this book is devoted to teaching these elements. Mastering them is the key to understand and interpret literature. There is nothing mysterious about the word *interpretation*, which simply means sharing with the reader what we grasp as the meaning of a literary work or a movie. The exercise of discovering, formulating, and discussing themes from literary works and movies is thus called interpretation. It involves critical thinking, analysis, and argumentation. Some works yield their meaning effortlessly while others are complex, and decoding them becomes a challenge. The skills and knowledge introduced in this chapter will help you meet that challenge. Interpretation is needed to access topics and themes in literary works and movies. It also comes into play in evaluating the elements of character, plot, and style if you can persuasively argue how they generate or reinforce themes. Interpretation, like argumentation, can be opinionated, harshly judgmental, and reactionary. Ideally, however, it should be viewed as cordial sharing that deepens the meaning of a literary work. It is this latter kind of interpretation that this book practices and recommends. Some necessary ground must first be covered toward that end.

Before getting further into a discussion of topics and themes, it is necessary to understand that not every single literary work may have a readily identifiable topic and theme and not all authors may start writing their works with a distinct topic or theme in mind. However, important topics and themes inevitably and naturally emerge from all literary works that matter.

The critic Roger Henkle's position seems to be reasonable and persuasive. It is this view that the chapters of this book mainly adhere to: "We expect to be manipulated to some extent in reading any . . . [literary work]; all writers assemble their materials with some plan of moving the reader toward certain insights or conclusions" (Henkle 72). The reader's task is to understand the author's plan and evaluate the insights and conclusions through careful interpretation.

To learn the skill of interpretation through critical thinking, analysis, and argumentation, we have to assume that literary works do have topics and themes and choose works with identifiable themes. In your interpretation, it is better to avoid overuse of the words *topics* and *themes*. You can interpret a work without using those words. They, however, should always remain in the back of your mind to give your analysis the right focus.

Theme and Its Central Place in Interpreting Literature and Film

The critic Allardyce Nicoll calls a theme the "central spirit" by which a literary work is inspired and which gives it "unity of impression." To interpret literary works and movies, understanding and recognizing their themes is paramount. All other features, including style, become incidental to *theme*, which may be defined as *the position an author or a work takes on a topic*. That position is often not self-evident. To access it, we need interpretation of the work's events, key statements, action, characters' values, the author's style, and similar elements. For example, an important topic in Edgar Allan Poe's short story "The Cask of Amontillado" is the nature of human conscience. The story's theme on that topic, derived through interpretation, is that *criminals may escape prosecution by law, but they cannot escape trial by their own conscience*. Poe does not make this statement of theme. He implies it through the story's plot and characters. Even though the story's narrator and main character Montresor has successfully escaped prosecution by law for his murder of Fortunato, the story shows that his conscience has finally caught up with him and he has to divulge his secret crime.

Formulation of a theme, thus, is an exercise in literary interpretation and reasoned analysis. It is not a purely subjective emotional response.

Theme as an awareness (and an invitation)

A theme thus is an awareness a work of art creates in us. When we put that awareness in the form of a thematic statement, as in the above example, it is of the nature of general, sometimes universal, application and captures the essence of a large part of the work being interpreted. Most literary works communicate their themes not overtly but through implications of plot, characters, and style (that is, the way in which an idea is expressed). On the topic of marriage, for example, an author may present interactions between characters' actions and their outcomes to suggest the theme that *marriage is not a panacea for personal shortcomings and that, to be successful, it requires constant hard work*. The preceding two examples of statements of theme (on the topics of conscience and marriage) demonstrate that when reading literature and viewing movies, we grasp their essence only if we go beyond surface meanings, beyond the story level, into the concepts and feelings that often animate literary and cinematic works.

Since the theme of a literary work is like an invitation to contemplate a view of life, grasping it brings a sense of fellowship with the author. By its very nature, a theme is a generalization and an abstraction, as in the aforementioned examples, but it is inherent in and based upon the work's specific and physical details, such as settings that create a mood, descriptions that tell of a background, events, characters, their actions, values, and outcomes. Understanding these details brings us closer to perceiving a literary work's theme(s) and thus gaining mastery over the ebb and flow of events and appearances presented in a work of art. A work can be read at several levels just as a movie can be viewed for its surface as well as subtler meanings. The heart of interpretation lies in recognizing the deeper themes imbedded in the seemingly chaotic cavalcade of characters and events in a work of art.

Theme-centered discussions are interpretations that involve an ideal synthesis of reading and writing. The ideas on which we write are derived from our reading of the work, and improvement in critical and analytical reading skills enhances our writing ability. Mina Shaughnessy, a well-known writing scholar, describes this essential connection between reading and writing:

"Reading in this way, the student begins to sense that the meaning of what he reads or writes resides not in the page nor in the reader but in the encounter between the two. This insight makes him a more careful writer and a more critical reader. As a writer, he must think about the kinds of responses his words are likely to arouse; as a reader, his growing critical stance encourages him to raise questions about what he reads, to infer the author's intent, and even to argue with him" (Shaughnessy 223).

"What's In It for Me?"
Personal Enrichment from Interpretive Reading

Enhancement of reading and writing skills, for many readers, is a good enough reason to warrant literary study, but a theme-centered approach to literature and film has an additional benefit: Many readers will find in this exercise a means of learning about themselves. In real life, when we are emotionally involved in an experience, our involvement often makes it difficult to have the detachment that is necessary to learn about ourselves. Movies and works of literature can provide us that detachment and objectivity through which we can examine the behavior and motives of literary characters who act or do not act like us. Roger Henkle is persuasive on this subject:

". . . there is no more sensitive and versatile laboratory for the understanding of individual or group behavior or for registering our own reactions, than literature" (Henkle 4).

According to the philosopher Martha Nussbaum, in literature, "we can have truly altruistic instincts, genuine acknowledgement of the otherness of others." Elaborating on Nussbaum's statement, the novelist Zadie Smith also feels that when "we read with fine attention, we find ourselves caring about people who are various, muddled, uncertain and not quite like us (and that is good)."

In *How Fiction Works*, James Wood also points out the value of literature: "Literature differs from life in that life is amorphously full of detail, and rarely directs us toward it, whereas literature teaches us to notice. . . . makes us better noticers of life; we get to practice on life itself; which in turn makes us better readers of detail in literature; which in turn makes us better readers of life" (65).

Experiencing literary or cinematic works through their themes takes us beyond ourselves by allowing us to live vicariously through the characters that we meet. We place ourselves in those characters' as well as their creators' positions and feel their emotions. In this way works of art broaden and sharpen our points of contact with humanity. Our ability to formulate themes also means that we can transmute our personal experiences into inferences, concepts, and observations of a philosophical nature. This training helps us learn from significant events and actions in life. Such learning, however, is possible only if we are able to step back from the intimacy of a situation and analyze it in order to grasp the essence of our experience. Theme-oriented study of literature thus adds immensely to our self-enrichment.

Distinguishing Topic from Theme

Now that we have covered some basic ground, let us study a few literary works to better understand the terms *topic* and *theme* and to see how full comprehension of them can enhance our enjoyment of literature. It needs no reiteration that the first requirement of interpretation is a clear grasp of these two terms. Without necessarily using these terms, an interpreter moves from topic identification to theme formulation, at least mentally. Without that process, it is difficult to move beyond merely summarizing the events and actions in a literary work. Summarizing is not interpretation. Initially, it is advisable to be explicit in identifying and using the terms *topic* and *theme*. Later, as they become a part of your thinking process when interpreting and analyzing literature, you will find yourself writing about *topics* and *themes* without necessarily using those terms.

Simply stated, a *topic* is an open-ended concept, such as aging. A *theme* is the position an author or a literary work takes on a topic. Identifying a topic does not involve the same amount of detail as a formal statement of theme. A topic is often introduced with words, such as *about, deals with, concerns,* etc. By their very nature such words do not introduce a complete thought. On the topic of aging, for example, a theme could be that *the process of aging, though inevitable, is seldom accepted cordially, especially in an excessively looks-conscious, youth-oriented society.* Arriving at a theme from a topic thus involves narrowing down the topic and completing the thought process. When we look at a topic and its open-ended nature, we are curious to see how it would be narrowed to a precise theme to satisfy the "What about it?" response. Identifying a topic leaves the author's/story's position on that topic unstated. The above-stated, italicized theme on the topic of aging removes the "What about it?" sense of incompleteness.

Compared with identifying a topic, a thematic statement thus demands more effort, greater risk in interpretation, and a clearer grasp of the ideas presented in the work. A literary work or a movie may have several themes; a distillation of all of them leads to the work's central theme. Some works do not strive for a central theme. We should also keep in mind that some topics, because of their elusive nature, may not yield precise themes. Another term, often used in conjunction with *topic* and *theme* is *thesis*, which is used to refer to the central idea in nonfiction prose, including expository and interpretive essays.

To understand the process of moving from an author's *topic* to *theme*, let us read Sylvia Plath's poem "Mirror."

Mirror

I am silver and exact. I have no preconceptions.
Whatever I see I swallow immediately
Just as it is, unmisted by love or dislike.
I am not cruel, only truthful —
The eye of a little god, four-cornered.   5
Most of the time I meditate on the opposite wall.
It is pink, with speckles. I have looked at it so long
I think it is a part of my heart. But it flickers.
Faces and darkness separate us over and over.
Now I am a lake. A woman bends over me,   10
Searching my reaches for what she really is.
Then she turns to those liars, the candles or the moon.
I see her back, and reflect it faithfully.
She rewards me with tears and an agitation of hands.
I am important to her. She comes and goes.   15
Each morning it is her face that replaces the darkness.
In me she has drowned a young girl, and in me an old woman
Rises toward her day after day, like a terrible fish.

Sylvia Plath (1932-1963)

The *topic* of Sylvia Plath's poem is the fear of aging. The poem's central *theme* (or the position the poem takes on that topic) may be stated in many ways, one of which is this: *Seeking self-worth through transient attributes, such as physical beauty and youth, does not lead to contentment.* Like most modern poets, Plath does not state her theme. We arrive at it through interpretation. Plath suggests this theme by the careful selection of the speaker, the setting, the main character's values, and imagery. After we understand how the elements that constitute the poem's physical details function in the poem, we can then infer its theme. On reading any literary work, we usually have at least a vague idea as to what the work is about. Transforming that vague, amorphous idea into a logically supported and valid interpretation is the challenge of this assignment.

Our formulation of the poem's theme comes after something like the following absorption of the poem's plot details or summary has taken place in our minds, if not on paper: *The speaker is a mirror that truthfully reflects the woman's appearance, which is undergoing inevitable changes as a result of aging. This woman is obsessed with the remembered image of her past youthfulness. Instead of accepting the natural process she struggles painfully and vainly to block out the truth. While searching for her youth that, she feels, has disappeared somewhere in the depths of the mirror, she finds "an old woman . . . [rising] toward her day after day, like a terrible fish"* (lines 17-18).

Interpretation also requires that we explain the complex parts of a work as in the following example: In the poem's last line, the image of an old woman rising "toward her day after day, like a terrible fish" signals the unavoidable -- a dead fish does rise to the surface. Her physical decay that she has been trying to hide will become unconcealable eventually.

The just-finished exercise of reading Sylvia Plath's poem would be regarded as a literary interpretation. The poem's broad *topic* of aging is narrowed down to the *theme* of the futility of seeking self-worth through transient attributes.

The preceding examples show that any supportable generalization made on a topic in a literary work could be regarded as a statement of theme. However, the quality of the thematic statement will depend on two accomplishments:

1. The extent to which your words cover an important idea or aspect of the work being discussed.

2. The precision of the words that you *add* to the topic to capture the scope and direction of your thought.

It will be helpful to remember that in grammatical terms, the topic is like the *subject* in a clause, and what you say about it is like the *predicate*. With this guideline in mind, let us analyze the following sentence: "Plath's position on the topic of aging is that aging is inevitable and efforts to fight or hide it are bound to be unsuccessful." In this statement of theme, *aging* is the *subject*, and the remaining words about its inevitability are the *predicate*. It is, moreover, not necessary that all themes in a literary work or a movie should relate to just one topic. Sometimes a work may have several different topics and many different themes that cannot be forced into the category of an overarching *central* theme. If one is so inclined, one may try to point out a *central* theme that intersects all themes.

A good example of this accomplishment is Augustus W. Schlegel's following interpretation of Shakespeare's complex play *Hamlet*:

> *Hamlet* is . . . a tragedy of thought inspired by continual and never-satisfied meditation
> on human destiny and the dark perplexity of the events of this world, and calculated to
> call forth the very same meditation in the minds of the spectators (Schlegel 404).

Schlegel's thematic statement captures the essence of *Hamlet*.

The First Major Challenge in Interpretion:
Distinguishing Between a Plot Summary
and a Statement of Theme

The problem of confusing plot summaries with themes is quite common in interpretations of literature and film. The fundamental rule is clear enough: *Fewest possible analytic, interpretive, and evaluative words in a summary and fewest possible plot details in a statement of theme.* In spite of this seemingly clear rule, the problem remains endemic. To overcome this hurdle, let us first read "The Man from Kabul," a short story by Indian author Rabindranath Tagore, then write its summary and formulate its themes.

The Man from Kabul

My five-year-old daughter, Mini, cannot live without chattering. I really believe that in all her life she has not wasted a minute in silence. Her mother is often vexed at this, and would like to stop her prattle, but I would not. For Mini to be quiet is unnatural, and I cannot bear it long. And so my own talk with her is always lively.

One morning, for instance, when I was in the midst of the seventeenth chapter of my new novel, my little Mini stole into the room, and putting her hand into mine, said, "Father! Ramdayal, the doorkeeper, calls a crow a crew! He doesn't know anything, does he?"

Before I could explain to her the difference between one language and another in this world, she had embarked on the full tide of another subject. "What do you think, Father? Bhola says there is an elephant in the clouds, blowing water out of his trunk, and that is why it rains!"

And then, darting off anew, while I sat still, trying to think of some reply to this: "Father, what relation is Mother to you?"

With a grave face I contrived to say, "Go and play with Bhola, Mini! I am busy!"

The window of my room overlooks the road. The child had seated herself at my feet near my table, and was playing softly, drumming on her knees. I was hard at work on my seventeenth chapter, in which Pratap Singh, the hero, has just caught Kanchanlata, the heroine, in his arms, and is about to escape with her by the third-story window of the castle, when suddenly Mini left her play and ran to the window, crying, "A Kabuliwallah! A Kabuliwallah!" And indeed, in the street below, there was a man from Kabul, walking slowly along. He wore the loose, soiled clothing of his people, and a tall turban; he carried a bag on his back and boxes of grapes in his hands.

I cannot tell what my daughter's feelings were when she saw this man, but she began to call him loudly. "Ah!" thought I. "He will come in, and my seventeenth chapter will never be finished!" At that very moment the Kabuliwallah turned and looked up at the child. When she saw this, she was overcome by terror, and running to her mother's protection, disappeared. She had a blind belief that inside the bag which the big man carried there were perhaps two or three other children like herself. The peddler meanwhile entered my doorway and greeted me with a smile.

So precarious was the position of my hero and my heroine that my first impulse was to stop and buy something, since Mini had called the man to the house. I made some small purchases, and we began to talk about Abdur Rahman, the Russians, the English, and the Frontier Policy.

As he was about to leave, he asked, "And where is the little girl, sir?" And then, thinking that Mini must get rid of her false fear, I had her brought out.

She stood by my chair and looked at the Kabuliwallah and his bag. He offered her nuts and raisins, but she would not be tempted, and only clung the closer to me, with all her doubts increased.

This was their first meeting.

A few mornings later, however, as I was leaving the house, I was startled to find Mini seated on a bench near the door, laughing and talking, with the great Kabuliwallah at her feet. In all her life, it appeared, my small daughter had never found so patient a listener, save her father. And already the corner of her little sari was stuffed with almonds and raisins, the gift of her visitor. "Why did you give her those?" I said, and taking out an eight-anna piece, I handed it to him. The man accepted the money without demur and put it into his pocket.

Alas, on my return, an hour later, I found the unfortunate coin had made twice its own worth of trouble! For the Kabuliwallah had given it to Mini; and her mother, catching sight of the bright round object, had pounced on the child with: "Where did you get that eight-anna piece?"

"The Kabuliwallah gave it to me," said Mini cheerfully.

"The Kabuliwallah gave it to you!" cried her mother, greatly shocked. "Oh, Mini! How could you take it from him?"

I entered at that moment, and saving her from impending disaster, proceeded to make my own inquiries.

It was not the first or the second time, I found, that the two had met. The Kabuliwallah had overcome the child's first terror by a judicious bribe of nuts and almonds, and the two were now great friends.

They had many quaint jokes, which amused them greatly. Mini would seat herself before him, look down on his gigantic frame in all her tiny dignity, and with her face rippling with laughter, would begin: "O Kabuliwallah! Kabuliwallah! What have you got in your bag?"

And he would reply, in the nasal accents of the mountaineer, "An elephant!" Not much cause for merriment, perhaps; but how they both enjoyed the fun! And for me, this child's talk with a grown-up man had always in it something strangely fascinating.

Then the Kabuliwallah, not to be behindhand, would take his turn: "Well, little one, and when are you going to your father-in-law's house?"

Now, nearly every small Bengali maiden had heard long ago about her father in-law's house; but we were a little newfangled, and had kept these things from our child, so that Mini at this question must have been a trifle bewildered. But she would not show it, and with ready tact, replied, "Are you going there?"

Amongst men of the Kabuliwallah's class, however, it is well known that the words "father-in-law's house" have a double meaning. It is a euphemism for jail, the place where we are well cared for, at no expense to ourselves. In this sense would the sturdy peddler take my daughter's question. "Oh," he would say, shaking his fist at an invisible policeman, "I will trash my father-in-law!" Hearing this, and picturing the poor discomfited relative, Mini would go off into peals of laughter in which her formidable friend would join.

These were autumn mornings, the very time of year when kings of old went forth to conquest; and I, without stirring from my little corner in Calcutta, would let my mind wander over the whole world. At the very name of another country, my heart would go out to it, and at the sight of a foreigner in the streets I would fall to weaving a network of dreams – the mountains, the glens, and the forests of his distant land, with his cottage in their midst, and the free and independent life, or faraway wilds. Perhaps scenes of travel are conjured up before me and pass and repass in my imagination all the more vividly because I lead an existence so like a vegetable that a call to travel would fall upon me like a thunderbolt. In the presence of this Kabuliwallah, I was immediately transported to the foot of arid mountain peaks, with narrow little defiles twisting in and out amongst their towering heights. I could see the string of camels bearing the merchandise, and the company of turbaned merchants, some carrying their queer old firearms, and some their spears, journeying downward toward the plains. I could see – But at some such point, Mini's mother would intervene, and implore me to "beware of that man."

Mini's mother is unfortunately very timid. Whenever she hears a noise in the street, or sees people coming toward the house, she always jumps to the conclusion that they are either thieves, or drunkards, or snakes, or tigers, or malaria, or cockroaches, or caterpillars. Even after all these years of experience, she is not able to overcome her terror. So she was full of doubts about the Kabuliwallah and used to beg me to keep a watchful eye on him. If I tried to laugh her fear gently away, she would turn around seriously, and ask me solemn questions: Were children never kidnapped? Was it not true that there was slavery in Kabul?

Was it so very absurd that this big man should be able to carry off a tiny child? I urged that though not impossible, it was very improbable. But this was not enough, and her dread persisted. But as it was a very vague dread, it did not seem right to forbid the man [from] the house, and the intimacy went unchecked.

Once a year, in the middle of January, Rahman, the Kabuliwallah, used to return to his own country, and as the time approached, he would be very busy, going from house to house collecting his debts. This year, however, he could always find time to come and see Mini. It might have seemed to a stranger that there was some conspiracy between the two, for when he could not come in the morning, he would appear in the evening.

Even to me it was a little startling, now and then, suddenly to surprise this tall, loose-garmented man, laden with his bags, in the corner of a dark room; but when Mini ran in, smiling, with her "O Kabuliwallah! Kabuliwallah!" and the two friends, so far apart in age, subsided into their old laughter and their old jokes, I felt reassured.

One morning, a few days before he had made up his mind to go, I was correcting proof sheets in my study. The weather was chilly. Through the window the rays of the sun touched my feet, and the slight warmth was very welcome. It was nearly eight o'clock and early pedestrians were returning home with their heads covered. Suddenly I heard an uproar in the street, and looking out, saw Rahman being led away bound between two policemen, and behind them a crowd of inquisitive boys. There were bloodstains on his clothes, and one of the policemen carried a knife. I hurried out, and stopping them, inquired what it all meant. Partly from one, partly from another, I gathered that a certain neighbor had owed the peddler something for a Rampuri shawl, but had denied buying it, and that in the course of the quarrel, Rahman had struck him. Now, in his excitement, the prisoner began calling his enemy all sorts of names, when suddenly in a veranda of my house appeared my little Mini, with her usual exclamation: "O Kabuliwallah! Kabuliwallah!" Rahman's face lighted up as he turned to her. He had no bag under his arm today, so that she could not talk about the elephant with him. She therefore at once proceeded to the next question: "Are you going to your father-in-law's house?" Rahman laughed and said, "That is just where I am going, little one!" Then seeing that the reply did not amuse the child, he held up his fettered hands. "Ah!" he said, "I would have thrashed that old father-in-law, but my hands are bound!"

On a charge of murderous assault, Rahman was sentenced to several years' imprisonment. Time passed, and he was forgotten. Our accustomed work in the accustomed place went on, and the thought of the once-free mountaineer spending his years in prison seldom or never occurred to us. Even my lighthearted Mini, I am ashamed to say, forgot her old friend. New companions filled her life. As she grew older, she spent more of her time with girls. So much, indeed, did she spend with them that she came no more, as she used to do, to her father's room, so that I rarely had any opportunity of speaking to her.

Years had passed away. It was once more autumn, and we had made arrangements for our Mini's marriage. It was to take place during the Puja holidays. With Durga returning to Kailas, the light of our home also would depart to her husband's house, and leave her father's in shadow.

The morning was bright. After the rains, it seemed as though the air had been washed clean and the rays of the sun looked like pure gold. So bright were they that they made even the sordid brick walls of our Calcutta lanes radiant, and at each burst of sound my own heart throbbed. The wail of the tune, "Bhairavi," seemed to intensify the pain I felt at the approaching separation. My Mini was to be married that night.

From early morning, noise and bustle had pervaded the house. In the courtyard there was the canopy to be slung on its bamboo poles; there were chandeliers with their tinkling sound to be hung in each room and veranda. There was endless hurry and excitement. I was sitting in my study, looking through the accounts, when someone entered, saluting respectfully, and stood before me. It was Rahman, the Kabuliwallah. At first I did not recognize him. He carried no bag, his long hair was cut short, and his old vigor seemed to have gone. But he smiled, and I knew him again. "When did you come, Rahman?" I asked him. "Last evening," he said, "I was released from jail."

The words struck harshly upon my ears. I had never before talked with one who had wounded his fellow man, and my heart shrank within itself when I realized this; for I felt that the day would have been better-omened had he not appeared.

"There are ceremonies going on," I said, "and I am busy. Perhaps you could come another day?"

He immediately turned to go; but as he reached the door, he hesitated, and said, "May I not see the little one, sir, for a moment?" It was his belief that Mini was still the same. He had pictured her running to him as she used to do, calling, "O Kabuliwallah! Kabuliwallah!" He had imagined, too, that they would laugh and talk together, just as of old. Indeed, in memory of former days, he had brought, carefully wrapped up in a paper, a few almonds and raisins and grapes, obtained somehow or other from a countryman; for what little money he had, had gone.

I repeated, "There is a ceremony in the house, and you will not be able to see anyone today."

The man's face fell. He looked wistfully at me for a moment, then said, "Good morning," and went out.

I felt a little sorry, and would have called him back, but I found he was returning of his own accord. He came close up to me and held out his offerings with the words: "I have brought these few things, sir, for the little one. Will you give them to her?"

I took them, and was going to pay him, but he caught my hand and said, "You are very kind, sir! Keep me in your memory. Do not offer me money! You have a little girl; I, too, have one like her in my own home. I think of her, and bring this fruit to your child -- not to make a profit for myself."

Saying this, he put his hand inside his big loose robe and brought out a small and dirty piece of paper. Unfolding it with great care, he smoothed it out with both hands on my table. It bore the impression of a little hand. Not a photograph. Not a drawing. Merely the impression of an ink-smeared hand laid flat on the paper. This touch of the hand of his own little daughter he had carried always next to his heart, as he had come year after year to Calcutta to sell his wares in the streets.

Tears came to my eyes. I forgot that he was a poor Kabuli fruit-seller, while I was – But no, what was I more than he? He also was a father.

That impression of the hand of his little Parvati in her distant mountain home reminded me of my own little Mini.

I sent for Mini immediately from the inner apartment. Many difficulties were raised, but I swept them aside. Clad in the red silk of her wedding day, with the sandal paste on her forehead, and adorned as a young bride, Mini came and stood modestly before me.

The Kabuliwallah seemed amazed at the apparition. He could not revive their old friendship. At last he smiled and said, "Little one, are you going to your father-in-law's house?"

But Mini now understood the meaning of the word "father-in-law," and she could not answer him as of old. She blushed at the question and stood before him with her bride like face bowed down.

I remembered the day when the Kabuliwallah and my Mini had first met, and I felt sad. When she had gone, Rahman sighed deeply and sat down on the floor. The idea had suddenly come to him that his daughter, too, must have grown up while he had been away so long, and that he would have to make friends anew with her, also. Assuredly he would not find her as she was when he left her. And besides, what might not have happened to her in these eight years?

The marriage pipes sounded, and the mild autumn sunlight streamed around us. But Rahman sat in the little Calcutta lane and saw before him the barren mountains of Afghanistan.

I took out a currency note, gave it to him, and said, "Go back to your daughter, Rahman, in your own country, and may the happiness of your meeting bring good fortune to my child!"

Having made this present, I had to curtail some of the festivities. I could not have the electric lights I had intended, nor the military band, and the ladies of the house were despondent about it. But to me the wedding feast was all the brighter for the thought that in a distant land a long-lost father had met again his only child.

Rabindranath Tagore (1861-1941)

Plot Summary
(with fewest possible analytic/interpretive comments)

In a plot summary, information is included about settings, characters, their significant deeds, events, conflicts, consequences, and similar matters. Comments of interpretive, analytic, and evaluative nature, which belong in a statement of theme, are excluded or, at least, kept to the very minimum. For easy recognition, analytic and interpretive words are italicized in this summary.

The man from Kabul – Abdur Rahman – is a street vendor. The little girl Mini, like her mother, is initially frightened of Rahman because of the prevailing myth that outsiders like him kidnap little children. However, with some encouragement from her father and with the help of little presents of almonds and raisins brought to her by Rahman, the little girl soon loses her fear and befriends him.

One day, just before Rahman's annual trip back home to Kabul, he is arrested for assaulting someone who refuses to pay him the money owed. Rahman is jailed, and when he is released after several years, he goes directly to see Mini. Her father is not pleased to see him and considers his sudden appearance on the day of Mini's marriage an ill omen.

Rahman's heartbreak on being denied his request to see Mini, *the initial insensitivity and harshness of Mini's father,* and the eventual *melting away of the barrier between the two men* are the story's *vital details.* We discover in the end that Rahman, too, has the loving heart of a father. Having been unable to see his daughter of Mini's age for many years, he has had to satisfy his longing for his daughter with a precious memento that he has always carried "next to his heart" inside his robe. This memento is the impression of his little girl's hand on an ink-smeared paper, *a poor man's substitute for a photograph.* When he shows it to the father-narrator and explains to him the reason for his closeness to Mini, the [*gulf between the two men disappears.* This was a brief plot summary of the story. Statements of the story's themes now follow.]

Theme Formulation
(with fewest possible plot summary details)

Statements of themes are analytic and interpretive in nature. They prevent an essay from sounding like a plot summary. In thematic statements, plot details are kept to a minimum. In the following sample of theme formulation, there are no plot summary details. However, such details can be used as long as they are kept subordinate to the themes.

The two topics of stereotyping and human ties lead to the following two themes in Tagore's story:

"The Man from Kabul" makes us realize that we have a tendency to stereotype people according to our imperfect knowledge of their backgrounds and cultures. From another closely related <u>direction that the story takes</u> *we learn that when the superficial barriers of class, caste, and origin are overcome, human beings are found to have the same fears, longings, needs, and concerns, thus emphasizing the element of common humanity that binds us all.* (In the preceding sentence the underlined words are a substitute for the word *theme*, just in case you want to avoid using that word too frequently).

The foregoing examples of converting topics into themes have demonstrated this simple and very practical method: To discover and formulate a theme, the first step is identifying an important topic and then determining the position or stand the literary work or movie takes on that topic. This is an easy, solid, and reliable way to access themes. These examples also show that readers often derive different themes from a topic, based on their own perceptions and interpretations.

Criteria for good statements of themes

Statements of themes are often made with insufficient regard to their wording. As a result, *themes* get confused with *topics* and plot summaries. The preceding section on "Distinguishing Topic and Theme," together with the guidelines for phrasing themes listed below, will solve the problem.

- Any theme that you formulate or identify should be supportable with textual evidence.

- Nothing in the text should contradict your statement of theme.

- A thematic statement should cover a substantial portion of the text's content.

- Avoid prefabricated expressions and cliches like the following: "The story's theme is that what goes around comes around." Being the product of someone else's thoughts, such cliches sound inauthentic and cannot be expected to carry the weight of a theme, nor can they evoke the reader's interest.

- Statements of themes are the culmination of your thinking as your mind interacts with the characters, events, and topics in the works you read.

- Write the themes in the present tense for these two reasons: First, the past tense is often associated with summaries, which a theme is not. Secondly and more importantly, the truth contained in themes is never dated and is, therefore, always relevant to the present.

Combining Skill with Creativity in Generating Statements of Themes

The preceding examples have demonstrated that formulating a statement of theme based on a literary work or film combines skill with creativity. Skill is needed to choose the appropriate word combination and sentence structure. Creativity comes into play in discovering connections between characters' values and their actions, between an author's style and the work's substance, between the work's title and its thought content, and working them into an engaging statement of theme. Undoubtedly, the process of discovering themes is somewhat like solving an intellectual puzzle, but, as Roger Henkle points out, there is a difference:

> Unlike a puzzle . . . some of the pieces are from your own experience, your past reading, or your own imagination, so it is to that extent a creative, not a mechanical operation (Henkle 15).

When making statements of themes, remember that such statements should be general. Therefore, names of particular characters are usually not mentioned in the statement to keep its relevance general and not limited to a few characters. If the character's name is mentioned, the phrasing of the theme should not limit the theme to the named character alone. The following examples from *Hamlet* will illustrate this point.

Weak: In his play, Shakespeare shows that Hamlet comes to grief because he expects too much out of life.

Comment: This statement is limited to Hamlet in its application.

Improved (1): In *Hamlet*, Shakespeare shows that a perfectionist is often unhappy in an imperfect world.

Comment: Here the theme is universal because it is applicable to perfectionists in general, not to just one perfectionist (Hamlet).

Improved (2): As an epitome of perfectionism, Hamlet demonstrates that it is tragic to be a perfectionist in an imperfect world.

Comment: Here the character's name is mentioned, but the relevance of this theme is not limited to him. He is used only as a representative of his type.

A rule of thumb

If all else fails, this rule of thumb will help you create a suitably worded thematic statement: A sentence containing a statement of theme requires a complete thought after the introductory words. Surprisingly, almost always the introductory part of a formal statement of theme ends with the words *that, is that, how,* or with a colon (not with *about, deals with,* or *concerns*). This part is then followed by a complete thought, which a theme always is. Both parts together make up a complete statement of theme.

For example, the topic of jealousy could yield three different themes. [*For easier recognition, I have placed the introductory words in square brackets and underlined the complete thought in all three* instances. Both parts – the words in brackets and the underlined words – make up a complete statement of theme.]

1. [A major theme in this story is that] the <u>feeling of jealousy stems from insecurity</u>.

2. [Several events in the story, moreover, dramatize the author's feeling that] <u>jealousy sometimes acts as a necessary spark to rekindle a dying relationship</u>.

3. [The author's next notable concern is with a curious irony that characterizes jealous people:] <u>even though jealousy is a common human feeling, the persons afflicted with it often deny being jealous</u>.

The third example above introduces a challenging way to formulate a theme.

A colon is placed after the introductory words that identify the literary work's/film's general topic. Then the author's/work's position on the topic, as perceived by the interpreter, appears in an independent clause.

Comment: The curious irony in jealousy is the topic in this example. The independent clause that follows the colon is the position the story takes on that topic. Both parts of the sentence, joined by the colon, make up the complete theme.

Alternative Ways of Stating Themes

Knowledge of appropriately phrasing themes is essential to accurate interpretation and analysis. However, there are several valid ways of stating themes. So far I have demonstrated only one of them that you can start with. Once you are comfortable with this basic format, feel free to do some experimentation. The primary goal is to grasp the substance of a work of art. Summarizing of supporting details poses no problem for the beginning student. The challenge lies in the phrasing of statements of themes. To make the task easier, you can use an alternative way of stating themes.

Since supporting details are easier to come by, you can start with them and make them the opening part of the statement of theme while still keeping the thematic statement general/universal. Sometimes the mere fact of finding the relevant supporting details can lead us to the related theme. Let us read Keith Douglas's poem "Vergissmeinnicht" to practice this alternative method of theme formulation.

The German title of this poem means "Forget me not." The author, an English poet, fought with a tank battalion in World War II.

Vergissmeinnicht

Three weeks gone and the combatants gone,
returning over the nightmare ground
we found the place again, and found
the soldier sprawling in the sun.
The frowning barrel of his gun
overshadowing. As we came on
that day, he hit my tank with one

like the entry of a demon.

Look. Here in the gunpit spoil
the dishonored picture of his girl
who has put: Steffi. Vergissmeinnicht
in a copybook gothic script.

We see him almost with content
abased, and seeming to have paid
and mocked at by his own equipment
that's hard and good when he's decayed.

But she would weep to see today
how on his skin the swart flies move;
the dust upon the paper eye
and the burst stomach like a cave.
For here the lover and killer are mingled
who had one body and one heart.
And death who had the soldier singled
has done the lover mortal hurt.

Keith Douglass (1920-1944)

Combining supporting details from the poem with the statement of theme, we may write: The picture of the dead German soldier's beloved (Stefi), found next to his body, poignantly conveys the theme that the *nameless, faceless soldier, who kills and dies on the battlefield, is someone's lover and beloved* (theme in italics).

The following sentence is another example of this different but valid style of stating a theme by mixing plot details (specific in nature) and thematic key words (general in nature): Since, as a consequence of his values, Hamlet meets a tragic end, we find in his fate a reiteration of the view that *perfectionists have a difficult time surviving in a corrupt system* (theme in italics).

This alternative style of theme formulation is the preferred format for writers who like to disguise their statements of themes in order to appear less deliberate. The important point to note is that the plot details are still subordinated to, and made to serve, the theme-bearing words, without which the result would be summarizing, not interpretation.

As you become comfortable with the basic format, you will discover that literary interpretation allows abundant room for creative experimentation.

Advice on experimentation

Before taking too many liberties with the structured approach to the craft of interpretive writing, you should first learn to observe its restraints; only then will your innovations be effective. There is no limit to successful creative experimentation.

Organization of an Interpretive Essay

Sylvia Plath's poem "Mirror" and Rabindranath Tagore's short story "The Man from Kabul" are the two literary works we have discussed in some depth so far. Since we identified only one topic – the fear of aging – and only one theme on that topic in Plath's poem, our thesis statement for the interpretive essay was stated as follows: Seeking self-worth through transient attributes, such as physical beauty and youth, does not lead to contentment. Using supporting details from the poem to support this thesis needed a simple organization. However, had we covered more than one topic and theme in Plath's poem, the thesis and organization would have been more complex as demonstrated in the interpretation of Tagore's multi-topic and multi-theme story.

To complete our interpretation of Tagore's story in the form of an essay, the following items would be needed. All examples are italicized for clarity.

1. A suitable *title* for the essay, such as "Education of the Educated" or "The Sanctity of Human Ties."

2. An *introduction*: A few points selected from the plot summary (already completed) can often serve as a good introduction, as in this example: *Tagore's "The Man from Kabul" is a story of two fathers – one rich, the other poor. It is Mini, the rich man's daughter, who makes the two men see their common humanity.*

3. The *thesis*: It has been already stated in the form of two statements of themes in the preceding section on "Theme Formulation," as follows: The two topics of stereotyping and human ties lead to the following two themes in Tagore's story:

   "The Man from Kabul" makes us realize that we have a tendency to stereotype people according to our imperfect knowledge of their backgrounds and cultures. In another closely related theme, the story demonstrates that when the superficial barriers of class, caste, and origin are overcome, human beings are found to have the same fears, longings, needs, and concerns, thus emphasizing the element of common humanity that binds us all.

4. *Supporting the thesis*: It consists of relevant plot details, controlled by topic sentences. Only those details from the story would be cited that illustrate Tagore's themes, stated in the interpreter's thesis. Supporting details come from plot summaries whom they resemble. Both are specific, unlike the statements of themes that are always general. Short quotations, combined with relevant plot details in your own words, are an effective way to support your thesis.

   Supporting details from Tagore's story: *The narrator's wife wants to protect their little daughter Mini from the street vendor of dry fruits – Rahman. Her fear is caused by her stereotypical thinking that men from Kabul kidnap little children. Encouraged by her father, who happens not to believe in the stereotype, Mini loses her fear of Rahman as she get to know him. The negative thinking about this outsider Rahman finally gets replaced by trust, and the questionable barrier is removed by Rahman's friendship with the family.*

   Relevant to the story's second theme that concerns the binding human ties between people of different classes and backgrounds, the upper-class narrator initially distances himself from the vendor Rahman because his return after many years coincides with the day of Mini's wedding. He considers it a bad omen and discourages Rahman from seeing her. He offers him some money for his gifts of dry fruit that he has brought for Mini. Rahman refuses to accept money, and a wrenching scene follows that transforms the narrator: Rahman tells the narrator that he brings Mini the gifts of nuts and raisins not because he wants to make a profit but because Mini reminds him of his own daughter whom he has not seen in many years. He pulls out from inside his robe the impression of his little daughter's ink-smeared hand on a sheet of paper (a poor man's substitute for a photograph). "This touch of the hand of his own little daughter he had carried always next to his heart, as he had come year after year to Calcutta to sell his wares in the streets." After this scene, the narrator's words show that he is a changed person: "Tears came to my eyes. I forgot that he was a poor Kabuli fruit-seller, while I was – But no, what was I more than he? He also was a father." The narrator not only lets Rahman see the bride but also gives him some money so that he can go back home and see his daughter. Giving Rahman the present of money necessitated curtailment of the wedding festivities, but to the narrator "the wedding feast was all the brighter for the thought that in a distant land a long-lost father had met his only child."

It is important to note that even though most of the words in the preceding paragraph are a summary of relevant parts of plot, the controlling words of the paragraph are the thematic words of the opening sentence – "binding human ties."

5. The *conclusion*: Reiteration of a crucial point, raising or answering an important question, mentioning any special insight the work has offered, bringing either a sense of closure to the work's interpretation or purposely leaving the conclusion open-ended.

   Sample conclusion: *In this work, Tagore shows his special gift of weaving profound themes into a simply told, compelling story. Impressive character development, credible character revelation, gripping suspense, and a deeply satisfying conclusion make "The Man from Kabul" an exemplary tale.*

   Evidently, the more themes an essay discusses the more sections are needed that increase the complexity of organization. However, observing the basic rules of organization explained above would keep your paper organized and coherent.

Placement of Statements of Themes

In an interpretive essay, thematic statements may appear in one cluster as they do in our sample thesis on "The Man from Kabul." Alternatively, thematic statements may be made and supported with textual evidence one by one until the discussion of all themes is completed. Whether they appear in one *concentrated* cluster or one at a time, statements of themes constitute the thesis of an interpretive essay and *control* its organization. As for their placement, they can appear anywhere – in the beginning, in the middle, or at the end of the section that they control. They may appear before the supporting details, after them, or may be mixed with them.

Length Ratio: Analysis *versus* Summarizing

In an interpretation, thematic statements and analytic, creative, and evaluative comments take up far less space than plot summaries (usually about one-third of the essay's total length), but they are the means to organize the more voluminous supporting details and give an interpretive essay its form. Analytic and interpretive statements often consist of the following:

- The title of an interpretive essay.

- Thesis: the most important component. In an interpretive essay, it consists of statements of themes from the literary work/movie.

- Connecting and transitional devices.

- Evaluative comments that link a work's stylistic and technical features to its themes.

- Conclusion.

How Supporting Details Are Organized

Every interpretation contains at least one statement of theme and many supporting details that are necessary to validate it. As was noted earlier, supporting details do not have to come *after* a statement of theme. They could precede and thus lead up to it, using the inductive method of organization, according to which the topic sentence comes at the end of the details that it controls. Inductive organization, that is, putting supporting details *before* the interpreting topic sentence, is especially suited to situations in which you expect resistance to your interpretation. Moreover, instead of separating them into distinct categories, most interpreters blend plot summaries (using specific supporting details) with themes harmoniously, and include direct quotations from the work sparingly. [*The structure of an interpretive essay is the focus of Chapter Seven. Only the absolutely necessary information is given here for clarity.*]

Works Ideally Suited to Interpretation: Explicit *Versus* Implied Themes

It is important to remember that not every literary work or film lends itself equally well to the exercise of interpretation. To write an interpretive essay, you should choose a literary work or a film that is rich in ideas and requires an effort on your part before yielding its meaning. Such works veil their themes in suggestive plot details and stylistic elements. In complex works, the author's position may be so disguised as to be almost inaccessible without the reader's deep engagement with the text, thus compounding both the difficulty of interpretation and the pleasure of discovering the theme.

Direct expression of theme, such as this one in Jean Toomer's "Fern," is rare in literature: ". . . men are apt to idolize or fear that which they cannot understand, especially if it be a woman" (Toomer 14). Most writers suggest their themes indirectly through choice of the title, dialogue, narrative voice, settings, atmosphere, imagery, figurative language, tone, characters, symbolism, allusion, and other elements of style (discussed in Chapter Four).

Modern fiction writers and film directors often prefer subtlety to direct statement and, therefore, rely on the power of suggestion. This absence of overt thematic statement does not mean that such works are lacking in ideas. Sometimes themes emerge from a pattern of images. For example, in Faulkner's "A Rose for Emily" (discussed in Chapter Three), imagery of tarnishing and decay subtly embody the theme of decline and decadence of Southern aristocracy.

Exercises to Test Your Mastery of Chapter One

The following questions have been answered in this chapter. The knowledge needed to answer them is essential to interpretation.

1. How is a *topic* different from a *theme*? Give an example of each term.

2. What are the two parts of a statement of theme? Give an example.

3. What are the criteria for good statements of themes?

4. List some of the ways to save an essay on themes of a work from sounding like a plot summary.

5. When you write an essay on themes from a literary work or a movie, what parts of the essay are called your analytical comments. These parts are the result of your interpretation of the work. Summarizing details and quotations from the work are tied and subordinated to these analytical comments.

6. Toward the end of the chapter, a way of stating themes is mentioned that is an alternative to the conventional form. This latter style mixes specific plot details with thematic words of a general nature while keeping the dominant *versus* subordinate nature of the two clear. Does the following example mix plot details with theme-bearing words in a valid, acceptable way? You need not be familiar with the story to answer this question. The theme-bearing words are italicized in the following example:

   In O Yong-Su's short story "Nami and the Taffyman" Nami's crafty and purposeful aloofness and the Taffyman's clumsy but sincere pursuit of her illustrate that *in the rituals of romantic love, it is men who are often called upon to take the initiative and risk rejection and ridicule.*

7. Mention some of the personal enrichment aspects of acquiring the know-how of discovering and formulating themes from literary works and movies.

8. If you expect resistance from your reader in a particular section of your paper, what method of organization would you use – inductive or deductive? Why?

C H A P T E R   T W O

CHARACTERS

Formulating statements of themes is not the only form of interpretation. Character and plot analysis also fall under that rubric. An understanding of the conventions relating to them, especially their role in theme embodiment, is necessary for literary interpretation. In this chapter, the focus is on basic concepts and conventions relating to characters, with demonstration of their fuller application appearing in the chapters on short stories, novel, drama, and poetry.

Character and *plot* go together. Actions and events make up the plot, whereas characters are people who perform actions and to whom events occur. These elements of literature, together with *theme* and *style*, are central to the study of all forms of literature and film. It is important to note that we are discussing these elements separately to understand them clearly and fully. In literature, they often blend into and complement one another.

People who inhabit the world of an imaginative work are called characters and include narrators in fiction. Along with plot, characters are essential to literary and cinematic creation. They also play an important role in the process of interpretation. Character-related topics range from simple to very complex. To make character-based discussions more than mere plot summaries, it is necessary to look at different possibilities of creative handling of this topic. As the sample essays in various chapters of this book will demonstrate, writing on characters can take many forms, the basic variety of which is summarizing characters' deeds and events that happen to them. Such sketches take little effort but are not the most rewarding kind of character study.

What Makes a Good Character Analysis?

For a character analysis to be meaningful, we need to consider as many of the following aspects as possible:

1. Characters' significant deeds

2. Cause and effect connection between their values and their fate

3. Events that characters cause to happen, events that happen to them, the influence they exert on and receive from other characters, their overall impact on the world they inhabit, and the impact of their milieu on them

4. The author's and narrator's tone and attitude toward the subject character: Authors reveal their tone by giving favorable or negative traits, words, and conduct to the subject characters.

5. Prominent characters' opinions of the character being evaluated

6. Characters' self-evaluation, keeping in mind their potential for self-deception as in the case of the main character (also the narrator) in E. M. Forster's short story "The Other Side of the Hedge," included at the end of this chapter

Since competing arguments about characters use the same evidence toward different ends, deciding which of the contending views has greater validity requires careful thought and comprehension. To guide you to interesting topics relating to characters, I have suggested and explained a few sample assignments. To facilitate your work, I have also shown how you might develop your essay responses to selected topics to enhance your reading, interpreting, and writing abilities while sharpening your critical thinking and analytic skills. Feel free to add more topics, including those from other works of your interest.

Characterization and Characters

Before enumerating character-related topics, it is necessary to understand the distinction between characters and characterization. Characters are persons, whereas characterization is the way in which authors create those persons, make them believable, and give them distinguishing traits, voice, and expression. Thus characters are a part of a work's content while characterization is an element of an author's style.

Character Sketch *versus* Character Analysis

Another important distinction that needs to be made is between character sketch and character analysis. A sketch is like a plot summary. As we have noticed in our discussions of literary works so far, the element of analytic and critical thinking is missing in a summary. The same is true of a character sketch. Like a summary, a character sketch reports, with minimum interpretation, what people do and what happens to them in a work. Our character sketch of Hamlet, for example, would mention that the hero is called upon to take revenge for the murder of his father. After many hurdles, he accomplishes that goal but loses his own life in the process.

A character analysis that involves interpretation, on the other hand, goes deeper than the physical details. Its basis is critical/analytic thinking. In interpreting the aforementioned plot details about what Hamlet does and what happens to him, we would say that the deaths of Ophelia, Gertrude, Laertes, Polonius, Rosencrantz, Guildenstern, along with those of the two combatants – Hamlet and Claudius – show that the destructive side effects of revenge are often unpredictable and far-reaching. Actor and author Steven Berkoff's words about Hamlet offer another example of interpretation on the basis of the character's actions and values:

"For whatever reason, and there are many, Hamlet is the accumulation of all our values and beliefs. In him are set out the rules for the perfect human, the perfect rationalist, plus the adventurer, all rolled into one. No other play gives an actor such words of compassion, charm, wisdom, wit, moral force, insight, and philosophy" (Berkoff vii).

From these examples it is apparent that whereas a character sketch simply demands remembering of plot details, character analysis requires interpretation and analysis of those details – a much more challenging and rewarding task. Furthermore, the details that sketch a character, like details in a plot summary, are indisputable, whereas analysis and interpretation often provoke debate.

CHARACTER-RELATED TOPICS

Just as in life, we tend to form opinions of the people we encounter in literature and movies. By tracing and analyzing the process of arriving at our opinions, we can generate interesting discussions.

We can form an idea of the immense range of character-based interpretations by glancing at the following topics and writing prompts, some of which are used to write sample essays in this book.

Interpretation through Comparing and Contrasting Characters

Comparing and/or contrasting two or more characters can take the form of a mere summary, or it can be a more challenging assignment requiring careful interpretation and going beyond the usual details concerning the similarities and/or differences between the characters' looks, deeds, attitudes, and outcomes. If we feel so inclined, we may reveal our preference for either of the characters compared, giving reasons for our opinion. If possible, we should also connect each character with a theme.

In comparing Laertes with Hamlet, for example, we would mention the expected details: The two characters have similar goals in that both are called upon to avenge their respective fathers' deaths. But there the similarities end, for no two characters could be more different in the way they carry out their revenge. Laertes is unthinking, impetuous, and even dishonorable in stooping to the use of poison to kill Hamlet and in his unsportsmanlike foul play during the duel with Hamlet. On the other hand, Hamlet is extremely cautious, conscientious, and honorable. He weighs and considers every step to avoid killing an innocent man. He is averse to taking Laertes' life but is forced into doing so after he realizes he, too, is dying as a result of Laertes' stabbing him with an envenomed weapon.

After we have pointed out the differences between the two characters, we could take on a more challenging task, that is, inferring from the two characters' conduct and fate the worth of each character as perceived by the author. We might argue that Hamlet does not resort to underhanded means, and even his archenemy, Claudius, regards him as "Most generous, and free from all contriving" (IV, vii, 148).

Therefore, Hamlet is at peace with himself in his dying moments. His last words, "The rest is silence," reflect his state of mind.

Laertes, on the other hand, dies a desperate man, with his dying breath putting all the blame on Claudius when, in fact, we know that Laertes himself had offered to touch the point of his dueling weapon with deadly poison. Nevertheless, we feel compassion for him, as does Hamlet, since we know Laertes has been manipulated by Claudius to get rid of Hamlet. If placed in that situation, Shakespeare seems to be implying, we should prefer to die like Hamlet, not like Laertes. This, of course, is a debatable point, and we should take a position that is supportable with relevant quotations and details from the play.

Our exploration of characters' psyches often becomes a gateway to the author's mind. By evaluating Hamlet and Laertes' motives and means to avenge their fathers' deaths, we are able to perceive the position the play/playwright takes as to which character's approach to revenge seems less offensive ethically. A simplistic sketching of each character, on the other hand, would have simply mentioned the two characters' positions in their families, listed their actions, and traced their careers. Such surface renditions of characters would be of limited value in interpreting the play's important themes on the topic of revenge.

Another variety of interpretation through comparison and contrast of characters relates to those works in which the protagonist is not clearly designated. It will be an interesting exercise, for example, to determine whether the protagonist in Hemingway's short story "Hills Like White Elephants" (Chapter Ten) is the man or the woman.

Interpretation through a Character's Self-Analysis

An interesting exercise in interpretation would be writing a character-revealing essay in the character's own voice, using the first person "I" and assuming the persona of that character. This exercise would sound like this:

I am Hamlet – the main character of Shakespeare's longest and most-discussed play. I know all of you have formed an opinion about me, and you are ready to put your life on the line to defend your position. That violently dogmatic attitude, frankly, scares me and causes me to hesitate in telling you truthfully who I really am.

The character's self-analysis could continue along these lines, focusing on Hamlet's character after that introduction.

If you choose the character of Ophelia for this exercise, you may wish to include her feelings of being trapped in a male-dominated society in which all three men in her life – her father, her brother, and her lover – bully her. Another interesting point of view to include would be Ophelia's own account of her insanity.

Stories in drama and fiction are told from the protagonist's perspective. Changing that focus to another point of view – from Hamlet's to that of Rosencrantz and Guildenstern, for example – would yield highly interesting results. These two friends of Hamlet are summoned by Claudius to spy on Hamlet. They are assigned the task of escorting Hamlet to England, where he is to be killed by the English King on Claudius's orders. However, suspecting foul play, Hamlet searches his escorts' belongings and secretly puts their names in the place of his name on the death warrant. After the scuffle with the sea pirates, Hamlet is brought back to Denmark whereas Rosencrantz and Guildenstern continue their voyage to England. At the end of the play, the news comes from England that Rosencrantz and Guildenstern have been put to death. A particularly gripping part of this exercise of self-analysis by the two characters would be their state of panic when, instead of the expected thanks, they receive death sentences. Their memoirs in the form of self-analysis promise an insightful reading. It is worth noting that Tom Stoppard's play *Rosencrantz and Guildenstern Are Dead* tells the *Hamlet* story from their points of view.

Among points that you can include in this kind of self-analysis is any startling revelation that affects the character profoundly. In *Hamlet*, the examples are Hamlet's finding out that his friends Rosencrantz and Guildenstern are working as spies for Claudius and his discovery that Ophelia has started to obey her father blindly to the point of denying Hamlet's access to her. In Albert Camus' novel *The Stranger* (discussed in Chapter Eleven), an example would be the protagonist Meursault's shattering realization that he had been wrong in assuming that he was like everyone else and that people accepted him as one of them.

Protagonist, Antagonist, Foil, and the Anti-hero

The **protagonist** is a character from whose perspective the action of a literary or cinematic work is presented. Hamlet is the protagonist in Shakespeare's play, as is Abdur Rahman in Tagore's "The Man from Kabul" (discussed in Chapter One). In some works it is not easy to determine who the protagonist is. For example, in Hemingway's "Hills Like White Elephants" (discussed in Chapter Ten), it is difficult to take a decisive position as to which of the two characters (the male or the female) is to be called the story's protagonist.

The **antagonist** is a character or force that resists and thwarts the protagonist in his or her quest. In a play such as *Hamlet*, the antagonist clearly is Claudius. In some works, such as Camus' *The Stranger*, for example, the antagonist may be the society in conflict with the protagonist's vision and values.

The **foil** is a character that is the opposite of another character. In E. M. Forster's story "The Other Side of the Hedge," discussed later in this chapter, the narrator, a selfish person, is drawn as the foil to his deceased brother who believed in using his energies on helping others. In *Hamlet*, Laertes, being impulse-driven, is a foil to the rational-minded, philosophical Hamlet.

The term **anti-hero** refers to characters who do not embody the qualities that are typically associated with heroic characters. Conventional heroic qualities usually consist of, but are not limited to, submission to a "higher" order in the light of self-knowledge gained by the hero. The rebellious tendencies in the hero are tamed into acquiescence. However, an anti-hero refuses to compromise – regardless of the consequences – when his or her deeply felt values are at stake. In Camus' *The Stranger*, Meursault, who embodies these traits, is a good example of an anti-hero.

Heroes and anti-heroes have existed side by side, sometimes in the same person, for thousands of years. Going back to ancient Greece, Oedipus, the protagonist of plays by Sophocles, may be seen to embody qualities of eventual acceptance after initial and dogged defiance of what his fate has decreed for him. In this sense, he fits the concept of a "hero." However, Prometheus, the protagonist of Sophocles' contemporary Aeschylus, epitomizes those attributes that we have associated throughout centuries with anti-heroes. His defiance of Jupiter-decreed cosmic laws brings on him this awfully bizarre eternal punishment: his liver is to be devoured by a vulture. Rene Marill (pseudonym Alberes) describes Promethean anti-heroes:

"They wish to be alone, and it is in this sense that they refuse, from the beginning, the solutions of other men, the guaranteed, proven solutions. . . . Solitude defines the conditions of the hero, and his heroism is that he has not been born to accept the help of proven formulae. Prometheus is alone because he is the only one to dare, and his solitude expresses only the audacity of his enterprise" (125-26).

Even though thousands of years separate Camus' anti-hero Meursault and Aeschylus' Prometheus, they show striking similarities.

Edith Hamilton's following description of the anti-heroes of Euripides, the third prominent dramatist of ancient Greece, is also applicable to the modern protagonists of Tennessee Williams:

"Above all, they care for human life and human things. . . . They suffer for mankind, and what preoccupies them is the problem of pain. They are peculiarly sensitized to 'the giant agony of the world.' What they see as needless misery around them and what they envisage as needless misery to come is intolerable to them. The world to them is made up of individuals, each with a terrible power to suffer (99)."

Flat, Round, and Fragmented Characters

When used to refer to literary characters, the words flat and round imply no favor or disfavor. **Flat** characters do not change during the events of a story; their values and attitudes remain constant. **Round** (complex) characters, on the other hand, undergo remarkable changes and are often multidimensional. Authors make their characters round or flat according to their plot requirements and themes. With very few exceptions, of the two varieties, flat characters are suited to detective/suspenseful fiction, satire, and allegory. In detective works the relentless pace of the story and layer-by-layer unraveling of plot are paramount, with attention to character assuming a secondary position. Satire also thrives on generalization for the purpose of ridicule, and flat characters, being types rather than individuals, lend themselves well to this treatment. The character of Polonius in Shakespeare's *Hamlet* exemplifies a flat character. His slow-witted responses to Hamlet's sharply astute comments make him well-suited for satiric treatment.

Since flat characters tend to be **abstractions** and qualities, **they** also fit the allegorical mode very well. The first-person narrator in E. M. Forster's allegory "The Other Side of the Hedge," for example, is a flat character because he remains unchanged. A novelist well-known for her engaging flat and round characters is Jane Austen. In *How Fiction Works*, James Wood makes a comment on Austen's heroines and minor characters which can be applied to literary works in general. Most of Austen's minor characters are flat. Playing a necessary, complementing role, they "belong to a certain stage of theatrical satire." They move with the currents and remain oblivious to the pressures faced by the protagonists.

Round characters are unpredictable; they appear in works with complex plots and difficult-to-resolve conflicts. James Wood has noted in *How Fiction Works* that Jane Austen's heroines, like most round characters, "possess the secret of consciousness" and "belong to the newly emergent, newly complex form of the novel" (131). Determining whether a character is flat or round would be an interesting exercise to acquire a full understanding of a character's role, motives, aspirations, and values, which, in turn, can lead us to the work's themes. Hamlet's gradually expanding awareness in so many ways – love and duty, permanence and change, death and eternal life – make him a round character.

Current scholarship, while still deeply indebted to E. M. Forster's pioneering work, *Aspects of the* Novel, has added some new insights. For example, in *How Fiction Works*, James Wood offers an interesting perspective on character classification and analysis:

"Spatial metaphors, of depth, shallowness, roundness, flatness, are inadequate. A better division . . . is between transparencies (relatively simple characters) and opacities (relative degrees of mysteriousness). Many of the most absorbing accounts of motive [as in *Hamlet*] are studies in mystery. . . . . Why does Lear test his daughters? Why can't Hamlet effectively avenge the death of his father? Why does Iago ruin Othello's life? The source texts that Shakespeare read all provided transparent answers (Iago was in love with Desdemona, Hamlet should kill Claudius . . .). But Shakespeare was not interested in such transparency" (129).

Along the same lines, Stephen Greenblatt, in *Will in the World: How Shakespeare Became Shakespeare*, maintains that Shakespeare's principle in creating his characters "was . . . the creation of a strategic opacity." Wood and Greenblatt thus emphasize artistic superiority of nuanced and complex motivation in characters as opposed to transparency.

Some characters are neither entirely flat nor round but **fragmentary** beings. Incomplete by themselves, they form part of a whole. An example is Vladimir and Estragon in Samuel Beckett's *Waiting for Godot*. Vladimir represents the intellectual and rational part while Estragon embodies the irrational and instinctual. The entire play is a record of their attempts to enter into a harmonious fullness. By themselves, they are like two broken, vulnerable halves. Beckett has used these fragmentary characters to dramatize a theme: Only when human beings resolve the conflict between instinctual and rational elements, can they live harmoniously. Given the atomized nature of today's life, we are likely to see a significant increase in fragmentary characters in all forms of artistic expression and an ability to recognize them as such will be essential.

Interpretation through Character Analysis:
Connecting Characters with Themes

This exercise is not the usual character sketch that requires only summarizing the part played by each character. For an in-depth discussion that involves interpretation through critical thinking, it is necessary to consider the values the characters represent, significant choices they make, and what happens to them or what they cause to come about as a result of their actions, motives, and attitudes. Through such analysis we can also arrive at the author's theme(s) since themes are often embedded in the characters' words and actions and in the events that happen to them. Each major theme is usually associated with at least one major character, sometimes with several prominent characters.

An understanding of characters, therefore, facilitates interpretation. By drawing a cause-and-effect link between characters' actions, values, and outcomes, we can perceive an author's thematic suggestions. For instance, Hamlet is a perfectionist who hesitates to act until he is absolutely sure about the rightness of his actions. Since, as a consequence of his values, he meets a tragic end, we find in his fate a reiteration of the view that perfectionists have a difficult time surviving in a corrupt system.

"The Short Happy Life of Francis Macomber"

A look at Ernest Hemingway's "The Short Happy Life of Francis Macomber" (included toward the end of Chapter Four) also shows how a cause-and-effect examination of the values and motives of significant characters and the ends to which those values drive them may suggest a theme. The cause of the unhappy union of Francis and Margot Macomber is revealed in the narrator's ironic comment: "They had a sound basis of union. Margot was too beautiful for Macomber to divorce her and Macomber had too much money for Margot ever to leave him." The relationship of this couple is based on exploitation, not on mutual love and respect. An analysis of these two characters' actions and outcomes helps us recognize a central theme in the story: A relationship based on calculation, manipulation, and exploitation does not bring fulfillment and often leads to disaster.

Women in Love: Creative *versus* Destructive Love

The character–theme connection plays out at its best in D.H. Lawrence's novel, *Women in Love*. As the novel's title suggests, love in its various manifestations is its subject expressed through several pairs of lovers. First, there is the conventional, possessive love of Hermione for Birkin. Based on the will to possess at any cost, this love allows little room for spontaneity. This love demands self-sacrifice and surrender from the lovers. In time, this kind of love leads to a feeling of entrapment and resentment.

The second kind of love, dramatized in the Gerald-Gudrun relationship, is passionate but ultimately sterile because the lovers engage in an unending struggle for domination and allow the disintegrating and negative influences from the environment to direct the course of their love. They play elaborate games of self-deception by aiming for invulnerability and holding back their true feelings at crucial moments.

An example of their last-mentioned trait is their refusal to admit fulfillment even when they feel greatly moved by each other. They fear that any admission of gratification would somehow lower them. With this conduct they make each other feel like emotional beggars, denying the other person the satisfaction of giving and receiving.

These two characters steel themselves against tenderness and hurt by becoming invulnerable. This tendency prevents their evolution toward a higher plane. Their relation remains physical, essentially wordless, and undefined – undefined because any attempt to define it might commit the lovers too much.

In spite of her perceptiveness, intelligence, and physical beauty, Gudrun comes across as a shallow character, interested only in the excitement of the hunt. She loses all interest in Gerald as soon as he declares his love for her. She indulges in sadistic games by first making Gerald declare his love and then mocking him for doing so.

Before his transformation from an unfeeling womanizer to a sensitive human being, Gerald represents the mechanical principle, a compulsion to dominate every form of life – from inert matter to human emotions. He treats human feelings the same way he handles his coal mining industry: Everything must yield to his inexorable will.

The novel's third pair of lovers – Ursula and Birkin – exemplify the growing, open, and somewhat freer variety of love. Not without its own peculiar brand of problems, this love, nevertheless, allows the lovers to progress toward maturity through dialogue, debate, and even sharp disagreement. The book leads us to believe that this kind of love holds the potential of fulfillment and evolution toward a higher, mystical union, as the lovers surrender not to each other but to the inexhaustible "Creative Mystery."

In the last manifestation of love to be discussed, the novel offers the healing power of nonsexual, Platonic love between friends, members of the same sex. (Some readers see elements of homoeroticism in the Birkin-Gerald relationship.) This love is in addition to the heterosexual marriage and is meant to complement that marriage. Birkin's and Gerald's love for each other has this potential, which, unfortunately, is never realized.

Though seeming to tilt toward hopelessness at the process that has made human relationships machine-like, the book does manage to strike a balance between hope and despair through one destructive and one constructive pair – that is Gerald-Gudrun and Birkin-Ursula respectively.

Themes extracted from the preceding character analysis

The novel expresses one of its major themes through the failed Birkin-Hermione and Gerald-Gudrun relationships: Any attempt to close up a deficiency within oneself by trying to possess the beloved (as Hermione tries to do) stifles love just as failure to communicate passionate feelings for fear of becoming vulnerable ultimately kills those feelings. (The Gerald-Gudrun relationship illustrates the latter part of the theme.) The positive relationship between Birkin and Ursula becomes the vehicle for another prominent theme: Successful love relationships are the result of hard work, mutual growth, compromise, and acceptance of each other's individuality. Still another notable theme, implied in the story and developed at length in Lawrence's complex novel, concerns the threat of excessive mechanization in every sphere of life: Ever since the industrial and technological revolutions, a subtle and often unrecognized process of mechanization has been making inroads even into the realm of emotions. Since the larger, outside culture exerts its inevitable influence on our inner, passional lives, we cannot afford to hide behind the smug attitude, believing that our emotions can remain inviolate if we keep them separate from our machine-dominated ambiance, for the two are inseparable and affect each other.

Two famous paragraphs from Lawrence's writings that lament our divorce from nature enhance our understanding of the impact of mechanization on our lives:

No flowers grow upon busy machinery, there is no sky to a routine, there is no space to a rotary motion. And all life was a rotary motion, mechanized, cut off from reality. . . . The soul was a prisoner within this sordid vast edifice of life. . . .

The sea they turned into a murderous alley and a soiled road of commerce, disputed like the dirty land of a city every inch of it. The air they claimed too, shared it up, parceled it out to certain owners, they trespassed in the air to fight for it. Everything was gone, walled in, with spikes on top of the walls, and one must ignominiously creep between the spiky walls through a labyrinth of life. (Lawrence 185)

Another character whose values and conduct reveal a prominent theme is the unnamed narrator and main character in E. M. Forster's short story "The Other Side of the Hedge." The following complete sample essay demonstrates this character-theme connection. The story is given first.

The Other Side of the Hedge

My pedometer told me that I was twenty-five; and, though it is a shocking thing to stop walking, I was so tired that I sat down on a milestone to rest. People outstripped me, jeering as they did so, but I was too apathetic to feel resentful, and even when Miss Eliza Dimbleby, the great educationist, swept past, exhorting me to persevere, I only smiled and raised my hat.

At first I thought I was going to be like my brother, whom I had had to leave by the roadside a year or two round the corner. He had wasted his breath on singing, and his strength on helping others. But I had travelled more wisely, and now it was only the monotony of the highway that oppressed me – dust under foot and brown crackling hedges on either side, ever since I could remember.

And I had already dropped several things – indeed, the road behind was strewn with the things we all had dropped; and the white dust was settling down on them, so that already they looked no better than stones. My muscles were so weary that I could not even bear the weight of those things I still carried. I slid off the milestone into the road, and lay there prostrate, with my face to the great parched hedge, praying that I might give up.

A little puff of air revived me. It seemed to come from the hedge; and, when I opened my eyes, there was a glint of light through the tangle of boughs and dead leaves. The hedge could not be as thick as usual. In my weak, morbid state, I longed to force my way in, and see what was on the other side. No one was in sight, or I should not have dared to try. For we of the road do not admit in conversation that there is another side at all.

I yielded to the temptation saying to myself that I would come back in a minute. The thorns scratched my face, and I had to use my arms as a shield, depending on my feet alone to push me for1ard. Half way through I would have gone back, for in the passage all the things I was carrying were scraped off me, and my clothes were torn. But I was so wedged that return was impossible, and I had to wriggle blindly forward expecting every moment that my strength would fail me, and that I should perish in the undergrowth.

Suddenly cold water closed round my head, and I seemed sinking down for ever. I had fallen out of the hedge into a deep pool. I rose to the surface at last crying for help, and I heard someone on the opposite bank laugh and say: "Another!" and then I was twitched out and laid panting on the dry ground.

Even when the water was out of my eyes, I was still dazed, for I had never been in so large a space, nor seen such grass and sunshine. The blue sky was no longer a strip, and beneath it the earth had risen gradually into hills – clean bare buttresses, with beech trees in their folds, and meadows and clear pools at their feet. But the hills were not high, and there was in the landscape a sense of human occupation --

so that one might have called it a park, or garden, if the words did not imply a certain triviality and constraint.

As soon as I got my breath, I turned to my rescuer and said: Where does this place lead to?"

"Nowhere, thank the Lord!" said he, and laughed. He was a man of fifty or sixty – just the kind of age we mistrust on the road -- but there was no anxiety in his manner, and his voice was that of a boy of eighteen.

"But it must lead somewhere!" I cried too much surprised at his answer to thank him for saving my life.

"He wants to know where it leads!" he shouted to some men on the hill side, and they laughed back, and waved their caps.

I noticed then that the pool into which I had fallen was really bent round to the left and to the right and that the hedge followed The hedge was green on this side – its roots showed through the clear water, and fish swam about in them – and it was wreathed over with dog-roses and Traveller's Joy. But it was a barrier, and in a moment I lost all pleasure in the grass, the sky, the trees, the happy men and women, and realized that the place was but a prison, for all its beauty and extent.

We moved away from the boundary, and then followed a path almost parallel to it, across the meadows. I found it difficult walking, for I was always trying to out-distance my companion, and there was no advantage in doing this if the place led nowhere. I had never kept step with anyone since I left my brother.

I amused him by stopping suddenly and saying disconsolately, "This is perfectly terrible. One cannot advance: one cannot progress. Now we of the road –"

"Yes. I know."

"I was going to say, we advance continually."

"I know."

"We are always learning, expanding, developing. Why, even in my short life I have seen a great deal of advance – the Transvaal War, the Fiscal Question, Christian Science, Radium. Here for example – "

I took out my pedometer, but it still marked twenty-five, not a degree more.

"Oh, it's stopped! I meant to show you. It should have registered all the time I was walking with you. But it makes me only twenty-five."

"Many things don't work in here," he said. "One day a man brought in a Lee-Metford, and that wouldn't work."

"The laws of science are universal in their application. It must be the water in the moat that has injured the machinery. In normal conditions everything works. Science and the spirit of emulation – those are the forces that have made us what we are."

I had to break off and acknowledge the pleasant greetings of people whom we passed. Some of them were singing, some talking, some engaged in gardening, haymaking, or other rudimentary industries. They all seemed happy; and I might have been happy, too, if I could have forgotten that the place led nowhere.

I was startled by a young man who came sprinting across our path, took a little fence in fine style, and went tearing over a ploughed field till he plunged into a lake, across which he began to swim. Here was true energy, and I exclaimed: "A cross-country race! Where are the others?"

"There are no others," my companion replied; and, later on, when we passed some long grass from which came the voice of a girl singing exquisitely to herself, he said again: "There are no others." I was bewildered at the waste in production and murmured to myself "What does it all mean?"

He said: "It means nothing but itself – and he repeated the words slowly, as if I were a child.

"I understand," I said quietly "but I do not agree. Every achievement is worthless unless it is a link in the chain of development. And I must not trespass on your kindness any longer. I must get back somehow to the road, and have my pedometer mended."

"First you must see the gates," he replied, "for we have gates, though we never use them."

I yielded politely, and before long we reached the moat again, at a point where it was spanned by a bridge. Over the bridge was a big gate, as white as ivory, which was fitted into a gap in the boundary hedge. The gate opened out- wards, and I exclaimed in amazement, for from it ran a road – just such a road as I had left – dusty under foot, with brown crackling hedges on either side as far as the eye could reach.

"That's my road!" I cried.

He shut the gate and said: "But not your part of the road. It is through this gate that humanity went out countless ages ago, when it was first seized with the desire to walk."

I denied this, observing that the part of the road I myself had left was not more than two miles off. But with obstinacy of his years he repeated: "It is the same road. This is the beginning, and though it seems to run straight away from us it doubles so often that it is never far from our boundary and sometimes touches it." He stopped down by the moat and traced on its moist margin an absurd figure like a maze. As we walked back through the meadows I tried to convince him of his mistake.

"The road sometimes doubles to be sure but that is part of our discipline. Who can doubt that its general tendency is onward? To what goal we know not – it may be to some mountain where we shall touch the sky, it may be over precipices into the sea. But that it goes forward – who can doubt that? It is the thought of that that makes us strive to excel, each in his own way and gives us an impetus which is lacking with you. Now that man who passed us – it's true he ran well, and jumped well, and swam well; but we have men who can run better and men who can swim better. Specialization has produced results which would surprise you. Similarly, that girl ___"

Here I interrupted myself to exclaim: "Good gracious me! I could have sworn it was Miss Eliza Dimbleby over there, with her feet in the fountain!"

He believed that it was.

"Impossible! I left her on the road, and she is due to lecture this evening at Tunbridge Wells. Why, her train leaves Cannon Street in – of course my watch has stopped like everything else. She is the last person to be here."

"People always are astonished at meeting each other. All kinds come through the hedge, and come at all times – when they are drawing ahead in the race, when they are lagging behind, when they are left for dead. I often stand near the boundary listening to the sounds of the road – you know what they are – and wonder if anyone will turn aside. It is my great happiness to help someone out of the moat as I helped you. For our country fills up slowly, though it was meant for all mankind."

"Mankind have other aims," I said gently, for I thought him well-meaning; "and I must join them." I bade him good evening, for the sun was declining, and I wished to be on the road by nightfall. To my alarm, he caught hold of me, crying:

"You are not to go yet!" I tried to shake him off, for we had no interests in common and his civility was becoming irksome to me. But for all my struggles the tiresome old man would not let go; and, as wrestling is not my specialty, I was obliged to follow him.

It was true that I could have never found alone the place where I came in, and I hoped that, when I had seen the other sights about which he was worrying, he would take me back to it. But I was determined not to sleep in the country, for I mistrusted it, and the people too, for all their friendliness. Hungry though I was, I would not join them in their evening meals of milk and fruit, and, when they gave me flowers, I flung them away as soon as I could do so unobserved. Already they were lying down for the night like cattle – some out on the bare hillside, others in groups under the beaches. In the light of an orange sunset I hurried on with my unwelcome guide, dead tired, faint for want of food, but murmuring indomitably: "Give me life, with its struggles and victories, with its failures and hatreds, with its deep moral meaning and its unknown goal!"

At last we came to a place where the encircling moat was spanned by another bridge, and where another gate interrupted the line of the boundary hedge. It was different from the first gate; for it as half transparent like horn, and opened inwards. But through it, in the waning light, I saw again just such a road as I had left – monotonous, dusty, with brown crackling hedges on either side, as far as the eye could reach.

I was strangely disquieted at the sight, which seemed to deprive me of all self-control. A man was passing us, returning for the night to the hills, with a scythe over his shoulder and a can of some liquid in his hand. I forgot the road that lay before my eyes, and I sprang at him, wrenched the can out of his hand, and began to drink.

It was nothing stronger than beer, but in my exhausted state it overcame me in a moment. As in a dream, I saw the old man shut the gate, and heard him say: "This is where your road ends, and through this gate humanity – all that is left of it – will come in to us."

Though my senses were sinking into oblivion, they seemed to expand ere they reached it. They perceived the magic song of nightingales, and the odour of invisible hay, and stars piercing the fading sky. The man whose beer I had stolen lowered me down gently to sleep off its effects, and, as he did so, I saw that he was my brother.

E.M. Forster (1879-1970)

Interpretation of E. M. Forster's "The Other Side of the Hedge" through Character Analysis

E. M. Forster's classic tale has been considered a fable for our times. This interpretation of the story demonstrates the method of reaching an author's themes through character analysis. Note that even though I have commented on Forster's symbolism and his allegorical mode in telling this story, I have maintained my focus on character analysis to arrive at the themes.

The Awakening of Forster's Imperfect Narrator
Sample essay by the author of this book

In E. M. Forster's famous work of short fiction "The Other Side of the Hedge," the main character is also the first-person narrator. A look at his values and lifestyle elucidates some of the reasons for his predicament – his incapacity for joy – which stems from his selfishness, distrust of others, and close-mindedness.

One of his notable traits is his selfishness, which makes him believe that helping others is a waste of one's time and energy. Of his humane brother, he has this to say: "I had . . . to leave [him] by the roadside. . . He had wasted his breath on singing, and his strength on helping others. But I had traveled more wisely." Ironically, however, his brother, whom he had left behind, gets ahead of him and helps him in the story's climactic moments.

During the course of a relentless, oppressively tedious, and boring foot race that seems to symbolize a way of life dominated by self-centered desire to get ahead of others, the narrator has been trying to outstrip the competitors. However, overcome by sheer exhaustion, he is forced to pause. It is during this forced halt on the road – symbolic of the road of life – that he thinks of crossing over to the other side of the hedge, where unknown wonders await him. As he crosses over, he falls into a moat, from which a kind stranger rescues him. This immersion seems to represent the narrator's baptism into his new life, in which he is compelled to reevaluate his ego-centered philosophy.

His other trait of distrusting everyone is revealed during his meeting with perfectly well-meaning and caring people who inhabit the paradise-like other side of the hedge. He proudly claims:

"... I was determined not to sleep in the country, for I mistrusted it, and the people too, for all their friendliness. Hungry though I was, I would not join them in their evening meals of milk and fruit, and, when they gave me flowers, I flung them away as soon as I could do so unobserved."

For the kindly guide who saved him from drowning, the narrator has this to say: "He was a man of fifty or sixty – just the kind of age we mistrust on the road."

Conditioned by his lifestyle to regard everyone as his competitor, he is incapable of relaxing to enjoy the peaceful, idyllic, and tension-free life on the other side of the hedge. He cannot enjoy walking with the host because he is so used to competing: "I found it difficult walking, for I was always trying to outdistance my companion." When he sees a young man sprinting across his path and thoroughly enjoying the activity, our narrator asks at once, "Where are the others?" He cannot conceive that someone might run for the sheer joy of running with no thought of competing with others. The fact that there are no competitors in that race disappoints him. On hearing "the voice of a girl singing exquisitely to herself," he has the same reaction: "I was bewildered at the waste in production, and murmured to myself, 'What does it all mean?' "

His close-mindedness is apparent from his refusal to believe that there could be another viable way of life besides his: "For we of the road do not admit in conversation that there is another side at all." When the guide, who knows the place well, tries to educate the narrator about life in the paradise-like garden – reminiscent of the Biblical Garden of Eden – the narrator continues to resist enlightenment. Pointing to the gate of ivory that opens outwards – symbolic of delusive dreams which we may pursue endlessly – the guide tells him: "It is through this gate that humanity went out countless ages ago, when it was first seized with the desire to walk." Since in this story walking also means competing, the word "seized" appropriately describes humanity's obsession with a competitive way of life and abandonment of a peaceful, tranquil, and fulfilling lifestyle. Instead of profiting from the guide's knowledge, the narrator remains imprisoned in his own narrow shell.

In a highly suggestive passage, full of symbolic meanings, what the guide tells the narrator is meant to be heard by all of us, who may be trapped in similar competitiveness. The guide explains that though the road "seems to run straight away from us, it doubles so often, that it is never far from our boundary and sometimes touches it." The dusty road of competition, we remember, is lined "with brown crackling hedges on either side as far as the eye could reach." Caught in this seemingly endless toil, we fail to notice that the other side – the other and a better way of life – is so close at hand. The guide's words serve to remind us that happiness is always within our reach even though we continue to believe that a life of fierce competition and constant battle to forge ahead of others is our only destiny.

The narrator of Forster's story refused to listen to the wise guide, and if we find ourselves in the same quandary as the story's narrator, we can infer that Forster's subtle allegorical tale, rich with symbolic meanings, seems to ask whether the narrator's failings are our failings as well.

Exercises to Test Your Mastery of Chapter Two

(Suggested length: 500 to 750 words)

Complete only those exercises that you are prepared to handle. You can return to the rest of them later after you have read other chapters.

1. Compare and/or contrast two characters from any work. Describe their values, their influence on those who are close to them and on those who come in contact with them, their overall impact on the world they inhabit and the impact of their environment on them. Mention these characters' significant deeds, values, and fate. If you feel inclined to say so, reveal your preference for either of the two characters compared, giving reasons for your opinion. If possible, also connect each character with a theme.

2. Write a character analysis that includes one or more critics' opinions. Some fictional characters draw strong responses from us. By tracing and analyzing the process of arriving at our opinions and by comparing our views with those of the critics, we can generate an interesting character study.

3. Analyze a literary or film character that comes close to representing you, your personal beliefs, and worldview.

4. Focusing on any work with a single major character, combine plot summary with theme-oriented character analysis as demonstrated in the sample essay on E. M. Forster's "The Other Side of the Hedge."

5. Select a modern literary work that is based on a myth or a mythic character from the past. Discuss any significant variations in characterization and theme that are introduced in the modern version, with possible reasons for those changes. One example is the play *Pygmalion* by George Bernard Shaw, which is discussed in Chapter Twelve. Another example is the short story "Pygmalion" by John Updike. That story and a sample essay are on my website content relating to Chapter Two. A third example is Eugene O'Neill's play *Mourning Becomes Electra*. This play is not discussed in this book.

6. Write an essay in which you analyze a flat, a round, and a fragmented character to demonstrate the characteristics of each type.

7. Define the concept of the anti-hero and relate it to one or two characters who fit your definition.

8. Discuss a character from a literary work or a movie as a tragic hero or heroine. Demonstrate how the selected character embodies the qualities that are characteristic of protagonists in tragic drama. Consult the list of fifteen elements that are considered central to tragedy. These elements are mentioned near the beginning of Chapter Twelve (Drama). You will find some of the listed elements more helpful than others in answering this question.

9. Characters are ultimately about human relationships. Arthur Miller wrote his play *After the Fall* subsequent to his divorce and his wife Marilyn Monroe's death. This play was also made into a movie with Christopher Plummer. Select a few sections of the play or movie that illuminate some of the challenges in human relationships, keeping your focus on Arthur Miller's personal life. Feel free to add other relevant information without losing that focus.

10. Arthur Miller wrote the screenplay for *The Misfits* for his wife Marilyn Monroe. The movie premiered in 1961 soon after the Millers' divorce in the same year. Marilyn Monroe and Clark Gable had the leading roles. Identify and analyze the character that seems to have been drawn after Miller himself and the character presumably representing the baseball legend Joe DiMaggio, to whom Marilyn was married before becoming Miller's wife. When completing this exercise, you may find it helpful to remember that the Miller-Monroe marriage has been interpreted as a "union between American icons representing everything from high and popular culture to the mind and the body, tragedy and comedy and intellect and sex" (Hurwitt A12). Give supporting reasons and facts for your views.

11. Write an obituary of a character whom you have come to know intimately through a literary work or movie. Besides anything you may wish to mention, include the values and principles the character stood for.

Timed, Self-Test Exercises
(Time allowed for each item: 50 minutes)

In the time allowed for this exercise, you should be able to write the first draft or at least create an outline for a 500 to 750 words long paper. Such timed exercises are a proven way to overcome the writer's block.

1. Using the advice given at the beginning of this chapter, write a character analysis (as distinguished from a character sketch), based on any literary work or movie.

2. Write a character-revealing piece in the character's own voice, assuming his or her personality and using the first-person pronoun "I" (for example: I am Hamlet).

3. Analyze a character in a literary work or movie to trace the source of his or her biased or racist views and point out how that character's awareness and tolerance of other cultures might be expanded. This exercise may be completed in the form of a letter to that character. Assume that the reader of your essay is unfamiliar with the work you are discussing so that you provide sufficient plot details to make your writing completely understandable.

4. Connect a character with a prominent theme in a play, novel, short story, or movie. In making this character-theme connection, give relevant details from the work to support your points.

CHAPTER THREE

PLOT

Plot is inseparable from character because a large part of plot is actions performed by characters. Since plot details, by definition, emphasize the link between cause and effect, we often discover themes by tracing connections between characters' deeds and their consequences. In this way, plot and character become linked with each other and with themes and style of a literary work. Perceiving this network of connections between these elements is necessary to fully appreciate literature. Plots give us details that are essential to our comprehension of a literary work. At a deeper level, plot becomes an instrument of an author's thematic design. Not just necessary mechanisms to make the story possible, even simple plot components, such as scene placement, also contribute to a work's theme formulation. For example, Shakespeare's placing of the humor-filled grave-diggers scene just before the catastrophic last scene of *Hamlet* makes us aware of the proximity of pleasure and pain in life.

The very word *plot* suggests a strategy or a plan to carry a work's content. How authors open and close their works, how they decide on the sequence of scenes, whether they use just one plot or add one or more sub-plots, how they pace and select events – these and similar options are parts of an author's plan. In this respect, plot seems closely related to an author's style. Plot, however, is also the story's outline. It is in this sense that we use the word *plot* when we ask, "What is the book's or the movie's plot?" Plot is thus also closely related to content. Whereas the word "what" goes with content and the word "how" goes with an author's style, plot answers to both "what" and "how." This duality of function (plot acting both as style and substance) will become clearer as we look at some definitions of plot and analyze its components. Familiarity with some plot-related theories and practices will help us appreciate their observance as well as rejection by authors. Departures from established conventions become meaningful only if we know what the dissenting and innovative authors are departing from.

Definitions and Essential Features of the Classical Plot

When looking for definitions of plot, E. M. Forster's famous book *Aspects of the Novel* is a good starting point because it not only makes helpful comments on the art of fiction but also offers valuable advice on how to read great literary works. Making a distinction between a story and a plot, he says that a story is "a narrative of events arranged in their time-sequence. A plot is also a narrative of events, the emphasis falling on causality" (Forster 86). To quote E. M. Forster's famous words, "The King died, and then the Queen died" is a story. "The king died, and then the queen died of grief" is a plot. In the definition of plot, the "time-sequence is preserved, but the sense of causality overshadows it" (86). To the random sequence of events of a story, a causal element is now added. In a story, the emphasis is on "and then?"; in a plot we ask "Why?" Plot therefore requires greater sophistication:

"A plot cannot be told to a gaping audience of cave-men. . . . They can only be kept awake by 'and then – and then – '. They can only supply curiosity. But a plot demands intelligence and memory also" (86).

The element of surprise or mystery "is of great importance in a plot. It occurs through a suspension of the time-sequence" (Forster 87). Mystery can occur crudely, as in "Why did the queen die?" Superior works have a more subtle kind of mystery. It exists "in half-explained gestures and words, the true meaning of which only dawns pages ahead. Mystery is essential to a plot, and cannot be appreciated without intelligence. To the curious it is just another 'and then –'. To appreciate a mystery, part of the mind must be left behind, brooding, while the other part goes marching on" (87).

Two more points from Forster's work are worth noting. Both of them are central to a good plot. The first concerns the interconnectedness of plot details that requires the reader to look at the work's totality: "The facts in a highly organized novel . . . are often of the nature of cross-correspondences and the ideal spectator cannot expect to view them properly until he is sitting up on a hill at the end" (87).

In this statement that places the reader/viewer "up on a hill" Forster is emphasizing a vision that takes in the totality of connections in plot details. That vision requires rising above the flux, the ebb and flow of actions and events that make up plot—a form of detachment that the author also needs to create good plots.

The second point addresses the question about what constitutes a superior plot. Forster favors the prophetic novel, such as Emily Bronte's Wuthering Heights. In such works, "what is implied is more important . . . than what is said." The emotions of the novel's two main characters – Heathcliffe and Catherine – function differently from ordinary emotions in fiction. "Instead of inhabiting the characters, they surround them like thunder clouds, and generate the explosions that fill the novel" (145). The two characters "cause the action by their separation: they close it by their union after death . . . . Even when they were alive their love and hate transcended them" (145).

In D. H. Lawrence's Women in Love, Forster finds another example of the prophetic novel. He refers specifically to a scene in which the protagonist Birkin repeatedly but unsuccessfully tries to shatter the moon's reflection on water. The rare "power of re-creation and evocation" is what he notes in Lawrence:

"What is valuable about him cannot be put into words; it is colour, gesture and outline in people and things, the usual stock-in-trade of the novelist, but evolved by such a different process that they belong to a new world" (144).

To Forster's view, we should add Richard M. Eastman's exegesis of plot in A Guide to the Novel. Unlike Forster, he does not offer criteria for an ideal plot or a superior novel. However, he does offer a comprehensive definition of plot and lists its essential features, most of which are also applicable to drama:

"Plot is indeed the structural principle of narration; without it, a narrative seems like a spineless heap of incidents. . . . Plot begins when the protagonist is displaced from an original equilibrium in which he has been reasonably well adjusted. . . . Once the plot is set going, it intensifies by a series of further steps, each of which basically and irreversibly alters the protagonist's fortunes, moral standards, or knowledge" (8).

Events add to the protagonist's disequilibrium, reaching the crisis or "the point of maximum instability," after which a new equilibrium is reached, followed by "the final state of affairs" or the denouement (Eastman 8-11). All definitions of plot, like those by Forster and Eastman, emphasize a cause-and-effect connection between narrative events, human deeds, and constantly changing human relationships. Plot, thus, becomes a vehicle for the plan of action carried in the narrative thread of fiction, drama, some forms of poetry, and film.

Most theories of plot are derived from Aristotle's theory that he offered in the context of discussing drama in *The Poetics*. As far back as fourth century B.C., he laid down the stringent requirements for a tightly structured plot in classical dramatic art:

". . . the plot being an imitation of an action, must imitate one action and that a whole, the structural union of the parts being such that, if any one of them is displaced or removed, the whole will be disjointed and disturbed. For a thing whose presence or absence makes no visible difference is not an organic part of the whole" (Butcher 35).

It is undeniable that Aristotle's ideal plot, with no loose ends and with its demanding concept of justification for inclusion and order of each plot detail yields aesthetic pleasure whenever implemented. The ideal plot can be seen in the Greek plays by Aeschylus, Sophocles, and Euripides, in most of Racine's plays (*Phaedra*, for example), some Shakespearean plays (*The Tempest*, for example), in Gustave Flaubert's novels (*Madame Bovary*, for instance), and in most of the meticulously crafted novels by Henry James.

The classical requirement of order and economy can also be applied to plots of short fiction. Edgar Allan Poe spoke of this type of plot: "In the whole composition there should be no word written, of which the tendency, direct or indirect, is not to the one pre-established design" (Fallon 48).

It is impossible to formulate a universally acceptable single definition of a perfect plot because authors have their own unique ways of organizing and presenting their material. However, some features seem common to successful plots:

1. All details are interconnected and have psychological and emotional linkage besides the cause-and-effect connection of logic, which sometimes may be suspended for impact.

2. Nothing is superfluous; all events, actions, and characters serve a purpose and contribute to the plot's unity.

3. Using the esthetics of omission, a plot may communicate its ideas through implication rather than by statement.

4. Keeping in mind the reader's/viewer's need for entertainment along with instruction, a plot may have the elements of mystery and suspense, which are often achieved through manipulation of chronology, point of view, flashback, premonition (flash forward), suspension of logic, parallelism, coincidence and similar strategies.

5. Its events, settings, moods, and questions reverberate in the reader's imagination long after the book is finished. In E. M. Forster's words, expansion "is the idea the novelist [or any literary artist] must cling to. Not completion. Not rounding off but opening out" (Forster 169).

Plot Variations: Simple, Complex, Episodic, Melodramatic, Inert, and Intuitive

Simple and Complex Plots

Not all authors follow the rigorous classical plot pattern. To look at other plot variations, starting with Aristotle would be the logical choice. His definition attempts to explain simple and complex plots:

"Plots are either simple or complex, since the actions they represent are naturally of this twofold description. The action, proceeding in the way defined, as one continuous whole, I call simple, when the change in the hero's fortunes takes place without Peripety or Discovery; and complex, when it involves one or the other, or both. These should each of them arise out of the structure of the Plot itself, so as to be the consequence, necessary or probable, of the antecedents" (Leech 1).

The term "peripety" means reversal in the hero's fortunes, from prosperity to adversity in tragic plays. "Discovery" is crucial new knowledge that usually occurs after the climax and leads toward the resolution.

Episodic Plots

Some plots are episodic – the opposite of the classical organic which has the attributes of a living organism with mutually interdependent and interconnected parts. Episodic plots are made up of a string of random incidents that befall the protagonist. Cervantes' *Don Quixote* and Daniel Defoe's *Moll Flanders* are two of the well-known examples. Both novels let the incidents and events structure the plot, giving the impression that there is no controlling and designing force behind the characters except life itself.

Melodramatic Plots

Melodramatic plots thrive on the audience's hunger for sensationalism. Byron's play *Manfred*, with its brooding, melancholy, and remorse-stricken but defiant Byronic hero, who carries the scars of forbidden passion, exemplifies the melodramatic type of plot. The word "melodrama" often carries negative connotations. It would, however, be questionable to consider melodrama as invariably inferior. It can combine with artistic gifts to good effects. We have, for example, V.S. Pritchett's following words on

Daphne Du Maurier's popular, melodramatic novel *Rebecca*: "Many a better novelist would give his eyes to be able to tell a story as Miss Du Maurier does, to make it move at such a pace and to go with such mastery from surprise to surprise . . . the melodrama is excellent" (Pritchett A-10).

Inert Plots

Another plot variation – one that has hardly anything dramatic in its action – is exemplified by Samuel Beckett's play *Waiting for Godot*. The central action in Beckett consists of the two main characters waiting for Godot, who never comes to relieve their misery. In the play all action is paralyzed; instead of dramatic action, we have complete inertia that blends with the play's theme of futility of waiting for a savior instead of taking control of one's life.

Intuitively Organized Plots

Some modern authors prefer organizing stories by a method that is more intuitive than the conventional plot. In *San Francisco Chronicle's* review of *The Best Books of 2004*, William Trevor arguably is rated "the greatest living writer of short stories." Commenting on Trevor's approach to fiction in his story collection *A Bit on the Side*, the reviewer notes:

"Trevor seems . . . willing . . . to forego the conventions of plot, preferring instead to tack his stories down with possessions, mementos or pawnshop bric-a-brac. These 12 stories seem as if they have been organized by a method more intuitive than plot, as if Trevor weren't so much telling a story as composing a collage of words that record the intersection of a particular insight or realization and its external circumstance. Like James Joyce before him, Trevor specializes in epiphanies, though Trevor's are more subtle, less overly literary, more appropriate for a contemporary Ireland where characters seek sanctuary in Japanese cafes as often as smoky public houses and cathedrals" (*San Francisco Chronicle* E-2).

As has been noted, between the two extremes of the tightly structured organic plots of the classical school and the intuitively rather than logically plotted narratives of authors like Trevor, there are numerous other variations that combine different plot-organizing strategies according to the structural needs of a literary work or a movie.

Plot Components

Whereas plots of fiction and modern drama have a wide range, classical drama has six major plot components.

1. Exposition: Setting, introduction of important characters and issues, establishing the primary plot-structuring device around which almost all of the plot details are organized, and conflict and its source are parts of the exposition.

2. Conflict: Often in the exposition part, an event or an issue sets off the opposing forces on their collision course. The warring forces could also exist within one character.

3. Rising Action: Events spiral and issues get complicated.

4. Climax is the story's high point, to which every development has been building up.

5. Falling action results from the climax and steers the plot movement toward an inevitable end.

6. Denouement is the resolution and cleansing of tensions created by the plot action. Like the opening part, the conclusion of a literary work also requires careful plotting and planning by the author regardless of the literary form.

These plot components are of a general nature. Authors introduce variations to suit their styles and goals, sometimes deviating from conventions to make a point. Even though these plot components primarily belong in classical drama, familiarity with them promotes understanding of all plots.

Illustration of Plot Components in *Hamlet*

The plot of a work is only a shell unless it is energized with appropriate content and means of organization. We can acquire a better understanding of the elements of plot by applying them to a specific play – *Hamlet* by William Shakespeare.

Shakespeare introduces all elements of *exposition* just as he handles other plot components with rare clarity. If handled unskillfully, the exposition part of plot can become confusing and unwieldy under the weight of details.

Shakespeare wastes no time to introduce all the important players of the main plot – Claudius, Gertrude, Hamlet, and the ghost of Hamlet's dead father (whose appearance functions as the primary plot structuring device). The characters of the sub-plot – Polonius, Laertes, and Ophelia – are also quickly presented. Horatio, the play's balancing force, is present from beginning to end.

The source of *conflict* – the murder of King Hamlet by his brother Claudius – and the primary plot-structuring device (the ghost's plea to Hamlet for revenge and rectification) are clearly established by the end of Act One. The play's *rising action* consists of Hamlet's playing the detective to verify the truth of the ghost's words. The climax may be Hamlet's unintended murder of Polonius, who was spying on him from behind the curtain in the Queen's bedroom. Hamlet thought it was Claudius.

This murder puts Hamlet at the mercy of Claudius, and thus ensues the *falling action*. The important components of this phase are Claudius's attempt to eliminate Hamlet by sending him to England under Rosencrantz and Guildenstern's escort with a warrant for his death, Hamlet's accidental encounter with the pirates, and his subsequent return to Denmark.

Hamlet's resolution phase consists of a huge pile of details unfolding with dizzying speed as if to make up for all lack of action until that point. For clarity, the details of the play's concluding phase can be listed as follows:

1. Perhaps the most exciting duel in the history of drama, in which both Laertes and Hamlet are mortally wounded
2. The Queen's death as a result of drinking from the poisoned refreshment prepared by Claudius for Hamlet
3. The murder of Claudius by Hamlet
4. Fortinbras' assuming the control of Denmark
5. Horatio's declaration to tell Hamlet's story

Shakespeare's handling of complex concluding details with dexterity is notable.

This overview of major elements of plot has revealed that each component can be further subdivided into narrower categories to understand how they blend artistically in a plot. With that goal in mind, let us evaluate Shakespeare's plot construction in *Hamlet* with an in-depth look at his use of the primary plot-making device (a part of *exposition*).

Plot-Structuring Devices

The Primary Plot-Structuring Device

How to organize a plot, what details to include, what to leave out – these are among the difficult challenges faced by all authors. They are also central to plot evaluation. In artistically appealing works, authors unify their plots by selecting just one item, usually an event, for their primary structuring device. Such an event or plot detail occurs early in a play and functions like the thesis statement in an expository essay. Since every major detail refers back to it, the play would be inconceivable without it.

An example of the primary plot-structuring device is the one-thousand dollar life insurance check that the Younger family is expected to receive on the death of their patriarch in Lorraine Hansberry's play *A Raisin in the Sun*. The competing dreams of family members as to the best use of that money generate the play's suspenseful, exciting, and well-designed plot.

Similarly, the phonetician Henry Higgins' bet that he will transform the flower girl Eliza Doolittle to speak like a duchess in a matter of months is the primary plot-setting device in George Bernard Shaw's play *Pygmalion*. All other details are held together by this wager between Higgins and Colonel Pickering, just as the audience is kept guessing whether Higgins will succeed in winning his bet or fail.

To fully understand the function of a primary plot-structuring detail, let us analyze its use in *Hamlet*. The appearance of King Hamlet's ghost in *Hamlet*, for example, is the main plot-structuring device because all actions and conflicts are traceable to that supernatural figure. In this scene, the secret of King Hamlet's murder by his own brother is divulged, and the strict conditions of Hamlet's revenge laid out. The ghost's appearance gives the starting push to the play's complex plot of interconnected, causally linked events.

Two elements, connected with the primary plot-structuring device in *Hamlet*, lift the play far above the revenge plays of his day and make it deeply philosophical: First, the conditions the ghost imposes on

Hamlet to make it a just revenge are almost impossible to meet: Hamlet is to kill Claudius without in any way hurting his wife (Hamlet's mother) Gertrude. Secondly, what makes this plot-setting device even more effective is the fact of Hamlet's skepticism. He is not sure whether the spirit he has seen is truly his father's ghost, or is it an evil spirit trying to mislead Hamlet into a heinous crime. To investigate the veracity of the ghost's words, Hamlet has to put on the mask of insanity and devise a play for Claudius and the court, re-enacting the way King Hamlet was murdered by Claudius according to the apparition. Once Hamlet himself is convinced of Claudius's crime, he has to convince the court before he can take action. Almost all of the events, actions, and conflicts in the play can be traced to the ghost's revelation. By its pivotal role in the play's action, the scene touches off the themes of revenge, crime, justice, punishment, innocence, and guilt. The play's central conflict and its themes are traceable to the plot-setting device.

Shakespeare's plotting strategy required a delicate arrangement and maneuvering of details. In his book *Conscience and the* King Bertram Joseph has noted the playwright's superb handling of this challenge:

> "[It is] not enough to kill Claudius; the king must also be unmistakably exposed for what he is. In the whole play there is only one moment when this [the exposure of the king's criminal acts] can happen; and when it happens it is a culmination of a long serpentine course of events."

The moment to which Joseph is referring occurs in the play's last scene, which exposes Claudius's predilection for poison as his favorite weapon to eliminate his opponents. He had used poison to kill his brother in order to seize the throne of Denmark, and now again he resorts to the same means to get rid of his nemesis – his nephew Hamlet. He is able to manipulate Laertes to conspire against Hamlet by using an unbated and poison-coated sword in the so-called friendly duel with Hamlet. He also prepares a poisoned refreshment that he offers to Hamlet during the duel but which Gertrude unknowingly drinks and dies. From the lips of the dying Queen and the mortally wounded Laertes comes the incriminating evidence against Claudius in the presence of important political figures of the Danish court. That is the moment of truth about Claudius's crime-filled career.

What the ghost asked Hamlet to do in the play's first Act had to be postponed until this moment of exposure in the play's last scene. The way Shakespeare has designed the plot, there was a necessity for this long delay. Hamlet could not have acted merely on the basis of the Ghost's word or even when Claudius acted guilty by stomping out of the play-within-the-play that Hamlet had devised to "catch the conscience of the king" (II,ii,617). These two sources could not be demonstrated before the public as conclusive proof of Claudius's crime of fratricide. The only evidence of the King's wrongdoing is his warrant ("commission") for Hamlet's death. However, only Hamlet knows about it. That commission is meant to be delivered to the English monarch by Hamlet's escorts – Rosencrantz and Guildenstern. That is the warrant that Hamlet intercepted and put the names of Rosencrantz and Guildenstern in the place of his name. By then, there is no doubt in Hamlet's mind that the King is guilty of more than one crime.

To carry out the ghost's command, two conditions had to be met: First, Hamlet himself had to be convinced of the truth; secondly, the moment had to be right to expose the King's crime publicly. The first of these two conditions – Hamlet's readiness – is met by the time he returns from the sea voyage. His words to Horatio leave us with no doubt:

> He that hath killed my king, and whored my mother,
> Popped in between th'election and my hopes,
> Thrown out his angle for my proper life,
> And with such cozenage – is't not perfect conscience
> To quit him with this arm? And is't not to be damned
> To let this canker of our nature come
> In further evil?   (V, ii, 64-70).

However, killing a reigning monarch is a huge undertaking, for which only the play's last scene offered the right moment. Through his superb handling of the play's plot with serpentine turns, Shakespeare is able to keep our interest in the characters, their actions and outcomes at an unusually high level of suspense and involvement. His artistry in weaving a plot of such complexity is, indeed, impressive. It comes close to the ideal plot in which, according to Aristotle, the scenes and details are so closely woven that even a slight transposition in order would cause the entire structure to crumble.

Secondary Plot-Structuring Devices

The single, *primary* plotting device is almost exclusively used in drama. Some writers of fiction also use this strategy, but their adherence to it is neither so visible nor as strictly enforced as in drama. In addition to this *primary* means of organization, authors also rely on secondary structuring devices. Along with characters' actions, events (that is, occurrences and what happens to characters) are a large part of what constitutes plot. Plot events can serve as both primary and secondary means of organization. It was noted earlier, in the context of discussing *Hamlet*, *Pygmalion*, and *A Raisin in the Sun*, how a special event can be the primary means of structuring a plot. Events serving as secondary structuring devices are too numerous to be listed. Suffice it to say that all events other than the one that serves as the primary means of plot structuring may be called the secondary plot-structuring devices.

Among secondary plot-organizing means other than events, notable are repetition of key details, setting, symbolism, irony, foreshadowing, parallelism, and the esthetics of omission. Since they are also categorized as elements of style, their explanation and discussion are postponed until the next chapter. Authors select from the secondary plot-structuring devices whatever they need.

The Three Unities of Classical Drama

Other plot-related matters, specifically relevant to action in drama and film (but also applicable to fiction) are the so-called three unities – of *action*, *time*, and *place* – that are often used to control plot. In *The Poetics*, Aristotle wrote about the importance of the unity of action. French and Italian authors of the sixteenth and seventeenth centuries established stringent guidelines for the unities of time and place. These three unities are meant to impose limits on plot design and increase the plausibility of dramatic action.

Simply explained, the unity of *action* means that the story line should move forward in a straight line without any distracting subplots. The concept of the unity of action also frowns on the mixing of tragedy with comedy, since it violates consistency in tone.

The unity of *time* asks dramatists to limit the action on stage to approximately twenty-four hours. The sixteenth- and seventeenth-century French and Italian dramatists tried to limit dramatic action to three hours – the amount of time it takes to present the play on stage. To satisfy this rule, authors would have to concentrate on a limited span of the protagonist's life and render on stage what transpires only in that brief duration. The audience received information on relevant past events through dialogue and soliloquies.

The third unity – that of *place* – refers to the setting for the plot action. Shifting the venue of action from place to place, especially between distant places, would, according to this view, reduce the story's credibility. Dramatists were, therefore, urged to use just one setting. Modern means of speedy transportation are likely to allow the author greater freedom with regard to the limitations of the unity of place.

It is undeniable that observance of these unities results in tighter plots, rapidity of action, and greater overall intensity. It is also undeniable that these unities impose too many restraints on the artist's creativity besides narrowing the play's scope. For this reason, since the daring example of Shakespeare, many authors refuse to submit to a literal observance of the unities.

In some of his plays (especially in *The Tempest*), Shakespeare observed the Aristotelian plot concept as if to show that he could do so if he wanted to. The plot details in this play are tightly woven; the entire action is limited to a few hours, and the setting is limited to just one island on which the old conflicts are reconciled. In most of his plays, however, he has created great dramatic works without strictly following the classical unities. For example, he mixes tragedy and comedy in *Hamlet*, which goes against the classical convention of the unity of action. Classical Greek plays were either pure comedies or pure tragedies. Thus it is not only the observance but also violation of any of the classical unities that could be the topic for an interesting and enlightening discussion.

Why does Shakespeare interject humorous moments in the midst of deeply tragic scenes? Hamlet's barbed wit, especially noticed in his repartee with Polonius, Rosencrantz, Guildenstern, and Claudius, is the source of humor throughout the play's solemn moments. One scene, in particular, stands out as an example of concentrated humor. This scene, with the graveyard for its setting, occurs just after

Ophelia's death and just before the catastrophic end of the play. It contains Shakespeare's highly comic use of parody to ridicule litigious lawyers' and politicians' use of legal jargon and inflated style of speech. Hamlet remarks on seeing the gravedigger toss around a skull:

"Why may not that be the skull of a lawyer? Where be his quiddities now, his quillets, his cases, his tenures, and his tricks? Why does he suffer this rude knave now to knock him about the sconce with a dirty shovel, and will not tell him of his action of battery? Hum, this fellow might be in's time a great buyer of land, with his statutes, his recognizances, his fines, his double vouchers, his recoveries. Is this the fine of his fines and the recovery of his recoveries, to have his fine pate full of fine dirt?" (V, I, 83-90)

These comic details occur just before the stage is covered with dead bodies. Scholars like John Dryden and Samuel Johnson have defended Shakespeare's mixture of tragedy and comedy as realistic, for tears and laughter do go together in real life. At the same time, it is undeniable that compression of details as a result of observing the classical unities lends special intensity to the plot action. Without undermining the value of either approach, a comparison of a Shakespearean play like *Hamlet* with a classical Greek work (such as Sophocles' *Oedipus the King*) will illuminate the respective merits of both practices.

Even though the concept of the three unities originally concerned drama, these rules can be and have been applied to novels, short stories, and film. Because of their short length and compression of detail, the short story and film are also suited to analysis from the point of view of the classical unities.

Use of Chance/Coincidence

The requirement of cause-and-effect connection between events does not discount the use of chance in plots. Here we enter a highly interesting and controversial point in literary criticism. Chance happenings and coincidences do take place in real life, and if literature and film are to mirror reality, the element of chance should have a place in plot.

Excessive use of chance to resolve complicated plots, however, would diminish the credibility of a work of art. Since they do not grow out of plot construction naturally, extraneous incidents introduced to resolve tangled situations are called *deus ex machina*, a Latin term meaning "god out of a machine," which refers to the practice of lowering a god onto the stage from up above with the help of a machine. The god settled the complicated problem which the author could not do. Some works today also resort to such forced mechanical endings, which are considered artistically inferior.

Careful authors minimize the credibility-reducing effect of the use of chance. In *Shakespearean Tragedy*, A.C. Bradley has demonstrated how in Shakespeare's plays "some things which look like accidents have really a connection with character, and are therefore not in the full sense accidents" (Bradley 23). For example, it only seems like an accident that Hamlet finds out the truth about his so-called friends Rosencrantz and Guildenstern, who are escorting him to his death in England. But is it really an accident? Closer analysis reveals a connection between Hamlet's character and his discovery of the plot against him. Hamlet is gifted with extraordinary powers of intuition. Sensing foul play, he searches Rosencrantz and Guildenstern's belongings and discovers his death warrant. This discovery can thus be traced to Hamlet's character. A less intuitive person in Hamlet's place might not have sensed any danger.

Shakespeare and other consummate writers use another precaution to make the element of chance artistically satisfying: "almost all the prominent accidents [in Shakespeare's works] occur when the action is well advanced and the impression of the casual sequence is too firmly fixed to be impaired" (Bradley 23).

Changing Concepts of Dramatic Action

Over the centuries, we have witnessed a gradual turning of the plot action inward. The locale of struggle seems to have changed, in most cases, from a physical arena to states of mind. The voyage of discovery leading to the classical recognition stage of self-knowledge and reconciliation may still be there. However, this voyage has become more and more mental; instead of traversing the earth and conquering hostile forces, the protagonist now struggles mainly to harmonize the warring tendencies within his/her own psyche. Shakespeare's Hamlet is a famous illustration of intellectualizing the protagonist in comparison with the classical Greek and Roman heroes. Classic conflicts between human beings and Nature, between individuals and social institutions, now also include individuals against themselves.

Changing concepts of plot action have raised an interesting question: Do plots with events that barely break through the subliminal layer of consciousness compensate for lack of traditional, action-filled plots. Among contemporary novelists, the British author Anita Brookner crafts her works with meticulous care and subtlety. Commenting on Brookner's *Latecomers* (Pantheon, 1989), Penelope Rowlands notes: "Her plots move so slowly as to seem surreptitious. By the end of one of her novels, the reader may have an odd sensation of feeling moved and yet not quite sure what's taken place" (Rowland 5). Plots of a very different kind characterize works that move at a rattling pace. Both types of plots – results of two different styles of pacing – merit study and meet the different demands of readers.

Movement of Plot Action

Tracing the movement of action in any plot can be illuminating, since action – an important ingredient of plot – is clearly visible in at least three stages of rising action, climax, and falling action.

Horizontal *versus* vertical movement

Maya Deren's classification of movement of plot details in film as horizontal or vertical helps us appreciate the two essential directions in which plots move in fiction and drama as well. The horizontal movement is forward and linear toward the story's anticipated end, satisfying the reader's curiosity as to what happens next. This unfolding of plot, the chief means of narrative pace, is subject to the limitations of time and space. The vertical dive, on the other hand, halts the forward movement. Ignoring time and space, it explores an idea or emotion. The emphasis shifts from "what" to "why" and "how." In these vertical dives, liberated from the constraints of time and space, characters unburden their souls, analyze their actions, weigh and consider their outcomes, and try to make some sense of life's enigmas. This vertical movement manifests itself in soliloquies of drama and reflective passages of fiction.

Classical movement of plot action

Plot movement is understood in another sense also. Most great tragedies, for instance, move from the tension of conflict through *catharsis* (Greek word for cleansing) of turmoil to the hero's apotheosis in the classical tradition. Applying this structural principle to *Hamlet*, we notice that the play's earlier scenes are filled with nervous anxiety of all characters. The rantings and ravings of these earlier scenes give way to the comparatively tranquil last parts highlighted by Hamlet's conversation with the grave digger about the reality of death, his acquiescence in the flow of fate, and his final expression of faith in

> . . . a divinity that shapes our ends, Rough-hew them how we will. (V, ii,10-11)

This change in the play's action is also signaled and reinforced by smooth and peaceful rhythm of Hamlet's speech:

> There is special providence in the fall of a sparrow. . . . The readiness is all. (V, ii,211, 214)

Gone is the compulsive, emotionally charged earlier manner of his speech:

> O that this too solid flesh would melt,
> Thaw, and resolve itself into a dew,
> Or that the Everlasting had not fixed
> His canon 'gainst self-slaughter. O God, God,
> How weary, stale, flat, and unprofitable
> Seem to me all the uses of this world!   (Act I, sc. ii, 131-136)

At the end of the play, there is even a suggestion of Hamlet's apotheosis in Horatio's eulogy to the dying Hamlet:

> Now cracks a noble heart. Good night, sweet Prince,
> And flights of angels sing thee to thy rest.

In comedy the movement of plot action is toward reintegration and reunion. Misunderstandings and conflicts of the past give way to the new order that brings back into its folds, the deviating, isolated, and rebellious characters. The atmosphere is very much secular and social, not other-worldly and mystical-spiritual as in tragedy. Shaw's romantic comedy *Pygmalion* exemplifies these traits of comedy to some extent. The play's essential plot consists of the flower girl Eliza's winning Higgins' bet that he would transform her speech into that of a duchess within a few months.

Plot movement in individual scenes

This principle of movement of plot action has a parallel movement of thought, which can be used to analyze individual scenes. If we focus, for example, on Hamlet's soliloquy starting with "To be, or not to be: that is the question" (one of the play's vertical dives), we notice Hamlet's progress from suicidal thoughts and psychological turmoil to philosophic composure. In this process of self-debate, which a soliloquy often is, he comes to an understanding that scruples of conscience bind every thinking person, sometimes to the point of paralysis:

> Thus conscience does make cowards of us all,
> And thus the native hue of resolution
> Is sicklied o'er with the pale cast of thought,
> And enterprises of great pitch and moment,
> With this regard their currents turn awry,
> And lose the name of action. (Act III, sc. i, 89-94)

The movement of this soliloquy takes Hamlet from despair to resignation. Hamlet comes to know that conscience, not cowardice, holds back a thoughtful person from impulsive action. The principle used to analyze this soliloquy from *Hamlet* can be applied to any important speech in any work.

Tips for Plot Analysis

Plots give us details that make cause-and-effect connections in the story's events and actions. Conventionally, plots also offer us insights into characters' motives for their actions in order to make thematic suggestions, such as connecting characters' happiness or unhappiness with their actions. Appreciating literary conventions requires vigilance on the reader's part. Perceiving the reasons behind an author's arrangement of scenes, use of plot-setting devices, pacing and placing of events, and opening and closing sections of a work contribute to our understanding of a work's craft and substance.

To see how various plot components are interrelated and to appreciate their role in theme formulation, the best way is to analyze the plot of a complete literary work. To that end, let us read a short story classic "A Rose for Emily" by William Faulkner (1897-1962). You can read the story online: http://flightline.highline.edu/tkim/Files/Lit100_SS2.pdf

As you read the story, note how Faulkner uses elements, such as setting, conflict, foreshadowing, chronology, and climax, to plot the story effectively.

Also read the questions given at the end of this chapter. One question gives you a link to Faulkner's own interpretation of the story. Read it carefully. If you can manage, it would also be helpful to watch the 27-minute long film adaptation of the story, directed by Lyndon Chubbuck, produced by Kaye Dyal, and starring Angelica Huston as Emily Grierson and John Carradine as Homer Baron.

Faulkner's Plotting Skill in "A Rose for Emily"
Sample essay by the author of this book

In this sample essay on Faulkner's plot in "A Rose for Emily," the observations of an interpretive nature are italicized to distinguish them from plot summary. Knowledge of principles gained from this plot analysis can be applied to other literary works. When analyzing any plot, relevant selected parts of the story can be retold with the reader's interpretive comments to show how those parts are organized.

Faulkner divides the story into five sections of almost uniform length, giving the work an impressive symmetry.

Part I

Opening with Emily's death, *the story is told in reverse chronology*. Emily's family lineage and the stubborn and "coquettish decay" of her house are described. *Her arrogance and dismissal of laws with impunity* are accepted by the older generation of Mayor Col. Sartoris. However, *the clash between the old and the new* occurs when the younger generation of mayors and aldermen confront Emily with their insistence that she pay her taxes. "I have no taxes in Jefferson" is all she tells the delegation, dismissing them with hauteur.

Part II

Faulkner opens the second part with the mention of an offensive smell around Emily's house – *an important clue whose impact is strengthened incrementally in the events the story unfolds*. The mysterious smell starts soon after Homer Barron, "her sweetheart – the one believed would marry her – had deserted her." Here again, as in the story's opening, *the end is given before the stages in the process are delineated, suggesting that somehow the narrator is anxious to impose a clarifying focus on Emily's story*. After her desertion, she is hardly ever seen by anyone, and the only sign of life around her house is the black man who does her errands and serves her faithfully. Too intimidated to confront Emily about the smell, the aldermen steal into her lawn and sprinkle lime to kill the foul-smelling odor. This part ends with the description of Emily's refusal to give up her father's body for three days after his death. *Emily's stature declines quickly from proud to pitiful*.

Part III

Part III describes the *vulnerability of the seemingly invincible Emily*. After her long illness, she looks "like a girl . . . sort of tragic and serene." Here the narrator picks up the details of the story of Emily and "her sweetheart," whose desertion of her was mentioned earlier. The construction company's foreman, the Yankee named Homer Barron, becomes Emily's companion, to the surprise of some and pitying disapproval of others – a southern aristocrat falling for a Northerner, a day laborer." In this climactic part of the story, she is described as "over thirty." As a plotting strategy, *Faulkner withholds from us further information about the Emily-Barron relationship*. We are not told what caused the souring of the relationship. Faulkner ends the chapter with Emily buying arsenic from a drug store.

71

Part IV

This part opens with the narrator's suggestion that Emily might have purchased the poison to kill herself because Homer Barron seemed interested not in Emily but in her aristocratic image. In view of the story's ending, *this apprehension of the townsfolk may be regarded as the false clue – a sort of red herring – to send the reader on the wrong trail.* We learn that Homer "liked men . . . drank with the younger men [and] . . . was not a marrying man." At this point in the story, *the plot becomes complicated with many possibilities, heightening suspense as to the outcome.*

When Emily goes to the jeweler and orders a "man's toilet set in silver, with the letters H.B. on each piece" and later buys men's clothing, the narrator and the town's people think that Emily is finally getting married. However, quite mysteriously, Homer vanishes. At the time when Emily seems to have been abandoned by Homer Barron and in need of our sympathy, *Faulkner introduces the detail about her giving lessons in china painting during her isolation. This detail about Emily's artistic talent gives her character a positive dimension.*

The story then lurches forward to Emily at age 74 at the time of her death with her hair turning "an even pepper-and-salt iron gray – *a detail that takes on immense importance when we read the story's concluding sentence in Part V.* This part of the story also mentions what may be considered her last act – *a defiant gesture of dismissal of what she might have considered the newfangled concept of "free postal delivery." She refused to have her house marked with metal numbers and a mailbox.*

Part V

The story's concluding part is a departure from the classical denouement (resolution) in that it unravels one tangled detail but creates a new complication. The mystery of Emily's lover Homer Barron's sudden disappearance is solved, but the story's concluding sentence leaves the reader not content but shocked. Let us first look at the disentanglement. After Emily's funeral, people notice a room that no one had seen in forty years. When the room is forced open, Homer's skeleton with its "fleshless grin" is found lying in bed "in the attitude of an embrace," with his collar and tie next to him "as if they had just been removed." The room had been "decked and furnished as for a bridal." The narrator, the other townsfolk, and the reader then understand the reason for Emily's purchase of poison. However, *the story's plot is so skillfully woven that its last sentence introduces yet another mystery as to Emily's bizarre necrophilia.* On a pillow next to Barron's skeleton "was the indentation of a head . . . [with] a long strand of iron-gray hair."

The story ends at this point physically but touches off numerous reverberations of thoughts and feelings – a trademark of effective plotting. The conclusion brings back to our minds the details about insanity in Emily's family, her desperate clinging to her father's dead body, and her vow never to yield! Faulkner frames the story with three deaths to enclose the plot details – that of Emily's father occurring a couple of years before Homer Barron's, and Emily's death happening nearly forty years afterward. The horror of how Emily might have spent those forty years dawns on us with the story's concluding sentence with the mention of what seems to be Emily's iron-gray hair on the pillow next to Barron's. The story's conclusion does not yield the feeling of contentment that is associated with classical denouement. On the contrary, it demonstrates E. M. Forster's idea of a good ending that opens out instead of closing in.

In the concluding part, the narrator makes a concentrated statement about the vanity of human arrogance and death's enduring reign. The words soon after the macabre description of Homer's skeleton in the "bridal" room are so well sculpted and so strategically placed that we may, with some validity, see in them the story's theme:

". . . now the long sleep that outlasts love, that conquers even the grimace of love, had cuckolded him . . . . upon him and upon the pillow beside him lay that even coating of the patient and biding dust."

Owing to Faulkner's way of arranging the story's details, the narrator's concluding comment comes to us as a successfully dramatized reality, not just an empty precept. The reason why "A Rose for Emily" has become such a classic is inherent not just in its themes relating to time and human nature but also because Faulkner has plotted the story with meticulous attention to maximize its effect through manipulation of chronology and by dropping hints as well as withholding information to heighten suspense and reader's involvement.

Plot Analysis of Longer Works

Plots of short stories can be discussed in their entirety because of their shorter length in comparison with novels and plays. The best way to appreciate an author's plotting skill in a longer work is to focus on just one scene to see how it relates to the whole, how it introduces or continues development of a theme, and how it reveals and tests a character, to name just a few angles of approach.

Analyzing a scene

Since scenes are the basic building blocks of plot, focusing on just one scene to analyze its function would certainly clarify several of the important points listed above. The duel scene from *Hamlet* would serve the purpose. This play by Shakespeare is held up as a famous example of an actionless play. However, even in this so-called all-talk-no-action play, we can identify three notable acts, out of which the duel between Hamlet and Laertes is the longest piece of sustained action. The other two significant acts are Hamlet's unintended murder of Polonius and his very last act of killing Claudius just before his own death.

Analyzing the duel scene, we notice that it has a carefully planned preface in which the long-winded but unintelligent courtier Osric brings to Hamlet an invitation from Claudius: Hamlet is to participate in a so-called friendly sporting duel with Laertes. In the close to 80 lines of conversation between Hamlet and Osric – with Horatio putting in just a few words – the mindlessness of political sycophants and opportunists like Osric is revealed.

The impact of Osric's offer on Hamlet is then revealed. After ridiculing Osric and his class to his heart's content, Hamlet has a disquieting intuition, of which he tells Horatio: "But thou wouldst not think how ill all's here about my heart – but it is no matter" (V,ii,185-186). When Horatio suggests informing Claudius that Hamlet does not feel well enough to participate in the sporting event planned by Claudius, Hamlet gives his famous "The readiness is all" speech, literally accepting the ultimate assignment of each individual – being ready for death. Hamlet's words do not sound like needless preoccupation with death because Shakespeare has so skillfully paralleled them with the conspiracy between Claudius and Laertes that would allow absolutely no possibility of escape for Hamlet.

The action-filled duel scene is among the most celebrated duels in drama. It reveals to the court and people of Denmark what the audience/reader has known all along about Claudius's criminal actions and plans and the gullible but impetuous Laertes' role in them. Before the duel scene ends, it is not just the two duelers who die but also Gertrude and Claudius, the death of Claudius at the hands of Hamlet being the most satisfying event for the audience, whose roller-coaster ride of emotions can finally subside in a sense of justice rightly served. However, there are seldom any neat resolutions in life, and the realist in Shakespeare makes the conclusion of the duel scene heart-wrenching by including two reconciliations – one between the dying Laertes and Hamlet and the other between Gertrude and Hamlet. These resolutions are somewhat satisfying to the audience but leave behind a lingering regret about the unfulfilled possibilities – about what might have been *versus* what actually happened.

Shakespeare's skillful designing of the duel scene thus becomes much more than an action-packed release of the cumulative pent-up frustrations of the characters and audience alike. It also becomes a vehicle to motivate us to complete each individual's required assignment of being ready for death.

Experimenting with Plot Design

Creating a missing scene

To appreciate the intricacies of plot design, it would be instructive to create a missing scene or to envision an opening or ending that is different from the existing one in a literary work or a movie. This exercise, which is somewhat like analyzing the esthetics of omission, will quickly sensitize you to an important part of plot design, whereby credible scenes are created. You may use dialogue with stage directions if you are creating a missing scene from a play or a movie. In the case of fiction, you may combine narration with dialogue. The scene should be compatible with the mood, tone, and language of the context in which it is created. Pay attention to matters of consistency and appropriateness of the characters' words and actions. Your creative exercise may be on any work. For example, to share with the reader an insight into the minds of Claudius and Gertrude in Shakespeare's *Hamlet*, you may attempt this exercise:

Write a dialogue of 10 to 15 lines between Gertrude and Claudius (in the form of poetry, prose, or a mixture of both), focusing on the following situation that is not dramatized in the play: After King Hamlet is killed by Claudius, the murderer tries to court and seduce Gertrude into marrying him. In creating this missing scene with dialogue, give Claudius and Gertrude words and actions that suit their personalities. You can reveal characters' actions and reactions in parentheses after their names, but use this method sparingly.

Changing the original ending

Another way to understand plot design is by playing the author by changing the concluding scene of any literary work or film. This exercise involves describing the original ending, making the change, and then giving your reasons for the change. You may either create a new ending or describe the ending that you would like along with your reasons for the change. If you rewrite an ending, remember to suit it to the tone and diction of the original. You can make it a creative writing exercise or simply explain what ending you would have liked better and why

Transition to the Next Chapter "Style"

With the background knowledge that this chapter has offered, you should be able to analyze and appreciate plot development and design of any work of art. After *topics* and *themes*, *characters*, and *plot*, the next major literary element to be studied to conclude Part One is that of style. As we make the important transition from plot to style in the next chapter, it is important to remember that good plots blend the style of a literary work with its content.

Exercises to Test Your Mastery of Chapter Three

Timed Self-Test Exercises
(Allow 50 minutes for each item)

To self-test your mastery of this chapter, you should be able to write the first draft or an outline for a 500- to 750-word essay on any one of the following plot-related items.

For items 1 through 16, choose any novel, movie (with literary merit), or play with your instructor's approval. Support your answers with examples from the literary work/movie.

1. Give a definition of plot and list its essential components with reference to a specific short story, novel, play, or movie.

2. Determine whether the plot of a selected work is episodic, organic/classical, melodramatic, inert, or intuitive.

3. Discuss various kinds of conflicts – individual *versus* society, individual *versus* nature, contrary forces warring within a person, or any such internal or external conflict. Demonstrate at least one of those conflicts with reference to a specific literary work.

4. Discuss any three structural devices that an author/film-maker has used to hold the plot together.

5. Focusing on any specific part, describe the movement of plot action – from despair to affirmation, from joy to resignation, horizontal movement, vertical movement, etc.

6. Comment on the effectiveness of an author's sequencing of scenes.

7. To appreciate the complexity of plotting, draw a time-line highlighting the various stages and the sequence of events along with causal links between them in any work. In this chapter, my essay on Faulkner's "A Rose for Emily" would serve as a sample.

8. Change the ending of any literary work or movie, or create a scene that is missing from a work. Give your reasons for the change/addition. Read this chapter's concluding section on "Experimenting with Plot Design" for help.

9. According to the classical concept, a plot should be constructed so tightly and with its various parts so interdependent that any transposition of scenes or removal of any scene would cause the entire network of the plot to collapse. Identify any such plot in a literary work or movie. Demonstrate with details how the work's various plot-components unite and sustain one another.

10. Select a scene from a literary work or movie to discuss how it introduces a topic, develops it into a theme, reveals a character, and serves a strategic function to control the audience response.

11. Identify the plot-structuring device in a literary work or movie that has not been discussed in this chapter. Add supporting details.

12. Evaluate an author's/film-maker's observance or disregard of the unities of action, time, and place in a selected work. Mention the gain or loss consequent to the observance or disregard of the unities.

13. Evaluate an author's use of flashback, parallelism, repetition, irony, or any other stylistic element as a plot-structuring device in any work of your choice. (These and other elements of style are discussed in the next chapter.) You may return to this question after you have read the next chapter.

14. Comment on an author's use of setting to organize the plot details.

15. Select a literary work or movie to discuss the author's/director's use of chance, coincidence, or accident. How does it affect the credibility of the plot?

16. Identify the turning point (climax) in any literary work and comment on the effectiveness of its placement.

17. Assume that you are writing a short story that is based on an event in the area where you live. Keep the balance between making your account engaging as well as truthful. After finishing your narrative, analyze it to determine if what you wrote is merely a story, or does it have a plot? Make use of E. M. Forster's distinction between plot and story given at the beginning of this chapter. Support your analysis with details from your narrative.

Timed Self-Test Topics

(Allow 30 minutes for each item)

To demonstrate your mastery of the contents of this chapter, you should be able to write from a paragraph to a page (about 250 words) of essential information on each of the following plot-related terms.

1. Definitions of plot

2. Essential plot components

3. Varieties of plot

4. Stages of action: exposition, development, climax, denouement

5. Cause-and-effect link between events

6. Use of chance/coincidence, flashback, and foreshadowing

7. Primary and secondary plot-structuring devices

8. Use of any specific item from a story's details (including a stylistic element) as structural devices

9. Arrangement and order of plot details in any specific literary work or movie

10. Appropriate openings and conclusions

11. The story's movement in a sequence-driven direction

12. Horizontal *versus* vertical movement of plot action

13. Movement of plot action in classical tragic drama

14. Movement of plot action in comedy

15. Management of narrative pace

16. Changes in the nature of dramatic action – from extroverted to introverted

17. The three unities (of action, time, and place).

C H A P T E R   F O U R

STYLE

Plot and *style* go together. In fact, some of the elements of style, such as parallelism, irony, contrast, the esthetics of omission, repetition, and flashback (to be discussed in this chapter) are often used as plot-structuring devices. Similarly, setting in terms of place and time is a part of plot, but *how* and *why* an author uses a particular setting is a matter of style. Along with characters and plot, style is an element that is present in every literary work. Of these three elements that complement one another and play a role in theme embodiment, style evaluation and grasping themes through style analysis are considered challenging forms of literary interpretation.

If not approached in the right spirit, teaching and learning the subtle intricacies of style can be a tedious undertaking. Gerald Graff tells us in *Professing Literature* that at one time professors of philology had "made the course in English prose style so 'heartily despised' that Berkeley students engaged for some years in annual burning of the textbook, Minto's *Manual of English Prose Literature*" (Graff 102). Besides avoiding book burning rituals of the kind described above, the discussion of style in this chapter is designed to give students the background knowledge and tools to appreciate and enjoy style in literature. Style conscious readers can also become style conscious writers by using tried and tested elements of style to make their own writing more effective.

Unfortunately, study of style does not receive adequate attention in literature courses, which tend to be content-based. Style analysis is regarded as too daunting a task for students. The difficulty of this aspect of literature is undeniable, but so is its importance. Since good writers take great pains in crafting their works, sensitivity to their use of language resources can bring us deeper understanding and greater esthetic pleasure. Moreover, since style is inseparable from content, inattention to style also means experiencing literature incompletely. Since language is the tool of thinking, neglect of style affects the quality of our thoughts as well.

In his review of Francine Prose's book *Reading Like a Writer: A Guide for People Who Love Books and for Those Who Want to Write Them*, Charles May captures well Prose's emphasis on the importance of style in literature:

". . . to be a good reader, one must be knowledgeable of, and sensitive to, those elements of writing that constitute the craft: words, sentences, character, dialogue and details. . . . Subject matter is not all that important, and what the writer most often wants to do is write great sentences" (May E6).

Without fully accepting Prose's view of priority of style over content, we can still understand the importance of style as an element in literature.

Definitions of Style

Perhaps the first step in the study of style should be getting rid of the notion that style is an embellishment. We should look upon style more as an instrument than a dress of thought. Defined simply, style is the *way* or *manner* in which authors communicate their ideas. *What* authors say relates to *content*. *How* they say it relates to *style*. Topics, ideas, feelings, characters, and events make up the *content* of literary works; the *way* the content is created belongs to *style*. Thus the plot of a literary work holds its content, and the way an author constructs the plot has to do with style. While characters are a part of *content*, characterization – the *way* an author creates characters (by giving them distinct idiosyncrasies of speech, appearance, and values) – belongs to style.

Looking at some articulate definitions of style would enhance our understanding of the concept and importance of style.

1. Donald Hall gives a clear definition of style in *The Modern Stylists*: "Style is the manner of a sentence, not its matter. But the distinction between manner and matter is a slippery one, for manner affects matter." Hall rightly points out that if we change Caesar's "I came; I saw; I conquered" to "I arrived on the scene of the battle; I observed the situation; I won the victory," the matter or content remains the same, "but Caesar's tone of arrogant dignity disappears in the pallid pedantry of the longer version. It is impossible to say that the matter is unaffected. But, let us say that this kind of difference, in the two versions of Caesar, is what we mean by style" (Hall 1).

2. In Truman Capote's view, style "is the mirror of an artist's sensibility – more so than the content of his work."

3. Rene Wellek's words from *Style in Language* offer the broadest definition of style:

   "Style may include all devices of speech that convey the attitude of the speaker . . . and all devices that aim to achieve rhetorical ends, all devices for securing emphasis or explicitness . . . [–] metaphor, rhetorical figures, syntactical patterns. Clearly, style embraces all speech and all writing" (Wellek 147).

4. Marshall McLuhan's often-quoted statement – "the medium is the message" – goes beyond implying a close connection between style and substance, between form and content, to the extent that in his view an author's style (or medium) *is* the message. Whether one agrees with McLuhan or not, one can see the connection between the manner (style) in which an idea is expressed and the matter (substance) of that idea.

5. In *Prose Style*, James Bennett shows how individual style is impacted by cultural environment:

   "While a good style is always individual, if the artist is to project the vision that is uniquely his, at the same time it is always conditioned by his culture, the choices available in his language in his time and place. Through the mating of a writer's individual style with styles of the past, a 'new style' is born" (Bennett ix).

Having looked at some of the concepts and definitions of style, we are now ready to focus on the study of literary style.

Do Authors *Choose* Their Stylistic Elements?

There is no agreement on the extent to which authors consciously *choose* artistic devices in literature. However, it is safe to assume that they choose their settings, atmosphere, and similar elements to provide a tentative framework for their creation. At this stage, an author's mind may be functioning at a conscious level. It is later that the powers of the unconscious take over, yet the conscious design tends to emerge now and then to meet the reader's need for clarity. Authors cannot afford to neglect this need since they are writing for others to read their work.

Comments by a few well-known authors would be helpful here. Edgar Allan Poe, a famous practitioner of the short story, supports the view of *design* in literature: The short-story writers have in their minds a definite effect that they intend to achieve, and in "the whole composition there should be no word written, of which the tendency, direct or indirect, is not to the one pre-established design" (Fallon 48). Without agreeing with Poe completely, one can still acknowledge the presence of a conscious design in works of art, according to which the function of every stylistic element, even every word, is to contribute toward an intended effect.

"The truth is, surely," said the novelist Zadie Smith, "that every variety of literary style attempts to enact in us a way of seeing, of reading, and this is never less than an ethical strategy" (*The Guardian*, Nov. 1, 2003). A slightly different emphasis in the novelist E. L. Doctorow's words from his book *Creationists* is also helpful in understanding the creative process:

"No matter what your plan or inspiration, or trembling recognition for an idea that you know belongs to you, the strange endowment you set loose by the act of writing is never entirely under your control." He acknowledges that creation is a mysterious thing: "And of course, finally, something comes off the pages that defies analysis" (Skloot E6)

As for the connection of *style* with *theme*, it may well be at the level of the unconscious. In an interview, E. L. Doctorow offers some insights into the mysterious ways in which authors come to their styles. When asked if he was aware at the time of writing his novel *Ragtime* that he was simulating in prose the actual ragtime music, Doctorow replied: "Well, that sort of thing can never be a conscious intention. I wasn't really aware until it was pointed out to me that *Ragtime* suggested the rhythm and form of the rag in its prose" (Doctorow 5). When asked whether he was trying to make the very form of his novel *Loon Lake* express its theme, Doctorow said:

"In the case of *Loon Lake*, I didn't realize either that what I wanted finally was for the book itself to be the lake. But a very good friend of mine, a wonderful reader and critic, said, 'Why, the way you tell the story, shifting time and place and voice, makes it just like the lake – shimmering, and reflecting, and refracting, and changing light and color.' And I said, 'Of course. That's what I must be doing'" (Doctorow 5).

Whereas novelists may move at a leisurely pace and let their artistic designs slowly emerge from the narration, short story writers, moving with much greater speed do not have that luxury. Their compressed time necessitates a different style.

What may help us understand the presence of at least some conscious design in literary style is the use of cinematographic devices in film, which are much more deliberate than their counterpart in literature. Leo Braudy's following words are revealing:

"When we are faced with a film, we should . . . assume everything has meaning because everything is the result of a choice – to write, cast, stage, act, shoot, edit, or score in a particular way – all dictated by formal necessities that in another art could seem disjunctive and fragmentary" (Braudy 9).

We may never come to an agreement about the extent to which an author's style is the result of conscious choice, but the preceding look at the writing process has offered some valid insights: In its journey beyond the embryonic stage, exactly when does an idea become full-limbed is not known. It is, however, obvious that for its satisfactory development, an idea needs nourishment of language. The quality of the idea, thus, is determined, to a large extent, by the quality of the language that sustains it.

Appreciating Literary Style

It is neither necessary nor possible to make a complete list of stylistic elements used in literature. Some stylistic practices do not even have a name. An author's choice of the title of his or her work, for example, is in itself an element of style and is significantly connected to the content. An example is Faulkner's "A Rose for Emily," in which the title suggests an offering made to the main character Emily. Since no rose is mentioned in the story, the title becomes a means of not only expanding the content but also challenging the reader into attention about the meaning of "rose" in the story's title: What does the rose symbolize, and who offers it to Emily? Other such nameless devices are an author's choice of characters' names (for example Meursault, meaning silly death in French), leaving a character nameless (the male character has no name and is called simply "the American" in Hemingway's "Hills Like White Elephants"), the way of opening and closing a work, and use of more dialogue or more narration. All of these practices have no names but are part of an author's style and may have close links with content. When discussing such "nameless" stylistic elements, we can simply describe what they are before evaluating them.

The protean nature of style is apparent from the fact that it has shared as well as unique features from one genre to another. Style in poetry is different from that of prose fiction and drama, and style in works of nonfiction tends to have its own uniqueness. In spite of this endless variety in style, there are some elements that are common to all forms of writing and serve similar ends. The brief discussion of frequently used stylistic elements in this chapter is by no means complete and is meant only for convenient reference.

A cardinal principle to be kept in mind when evaluating style is that the effectiveness of an element of style is determined by the naturalness and spontaneity with which it appears in a given context. In exercising this standard, the words of Virginia Woolf, Hemingway, and William Butler Yeats can be our guide. Woolf astutely diagnoses the reason for abuse of style: "The temptation to decorate is great where the theme may be of the slightest" (Woolf 298). Hemingway's words on the same topic are an apt reminder of the true *versus* false style:

"No matter how good a phrase or a simile he [any author] may have[,] if he puts it in where it is not absolutely necessary and irreplaceable[,] he is spoiling his work for egotism. Prose is architecture, not interior decoration" (Hemingway 191).

The word style, unfortunately, has become associated with ornamentation. Effective style, however, is so charged with its content that it never intrusively draws attention to itself. William Butler Yeats's words from his poem "Adam's Curse" reveal the paradoxical nature of writing: The goal of putting in great effort in writing is to achieve the effect of effortlessness that characterizes good writing.

> A line will take us hours maybe;
> Yet if it does not seem a moment's thought,
> Our stitching and unstitching has been naught.

Analyzing Style in Literature

After the preceding discussion of definitions of style and the nature of creative process, we are better equipped to analyze style and reduce the mystery that surrounds it. Clearly, acquiring the ability to appreciate style takes time. Proceeding methodically can make the task easier. The format for style appreciation consists of three steps: (1) identifying the element of style, (2) giving an example from the work being discussed, and (3) commenting on the function/effectiveness of the element of style.

Of the three items listed above, determining and evaluating the function of an element of style is the most difficult part. It may help to remember that an author's choice of stylistic elements may serve any of the following and similar functions:

1. Dramatizing and reinforcing a theme

2. Creating a mood

3. Revealing and developing a character

4. Jolting the reader into a new awareness or giving the reader new eyes to see an apparently everyday occurrence

5. Bringing to the reader dramatic illumination of a complex idea or feeling

6. Reversing the expected response through situational irony

7. Adding sensory dimensions to the intellectual content through imagery and figurative language

8. Adding extra layers of meanings through verbal or dramatic irony

9. Giving delight through ingenious formations of phrases, sometimes transporting the reader to a different realm with the magic of words and sounds.

When reading literature for style analysis, paying attention to and taking notes on the following and similar features is necessary.

- Thematically significant flashbacks, flashforwards, arrangements of scenes, imagery, symbolism, and allusion
- Use of dramatic as well as verbal irony, understatement, paradox, repartee, sarcasm, and similar devices in the dialogue. (In addition to entertaining us with their artistry, these elements of style are also often connected with themes and topics.)
- Any striking and effective words, phrases, images, sounds, and any other notable elements of style, such as symbol, allusion, analogy, personification, and figurative language
- Functions of the stylistic features that you choose to discuss

Such notes will lead to impressions that will later be of great help in interpretation.

Maintaining Correct Focus

When analyzing style, it is necessary to keep your focus on the *way* authors express an idea or a feeling, not on *what* they are expressing. To maintain this focus, treat authors as active makers of their work who use stylistic elements to elicit desired responses from the reader. Here are some examples of the ways to improve your focus.

Example of vague focus: The allusion to *Hamlet* in Eliot's poem is a reminder of Prufrock's indecisiveness.

Example of improved focus: Eliot selects his allusions carefully to make them serve specific functions. His allusion to Hamlet, for example, dramatizes and puts into sharper focus Prufrock's inability to make up his mind (just like Hamlet in Shakespeare's play)

Comment. In the first example, the allusion just happens. In the improved focus of the second example, the poet is shown to be choosing the allusion to develop a theme and reveal character.

Style-Theme Connection

Besides playing a role in sculpting plot and characters, style sometimes functions as the primary means to suggest, reinforce, and embody themes. William Faulkner's choice of images of "tarnished" objects in "A Rose for Emily," for example, strengthens the theme of decay of the Southern aristocracy. Hemingway's setting (an African jungle) in "The Short Happy Life of Francis Macomber" helps embody the themes of fear, danger, and courage, whereas his detached, matter-of-fact tone feeds the theme of petrification of feelings that afflicts the story's characters. Elements of style, however, have other functions besides theme embodiment. Later in this chapter, the section on "Elements of Style Common to All Literary Works" contains a detailed discussion of this topic.

After this general introduction, it is necessary to break down style into three categories for easier comprehension:

- Style in drama and fiction
- Style in poetry
- Nonfiction prose style, which relates to students' own writing (covered in Chapter Eight on "Revising")

ELEMENTS OF STYLE OFTEN USED IN DRAMA AND FICTION

To evaluate style in drama and fiction, those elements are selected that, like the plot-structuring devices, impact the entire work, not just a part of it. Since *styling* and *plotting* do mean the *way* a work is put together, style's connection with plot is reiterated in the discussion of the following six elements that are shared by both plot and style: the esthetics of omission, dramatic and situational irony, refrain-like repetition, setting and atmosphere, foreshadowing, and parallelism.

1. The Esthetics of Omission

To meet the challenge of inclusion/exclusion of details and to communicate important themes, authors sometime rely on omission, whereby they emphasize a point by conspicuously leaving it out. This element belongs both to plot and to an author's style. For this reason, it may be considered a theme-embodying feature of both plot and style. If a scene seems to be inconclusive and fragmentary, we should try to see a connection between the fragmented style and the author's thematic concern. Using this method, authors communicate ideas by withholding the expected information.

In Camus' *The Stranger*, for example, Meursault's real reason for going to bed without supper is not what he says but what he hides. He says that he went without food because he had to get up early the next morning to go to work and that he was not hungry. However, we know the real reason: Meursault has heard his neighbor Salamano crying over his dog's disappearance. For some reason, he admits, it reminded him of his recently deceased mother. Meursault refuses to make any connection between the two events – his hearing the old man crying and his going to bed without supper. However, the author's use of this style of esthetics of omission invites the reader to fill in the missing details.

To take another example, at the end of *The Great Gatsby*, Fitzgerald uses omission by withholding from us the narrator Nick Carraway's motive for not telling the truth that it was Daisy, not Gatsby, who was driving the car that hit and killed Myrtle. This omission irritates the reader momentarily but forces us to think deeper for possible reasons for Nick's silence on such a crucial issue. We speculate that perhaps Nick wanted to be true to his friend Gatsby's spirit and did what Gatsby himself would have done in that situation, that is, taking the blame for Myrtle's death to protect Daisy. Some readers, coming to a different inference, may feel that Nick must have realized the futility of trying to tell the truth when he knew that he did not have a chance to convince anyone because Tom Buchanan and Daisy were just too powerful to be questioned even in their lies. Nick, therefore, had to take refuge in silence and withdrawal from the scene. Fitzgerald's omission of key details that are expected by the reader thus has the effect of enriching the narrative and eliciting greater reader involvement.

Another form of omission many authors favor is leaving the work's central conflict unresolved, thus empowering readers to become co-authors to create their own conclusions. In Hemingway's "Hills Like White Elephants," for example, there is an apparent conflict and an unstated deeper conflict. Almost the entire story is in the form of dialogue with very little narration, as if Hemingway refuses to hold the reader's hand. From the conversation between the man and the girl, we gather that she would not like to abort the baby she is carrying, whereas the man is insistent that abortion is necessary for their relationship to continue as before. Hemingway does not give us the *real* reasons why they feel the way they do, and the story ends without a neat resolution. Underneath their surface disagreement, there seems to be a deeper one, but we are not sure what it is. What heightens our suspense is the uncertainty whether they are traveling together, or is it the parting of their ways.

By using a railway station in Spain for the story's setting and compressing the couple's important conversation in the short time span before the train's imminent arrival, Hemingway has maximized the effect of his esthetics of omission. He leaves us hungering for more of the couple's conversation in the hope that they can resolve their conflict to their mutual satisfaction. The objectivity and sparseness of the narrative makes it difficult to come to a clear conclusion about the narrator's position. Just the fact that the story's title "Hills Like White Elephants" is based on a phrase used by the girl gives us a hint of the author's partiality for her, but this conclusion is moot.

2. Dramatic and Situational Irony

Issues of structure, organization, and style sometimes become so closely interconnected that it is difficult to see them as separate elements. If, for instance, we perceive that *Hamlet's* plot structure derives from a series of crimes committed by Claudius to gain and retain sovereignty, the play's action becomes an illustration of both dramatic and situational irony. In dramatic irony, the character does not know the full implications of what he or she is doing. In situational irony, what happens is the opposite of what was expected. With each step that Claudius takes and with each crime that he commits, he feels he is strengthening his hold on his unlawfully and immorally acquired position of power (dramatic irony). However, the truth, unknown to him, is that the noose around his neck becomes tighter with every step he takes to consolidate his position until his final, pathetic but well-deserved end that he had never expected (situational irony). The play's ending is also an illustration of situational irony because neither Claudius nor Hamlet survives, and the kingship passes to Fortinbras of the neighboring country of Norway. In this example, the stylistic element of situational irony becomes a plot-structuring device.

Kate Chopin uses dramatic irony effectively in "The Story of an Hour." The doctors and other characters in the story think that Louise died because her ailing heart could not bear the shock of joy on seeing her husband alive. Through the author's use of dramatic irony, however, the reader knows more than the characters. Soon after she hears the news of her husband's death in a railroad accident, Louise starts analyzing the quality of her married life. Even though she mourns her loss, she feels that the death of her husband will allow her the freedom to live her life the way she would like – a luxury denied to her during her marriage. When the news of her husband's death turns out to be false and he appears before Louise, she dies. The reader who thinks that her death was caused by the shock of pain, not of joy may resent the failure of characters in the story to recognize Louise's marital oppression and the true cause of her death.

Dramatic irony at the end of this story thus may make some readers feel that since wrongs, such as Louise's suffering, go unnoticed, there is little chance of mending the problem. In this way, this stylistic and plot-structuring device becomes a powerful instrument to make people question the veracity of what they are told and whets their desire to take corrective action.

As a plot-designing strategy, dramatists use dramatic irony in which the words spoken by a character have one meaning for the speaker but a very different meaning for the better-informed audience/reader. In Sophocles' *Oedipus the King*, Oedipus keeps insisting that he will find and punish the murderer of King Laius, not realizing that he himself has been that murderer in a chance encounter. His pursuit of himself and his eventual self-conviction and self-punishment make the play a wrenching tragedy. Use of the ambiguous language of dramatic irony keeps alive the possibility of the hero's victory – a flicker of hope – even when the protagonists go to their inevitable doom. Once again *Oedipus the King* offers a good example. In that play, until the very end, there is a possibility that Oedipus may escape the terrible fate prophesied about him by the oracle. Jocasta keeps telling him (and us indirectly) that oracles are not to be trusted. Through dramatic irony, Sophocles gives Oedipus and other characters hope that he is running away from his terrible fate while, in fact, he has been galloping toward it all along.

3. Repetition of Key Plot Details

To organize as well as connect various sections, authors use the strategy of repeating a key plot detail. The opening, middle, and concluding sections of Manto's short story "Odor" exemplify this stylistic element of repetition that also functions as a plot-structuring device. We notice how the monsoons – the patter of rain drops on quivering pipal leaves – function to hold together the plot details as well as to signal the passage of time. The story opens with this sentence: "It was again the monsoon season." Near the middle of the story, the narrator tells us: "It was again the season of rains." A little later, we are again reminded: "The monsoons were back again." The same refrain introduces the story's last section: "It was the same season of the monsoons." Manto's use of flashbacks of the monsoon season that bring the protagonist (Randhir) the achingly intense memory of his encounter with the Ghatan girl not only holds the narrative together but also keeps the emotion at a hightened level throughout this tale of obsessive, nostalgic longings.

Both E. M. Forster (in *A Passage to India*) and Albert Camus (in *The Stranger*) use the harsh sunlight and heat to signal unpleasant occurrences and experiences for their major characters in several scenes. Evenings, nights, and water in the two novels are associated repeatedly with peace and harmony. In *A Passage to India*, for example, the major conflicts between characters occur in the hot weather. At one point the narrator says, "It was as if irritation exuded from the very soil" (Forster 78). In such weather, even evenings bring no relief:

"Never tranquil, never perfectly dark, the night wore itself away, distinguished from other nights by two or three blasts of wind, which seemed to fall perpendicularly out of the sky and to bounce back into it, hard and compact, leaving no freshness behind them: *the hot weather was approaching*" (Forster 100, italics added). Dr. Aziz, the novel's protagonist, is worried about the English lady Mrs. Moore's coming to visit India "just as the cold weather is ending" and warns her, "It will soon be so unhealthy for you!" (Forster 21) In *The Stranger*, the narrator describes his experience of attending his mother's funeral: "The sun was beginning to bear down on the earth and it was getting hotter by the minute. . . . with the sun . . . making the whole landscape shimmer with heat, it was inhuman and oppressive" (Camus 15).

In fact, Camus' protagonist Meursault attributes his totally unpremeditated and senseless murder to the "cymbals of sunlight crashing on my forehead" (Camus 59). His earlier descriptions leave no doubt that he took the fatal step toward the armed adversary because of the sensory befuddlement caused by the sun:

"the whole beach, throbbing in the sun, was pressing on my back . . . . my forehead especially was hurting me, all the veins in it throbbing under the skin. It was this burning, which I couldn't stand anymore, that made me move forward" (Camus 58-59).

Conversely, in both novels, it is away from the harmful sun that reconciliations occur. In Forster's novel, it is a night scene in which Mrs. Moore, a major character in the novel, has this mystical experience of unity:

"She watched the moon, whose radiance stained with primrose the purple of the surrounding sky . . . [the moon] was caught in the shawl of night together with earth and all the other stars. A sudden sense of unity, of kinship with the heavenly bodies, passed into the old woman . . . leaving a strange freshness behind" (Forster 29-30).

Camus' protagonist makes his peace with life and approaching death in a moving nocturnal scene:

". . . in that night alive with signs and stars, I opened myself to the gentle indifference of the world. Finding it so much like myself – so like a brother, really – I felt that I had been happy and that I was happy again" (Camus 122-123).

Water also functions as a positive symbol in both novels. The tranquil ending of Forster's novel takes place during the rainy monsoon season, and swimming in Camus' novel is almost like a vitalizing ritual.

By using the stylistic element of repeating these contrasting images of heat and coolness, of day and night, of dryness and water, the two authors are able to unify a great deal of plot details. These images also serve as a means of foreshadowing and suspense. Once this pattern is established, the readers automatically start anticipating pleasant or unpleasant experiences, depending on the images that are introduced.

What the monsoons do for Manto and what imagery accomplishes for Forster and Camus, repeating the use of poison does for Shakespeare in *Hamlet*. Shakespeare uses poison as a means to unify several sections of the play. The play's action opens with Claudius having already killed his brother, King Hamlet, by poisoning him. Prince Hamlet probes his uncle's guilty conscience by interjecting in the play within the play a scene that re-enacts Claudius's act of pouring poison in his sleeping brother's ear. Later, Claudius schemes with Laertes to kill Hamlet with a poisoned drink. At the end of the play, Hamlet forces Claudius to drink from the same poisoned chalice that he has prepared for Hamlet and which has already killed Gertrude. There are other uses of poison as well: Laertes puts lethal poison on the weapon that he uses in the so-called "friendly" duel with Hamlet that Claudius arranges to get rid of the Prince. That poison kills not only Hamlet but also Laertes. These poison-related scenes hold together a substantial part of the plot in *Hamlet.*

4. Setting and Atmosphere

These two elements go together. *Setting* is the source of atmosphere – the dominant mood and feeling a work evokes. Setting in terms of time refers to the period during which the action of a literary work takes place. Depending on the author's intentions, the setting of a literary work could be the remote or recent past, the present, or the distant future. Setting in terms of place refers to the physical location where the events of a work occur. It is not necessary that there be only one setting in a work. Authors use more than one setting to suit their purposes.

Both settings of time and place are associated with creating an atmosphere (predominant mood) that the author needs to sustain a theme. In his poem "Horses," Edwin Muir creates an anti-war and anti-machine atmosphere with the help of a futuristic setting when humanity's drive toward self-destruction has almost completely annihilated the world, and after making centuries of technological progress, we revert to the beginning, as the horses take the place of tractors and other machines.[1] For another example of setting serving a thematic function, Hemingway's story "The Short Happy Life of Francis Macomber" takes place in an African jungle, which helps embody the themes of fear, danger, and courage.

The setting of a work, especially when combined with symbolism (a term to be discussed later), plays a significant role in helping authors control and organize plot details. E.M. Forster's "The Other Side of the Hedge" is structured like a parable. The author presents the other side of the hedge as symbolic of paradise. *This* side in the story symbolizes our world of materialism, fierce competition, toil, and selfishness. However, Forster makes the two contrasting sides very close to each other. Through this ingenuity in the choice of setting, Forster makes us aware of our responsibility to take advantage of our proximity to a life of tranquil joy. This setting supports the theme that the possibility of happiness is always close by if we are willing to take the initiative and explore alternative possibilities beyond the narrow confines of self-centered toil.

---

[1] Read Muir's fascinating poem, using this link: www.poemhunter.com/poem/the-horses/

Atmosphere becomes more than mood when it serves as a gauge to register hidden motives of characters. Poe's setting in "The Cask of Amontillado" is a good example. The story's concluding scene takes place in the catacombs underneath the house of Montresor as he lures his intended victim Fortunato on the pretext of letting him taste the rare amontillado from the cellar. The damp and murky subterranean vaults – emblems of Montresor's mind – create an eerie atmosphere suited to the story's macabre end.

5. Foreshadowing

Another stylistic element relevant to the timing and arrangement of details is foreshadowing, which consists of the use of innuendoes to drop hints about events to come. This device, sometimes used in conjunction with irony, captures and retains the reader's/viewer's interest, rouses curiosity, and intensifies anticipation. In Sophocles' *Oedipus the King*, through foreshadowing in the form of an acrimonious exchange of words between Oedipus and the blind sage Tiresias early in the play, it is suggested that in spite of his best efforts, Oedipus may meet a tragic end.

In F. Scott Fitzgerald's *The Great Gatsby*, the narrator Nick Carraway's foreshadowing words create an uncomfortable sense of foreboding that Gatsby might fail in achieving his dream just as the builder of his home had failed before him:

"There was nothing to look at from under the tree except Gatsby's enormous house so I stared at it, like Kant at his church steeple, for half an hour. A   brewer had built it early in the 'period' craze, a decade before, and there was a story that he'd agreed to pay five years' taxes on all the neighboring cottages if the owners would have their roofs thatched with straw. Perhaps their refusal took the heart out of his plan to Found a Family – he went into an immediate decline. His children sold his house with the black wreath still on the door" (Fitzgerald 93).

6. Parallelism

Parallelism is another element that authors use frequently as a stylistic and structural tool. Elements of style sometime overlap, and the example of foreshadowing from *Gatsby* cited above is also an example of parallelism in that the fates of the two dreamers – the brewer and Gatsby – are parallel in their failure. Another example of parallelism from *Gatsby* is introduced in the context of showing how the situations of the extremely affluent Tom Buchanan and the pathetically poor George Wilson are identical (parallel): Wilson has just discovered that his wife had a liaison with another man just as Buchanan has found out about his wife Daisy's connection with Gatsby. In Nick's words, "I stared at him [Wilson] and then at Tom, who had made a parallel discovery less than an hour before – and it occurred to me that there was no difference between men, in intelligence or race, so profound as the difference between the sick and the well" (Fitzgerald 130-131).

An example of parallelism from *Hamlet* is the similar situations of Hamlet, Laertes, and Fortinbras. Fathers of these three characters are killed, and the sons are driven to take revenge. From this perspective, the play becomes a record of the three different ways in which these three characters approach the task of revenge. In the process, by implication, Shakespeare invites us to think for ourselves as to whose approach to revenge is least offensive.

Having understood the nature and functions of the six elements that plot and style share, we are now ready to look at style in poetry.

STYLE IN POETRY

All six elements of style, presented in the context of drama and fiction in the preceding section can also be used in poetry. Henry Reed's use of contrast, tone, and imagery in his poem "Naming of Parts," for example, is discussed in Chapter Five under "Hard to Explicate Works." However, there are some elements, such as allusion, that appear more frequently in poetry than in any other genre. They are used to compress and communicate meanings. It is allusion that is the focus of the section that follows. The poem used to elucidate the impact of allusion is Muhammad Iqbal's poem of truly universal meanings – "The Story of Adam" (text near the end of Chapter Thirteen).

The poem's speaker "I" represents the whole of humanity. Almost every line of the poem alludes to something of religious or historical significance, an understanding of which is essential to fully appreciate the poem's unusually rich content. The words "foreign lands" in line 2 refer to Adam in this world. His original home was Paradise. Therefore, the countries of this world are "foreign lands" to him.

The "story of the First Covenant" is an allusion to the Quran (7:172), according to which there was a covenant between human beings and God that there is only one God for all human beings. The "fiery cup of awareness" (line 5) is a reference to Adam's eating of the forbidden fruit from the tree of life in Paradise. The word "awareness" makes it a positive act in the tradition of "felix culpa," or happy mistake, in that it bestows him with a questioning and thinking mind. The "Fiery cup of awareness" that makes him uneasy serves both as allusion and double entendre. It alludes to Satan, who was created out of fire. It also means Adam's ardent desire to seek knowledge.

The Prophet Muhammad introduced the Abrahamic idea of monotheism and cleared the Kabah in Arabia of "stone idols" (line 10). "Mount Sinai" of line 12 is a reference to Moses in conversation with God on that mountain. The "eternal light in the folds of my sleeve" is also associated with Moses. According to the Bible and the Quran, God granted Moses the power to perform several miracles against the pharaoh. When Moses brought his hand out of his sleeve, it had shining light.

"By my own people I was hung on the cross" (line 14) is an obvious reference to the Crucifixion of Christ. The next line is both an allusion and a double entendre. It continues the reference to Christ's spirit ascending to Heaven. It may also refer to the Prophet Muhammad's Night Journey, during which he was taken up to Heaven and then brought back to earth. "Cave of Hira" is a reference to the cave, to which Prophet Muhammad used to retire for meditation before his prophethood. "I served the world its last cup of wine" may be alluding to Prophet Muhammad's words that he has completed the work of transmitting God's words to humanity – the same message that earlier prophets of Judaism and Christianity brought but which was forgotten with the passage of time. "Divine Song" (line 18) refers to the Hindus' holy book *The Bhagavat Gita* (The Song of the Lord). Buddhism came out of Hinduism but was rejected by the upper-caste Brahmins and, therefore, travelled to China and Japan.

At this point in the poem, there is a major shift from religious to secular knowledge. These two lines mark this transition:

> I saw the world composed of atoms,
> Contrary to what the men of faith taught. (Lines 22-23)

The history of religion as a reason for wars and bloodshed is captured in these two lines:

> By stirring up the conflict between reason and faith,
> I soaked in blood hundreds of lands. (Lines 24-25)

The poem packs the concluding lines with allusions to scientific discoveries that were based on reason, not on faith. In quick succession are mentioned the major breakthroughs in astronomy, the knowledge of gravity associated with Isaac Newton (1642-1727), Nicolaus Copernicus' discovery that it is the earth that revolves around the sun and not the other way about, the x-ray invention by the German physicist Wilhelm Conrad Rontgen, and the heroes of science, such as the Italian philosopher Giordano Bruno, who was burnt at the stake (1600) for refusing to retract statements that he believed to be true but which the Church found heretical and the astronomer and physicist Galilei Galileo (1564-1642), who was imprisoned by the Inquisition for advocating heliocentricity. Restless lightning alludes to electricity invented by the English scientist Michael Faraday (1791-1867).

All of these scientific discoveries and advancements made "this earth the envy of paradise" (line 33). This line exemplifies the classic reversal as well as situational irony. Instead of finding Adam miserable as a result of his Fall, the human mind has made the earth "the envy of paradise." Adam's expulsion from Paradise ends on a positive note. The poem ends with the speaker's discovery that to know "the secret of existence," all he had to do was look inward, into "the mansion of my heart." It is in such heart-based compassionate humanism that the secret of human unity and brotherhood lies.

The poet's extensive and effective use of allusion compresses maximum meaning in minimum space. The stylistic element of allusion requires that readers who are not familiar with the reference should look it up and thus expand their knowledge and comprehend the poet's meaning. One major benefit of style analysis – if carried out with correct emphasis – is that it brings the reader closer to the literary work's meaning.

ELEMENTS OF STYLE COMMON TO ALL LITERARY WORKS

After the study of style in fiction, drama, and poetry, we need to look at additional elements that are common to all forms of literature. This knowledge is necessary for interpretation and evaluation of literary works because elements of style often suggest, establish, and develop themes. Only the most commonly used elements are listed below, along with their definitions, examples, and functions usually associated with them. They are introduced according to their connection with each other, not alphabetically. For example, simile, metaphor, and analogy follow one another because all of them are comparisons of one kind or another. Not included here are the following stylistic elements that were discussed earlier in this chapter under "Style in Drama and Fiction": the esthetics of omission, dramatic and situational irony, refrain-like repetition, setting and atmosphere, foreshadowing, and parallelism. For more detailed information, consult *Handbook of Literary Terms: Literature, Language, Theory* by X. J. Kennedy, Dana Gioia, and Mark Bauerlein, M. H. Abrams' *A Glossary of Literary Terms*, or a similar book. Even though the listed elements are discussed primarily in their literary context, they can be replicated in your own writing with appropriate content.

Imagery

Presenting sensory experience through mostly iconic language, *imagery* is used to elicit appropriate tactile, visual, gustatory, aural, and olfactory responses that engage our senses of touch, sight, taste, hearing, and smell respectively. As direct expression of theme becomes less prevalent, imagery performs the important function of carrying the author's meanings indirectly through images. William Faulkner's choice of images of "tarnished" objects in "A Rose for Emily," for example, suggests the theme of decay of the Southern aristocracy.

In "Odor," Manto uses elements-related imagery to depict the protagonist's instinct-driven passion. Images of earth, water, and fire nourish this tale of Randhir's ever-burning, never-satisfied longing for the Ghatan girl, with whom he had spent a monsoon-drenched night. The Ghatan girl's odor, "was like the fresh smell of earth sprinkled with water." The "luminous gray clouds . . . had a strange glow like the one that had lurked in the Ghatan girl's breasts." Earth, water, and fire images are appropriate for this tale of passion.

Imagery appears in all literary genres but plays a central role in poetry. English poet Robert Browning's short love poem "Meeting at Night" is a notable example of concentrated imagery.

Meeting at Night

> The gray sea and the long black land;
> And the yellow half-moon large and low;
> And the startled little waves that leap
> In fiery ringlets from their sleep,
> As I gain the cove with pushing prow,
> And quench its speed i' the slushy sand.
>
> Then a mile of warm sea-scented beach;
> Three fields to cross till a farm appears;
> A tap at the pane, the quick sharp scratch
> And blue spurt of a lighted match,
> And a voice less loud, through its joys and fears,
> Then the two hearts beating each to each!"

> Robert Browning (1812-1889)

The title makes it clear that the poem is about a meeting of lovers at night. Instead of narrating the event as a report, the speaker recreates the images of sight (lines 1-4), sound (lines 6, 9, 11-12), and smell (line 7). There is a touch of personification in the image of sleepy waves that leap in "fiery ringlets." This image parallels the awakening passion of the two lovers, and the sound that dominates the poem at the end is that of their "hearts beating each to each!" Imagery is a broad term that often includes simile, metaphor, and analogy.

Simile

Simile is a comparison in which similarities are pointed out between two things that are essentially unlike. For a comparison to qualify as a simile, the two items compared should be drawn from different categories. For instance, if we compare a human being with another human, it will be a straightforward comparison, not a simile or metaphor. However, if we compare a human being with an animal or with an inanimate object, we will have a simile or metaphor. This description of a nocturnal scene uses simile: *From my vantage point at night, the lights on the San Francisco-Bay Bridge look like a string of pearls across the dark body of the Bay.*

Annie Dillard uses simile to describe a solar eclipse: "The sky snapped over the sun like a lens cover" (Dillard 168). In *The Great Gatsby*, Fitzgerald's simile captures the ambience of Gatsby's parties that plain language could not have done: "In his blue gardens men and girls came and went like moths among the whisperings and the champagne and the stars" (Fitzgerald 43). In his poem "On Seeing the Elgin Marbles," John Keats's simile captures intense, unsatisfied longing when the ailing speaker, sensing the brevity of his life span, says: he "must die like a sick eagle looking at the sky" (4-5).

Simile is a simple but powerful tool to vitalize writing and to cure dullness, monotony, and flatness of language. There is something magical about these little comparisons that bring about big effects.

Metaphor

Metaphor is also a comparison (an implied one) in which similarities are pointed out between two things that are essentially unlike. The only difference is that whereas simile uses words, such as *like, as, seem,* or their equivalents to make a comparison, in a metaphor such words are left out. Instead of saying that A is like B, A is *identified* with B. For this reason, metaphors are more condensed comparisons than similes. In its broadest definition, any statement that cannot be taken literally is a metaphor. An example would be this description of cascading papers: The pile on my desk is so high that even a slight shuffling of unevenly stacked papers can set off an avalanche. In *English Prose Style*, Herbert Read defines metaphor as "the swift illumination of an equivalence. Two images, or an idea and an image, stand equal and opposite, clash together and respond significantly surprising the reader with a sudden light" (Read 25). Paul Roberts metaphorically describes the role of words in writing: "The writer builds with words, and no builder uses raw material more slippery, elusive, and treacherous" (McCuen and Winkler 261).

Shakespeare is famous for using sustained metaphoric language, as in this example from Macbeth:

> Life's but a walking shadow
> A poor player that struts and frets his hour upon the stage

Similes and metaphors, when used well, bring freshness and concreteness to one's expression and transform fatigued language into lively expression. Best known for their pictorial effects they contribute to vividness and create refreshing linguistic surprise and drama in one's expression. They accomplish these effects by showing striking similarities between dissimilar things. On the effect of these two forms of figurative language, F. L. Lucas's words are illuminating:

"Why such magic power should reside in simply saying, or implying, that A is like B remains a little mysterious. . . . language often tends to lose itself in clouds of vaporous abstraction, and simile or metaphor can bring it back to concrete solidity; . . . such imagery can gild the gray flats of prose with sudden sun-glints of poetry" (McCuen and Winkler 625).

Analogy

An analogy is an extended comparison between two dissimilar items that are taken from different categories but have surprising similarities. It often begins with a simile or metaphor that is developed further to continue the comparison. The comparison proceeds from the easily recognizable known to the hard-to-grasp unknown that good analogies help us understand. Analogies can be short like the examples below, or they can continue the length of a paragraph or even a complete essay or poem. If the differences between the compared items are greater than their similarities, the analogy is considered false. The main function of an analogy is clarification of a complex point. If an idea seems abstract and hard to grasp, an analogy solves the problem. John Ciardi's following analogy (not an exact quotation), for example, elucidates the challenging concept of free will *versus* determinism: *Free will and determinism are like a game of cards. The hand we are dealt represents determinism, and the way we play those cards represents free will.*

The psychologist Carl Jung was able to explain the difficult concepts of the conscious and the unconscious parts of the human mind with the help of his familiar analogy: *The mind is like an iceberg. The conscious part is like the smaller, visible part of the iceberg, whereas the unconscious is comparable to the larger, hidden part.* This analogy can be developed further by equating the unconscious with the more dangerous, submerged-in-water and invisible part of the iceberg, whereas the conscious part is comparable to the smaller, visible, and thus less threatening part. Shakespeare's famous analogy compares life to a stage: "All the world is a stage. . . ." The first two examples started with a simile; Shakespeare's analogy started with a metaphor. The compared items were then further explained in all examples.

For our last example, let us enjoy Mina Shaughnessy's analogy that compares crocheting with writing:

"Much as the person who crochets creates, by a deft looping and interlocking of a single thread, a design of great intricacy, so the writer beginning with the thread of his idea slowly 'works' it into a paragraph or an article or a book. But for him, the pattern as well as the product is being developed as he goes. Each sentence, each turn of thought, leaves a deposit out of which the next sentence or thought is generated. . . . The writer, if he cannot know precisely where he is going, must nonetheless know where he has been so that he can mark the pattern of his thought for his reader" (Shaughnessy 244).

In this example, Shaughnessy starts with a simile that compares writing to crocheting, but she introduces several metaphors in the course of developing this comparison into an analogy. For one, "The writer begins sewing with the *thread of his idea*" is a metaphor (italicized words).

Analogies are harder to create than similes and metaphors, but since analogy is a very useful tool to clarify difficult points, the hard work is worth the trouble. One convenient method to acquire this skill is attempting to develop a simile or metaphor into an analogy. For example, the simile "The world is like a play" can be made into the following analogy: *The world is like a play whose author chose not to write the stage directions, thus leaving every player free to act out his or her role in accordance with the performer's understanding of the role.*

Synesthesia

Synesthesia is a special kind of metaphor that engages more than one sensory impression simultaneously through one image. *The air show was a V-shaped screeching.* This image combines two senses – visual and auditory – just as Fitzgerald does in this example from *The Great Gatsby*: *the orchestra was "playing yellow cocktail music"* (Fitzgerald 44). In the same novel, Fitzgerald compresses two senses, this time of touch and sight, in one image: *"the moon soaked with wet light his tangled clothes upon the floor"* (105). The phrase "wet light" is an example of synesthesia; so is the "bed of crimson joy" in William Blake's poem. He gives color to the feeling of joy.

Describing one kind of sensation in terms of another – shape as sound, sound as color, and sight as touch – synesthesia has the effect of intensifying and compressing an image just as imagery compresses ordinary language to generate extraordinary feelings.

Diction

No literary work can be created without language, and *diction* is the author's choice of words to obtain the desired effects. In order to be effective, words should have the right *connotations*, which are the meanings and feelings associated with a word, not its denotative or literal meaning. On the importance of word choice, Mark Twain's words remain unsurpassed: "The difference between an exact word and an almost accurate word is the difference between lightning and lightning bug."

To get a sense of the importance of exact word choice, let us look at some examples. In "Hunting Season," Joanne Greenberg uses the following words to describe the "cruel season" of hunting:

"How she hated and feared those old mine shafts! These hills were full of *raped land* the takers had plundered and left unhealed. Mines and quarries still poured *yellow trailings from their wounds*. She heard a gun, then another. Now the hunters too. A world of *rape and murder*, a whole world" (Greenberg 134).

The author's diction, especially the italicized phrases, effectively evokes a feeling of destruction of natural life by predatory machines and predatory hunters. Word choice can have a variety of different effects, such as suggesting a theme, creating a mood, enriching the narrative with desired connotations, and revealing a character.

F. Scott Fitzgerald has a reputation for handling romantic love and nostalgia particularly well. A look at his choice of words – *grail, benediction*, and *personal* in particular – shows how he achieves that goal in *The Great Gatsby*. In describing Gatsby's pursuit of Daisy, the narrator Nick Carraway tells us that "he [Gatsby] had committed himself to the following of a *grail*. . . . She vanished into her rich house, into her rich, full life, leaving Gatsby – nothing. He felt married to her, that was all" (Fitzgerald 156-157). Use of the word *grail*, which is usually reserved for sacred contexts, adds an aura of holiness and reverence to Gatsby's quest and lifts it above the purely erotic.

Fitzgerald's use of the word *benediction* a few pages later in the novel is also noteworthy. This is how the narrator describes Gatsby's sentimental journey to Louisville after Daisy is gone from that city as a result of her marriage to Tom Buchanan. He walked "the streets where their footsteps had clicked together . . . revisiting the out-of-the-way places to which they had driven in her white car." As Gatsby was leaving the city that he felt "was pervaded with a melancholy beauty," he scrutinized the people in it "who might once have seen the pale magic of her face along the casual street." At that moment, he noticed that the sun "seemed to spread itself in *benediction* over the vanishing city where she had drawn her breath. He stretched out his hand desperately as if to snatch only a wisp of air, to save a fragment of the spot that she had made lovely for him" (160). These passages are a record of the triumph of simple elegance of Fitzgerald's language in capturing Gatsby's romanticism, and his choice of the word *benediction* lifts Daisy out of ordinary humanity into the realm of sacred symbology in Gatsby's mind.

The last of the three words chosen for this diction analysis is *personal*. As used by Gatsby himself, the word seems odd and unclear at first. When Nick tries to reason with Gatsby that Daisy might have loved Tom Buchanan also and that one could not repeat the past, Gatsby vehemently dismisses both suggestions and comes up with a curious remark to describe Tom's love for Daisy: "In any case, . . . it was just personal" (160). This odd expression on Gatsby's part, however, is revealing because it shows how his love for Daisy is different from that of Tom, who loves her only as a person. That is why Tom's love, according to Gatsby, is just *personal*. However, Gatsby loves her as an idea and as the epitome of all that love in its highest sense represents. Thus, to him, his love for Daisy is far superior to Tom's.

Even though word choice is important in all literary forms, it is particularly crucial in poetry. Poetic language thrives not only on iconic, connotative, and sense-stirring words but also on their sound effects. In analyzing Browning's love poem "Meeting at Night" in the section on "Imagery," we noted the poet's use of language that engages our senses of sight, smell, and sound. Some words in poetry are chosen for their sound. This device is called *onomatopoeia* – use of words whose sound suggests their meaning. In Browning's poem, the phrase "*slushy sand*" is onomatopoetic. It describes the lover's docking of the boat at the eagerly awaited end of his journey that will take him into his beloved's waiting arms.

Another unique feature of poetic language is that its use of intentional ambiguity is considered a virtue, not a failing. In Henry Reed's poem "Naming of Parts," for example, several phrases have a double meaning. In "The early bees are assaulting and fumbling the flowers" (line 3) the words "assaulting and fumbling" have both a negative and a positive meaning. Initially, the words connect with the military language, in which "assault" has the clear sense of destruction. However, since it is the bees that are assaulting the flowers, the second meaning is positive because the bees are cross-pollinating the flowers to create new life. Similarly, at first, the phrase "easing the Spring" (line 24) reminds us of the spring of a gun, since the poem is about the training of conscripted youth in a boot camp setting. When that spring is eased, it means the gun is fired. However, the poem emphasizes the opposite, positive meaning of the capitalized word "Spring." In its second meaning, "easing the Spring" suggests that by assaulting and fumbling the flowers, the bees are causing the release of Spring's pent-up life-giving energy. Another phrase with two different meanings is "the point of balance" (line 27). The phrase is ostensibly a reference to the point on the rifle at which it is balanced on the finger. The other meaning is the point of balance in the lives of the young, amateur soldiers. It is this "point of balance" that the soldiers say, regretfully, they "have not got" (line 28). Thus ambiguity in language, which may be a drawback in other forms of writing, becomes an asset in poetry. "Naming of Parts" is also discussed in Chapter Five.

Symbolism

Unlike metaphors and similes, both of which are comparisons that show similarities between unlike objects, a symbol is not a comparison. It is often a concrete object that represents an abstraction. It stands for something much larger than itself. In Christianity, the cross, for example, represents the burden of humanity that Christ carried in his crucifixion. In *The Great Gatsby*, the valley of ashes – a stretch of land that separates the elegant suburbia from the depressing stretch of nothingness – symbolizes the blight of uncontrolled urbanization destroying wholesome Nature. Instead of life-sustaining crops, the soil seems to produce only ashes.

In Poe's "The Cask of Amontillado," Montresor's coat-of-arms – a foot crushing "a serpent whose fangs are imbedded in the heel" – symbolizes the destructive Montresor-Fortunato relationship. It also reflects Montresor's struggle with his conscience after his crime of killing Fortunato. The foot crushing the snake symbolizes Montresor destroying Fortunato. The fangs of the snake in the heel of Montresor suggest that even though the snake is crushed, its poison has entered the heel. This symbol thus becomes a lucid expression of the need of Montresor to confess his crime to relieve his guilt. It is this symbol that strengthens the interpretation of the story as Montresor's confession before a priest, before the police, or before his own conscience.

As a source of enrichment and expansion of meaning, a symbol summons feelings and ideas which, over a long period, become associated with it in folklore, legend, history, religion, art, literature, science, technology, or any other similar record of humanity. Surrounded as it is by a fund of knowledge shared not only by the reader and the writer but also by a sizeable section of humanity, a symbol has the power of condensing the intended meaning much more effectively than a straightforward exposition of the same meaning through ordinary, non-symbolic language. Skillful use of symbol can thus add considerable emotive force to a work because a symbol has a whole history behind it and functions through recollection which, by itself, triggers emotion.

By their very nature, symbols are susceptible of multiple interpretations. Whereas similes and metaphors emphasize exactness in the terms of comparison, a symbol thrives on layers of seemingly endless nuances.

Allegory

A set of related symbols in a literary work often lead to allegory that may be defined as a narrative with two levels of meanings – one literal and the other symbolic. Aesop's fables, in which animals take on human characteristics, are a well-known example of classical allegory. For a modern example, the allegorical poem "Curiosity" by Alastair Reid is literally about cats and dogs. Its true meaning, which is also the allegorical meaning, however, is revealed through an interpretation of the two symbols: cats symbolize people who are curious and lead intense and adventurous lives. Dogs, on the other hand, symbolize people who are incurious and therefore dull. Thus the poem is about cats and dogs only literally and superficially. Its real subject is the curious and incurious people.

It should be noted that symbols do not always have to be used in connected clusters. An author may use just one symbol in an entire work. But only when symbols appear according to a plan and in an interconnected series do they lead to an allegory.

Allusion

Inviting the reader to share something from the past, an allusion is a reference to a famous person, place, or event from mythology, history, religion, art, or literature. Through association with the object of reference and by relying on the pool of assumed common knowledge, an allusion becomes a short cut to expansion and enrichment of the author's meaning. Its other important functions are economy of expression by condensing information, and evoking a desired feeling. In this respect, it is like a symbol. Since authors cannot be expected to limit themselves to the range of the reader's knowledge, an encyclopedia or some other source book should be consulted to understand unfamiliar allusions. Full communication between the author and the reader cannot take place without an understanding of the allusion being used.

An effective use of allusion is provided by Rona Jaffe in her story "Rima the Bird Girl" when she alludes to the mythical bird phoenix of Egyptian mythology: "The death of love leads to the rebirth of another love, for love is a phoenix" (Ferguson 287). With the help of this allusion, the author is able to convey the feeling that the flame of love continues to rekindle in spite of many extinctions just as the phoenix rises from its ashes after being consumed by fire at the end of its renewable life cycle. In an earlier section of this chapter under "Style in Poetry," Muhammad Iqbal's masterly use of allusion receives an in-depth discussion.

Personification and Animation

Personification consists of giving human attributes to abstractions, ideas, and inanimate or non-human beings. If an inanimate object is given an emotion that is common to both animals and human beings (such as anger and affection), it could be called personification: *The tired, yellow flame tried to project its light.* In this example, a non-human object (a flame) is given the human (or animal) attribute of having a sentient nature. The key word *tired* makes this statement a personification. This element of style is not uncommon in everyday use. *Our car was determined to teach us a lesson* is an example.

Using personification, this is how we may describe the outcome of a mudslide: *It seems that the ancient, long abandoned home on top of the hill got tired of being isolated for so long and decided to slide down to seek the company of other homes down below.*

When something is imbued with non-human life, the device may be called *animation*, not personification. In his poem "Fog," Carl Sandburg uses animation by making fog act like an animal (cat):

> The fog comes on little cat feet. It sits looking over the harbor and city
> on silent haunches and then moves on.

Ordinarily overlooked, this distinction between personification and animation is necessary for precision.

Since personification gives body to abstract concepts and animation to lifeless objects, it adds vitality and vigor to an author's style. It may be viewed as an aid to understanding through rendition of abstractions in human terms. However, it is an indication of the versatility of this element of style that in addition to the animating touch often associated with personification, this device can be used with equal success to reinforce a mood of loneliness, isolation, and alienation. In John Steinbeck's description from the short story "Flight" – "the wind went sighing through the underbrush" – the personifying touch in "sighing" captures the young, pursued protagonist's suppressed sadness as well as Nature's sympathy for his predicament.

Narrative Point of View

Narrative point of view in fiction is the perspective or angle from which the story is told. An author may use either the first-person or third-person point of view. Both have their merits as well as shortcomings, and one is chosen over the other in keeping with the effects desired by the author. Authors create narrators just as they create characters. Even though many times narrators have served as the authors' spokespersons, neither characters nor narrators are to be equated with the author. We should also be open to the possibility of an imperfect narrator, whose views and actions the author may want us to avoid rather than emulate. An example is the first-person narrator in E. M. Forster's story "The Other Side of the Hedge," discussed in Chapter Two. His selfishness makes him regard his well-wishers with suspicion and distrust to his own detriment.

First-person point of view. The first-person narration describes events and characters as filtered through the consciousness of a single, non-omniscient person. It is often more dramatic and credible because the people telling their stories have been participants in the action. Their words come to us directly without the interference of an intermediary as in the third person narration. If a person, for instance, has had a close encounter with death but escaped, the story would be more effective in that person's own voice rather than from a third person's point of view. This point of view, suited to stories that need the reader's involvement rather than detachment, works well in mysteries and fiction involving deception, ambiguity, or illusion. The fragile tentativeness of the first-person narrator (as in Camus' *The Stranger*) is often more compelling than the omniscient narrator's certainties.

Ernest Gaines' story "The Sky Is Gray" is told from the young boy James' first-person point of view. Its appeal would be diminished considerably had it been told from the point of view of a third person. James' swift transition from the state of innocence to that of experience is best chronicled in his own words. His concern for his mother and his dreams of making her happy one day are more poignant as narrated directly by James.

However, by its very nature, the first-person point of view has certain limitations: It tends to be subjective and when compared with the omniscient third-person narrator, it is limited in its range, since it can only report one person's point of view.

Third-person point of view. When no single character can become the author's consciousness or when several characters may have an equal claim to that distinction (as in E. M. Forster's novel *A Passage to India*), authors use the third-person narrative point of view. This way of storytelling is also called omniscient because in it the narrator takes on the almost divine stature in terms of knowing even the characters' innermost thoughts and feelings. The chief strength of the third-person omniscient point of view is its unlimited range in comparison with the first-person narration. This narrative strategy has been often used for philosophical, psychological, and historical fiction because it allows greater scope and objectivity. It also permits the author's interpretation of fictional reality.

A weakness of the third-person point of view, however, is that it does not achieve the reader's immediate involvement and credibility. If not used with caution, this narrative style can appear arbitrary and somewhat "stagey" since no single person is expected to know everything. This method is especially unsuitable for suspense for the simple reason that since the narrator is all-knowing, s/he can create suspense only by withholding some key information and thus deceiving the reader. This deficiency of the omniscient method has led to the use of a third-person narrator who is only partially aware of the characters' activities and thoughts.

An author's choice of the narrative point of view is not random and, like the elements of setting and atmosphere, it is meant to achieve the intended effects. Mark Twain, for instance, revolutionized the concept of the narrative point of view in *The Adventures of Huckleberry Finn* by choosing a narrator who is nine years old. The task is indeed enormously difficult because Mark Twain, after making that choice, had to limit himself to the experiences and vocabulary of a nine-year old boy. In the hands of Mark Twain, however, this limitation actually became a means of enrichment, for we read the novel at two levels throughout: One level is obvious and literal – that of the young narrator. The other, more significant, is the ironic, deeper level at which the adult reader perceives the boy's racist remarks that drop innocently from his lips because he is not yet aware of their prejudicial implications. Not the least important aspect of Twain's choice of the narrator is the humor with which the novel scintillates even in the midst of grim situations. An adult narrator would not have been able to accomplish those artistic goals as well.

Other Narrative Styles

In addition to the two narrative styles explained above, authors are sometimes compelled to create alternative ways to narrate their stories, notable among which are the following:

1. **Third-person narrator who is not omniscient.** This narrative style limits the third-person narrator's range of knowledge to make it realistic. Kate Chopin's "The Story of an Hour" (Chapter Seven) exemplifies this strategy. The story is told mostly through the consciousness of the protagonist Louise Mallard. Limited knowledge on the narrator's part allows suspense to build up without deceiving the reader because the third-person narrator in this particular work is not all-

knowing. The use of irony on the author's part combines well with this variety of third-person limited omniscience to convey two conflicting messages about the cause of Louise's death. The characters in the story believe that she died of the shock of joy that her ailing heart could not withstand on seeing her presumably dead husband alive. This, however, may not be the true reason for her death, which might have been caused by the shock of pain to see her husband alive after she had found, with thorough self-analysis, a new direction in her life. She had finally understood the true nature of her relationship with her husband in an oppressive marriage. These two very different readings of the story's conclusion would not be possible with a truly omniscient narrator because in that case the all-knowing narrator would have to reveal the exact cause of Louise's death.

2. **The objective or dramatic point of view.** This most restricted form of narration is almost all dialogue, as in "Hills Like White Elephants" by Hemingway (Chapter Ten). Suitable for situations in which the author and narrator refuse to take sides, this point of view comes very close to drama. Hemingway's story is mostly dialogue between two young lovers who have reached a point of conflict in their relationship.

3. **Use of multiple narrators.** Sometimes authors use more than one narrator to achieve more credibility. In *The Great Gatsby* (Chapter Eleven), for example, Nick Carraway is the main first-person narrator. Not being an omniscient narrator, he cannot know everything. Fitzgerald, therefore, gives Jordan Baker a brief narrative role to introduce the details about Gatsby's background that Nick could not have known, specifically, the beginning of Gatsby's relationship with Daisy, his prolonged absence caused by the war, and Daisy's marriage to Tom Buchanan. Jordan Baker is a character, not a narrator, and her words are addressed to Nick, not to the reader. Nevertheless, her above-noted narrative input contributes toward making the story more authentic.

4. **Rarely used narration in the second person.** In this rare form, the narrator talks to herself or himself as in Chitra Divakaruni's story "The Word Love" (Chapter Ten). This style is suited to situations involving isolation when the person is forced into self-analysis by talking to oneself in the absence of a listener. This style is like a long soliloquy with the protagonist's inner struggle, conflict, and possible resolution dramatized before a hopefully sympathetic reader as the only audience.

Tone and Verbal Irony

Tone is related to point of view, since it reveals the author's and narrator's attitude toward the audience, subject, characters, their actions, and values. Tone is present in many elements of style, such as the author's choice of words, imagery, characterization, irony, understatement, paradox, sarcasm, and humor. Understanding of tone is critical to grasping the meaning intended by the author. Failing to perceive verbal irony in a statement, for example, would result in completely misunderstanding the author's intended meaning.

The title of Paul Roberts' highly entertaining piece "How to Say Nothing in 500 Words" is an example of verbal irony, which consists of saying the opposite of what is actually meant or intended. As we know from the content of his essay, Roberts' real intention is to teach us how to avoid saying nothing in 500 words. The title of his essay is thus an example of verbal irony.

A famous literary example is Jonathan Swift's masterpiece of verbal irony, "A Modest Proposal." Because some readers completely misunderstood Swift's tone of irony in the essay, a warrant for his arrest was about to be issued on the charge that the author was propagating cannibalism. Fortunately for Swift, some friends were able to persuade the authorities that what he wrote in the essay was ironic and not meant to be taken literally. After several unsuccessful attempts to persuade the British government to treat the poverty-stricken Irish Catholics humanely, Swift wrote his stinging ironic piece.

Pretending to be only a well-wisher of the British government and supporter of its policies, Swift stated that the poor Irish were to blame for their misery and that they were an unjust burden on the rich British citizens. To remedy the situation, he offered his "modest" proposal: All one-year old Irish Catholic children should be slaughtered and served as food for the British landlords. Using verbal irony, he suggested that his proposal was "a fair, cheap, and easy method of making these children sound, useful members of the commonwealth" (McCuen and Winkler 525).

Some readers misinterpreted Swift's ironic tone and did not pay enough attention to sentences that reveal the author's true intention. Angry at the greedy landlords, he had also said that they had "the best title to the children," since "they have already devoured most of the parents" (527). Swift's example shows that out of all elements that go under "tone," verbal irony is the most difficult one in terms of understanding the author's true meaning. Other elements do not offer so great a challenge.

The function or effect usually associated with verbal irony is that it offers an opportunity for humor even in grim, humorless situations and thus prevents an author from becoming overly serious.

Summing up irony. By now you have been introduced to all three forms of irony – verbal irony in this section and dramatic and situational irony in this chapter's earlier section on "Style in Drama and Fiction." All three forms center on some form of discrepancy. Verbal irony has to do with the use of words in a statement, situational irony is connected with a situation, and dramatic irony points out the discrepancy between what a character says and what the author wants the audience to understand from that statement.

Use of irony is associated with the following effects:

1. Verbal irony provides a chance for humor even in grim situations. It also functions as a safeguard against excessive emotionalism and mawkishness.

2. It enriches the content by asking for at least two possible interpretations of a statement – one literal and the other intended.

3. Verbal irony also challenges the reader to become more deeply involved with what s/he is reading because if the irony is not understood, the reader will walk away with a meaning that is the opposite of the author's intended meaning.

4. In tragic plays, situational irony makes us aware that life can sometimes run counter to our expectations, with unexpected and tragic consequences. By reversing the expected outcome, irony thus brings new awareness of the disparity between what we want or expect and what we get – between desire and denial. In comedy, situational irony introduces unexpected good luck and happy resolution of conflicts

5. Dramatic irony has the power to orchestrate the audience sympathy for the hero, who may be inevitably moving toward disaster while thinking that s/he is running away from it.

Contrast

Contrast may be defined as a study in differences, just as comparison is a study in similarities. Used as a plot-structuring device, a strategy for characterization, and juxtaposition of details for thematic purposes, the element of contrast stands out in frequency of use. As an example, Shakespeare's effective use of contrast for characterization is especially notable in *Hamlet*, in which he uses this strategy to develop the three major revenge-seeking characters – Hamlet, Fortinbras, and Laertes.

Contrast is also Shakespeare's means to delineate the vastly different values of Ophelia and Gertrude, King Hamlet and Claudius, Prince Hamlet and Claudius, and Horatio *versus* Rosencrantz and Guildenstern.

The element of contrast is also found to be crucial in discovering the elusive themes of Henry Reed's poem "Naming of Parts" in Chapter Five under "Hard to Explicate Works." Contrast, moreover, becomes a principal means to access a theme in Alberto Moravia's short story "The Chase" (end of Chapter Seven), in which the narrator's boyhood experience of hunting is contrasted with his father's attitude. More importantly, the narrator's atypical, idealistic conduct, when confronted with the shock of his wife's infidelity, is etched in sharp contrast with the prevailing norms.

Understatement

This device is similar to the esthetics of omission in some ways. By saying far less than expected, saying nothing when something is expected, or holding back on emotion, *understatement* has the effect of emphasizing a point by conspicuously and deliberately de-emphasizing it. Referring to an inarticulate person, if we say that he or she is *not an orator*, we would be using understatement. It would also be an understatement to say that *reading all of Shakespeare's plays in one day is hard* because, in this example, we are understating what is impossible as if it were merely difficult. Similarly, saying that the story of *Hamlet* is not a happy one is understating the truth. The play is much more than a story that is not happy. It is a painful tragedy. Another easy-to-understand example is this: If you put your hand in an oven preheated to 500 degrees, you will feel an *unpleasant sensation of heat*. The italicized words understate the severity of the burn. If we had said that your hand would be reduced to cinders, we would be using hyperbole (exaggeration), which is the opposite of understatement.

Understatement is the poets' favorite, and they use it with notable impact. In these lines from Shakespeare, the understatement consists of the simile – "like a winter" – which captures the painful absence of warmth during the separation of lovers:

> How *like a winter* hath my absence been
> From thee, the pleasure of the fleeting year!" (Sonnet 97)

Robert Frost uses understatement with tremendous effect at the end of his poem "Out, Out." The poem describes a fatal accident in which a young boy loses his arm. Here is how Frost describes the tragic loss and the bewilderment of the bereaved:

> . . . They listened at his heart,
> Little – less – nothing! – and that ended it.
> No more to build on there. And they, since they
> Were not the one dead, turned to their affairs.

The concluding phrase "turned to their affairs" poignantly shows that those who witnessed this tragedy did not even have the luxury of mourning properly. They were hurriedly pulled away to "their affairs." The understatement in the last two lines draws our attention to the painful reality of life's urgent demands on the living.

Another memorable example of understatement, this one from Fitzgerald's short story "The Last of the Belles," describes the returning war heroes: "And now the young men of Tarleton began drifting back from the end of the earth – some with Canadian uniforms, some with crutches or *empty sleeves*" (Ferguson 260). The little phrase "empty sleeves" says it all. As we can see, understatement can be used for both serious and comic effects.

A memorable comic example is from Oscar Wilde's play *The Importance of Being Earnest*: "To lose one parent, Mr. Worthing, may be regarded as a misfortune; to lose both looks like carelessness." Another well-known example is from satirist Jonathan Swift: "The other day I saw a woman flayed. It changed her appearance for the worse."

Like verbal irony, understatement needs appropriate build-up to be effective. Here is how it usually works: In 1863, Abraham Lincoln's Emancipation Proclamation freed the slaves, but it took the country one hundred years to pass the Civil Rights laws. Obviously, the country *did not act promptly* to implement the promise of Lincoln's Proclamation. The understatement is italicized in this sentence. Another understated way to express the same idea would be this sentence: The country had been *somewhat slow* in enforcing the new law.

Demonstrating its close relation to verbal irony, we can convert the above-noted sentence into irony as follows: In 1863, Abraham Lincoln's Emancipation Proclamation freed the slaves, but it took the country one hundred years to pass the Civil Rights laws. Legal reforms have seldom been carried out with such *dazzling speed*.

Paradox

Paradox at first seems like a self-contradictory statement that turns out to be valid when examined closely. Mark Twain's often-heard remark – "*The coldest winter I ever had was a summer in San Francisco*" – is a paradox because one would expect warmer, not colder weather in the summer. However, those who are familiar with the cold, foggy summers of San Francisco would have no trouble understanding Twain's paradox. An *oxymoron* is a special kind of paradox in which the conflicting words appear next to each other, as in "cruel joy" and "eloquent silence." Appreciation and use of paradox requires the ability to perceive truth in a *seemingly* untrue statement.

In Henry David Thoreau's famous oxymoron – "Most men lead lives of quiet desperation" – the last two words are paradoxical. Ordinarily, we do not associate desperation with quiet. Screaming, not silence, seems to be the expected response to desperation. However, the validity of Thoreau's paradox is obvious from our routine response of "OK" or "fine" when someone asks us, "How are you?" Our routine response is expected of us regardless of our true feelings when we are asked that question. It would, indeed, be a rare person who felt OK or fine all the time, yet all of us, even in a state of desperation, respond quietly as expected. Thoreau's paradox startles us as it uncovers a state of being more effectively than straightforward language could have done.

In another well-known example, George Orwell opens his essay "Shooting an Elephant" with a paradox: "In Moulmein, in Lower Burma, I was hated by large numbers of people – the only time in my life that I have been important enough for this to happen to me. I was sub-divisional police officer of the town" (Muller 43). The surface contradiction in this statement seems to be between importance and hatred. It has an unsettling effect on the reader because ordinarily, we associate popularity, not hatred with important people. However, if we examine the statement closely and analytically, it proves to be a valid observation because it is the important people who end up being hated by a large number of people. Hitler, Mussolini, and Stalin were important people, whom many people despise because of their extremist ideologies and inhumane practices. This new insight into the drawbacks of being an important person is at the heart of Orwell's essay.

An analysis of the often-heard paradoxes – "torment of hope" and "cruel joy" – brings further awareness of the power of paradox. Usually torment is not associated with hope; joy is. But it does not take much thought to realize the validity of the idea that in despair the feelings may be numbed, but in hope the very expectation and anticipation may keep the hopeful in a state of unrest. In "cruel joy," a joy that brings self-consciousness and an awareness of its impermanence can indeed be cruel, for in the very moment of joy, it introduces the awareness of its ephemeral nature.

From these examples, it is apparent that paradox is not an embellishment but rather a means to more inclusive version of truth and a gateway to a better understanding of human nature. It shows the reader ways to find new meanings in a truism or a commonplace occurrence. By its seeming impossibility, it startles the reader into attention. Its special appeal lies in the shock of surprise that results from its juxtaposition of opposites. As a result, it succeeds in evoking a response when other devices may prove less effective.

Paradox shares with irony a special place in modern discourse. Because of their de-sentimentalizing, enriching, and startling effect, along with their potential for humor even when the subject matter is serious, these two devices have become inseparable from modern consciousness in which demarcations between right and wrong are so often blurred and in which conflicting tendencies strive for synthesis.

Characterization

Characterization is the technique by which authors create various characters and give them distinguishing traits, unique words, ideas, gestures, and actions in order to control our perception of them and to make them believable and distinct from one another. The ability to create characters is related to the artistic temperament, on which John Keats made a perceptive statement. An artist, says

Keats, has no self because he is constantly becoming the character that he is trying to create. Such freedom from self-consciousness in creating characters is, indeed, an admirable quality.

One of the reasons for Shakespeare's success as a playwright is that he is able to create a vast variety of believable, true-to-life characters. He can give them not only distinguishing traits but also distinct speech. It has been correctly noted that after reading a few scenes of a play by Shakespeare, we may hide the character's name speaking the lines and still be able to identify the speaker on the basis of the language, tone, and rhythm he or she is given.

The words of Prince Hamlet, for example, are indicative of struggle and marked by exclamation points, as if the language has to be stretched beyond limit for him to express himself. These words from his first soliloquy are a good example:

> O that this too solid flesh would melt,
> Thaw, and resolve itself into a dew,
> Or that the Everlasting had not fixed
> His canon 'gainst self-slaughter. O God, God,
> How weary, stale, flat, and unprofitable
> Seem to me all the uses of this world! (I,ii,131-136)

The language of Claudius, on the other hand, is marked by the balancing contrast of paradox and the controlling rhythm of carefully chosen syntax. He opens his coronation address to the court with long periodic sentences (explained in Chapter Eight), the second one studded with paradoxes, speaking like someone who is in control – a successful manipulator of language and a crafty planner:

> Though yet of Hamlet our dear brother's death
> The memory be green, and that it us befitted
> To bear our hearts in grief, and our whole kingdom
> To be contracted in one brow of woe,
> Yet so far hath discretion fought with nature
> That we with wisest sorrow think on him . . .
> Therefore our sometime sister, now our Queen, . . .
> Have we, as 'twere, with a defeated joy,
> With an auspicious and a dropping eye,
> With mirth in funeral, and with dirge in marriage,
> In equal scale weighing delight and dole,
> Taken to wife (I,ii,1-14).

Besides this marked difference between the language given to these two characters, the speech patterns, diction, and rhythm of all other characters – Polonius, Ophelia, Laertes, Gertrude, Horatio, etc. – are distinct from one another. In creative writing exercises that involve characterization, if the characters we create talk alike, that is the sign of a novice. Indeed, the proof of successful writing is the ability to create interesting, credible, varied, and distinct characters.

STYLISTIC ELEMENTS WORK IN COMBINATION

It was necessary to study the elements of style one by one for clarity and comprehension. However, it is important to know that in literary works, they seldom work in isolation. They usually appear in combination with other elements. Reading of English poet Gerard Hopkins' sonnet "God's Grandeur" from the perspective of style can be instructive to see how the elements of diction, repetition, symbolism, and imagery combine to convey the poem's theme.

God's Grandeur

The world is charged with the grandeur of God.
    It will flame out, like shining from shook foil;
    It gathers to a greatness, like the ooze of oil
Crushed. Why do men then now not reck his rod?
Generations have trod, have trod, have trod;
    And all is seared with trade; bleared, smeared with toil;
    And wears man's smudge and shares man's smell: the soil
Is bare now, nor can foot feel, being shod.

And for all this, nature is never spent;
    There lives the dearest freshness deep down things;
And though the last lights off the black West went
    Oh, morning, at the brown brink eastward, springs –
Because the Holy Ghost over the bent
    World broods with warm breast and with ah! bright wings.

Gerard Manley Hopkins (1844-1889)

Hopkins' word choice, use of repetition, symbolism, and imagery effectively convey his feelings. The words "charged" and "flame out" in the opening lines create an ecstatic mood to celebrate God's grandeur. "Seared," "bleared," "smeared," and smudge" (lines 6-7) are appropriate words to describe man in his fallen state, steeped in materialism. To express Nature's infinite resources, the poet uses appropriately simple, natural, and basic diction: "And for all this, nature is never spent" (line 9).

The repeated use of "have trod" three times (line 5) is very effective in capturing the entrapment of humanity in its mechanical round that threatens Nature's harmony.

Among the poem's notable symbols, the "shod" foot that cannot feel the earth below becomes a symbol of divorce between humanity and Nature. "The ooze" of crushed oil gathering to a greatness (line 3) conveys human efforts to blot out God from their minds, but their attempts have resulted only in augmenting God's splendor. The cyclical, never-ending movement of light – from "the black West" to the East (line 10) – is symbolic of the universal order far above the puny human efforts of self-destruction. The poet draws the picture of the toiling masses (totally consumed by their backbreaking labor) with his portrayal of the world as "bent" (line 13). These symbols help to condense and intensify the poet's feelings.

Nature's/God's protective warmth for the lost and toiling masses is well captured in the poem's final image of the "warm breast" and "bright wings" of the Holy Ghost who oversees and shields the world.

In this poem about human relationship with Nature and God, Hopkins' style empowers him to affirm his faith that in spite of humanity's recklessness, Nature continues to protect and provide for human beings.

Interconnectedness of Theme, Character, Plot, and Style

Part One of this book has been a study of the following major elements of literature:

- Topics and themes
- Characters
- Plot
- Style

In order to appreciate the interconnected nature of these elements, it is necessary to see how they complement one another in a literary work. Writing an interpretation of a short story by analyzing theme-embodying functions of *all three elements* of characters, plot, and style seems like an appropriate way to end Part One. Hemingway's story "The Short Happy Life of Francis Macomber" promises an interesting discussion from this perspective. Read the story online before reading my analysis. Use this link:

http://www.tarleton.edu/Faculty/sword/Short%20Story/The%20Short%20Happy%20Life%20of%20Francis%20Macomber.pdf

Characters, Plot, and Style in Hemingway's "The Short Happy Life of Francis Macomber" Essay by the author of this book

By analyzing characters, plot, and style in American writer Ernest Hemingway's "The Short Happy Life of Francis Macomber," we can gain insights into his modes of creation and see how authors blend action, narration, and ideas together. *This essay contains italicized explanations of the analyzed elements for clarity.*

Formulating a theme through character analysis

[*We can approach the story, using character analysis to discover themes.*]   A cause-and-effect examination of the values and motives of significant characters and the ends to which those values drive them may suggest a theme. Let us, for instance, look for the causes of the unhappy situation that prevails in the story by asking a simple question: Why are Mr. and Mrs. Macomber still together? The answer may lead us to one of the themes in this story. Hemingway's narrator makes an ironic comment which answers the above question: "They had a sound basis of union. Margot was too beautiful for Macomber to divorce her and Macomber had too much money for Margot ever to leave him." This statement is obviously ironic, since the basis of the union of these two characters is anything but "sound." Perhaps here, in this casually made remark, lies the reason for the Macombers' misery. They have entered into a relationship for the wrong reasons. If we analyze their actions in the story's main events, we come to recognize a central theme of the story: *a drawn-out relationship – based on calculation, manipulation, and exploitation – deadens people's emotions.*

Formulating a theme through plot analysis

[*Another method of theme recognition and interpretation is to focus on just one theme-revealing plot detail, such as a prominent scene or event that the author has placed strategically in the story.*] The story's concluding scene always generates controversial reactions. Did Margot shoot her husband accidentally or deliberately? Hemingway's obscuring of Margot's motive in this scene points to a significant theme that may be phrased as follows: *Our patterns of behavior become so fixed with time that any move against them,* (like Macomber's moving away from Margot's control), *triggers an automatic reaction to preserve the established pattern* (of domination and submission in this case).

This theme is clearly demonstrated by Margot's violent and desperate termination of her husband's short, happy life, which began as soon as he shuffled off his emotional vulnerability and became fearless.

Theme formulation through style analysis

[*Hemingway's style of "less is more" consists of using simple words that become thematic when used in specific settings.*] In the story, Wilson, a hunter makes the following statement in the course of a typical Hemingway dialogue that suggests much more than what it says: "We all take a beating every day . . . one way or another." When *these words* are uttered by Wilson, they do not seem significant thematically, but when we look at them in the story's total context, they *stand out as a prominent theme.*

Hemingway uses an African safari as *the setting* for this story in which the main characters – Francis Macomber, his wife (Margot), and their guide (Wilson) – face their demons. *The unrelieved conflict between the major characters is paralleled and reinforced by the tension of a safari in the perilous jungles of Africa. The domestic tension of the Macombers is magnified by the harsh environment.* In this milieu, Wilson's foreboding words assume significance: everyone *does* get a beating one way or another. Wilson gets his beating by having to lead a pathetic couple like the Macombers; Margot gets her beating by resorting to the pettiness of trying to make her husband jealous and insecure with her actions; Macomber gets his beating by having to put up with a beautiful but unfaithful and domineering woman. *Hemingway's use of this setting thus combines with a seemingly casual remark to formulate an important theme.* Such combination of setting and matter-of-fact dialogue has become so famous that it has added a new word "Hemingwayesque" to the vocabulary of literary style.

An analysis of Hemingway's stylistic element of tone also reveals a thematic function. The author uses understatement and detachment in Margot's and Wilson's response to the final catastrophe in the story. Wilson comes up with this curious remark to Margot after she has "accidentally" shot her husband: "That was a pretty thing to do," he said in a toneless voice. "He would have left you too." Wilson's cold remark implies that Margot's shooting of her husband was the fulfillment of her wish to keep Macomber, especially his money, under her control at any cost. His leaving her would mean her losing all his money. To her, he is worth more dead than alive.

Wilson's later remark is even more outrageous in revealing his cold detachment: "Why didn't you poison him? That's what they do in England." Had she finished Macomber off by poisoning him, Wilson would have been spared this forced participation in this serio-farcical domestic tragedy of the Macombers. All Wilson seems to feel is annoyance. He is too detached to feel compassion.

Margot's response to her husband's death is equally puzzling. After her initial, "hysterical crying" brought on probably by guilt and regret (just the night before she had slept with Wilson to humiliate her husband), she appears devoid of any genuine emotion. All she manages to say in reply to Wilson's cutting remarks is, "Stop it." *Her lack of expression, emphasized in Hemingway's use of understatement, reveals the theme that obsession with power and control leaves no room for tenderness in a relationship.*

Through Wilson's bantering and sarcastic words, which are as icy as his "flat blue eyes," and through Margot's response to the situation, Hemingway ends his story on an appropriately cold note that goes with the relationship between the major characters. *The author's stylistic devices of understatement, sarcasm, and irony create a tone that is appropriate to portray the theme of twisted passions.* Through examining elements of style that reflect important characters' values and traits, we are granted access to an author's themes.

On the surface, this story is about adventures in an African setting. Underneath the adventure, however, the author explores the ever-changing nature of human relationships, patterns of dominance and submission, and the innate human desire for freedom and respect – exciting themes running through both life and great literature.

Summary

Looking back at this reading of Hemingway's story, we can see how themes (the essence of interpretation) can be discovered by:

- tracing a cause-and-effect link between characters' actions and their consequences
- focusing on just one theme-bearing event or scene
- catching the significance of a seemingly casual remark made by a character
- finding a theme-reinforcing element of style, such as Hemingway's use of setting and tone.

After studying the important elements of *theme, characters, plot,* and *style* in Part One, we can now move on to Part Two of this book, which gives further advice on reading literature and writing about it. That advice is applicable to all genres of literature.

Exercises to Test Your Mastery of Chapter Four

1. Of all the definitions of style given in the chapter, which one do you like the best? Why? Apply that definition to a specific literary work to demonstrate the impact of an author's style on his or her content.

2. Discuss the extent to which authors *choose* their stylistic elements. Points to consider include:

   A. The role of deliberate design.

   B. Choice of elements of style in artistic creation.

   C. The extent to which this craft-related prowess controls the powers of the unconscious.

3. Under "Analyzing Style in Literature" (in an earlier part of this chapter) several different functions of style are mentioned. Add two more functions on your own.

4. Discuss a literary work that clearly demonstrates the theme-embodying role of style. You may want to analyze a poem whose theme can be grasped primarily through the author's style, as was demonstrated in this chapter's analysis of Henry Reed's poem "Naming of Parts."

5. Explain the artistic device known as the esthetics of omission, which consists of revelation of feelings and ideas not by expressing them but by conspicuously withholding the expected information. Demonstrate your knowledge of this device preferably with reference to works other than those discussed in the chapter.

6. Discuss the following elements in their plot-structuring and/or theme-embodying roles:

   A. Setting

   B. Symbolism

   C. Parallelism

7. Discuss the impact of an author's choice of the narrative point of view on the story being told. How do first-person and third-person narrative styles affect the story and its message?

8. Discuss the effectiveness of an author's choice of using an unknowing and hence unreliable narrator in any literary work. This literary style was popularized by Edgar Allan Poe and used extensively by authors like Dostoevsky and later by Ford Maddox Ford (as in *The Good Soldier*). Narrators in fiction are called speakers in poetry and drama.

9. Imagery adds a sensory dimension to the intellectual content in literature. Discuss a literary work that gains its impact and richness through imagery. Keats's poem "To Autumn," for example, is known for its theme-enhancing imagery. Look for a similar work for this exercise.

10. Discuss the role of foreshadowing and flashback in controlling the pace of a narrative.

11. How is the stream-of-consciousness technique of writing different from the straightforward narration in rendering events and characters' states of mind. Comment on its effectiveness.

12. Connotation is a means to invest words with meanings and emotions that go beyond their literal meanings. Demonstrate this function of connotation with reference to a specific literary work.

13. Paradox, verbal irony, and understatement are considered the hallmarks of modern artistic expression and referred to as the "holy trinity of style." How do you account for their special appeal and relevance to modern sensibility.

14. What form of irony is being used in the following sentences?

   A. "You are really wide awake." You tell this to someone who is falling asleep.

   B. When discussing *The Great Gatsby*, we say that Tom Buchannan is an ideal husband (after we have learned of his extra-marital affairs).

   C. A speaker expects applause from the audience, but receives censure.

   D. Contrary to all audience expectations that Oedipus would be able to avoid the terrible fate that awaits him according to the oracle, Oedipus ends up meeting that exact fate.

   E. In which form of irony, is the significance of a character's words far greater than his or her understanding of them? Consider this proclamation by Oedipus as an example: "I shall fight for him [the dead Laius] as if he were my own father." At this point, Oedipus did not know that Laius was his father whom he had killed in an encounter.

   F. In which form of irony does a character's statement mean more to the audience than to the speaker?

15. Explain the meaning of this quotation from Alexander Pope: "True wit is nature to advantage dressed,/What oft was thought, but ne'er so well expressed" ("Essay on Criticism").

Part Two

Reading and Writing Advice

Applicable to all Genres

C H A P T E R   F I V E

READING SKILLS FOR INTERPRETATION: GUIDELINES AND SAMPLES

Interpretation requires an ability to recognize themes and understand the ways in which authors embody them. This skill is acquired through experiencing works of art carefully and critically. A skilled reader can reach deeper layers of meanings in a literary work more readily than an unskilled reader. Similarly, some film viewers can grasp themes with less effort than is necessary for others, but everyone improves with practice. With this improvement comes deeper appreciation and greater enjoyment of literary works and movies, not to mention the ability one acquires to relate art to one's personal as well as larger contemporary concerns.

Some important prerequisites to achieving these goals are an active reading style and the skills of explication and analysis.

First Requirement: Active Reading Style and Taking Mental Notes

For the purpose of interpretation, it is necessary to keep an active mind when reading a literary work or viewing a film. Reading well requires empathetic identification with authors and their characters. This ability, which comes naturally with the study of literature, can be acquired quickly if one starts pondering the kind of questions and suggestions listed below.

What kind of world – peaceful, violent, friendly, hostile – is presented in the literary work/movie?

What is the setting?

What are the values, aspirations, fears, and motives of prominent characters?

What are the characters' significant deeds, and what happens to them as a result of their values, attitudes, and actions?

What appears to be the work's central topic?

Annotating the pages that you read

Active Reading

Reading is a conversation between the author and the reader. It is note taking that makes it a two-way process. To understand complex writing, being on the receiving end is never enough. Your notes become a gateway to the knowledge that the author wants to share with you. On the importance and value of note taking, keep in mind Mortimer Adler's words: "You know you have to read 'between the lines' to get the most out of anything. I want to persuade you . . . to 'write between the lines.' Unless you do, you are not likely to do the most efficient kind of reading" (McCuen and Winkler 245).

If you are reading a literary work for discussion or for writing an essay about it, it would be helpful to establish a method of note taking to supplement your "mental notes." If you do not have a satisfactory method, try this one:

For **content** (topics, themes, significant events, deeds, consequences, etc.), put a dot with a pencil in the margin of the page that you are reading. If something looks unusually significant, put two dots in the margin. Reserve three dots for only concentrated statements of content. Putting these dots will not slow down your reading.

When you finish reading the essay, story, chapter, poem, etc., go back to the dots and convert them into numbers. Put a number in the margin. On top of the page put a corresponding number and write a few words to explain to yourself what content the number signifies. For example, if you put a number 1 in the margin, that number on top of the page should say something like "a major topic, a notable theme, a crucial event, or a significant deed, etc." When you revisit the text later for discussion or for a paper assignment, you will only have to look at the annotated numbers on top of the page to take you back to relevant details in the work. To annotate online texts, open a new document; copy relevant lines and paste them with your brief comments.

When analyzing an author's **style** (covered in the preceding Chapter Four), note the following by using capital alphabets rather than numerals for annotations. This way you will be able to separate style notes from content notes easily.

- Note thematically significant flashbacks, flashforwards, arrangements of scenes, imagery, symbolism, and allusion.

- In film, also note lighting, colors, costumes, camera angles, close-ups, music, etc.

- Be attentive to the use of dramatic as well as verbal irony, understatement, paradox, repartee, sarcasm, and similar devices. These elements of style are often connected with themes and topics.

Such questions and notes will help you later in your interpretations.

Second Requirement: Learning the Skill of Explication

Explication and analysis are two of the commonly used methods of interpretation. Whereas analysis imposes no restrictions as to the order in which we select details for discussion, explication requires our adhering to the order in which those details appear in the literary work. Both can be learned with the help of close textual reading as the rest of this chapter will demonstrate.

Explication

Explication – a line-by-line reading – is best suited to complex short poems but may also be used to elucidate sections of long poems and short stories. To get a feel for this method of interpretation, let us read the student Ayana Summers' reading of English poet William Blake's poem "London."

London

I wander thro' each charter'd street,
Near where the charter'd Thames does flow,
And mark in every face I meet
Marks of weakness, marks of woe.
In every cry of every Man,
In every Infant's cry of fear,
In every voice, in every ban,
The mind-forg'd manacles I hear.
How the Chimney-sweeper's cry
Every blackening Church appalls;
And the hapless Soldier's sigh
Runs in blood down Palace walls.

But most thro' midnight streets I hear
How the youthful Harlot's curse
Blasts the new-born Infant's tear,
And blights with plagues the Marriage hearse.

William Blake (1757-1827)

Student author: Ayana Summers

William Blake resided in London, a metropolis of England, all his life, except for three years in Felpham, a village on the south coast of West Sussex. Blake loved London, but at the same time was outraged by the suffering its society inflicted on the oppressed. To Blake, London was a dark place with depressing pillars of smoke from the mills and degradation of its people. His poem "London" chronicles those feelings.

"London" is one of Blake's greatest prophetic lyrics. Based on the Bible's Book of Ezekiel, it associates London under British Prime Minister William Pitt's counter-revolutionary repression with Jerusalem waiting for its destruction. Whereas the third stanza focuses on societal repression, the other three manifest Blake's sense of loss of freedom, pleasure, and liberty.

In the first stanza, Blake begins the cycle of corruption and degradation, from which there is possibly no escape: The word "charter'd" has multiple meanings. It refers to the "charter'd rights of Englishmen" which have been curtailed by Pitt, but it also refers to commercial chartering of the River Thames. The spirit of London's inhabitants has been restricted, bound, "charter'd" by commercialism which has abused regulations to stifle freedom. This abuse marks every face Blake sees, but the people are too weak and too fearful to rebuke the system. Blake also echoes Ezekiel (9:4), where God says: "Go through the midst of the city, through the midst of Jerusalem, and set a mark upon the foreheads of the men that sigh and cry for all the abominations that be done in the midst thereof."

Fear is prevalent in the second stanza, for it is what makes "every" person a prisoner, a victim of the system. The repetition of "every" three times wields incredible power. It shows that human misery is widespread. The frightening fact is that human mind – ideally an instrument of freedom – has become the source of imprisonment in that the manacles worn by Blake's Londoners are "mind-forg'd." In this vision of endemic desolation, freedom, pleasure, and liberty have no place.

Stanza three is Blake's most focused indictment of society: The blackening of the churches is literal, for London was becoming a dark place with soot from countless chimneys showering its questionable blessings on the city. The real dark spot was the Church's complacent attitude toward its children – the chimney sweepers. These children were condemned to a miserable life under the very eye of the Church of England. The "hapless Soldier's sigh" that "Runs in blood down Palace walls" is a strong symbol. It is an indictment of the royal palaces that send these young men to wars of questionable validity to be slaughtered. It points an accusing finger at the court's guilt surrounding the bloodshed of its soldiers. Blake viewed the chimney-sweeping children and soldiers as victims of an abusive system.

The most pathetic victim (in Blake's vision) was the young harlot, who is described in the poem's final stanza. Blake comments on the condition of the harlot, who has killed married life and infected mothers and children with disease. Her plight seems to be forced on her by economic injustice. Her presence destroys the ideals of marriage that have been transformed from a celebration into a funeral. The marriage coach becomes a "Marriage hearse" when disease-stricken harlots, themselves victims of economic injustice, roam the streets of London to spread their disease to others.

Though triggered by depressing events, Blake's "London" is highly lyrical. Yet the oppressive tone of the poem cannot be overshadowed by lyrical style. "London" is Blake's criticism of society. Outraged, he chose some of the most oppressed Londoners to record his vision of loss: the child chimney sweep, the soldier and the harlot. Exposing the truth yet providing no resolution, Blake's microcosm of London is an unhappy one.

Sample explication of a section from a complex, longer poem

T.S. Eliot's "The Love Song of J. Alfred Prufrock" is one of the most highly regarded poems of the twentieth century. The complexity of the poem's meanings sometimes seems impossible to overcome. However, explicating a key section can make the poem seem more accessible. Let us read the famous lines that describe the London fog and smoke:

> The yellow fog that rubs its back upon the window-panes,
> The yellow smoke that rubs its muzzle on the window-panes
> Licked its tongue into the corners of the evening,
> Lingered upon the pools that stand in drains,
> Let fall upon its back the soot that falls from chimneys,
> Slipped by the terrace, made a sudden leap,
> And seeing that it was a soft October night,
> Curled once about the house, and fell asleep.

Can we perceive a connection between Prufrock (the poem's speaker and main character) and the "yellow smoke"? Is there a likeness between the lazy, indolent, cat-like, and spasmodic movements of the yellow smoke and Prufrock's similar failure to break away from the inertia and his paralysis of will? The yellow smoke tries to rise but realizing "it's a soft October night," gives in to inertia. It curls once about the house and falls asleep. Does Prufrock do something similar? His unacted desire to go to a tea party and make a crucial declaration mirrors the smoke's inertia. Like the smoke, he, too, surrenders to indolence. At the end of the poem, we find him exactly where he was at the beginning. If, through explication, we can capture the poet's suggested analogy, we are closer to grasping the poem's elusive meanings. [*The complete poem and its interpretation are in Chapter Thirteen.*]

Sample explication of a section from a short story

The skill of explication can also be applied to selected sections of fiction. The enigmatic ending of Kate Chopin's "The Story of an Hour" invites speculation. The last scene presents the just-widowed protagonist Louise Mallard emerging from her seclusion on her sister's insistence. Just as it seems that Louise has not only weathered her grief but also found something positive in her bereavement, her supposedly dead husband Bentley Mallard shows up, and Louise drops dead:

"She rose at length and opened the door to her sister's importunities. There was a feverish triumph in her eyes, and she carried herself unwittingly like a goddess of Victory. . . . Someone was opening the front door with a latchkey. It was Bentley Mallard who entered . . . He had been away from the scene of the accident, and did not even know there had been one. He stood amazed at Josephine's piercing cry; at Richards' quick motion to screen him from the view of his wife. But Richards was too late."

"When the doctors came they said she had died of heart disease – of joy that kills." The doctors think that Louise was so overjoyed to see her reportedly dead husband that her ailing heart could not cope with the rush of excitement. However, a careful reading of the third-person narrator's words from earlier parts of the story – "feverish triumph" – and the comparison of Louise with "a goddess of

Victory" tells us another reason why she might have died: The husband's totally unexpected appearance shatters the citadel of liberty that she had so carefully constructed during her hour of seclusion. She was going to "live for herself," free from the husband's "powerful will bending hers in . . . blind persistence." With that dream of freedom now gone, she dies of a painful shock. The doctors and the other characters in the story may be mistaken in assuming that her weak heart failed to bear the sudden excitement of joy. An explication that is attentive to such details can make our interpretation convincing and bring us closer to grasping the theme of subtly oppressive marital relationships. [*Kate Chopin's complete story and its comprehensive interpretation are in Chapter Seven.*]

Hard to Explicate Works

A clear explication of the ending of "The Story of an Hour" was possible because the author offered some clues. However, in some works authors' themes are so elusive that they are accessible mainly through their elements of style, as is the case in Henry Reed's poem "Naming of Parts."

Naming of Parts[1]

Today we have naming of parts. Yesterday,
We had daily cleaning. And tomorrow morning,
We shall have what to do after firing. But today,
Today we have naming of parts. Japonica
Glistens like coral in all of the neighboring gardens,   5
    And today we have naming of parts.

This is the lower sling swivel. And this
Is the upper sling swivel, whose use you will see,
When you are given your slings. And this is the piling swivel,
Which in your case you have not got. The branches   10
Hold in the gardens their silent, eloquent gestures,
    Which in our case we have not got.

---

1. Read this poem's discussion in any source of literary criticism to add to your understanding of the poem. One convenient resource is the *Explicator* – available both in print and online formats. For online access, use this link:
http://www.solearabiantree.net/namingofparts/explicator.html.
Another widely used and convenient site is Gale Literature Resource Center. Narrow down your search by first clicking on the following link:
http://www.pulaskitech.edu/library/content/DB_Search_Tips_Literature_Resource_Center.pdf.

This is the safety-catch, which is always released
With an easy flick of the thumb. And please do not let me
See anyone using his finger. You can do it quite easy
If you have any strength in your thumb. The blossoms
Are fragile and motionless, never letting anyone see
    Any of them using their finger.

And this you can see is the bolt. The purpose of this
Is to open the breech, as you see. We can slide it   20
Rapidly backwards and forwards: We call this
Easing the spring. And rapidly backwards and forwards
The early bees are assaulting and fumbling the flowers:
    They call it easing the Spring.

They call it easing the Spring: it is perfectly easy   25
If you have any strength in your thumb: like the bolt,
And the breech, and the cocking-piece, and the point of balance,
Which in our case we have not got; and the almond-blossom
Silent in all of the gardens and the bees going backwards and forwards,
    For today we have naming of parts.   30

Henry Reed (1914-1986)

Explication

The challenge of this poem is that there are no lines that can be considered thematic. However, a look at its style, specifically, the elements of contrast, tone, and imagery, allows access to its themes. Contrast is noticed in the fourth line of each stanza. Those lines introduce a sharp difference in tone and imagery. The stanzas open with monotonously catalogued details of the routine drill in what seems to be a hastily organized boot camp to train young, inexperienced, and possibly uninterested recruits.

Today we have naming of parts. Yesterday,
We had daily cleaning. And to-morrow morning,
We shall have what to do after firing.

Both the tone and imagery change in the fourth line of each stanza. The tone changes from strident and commanding to one that is meditative and full of melancholy longing.

Japonica/Glistens like coral in all of the neighboring gardens (lines 4-5)

The images change from enumeration of life-threatening parts of the gun to the life-giving activities and aspects of Nature:

The branches/Hold in the gardens their silent, eloquent gestures (10-11)
The blossoms/Are fragile and motionless (16-17)
and the almond blossom/Silent in all of the gardens and the bees going
    backwards and forwards (28-29).

Once we have detected the elements of style known as tone, contrast, and imagery, we can access at least one theme: When human acts of violence run counter to Nature's life-sustaining designs, the result is confusion and despair. The poem was one of the three poems that the poet included under the heading "Lessons of War." Human actions in this war setting are regimented, restricting, and menacing. Nature, on the contrary, with its "eloquent gestures," Japonica, blossoms, and cross-pollinating bees, is liberating and reassuring, promising renewal. The first part of each stanza with human-made details create fear; the last part of each stanza with details from Nature offers hope.

After grasping this theme, we can go deeper into analyzing the poet's style, this time focusing on the speaker and the stylistic element known as the point of view. Does the poem have only one speaker or two? Are the opening lines of each stanza spoken by a captain in charge of the training camp, with the stanza's last lines representing the unspoken thoughts of the young recruits – the draftees? Or do the two parts represent the speaker's multidimensional personality? Interestingly enough, with the goal of making the poem easier to understand, Laurence Perrine, editor of the poetry anthology *Sound and Sense*, asked for the poet's permission to enclose in quotation marks the contrasting words at the end of each stanza to make a clear distinction between the two contrasting voices in the poem. Henry Reed vehemently opposed any such tinkering with his poem, thus validating and honoring the reader's independent interpretation.

Having reached this point in style awareness and analysis, we may, if we so desire, venture further into inferring yet another theme: however grim and humorless the reality may be, human mind offers through imagination an escape route for the afflicted. The simultaneity and coexistence of both negative and positive details in the poem's stanzas suggest this theme.

One unique advantage of style analysis in poetry – if carried out with correct emphasis – is that it brings the reader closer to the poem's meaning.

Third Requirement: Learning the Skill of Analysis

Sample Interpretations through Analysis

Analyzing techniques include looking at selected parts or features of a literary work to see how they contribute to its totality. This frequently used method of interpretation is demonstrated in the sample readings of Native American poet Carter Revard's poem "Discovery of the New World" by two students and in my reading of William Faulkner's story, "A Rose for Emily."[2]

---

2. Read the text of Faulkner's story online using this link:
http://flightline.highline.edu/tkim/Files/Lit100_SS2.pdf

Discovery of the New World

The creatures that we met this morning
marveled at our green skins
and scarlet eyes.
They lack antennae
and can't be made to grasp   5
your proclamation that they are
our lawful food and prey and slaves,
nor can they seem to learn
their body-space is needed to materialize
our oxygen absorbers —   10
which they conceive are breathing
and thinking creatures whom they implore
at first as angels or (later) as devils
when they are being snuffed out
by an absorber swelling   15
into their space.
Their history bled from one this morning
while we were tasting his brain
in holographic rainbows
which we assembled into quite an interesting   20
set of legends –
that's all it came to, though
the colors were quite lovely before we
poured them into our time;
the blue shift bleached away   25
meaningless circumstance and they would not fit
any of our truth-matrices –
there was, however,
a curious visual echo in their history
of our own coming to their earth;   30
a certain General Sherman
had said concerning a group of them
exactly what we were saying to you about these creatures:
it is our destiny to asterize this planet,   35
and they will not be asterized,
so they must be wiped out. We need their space and oxygen
which they do not know how to use,
yet they will not give up their gas unforced,   40
and we feel sure,
whatever our "agreements" made this morning,
we'll have to kill them all:
the more we cook this orbit,
the fewer next time around.   45
We've finished burning all their crops

and killed their cattle.
They'll have to come into our pens
and then we'll get to study
the way our heart attacks and cancers spread among them,   50
since they seem not immune to these.
If we didn't have this mission it might be sad
to see such helpless creatures die,
but never fear,
the riches of this place are ours   55
and worth whatever pain others may have to feel.
We'll soon have it cleared
as in fact it is already, at the poles.
Then we will be safe, and rich, and happy here forever.

Carter Revard (b. 1931)

Interpretations of Revard's poem "Discovery of the New World"

The Aliens Among Us
Student author: Laura F. Franklin

Revard's poem "Discovery of the New World" allegorizes the subjugation of the Native American people by white colonists during the nineteenth century; he does this by presenting the story of an alien race that colonizes the earth and dominates the existing native culture for their own needs, ignoring the physical and psychological harm it will do to the native race.

This poem has a clear message: in order for humanity to evolve and gain wisdom, we must restrain ourselves from dominating other peoples, and the earth, for personal profit.

Revard challenges the reader's perceptions of their own reality: Are we the oppressors, or could we become the oppressed? The poem is narrated by a technologically-superior alien being whose relationship with the human race parallels that historical relationship between Native Americans and white colonists. In this way Revard effectively manipulates the reader into identifying with the oppressed, while simultaneously allowing the reader to feel related to the historical legacy of being an oppressor. Like those white colonists, the alien invaders are morally and philosophically bankrupt, despite their technological superiority.

The alien invaders' actions, and their attitudes towards the conquered race, are a reflection of our own history. Revard shows the invaders' conscious choice to remain ignorant of the natives' intelligence, culture and feelings. The alien speaker feels a twinge of guilt, but justifies the subjugation of the natives by deeming them inferior. The speaker's mission, comfort, and needs far outweigh the suffering of the indigenous race.

The poem parallels historical events in the United States when white colonists took the land from the Native Americans. There are many allusions in the poem that make direct references to events in

American history. The lines, "marveled at our green skin, and scarlet eyes" (2-3) is a reference to the reaction Native Americans had to the colonists' white skin, and blue eyes. Other allusions are made: false agreements with the natives (broken treaties); killing their cattle (buffalo); placing them into pens under alien control (governmentally enforced reservations); and the natives' lack of immunity to the invaders' diseases. Unable to relate to the native people, the alien invaders excuse themselves from moral responsibility by claiming that the natives are inferior – based on the differences in culture and language:

> They lack antennae
> and can't be made to grasp
> your proclamation that they are
> our lawful food and prey and slaves,
> nor can they seem to learn. (4-8)

The poem also alludes to a time in the American history when humans abused and exploited others of their own species:

> there was, . . .
> a curious visual echo in their history
> of our own coming to earth;
> a certain General Sherman
> had said concerning a group of them
> exactly what we were saying to you
> about these creatures:
> it is our destiny to asterize this planet,
> and they will not be asterized,
> so they must be wiped out. (28-37)

The invaders are aware of the native's history; they even see the irony of the historical situation. Yet that knowledge has little effect on the invading civilization, and they choose to exploit, ostracize, and finally destroy the native culture. With their own version of manifest destiny, the aliens justify their need to acquire and conquer:

> If we didn't have this mission it might be sad
> to see such helpless creatures die
> but never fear
> the riches of this place are ours
> and worth whatever pain others may have to feel. (52-56)

The aliens are comfortable with their certainty of superiority: "Then we will be safe, and rich, and happy here forever" (59). Or at least until history repeats itself.

Revard's imaginative use of words implies the other-worldly origins of the speaker: "oxygen absorbers" (10), "truth matrices" (27) and, "asterize" (35). The words "Their history bled from one this morning"

(17) are an effective symbol of the blood which spilled from Native Americans when the white colonists forcibly took their land.

Revard's poem persuades the reader to contemplate history and humanity. He also suggests that perhaps the only way to stop the oppression of others is to learn to identify with those that are oppressed.

Student author: Janey Skinner

This poem describes colonial genocide in the wake of an invasion from the point of view of the victor, with irony using an extended metaphor of alien invasion of the planet Earth to evoke the actual invasion of Native America by Europeans and their descendents in the United States.

One theme in this poem is the capacity of intelligent beings to justify their actions, no matter how brutal, given sufficient incentive (such as valuable natural resources). The invaders in this poem, the aliens, are clearly intelligent, articulate, even with some aesthetic appreciation of the legends and history of the people they are about to obliterate. Yet their "truth-matrices" (a powerful image!) do not admit the history of their victims; the very colors of that history (facts, meaning, analysis) are bleached away. Literally, they cannot be seen. The image of the holographic rainbows and the "blue shift" in the poem makes me think of how narrow a range of light frequencies are visible to the naked human eye – if you shift the frequency of light only slightly toward red or toward blue, we no longer see any color. Surely, there are colors in other frequencies of light, perceptible, for example, to honeybees, but not perceptible to us. Similarly, the alien invaders (whether extraterrestrials or white people) cannot perceive the history, or more importantly, the humanity of the original inhabitants. This blindness is only one of the justifications suggested in the poem. Others include the idea of manifest destiny (here voiced by General Sherman); avoidance of future conflict ("the more we cook this orbit, the fewer next time around"); scientific inquiry ("and then we'll get to study..."); the riches to be gained (which are "worth whatever pain others may have to feel"); and utopian ideals ("we will be safe, and rich, and happy here forever"). All of these justifications were and are fully present in the colonization of the Americas.

Using Analysis to Interpret Fiction

The skill of analysis that was applied to poetry can also be used to interpret works of fiction. For this exercise, Faulkner's short story "A Rose for Emily," which was discussed in greater detail in Chapter Three, is especially suitable because it offers some challenges that can be met through careful analytic reading.

Interpretation of William Faulkner's "A Rose for Emily" by the author of this book

Faulkner's story is an example of implying themes through elements of style rather than stating them in the narrator's or a character's words. There are hardly any overtly thematic statements in the story; however, by analyzing its stylistic elements of setting and imagery and by connecting the story's title to its content, we can formulate its themes. Understanding the implications of an author's choice of the title, which could be considered a part of style, often helps, as it does in the case of Faulkner's story, in grasping the work's thematic substance.

Besides this approach to theme extraction through an author's style, the method of character analysis to discover themes — exemplified in the interpretation of Forster's story "The Other Side of the Hedge" in Chapter Two — can also be applied to "A Rose for Emily." By focusing on the values and actions of the main characters and making cause-and-effect connections between their significant deeds and their fates, we can formulate statements of themes. The following interpretation of Faulkner's story uses both methods of style analysis and character analysis for theme recognition and theme formulation.

Interpretation through style analysis

In "A Rose for Emily," the story's setting becomes the background for themes that are connected with the futility of clinging to a dead past. Emily's house, once glorious but now in decay, is an odd but imposing presence representing an anomaly: "Miss Emily's house was left, lifting its stubborn and coquettish decay above the cotton wagons and the gasoline pumps." This house represents Emily's aristocratic past, to which she clings desperately and unreasonably, disregarding the fact that it is out of place in her day and age.

In addition to setting, another stylistic feature that expresses the theme of decay is the author's choice of imagery. The "tarnished gilt easel" on which stands a portrait of Emily's father, the ebony cane "with a tarnished gold head" on which Emily leans, the smell of "dust and disuse — a close, dank smell," and the "faint dust" that rises sluggishly in Emily's room, all reinforce the story's theme of decline and disintegration.

Interpretation through character analysis

Searching for Faulkner's thematic emphasis through his characters, we may find the story's title, in itself, to be significantly suggestive. Since there is no rose in the story, why did Faulkner use it in the title? One possibility is that the narrator's attitude toward Emily may be different from that of the other townsfolk. Perhaps Emily's spurning of the tyranny of time and its fads leaves an impression on the narrator, who might also have attributed Emily's bizarre and criminal conduct to mental illness rather than any inherent evil in her. The story does refer to the evidence of mental illness in the family. The casually mentioned detail of Emily's giving china painting lessons during the miserable days of her isolation could also be viewed positively. The narrator's pity for Emily's plight is mixed with recognition of her stubbornness, displayed in her choice to live on her own terms opposing any new system. Her strength is suggested by the image of her "vigorous iron-gray" hair. Since it was not Emily's fate to receive a rose of love or happiness – illustrated by her abortive relationship with Homer Barron – the narrator gives her the rose of pathetic remembrance in the form of this story.

Speculation about the meaning of the story's title in relation to the character's values leads us to one of the possible themes: *human beings are multidimensional; with a little empathy, we can muster some compassion even in the most unappealing of human beings (such as Emily).*

Drawing a cause-and-effect connection between Emily's actions and their outcome, between her stubborn, unchanging ways and her dilemma, we also learn that *when the present seems threatening, one is likely to cling to the past, thereby diminishing the chances of a satisfactory compromise with life.*

These interpretive comments on Faulkner's "A Rose for Emily" are just a few of the many possible readings, all of which may be validated with supporting details from the story. Complete analysis of its plot is in Chapter Three.

The Process of Discovering Themes:
Summing Up the Chapter

In writing the sample interpretations of this chapter, all interpreters relied on the skills that have been explained and exemplified in this chapter:

- taking mental notes when reading a literary work
- using explication and analysis to elucidate themes

Armed with these skills, we can enjoy the luxury of simply following the feelings that different parts of literary works/movies evoke in us. In the course of tracing the sources of our feelings, we are led to the creation of themes. This process develops our interpretation skill through analysis and critical thinking, together with persuasive and structured writing. The following list of clues and aids to theme recognition can facilitate literary interpretation and analysis.

Summary of Clues to Recognizing Themes in Literature and Film with Additional Aids to Interpretation

1. Look for direct statements of themes by narrators and characters.

2. Keep in mind that every literary work and film usually concerns at least one major topic. By determining the position or stand the work takes on that topic, we can arrive at its theme.

3. Go beyond the surface meaning of the literary work and the film. You can do so by following your feelings evoked by actions, events, statements, settings, etc., and by asking such questions: Did the characters deserve their fate? Was there a cause-and-effect relationship between the characters' deeds and the outcome? What kind of world does the literary work or movie present? Is it comforting, reassuring, frightening, or indifferent? How would you feel being part of that world?

4. Analyze significant events and experiences for their theme-bearing function.

5. Analyze various stylistic devices used by the author. Some devices, such as setting, atmosphere, tone, allusion, and symbol may be connected with themes. For example, a theme may grow out of imagery. In a work of this nature, the author's theme, (intended meaning) or purpose, (intended effect) could be surmised through a careful study of the central images or sense impressions that expand into a thematic design.

6. Think of literary works, personal experiences, and films with which you are already familiar that stirred feelings similar to those created by the work you are studying. Such analogues are often variations on the same theme.

7. Authors and film directors connect their main themes with the work's major characters and events. The search for a work's main themes should not overlook these two elements. To use this method, go beyond external events and actions that issue from characters. Try to grasp the values that characters represent. An understanding of those values and a discovery of a cause-and-effect connection between the values and their impact on the fate of the characters could suggest a theme.

8. Often a quick access to a story's or film's world of ideas can be gained by asking a few probing questions about the outcome of the story in relation to the narrator's and characters' motives, actions, fears, and aspirations. For example, do the characters deserve what happens to them? Do the outcomes suggest the existence of a just order that rules the world presented in the literary work? If a virtuous character comes to grief, does this outcome suggest that virtue does not guarantee prosperity? Concluding parts of literary works often provoke such thoughts that we can use for our theme formulations.

9. Sometimes you may have to rely on inferences that you can draw from reading between the lines. Since inferences are always of a tenuous nature, you must exercise caution when using this method of interpretation.

Themes derived through inferences may not be supportable by evidence in the form of direct quotations or identifiable elements from the literary or cinematic work. However, such themes may be suggested by intuitive perception. All the same, to validate your statements of theme(s) you must state exactly what in the literary work/movie is the source of your perceptions and inferences. Test your inferences with an eye on the entire work, not just a portion of it.

Just as interpretation requires going a step beyond comprehension, getting at themes through inference sometimes requires going beyond reliance on readily verifiable elements in the given text. My formulation of a theme on the basis of the title of Faulkner's "A Rose for Emily" earlier in this chapter is an illustration of using inference, which is supported by the narrator's tribute to Emily.

10. Pay attention to the aesthetics of omission. Unexpected omissions in statements, events, and responses can be significant in creating themes. Using this method, an author can convey a theme as an artist might shape an image with the use of empty space in a painting. When a character, for example, does not say or feel what is expected of him/her, it may be the author's way of drawing our attention to an important idea. Classic examples of this elusive style of theme formulation are Albert Camus' short story "The Guest" and his novel *The Stranger*, in which the characters express many of their feelings by concealing them.

11. Read the opening and closing paragraphs carefully and pay special attention to all those words and details that relate to the work's title. Similarly, when watching movies, view the opening and concluding scenes closely and make a mental note of all those scenes that appear to have a connection with the film's title.

12. To determine the importance of a theme, pay attention to the amount of space devoted to its presentation and development. Unless a narrator or a character states the importance of a theme clearly (which is rarely the case), the usual way of measuring a theme's significance is the amount of space allocated to it, together with its repetition in the literary work/film.

Exercises to Test Your Mastery of Chapter Five

1. This chapter ended with many clues or aids to discovering themes in literature and film. Add two more aids on your own.

2. When reading literature for interpretation, what kind of mental notes prove helpful to the reader?

3. How is explication different from analysis? Are these two skills equally suited to all literary works, or do certain works require one skill rather than the other? Write an explication of an especially complex poem, short story, or section of a novel or play.

4. Describe a few steps in the process of discovering themes in literature and film. Support your points by referring to a specific work.

5. What advice would you give someone who has difficulty going beyond the surface meaning of a literary work or movie? Support your answer with examples.

CHAPTER SIX

INFORMAL INTERPRETATION
Using the Journal Format

Journaling as a Passport to Good Writing

Journals are a way to intimacy with literature. They can be an informal and highly interesting way to study literature and film. The journaling technique is introduced in this chapter with these objectives in mind:

1. Becoming more familiar with various literary forms: this knowledge is necessary because each form comes with its own unique style and ways of theme embodiment.

2. Feeling comfortable with works of art through the inviting informality of the journal format: It has been noticed that those students who find the formality of writing literary essays forbidding welcome the inviting informality of journals. They can engage in literary criticism without the trepidation that they usually associate with writing about poems, short stories, novels, drama, and film.

3. By collecting ideas for future papers, students can use journals as precursors to complete interpretive essays.

4. Using the journals' potential as conditioning and warm-up mental calisthenics, thereby building up our emotional and intellectual stamina before we face the rigor of writing formal literary essays.

Definitions of Literary Forms

Use of the two journal formats explained in this chapter will greatly facilitate access to any literary work or film. Before starting journal entries, however, it is necessary to have a basic understanding of various literary forms.

Both the novel and the short story can be defined as narratives in which a cause-and-effect sequence of events illuminates an aspect of human nature. Film is also typically a narrative but with the difference that it is primarily a story told through visual representation.

Drama and poetry also comment on and embody the human condition. The distinguishing mark of drama is that it is a portrayal of life by means of action, speech (dialogue and soliloquies), and nonverbal elements, such as scenery, setting, sound effects, gestures, costumes, color, etc. In drama the narrative voice of fiction is replaced with the dramatist's brief stage directions, noticed only when we read a play. Thus drama shares with fiction and film the characteristic of telling a story, but with the difference of people acting and talking on a stage.

The defining characteristic of poetry is that it is usually the most condensed form of literature that relies on connotative language, allusion, image, and sound more than any other genre. All of the preceding forms of literature require interpretation to understand the author's concerns, emphasis, and themes. Works of nonfiction, which include essays, memoirs, and literary criticism, do not require as much in-depth interpretation in order to be understood, as the author's main point is either implied in a recognizable manner or given clearly in the form of a thesis, which is supported with facts, arguments, and examples.

Steps in Journaling

Journal entries can be an inviting way to respond to selected literary works and films. When making your selections, start with simpler works and build up to more complex works that require greater effort (in some cases even research) to be understood. You can journal just about anywhere. Set aside a spiral notebook or smaller size journal specifically for your writing exercises. Journals can cover short stories and poems in their entirety. However, when recording your response to a novel or a play, try to limit each journal to a specific topic and theme in the work or to a major character that carries the theme; otherwise, your journal entry may become too long. Your summary of the novel/play should also be directed mainly to those details that relate to your selected topic.

When reading lengthy and complex works, you will find it helpful to make a tentative list of topics and themes in your journal, noting the page numbers where they are introduced, as you proceed with your reading. You will need to include quotations/details to support your points. Keep a record of events that may suggest a theme and notice the values represented by each major character, for they may have thematic implications. These rough notes can then yield more concise and focused responses. The ease with which journals allow access to complex works is proof of their usefulness in literary study. However, simplicity of the journal format does not mean that it is less valuable than a formal essay to explore literary works. Sample journal entries in this chapter will substantiate this point.

Two Journal Formats

Two journal formats are suggested, with differing gradations of informality and subjectivity.

Informal and free flowing

All or any number of the five basic journal components – *summary, topic, theme, supporting details, and style* – may be covered without necessarily using those labels in this type of journal entry. Initially, evaluation of an author's style of writing is optional in this format. Whether the five components are labeled or not, their treatment in the informal responses is not as detailed as in the more structured variety of the journal.

Structured format

This format treats the selected works in greater depth – a precursor to formal literary essays. All five basic components of a journal (listed above) are covered and labeled as subheadings. Some responses may also include comments on any of the following additional items:

1. Personal enrichment that the work has brought you
2. Inclusion of a critic's helpful evaluative comment on the work being studied
3. Insights offered into the culture(s) that the work examines
4. A concluding comment

Most writing samples in this chapter adhere to the structured format. Only a few examples of the informal journal are included. You may start with the format that you are more comfortable with, but practice both varieties. Before reading the sample journal entries, become familiar with the works being discussed. More poems and stories are included than other genres for two reasons: They are shorter in length and constitute a large portion of literature courses. They are also an attractive means to introduce cultural diversity.

Rationale for including more than usual sample essays and literary works in this chapter

The principles of formatting journal entries can be learned quickly by reading the opening pages of this chapter and just a few samples of each of the two kinds of journals – informal and structured. A few words are therefore necessary to explain the rationale behind the abundance of students' writing samples and the accompanying literary works. Reading other students' interpretations of literary masterpieces – learning from peers – is an interesting and effective way to increase your knowledge of literature and improve your writing. Secondly, when completing the assignments in this book, students chose literary works that are either actual or potential masterpieces. Reading them is a good investment of your time. The more writing samples you read, the greater awareness you acquire of the variety of writing options available. And, finally, the rich variety of literary works and different ways to capture their beauty required more samples.

THE INFORMAL JOURNAL

This format encourages personal interaction with literary works. It results in subjective responses, self-debate, thinking aloud, and asking questions, along with speculations about the answers. Such readings – valid literary exercises in their own right – may lead to the structured journal and formal interpretive essays.

STUDENTS' JOURNAL RESPONSES

The students whose journal entries I have included here were enrolled in my introduction to literature classes just like other student authors featured in this book. If more than one sample appears on the same work, it is to show how readers and viewers can arrive at different, equally valid interpretations of the same work. In the informal journal samples, labels of "summary," "topic," "theme," "supporting details," and "style" are not used. However, the organization follows that pattern.

Informal Journal Responses to Poems

In all journal entries, the poems precede the responses to them. In cases of high permission costs, only the links to those poems are given.

Constantly Risking Absurdity
by Lawrence Ferlinghetti (b. 1919)

Read this poem on the internet before reading the journal entry on it. Use this link:

http://www.poemhunter.com/poem/constantly-risking-absurdity/

Student author: Mara McCain

This poem compares the feet of an acrobat with the poet's metrical feet. Both must use precision and skill, timing and balance, and both teeter on threads before a "sea of faces," risking their reputation. Neither can make even a small mistake, always one step from peril. They are both trying to give pleasure, but the poet is particularly concerned with truth, "for he is the super realist."

The subject is the extraordinary skill needed in performing meaningful work under the pressure of performance and scrutiny. The fine line between beauty and triviality, the delicate balance between success and failure are risks omnipresent in the tasks of the artist, who must make something out of nothing.

> The poet like an acrobat
>   climbs on rime
>   to a high wire of his own making.

The positioning of the lines is demonstrative, creating a feeling of the tension of the rope, tightness of word selection. It shows the steps taken by both the acrobat and the poet. Ferlinghetti uses the personification of beauty standing there waiting.

> where Beauty stands and waits
> > with gravity
> > > to start her death defying leap.

The word "gravity" has double meanings. It is the force trying to pull the poet and the acrobat down, but gravity also represents the seriousness with which a poet approaches his subject. The double meanings and implications are a stylistic feature throughout the poem.

Not Waving but Drowning

Nobody heard him, the dead man,
But still he lay moaning:
I was much further out than you thought
And not waving but drowning.

Poor chap, he always loved larking
And now he's dead
It must have been too cold for him his heart gave way,
They said.

Oh, no no no, it was too cold always
(Still the dead one lay moaning)
I was much too far out all my life
And not waving but drowning.

Stevie Smith (1902-1971)

Student author: Laurian Rhodes

This poem describes the dilemma of a man whose desperate cries for help are misconstrued as just waving by the onlookers. He moans as he is drowning, but no one takes his gestures and pleas seriously. The poem's message becomes even more alarming when it is revealed that the man's drowning was not sudden, for he had been drowning all his life while trying to send out messages for help.

Thus the poem is about the signals that people send out – signals that are often misperceived. "Not Waving but Drowning" is a vivid illustration of the apathy with which we view our fellow humans' sufferings and choose to either ignore them or deliberately misinterpret them so as to stay uninvolved in their problems.

"I was much too far out all my life, and not waving but drowning." This starkly visual line urges us to distinguish between waving and drowning. It reminds us of the connection between the drowning man and us. At one time or another, we have all felt "too far out" and in too much pain, while those in a position to help chose to ignore our cries for help.

The next poem by Robert Hayden introduces the sonnet form of poetry.

Those Winter Sundays

Sundays too my father got up early
and put his clothes on in the blue black cold,
then with cracked hands that ache
from labor in the weekday weather made
banked fires blaze. No one ever thanked him.
I'd wake and hear the cold splintering, breaking.
When the rooms were warm, he'd call,
And slowly I would rise and dress,
Fearing the chronic angers of that house,
Speaking indifferently to him.
who had driven out the cold
and polished my good shoes as well.
What did I know, what did I know
of love's austere and lonely offices?

Robert Hayden (1913-1980)

Student author: Larry Devich

This brief poem about paternal love by Hayden illustrates wonderfully that very often the love of a father is subtle and difficult for a child to see, especially when he is caused to be afraid by the often angry behavior of that same father.

Hayden begins his poem by describing the dedication of the father. "Sundays too my father got up early" indicates that every day the father was the first to rise and make the house comfortable for the family. "When the rooms were warm, he'd call." The speaker is unable to interpret this act as an act of love because of fear: "and slowly I would rise and dress,/fearing the chronic angers of that house." That the love of the father went unnoticed is seen in line 5 where the poet writes, "No one ever thanked him" and in line 10, "Speaking indifferently to him/ who had driven out the cold/ and polished my good shoes as well." In the end the son has at last realized (perhaps too late?) that he had missed an important aspect of his father's being, "What did I know, what did I know/ of love's austere and lonely offices?"

Informal Journal Responses to Short Stories

Lullaby
by Leslie Marmon Silko (b. 1948)

The text of the story is in Chapter Ten.

Student author: Maxwell Lynch

In "Lullaby," Leslie Marmon Silko explores the loss of culture by exposing the chasm between her true Native American identity and the one forced upon her by the injustices deferred from the initial subjugation of her people centuries prior – all set in motion by the intrusion of Europeans. The main tragedies of her life are the loss of her son to the war, her children to doctors (presumably for their TB infection) and her vacuous relationship with her husband, Chato.

Throughout the story, she has flashbacks, or memories of the joys she once had – bittersweet memories of her old life. They seem to at once haunt and comfort her, as if her daily life has become a waking nightmare. The only salve is the easily triggered memory of a more harmonious past. A carefully orchestrated dichotomy in the narrative reveals these memories, as the line between reality and reverie is constantly traversed. Visual and olfactory cues set off the remembrances that buoy this aspect of the narrative, each triggering a moment from her past that paints a stark contrast between her authentic identity and her bastardized one.

Despite the deep sadness over her losses, there is an undercurrent of defiance and perseverance that permeates the surface of her story. It suggests that no matter the devastation of her Native American cultural identity, nothing can take away her memories, the shared collective thread to her people that has survived generations of persecution. This concept is most cogently expressed as she recites her family's song, its final line the most striking: "We are together always/There never was a time when this was not so."

Informal Journal Responses to Novels

As we move to the journaling of novels, we face the challenge of keeping our entries manageable by restricting our coverage to just one or two major topics covered in the book. The novels – The Great Gatsby and Wuthering Heights– could not be included in this book because of their size; you can read them online or from a library.

SAMPLE ESSAYS

The Great Gatsby
by F. Scott Fitzgerald (1896-1940)
http://ebooks.adelaide.edu.au/f/fitzgerald/f_scott/gatsby/contents.html

Sample journal response by the author of this book

Informal journal entries can take some unusually interesting forms. For example, in the form of self-debate one could ponder the ending of *The Great Gatsby* by F. Scott Fitzgerald, in this way:

I have always wondered why Nick Carraway, Gatsby's friend and the novel's narrator, did not set the record straight. We, as readers of the novel, know that it was Daisy, not Gatsby who ran over Myrtle and killed her. However, Tom Buchanan (Daisy's husband and Gatsby's rival) misinforms Myrtle's husband George Wilson about Gatsby's role in the car accident. Wilson ends up killing the innocent Gatsby.

I have never liked Nick's failure to speak up and protect his friend Gatsby against a damning, false accusation. However, reading the novel this time, I became aware of possible reasons for Nick's silence on this crucial issue. Is it possible that Nick did not divulge Daisy's culpability because that is exactly what Gatsby himself would have done to protect Daisy? By keeping quiet and thus protecting Daisy, Nick might be honoring Gatsby. Yet another possibility for Nick's silence might be that he is fully aware of his own powerlessness in the face of Tom Buchanan's power and influence. Perhaps a sense of the futility of his effort might have forced him not to attempt what he might have considered impossible. Tom blatantly and shamelessly says to Nick that Gatsby killed Myrtle – a complete lie. So it comes down to Nick's word against Tom's.

After going through this self-debate and reflection, I no longer judge Nick's silence harshly, and his leaving of the East coast glamour for the simple securities of his ancestral rural Midwest begins to make sense.

Wuthering Heights
by Emily Bronte (1818-1848)
http://www.online-literature.com/bronte/wuthering/

Sample journal response by the author of this book

Emily Bronte's famous novel, *Wuthering Heights*, is a story of two of the most passionate lovers in literature – Catherine Earnshaw and Heathcliff. Heathcliff is a waif, whom Catherine's father brings home to be looked after. Catherine is a willful girl. A strong love develops between them, nurtured by the wild moors that they roam together. Later, however, Cathy tries to suppress her love out of forced conformity to conventions and because someone with better means and a better name than Heathcliff wins her away from him.

We shudder with horror at the frenzy of Heathcliff's revenge after he returns from America, having made his fortune. During his absence, Catherine has yielded to the ethics of "sensibleness" by marrying Edgar Linton – someone of her own class. Heathcliff gains control of Wuthering Heights by taking advantage of Catherine's brother Hindley's dwindling fortunes. He also marries Edgar's sister (Isabella) just to spite and control Edgar and Catherine.

Despite having been suppressed and denied first by Cathy, then by Heathcliff, their love finally overcomes everything – both lovers, their marriage partners, their families, even their physical deaths – for even after Cathy and Heathcliff are no longer alive, their spirits haunt the wilderness of the moors. Like the dwellers of Wuthering Heights and Thrushcross Grange, we come into contact with this strange, fierce, and death-defying passion. In their re-absorption into the wild moor that had nurtured their love, we witness this strange apotheosis.

Informal Journal Responses to Plays

When responding to plays (in fact, to any literary work or movie), we have several options to write informally about the issues raised in the work. Some of them are the following:

1. Writing in a character's own voice.
2. Writing a letter to a character, advising him or her to either take or not take an action for his/her own good.
3. Copying from the play a statement (has to be a direct quotation) that communicates a great idea. What you choose should be understandable on its own (without the necessity of having to read the play first). It will be necessary to explain how your choice is an example of a great idea.

Example of no.1. I am Hamlet, and I am here to set the record straight. Everyone has formed strong opinions about me and claims to know the deepest recesses of my mind. Professional critics seem to be the worst offenders. Who can know more about me – Hamlet – than my own self? So let me tell you about the great ideas Shakespeare wished to communicate to humanity through me. And no, they are not exactly the same ideas that are often attributed to me.

This informal journal exercise could continue along these lines.

Explanation of no. 2. If a character is guilty of an error of judgment, bias, or any such failing, you can offer help in the form of a letter of advice for self-appraisal and corrective action. For example, if you chose Lorraine Hansberry's play *A Raisin in the Sun* for this exercise, you could address your letter to the character Karl Lindner, who thinks highly of himself and is not aware of his racism. You could make him aware of this failing. A sample letter by Aaron Nathan, titled "Flourishing Without Roots," is in the essays that are linked to the website connected to this book.

Example of no. 3. "Madness in great ones must not unwatched go" (Hamlet). Insane policies of just one powerful person can cause havoc not only in a country but in the whole world.

STRUCTURED, IN-DEPTH JOURNAL ENTRIES

The journal format explained below and observed in most of the samples that follow is of a more demanding variety that brings it closer to the formal literary essay.

Summary

In about 50 words for poems and 100 words for longer works, summarize the work's essential content, focusing on main events, actions and interactions of major characters, values and motives of important characters, and the conclusion. This is a valuable exercise because writing succinct summaries is going to be a part of most of your writing assignments on literary works and films. Avoid analyzing, interpreting, and evaluating the works in this part of the journal.

Topic

In no more than one sentence, identify the literary work's/movie's broad topic (that is, what the work is about). As per advice of Chapter One, do not use specific details, such as names of characters and places, to keep your statement general/universal.

Theme

In this part of the exercise, write one or two sentences to narrow the topic down to a theme, which often is your perception of the author's/filmmaker's position on the topic. Identifying one theme is enough, but if you like, you may mention and support more than one theme. The theme or the author's position is discovered through interpretation of the work's events, key statements, action, characters' values, and similar elements. You have learned from the advice on theme formulation in Chapter One that a formal statement of theme consists of two parts:

- the introductory part of the sentence often ending with "is that," "that," "how," or a colon, and
- a complete thought that follows the introductory part.

The introductory part may be omitted sometimes if clarity is not compromised. Review the relevant part of Chapter One if necessary. Variety of phrasing is necessary in thematic statements. The usual criteria for a good statement of theme are as follows:

1. Like the statement of topic, a thematic statement is free of specific details, such as characters' names, place names, etc. Being of general, sometimes universal, application, a theme is not limited to just the characters and places in a work.
2. It covers most of the literary/cinematic work – events as well as characters.
3. It is phrased attractively and clearly.
4. It does not reduce the rich complexity of a work to a superficial, crude, and cliché-like expression.
5. It is written in the present tense in the form of complete sentences.
6. It assumes that the reader is not familiar with the literary work or movie being discussed and uses that assumption in phrasing themes to make them understandable to readers.

Supporting details

A statement of theme must be supported with evidence from the work. The evidence should consist of three or four sentences containing direct quotations mixed with a summary of relevant details in your own words. When writing this part, remember to assume that the reader is not familiar with the work. Always include explanatory and clarifying details.

Elements of style

In a few sentences for short poems and at greater length for longer works, point out the striking and effective words, phrases, images, sounds, and any other notable elements of style, such as symbol, allusion, irony, paradox, understatement, analogy, personification, and figurative language. Include a brief comment on the function of the stylistic features that you choose to discuss. Chapter Four of this book covered style in a comprehensive manner. The following points, meant to reduce the mystery that surrounds "style," are taken from that chapter.

Advice on Appreciating an Author's Style

The ability to appreciate and articulate how style plays a part in literary works takes time. Therefore, coverage of style need not be elaborate at this point. Your format for style appreciation may consist of three steps:

1. Identifying the element of style being used
2. Giving one or two examples from the work being discussed
3. Commenting on the function/effectiveness of the element of style

Of the three items listed above, number 3 is the most difficult part. It would be helpful to remember that an author's choice of stylistic elements may serve any of the following and similar functions:

- Dramatizing and reinforcing a theme
- Creating a mood
- Revealing and developing a character
- Jolting the reader into a new awareness or giving the reader new eyes to see an apparently everyday occurrence
- Bringing to the reader dramatic illumination of a complex idea or feeling
- Reversing the expected response through situational irony
- Adding sensory dimensions to intellectual content through imagery and figurative language
- Adding extra layers of meanings through verbal or dramatic irony
- Giving delight through ingenious formations of phrases, sometimes transporting the reader to a different realm with magical words and sounds.

Importance of focus

When you are appreciating an author's style, keep your focus on the way he or she expresses an idea or a feeling, not on what he/she is expressing. To maintain correct focus, treat the author as an active maker of the work – someone who is using stylistic elements to enhance his/her ideas and feelings.

Example of vague focus: The allusion to Hamlet in Eliot's poem is a reminder of Prufrock's indecisiveness.

Example of improved focus: Eliot selects his allusions carefully to make them serve specific functions. His allusion to Hamlet, for example, dramatizes and puts into sharper focus Prufrock's inability to make up his mind (just like Hamlet in Shakespeare's play).

Optional Items in Structured Journals

Personal enrichment the work has brought you

In a few sentences, record your personal response to the world the work has presented. Write your feelings about the characters and their values. Identify characters and events that serve as a contrast or a parallel to you or to situations you are familiar with. You have already implied in your statement of theme the new awareness or insight the work has brought to you. Keep that knowledge in mind when writing this part.

Research input

This part is only for selected works, especially those that prove difficult to understand. One convenient and valuable way to include research material is copying a quotation from a scholarly work – a quotation that captures the work's essence. For example, if your journal entry is on Shakespeare's *Hamlet*, you may quote A. W. Schlegel's following words:

Hamlet is . . . a tragedy of thought inspired by continual and never-satisfied meditation on human destiny and the dark perplexity of the events of this world, and calculated to call forth the very same meditation in the minds of the spectators (Schlegel 404).

Cultural insight

Acknowledge the insights that the author has offered into the culture(s) represented in the work. An example is the student Noah Reinhertz' interpretation of the short story, titled "On the Market Day" (the first sample essay in Chapter Ten). He makes several comments to enhance our awareness about life in a part of Africa, its huge challenges and small pleasures. Another example of cultural insight is the concluding paragraph of the journal entry on the movie *Samapti* at the end of this chapter.

A concluding comment

Include this comment on the literary work's overall achievement only if it will not repeat what was stated earlier in the journal entry.

Keeping a journal along the lines suggested above will prepare you in a systematic way to respond to literary works and movies in an informed and pleasing way. Remember to start with simpler, shorter works, such as poems or short stories. Later you can advance to longer and more complex works like novels, movies, and plays.

Structured Journal Responses to Poems

Those Winter Sundays
Three readings of the poem by the author of this book

The text of the poem is in the Informal Journals section of this chapter.

In giving different interpretations of Robert Hayden's poem, I have tried to show how we can arrive at several different but valid themes through interpretation. A theme is valid if it is supported with convincing evidence from the work itself. Evaluation of the poet's style is included to make this formal journal entry complete.

First interpretation of the poem

Summary
The speaker, now an adult, is reminiscing about his childhood. He blames his lack of knowledge and perception, ("What did I know, what did I know") for his failure to understand and appreciate the love his father offered. This love did not consist of soft words; it was shown in actions, such as getting up early even on Sundays to build a fire to drive out the cold, polishing the speaker's shoes, and doing extremely hard manual work (his cracked hands ached from labor) to provide for the family.

Topic
The importance of expressing feelings

Theme
Hayden's poem is a moving reminder that we should communicate our feelings before time takes away the opportunity.

Supporting details
The speaker regrets too late, "What did I know, what did I know/ Of love's austere and lonely offices." The father, whom the speaker would like to thank, is most likely dead by the time the speaker thinks of showing his appreciation.

Second interpretation of the same poem

Summary
(The summary could be the same as in the interpretation above.)

Topic
Confusion between love and duty

Theme
Caring acts, when carried out in a mechanical and undemonstrative manner, can be mistaken for duties and obligations, performance of which is a thankless job, often taken for granted by those whom those acts are meant to serve.

145

Supporting details

The child in this poem saw no love – only "chronic angers" and resentful performance of duties – in his father's everyday acts of concern and sacrifice: getting up early even on Sundays to make a fire to drive out the cold, polishing the speaker's shoes, and doing extremely hard manual work to provide for the family, evidenced by his "cracked hands that ached from labor." The father's alienation is conveyed by the words, "No one ever thanked him." The implication is that there were others in the house beside the father and the speaker, but no one appreciated the father's sacrifices.

Third interpretation of the same poem

Summary
(Same as in the earlier interpretation)

Topic
Delayed awareness of love

Theme
It is tragic and painful when awareness of an important truth comes too late.

Supporting details
As a child the speaker noticed the sullen atmosphere – "the chronic angers of the house" – but failed to perceive love in his father's everyday small acts of self-sacrifice. The child neither understood nor appreciated what his father did for the family. Now as an adult he can understand his father's acts of sacrifice as love but regrets his former lack of understanding of "love's austere and lonely offices."

Style (applies to all three examples)
The poet has compressed a lot of feelings in this 14-line poem. The first notable element of style is the repetition of "What did I know" in line 13. Since the speaker uses words sparingly, this repetition stands out and helps to emphasize the speaker's realization of his lack of understanding of the complexity of love.

Another striking stylistic element is the paradox in "love's austere and lonely offices" that concludes the poem. The paradox is inherent in the fact that ordinarily we associate love with giving, not with the austerity of holding back, and we think of love as a cure, not a cause of loneliness. However, in the context and circumstances of the poem, love is displayed through small everyday actions, through holding back emotion (exercising austerity in displaying emotion), and through suffering from isolation as a result of finding no appreciation for this kind of love. This device effectively captures the paradoxical nature of such love that consists of withholding rather than giving and which, instead of curing loneliness, leads to it. Nevertheless, this austere form of the father's expression of love can best prepare the youth for the harsh world outside, where love is not always present.

Conclusion
In fourteen lines, using emotionally charged language, Robert Hayden has taken us through a person's memories of childhood, his failure to appreciate his father's sacrifices for the family, and his eventual

enlightenment about the difficult role of his father. The poem thus becomes a memorial, a monument to the spiritual father-child bond that overrides their imperfect ways to express it.

The just-concluded sample journal entry would be enough to give you a clear idea of the structured journaling format.

STUDENTS' JOURNAL RESPONSES

Structured journal responses to poems

For the next journal entry the student Dana Gong chose Matthew Arnold's "Dover Beach," a poem that is famous for its anti-war and pro-love stance.

Dover Beach

The sea is calm tonight,
The tide is full, the moon lies fair
Upon the straits;—on the French coast the light
Gleams and is gone; the cliffs of England stand,
Glimmering and vast, out in the tranquil bay.
Come to the window, sweet is the night-air!
Only, from the long line of spray
Where the sea meets the moon-blanched land,
Listen! you hear the grating roar
Of pebbles which the waves draw back, and fling,
At their return, up the high strand,
Begin, and cease, and then again begin,
With tremulous cadence slow, and bring
The eternal note of sadness in.

Sophocles long ago
Heard it on the Aegean, and it brought
Into his mind the turbid ebb and flow
Of human misery; we
Find also in the sound a thought,
Hearing it by this distant northern sea.
The Sea of Faith
Was once, too, at the full, and round earth's shore
Lay like the folds of a bright girdle furled.
But now I only hear
Its melancholy, long, withdrawing roar,

Retreating, to the breath
Of the night-wind, down the vast edges drear
And naked shingles of the world.

Ah, love, let us be true
To one another! for the world, which seems
To lie before us like a land of dreams,
So various, so beautiful, so new,
Hath really neither joy, nor love, nor light,
Nor certitude, nor peace, nor help for pain;
And we are here as on a darkling plain
Swept with confused alarms of struggle and flight,
Where ignorant armies clash by night.

Matthew Arnold (1822-1888)

Student author: Dana Gong

Summary

The speaker's senses are heightened as he describes a vivid, fluid scene of the ocean meeting the land. The flow of the waves, although alluring, reminds the speaker of the human condition – the turbid ebb and flow of human misery. According to the speaker, the world is a melancholy and apathetic place due to the decline of religious faith and because of pointless violence. Ignorance, pain, and apathy are the underlying forces. The speaker retreats, solemn and pessimistic, into the solace of love.

Topic

Decline of faith and presence of inexplicable violence

Theme

Although humanity is lacking in faith, bombarded by misery and uncertainty, love can still offer a solution.

Support

The waves of the sea with their "tremulous cadence slow," their "melancholy, long, withdrawing roar," and their "eternal note of sadness" reflect the solemn condition of the human faith. On the surface, the world seems a beautiful place, but underneath lies uncertainty and confusion:

. . . for the world, which seems
To lie before us like a land of dreams,
So various, so beautiful, so new,
Hath really neither joy, nor love, nor light
Nor certitude, nor peace, nor help for pain (line 30-34)

The only answer to this dilemma, the speaker feels, is being true to one another in a trusting and sincere love:

> Ah, love, let us be true
> To one another!

Style

Rhythm and symbolism are two of the poet's notable stylistic elements. As seen in each of the five stanzas, the rhythm of the poem captures the rhythm of the waves. Arnold's imagery, the "to-and-fro" movement within the poem emulates the "to-and-fro" movement of the ocean. An example is lines 10-12:

> . . . Of pebbles which the waves drawback, and fling,
> At their return, up the high strand,
> Begin, and cease, and then again begin. . .

Symbolism is noticed in Arnold's phrasing. The "The Sea of Faith" is symbolic of collective religious faith and is personified in lines 25-26 with "Its melancholy, long, withdrawing roar,/ Retreating, to the breath of the night wind." The implication is that humanity's faith in religion has retreated like the melancholy notes of the sea. As a result, instead of the protective "folds of a bright girdle" (symbolic of a comforting faith) humanity is left with "naked shingles" that are symbolic of a bleak, harsh, and uncaring universe of objects.

Mirror
by Sylvia Plath

The text of this poem has already been included in Chapter One. Caroline Alcantara's reading of the poem capture's its theme of aging.

Student author: Caroline Alcantara

Summary

In this poem, a young woman seeks affirmation of her youth, her beauty, and her very worth from a silver-framed mirror, projecting a reflection of her face, a reflection that bears the lines and creases of age. Plath explores the relationship between the woman and the detached, indifferent mirror, whose perpetual state of meditation on the opposite wall is constantly interrupted by the woman's face. The poem is also about the woman's daily pilgrimage to the four-cornered little god, whom she approaches in desperate hope of finding a miracle – emergence of the youthful beauty she once had, which, she feels, has somehow disappeared in the depths of the mirror.

Topic

Plath depicts an all-too-common, yet unrealistic attitude toward aging.

Themes

From Plath's poem we learn that vanity makes us seek flattering lies rather than face bitter truths. Moreover, even though aging is a natural and inevitable process, we have a tendency to run away from its reality. Still another feeling embodied in this poem comes in the form of an indirect exhortation: To be content with life, we should not base our self-worth on transient attributes, such as physical beauty and youth.

Supporting details

The woman in this poem cannot accept the facts about her aging and turns from the harsh reality to the false reassurance of the wrinkle-concealing, soft glow of "those liars, the candles or the moon" (line 12). Like a devout pilgrim, she submits to the daily, hallowed ritual of appearing before the truthful mirror in the hope of having her silent prayers answered. Day after day, with desperate faith, she submits to what she perceives as the "eye of a little god" (line 5), hoping to find the lost image of her face as unblemished by time. Day after day she loses her youth and advances rapidly and miserably toward old age. This woman's false set of values, unfortunately based on and sanctioned by societal standards, has attached too much importance to youth. As a consequence, she is reduced to desperation as her "tears and . . . agitation of hands" demonstrate (line 14).

Style

Sylvia Plath's use of personification is an outstanding feature in this poem. She gives the mirror personality, consciousness, and awareness. The mirror claims to have no preconceptions; it reflects truthfully whatever it sees: "I am not cruel, only truthful" (line 4).

By making the mirror into a lake in the second stanza, Plath gives it an added dimension of depth, thus effectively making it a repository of the images of the woman's past youth. This device enhances the futility of this woman's quest. While she is busy searching for her lost youth in the depth of the mirror/lake, precious moments of her life are slipping away.

Conclusion

"Mirror" reminds me of a cherished poem, "Desiderata," which speaks of wisdom on the subject of aging in one line: "Take kindly the counsel of the years, gracefully surrendering the things of youth."

However much one may not want to hear about the art of losing, the next poem "One Art" by Elizabeth Bishop treats that same topic of coping with loss.

One Art

The art of losing isn't hard to master;
so many things seem filled with the intent
to be lost that their loss is no disaster.
Lose something every day. Accept the fluster
of lost door keys, the hour badly spent.
The art of losing isn't hard to master.
Then practice losing farther, losing faster:
places, and names, and where it was you meant
to travel. None of these will bring disaster

I lost my mother's watch. And look! my last, or
next-to-last, of three loved houses went.
The art of losing isn't hard to master.

I lost two cities, lovely ones. And, vaster,
some realms I owned, two rivers, a continent.
I miss them, but it wasn't a disaster.

--Even losing you (the joking voice, a gesture
I love) I shan't have lied. It's evident
the art of losing's not too hard to master
though it may look like (*Write* it!) like disaster.

Elizabeth Bishop (1911-1979)

Student author: Paul Brandt

Summary

The speaker in Bishop's poem mentions many things she has lost. Describing losing things as an "art," she explains it as something that can be mastered. By accepting the loss of less significant things, both the tangible and intangible, she explains that more important things can be lost without "disaster." In the last stanza the speaker addresses a person whom she has "lost" and, despite the regret she seems to indicate, tries to convince herself that the loss is not a disaster.

Topic

The subject of the poem is the hardening of one's heart and emotional indifference to loss.

Theme

Bishop's poem comments on a side effect of modern life. She illustrates that the conveniences of a prosperous society condition a person to not become attached to many things – that such things are replaceable and dispensable; the resulting disposition can permeate and influence a person's actions and their entire lives, even their relationships.

Supporting details

In the first stanza the speaker explains that "so many things seem filled with the intent/to be lost that their loss is no disaster" (2-3). She suggests that accepting the loss of keys or "an hour badly spent" (5) is not unlike a conditioning exercise: "then practice losing farther, losing faster" (7-8). The irony of the speaker's tone is clear from the beginning, but becomes more obvious as she describes losing things of great sentimental value: "I lost my mother's watch. And look! My last...of three loved houses went" (10-11). The dialogue that the speaker has within herself in the last line of the poem shows that everything said in the poem is an attempt to rationalize or to understand her actions and attitude: "even losing you (the joking voice, a gesture/I love) I shan't have lied. It's evident / the art of losing's not too hard to master though it may look like (Write it!) like disaster" (16-19).

Style

Bishop's use of verbal irony to portray the speaker's attitude illustrates the disdain the speaker feels for her own actions. She feels detached from what she has done; her casual acceptance of losing so many things has influenced her to let go of an important relationship. The situation that the poem presents illustrates the unnatural ease with which people are able to discard significant things in their lives. It narrates a possible effect of such an acquired indifference – an emotional outlook that would sooner let go of a relationship than work out its problems.

Alexander Pope's idea of "damning with faint praise," seems to apply to "Mr. Z" by M. Carl Holman, as demonstrated by the student author Julie Doyle.

Mr. Z

Taught early that his mother's skin was the sign of error,
He dressed and spoke the perfect part of honor;
Won scholarships, attended the best schools,
Disclaimed kinship with jazz and spirituals;
Chose prudent, raceless views of each situation,
Or when he could not cleanly skirt dissension,
Faced up to the dilemma, firmly seized
Whatever ground was Anglo-Saxonized.

 In diet, too, his practice was exemplary:
Of pork in its profane forms he was wary;
Expert in vintage wines, sauces and salads,
His palate shrank from cornbread, yams and collards.

He was as careful whom he chose to kiss:
His bride had somewhere lost her Jewishness,
But kept her blue eyes; an Episcopalian
Prelate proclaimed them matched chameleon.
Choosing the right addresses, here, abroad,
They shunned those places where they might be barred;
Even less anxious to be asked to dine
Where hosts catered to kosher accent or exotic skin.

And so he climbed, unclogged by ethnic weights,
An airborne plant, flourishing without roots.
Not one false note was struck—until he died:
His subtly grieving widow could have flaye
The obit writers, ringing crude changes on a clumsy phrase:
"One of the most distinguished members of his race."

M. Carl Holman (1919-1988)

Student author: Julie W. Doyle

Summary

M. Carl Holman's poem, "Mr. Z," portrays a black man who has disowned his race early in life. The man adopts White Anglo-Saxon Protestant values to attain distinction in the white world. He marries a Jewish woman, who, like himself, disclaims her heritage. They avoid controversial situations and all goes well until he dies. The obituary notice praises Mr. Z and states that he was a credit to his race. Holman cleverly notes here that Mr. Z was not as successful as he thought he was at covering up his identity.

Topic

The subtle and pervasive nature of racial prejudice

Theme

Holman's poem mirrors an unpleasant reality that needs to be confronted and rectified: Self-deluding individuals who try to hide their true identity are products of complex racism.

Supporting details

The poet does not give Mr. Z an identity because he has turned his back on his own cultural identity. The poem blames American society for teaching Mr. Z when he was very young that there was something wrong with his race. But it is not only the black race Holman refers to in his poem; it is anyone who is not a White Anglo-Saxon Protestant. In the poet's view, WASP society in America created Mr. Z and those who are like him.

The poet describes in unmistakable terms Mr. Z's rejection of his roots in the hope of social climbing: "Mr. Z was "an airborne plant, flourishing without roots" (line 22). His aversion to African-American cuisine and music are described: "his palate shrank from cornbread, yams and collards" (line 12); he "disclaimed kinship with jazz and spirituals" (line 4).

Holman does not feel this alienation and self-deception was purely Mr. Z's fault because he was "taught early that his mother's skin was the sign of error" (line 1).

Style

The dominant stylistic element in this poem is the effective and pervasive use of irony. All his life Mr. Z thought he successfully concealed the fact of his cultural identity by espousing the tastes and values of the majority culture. However, on his death, the obituary writers called him "One of the most distinguished members of *his* race" (line 26; italics added for emphasis). This defining emphasis on his blackness leveled, with one stroke of the pen, his lifelong effort to dissociate from his roots and belong completely to the mainstream culture of success and power.

Other notable examples of irony occur in the context of describing as "exemplary" Mr. Z's dietary practice of shunning ethnic food and describing as "raceless" (line 5) what were obviously his racist views. How can we regard his views as "raceless" when they clearly degrade the black race? Such conduct is racist even when practiced by a black man against his own race. It is also clear that the word "exemplary" has a double meaning – one of them ironic: If anything, Mr. Z's life story is an example of what should be avoided, not what should be done.

Another effective stylistic element used by Holman is the sustained metaphoric language – *"climbed,"* *"unclogged,"* and *"airborne plant"* – that describes Mr. Z's struggle for upward mobility:

> And so he climbed, unclogged by ethnic weights,
> An airborne plant, flourishing without roots.   (lines 21-22)

The word "climb" is an apt choice because Mr. Z has been a social climber his entire adult life. With remarkable brevity and evocative power of metaphor, Holman sums up Mr. Z's character and the story of his life in the two lines just cited.

For the final journal sample on poetry, we turn to student author Nancy Brill's choice of John Keats's celebrated ode. Nancy follows the format of summary, theme, supporting details, and style without labeling the individual parts. This sample shows how easily a journal entry can be developed into an essay.

To Autumn

> Season of mists and mellow fruitfulness,
> Close bosom-friend of the maturing sun;
> Conspiring with him how to load and bless
> With fruit the vines that round the thatch-eaves run;
> To bend with apples the mossed cottage-trees
> And fill all fruit with ripeness to the core;
> To swell the gourd, and plump the hazel shells
> With a sweet kernel; to set budding more,
> And still more, later flowers for the bees,
> Until they think warm days will never cease,
> For summer has o'er-brimmed their clammy cells.
>
> Who hath not seen thee oft amid thy store?
> Sometimes whoever seeks abroad may find
> Thee sitting careless on a granary floor,
> Thy hair soft-lifted by the winnowing wind
> Or on a half-reaped furrow sound asleep,
> Drowsed with the fume of poppies, while thy hook
> Spares the next swath and all its twined flowers
> And sometimes like a gleaner thou dost keep
> Steady thy laden head across a brook;
> Or by a cider-press, with patient look,
> Thou watchest the last oozings hours by hours.
>
> Where are the songs of spring? Ay, where are they?
> Think not of them, thou hast thy music too,—
> While barred clouds bloom the soft-dying day,
> And touch the stubble-plains with rosy hue;
> Then in a wailful choir the small gnats mourn

Among the river sallows, borne aloft
Or sinking as the light wind lives or dies;
And full-grown lambs loud bleat from hilly bourn;
Hedge-crickets sing; and now with treble soft
The red-breast whistles from a garden-croft;
And gathering swallows twitter in the skies.

John Keats (1795-1821)

Student author: Nancy Brill

In this poem, Keats describes the season of autumn, beginning with the ripening of fruits and vegetables, continuing on with the harvest, and then moving through to the end of the season. Along with the cycle of autumn, the cycle of a day, from sunrise to sunset, is also described. Each stanza expresses a different point in time. The poem is itself a tribute to the season of fall, underscoring that spring is not the only season worthy of mention regardless of the fact that spring is often used in literature as a symbol of beauty, love, and passion.

Composed as a tribute to autumn, the poem suggests that this season has a distinct and unique beauty all its own, providing humanity with a hearty and bountiful harvest of nature's offerings. Several lines in the poem support this theme:

Where are the songs of spring? Ay, where are they?
Think not of them, thou hast thy music too" (23-24) [and]

Conspiring with him [the sun] how to load and bless
With fruit the vines that round the thatch-eaves run (3-4).

The question "where are the songs of spring?" reminds us that spring is over and that autumn has its own "music," with a different melody from that of spring's. Its song is somber and pensive rather than vibrant and carefree; nevertheless, autumn's song is lovely.

The bounty of the harvest is embodied in the descriptions of fruit ripening:

And fill all fruit with ripeness to the core;
To swell the gourd, and plump the hazel shells
With a sweet kernel; to set budding more (6-8).

The poem emphasizes that not only will this season produce crops, but the next season's produce is also guaranteed by the "sweet kernel" that promises more buds in the future.

The overall tone of this poem is solemn and dignified. Keats remarks on the fertility and beauty of this season with a graceful subtlety unlike the common, virtually overused, and overemphasized references to spring by other writers. Each stanza progresses along the time line of autumn and records the events of a single day. In the famous lines,

While barred clouds bloom the soft-dying day,
And touch the stubble-plains with rosy hue (25-26).

Keats again emphasizes the fertility of autumn by choosing the word "bloom" rather than "roam" or "drift" to describe the activity of the clouds. As the season is ending and "stubble-plains" remain, there is still an optimistic "rosy-hue" cast on the empty fields as though the poet views this season through a pair of rose-colored glasses. Keats elegantly conveys his respect and love for this nurturing season.

Structured journal responses to short stories

Having read the journal entries on many poems, we can apply the same guidelines to short stories, novels, plays, and movies. Let us begin with short stories. Each of the four sample readings carries a different set of expectations. Fewer journal entries are included for the novel, drama, and film because of their relatively greater length.

At this point, you should start experimenting with timed journal entries to gauge your reading comprehension, your writing speed, and your sensitivity to an author's style of writing.

Four Kinds of Journal Responses, Including Timed, Self-testing, Reading and Writing Exercises

1. A short story that you read for the first time and interpret in a journal format
(suggested time limit: for a shorter response, one hour; 90 minutes for a more detailed discussion)
2. A longer story that you read for the first time for journaling
(suggested time limit: 90 minutes)
3. A story that you have already read.
(you are asked to write your response to that story in 30 minutes.)
4. Demonstration of the process of moving from a journal to an essay
(written outside class)

The stories chosen for the first two exercises should be those that you have never read before. The time limit (within which the stories have to be read and discussed) will vary according to the length of the story. The first sample exercise (on Sadaat Manto's "Odor"), for example, took one hour, whereas completion of the second exercise (on Carson McCullers' "The Sojourner") took one and a half hours. In the journal response on Albert Camus' "The Guest," the time limit for writing on an already read story was 30 minutes. The final entry, on Jorge Luis Borges' challenging story "Tlon, Uqbal, Orbus Tertius," shows how journals are potential essays.

Instructions and Suggested Format

These instructions are the abbreviated form of the detailed structured journal format given earlier in this chapter. Use the following format to show your understanding of the story:

Summary (about 50 words)

Summarize the story's essential content, that is, setting, characters, significant events, and deeds with their consequences.

1. Identify the story's general subject or **topic** in one sentence.
2. State the story's **central idea/theme**, using appropriate form. You may state more than one theme if you so desire (one or two sentences).
3. **Supporting evidence** (three or four sentences). Give supporting details for the stated central idea(s) by combining direct quotations with relevant summarizing details in your own words. (50 words).
4. Evaluation of the author's **style** (about 50 words). Advice on style evaluation was given earlier in this chapter in the context of explaining the structured journal format, style being an important part of it. It will be adequate to cover the following points: Identify one or two outstanding elements in the author's style of writing. Give one or two examples of each; then discuss the function or effectiveness of the selected element(s) of style.

STUDENTS' TIMED JOURNAL ENTRIES

First Kind of Journal Responses

Two samples with time limits. *Two students' timed journal entries on "Odor" – a short story masterpiece by Saadat Hasan Manto are a good starting point because the story always generates an interesting and passionate discussion. The students read this story for the first time and wrote about it within the allowed time limit, using the suggested format. This assignment, like all timed journal writings, tests students' reading speed, comprehension depth, and ability to evaluate an author's style. The story precedes the journal entries.*

Odor

It was again the monsoon season.

Drops of rain had begun their patter on the leaves of the pipal tree near the window. Inside lay the teak bed on which a Ghatan girl [from the Ghat mountain ranges in South India] had slept with Randhir.

Beyond the window, in the night's milky darkness, the pipal leaves bathed in the rain, quivering like earrings.

On the spring mattress of the bed, the Ghatan girl had clung to Randhir like gooseflesh. Some hours earlier, he had seen her under the tamarind tree, sheltering from the downpour. She probably worked in the rope factory nearby. Randhir had watched her from his balcony, where he had come for a change from the mustiness of his room. He had wanted a diversion, for all afternoon he had done nothing but read the same newspaper again and again. He had cleared his throat and coughed. This had attracted her attention and he had beckoned her to come up.

For several days he had been feeling very lonely and dejected. One reason was the war, which had put beyond his reach those Anglo-Indian girls who used to come out with him for the evening and even for the night. They were not expensive and because of his English education he had preferred to date them rather than go to the brothels. With the coming of the war, some of them had enlisted in the Women's

Auxiliary Corps, others had joined the newly opened dancing schools in the Port areas. As only Tommies were admitted to these schools, Randhir had felt frustrated. His favorite girls had gone off the market. The only ones available were in the dancing schools, where white skin was the passport for admission; nothing else mattered. This had made Randhir very bitter, for he had felt that he was better educated, more refined, and healthier than the average Tommy.

Before the war Randhir had had many a rendezvous with his girl friends of the Nagpada and Taj Mahal Hotel areas. He knew more about these girls, physically, than did the Christian boys with whom they flirted, until they married the most gullible of them.

Randhir had often wondered why he was so attracted by girls like Hazel. Was it because they made themselves physically attractive by accentuating their curves and contours, or was it for their lack of inhibitions? They never felt abashed at referring to their menstrual irregularities, they told stories about their former lovers, their feet automatically tapped the floor on hearing a dance tune, and in bed they were like patent medicine with directions for use.

When Randhir had beckoned the Ghatan girl, he did not have any intention of taking her to bed. Noticing her drenched clothes, he had thought that the poor girl might get pneumonia, and had said, "Take off these wet clothes, you may catch a cold."

She had understood him, though she did not know his language. Red webs of shame had suddenly floated in her eyes. When Randhir had handed her a fresh white dhoti, she had hesitated for a moment, and then abruptly she had loosened her dirty coarse kashta, made filthier by the rain. As the soaked garment collapsed around her legs, she had swiftly covered her thighs with the dhoti. She had then tried to take off her tight choli by opening a tiny knot almost embedded in the deep and narrow hollow between her breasts.

Her worn-out nails had pecked at the tiny wet knot several times but had failed to loosen it. In despair, she had said something to Randhir in Marathi which meant, "What am I to do; it won't open?"

Randhir had sat down beside her and investigated the knot. But soon he had lost his patience, and gripping the strings on either side of the knot, he had given a sudden jerk. At once the string had snapped, and his hands had brushed over her breasts, which had come trembling into view. For a moment Randhir had felt like a potter, using freshly kneaded clay, who had suddenly molded two cups on the Ghattan girl's chest. Her breasts had the pliancy, the moist roughness, and the cooling warmth of vessels that have just come off the potter's wheel. Spotless and mud-colored, they had shone dully with a strange glow which seemed to come from a luminous layer beneath her translucent skin. Her uplifted breasts had looked like lamps lit at the bottom of a muddy pool.

It was again the season of rains.

Beyond the window the pipal leaves had dripped with rain. The Ghatan girl's soaked, two-piece dress was on the floor in a filthy heap. The girl had clung to Randhir. The warmth of her nude, unwashed body had reminded him of a hot bath in winter in a filthy public hamam.

All night she had clung to Randhir, as if they were one. They had hardly exchanged a word or two, for their panting was as eloquent as their lips and hands were expressive. All night Randhir's hands had fondled her breasts, like the caress of the breeze. Occasionally, her dark areolas, with their coarse grain and the tiny nipples, had stiffened and started a tremor that would streak through her body and communicate itself even to Randhir.

Randhir had experienced such tremors hundreds of times, and was familiar with the delicious sensation they imparted. He had spent many nights with girls, clasping their taut or soft breasts against her own. He had slept with all sorts of girls, simple and talkative ones who gave him information about their families that no stranger should know, and the type who bore all the physical burden in bed and would not let him exert himself. But this Ghatan girl, who had come up to his float from her shelter under the tamarind tree, had been quite different.

All night Randhir had inhaled a strange odor from her body, an odor both unpleasant and pleasant. He had sought for it in her armpits, her hair, breasts, navel, and in every other part of her body where it could pervade his nose. He had thought that he would never have felt the nearness of the girl but for this odor which had penetrated every layer of his mind and had seeped through his memories, new and old.

For one night Randhir and the girl had been fused together by this odor; they had merged into each other and slipped down to fathomless depths where they had been transformed into pure ecstasy, a state which they thought would be perpetual in spite of its evanescence, and still and stable even though there were fluctuations. They had been like a little bird that soars into the blueness of the sky, higher and higher, until it becomes a motionless dot.

Randhir was familiar with the odor that had exhaled from every pore of the Ghatan girl's body, but he had not been able to analyze it. It was like the fresh smell of earth sprinkled with water- but no, this odor was different. It was not an artificial smell like that of lavender or attar, but something natural and eternal, like the relationship that has existed between man and woman since the beginning of time.

Randhir hated perspiration. After a bath he usually powdered his armpits or used deodorants. It was surprising that he had kissed the hairy armpits of the Ghatan girl many times – yes, many times – and had felt no aversion. In fact, it had given him a peculiar feeling of pleasure. The tiny hair in the armpits, bedewed with perspiration, had given off the same odor that had been obvious and yet so incomprehensible. Randhir had felt that he knew this odor, that he recognized it, understood it, but he could not describe it to anyone else.

The monsoons are back again.

Randhir looked out of the window and saw the swaying pipal leaves bathing in the rain, the sound of their rustle and patter merging in the atmosphere. The night was dark, not pitch dark but of the darkness that seemed to have absorbed some subdued pearly light washed down from the stars by the raindrops. The season was the same when there was only one teak bed in the room, but now another lay beside it. In the corner stood a new dressing table.

It was again the seasons of rains, the season of marriages.

The raindrops were flushing the stars of their milky light, but the atmosphere was filled with the strong perfume of henna. One of the beds was empty. On the other lay Randhir, looking beyond the window at the dance of the raindrops on the swaying pipal leaves. By his side was a milky-white girl who had fallen asleep trying unsuccessfully to cover her nakedness. Her red silk shalwar lay on the other bed, one end of its dark-red cord dangling by its side. Also flung on this bed were the other clothes of which she had been stripped, her green shirt with red flowers to match the shalwar, her brassiére, underwear, and dupatta. All were red, marriage red, and scented with henna.

Gold powder lay in the girl's black hair, like dust. The blurred make-up on her face, a mixture of gold dust, powder, and rouge, was like a pallid mask of death. Her creamy breasts were blotched with the color of her red brassiere.

Her breasts were as white as milk, a whiteness that has a faint tinge of blue. Randhir glanced at the girl several times and thought; "It seems as if I have just pulled out the nails from a crate and lifted her out," for she had scratches on her body like packing marks on books and crockery. When Randhir had unknotted the cord of her tight-fitting brassiére, he had felt the ribbing on the soft flesh of her back and bosom, and the creased imprint left around her waist by the cord of her shalwar. A heavy and sharp-edged gold necklace, set with jewels, had bruised her breast as if it had been scratched wildly with nails.

It was the same season of the monsoons.

Countless raindrops were falling again on the soft, delicate pipal leaves. Randhir heard the familiar patter throughout the night. It was a pleasant season. A cool breeze was blowing, but it carried with it the scent of henna. For a long time Randhir's hands stroked the girl's bosom, white as fresh milk. They brushed her breasts gently, like the caress of the breeze. His fingers roving over her soft, milky body felt racing tremors and stirred suppressed passions. When he pressed his breast to the girl's bosom, every pore of his body heard the twanging of the girl's strummed emotions- but where was that note, that call of the Ghatan girl's odor, which had been more compelling than the cry of a suckling baby, that cry which had gone beyond the limits of sound and for him, somehow, had become a nameless perfume.

Randhir was looking out through the bars of the window. Close by, the pipal leaves were rustling, but he was trying to look beyond, far beyond them, at the luminous gray clouds. They had a strange glow like the one that had lurked in the Ghattan girl's breasts, a glow that was hidden like a secret object but yet was discernible.

By his side lay a girl whose body was as white as flour kneaded with milk and ghee. Her sleeping body gave off the perfume of henna, which had now grown faint. Randhir felt a sudden aversion for this dying perfume. It had a peculiar tang, like the taste of the mouth after belching —unsavory and insipid.

Randhir looked at the girl by his side. He found her skirt covering her body like whitish curdled grains of sour milk floating without life in a colorless liquid. His senses were permeated with the odor which had exhaled effortlessly from the body of the Ghattan girl. It was an odor lighter but more penetrating than the attar of henna, reaching the olfactory organs without even the intake of the breath.

Randhir rallied and stroked the milky body of the girl. His hand countered numbness; there was no responsive tremor. His new bride, the daughter of a magistrate, a graduate, the heartthrob of the boys of her college, had failed to kindle his masculine interest. In the dying perfume of henna attar, he continued to grope for the odor of the Ghattan girl, the odor he had inhaled from her unwashed body in these very days of the monsoons, when the pipal leaves had bathed
in the rain.

Sadaat Hasan Manto (1912-1955)

First Entry (time allowed: 1 hour)
Student author: Samantha Gibson

Summary
"Odor" is a story about a well-educated man, Randhir, who seems to question his attraction to seemingly uninhibited and attractive Anglo women. As a result of a night spent with an Indian Ghatan girl, he acquires an understanding of what a real and natural relationship between a man and a woman should be. He does not realize the extent of the ramifications of this encounter until it is too late. His awakening comes after he has married an upper-class light-skinned woman, apparently for the sake of prestige.

Topic
Superficial *versus* deeper attraction

Theme
The major theme in "Odor" is that fulfillment does not come from striving to attain what one is superficially attracted to as opposed to what is truly meaningful and real.

Support
Manto supports his theme by bringing the special qualities of the Ghatan girl to the reader's attention in contrast to the women Randhir normally associates with. The following passage illustrates this point: "It [the Ghatan girl's odor] was like the fresh smell of earth sprinkled with water. . . . It was not an artificial smell . . . but something natural and eternal, like the relationship that has existed between man and woman since the beginning of time."

Style
The stylistic element that also strengthens Manto's theme is contrast. The Ghatan girl is always referred to as natural. The women Randhir normally sees are lovely but mechanical in their camouflaged smells and clothes: ". . . in bed they were like patent medicines with directions for use."

The preceding exercise was completed in 50 minutes. However, if one had more time, the response to this short story could have explored various possible interpretations, as is exemplified in the sample essay on this story in Chapter Ten.

Second Entry (time allowed: 90 minutes)
Student author: Arienne Aramchikova

Arienne followed the suggested format without labeling the sections. This entry reads almost like a complete essay, demonstrating how easily journal notes can lead to essays.

Saadat Hasan Manto's "Odor" is a story of an Indian man caught between his superficial lust for white-skinned British women and his deeper emotions of desire for a lower-caste woman from his native country. The story takes place during the monsoon season in India. After having his amorous access to Anglo-Indian women reduced since the start of the war, Randhir, a British-educated Indian bachelor, feels lonely and frustrated. From the window of his apartment, he spots a cold and wet "Ghantan" girl caught in the heavy downpour. He invites her up and they have sex. Randhir is intoxicated by her natural scent and spontaneity which are quite different from the perfumed and robotic "Anglo-Indian girls" to whom he is accustomed. A year later, Randhir marries. His new bride is white and comes from an upper-class family, yet his passion for her is non-existent in comparison to the sensual bond he felt with the dark-skinned factory girl.

"Odor" is about the immutable nature of desire. The body's truest passions cannot and will not follow the socially-conceived artificial webs of classism and racism. Randhir, having an "English education" demonstrates his unreasoned compliance with the Anglo-centric institutional racism by being preoccupied with the white flesh of "Anglo-Indian girls." When he is denied access to these white women because of his skin color, he does not question this system that segregates him, nor does he check his own racism towards women of his own ethnic background. He believes he is "better than the average Tommy" because of his higher education and better looks. When he attempts to analyze his desire to have sex with white-skinned Europeanized Indian women, he finds nothing passionate about them, merely that "they were like patent medicines with directions for use."

When suddenly he finds himself in bed with the Ghantan girl, Randhir is overwhelmed with lust and desire unlike anything he has experienced with the higher class Anglo-Indian girls. He becomes obsessed with her unwashed body odor, finding that "it had penetrated every layer of his mind and had seeped through his memories, new and old." Unable to analyze this odor that has him so enrapt, he can only feel its effect, one that reminds him of "the relationship that has existed between men and women since the beginning of time."

A year later, Randhir marries a white woman, and the passion he felt with the Ghatan girl is absent. Although his new bride, daughter of a magistrate, is from a wealthy anglicized family, the penetrating bodily desire he experienced one night with the Ghantan girl is completely absent. As he touches the new bride's body, "his hand countered numbness." He finds he longs for the odor of the Ghatan girl; his white bride fails "to kindle his masculine interest."

Manto uses symbolism, simile, and a tragic dramatic irony to demonstrate Randhir's instinctual feelings towards the Ghatan woman. Randhir finds the Ghatan woman under a "tamarind tree." The tamarind tree is native to India. Its ripe brown fruit, used by the Hindus "to appease the cravings of nature," (Oxford English Dictionary) is symbolic of the natural sensual attributes of the brown native girl.

Similes of sensual imagery describe the innate reactions of Randhir towards the two women of the story. The Ghatan girl's odor "is like the fresh smell of earth sprinkled with water." This, like the symbolic tamarind tree, underscores the natural element that bonds Randhir with the lower-caste girl. The scent of the magistrate's daughter is quite different. The flavor of her odor is "like the taste of the mouth after belching."

These contrasting physical descriptions uphold the tragic irony of the protagonist's feelings. Randhir, in describing his frustration towards the segregation which bars him from mingling with white girls, fails to understand his own extension of that racism. His "English education" has projected its racism onto Randhir, and Randhir accepts its precepts in choosing his own wife. He never rejects this socially proliferated classism, even when he is its victim, nor when he finds he has married a woman with whom he shares no spiritual or sensual union.

Second Kind of Journal Responses

In-class timed journal response to a longer story that students read for the first time in class
(Time allowed: 90 minutes for both reading the story and writing about it)

This assignment tests students' reading speed, depth of comprehension, and ability to evaluate an author's style. Carson McCullers's story "The Sojourner" was chosen for this exercise.

The Sojourner

THE TWILIGHT BORDER between sleep and waking was a Roman one this morning: splashing fountains and arched, narrow streets, the golden lavish city of blossoms and age-soft stone. Sometimes in this semi-consciousness he sojourned again in Paris, or war German rubble, or Swiss skiing and a snow hotel. Sometimes, also, in a fallow Georgia field at hunting dawn. Rome it was this morning in the yearless region of dreams.

John Ferris awoke in a room in a New York hotel. He had the feeling that something unpleasant was awaiting him – what it was, he did not know. The feeling, submerged by matinal necessities, lingered even after he had dressed and gone downstairs. It was a cloudless autumn day and the pale sunlight sliced between the pastel skyscrapers. Ferris went to the window glass that overlooked the sidewalk. He ordered an American breakfast with scrambled eggs and sausage.

Ferris had come from Paris to his father's funeral which had taken place the week before in his home town in Georgia. The shock of death had made him aware of youth already passed. His hair was receding and the veins in his now naked temples were pulsing and prominent and his body was spare except for an incipient belly bulge. Ferris had loved his father and the bond between them had once been extraordinarily close – but the years had somehow unraveled this filial devotion; the death, expected for a long time, had left him with an unforeseen dismay. He had stayed as long as possible to be near his mother and brothers at home. His plane for Paris was to leave the next morning.

Ferris pulled out his address book to verify a number. He turned the pages with growing attentiveness. Names and addresses from New York, the capitals of Europe, a few faint ones from his home state in the South. Faded, printed names, sprawled drunken ones. Betty Wills: a random love, married now. Charlie Williams: wounded in the Hurtgen Forest, unheard of since. Grand old Williams – did he live or die? Don Walker: a B.T.O. in television, getting rich. Henry Green: hit the skids after the war, in a sanitarium now, they say. Cozie Hall: he had heard that she was dead. Heedless, laughing Cozie – it was strange to think that she too, silly girl, could die. As Ferris closed the address book, he suffered a sense of hazard, transience, almost fear.

It was then that his body jerked suddenly. He was staring out of the window when there, on the sidewalk, passing by, was his ex-wife. Elizabeth passed quite close to him, walking slowly. He could not understand the wild quiver of his heart, nor the following sense of recklessness and grace that lingered after she was gone.

Quickly Ferris paid his check and rushed out to the sidewalk. Elizabeth stood on the corner waiting to cross Fifth Avenue. He hurried toward her meaning to speak, but the lights changed and she crossed the street before he reached her. Ferris followed. On the other side he could easily have overtaken her, but he found himself lagging unaccountably. Her fair brown hair was plainly rolled, and as he watched her Ferris recalled that once his father had remarked that Elizabeth had a 'beautiful carriage.' She turned at the next corner and Ferris followed, although by now his intention to overtake her had disappeared. Ferris questioned the bodily disturbance that the sight of Elizabeth aroused in him, the dampness of his hands, the hard heartstrokes.

It was eight years since Ferris had last seen his ex-wife. He knew that long ago she had married again. And there were children. During recent years he had seldom thought of her. But at first, after the divorce, the loss had almost destroyed him. Then after the anodyne of time, he had loved again, and then again. Jeannine, she was now. Certainly his love for his ex-wife was long since past. So why the unhinged body, the shaken mind? He knew only that his clouded heart was oddly dissonant with the sunny, candid autumn day. Ferris wheeled suddenly and, walking with long strides, almost running, hurried back to the hotel.

Ferris poured himself a drink, although it was not yet eleven o'clock. He sprawled out in an armchair like a man exhausted, nursing his glass of bourbon and water. He had a full day ahead of him as he was leaving by plane the next morning for Paris. He checked over his obligations: take luggage to Air France, lunch with his boss, buy shoes and an overcoat. And something – wasn't there something else? Ferris finished his drink and opened the telephone directory.

His decision to call his ex-wife was impulsive. The number was under Bailey, the husband's name, and he called before he had much time for self-debate. He and Elizabeth had exchanged cards at Christmastime, and Ferris had sent a carving set when he received the announcement of her wedding.

There was no reason not to call. But as he waited, listening to the ring at the other end, misgiving fretted him.

Elizabeth answered; her familiar voice was a fresh shock to him. Twice he had to repeat his name, but when he was identified, she sounded glad. He explained he was only in town for that day. They had a theater engagement, she said – but she wondered if he would come by for an early dinner. Ferris said he would be delighted.

As he went from one engagement to another, he was still bothered at odd moments by the feeling that something necessary was forgotten. Ferris bathed and changed in the late afternoon, often thinking about Jeannine: he would be with her the following night. 'Jeannine,' he would say, 'I happened to run into my ex-wife when I was in New York. Had dinner with her. And her husband, of course. It was strange seeing her after all these years.'

Elizabeth lived in the East Fifties, and as Ferris taxied uptown he glimpsed at intersections the lingering sunset, but by the time he reached his destination it was already autumn dark. The place was a building with a marquee and a doorman, and the apartment was on the seventh floor.

'Come in, Mr. Ferris.'

Braced for Elizabeth or even the unimagined husband, Ferris was astonished by the freckled red-haired child; he had known of the children, but his mind had failed somehow to acknowledge them. Surprise made him step back awkwardly.

'This is our apartment,' the child said politely. 'Aren't you Mr. Ferris? I'm Billy. Come in.

In the living room beyond the hall, the husband provided another surprise; he too had not been acknowledged emotionally. Bailey was a lumbering red-haired man with a deliberate manner. He rose and extended a welcoming hand.

'I'm Bill Bailey. Glad to see you. Elizabeth will be in, in a minute. She's finishing dressing.'

The last words struck a gliding series of vibrations, memories of the other years. Fair Elizabeth, rosy and naked before her bath. Half-dressed before the mirror of her dressing table, brushing her fine, chestnut hair. Sweet casual intimacy, the soft-fleshed loveliness indisputably possessed. Ferris shrank from the unbidden memories and compelled himself to meet Bill Bailey's gaze.

Billy, will you please bring that tray of drinks from the kitchen table?'

The child obeyed promptly, and when he was gone Ferris remarked conversationally, 'Fine boy you have there.'

'We think so.'

Flat silence until the child returned with a tray of glasses and a cocktail shaker of Martinis. With the priming drinks they pumped up conversation: Russia, they spoke of, and the New York rain-making, and the apartment situation in Manhattan and Paris.

'Mr. Ferris is flying all the way across the ocean tomorrow,' Bailey said to the little boy who was perched on the arm or his chair, quiet and well behaved. 'I bet you would like to be a stowaway in his suitcase.'

Billy pushed back his limp bangs. 'I want to fly in an airplane and be a newspaperman like Mr. Ferris.' He added with sudden assurance, 'That's what I would like to do when I am big.'

Bailey said, 'I thought you wanted to be a doctor.'

'I do!' said Billy. 'I would like to be both. I want to be an atom-bomb scientist too.'

Elizabeth came in carrying in her arms a baby girl.

'Oh, John!' she said. She settled the baby in the father's lap. 'It's grand to see you, I'm awfully glad you could come.'

The little girl sat demurely on Bailey's knees. She wore a pale pink crepe de Chine frock, smocked around the yoke with rose, and a matching silk hair ribbon tying back her pale soft curls. Her skin was summer tanned and her brown eyes flecked with gold and laughing. When she reached up and fingered her father's horn rimmed glasses, he took them off and let her look through them a moment. 'How's my old Candy?'

Elizabeth was very beautiful, more beautiful perhaps than he had ever realized. Her straight clean hair was shining. Her face was softer, glowing and serene. It was a madonna loveliness, dependent on the family ambiance.

'You've hardly changed at all,' Elizabeth said, 'but it has been a long time.'

'Eight years.' His hand touched his thinning hair self-consciously while further amenities were exchanged.

Ferris felt himself suddenly a spectator – an interloper among these Baileys. Why had he come? He suffered. His own life seemed so solitary, a fragile column supporting nothing amidst the wreckage of the years. He felt he could not bear much longer to stay in the family room.

He glanced at his watch. ''You're going to the theater?'

'It's a shame,' Elizabeth said, 'but we've had this engagement for more than a month. But surely, John, you'll be staying home one of these days before long. You're not going to be an expatriate, are you?'

'Expatriate,' Ferris repeated. 'I don't much like the word.'

'What's a better word?' she asked.

He thought for a moment. 'Sojourner might do.'

Ferris glanced at his watch, and again Elizabeth apologized. 'If only we had known ahead of time –'

'I just had this day in town. I came home unexpectedly. You see, Papa died last week.'

'Papa Ferris is dead? '

Yes, at Johns-Hopkins. He had been sick there nearly a year. The funeral was down home in Georgia.'

'Oh, I'm so sorry, John. Papa Ferris was always one of my favorite people.'

The little boy moved from behind the chair so that he could look into his mother's face. He asked, 'Who is dead?'

Ferris was oblivious to apprehension; he was thinking of his father's death. He saw again the outstretched body on the quilted silk within the coffin. The corpse flesh was bizarrely rouged and the familiar hands lay massive and joined above a spread of funeral roses. The memory closed and Ferris awakened to Elizabeth's calm voice.

'Mr. Ferris's father, Billy. A really grand person. Somebody you didn't know.'

'But why did you call him Papa Ferris?'

Bailey and Elizabeth exchanged a trapped look. It was Bailey who answered the questioning child. 'A long time age,' he said, 'your mother and Mr. Ferris were once married. Before you were born – a long time ago.'

'Mr. Ferris?'

The little boy stared at Ferris, amazed and unbelieving. And Ferris's eyes, as he returned the gaze, were somehow unbelieving too. Was it indeed true that at one time he had called this stranger, Elizabeth, Little Butterduck during nights of love, that they had lived together, shared perhaps a thousand days and nights and – finally – endured in the misery of sudden solitude the fiber by fiber (jealousy, alcohol and money quarrels) destruction of the fabric of married love.

Bailey said to the children, 'It's somebody's suppertime. Come on now.'

'But Daddy! Mama and Mr. Ferris – I – '

Billy's everlasting eyes – perplexed and with a glimmer of hostility – reminded Ferris of the gaze of another child. It was the young son of Jeannine – a boy of seven with a shadowed little face and knobby knees whom Ferris avoided and usually forgot.

'Quick march,' Bailey gently turned Billy toward the door. 'Say good night now, son.'

'Good night, Mr. Ferris.' He added resentfully, 'I thought I was staying up for the cake.'

'You can come in afterward for the cake,' Elizabeth said. 'Run along now with Daddy for your supper.'

Ferris and Elizabeth were alone. The weight of the situation descended on those first moments of silence. Ferris asked permission to pour himself another drink and Elizabeth set the cocktail shaker on the table at his side. He looked at the grand piano and noticed the music on the rack.

'Do you still play as beautifully as you used to?'

'I still enjoy it.'

'Please play, Elizabeth.'

Elizabeth arose immediately. Her readiness to perform when asked had always been one of her amiabilities; she never hung back, apologized. Now as she approached the piano there was the added readiness of relief.

She began with a Bach prelude and fugue. The prelude was as gaily iridescent as a prism in a morning room. The first voice of the fugue, an announcement pure and solitary, was repeated intermingling with a second voice, and again repeated within an elaborated frame, the multiple music, horizontal and serene, flowed with unhurried majesty. The principal melody was woven with two other voices, embellished with countless ingenuities – now dominant, again submerged, it had the sublimity of a single thing that does not fear surrender to the whole. Toward the end, the density of the material gathered for the last enriched insistence on the dominant first motif and with a chorded final statement the fugue ended. Ferris rested his head on the chair back and closed his eyes. In the following silence a clear, high voice came from the room down the hall.

'Daddy, how could Mama and Mr. Ferris –' A door was closed.

The piano began again – what was this music? Unplaced, familiar, the limpid melody had lain a long while dormant in his heart. Now it spoke to him of another time, another place – it was the music Elizabeth used to play. The delicate air summoned a wilderness of memory. Ferris was lost in the riot of past longings, conflicts, ambivalent desires. Strange that the music, catalyst for this tumultuous anarchy, was so serene and clear. The singing melody was broken off by the appearance of the maid.

'Miz Bailey, dinner is out on the table now.'

Even after Ferris was seated at the table between his host and hostess, the unfinished music still overcast his mood. He was a little drunk.

'L'improvisation de la vie humaine,' he said. 'There's nothing that makes you so aware of the improvisation of human existence as a song unfinished. Or an old address book.'

'Address book?' repeated Bailey. Then he stopped, non-committal and polite.

'You're still the same old boy, Johnny,' Elizabeth said with a trace of the old tenderness.

It was a Southern dinner that evening, and the dishes were his old favorites. They had fried chicken and corn pudding and rich, glazed candied sweet potatoes. During the meal Elizabeth kept alive a conversation when the silences were overlong. And it came about that Ferris was led to speak of Jeannine.

'I first knew Jeannine last autumn – about this time of the year – in Italy. She's a singer and she had an engagement in Rome. I expect we will be married soon.'

The words seemed so true, inevitable, that Ferris did not at first acknowledge to himself the lie. He and Jeannine had never in that year spoken of marriage. And indeed, she was still married – to a White Russian money-changer in Paris from whom she had been separated for five years. But it was too late to correct the lie. Already Elizabeth was saying: 'This really makes me glad to know. Congratulations, Johnny.'

He tried to make amends with truth. 'The Roman autumn is so beautiful. Balmy and blossoming.' He added, 'Jeannine has a little boy of six. A curious trilingual little fellow. We go to the Tuileries sometimes.'

A lie again. He had taken the boy once to the gardens. The sallow foreign child in shorts that bared his spindly legs had sailed his boat in the concrete pond and ridden the pony. The child had wanted to go in to the puppet show. But there was not time, for Ferris had an engagement at the Scribe Hotel. He had promised they would go to the guignol another afternoon. Only once had he taken Valentin to the Tuileries.

There was a stir. The maid brought in a white-frosted cake with pink candles. The children entered in their night clothes. Ferris still did not understand.

'Happy birthday, John,' Elizabeth said. Blow out the candles.'

Ferris recognized his birthday date. The candles blew out lingeringly and there was the smell of burning wax. Ferris was thirty-eight years old. The veins in his temples darkened and pulsed visibly.

'It's time you started for the theater.'

Ferris thanked Elizabeth for the birthday dinner and said the appropriate good-byes. The whole family saw him to the door.

A high, thin moon shone above the jagged, dark sky-scrapers. The streets were windy, cold. Ferris hurried to Third Avenue and hailed a cab. He gazed at the nocturnal city with the deliberate attentiveness of departure and perhaps farewell. He was alone. He longed for flight time and the coming journey.

The next day he looked down on the city from the air, burnished in sunlight, toylike, precise. Then America was left behind and there was only the Atlantic and the distant European shore. The ocean was milky pale and placid beneath the clouds. Ferris dozed most of the day. Toward dark he was thinking of Elizabeth and the visit of the previous evening. He thought of Elizabeth among her family with longing, gentle envy and inexplicable regret. He sought the melody, the unfinished air, that had so moved him. The cadence, some unrelated tones, were all that remained; the melody itself evaded him. He had found instead the first voice of the fugue that Elizabeth had played – it came to him, inverted mockingly and in a minor key. Suspended above the ocean the anxieties of transience and solitude no longer troubled him and he thought of his father's death with equanimity. During the dinner hour the plane reached the shore of France.

At midnight Ferris was in a taxi crossing Paris. It was a clouded night and mist wreathed the lights of the Place de la Concorde. The midnight bistros gleamed on the wet pavements. As always after a trans-ocean flight the change of continents was too sudden. New York at morning, this midnight Paris. Ferris glimpsed the disorder of his life: the succession of cities, of transitory loves; and time, the sinister glissando of the years, time always.

'Vite! Vite!'' he called in terror. 'Depechez-vous.'

Valentin opened the door to him. The little boy wore pajamas and an outgrown red robe. His grey eyes were shadowed and, as Ferris passed into the flat, they flickered momentarily.

'J'attends Maman.'

Jeannine was singing in a night club. She would not be home before another hour. Valentin returned to a drawing, squatting with his crayons over the paper on the floor. Ferris looked down at the drawing – it was a banjo player with notes and wavy lines inside a comic-strip balloon.

'We will go again to the Tuileries.'

The child looked up and Ferris drew him closer to his knees. The melody, the unfinished music that Elizabeth had played, came to him suddenly. Unsought the load of memory jettisoned – this time bringing only recognition and sudden joy.

'Monsieur Jean,' the child said, 'did you see him?'

Confused, Ferris thought only of another child – the freckled, family-loved boy. 'See who, Valentin?'

'Your dead papa in Georgia.' The child added, 'Was he okay?'

Ferris spoke with rapid urgency: 'We will go often to the Tuileries. Ride the pony and we will go into the guignol. We will see the puppet show and never be in a hurry any more.'

'Monsielr Jean,' Valentin said. 'The guignol is now closed.'

Again, the terror, the acknowledgment of wasted years and death. Valentin, responsive and confident, still nestled in his arms. His cheek touched the soft cheek and felt the brush of the delicate eyelashes. With inner desperation he pressed the child close – as though an emotion as protean as his love could dominate the pulse of time.

Carson McCullers (1917-1967)

Student author: Serrana Smith-Kassamali

Serrana's journal response to this challenging assignment is lucid and persuasive.

Summary

"The Sojourner" is a story of awareness. Through a succession of events, the main character, John Ferris, begins to realize how the seemingly unrelated pieces of his life are interconnected. In his awareness, he starts to assess the meaning of his existence. First, the death of his father, then a chance encounter with his ex-wife, and finally, a consciously executed, though initially quite unplanned visit to his ex-wife's home in New York, form the fabric of Ferris's changing awareness.

Topic

Completion of life's journey

Theme

The author points out that a life lived through unattached sequences of events can often lead to dismay or even emptiness. Put another way, a sojourner might enjoy each of life's episodes, but without evaluating the role of individual pieces, the whole can lack meaning.

Supporting details

Several thematic details surface throughout the story: "As Ferris closed the address book, he suffered a sense of hazard, transience, almost fear." This statement alludes to the feeling of emptiness associated with Ferris's life. Yet another line from the story, "He felt he could not bear much longer to stay in the family room," sums up the context of Ferris' own life amidst the realities of his ex-wife's current life. An awareness of his unfulfilled life dawns on him.

Style

The author uses rapid pacing and compressed time to dramatize events in this story. In essence, she juxtaposes the whole of Ferris' life with the events of one day to convey the weight of life's lessons. Ferris has an insight into the nature of his relationships as he commutes between the past and the present of his intercontinental life. By bringing characters from different eras and different continents together in a day's business, the author makes Ferris confront those truths that he has been avoiding so far. As he is, and as he was, melt into a discernible whole because in one "hurry-up" day, filled with intense activities and encounters, he *truly sees* the people in his life. In seeing what he is and what he has been, Ferris also sees what he lacks.

Third Kind of Journal Responses

An in-class, timed journal response to a story that had been read outside class

(Time allowed: 30 minutes)

Several interpretations of the story are included to show how readers can come to different yet valid conclusions. All responses by students were completed within the 30-minute time limit. You can read the text of "The Guest" by Albert Camus in Chapter Ten. Six more journal responses by students are placed on my website.

Student author: Jeff Neilson

Summary

Albert Camus' "The Guest" concerns a rural schoolmaster Daru, who is given the task of transporting a prisoner (who is accused of murder) to the authorities. Daru does not want the responsibility, but when the prisoner is left with him anyway, he decides to give him the choice to either go free or go to the police. The prisoner opts to go to the police.

Theme

The theme of the story seems to be that each person should take responsibility for his or her actions and do the right thing; this responsibility should not be governed by others.

Support

All three characters show respect for one another. The gendarme, Balducci, shows respect for the prisoner by handling him gently, and for Daru for not denouncing him. The prisoner shows respect for Daru by not escaping during the night and by going to the police. Daru shows respect for the prisoner by treating him well and giving him control of his destiny. By making each character do the right thing, Camus has shown us that anyone, regardless of his or her station, can be honorable.

Style

Camus' subtle style adds greatly to the story. He paints a vivid picture of the setting of the story, describing the environment as being covered with "dirty white snow" and illuminated by a "dirty light." He also describes Daru's "empty, frigid classroom." By using such a bleak, ravaged tone, Camus tells much about the lives of these characters.

Another of Camus' trademarks, his "less is more" technique, employs brevity to create the muted tone of the story. He tells a lot with a few words, such as when he unveils all we need to know about the "guest" with the following sentence: "Balducci was holding on the end of a rope an Arab who was walking behind him with hands bound and head lowered." This brief yet complete description mirrors the bleakness of the setting in creating an austere tone and defined purpose of the story.

Student author: Victoria Candau

Among several rich themes in Camus' "The Guest," a particularly notable one is that despite one's most earnest intentions, a person may only remain detached for so long before he encounters the pull of brotherhood and the sting of ostracization imposed upon his solitude by the outside world.

The unwelcome gnawing of conscience comes with hurting another, especially without such an intention. An example is Daru's rumination on his exchange with Balducci. "He had hurt [Balducci], for he had sent him off in a way as if he didn't want to be associated with him. He could still hear the gendarme's farewell and, without knowing why, he felt strangely empty and vulnerable." His attempt to stay clear of people's wars, hate, and blood lust has not been successful because he is being entrusted with the unpleasant duty of handing over the Arab prisoner to the police.

The Arab's presence "bothered [Daru] by imposing on him a sort of brotherhood [;] he knew it well but refused to accept it in the present circumstances."

Interpretation by the author of this book

In "The Guest" Albert Camus demonstrates painful limits on human freedom: In spite of one's best efforts to stay uninvolved with unpleasant human affairs, life does not allow that luxury to anyone for very long. In the story Daru chooses to remove himself from the turmoil and violence of the Algerian civil war. He lives in a small town, where he teaches poor Arab children and gives out rationed food to their families. His peaceful life is interrupted when Balducci, the gendarme, brings to him an Arab prisoner with orders from the authorities to hand him over to the police – something that Daru intensely dislikes getting involved with. Because of his approach of staying clear of violent human affairs and rendering only humanitarian service to the needy, Daru is brusque in treating Balducci, who brings Daru an assignment that goes against his grain. Nevertheless after Balducci leaves, Daru feels that he has hurt [Balducci], for he had sent him off in a way as if he didn't want to be associated with him. He could still hear the Gendarme's farewell and, without knowing why, he felt strangely empty and vulnerable."

A related theme demonstrates that in life's unexpected twists and turns, sometimes a painfully absurd disparity may exist between our intentions and their misperception by others. Even though Daru treats the Arab prisoner humanely, gives him food and money and the freedom to choose between escape and prison, the friends of the Arab leave Daru this threatening note: "You handed over our brother. You will pay for this." Demonstrating honorable conduct and concern for Daru's well-being, the Arab had not run away. He had chosen to go to the police. However, the Arab's friends did not know about his voluntary surrender to the police and wrongly held Daru responsible. The story's conclusion thus delineates Daru's tragic dilemma: The very people whom he has chosen to help misunderstand his actions completely.

[*Chapter Ten contains a full-length essay by a student on this story.*]

Fourth Kind of Journal Responses

Completed outside class, demonstrating the journal to essay transformation (no time limit)

It is easy to develop a journal into a complete essay. Any journal entry can become an essay by removing the labels of "summary," "topic," "theme," "supporting details," and "style" and adding transitions between those sections. The summary in a journal can become the *introduction* of an essay, statements of themes become the *thesis*, and all supporting details, controlled by the thematic statements, constitute the *main body*. When writing an essay, one can choose to focus on just one major theme or discuss a few related themes. This journal-to-essay transformation is exemplified by student author John Coetzee's interpretation of Jorge Luis Borges' "Tlon, Uqbar, Orbus Tertius."

Tlon, Uqbar, Orbus Tertius
by Jorge Luis Borges (1899-1986)

Jorge Luis Borges' fascinating tale of the triumph of the possibilities of a better life through imagination and fantasy over dreadfully limiting reality finds in John an able interpreter. His clear analysis of the author's playful style of magical realism makes the story's recondite episodes understandable. John's original journal entry consisted of the following components that were clearly labeled: Introduction, plot summary, topic, theme, supporting evidence for theme, style evaluation, cultural insight, and reasons for the story's greatness. A comprehensive journal entry like this takes little effort to make it into a well-

crafted and engaging essay. Read this story online. Here is the link for free access to the text http://www.coldbacon.com/writing/borges-tlon.html

Student author: John Coetzee

In "Tlön, Uqbar, Orbus Tertius," first published in 1941, Jorge Luis Borges displays his flair for labyrinthine narrative, challenges the reader's expectations, and indulges his penchant for metaphysics. A strange quote leads the speaker to search for an article on the nation of Uqbar in the Anglo-American Cyclopedia. He is unable to find it, but his friend's edition of the same encyclopedia, bought at a book sale years ago, does contain it. Strangely, Uqbar is not accounted for by the alphabetic cipher on the spine of the volume.

The speaker is troubled by the underlying vagueness of the article. Even Uqbar's location is ambiguous. Also, the article mentions that the literature of Uqbar is "fantastic, and never refers to reality, but to the two imaginary regions of Tlön and Mlejnan." Further research uncovers nothing.

Soon after, the death of an old friend, Herbert Ashe, leads to the speaker's discovery of the First Encyclopedia of Tlön, which contains highly detailed descriptions of the imaginary world referred to by the Uqbar article. The speaker becomes part of an international society of Tlönists who work, unsuccessfully, to uncover the mysterious origins of the book. The speaker then devotes several pages to describing the curious languages, cultures, and philosophies of Tlön, which seem extremely idealistic.

Another letter addressed to the deceased Ashe is discovered, and it tells that Tlön was created by a "benevolent secret society" and funded by an American "millionaire ascetic" named Ezra Buckley. "Orbus Tertius" is the provisional name given to the project. Then the imaginary world of Tlön begins to "intrude" into the real world. A Tlönian compass and a small, heavy cone made of Tlönian metal are discovered. Soon afterwards, the full 40 volumes of the Tlön encyclopedia are found. This leads to a far-reaching enthusiasm for Tlön, causing people all over the world to abandon their own cultures, which they replace with a fervent study of Tlön. In the end, the speaker observes that "contact with Tlön and the ways of Tlön have disintegrated this world."

In a most general way, the story is about the conflict between imagination and reality. This is constantly addressed, from the speaker's mistrust of Bioy's story, to the dubiousness of the Uqbar article, to the philosophies of Tlön, to the characterization of Ashe, and culminates in the "conquest" of humanity by Tlön. All these details become the foundation of the story's theme that imagination and fantasy are stronger than reality.

This reading of the story is supported by the speaker's emotions, the culture of Tlön, Tlön's physical intrusion into our world, and Tlön's eventual triumph over earthly culture. First, there is the speaker's own reaction to Uqbar and Tlön. When he first hears about Uqbar, he displays only mild curiosity and a mistrust of his friend, "I supposed that this undocumented country and its anonymous heresiarch had been deliberately invented by Bioy out of modesty, to substantiate a phrase". But as the mystery deepens, his fascination grows. When he discovers the First Encyclopedia of Tlön, his reaction is one of almost religious rapture, saying, "in the Islamic world, there is one night, called the Night of Nights, on which the secret gates of the sky open wide and the water in the jugs tastes sweeter; if those gates were to open, I would not feel what I felt that afternoon." Soon afterwards he joins (or forms) an international society of Tlön enthusiasts, and the study of this imaginary planet becomes the center of his life.

Then, there is the culture and philosophy of Tlön itself. With its lack of nouns, its dismissal of materialism, and its emphasis on idealism, the "association of ideas," and poetry, Tlon strongly favors imagination over conventional western concepts of reality, and seems to derive much of its attraction from this trait. As the speaker says, "this monism, or extreme idealism, completely invalidates science . . . the metaphysicians of Tlön are not looking for truth, nor even for an approximation of it; they are after a kind of amazement."

Perhaps the strangest moment of the story is when the world of Tlön begins to "intrude" upon the actual world. The two incidents are the discovery of a Tlönian compass by the Princess of Faucigny Lucinge, and of a heavy metal cone by the speaker. At first it seems that these objects may have simply been constructed by Tlön enthusiasts, but the speaker states that the heavy cone is "made of a metal which does not exist in this world." This suggests that the Tlön fantasy is so powerful that it can even overcome the physical laws of our universe!

But Tlön's real victory is in the hearts and minds of the people. As fascination with the meticulously crafted world of Tlön spreads, it causes people to lose interest in the cultures, histories, and philosophies of their own world, and refocuses all attention on itself. As the speaker says, "contact with Tlön and the ways of Tlön have disintegrated this world." In essence, Tlön conquers the known world.

Borges embodies his themes in a distinctive style. Let us look at his use of unfollowed references and caricature. The story seems to be written in a very dense, ornate manner. Much of this effect is due to the frequent dropping of references to objects or events within the story which are never further elaborated on, as if the author is constantly starting off in ten directions at once. For example, after the Princess of Faucigny Lucinge finds the Tlönian compass, she is never referred to again. It is never explained what her relation is to the speaker, or to anything else in the story, nor even where "Faucigny Lucinge" is. The same is true of the "etymology of the word gaucho," and of Herbert Ashe's "sundial and some oak trees."

Borges' characters are very spare and undeveloped. Not merely flat, we could say they are caricatures, for what little information we are given seems more concerned with emphasizing the unusualness of the character than with creating a believable person. For example, Herbert Ashe visits England and photographs only sundials and oak trees, and spends his days playing chess in total silence. Ezra Buckley is a millionaire ascetic, an apologist for slavery, and a freethinking nihilist who devotes his fortune to the creation of an imaginary world simply to "demonstrate to the nonexistent God that mortal men were capable of conceiving a world." This way of writing is consistent with the Latin American literary style known as magical realism.

Borges' primary insight is about western civilization itself. He seems to be saying that the kind of dry rational thought preferred by western civilization is deeply unsatisfying to the human imagination, which hungers for the fantastic and will jump at it if given the chance. This is evident in the enthusiastic way that the peoples of earth abandon their own cultures to study the imaginary world of Tlön, in which fantasy and amazement, instead of truth, are considered the superior values.

To my mind, this is a great story because it stimulates my imagination, challenges my intellect, upsets my preconceptions, and yet retains a sense of playfulness about the strange images that it creates.

Structured Journal Responses to Novels, Drama, Nonfiction, and Movies
(written outside class)

As was stated earlier, fewer journal samples are included on these genres because of their relatively greater length.

Novels

As we move to the journaling of novels, we face the challenge of keeping our entries manageable by restricting our coverage to just one or two major topics covered in the book. The novels could not be included in this text because of their size; you can read them on your own.

Student author Katherine Allen writes a structured response covering just one topic from Shusaku Endo's novel, Deep River.

Deep River
by Shusaku Endo (1923-1996)

This entry exemplifies a structured response to a novel, covering just one topic.

Student author: Katherine Allen

Summary

This novel by Shusaku Endo chronicles the lives of five Japanese individuals who are looking for answers to their dilemmas. Their search takes them to India, where they hope to find their answers by the Hindus' sacred river Ganges – the "Deep River" of the novel's title. Isobe is shaken out of his self-absorption when his wife Keiko is dying of cancer. Having failed to give her happiness while she was alive, taking her presence for granted, he wants to fulfill his promise to her by finding her reincarnated self in India.

Naruse Mitsuko considers herself selfish and insincere. With a short-lived abortive marriage to her credit, she has been unable to love anyone. She works as a volunteer at the hospital where Isobe's wife is admitted and receives Mitsuko's care. Not sure what she wants out of life, she hopes to find her direction in India.

Otsu is a devout church-going Catholic, whom, during his college days in Japan, Mitsuko had seduced and of whom she had demanded that he give up his God for her. After their parting, they meet again in France and then finally in India. He finds consolation for his past woes by working at the cremation grounds and assisting the dying people in completing their difficult pilgrimage to the Ganges. He insists that love is the most important value.

Numada, another of the five Japanese seekers, is an author of children's stories with animals as heroes. He chooses to go to India to experience the peacefulness of people and animals living together harmoniously.

Kiguchi, a Japanese World War II veteran, is tortured by the memory of taking so many human lives, many of them Indians. His mission in India is to have a memorial service to honor all soldiers, "friend and foe," that died in the war. He believes he can find peace through this ceremony.

Topic
Wrestling with the past to seek ways to achieve peace is an important topic in the novel.

Themes
Human suffering has to be understood and confronted in terms of its sources and possible solutions. Other themes concern the common mistake of taking people's companionship for granted and thus devaluing it out of shallow self-absorption.

Supporting details
The actions and states of mind of all five characters (described in the summary) illustrate the novel's themes. Isobe realizes too late how much his wife's cheerful presence has been a source of comfort and balance in his life. She had been so full of life that she yearns for and expects a rebirth somewhere in India. Her dying words bring Isobe to India looking for her reincarnation:

"I know for sure . . . I'll be reborn somewhere in this world. Look for Me . . . find me . . . find me . . . promise . . . promise!"

Mitsuko learns about the ultimate futility of power and control over others. Her love-hate relationship with Otsu, the devout Catholic, takes up a large part of the plot. Otsu's strong humanistic faith inspires Mitsuko to join the stream of humanity instead of always trying to rise above it. She puts on a sari and joins the other bathers in the river, affirming "I believe that the river embraces the people and carries them away. A river of humanity. The sorrows of this deep river of humanity. And I am part of it."

Style
A pervasive stylistic element in Endo's novel is symbolism. The river Ganges, which gives the novel its title, becomes a symbol of human unity and oneness. The river water is everywhere at once – at the point of its origin, at the point of its long journey toward the sea, and finally at the point of its merging with the sea. The river is also an appropriate symbol of transcendence and perpetual return as in the

Hindu concept of reincarnation. The river water becomes vapor, clouds, and rain that eventually becomes the river and continues the never-ending cycle.

Cultural insight

The novel brings home to the reader the special spiritual value and symbolism of the river Ganges. The appeal of this sacred river touches people far beyond India's borders. Besides this great tribute by a major Japanese author, the famous French filmmaker Jean Renoir made a movie *The River* on the same topic.

A Passage to India
by E. M. Forster (1879-1970)
http://archive.org/stream/APassageToIndia_109/APassageToIndia_djvu.txt

For those unfamiliar with this novel by the English author E. M. Forster, the film adaptation by Richard Attenborough gives a quick introduction. The film follows the novel faithfully.

A structured journal entry on this novel in Chapter Eleven demonstrates the journal-to-essay progress.

Structured journal responses to plays

Hamlet
by William Shakespeare (1564-1616)
http://shakespeare.mit.edu/hamlet/full.html

Before reading this journal entry, some knowledge of this play would be helpful. You can read the play using the above link. Chapter Three gives a brief summary in the context of discussing plot. If you do not have time to read the complete play by William Shakespeare (online or on your own), you can become familiar with the plot from the information given in Chapter Three. Preferably you should also watch a good film adaptation, starring actors such as Laurence Olivier, Richard Burton, Richard Chamberlain, Ian McClellan, or others.

Ideally, a play needs to be watched on stage, and complex works like Hamlet also need to be read. Evaluation of Shakespeare's style that needs comprehensive coverage is not included in this journal exercise. It is taken up in the chapter on drama.

Journal entry by the author of this book

Summary

Hamlet is Shakespeare's longest, most discussed, and most complex play. It bristles with probing questions and profound observations on the human condition. Its deeply meditative nature and inexhaustible wealth of ideas are apparent in every scene. In its rich array of characters and topics, the play has an idealistic protagonist in Hamlet, an evil but bright antagonist Claudius, a true friend Horatio, false friends like Rosencrantz and Guildenstern, honorable soldiers like Fortinbras, and impetuous and exploitable youths like Laertes. Also notable are the foolish wisdom of Polonius, the innocent love of Ophelia and not so innocent love of Gertrude, humor of the grave-diggers, and the ghost of former King Hamlet, who comes from the dead to seek revenge for his foul murder. These elements and characters combine to make *Hamlet* a murder mystery, a detective story, and a great philosophical drama – squeezed together into one play.

Topics
Among the play's important topics, notable are the fate of idealism, evil's finite reign, and the nature of human conscience.

Themes
From *Hamlet*'s rich thematic offerings, we learn that trying to achieve perfection in an imperfect world is bound to be frustrating. Another idea that repeatedly surfaces in the play is that in spite of initial victories, evil's reign is finite. The play, moreover, makes a profound observation on the nature of human conscience: the criminal may escape the law but cannot circumvent his or her conscience, which invariably brings the criminal to trial.

Supporting details
Prince Hamlet's tragic flaw seems to be his perfectionism and high morals in an imperfect and corrupt world. After Claudius's crime of murdering King Hamlet is revealed to Prince Hamlet by the spirit of his father, Hamlet tries painstakingly to verify the truth of the Ghost's words before avenging the death of his father. He does not rush to revenge in an impetuous manner, and this obsession with doing things right leads to his tragedy.

On a more positive note, Shakespeare's play does show evil to be finite. King Claudius – the epitome and source of evil in the play – can impose himself on the people of Denmark for only a short time. In the end his evil perishes with him, thus clearing the way for a new and better order.

Another theme in the play concerns the nature of human conscience. Even though Hamlet cannot legally prove Claudius' crime of fratricide, the guilty conscience haunts Claudius and forces him to betray his crime. In the play-within-the-play, he loses his characteristic self-control. We wonder why this "smiling, damned villain" cannot continue to pretend that he has done no evil. At the crucial moment, when the players re-enact the circumstances of King Hamlet's death by poisoning, he cannot maintain his composure. His conscience forces him to betray his guilt as he suddenly orders the play stopped.

Claudius' conscience tortures him at other moments as well, specifically in the scene in which he tries to pray unsuccessfully after publicly revealing his guilt during the play-within-the-play. Human conscience thus becomes an instrument of good, keeping evil in check.

Sample of limited coverage of the same play
Journal entry by the author of this book

This sample journal entry covers just one specific topic from the play unlike the previous, relatively comprehensive response.

Summary

Hamlet is unusual in many ways. Its one distinctive feature is that the protagonist – Hamlet – seeks no heroics, does not think of himself as a superhuman being, but is pulled into a vortex over which he has no control. Hamlet faces every challenge with utmost heroism but is unhappy about having to shoulder the crushing burden of responsibilities he finds himself saddled with.

Topic

One of the many notable topics in this play concerns the conflict between desire and duty.

Theme

Hamlet dramatizes the tragedy of having to play a role that conflicts with one's essential nature.

Supporting details

Hamlet would probably have been happy doing what he had been doing before the play opened – pursuing his scholarly goals, loving Ophelia, and enjoying great plays. However, fate had something else in store for him. Evidence for this view is in Hamlet's speech at the end of Act I right after he learns (from the ghost of his dead father) about the circumstances of King Hamlet's murder by Claudius and the possible guilt of Hamlet's mother (Gertrude):

The time is out of joint. O cursed spite,
That ever I was born to set it right!

Hamlet's words clearly show that he does not wish to be the moral rectifier of such a corrupt world. He is pushed by circumstances into this not only unpleasant but seemingly impossible role with tragic consequences.

Structured journal responses to essays

Courtship Through the Ages
by James Thurber (1894-1961)

Thurber's essay is in Chapter Fifteen.

Sample journal entry by the author of this book

Topic Courting rituals

Thesis

"None of the females of any of the species that she [Nature] created really cared very much for the male" and males of all species must perform rituals of "sorrowful lengths . . . to arouse the interest of a lady."

Support

Thurber's humorous essay focuses on the comically elaborate courtship rituals in the animal world with parallels among human beings to support his thesis. He finds it comforting that it is not just men who have to make up for the annoyance that their whiskers and mustaches cause women. The peacock, too, despite "all his gorgeous plumage, does not have a particularly easy time in courtship." Since the peacock's beautiful plumage failed to stir the peahen, "he had to learn to vibrate his quills so as to make a rustling sound."

Comparing this "love display" among the animals with similar rituals among humans, Thurber writes: "In ancient times man himself, observing the ways of the peacock, probably tried vibrating his whiskers to make a rustling sound; if so, it didn't get him anywhere. He had to invent new ways, such as gift giving, to attract the lady – something that he learned from flies and birds "who were making no headway at all with rustling sounds."

Thurber next compares the courtship woes of the male bowerbird with those of human males. The female bowerbird insists on an elaborate nest, filled with a great many gifts of rose petals, berries, red leaves, silvery leaves, etc. Only after the impressive nest is made with a specially built bower at the entrance and furnished with all kinds of showy paraphernalia and a playground, the female bowerbird consents to show up, but only for "a handshake." Using comic exaggeration, Thurber comes to the conclusion that he would not be surprised if all the male bowerbirds "became nervous wrecks within the next ten or fifteen years." Human males run the same risk. In Thurber's words, "A male bowerbird is as exhausted as a night-club habitué before he is out of his twenties."

To attract a female, the male fiddler crab "has to stand on tiptoe and brandish his claw in the air. . . . By nightfall of an average courting day, a fiddler crab . . . who has been standing on tiptoe for eight or ten hours waving a heavy claw in the air is in pretty sad shape. As in the case of the human male, however, he gets out of bed next morning, dashes some water on his face, and tries again."

Male web-spinning spiders are the worst sufferers in courtship rituals because they often end up losing their lives. The female web-spinning spiders have very poor eyesight. "If a male lands on a female web, she kills him before he has time to lay down his cane and gloves, mistaking him for a fly or a bumblebee who has tumbled into her trap." If Thurber's narrative were factual, it would be extremely sad. The only reason it makes us laugh is that it is untrue.

Perhaps the most comic example that blends the animal and human worlds is the one Thurber uses to close what he calls his "investigation into the mournful burdens of the male." In this case a man asks for his wife's attention to read to her his favorite poem. The wife is more interested in her magazine with detective stories. He is pleased to notice that she consents. Halfway through his recitation performance, he hears a sharp interrupting sound that brought his ritual to an unexpected end. He discovered that instead of paying any attention to the poem, his wife had been focusing on a circling mosquito and had finally succeeded in squishing it between the palms of her hands. Thurber's own words sum up the main thrust of his essay:

So it goes, through the long list of animals, from the bristle worm and his rudimentary dance steps to man and his gifts of diamonds and sapphires.

Style

To prevent the reader's confusing his imaginary details with facts, Thurber keeps using "I believe," "I imagine," etc., when introducing his hyperbolic figures and data throughout the essay. This device is important for keeping fiction and fact separate.

The humor-making devices that Thurber has used throughout this essay are comic exaggeration and fanciful inventions that, by their nature, cannot be mistaken for truth but are effective in creating laughter. An example is the fiddler crab who has to stand on his tiptoe for hours, waving his heavy claw, to attract a female – often to no avail. Thurber's essay is a catalogue of such humorous episodes.

Another stylistic element that Thurber has used well is situational irony, whereby what happens is the opposite of what was expected. Among many examples is that of the male web-spinning spider who gets murdered. The female web-spinning spider, because of her very poor eyesight, mistakes him for a fly or a bumblebee and kills him. The poor male web-spinning spider was expecting a better welcome in his courtship ritual.

Structured journal responses to movies

Samapti *(meaning* Conclusion*), directed by Satyajit Ray, is a faithful rendition of a story by Rabindranath Tagore, and* A Prince Among Slaves, *is a documentary directed by the independent filmmaker Andrea Kalin. You can watch clips from those movies* online.

A Prince Among Slaves
directed by Andrea Kalin

You may read about this documentary film and watch clips at these websites:

http://www.pbs.org/programs/prince-among-slaves/

http://www.princeamongslaves.org/

Student author: Maxwell Lynch

Topic
Perseverance

Theme
An enslaved king discovers that despite decades of perseverance, his modest dream of a homecoming is prevented by racist hatred and political cynicism.

Support
"Racist hatred" and "political cynicism" are quite obvious terms to use when describing anything related to slavery, but it helps bring into focus the plight of Abdul Rahman. Abdul Rahman was taken from Futa Jallon, a place said to be "two moons from Timbuktu" in 1778. After coming to terms with his stolen freedom, Rahman toiled on Foster's farm for decades -- but never gave up hope that he and his children might be able to return home. When the chance did come for the American administration to do the right thing, they did so only in hopes that it would be seen as a great diplomatic gesture. Herein lies the political cynicism surrounding Rahman: President Adams, and many others were under the false impression that Rahman was a Moroccan prince – thus, returning him to Morocco would earn them political capital. Of course, when he appealed to Adams himself for help, his honesty got the better of him. The truth of his heritage came out, and Adams could not overcome his own racist ideology or cynical politics to make a small gesture of goodwill. It is not surprising that a former African slave would be treated this way at that time, but it is strikingly depressing when one thinks of the archetypal concept of human perseverance, and how it is so often rewarded. Specifically, that the ugliness of racist hatred is such that it can extinguish nearly every aspect of human compassion – that is, not even a story of perseverance and human spirit (like Rahman's) could sway the President of the United States an inch.

Samapti (Conclusion)
directed by Satyajit Ray (1921-1992)

http://www.youtube.com/watch?v=lmBSdWRwHrs

Satyajit Ray's film Samapti (Bengali word for conclusion) is based on a short story by the Nobel laureate Rabindranath Tagore. Here we have the ideal combination of a brilliant filmmaker and a consummate author. Presenting universal themes with optimism, the movie reaffirms the power of love and kindness in resolving human conflicts. It also treats the topic of women's oppression in the form of denying them freedom to choose their husbands.

Journal entry by the author of this book

Summary

The setting of this movie is a small village in India. The young man Amulya, the only son of a doting mother, returns home after finishing his studies. His mother has already selected a girl for him to marry; she is educated and belongs to a respectable family. However, Amulya is not interested in her and shocks his mother when he reveals that he would like to marry Minu (nicknamed Puglee, meaning "crazy") who is the village tomboy with a reputation for wild, carefree ways.

After the mother gets over her shock, she agrees to Amulya's marriage to Minu. On the wedding night, Minu objects to the fact that her feelings were not taken into consideration at all in the process of deciding their match. In her view, the fact that Amulya wanted to marry her is not enough of a reason for marriage. Amulya is very puzzled at her attitude, but acts wisely in opposition to everyone's advice that he control his wife forcefully. He leaves her with the option to write to him if and when she wants him to come back to her.

Many months later, Amulya's mother sends for her son on the pretext that she is critically ill – a well-intentioned trick on her part to have him come back and work on reconciliation with his estranged wife. By that time, after going through hardships and soul searching, and convinced of Amulya's kind and considerate nature, Minu has changed. She writes a note to Amulya, asking him to come back.

Topic

This movie concerns a timeless issue: What are the components of a good marriage?

Theme

In addition to mutual interest in a union, kindness and regard for each other's feelings is essential to a good marriage.

Supporting details

Minu initially rebels against the marriage because her consent was not sought. Her family regarded themselves fortunate that a man of Amulya's family background, education, and stature had asked for Minu's hand in marriage. After her conflict with Amulya, she hurls several household items all over the room and expects to be beaten by Amulya. In opposition to everyone's advice that he should teach her a lesson by punishing her, Amulya acts with extreme kindness. Entrusting the fate of their marriage to Minu's hands, he leaves her free to choose how she would like to live. When Amulya is summoned back to the village by his mother's feigned illness, he is told of Minu's unhappiness and sudden disappearance. He searches for her frantically in the midst of a fierce rainstorm, but in vain. When Minu becomes convinced of Amulya's love for her and his extremely kind nature, she sends him a note asking him to come back to her, and the story ends with their reconciliation.

Cultural insight

The movie depicts the social pressures in a changing society, especially for independent-minded individuals, such as the two main characters in this story. With regard to the prevailing custom and problems of arranged marriages, as societies evolve toward fewer restrictions, it is becoming increasingly necessary that even though the parents may arrange a marriage, the two persons getting married have to be agreeable to the arrangement. Amulya, in this movie, acts like an ideal (not typical) husband in that he refuses to surrender to the custom of male domination. By showing sensitivity to his wife's feelings, he wins her love.

Exercises to Test Your Mastery of Chapter Six

1. Describe a typical informal journal entry. Give examples when needed for clarity.

2. Describe a typical structured (more in-depth) journal entry. Add necessary examples.

3. With a time limit of 30 minutes, write an informal journal entry on a work you are familiar with.

4. With a time limit of one hour, write a structured journal entry on a work you have already read.

5. Within the time limit of 90 minutes, read an unfamiliar short story and make a structured journal entry on it.

6. Observing the time limit of one hour, read an unfamiliar poem (no longer than three pages) and make a structured or informal journal entry on it.

7. Make a structured journal entry on a novel, play, or movie, focusing on just one major topic from the work.

8. What are the defining, distinguishing traits of fiction, poetry, drama, and nonfiction? One sentence on each genre would be enough.

9. How would your journal responses to longer literary works differ from your journal entries on short stories and poems? On what part of the longer work should your summary focus, since you cannot summarize the entire work?

CHAPTER SEVEN

FORMAL INTERPRETATION

Writing Assignments with Step-by-Step Instructions and Advice

The instructions and advice given in this chapter are designed to help you master some basic time-honored conventions that you can use as a means to clear thinking and writing. They should, in no way, inhibit your creativity. You will learn the necessary skills by completing two assignments – one on themes and the other on style in a literary work. The style assignment is meant for more advanced students. If you do not yet feel ready for it, you can return to it later. Even though the step-by-step instructions of this chapter appear in the context of writing interpretations of short stories, they also apply to interpreting novels, plays, poems, and movies – the focus of Chapters Eleven, Twelve, Thirteen, and Fourteen respectively. Therefore, when completing assignments on interpretation in those chapters, you may need to refer back to the step-by-step instructions of this chapter.

A note on the amount of instructions is in order. Some of you need more instructions than others. For that reason, I have tried to strike a balance between too little and too much. When too many questions about organization and strategy remain unanswered, you are left hungering for more information. However, if you are the kind that learns better from samples than instructions, you can skip to the chapter's two sample essays without lingering too long at the writing advice. Use instructions and advice on an "as-needed" basis. However, you should pay careful attention to the advice on writing effective thesis statements (both cluster and part-by-part varieties), crafting good topic sentences, careful marshaling of supporting evidence, use of focusing strategies, and transitions.

Structure and Organization

Even though there is no fixed form for a literary essay, most essays share some common features, mastery of which will greatly facilitate your writing about literature. After feeling secure that you have mastered the basic essay structure, feel free to use your creative imagination to introduce variety that promises pleasant reading and clear organization of your ideas. When writing essays, keep in mind Virginia Woolf's following words: "The principle which controls it is simply that it should give us pleasure; the desire which impels us when we take it from the shelf is simply to receive pleasure. Everything in an essay must be subdued to that end" (Scholes 4). The pleasure that Woolf speaks of comes from the pleasing form with which you shape your ideas. After you have learned how to organize a literature-based essay, you can apply the same knowledge to any essay on any topic – literary or non-literary – because the principles of organization, generating the thesis, and proving major points remain unchanged. The advice of this chapter will give you means to conceptualize effective ways to write all types of essays. The main difference between a literary and non-literary essay is that in the latter, support for the thesis comes from facts, data, and examples that the writer gathers and generates on his/her own. In a literature-based essay, however, support for the thesis comes primarily from relevant details from the work itself. Such details serve as supporting evidence for your interpretive and analytic comments.

The conventional form of the essay – consisting of a title, introduction, thesis, main body, and conclusion – has suffered from decrease in popularity. Nevertheless, its value as a structuring and organizing tool cannot be denied. Moreover, only after mastering it can one try to introduce innovations and variations on this basic formula. The step-by-step instructions in this chapter blend conventional advice with innovative approaches.

THE SHORT STORY

Of the various forms of literature – fiction, drama, poetry – the short story is likely to be most familiar to you. Among various elements of short fictional works – themes, characters, plot, and style – writing on an author's major themes is a good starting point. Since interesting topics and theme-bearing details are already embedded in the action and events of short stories, at the outset of your development as a literary critic, you will appreciate this abundant yield of topics for interpretation. Stories, moreover, engage our innate emotions and create in us a desire to share those feelings with others. This *sharing* is central to interpretation.

First Assignment:
Writing on Themes of a Literary Work

With the requirements of this assignment in mind, the entire class should read a complex story that demands interpretation in order to be understood. The steps, process, and challenges involved in completing this assignment may be covered in instructor-led group discussions. Such discussions, *which can also take place in an on-line course,* are very helpful and may be made a required part of tackling any major assignment.

Before starting the paper, pay close attention to the wording of the assignment. Keep consulting this chapter's sample essay on Kate Chopin's "The Story of an Hour" to get help with every part of the assignment. Feel free to modify the format of the sample essay to suit your style. The main goal to be kept in mind is an engaging, easy-to-read, clearly organized, and well-written paper to capture a story's thematic richness.

Select a short story of some complexity that deeply engages your feelings. Develop an essay of about 750 words on the story's major themes. To avoid pointless repetition, do not write on a work that has been discussed in class unless you can present original ideas. If the story you choose is considered a classic, briefly mention in your essay's opening or concluding section the reasons for its reputation. If what you select is not yet a classic, give reasons why it should be regarded as a superior work.

Optional: Try using these suggested elements of style in your own writing while completing this assignment.

When revising the first draft, strengthen your style with figurative language by using in the paper those of the following elements that your style permits: simile, metaphor, analogy, and personification. In addition, use a semicolon, an explanatory dash, and an explanatory colon – effective ways to eliminate wordiness and to introduce variety in writing. In any pre-final draft, prominently footnote or endnote only one (your best) example of each element of style that you use from the suggested list. These footnotes/endnotes should preferably be left out of the final draft. Attach to your final copy the draft that has these style footnotes/endnotes so that the reader of your paper can appreciate your attempt at style improvement through revision.

[End of the assignment]

Advantages of Writing on Several Themes from a Story

Besides being an exercise in interpretation, writing an essay on more than one theme in a story teaches the skill of organizing various sections of a composition. For example, writing on two or three themes from a literary work rather than on just one theme would give you the opportunity to learn how to manage multiple subdivisions of your essay and make you more keenly aware of organizing strategies. Writing on only one theme in a literary work or a movie is perfectly valid as long as you understand its following limitations as a learning tool:

1. One theme will seldom cover the entire work.

2. Your paper will have just one set of supporting details to go with the one theme. This format will, therefore, not give you the learning opportunity to manage a paper of several sections – one for each theme – and use transitions, subdivisions, and topic sentences for effective organization.

The benefit of writing on multiple themes to master your organizing skills is, therefore, evident. However, if your creative impulse leads you in the direction of just one central theme, feel free to obey yourself. This chapter's sample essay demonstrates how to write on three significant themes. I could have written on just one of them, but then I would not have been able to show you ways of meeting challenges of organization and focus posed by a multi-thematic topic. To preserve unity in your paper, it is advisable that if you write on more than one theme, try to write on themes that seem to be related to one another in some way. They can be distinct yet related. With such unity of thesis one major idea will lead to the other in a logical sequence.

Step-by-Step Instructions

These instructions are meant to cover almost every aspect of an essay, *including essays that are not based on literature and film.* The writing advice given here may *seem* too detailed; however, every piece of information has a purpose. If you have already mastered the skills taught in these instructions, take a quick look at them and go to the sample essay.

TITLE

Formulate a clear title that reveals your focus. It could be as simple as "Major Themes in Kate Chopin's 'The Story of an Hour';" or it could be on the more creative side, as in "The Short Happy Life of Louise Mallard in Kate Chopin's 'The Story of an Hour'." Remember that if you choose the latter kind of title, all themes discussed in the paper should relate to the focus of that title; otherwise the phrasing of the title, which limits the story's themes to just one topic, will be misleading. The first-mentioned variety of title is easier to manage because it allows you the freedom to write on many different themes that do not have to come out of one topic; instead, they could be developed out of several different topics. Both title options organize the main body of the essay in convenient sections – one section per theme. The title that you choose will direct your thesis, which, in turn, will control the main body.

INTRODUCTION (50 to 100 words)

Your introduction may be in the form of a summary of the story's significant details, such as the setting, main events, important characters and their actions, consequences of their actions, conflict, etc. If it is possible and meaningful to do so, relate the story's title to its topic. One of the many possible ways to end this summary is by pointing out the topic or topics that figure prominently in the story. Most importantly, the ending of the introductory paragraph should lead to the thesis, which is the next component of your paper. In writing your essay, assume that your reader is not familiar with the story so that you may include a sufficient amount of explanatory and clarifying details.

THESIS (30 to 100 words, depending on the kind of thesis used—cluster or part-by-part)

This is how you may create the thesis of an interpretive essay: Narrow down major topics from the literary work into clear statements of the author's/literary work's position on those topics, as perceived by you. If a story, for example, concerns the topic of marriage, to reach the *theme*, you need to state the author's/work's position on that *topic*. The theme could be that *marriage is not a panacea for personal shortcomings and that, to be successful, it requires constant hard work.* From this example, we can see that formulating a theme requires more thought than identifying a topic. The topic is easier to recognize, but interpreting the complete work to arrive at the *theme* on that topic is far more challenging. If necessary, review in Chapter Five the advice on how to discover themes and acceptable ways to formulate them.

As in other forms of structured writing, there are two kinds of theses that an interpretive essay can use – **part-by-part thesis** and **cluster thesis**. Choosing one form of thesis over the other is a matter of preference.

Part-by-part variety of thesis (used in the sample essay on "The Story of an Hour")

This kind of thesis introduces only one of its component parts at a time, as in the following example: *A major theme of Kate Chopin's "The Story of an Hour" is that desire for self-worth and a deep hunger for freedom surpass considerations of love.* If the wording of the theme seems too formulaic, you may use some other form. One of the many options is this: The values of self-worth and freedom receive special emphasis in Kate Chopin's "The Story of an Hour." Your statement of the first theme becomes the first part of your thesis as well as your first topic sentence. Specific supporting details from the story are then included.

The next theme is then stated (as the second part of your thesis), followed by supporting details and discussion. This pattern continues until you have stated and supported all themes. If you choose this part-by-part variety to organize your paper on three themes, your complete thesis will consist of your statements of the three themes, but these statements will be spread over three sections, not concentrated in one paragraph.

An important point to remember is that in a part-by-part thesis, there is no clearly visible separation between the thesis and the main body of your essay because the supporting details and partial thesis are combined in one unit of organization. Your statements of the story's themes, regardless of their location, become your thesis and control the entire interpretive essay. In papers that are not written in response to literature and film, we take it for granted that the thesis statement is the controlling and unifying device. We need to become aware that in interpretive essays, the statements of themes, functioning as a thesis, serve the same purpose.

Cluster variety of thesis

As its name suggests, the cluster thesis states the story's themes one after another in the same paragraph, using appropriate transitions between statements of themes. This essay structure is demonstrated in two places in this chapter:

- Right after the end of the complete sample essay that uses a part-by-part or non-cluster variety of thesis.
- As the main sample essay on an author's style (Moravia's style in "The Chase")

Necessity of varying the introductory parts of your statements of themes
[*If you feel you do not need this advice, skip to the next part* – **Support**]

When creating your thesis and topic sentences with the help of statements of themes, avoid monotony and awkward repetition, by varying the wording of your introductory phrases and clauses that precede the statement of theme. Your wording of the theme itself will, of course, vary according to the theme's substance. In an assignment like this, the problem of repetition often occurs in the phrases and clauses that introduce the themes.

For example, in writing a concentrated thesis paragraph for an essay on the themes in a literary work, you should introduce each theme differently. Words like *"A major theme in this story is that . . ."* should be used no more than once in the cluster thesis to avoid repetition. There are many ways to introduce themes. In the following examples when both the introductory words and the theme appear together, the introductory part is italicized for clarity. Use your imagination and creativity to add to this list.

1. *The story leaves the reader with a feeling that life is a series of ever-changing new goals.*

2. The author questions the commonly held belief that . . .

3. The story touches on the idea that . . .

4. *The fact that* many people continue to reach for the unattainable despite the impossibilities of their success *illustrates the author's major theme.*

5. The story is an expression of relief, regret, etc., that . . .

6. *The author dramatizes the consequences of submission*: molding one's life according to an image is fatal to one's freedom.

7. From this story we learn that . . .

8. Sometime people underestimate their actions as unimportant only to find out later just how important the actions actually were. *Phelps illustrates this theme through a character's dream.* [In the reversed structure of No.8, the theme is given first as a complete thought in a sentence. What is usually the introductory part then follows in a separate sentence.]

9. Selfish lovers act self-righteously at the end of a failed relationship. *This theme seems to pervade Fitzgerald's* The Great Gatsby.

10. Also vital to the story is the idea that . . .

11. The author's next theme, which concerns _____ [Use a word or phrase to identify the topic, such as love, marriage, friendship, etc.] leaves us looking for an answer.

12. *Some significant scenes in the story dramatize a common human trait*: in our pursuit of self-gratification, we sometimes trample on the needs and desires of others.

Avoid repeating the word *theme*

In an essay on themes from any work of art, *theme* is a key word and will have to be repeated at strategic points for maintaining correct focus and coherence. For example, the word theme or its equivalent is likely to appear in the title, thesis, topic sentences, and conclusion of such a paper.

However, in writing your thesis paragraph, which in the case of an interpretive essay on a literary work may take the form of your stating the work's themes one after the other (in the cluster thesis variety), you should avoid repetitive use of the word *theme*. Use it or its equivalent (*idea, view, belief, point*, etc.) only once as I have done in the following example of a cluster thesis.

A major theme in this story is that a relationship based on the convenience of one partner alone is never completely fulfilling to the other partner. The story also reveals that suspicion and mistrust act as corrosives in a relationship. Several events in the story, moreover, dramatize a common human trait: by using the word love indiscriminately, we vulgarize this sublime emotion.

Crafting attractively phrased statements of themes comes with practice. However, once you have crossed this hurdle, your task becomes easier in the main body.

SUPPORT (200 to 300 words)

In interpretations that use the cluster thesis, the term "main body" is sometimes used to describe the supporting evidence. However, in the thesis variety known as part-by-part format, the "body" does not stand out as a section by itself. Instead of one "main" body, we have different sections, each a self-contained unit controlled by a topic sentence. This chapter covers both the cluster and non-cluster thesis varieties.

After stating the literary work's/movie's theme(s) in the thesis, your next task is providing evidence (*proof* or *support*) from the work that your statements of themes are valid. In essence, you will be showing the reader how you arrived at your formulation of themes. It is here – in the process of presenting proof – that papers begin to sound like plot summaries and lose their identity as an essay. Digression from the topic is another problem that often occurs during this stage of the composing process.

Suggested Solutions

There are a few convenient means to prevent essays from sounding like a summary. Avoid the past tense as much as possible. This tense automatically signals narrative rather than expository writing. Short stories and novels are narrative writing, whereas their interpretations (such as your papers) are of an expository nature.

1. Avoid organizing the analysis chronologically so that you are not tempted to lapse into event-by-event summarizing.

2. Do not end any section of the essay with an unexplained or unexamined quotation from the literary work or with an isolated summary of any part of it. Everything you write should have a connection. Analytic and explanatory details – whether they precede or follow direct quotations – form the nucleus of interpretive writing. They keep summarizing details subordinate to topic sentences and give the essay its identity and unity.

3. Use well-phrased topic sentences throughout the essay and keep all supporting details tied to them.

Typical Structure of the Main Body in an Essay with a Cluster Thesis

The first major topic sentence in the main body, followed by supporting details. In an essay using a cluster thesis, your first major topic sentence for the main body will introduce the first part of the thesis and control its discussion.

Supporting details. The evidence to support the thesis is in the form of relevant quotations and summary of connected details. Each part of the thesis requires this support. It is important to remember that literary works often provide only details, such as setting, atmosphere, events, characters, significant deeds and their consequences. Seldom do they openly state themes, which have to be grasped through interpretation of those details. It is advisable to use one direct quotation to support each major theme. Include some analysis of the selected quotation or details and their connection to the theme that you are supporting. Introduce quotations with a variety of introductory words. Quotations should be brief and absolutely relevant. Leave out nonessential words from quotations by using ellipsis dots to indicate omission. Indent and set off from the text those quotations that are longer than three lines. Since all quoted material should read coherently with your statements, use square brackets to add clarifying editorial comments. Inside a quotation, you can use square brackets to enclose any words you need for clarity.

Refer specifically to theme-bearing statements, events, actions, characters, stylistic elements, etc. Whereas in the thesis paragraph you were writing in general or universal terms, here, in the discussion part of the main body, you support those generalizations with specific details from the literary work. Add explanatory details wherever they may be helpful to the reader. *Assume that the reader is not familiar with the story/work that you are discussing.* Add explanations and clarifying details accordingly. For example, if you mention a character's name, add a phrase or a clause that will give the reader an idea about that character's place in the story. If, for instance, you are mentioning the character Andy in Fitzgerald's story "The Last of the Belles," explain, in a phrase, that *Andy is the main male character as well as the narrator of the story*. If you are showing how an author's style is suggesting or strengthening a theme, include an example of that element of style from the work being discussed. Such explanatory details are essential for clarity.

Steps for clarity of focus:

- To prevent your paper from sounding like a summary of the literary work and to maintain correct focus, keep summarizing details tied and subordinate to the topic sentence by referring to the controlling idea of the section at strategic points. Returning to the controlling idea of the topic sentence at the end of a paragraph or section will also help maintain the desired focus.

- When using quotations, do not leave the reader confused by ending a section with an unexplained quotation, the point of which you have not explained.

The second major topic sentence and supporting details. After finishing the discussion of the author's first theme, open your next section (in which you are to take up the next theme) with a topic sentence. For the sake of variety, your phrasing of this topic sentence should be different from the wording of the preceding section's topic sentence. It should also include a transitional word or phrase to show that you are moving from one theme to another. Such transitional words are needed for coherence. Vary your word choice and sentence structure to introduce the topic sentence of each paragraph.

Add relevant details as was done to support the first major topic sentence.

The third major topic sentence and supporting details. When you reach the discussion of the author's third and last theme (in the case of this assignment), you should remember the need for style variation in phrasing the topic sentence. (This chapter's sample essay on Kate Chopin's story provides a clear example of topic sentence variety.)

Add relevant supporting details as before.

CONCLUSION (50 to 100 words)

The final step of the process is to compose a satisfactory conclusion, which may be a comment on the author's achievement, an acknowledgment of the enriching insights the work has brought you, or a remark on the validity of the author's view or philosophy as it bears on a common human condition, problem, aspiration, fear, etc. You may wish to acknowledge the author's contribution in sensitizing you to the validity of those views to which you have been less receptive, or enabling you to experience and understand an unfamiliar culture. Another way to conclude your essay is to comment on the author's ability to suggest a solution to a recurrent problem. If the work offers no solution, you may acknowledge the author's dramatization of the problem in a way that enhances your awareness of the problem.

Summary of advice on conclusions in essays on literary works

Of the many ways to conclude an essay on themes of a literary work, the following seem effective:

1. Acknowledging the emotional and intellectual enrichment the literary work has brought to you.

2. Attempting to answer a question raised but left unanswered in the literary selection, or giving an answer or solution different from the one offered in the work.

3. Relating the literary work to another work or movie that embodies similar themes and raises similar questions.

4. Pointing out a flaw in the author's, the narrator's, or a character's perception of a situation.

5. Commenting on the literary work's impact and on the author's accomplishment (in your own words or in the words of a critic).

Advice on conclusions applicable to most situations (not limited to literature-based essays)

It is almost easier to say how *not* to end a paper than to offer advice on how to end it. Therefore, only a few of the numerous ways to conclude a paper are mentioned here.

1.   Avoid introducing a new topic at the end of an essay. Doing so will confuse the reader and reduce the paper's impact.

2.   The conclusion is the last chance to impress upon the reader the goal and point of the essay. Therefore, no statements should be made that take the reader away from the thesis directly or indirectly. The thesis was the place where you declared your intentions, defined your scope, assumed your stance, mentioned your focal point, and invited the reader to enter the world of your composition. The conclusion is the place where you see your guest off with utmost clarity and no clutter.

3.   Another important point to remember is that ending the paper abruptly leaves the reader with a dissatisfied feeling of unanswered questions or unexplained statements. Such abruptness in ending is criticized in the often-heard remark that some papers do not conclude; they just come to a STOP.

4.   It is not a good idea to apologize to the reader for something left undone in the paper or for our lack of knowledge, skill, etc. These matters are best left to the reader's judgment.

5.   The conclusion should not be a mechanical repetition of the thesis. Some repetition is acceptable, even desirable for clarity, coherence, and for making a point, but literal repetition bores the reader with its redundancy.

6.   Concluding a paper with an apt supporting quotation is acceptable if we are not using that quotation as a substitute for a clearly written argument of our own to make a point.

7.   Of the numerous other ways of concluding a paper, notable are:

   • Reiterating the main point
   • Asking a provocative question
   • Pondering some other possible responses to the issue raised or the problem discussed in the paper
   • Presenting a generalization or an inference based on the evidence the paper has presented
   • Using a brief, relevant anecdote to emphasize a point.

Strategies for Coherence and Organization

At every step in the process of composing an essay – in the introduction, the thesis, the main body, and the conclusion, and especially at every significant turn of thought – we need devices to keep our writing coherent and unified.

Maximum readability should be the uppermost goal when selecting strategies for coherence and methods of organization. Here are a few suggestions.

Transitions

One of the primary functions of transitional expressions is joining one part of an essay with a preceding and/or following part. These connecting links are indispensable, especially between independent sections, in order to show orderly progression and the direction of your thought. Transitional words/phrases should be placed at the beginning of a paragraph and can be a part of a topic sentence. Sometimes in long essays, an entire paragraph may be used to serve a transitional purpose. Some transitions are obvious – words like *however, therefore, thus, consequently, on the other hand, on the contrary,* etc. Other transitions may be more subtle and depend on semantic, psychological, and emotional triggers rather than an evident connection between two sections.

For instance, if you have discussed in one section the difficulty involved in having to make a critical decision, you could open the next section in this way: *Sometimes we become so consumed with the fear of pain in making crucial decisions that we forget the relief that comes from overcoming indecisiveness.* The subtle but clear transition in this case will be from the difficulty of decision making to the relief that comes once a decision is made. The italicized sentence would thus sum up what was said in the preceding section and introduce the controlling idea of the new section. Try using both subtle and obvious transitions for variety.

Repetition of Key Words

Besides transitions, repetition of key words is another device for coherence. The key words that need repetition in an essay on an author's themes, for example, would be *author* (or the author's name) and *theme*, since these or their equivalents are the central words in the title of your paper. Similarly, in a paper on an author's style of writing, you will need to repeat the word *style* whenever necessary for clarity of focus and a means of organization. The same principle holds for writing on non-literary topics: you are required to refer to the title of your paper through your topic sentences.

Paying Attention to the Nature of Your Subject

Most often the nature of your subject itself furnishes the most appropriate devices for coherence and organization. For example, you may hold one section together by arranging its details in the order of their ascending or descending importance, using the climactic order. Chronological or temporal order, on the other hand, requires that you mention the themes in the order in which they appear in the literary work/film. If the position that you take on an issue is fairly well-accepted, you may use the deductive method of organizing details in your reasoning process. According to this method, one proceeds from general to specific, which means that your statements of themes or thesis (that are always general in nature) will come before your supporting details (that are always specific in nature). However, your view or interpretation may be controversial and likely to invite resistance or opposition from the reader. In that case, it would be more effective to organize your presentation inductively, according to which, verifiable supporting evidence (specific in nature) is presented *before* the point or generalization is made to minimize the reader's resistance to your reasoning. These methods of organization could also be used in the main body to arrange the supporting and summarizing details coherently. Once you know your organizational choices, you can select the method that seems most suitable.

Your subject, audience, and purpose determine the best choice of organization. Maximum clarity for the reader should be your first consideration in choosing your transitions and methods of organization. Style variation also demands that you avoid yielding to readily available visible transitions all the time; instead, you should rely on good judgment to choose the most appropriate strategies for connecting various parts of your essay.

Advice on Creating Good Topic Sentences

Topic sentences are the means to organize an essay and prevent digression. Each major topic sentence introduces and controls a part or aspect of a thesis. A paper on an author's three prominent themes, for example, would consist of at least three main sections – one for each theme.

To avoid making an essay sound like a summary, a suitably worded topic sentence would be needed in each main section, usually at the beginning of the section, to control the relevant plot summary. For variety, you may move the position of the topic sentence to the middle or end of the section as long as clarity and focus are not compromised. At first, however, it is advisable to stay with the convention of putting your topic sentence at the beginning of each section.

In an essay on just one theme from a work, topic sentences would still be needed to introduce various aspects of that one theme. Thus your discussion of an author's themes would mainly consist of *a few* analytic comments that are often placed in topic sentences and in all those parts that contain your interpretation and reasoning. Relevant plot details and summaries will appear in your discussion as supporting evidence that you should always keep subordinate to your controlling analytic comments. The controlling ideas for topic sentences, just as for the thesis, come from the interpreter's reading and perception of the literary work's details. Topic sentences, thus, are directly connected with the thesis, which, in turn, is directly connected with the essay's title. Omission of topic sentences makes one's writing sound like a mere summary (retelling) of the literary work.

It will help to think of topic sentences as signposts that keep the writer as well as the reader on track. Like their progenitor (the thesis), topic sentences should be eloquent, precise, and eminently readable. Whether they introduce a step in a process, sum up a preceding thought, or simply allow the writer a smooth access to supporting facts and data, good topic sentences have the tenacious quality of staying in the reader's mind.

In an interpretive essay on themes from a literary work or movie, each topic sentence will control the discussion of a theme. It is, therefore, necessary to have a topic sentence for each section of the essay. By announcing the main point (also called the controlling idea), topic sentences obligate the writer to stay on course. They are, therefore, essential for coherence and focus.

Steps in creating good topic sentences in deductive and inductive paragraphs/sections

1. It is important to remember that the *function of a topic sentence* is to introduce the idea that is being discussed in a specific paragraph or section. In a deductively organized paragraph, in which the writer proceeds from a valid generalization to examine the specifics that support it, the topic sentence appears at the beginning or somewhere near the beginning of the paragraph. Very often the valid generalization *is* the topic sentence.

2. In an inductive arrangement of details, in which the writer first gives specific supporting details before the generalization, the topic sentence is placed at the end of a section/paragraph *after* the evidence on which the topic sentence and its controlling idea are based. Most essays use both varieties of organization. However, *deduction* is the more prevalent form, and *inductive* arrangement of details is often reserved for situations in which the writer expects opposition to his/her point of view. Whatever its location, a topic sentence always controls the entire paragraph or section and regardless of the nature of your essay, the principles of generating good topic sentences remain the same.

3. Besides showing the direction of thought, a topic sentence should also serve the important function of suggesting the material and facts that the writer can draw on to develop a point. The words "The story's significant events" in the following topic sentence, for example, would enable you to introduce in your discussion a significant part of the story. *"**The story's significant events** support the theme that self-worth and freedom are greater human needs than love."*

4. Variety is essential in structuring topic sentences. The problem of repetition often occurs in papers with a cluster thesis (which consists of all themes stated one after the other). To avoid repetition, phrase topic sentences differently from the statements of themes. In a topic sentence, we need only the key words from the statement of theme instead of repeating the entire theme.

Examples of compressing a statement of theme into a topic sentence. Compressed statements become topic sentences in the body of an essay with a cluster thesis:

> **Statement of theme** (part of the interpreter's cluster thesis*):*
> *The story illustrates that a relationship based on the convenience of one partner alone is never fulfilling to the other partner.*

> **Compression of this theme into a topic sentence:**
> *The theme of one-sided relationships appears many times in the story's events and statements.* The entire theme is here compressed in one key phrase, *"one-sided relationships."*

A General Reminder on the Form of Organized Writing

Various parts of a structured piece of writing are closely connected. The following outline will give you an idea of the interconnectedness of the components of a well-organized composition.

TITLE: A good title is clear and inviting.

INTRODUCTION: The introduction is a clarification and expansion of the title.

THESIS: The thesis, which could be a part of the introduction, controls the entire essay. Any detail that does not relate to the thesis is regarded as irrelevant. A good thesis has the potential of generating many relevant details. In the cluster variety, the thesis is given at once; in the part-by-part variety, only a part of the thesis is introduced at one time, followed by the evidence that supports it. Regardless of the kind of thesis used, it controls the entire essay.

BODY: The body *proves* what the thesis *claimed.* In the part-by-part form, the thesis and the body are not separate as they are in the cluster thesis. In this variation, a part of the thesis and its supporting details form one bloc of details.

Topic sentence to introduce the discussion of the first part/aspect of the thesis.
Supporting details

Topic sentence to introduce the discussion of the next part/aspect of the thesis.
Supporting details

Continuing this pattern until completion of the main body.

CONCLUSION: Wrapping things up by summarizing the main points, reiterating the important point, asking a question that invites reflection, or presenting a generalization or an inference based on the evidence of the main body.

Creative Ways to Introduce Variety in Form

After gaining confidence in your ability to compose in a coherent and organized fashion, you should feel free to do some experimentation. You may, for instance:

1. Choose not to write the thesis statement of your essay at the beginning of the paper. Using the inductive method of organization, you may put the thesis at the end instead.

2. Use the part-by-part format to spread your thesis over various parts of the essay instead of including all of it in one concentrated statement or paragraph.

3. Move the place of a topic sentence to the middle or end of a section. Placing the topic sentence at the *end* of a paragraph is the normal practice in the *inductive* form of organization.

4. Avoid those transitional devices that seem too obvious; rely, instead, on subtle transitions.

The sample essays of this chapter exemplify these and other variations of form.

SAMPLE ESSAYS

The structure of my essay on major themes in Kate Chopin's "The Story of an Hour" corresponds to the organization that goes with a part-by-part, non-cluster thesis, which has been explained in the preceding section. This sample contains examples of each component of the assignment. The headings "Title," "Introduction," "Thesis," "Supporting details, and "Conclusion" are only to demonstrate the various parts of the essay. Do not use these headings in your paper. I have labeled topic sentences and supporting details for clearer demonstration of the components of this kind of writing. Read the following short story before reading the sample essay on it.

The Story of an Hour

Knowing that Mrs. Mallard was afflicted with a heart trouble, great cause was taken to break to her as gently as possible the news of her husband's death. It was her sister Josephine who told her, in broken sentences; veiled hints that revealed in half concealing. Her husband's friend Richard was there, too, near her. It was her who had been in the newspaper office when intelligence of the railroad disaster was received, with Bentley Mallard's name leading the list of "killed." He had only taken the time to assure himself of its truth by a second telegram, and had hastened to forestall any less careful, less tender friend in bearing the sad message.

She did not hear the story as many women have heard the same, with a paralyzed inability to accept its significance. She wept at once, with sudden, wild abandonment, in her sister's arms. When the storm of grief had spent itself she went away to her room alone. She would have no one follow her.

There stood, facing the open window, a comfortable, roomy armchair. Into this she sank, pressed down by a physical exhaustion that haunted her body and seemed to reach into her soul.

She could see in the open square before her house the tops of trees that were all aquiver with the new spring life. The delicious breath of rain was in the air. In the street below a peddler was crying his wares. The notes of a distant song which some one was singing reached her faintly, and countless sparrows were twittering in the eaves.

There were patches of blue sky showing here and there through the clouds that had met and piled one above the other in the west facing her window.

She sat with her head thrown back upon the cushion of the chair, quite motionless, except when a sob came up into her throat and shook her, as a child who has cried itself to sleep continues to sob in its dreams.

She was young, with a fair, calm face, whose lines bespoke repression and even a certain strength. But now there was a dull stare in her eyes, whose gaze was fixed away off yonder on one of those patches of blue sky. It was not a glance of reflection, but rather indicated a suspension of intelligent thought.

There was something coming to her and she was waiting for it, fearfully. What was it? She did not know; it was too subtle and elusive to name. But she felt it, creeping out of the sky, reaching toward her through the sounds, the scents, the color that filled the air.

Now her bosom rose and fell tumultuously. She was beginning to recognize this thing that was approaching to possess her, and she was striving to beat it back with her will – as powerless as her two white slender hands would have been.

When she abandoned herself a little whispered word escaped her slightly parted lips. She said it over and over under her breath: "free, free, free!" The vacant stare and the look of terror that had followed it went from her eyes. They stayed keen and bright. Her pulses beat fast, and the coursing blood warmed and relaxed every inch of her body.

She did not stop to ask if it were or were not a monstrous joy that held her. A clear and exalted perception enabled her to dismiss the suggestion as trivial.

She knew that she would weep again when she saw the kind, tender hands folded in death; the face that had never looked save with love upon her, fixed and gray and dead. But she saw beyond that bitter moment a long procession of years to come that would belong to her absolutely. And she opened and spread her arms out to them in welcome.

There would be no one to live for her during those coming years; she would live for herself. There would be no powerful will bending hers in that blind persistence with which men and women believe they have a right to impose a private will upon a fellow-creature. A kind intention or a cruel intention made the act seem no less a crime as she looked upon it in that brief moment of illumination.

And yet she had loved him – sometimes. Often she had not. What did it matter! What could love, the unsolved mystery, count for in face of this possession of self-assertion which she suddenly recognized as the strongest impulse of her being!

"Free! Body and soul free!" she kept whispering.

Josephine was kneeling before the closed door with her lips to the keyhole, imploring for admission. "Louise, open the door! I beg; open the door – you will make yourself ill. What are you doing, Louise? For heaven's sake upon the door."

"Go away. I am not making myself ill." No; she was drinking in a very elixir of life through that open window.

Her fancy was running riot along those days ahead of her. Spring days, and summer days, and all sorts of days that would be her own. She breathed a quick prayer that life might be long. It was only yesterday she had thought with a shudder that life might be long.

She rose at length and opened the door to her sister's importunities. There was a feverish triumph in her eyes, and she carried herself unwittingly like a goddess of Victory. She clasped her sister's waist, and together they descended the stairs. Richards stood waiting for them at the bottom.

Someone was opening the front door with a latchkey. It was Bentley Mallard who entered, a little travel-stained, composedly carrying his grip-sack and umbrella. He had been far from the scene of the accident, and did not even know there had been one. He stood amazed at Josephine's piercing cry; at Richard's quick motion to screen him from the view of his wife.

But Richards was too late.

When the doctors came they said she had died of heart disease – of joy that kills.

Kate Chopin (1850-1904)

Sample essay by the author of this book

This essay uses the non-cluster, part-by-part thesis.

Title: The Short Happy Life of Louise Mallard

Introduction

In Kate Chopin's brief narrative, the main character, Louise Mallard, who is "afflicted with a heart trouble," receives news of her husband Bentley Mallard's death in a railroad accident. In view of Louise's heart condition, her sister (Josephine) breaks the sad news to her as gently as possible. After weeping over her husband's unexpected death, she soon begins to feel a sense of relief and freedom at this sudden termination of an oppressive relationship. When the news of her husband's death turns out to be incorrect and he walks into the house, Louise dies. The characters in the story feel that she died because her ailing heart could not withstand the shock of joy on seeing her husband alive. However, the story's readers may come to a different conclusion. This shocking story raises many important questions, some of which concern the subtle nature of exploitation and oppression that characterize many relationships. [***End of the introduction***]

Thesis (part-by-part, non-cluster format)

The first part of the thesis *is in the form of statement of one theme. In this part-by-part format, that statement also serves as the topic sentence to introduce and control the discussion of this part of the thesis.*

From "The Story of an Hour" we learn that personal weaknesses and oppressive routines sometimes force people to continue as passive sufferers in unhealthy relationships. When such bonds are terminated unexpectedly, the repressed party is left with conflicting feelings – relief from oppression, combined with guilt for feeling relief. [***End of the first statement of theme***]

Supporting details for the first part of the thesis. Louise weeps upon hearing the news of her husband's death and withdraws into a room, asking to be left alone. During her brief seclusion – it is the story of just one hour – she goes through conflicting emotions with amazing rapidity. As she gazes out of the window at the symbols of vibrant life – "the tops of trees . . . all aquiver with the new spring life" and the "delicious breath of rain . . . in the air," her initial grief on losing her husband turns into a feeling of freedom. This change and the narrator's following words reveal that Louise has been leading a repressed life: "She was young, with a fair, calm face, whose lines bespoke repression and even a certain strength." Louise's guilt on feeling a sense of relief on her husband's death is a conditioned response. Her husband's death, Louise realizes, would give her the strength to emerge from her repression.

The second part of the thesis *is in the form of a statement of the second theme. That statement also serves as the topic sentence to introduce and control its discussion.*

Another notable theme in the story is that desire for self-worth and a deep hunger for freedom surpass considerations of love. [***End of the second statement of theme, which is also the second part of the three-part thesis***]

Supporting details for the second part of the thesis

Louise tries in vain to stifle the new stirrings of freedom she feels in her new situation:

"When she abandoned herself a little whispered word escaped her slightly parted lips. She said it over and over under her breath: 'free, free, free!' The vacant stare and the look of terror that had followed it went from her eyes. They stayed keen and bright. Her pulses beat fast, and the coursing blood warmed and relaxed every inch of her body."

Later we learn that she kept whispering "Free! Body and soul free!" Underscoring the importance of freedom to Louise is the fact that in the entire story, she speaks very few words (no more than sixteen altogether), but those that she utters are about freedom.

The narrator uses a very revealing phrase – "monstrous joy" – to describe Louise's guilt-laced elation. This monstrous joy overpowers her guilty conscience. Beyond the "bitter moment" of her husband's death, she sees "a long procession of years to come that would belong to her absolutely. And she opened and spread her arms out to them in welcome." Clearly, Louise is possessed by a force much stronger than her conditioned conscience, and that force is freedom.

Louise finally asserts her strength and her self-worth when she tells her sister, "Go away. I am not making myself ill." Her sister has been afraid that, in her seclusion, Louise is destroying herself with grief. The truth, however, is that Louise has been "drinking in a very elixir of life through that open window." Wishing herself a long life of freedom and moving with a "feverish triumph in her eyes" like a "goddess of Victory," Louise opens the door and emerges from her seclusion. Her transformation from a repressed wife into a free woman is complete: "Her fancy was running riot along those days ahead of her. Spring days, and summer days, and all sorts of days that would be her own." Even though her elation is short-lived – she dies upon seeing her supposedly dead husband walk into the house – her thoughts and emotions leave us in no doubt about Louise's joy at breaking her chain of oppression. It seems strange but perfectly understandable that she becomes aware of the full extent of her enslavement only after the source of her repression is removed. [***End of discussion of the second theme***]

The third part of the thesis *is in the form of a statement of the third theme. That statement also serves as the topic sentence to introduce and control its discussion.*

What Kate Chopin describes as the main character Louise Mallard's "brief moment of illumination" constitutes still another major point of the story: it is a crime to impose one's "private will upon a fellow-creature" even when the oppressor has the best of intentions. [***End of the third statement of theme, also end of the thesis***]

Supporting details for the third and last part of the thesis

Louise does not know whether or not she loved her husband. She first thinks "she would weep again when she saw the kind, tender hands [of her husband] folded in death; the face that had never looked save with love upon her, fixed and gray and dead." In the next breath, however, she feels relieved that there "would be no powerful will bending hers in that blind persistence with which men and women believe they have a right to impose a private will upon a fellow- creature. A kind intention or a cruel intention made the act seem no less a crime as she looked upon it in that brief moment of illumination."

A direct statement of Louise's confused feelings appears in the narrator's words: "And yet she had loved him – sometimes. Often she had not. What did it matter!" Toward the end of the story, Louise does move past this confusion. The narrator allows us a glimpse into Louise's new system of values that allots the first place to freedom and relegates "love" to a position of far less and dubious importance: "What could love, the unresolved mystery, count for in face of this possession of self-assertion which she suddenly recognized as the strongest impulse of her being!"

Louise's self-assertion, however, comes too late. The story's ending is disturbing not only because Louise dies and her husband continues to live, but also, and more importantly, because no one in the story – the doctors, the husband, the husband's friend, and Louise's sister – understands the true cause of Louise's death. The pattern of repression threatens to continue unquestioned. In fact, ironically, some observers may get a message contrary to the truth: they may feel that Louise had loved her husband so much that her joy on seeing him alive was unbearable, and this shock of joy proved fatal to this heart patient. The story's ambiguous ending is likely to elicit different interpretations. [***End of discussion of the third theme, also end of the main part of the essay***]

Conclusion (commenting on the story's impact)

The impact of Kate Chopin's story spreads far beyond its pages. Since Louise could not live long enough to tell her story, the reader feels compelled to complete Louise's tale by acknowledging and then communicating her important discoveries that are too crucial to die with her. By using this device of incomplete and inexact communication among the story's characters, Kate Chopin succeeds in getting the reader's maximum involvement – perhaps even a commitment from the reader to set the record straight about Louise by keeping her "brief moment of illumination" alive. It is by making the reader an active "co-author" that Chopin manages to enrich her brief narrative with so many ideas. [***End of the sample essay with a part-by-part thesis***]

Format for an Essay with a Cluster Thesis

The title, introduction, and the conclusion would be the same as in the essay with a part-by-part thesis. The thesis and the main body would be different.

Cluster Thesis

From "The Story of an Hour" we learn that personal weaknesses and oppressive routines sometimes force people to continue as passive sufferers in unhealthy relationships. When such bonds are terminated unexpectedly, the repressed party is left with conflicting feelings – relief from oppression, combined with guilt for feeling relief [*End of the first statement of theme*]. Another notable theme in the story is that desire for self-worth and a deep hunger for freedom surpass considerations of love. [*End of the second statement of theme*]   What Kate Chopin describes as the main character Louise Mallard's "brief moment of illumination" constitutes still another major point of the story: it is a crime to impose one's "private will upon a fellow-creature" even when the oppressor has the best of intentions. [***End of the third statement of theme, also end of the thesis paragraph***]

Main Body

The main body will consist of three sections – one for the discussion of each theme. Each section will open with a topic sentence to introduce and control the discussion of the theme for that section. Since the themes have already been stated in the thesis paragraph, their discussion will be introduced in an abridged form in the topic sentences.

Topic sentence to introduce the discussion of the first theme: The main character Louise Mallard's conflicting emotions about her husband's death refer to the theme of exploitive relationships that thrive on personal weakness and repression of one of the two partners. [*End of the topic sentence*]

Details and quotations to support the first theme: *Same as in the essay with a part-by-part thesis*

Topic sentence to introduce the discussion of the second theme: Self-worth and freedom as greater needs than love is the essence of the next prominent theme in Kate Chopin's story. [*End of the topic sentence*]

Details and quotations to support the second theme: *Same as in the essay with a part-by-part thesis*

Topic sentence to introduce the discussion of the third theme: Many statements and events in the story support the third theme that concerns the symptoms of repression and the dangers of repressed persons' inability to know and project their true feelings. [*End of the topic sentence*]

Details and quotations to support the third theme: *Same as in the essay with a part-by-part thesis*

Conclusion. *Same as in the essay with a part-by-part thesis*

*[**End of the sample essay with a cluster thesis**]*

Second and Last Assignment of the Chapter: Writing on an Author's Style

After this chapter's detailed instructions and the just-completed sample for writing on themes in a literary work, we now need to prepare for the more demanding assignment that concerns an author's *style* of writing. The challenge of style evaluation is that it requires not only an understanding of an author's themes but also an appreciation of his/her choice of *stylistic devices* used to communicate themes and bring characters to life. This is a challenging assignment. If you are not quite ready for it yet, you can return to it later.

Since detailed instructions for writing on an author's themes have already been given in the preceding section, advice relating to writing on an author's style, though necessary, need not be as detailed. The main difference between these two assignments is that of focus. In the preceding essay, the focal point was themes; here the focus is on the author's style. Whether we discuss content or style, the principles of organized writing remain the same, namely:

- Capturing the substance of your essay in a clearly stated thesis
- Dividing a complex topic into its component parts for easier handling
- Using topic sentences to organize each new section in an essay
- Developing each point completely
- Staying focused on the assignment
- Introducing supporting details clearly and connecting them with the point being supported
- Using transitions to connect various sections of the essay and to keep the flow of thought unobstructed.

The following assignment and the step-by-step instructions lead to the sample essay that demonstrates how style impacts and shapes content – a skill that is integral to interpretation.

Assignment

Write an essay of about 500 to 750 words on an author's style of writing in a literary work from the choices available to you. Discuss at least three elements of style used by the author. Relate one of the elements to a significant theme or topic by showing how that particular stylistic device expresses or reinforces the theme/topic. The remaining two elements of style may be discussed in terms of their function in the immediate context in which they appear. You could, for example, comment on the power of a stylistic element to create a mood, reveal or develop a character, create suspense, or elicit any other desired response from the reader. Keep your focus on the author's style, not on themes.

If it is possible to do so, you may, of course, discuss all three stylistic devices by connecting them with three different themes in the literary work and by showing how these devices are effective in suggesting or reinforcing those themes. However, not all literary works (especially shorter ones, such as short stories and poems) may have this potential.

Step-by-Step Instructions

TITLE

Give a clear title for your essay. It could be as simple as this: Hemingway's Style of Writing in "The Short Happy Life of Francis Macomber." If you choose to limit your discussion to just one element of style, you could say, "Hemingway's use of Irony in 'The Short Happy Life of Francis Macomber'."

INTRODUCTION

Make an introductory comment on the significance of style *in general terms*, not restricting yourself to any one particular author. Mention the close connection that exists between style and content, that is to say, between *what* an author says and *how* s/he says it. Make a statement to the effect that the appeal of a literary work depends, to a considerable degree, on the *way* in which it communicates its substance, in other words, on its *style*.

THESIS PARAGRAPH (cluster thesis)

Use a transition before starting the thesis paragraph. This transition should direct our thoughts from general observations on the importance of style to the function and impact of an author's style in a *specific* work. Identify in just one sentence (if you like) three outstanding stylistic devices used by the author in the selected literary work. In the same paragraph, relate (in just one brief statement) one of the aforementioned stylistic elements to a significant theme or topic in the literary work.

Continuing your thesis paragraph, relate the second element of style to a major theme or topic if you can do so just as you did with the first stylistic device. Otherwise, evaluate the function of this or any element of style with the help of the following tips.

Besides suggesting, reinforcing, or dramatizing a theme or topic, stylistic devices may also have any of the following effects/functions:

- Creating an appropriate mood
- Revealing or developing a character
- Depicting a scene vibrantly
- Creating suspense through devices, such as foreshadowing, parallel sets of situations and characters, etc.
- Manipulating time so as to increase or decrease the speed of the narrative
- Engaging the reader's senses through imagery for emotional effect
- Molding the reader's response with appropriate diction, characterization, tone, etc.

As the last part of your thesis paragraph, state the function of the third stylistic device in either of the two ways in which you handled the first and second elements of style.

Keep in mind that connecting an element of style to a theme is more demanding because the theme often permeates the whole literary work. By contrast, it is easier to discuss the effectiveness of an element of style in its immediate and limited context along the lines just explained.

It is also important to remember that in the thesis paragraph you simply make assertions which you prove later in the main body. Therefore, discussions, examples, and lengthy arguments do not belong in a thesis paragraph.

Note:

1. *If you use the part-by-part thesis format, which was explained in the instructions for writing on an author's themes, you will mention only one element of style at a time, followed by its discussion, before introducing the next stylistic element.*

2. *If you choose to write this paper on just one outstanding stylistic element, use the same format as for three elements of style. The only difference will be that in this case you will analyze different functions of just one stylistic device.*

SUPPORT (Analysis of the stylistic elements that were only mentioned, not discussed, in the thesis)

A. Write a topic sentence for the discussion of the author's first stylistic device in this way: Mention/identify the element of style that you are going to discuss in this section in synthesis with what you said about this device in your thesis paragraph. Avoid repetitious style when connecting the topic sentence with the thesis.

After writing the topic sentence, discuss the selected stylistic device in the following manner:

1. Give at least one example of this device in the form of a quotation or details from the literary work. Introduce the quotations/details appropriately and comment on their connection with the point being made. If direct quotation is not possible, refer to the relevant stylistic details to illustrate your point. *Never end a section with an unexamined quotation or unanalyzed details. Quotations and details should be connected to the point of the section.*

2. In discussing this first stylistic device, show how it helps the author in expressing or reinforcing a significant theme or topic. Specify the connection between the stylistic device and the theme/topic. Keep your focus on the author's style, not on the theme. To do so, you should place the author's element of style prominently in your key sentences, especially in the topic sentences. You will be using many details to summarize the literary work's relevant content, but to maintain correct focus, keep these details subordinate to your comments on the author's style.

B. Write a topic sentence for the discussion of the author's second stylistic device in this manner: Mention the element of style that you are going to discuss in this section along the lines of what you said about this stylistic device in your thesis paragraph. After writing the topic sentence, discuss this stylistic device as follows:

1. Repeat step A-1 that asks for an example of the stylistic device to be discussed.

2. Since you are not required to connect this stylistic device to a theme or topic that pervades the whole story, here you may point out the function of this element of style in its limited and/or immediate context by connecting it to effective rendition of an event, character, mood, scene, etc. Again, keep your focus on the author's style.

C. Write a topic sentence for the discussion of the author's third element of style and discuss it in the same manner in which you wrote your second topic sentence and discussed the author's second stylistic device; that is to say, repeat IV: B and parts 1 and 2 of B.

CONCLUSION

Comment on the author's overall stylistic accomplishment. Here are some of the many possible varieties of conclusion:

1. Summation of the effectiveness of the three stylistic devices which have been the subject of your paper
2. A well-known remark on style and how that remark applies to the work you have evaluated
3. Speculation as to what might have been lost in impact had the author not used appropriate stylistic elements
4. A reiteration of the close connection between style and content with a demonstration referring back to the main body.

Alberto Moravia's Style of Writing in "The Chase"
Sample essay by the author of this book

You will find my sample essay on this story in Chapter-Seven-related material on my website. For additional help with style evaluation read Jeffery Tarbell's essay on Hemingway's style and my annotations on Tarbell's essay in Chapter Ten.

Complete Preparation to Interpret *any* Work

Having learned from this chapter how to write on a literary work's themes as well as style, you are now fully prepared to interpret any literary work or movie. The chapter's demonstration of the interconnectedness of various parts of the essay and of the principle of subordinating summarizing details to interpretive and analytic comments will enable you to give a clear identity to your writings as essays, not mere plot summaries. For variety in organization, you will be able to use either the cluster or part-by-part thesis. Using the advice of this chapter, you will also be able to create effective topic sentences and move their position around to compose deductive or inductive paragraphs for maximum effect. Many of the elements of style, such as sentence variation, simile, metaphor, and analogy that you thought belonged only to professional writing will now find a place in your own work. The advice and samples of this chapter are applicable to *all* genres. Systematic, chapter-by-chapter study of each genre awaits the completion of just one more step – that of revising.

Exercises to Test Your Mastery of Chapter Seven

1. Readers can differ in their interpretations of a literary work. What are some of the requirements of a valid interpretation?

2. Kate Chopin's "The Story of an Hour" has been made into a short film (26 minutes). Produced by Themes Colour Productions and titled "Five Stories of an Hour," it has been directed by Paul Kafno and David Hodgson. Dramatization is by Kathleen Potter, David Stafford, and Michelene Wandor. Distributors are Films for the Humanities and Sciences (1-800-257-5126). The five versions of the same story include the husband's perspective on what his life has been with his now deceased wife. Which of the perspectives do you consider most defensible? Why?

3. What are the main components of an interpretive essay?

4. Delineate the ways in which formal interpretation differs from informal reading of a work.

5. How does a cluster thesis differ from a part-by-part thesis? Which variety do you use more frequently? What determines your choice? What is the effect of the choice of thesis on the essay's main body?

6. Just before the chapter's sample essay on Kate Chopin's "The Story of an Hour," four ways are mentioned to introduce variety in the essay form. Add one more to that list.

7. The chapter guides you step by step through the process of writing two papers – one on themes and the other on style of a literary work. Can one write meaningfully about an author's style without discussing the work's content (that is, themes and topics)? Support your answer with reasons.

8. If you expect opposition or resistance from your reader/audience in a particular section of your paper, which method of organization would you consider more suitable – inductive or deductive? Why?

9. After reading a story with which you are not familiar, write a *cluster thesis* that should consist of your formally stating the story's three major themes one after the other. Use transitions between statements of themes. Do not use the word *theme* more than once in the entire thesis paragraph.

10. Summarize the advice on conclusions given in this chapter; then offer at least one suggestion of your own to effectively conclude an essay. Add a suggestion on how not to write a conclusion.

11. Good topic sentences hold an essay together and keep it connected to the thesis. Summarize the advice given in this chapter to create good topic sentences. Add one or two suggestions of your own.

12. To the suggestions for coherence and organization mentioned in this chapter, add one or two suggestions of your own.

CHAPTER EIGHT

REVISING

Revision has a pivotal place among the prerequisites of effective writing. Good style is the result of rewriting, and sometimes several revisions of the first draft are necessary. At the very least, it needs to be understood that the first draft is for expression, the second for clarity, and the third for impact. Without this understanding, one can neither create nor appreciate good writing. On the importance of revising, Donald Hall's words are noteworthy: "Almost all writers, almost all the time, need to revise. We need to revise because spontaneity is never adequate. Writing that is merely emotional release for the writer becomes emotional chaos for the reader" (Hall 6). Here Hall is echoing Richard B. Sheridan's view: "Easy writing's vile hard reading." Isaac B. Singer expresses a similar view when he says that a writer's best friend is the waste basket. Richard Eastman warns that rewriting, "usually shirked at reckless cost, is not neat-work, but the extension and final thrust of discovery" (Eastman ix). There is a big difference between writing well and just getting the meaning across somehow. The first choice results in writing that is a pleasure to read; the second choice leads to torture for the reader:

"My students argue when I correct them in . . . writing: 'You got the meaning, didn't you?' Yes, I did, and so do we all get the meaning when a newspaper, a magazine, a set of directions stammers out its message. And I suppose, too, we could travel by ox-cart, or dress in burlap, or drive around with rattling fenders, and still get through a day" (Leonard and McGuire 211).

Revision, in short, is necessary to achieve clarity and brevity – two minimum requirements of good writing. The concept of clarity includes unity and clear organization of ideas with the help of a clear title, introduction, thesis, and topic sentences. Good style also requires suitable diction, variety in sentence structure and sentence length, and creative use of other language resources.

In "Theories of Style and Their Implications for the Teaching of Composition," Louis T. Milic points out that to be effective, a writer should be able to choose carefully from alternative utterances: "The writer intends to express something (idea) and he struggles with possibilities until he finds the formulation which best expresses it" (Love & Payne 15). According to Winston Weathers, style is

"the art of choosing, and one of our tasks . . . is to identify as many compositional choices as possible. Our comprehension – and practice – of style improves as we recognize verbal locutions and construction into areas of choice and indicate how the choice within any given area is to be made. Any such exercise seems valid, even if our conclusions are not always definitive or absolute" (Love & Payne 21).

Milic's and Weathers' views rightly emphasize the writer's need not only for sound ideas but also for several combinations of phrases, several styles of expression out of which to choose the best one. Increasing those choices is the goal of this chapter.

Achieving Clarity and Brevity

When revising, remember F. L. Lucas's words from his essay "What Is Style": "One should aim at being impossible to misunderstand," remembering that our "capacity for misunderstanding approaches infinity" (McCuen and Winkler 624). The readers should be spared the task of having to rearrange in their head the order of ideas and sentences in order to understand them. On the need to economize for brevity and to avoid wordiness, Lucas warns, "it is boorish to waste your reader's time. People who would not dream of stealing a penny of one's money turn not a hair at stealing hours of one's life" (McCuen and Winkler 624). The point of emphasis here is that we should not use even one word that is unnecessary.

To Lucas's advice, we should add John Trimble's valuable suggestion from *Writing with Style*: "Read your prose aloud. . . . If it sounds as if it's come out of a machine or a social scientist's report (which is approximately the same thing), spare your reader and rewrite it" (Trimble 80). One more piece of advice when revising, this one by Morris Freedman, is to delete those big words that sound pretentious, especially when smaller, simpler words convey the point more clearly. "There is nothing wrong with big words in themselves, provided they are the best ones for the job. A steam shovel is right for moving a boulder, ridiculous for picking up a handkerchief."

Alexander Pope's words from his poem "Essay on Criticism" also warn against wordiness:

> Words are like leaves; and where they most abound,
> Much fruit of sense beneath is rarely found.

Finding Your Own Voice

Besides economy, clarity, and variety in style, it is also important to find one's own voice in writing. Peter Elbow makes a helpful comment:

"My main argument for sincerity . . . is simply that a terrific liberation occurs when a writer finds his voice. . . . Writing . . . is characteristically unclear because it so often consists of using one's voice while at the same time shrinking from the use of it and thus disguising it. A person writes consistently and well only when he becomes comfortable with the sound of his true voice" (Elbow 594).

In *Making the Point*, J. Alexander Scharbach and Carl Markgraf also stress the importance of voice:

> . . . when you do not believe in what you are trying to say, a writing assignment becomes a torturous ordeal. Sincerity and voice are thus tied in with one's personality, one's basic character, viewpoints, tastes, and self-image.

The Role of Stylistic Elements in the Writing Process

An understanding of the composing process helps us appreciate the connection between revision and appropriate style. The process of careful revision begins after you have completed the first draft, which is seldom more than laborious self-expression with several unclear, undeveloped, and easily improvable parts. This "struggle" stage typically results in many needless repetitions, wordiness, poor word choice, lack of precision, monotonous sentence structure, and similar ills. In first drafts, we often yield to the temptation of throwing in everything that crosses our mind. This freedom is acceptable, even necessary, to overcome the infamous yet common writer's block, but it is dangerously out of place in the finished version.

The second draft brings you closer to the goals of brevity and clarity. Through scrupulous revisions, conscientious writers put themselves in the reader's place constantly and edit out items that hinder the communication of their ideas. To get rid of monotonous and overburdened sentences, attention is paid to variety in sentence structure and sentence length, and an effort is made to find the best words for our ideas. The movement is away from the "struggle" stage toward clarity and pleasing style. Revision of weak, usually perfunctory, sections of the first draft is necessary and may involve cutting out complete ideas and sentences. Samuel Johnson said, "What is written without effort is in general read without pleasure" (Williams 107). Commenting on Johnson's statement, Joseph Williams says in *Ten Lessons in Clarity and Grace* that the effort is more in the editing than in the writing.

Whereas it is indisputable that successful writing is often the result of several rewritings, it is not as easily understood that effective revision would be impossible without an awareness of what constitutes good style. In the process of revising and polishing our writing, we draw upon the available language resources, and the power of our expression is determined by the vastness of our range to give appropriate shape to our ideas. Stylistic elements go hand in hand with content and have specific effects associated with them. This knowledge can serve us well to maximize writing effectiveness.

Greater command of stylistic elements and linguistic choices could reduce your reliance on accidentally hitting on a felicitous phrase. On the question of craft *versus* chance, Alexander Pope's words remain unsurpassed:

> "True ease in writing comes from art, not chance,
> As those move easiest who have learned to dance."

It is evident that the charm of good writing and good conversation is inherent in a facility with the language that can be gained only through constant study and exercise. It is also evident that an engaging style is the result of these prerequisites: solid ideas, mastery of stylistic options, and a discriminating taste. This taste is *acquired*; one cannot stumble upon it by accident.

Steps for Style Improvement

Your quest for style improvement can start modestly with appropriate use of some of the following elements:

- A clear thesis
- Careful word choice
- Verbal economy – using only the necessary words
- Staying on the topic
- Variety in sentence length
- Mixing of simple, compound, and complex sentences
- Using semicolon, explanatory dash, and explanatory colon – effective punctuation symbols to eliminate wordiness
- Using paragraphs that are neither too long nor too short – just long enough to complete a point
- No more than one topic sentence per paragraph: sometimes one topic sentence may control more than one paragraph, but there should be only one topic sentence in a paragraph for clarity of focus.

Later in the process of revising you can try using more challenging elements:

- Figurative language in the form of simile and metaphor

- Variety in sentence structure by using as many of the following as seem appropriate: anaphora, isocolon, periodic/suspended sentence structure, balanced, antithetical, and cumulative sentences

- Variety in paragraph organization: use of some inductively organized paragraphs in which the topic sentence is placed at the end *after* the evidence that supports the controlling idea of the topic sentence.

  Some of the outstanding sample essays by students in this book demonstrate how this approach to style improvement may be implemented.

To supplement the advice of this chapter, a college dictionary will have definitions and examples of most of the terms. Additional resources can be found in standard works, such as *A Glossary of Literary Terms* by M. H. Abrams and *Handbook of Literary Terms: Literature, Language, Theory* by X. J. Kennedy, Dana Gioia, and Mark Bauerlein. There are also many handbooks that answer questions concerning punctuation, such as semicolon, colon, and dash, all of which affect style. For a quick reference to issues of grammar, usage, research, and documentation, McGraw Hill's *A Writer's Resource: A Handbook for Writing and Research* by Elaine Maimon and Janice Peritz or any similar handbook will meet the need. Libraries are also good sources of material on writing and style. Besides a current college dictionary, a thesaurus will be needed to hunt for appropriate diction.

The apparent lesson that we learn from students' writing practices and scholars' perceptive observations is that to learn and maintain good writing skills, you have to do no less than professional authors. All writers have to aim for the best possible expression that has economy, variety, rhythm, and appeal. They have to read with sensitivity to style and remain in constant writing practice, for the gems of yesterday become clichés of today all too soon.

To accommodate your varying needs and styles, the remaining discussion of revision is divided into two sections – compulsory revision and optional revision.

COMPULSORY REVISION

It is a known fact that many good ideas lose their effectiveness if we express them without adequate attention to some basic requirements of revision. Failure to tap the available language resources can impoverish our expression. Fortunately, this kind of poverty is avoidable if inspiration to write is matched with proficiency in the craft of writing. Without adequate mastery of that craft, one's expression will be lacking in style, clarity, and appeal. The notion that the subject automatically leads the writer to appropriate style is misleading because such happy union of style and substance can only occur if the writer is first equipped with the knowledge of available stylistic options. Even then, the writer has to be willing to take pains with revising. In his book, appropriately titled *Style*, Richard Eastman rightly stresses the importance of looking at "the issues of vocabulary, syntax, audience, structure, etc. not as pitfalls to be skirted, but as ways to expand . . . [our] powers of discovery" (Eastman ix). In his highly amusing and informative essay "How to Say Nothing in 500 Words," Paul Roberts tells us that the "writer's job is to find the argument, the approach, the angle, the wording that will take the reader with him" (Winkler and McCuen 254). Judicious use of relevant information from the language resources and options listed below will help expand your range of expression to make your writing more effective.

Requirements of Good Writing

Meeting as many of the following needs as possible will have a remarkable effect on your writing performance.

1. **Attention to the wording of the assignment**: Careful reading of the assignment cannot be overemphasized to meet the expected requirements.
2. **Having something to say:** Good writing is impossible without good ideas. In the words of F. L. Lucas, "writing from an empty head is futile anguish" (McCuen and Winkler 621).
3. **Adequate vocabulary:** After the goal of content is met, the next need is for appropriate diction. Mark Twain famously cautioned that "the difference between an exact word and an almost accurate word is the difference between lightning and lightning bug." Vocabulary building is a natural by-product of reading, and there is no substitute for it. However, you can speed up the process by learning at least one new word every day. These days, the internet also offers a convenient resource.

Among several possibilities, one is signing up to be on the e-mail list of a dictionary vendor, such as Miriam Webster, to receive one word a day with its complete definition, example, and etymology.

4. **Using appropriate tone:** One need that can be met easily is that of using the right tone to suit the audience. The same tone will not be suitable for peers, friends, family, and general public.

5. **Reading with the writer's eye:** One very successful way to improve your style and organization is acquiring the habit of reading with the writer's eye to see how good writers, both among peers and professional authors, craft their writing.

6. **Using feedback:** Getting your work critiqued by a qualified peer is yet another very helpful resource in the quest for style improvement.

7. **Familiarity with elements of style:** Some stylistic elements are considered essential to good writing. Among them are simile, metaphor, analogy, paradox, verbal irony, understatement, and allusion. These and other elements have been introduced in Chapter Four.

8. **Sentence variety and organization strategies:** Other important needs that require a methodical approach are variety in sentence structure and sentence length, along with effective strategies for organization. Their definitions, examples, and functions are given next. Use them on an "as-needed" basis in your writing to match your ideas. For writing well, having something to say is not enough. We need various ways – different combinations of words, phrases, and sentences – to express ourselves. Practical knowledge of the elements of style (discussed in Chapter Four) and sentence structure variations that follow have the potential to transform average into excellent writing.

Definitions and Examples of Sentence Structure Variations

Like other stylistic elements, syntax variations also tend to overlap sometimes, yet they have their own distinct features.

Loose sentence

Meant to give information and develop a point in a straightforward manner with hardly any design except clarity for the reader, the loose sentence is the most commonly used variety. It goes directly to the point. When used in the rhetorical sense, the word "loose" has no negative connotations. It is like furnishings in a room, used as a part of the setting. Though not the most conspicuous, they are the most abundant. It would be more accurate to call his type of sentence a "straightforward" sentence.

Example: Our English textbook has many useful chapters.

Cumulative sentence

As its name implies, a cumulative sentence is long. It unfolds its meaning very much like the loose sentence. Its distinctive feature is pouring forth and piling one detail upon another in an easy-flowing, straightforward structure.

A cumulative sentence usually opens with the main clause, to which are added many other clauses to modify and expand the meaning. This style is ideal for summation and for achieving an inspirational tone.

Example: "You can ignore the news and shun the headlines and close your eyes to the bloody gruesome photos and go about your work and play in the park with your dog and read only *US Weekly* and 'Boing Boing' and pretend that all this horrible global tragedy, these hurricanes and earthquakes and various planetary abuses, the appalling death tolls and severed limbs and blood-drenched streets, they never really happen on the same planet you inhabit" (Morford E8).

Periodic or suspended sentence

An exact opposite of the loose sentence, the periodic or suspended sentence is a strategically crafted variety, whose author uses the art of rhetoric to control the reader's mind. It has two common varieties.

1. The first kind consists of breaking up the main clause in such a way as to temporarily suspend the completion of its meaning by separating the two parts of the main clause (as separating the subject from the verb).

   Example: *"The authors of the best sellers*, after exhausting all the possibilities of sex in its normal and abnormal forms and all the variations of alcoholism and drug addiction, *are about to invade the recesses of the hospitals"* (Simpson in McCuen and Winkler 140). The main clause is italicized for clarity.

   The same idea, in the form of a loose sentence, would be as follows: The authors of the best sellers are about to invade the recesses of the hospitals after exhausting all the possibilities of sex in its normal and abnormal forms and all variations of alcoholism and drug addiction.

2. In the other common variation of the periodic structure, the main point is introduced at the very end of the sentence after a series of clauses starting with "If," "Though," "When," etc. The subordinate clauses before the main clause enhance anticipation of the main point and allow a build-up.

   Example: "If you want life to be lived on a dream cloud of love, constant intimacy and magic – if you expect the simple act of marriage to give focus and meaning to your life, to answer all of life's basic questions – you are going to be disappointed" (Kochakian B6).

   We can craft the second-mentioned variety of periodic sentence without "if," "when," and "though" clauses. All that is necessary is a series of phrases with details that create in the reader an anticipation of the emphatic point held back until the end. This style is ideal if the intent is to engage the reader's attention and generate suspense to achieve maximum involvement and a gradual build-up, as the following example demonstrates: *Buffeted by the winds of change, threatened by unforeseen challenges, unsure of its direction, the ship of our state somehow keeps moving on.*

Balanced sentence structure

In a balanced sentence, various parts complement each other and have approximately equal length. Isocolon, that is, use of phrases of equal length in succession, is a part of this type of sentence.

Example 1: "With his handsome face, his fiery glance, his strong supple body, his purple and gold cloak, and his air of destiny, he [Alexander] moved through the parting crowd . . ." (Highet in McCuen and Winkler 411).

This example of the balanced sentence also contains the element of periodicity because the subject is introduced toward the end. In the balanced as well as the following antithetical variety, the very structure of the sentence, to some extent, determines its content. One part of the sentence is balanced or contrasted by its other part not only in structure but also in meaning.

Example 2 of balance with isocolon: ". . . it was innovation in Muslim communities that developed the order of algebra; our magnetic compass and tools of navigation; our mastery of pens and printing; our understanding of how disease spreads and how it can be healed. Islamic culture has given us majestic arches and soaring spires; timeless poetry and cherished music; elegant calligraphy and places of peaceful contemplation. And throughout history, Islam has demonstrated through words and deeds the possibilities of religious tolerance and racial equality" (Obama, June, 4, 2009).

Antithetical sentence structure

Various parts of the antithetical sentence *contrast* with each other. Whereas one pair of contrasts will create basic antithetical effect, two or more pairs will make the rhythmic balance more pronounced and effective. Antithetical phrases or clauses should be of approximately equal length and should have *contrasting* content. Isocolon, therefore, is used in crafting an antithetical sentence. In the words of Herbert Read, "Antithesis operates by tension or suspense between two ideas: the sentence becomes a balance between equal but opposite forces." When used with discretion, this device of antithesis "adds point and vivacity to expression, but when abused it becomes tedious and artificial" (Read 43). In the following example, Marya Mannes emphasizes the importance of meaningful evaluation of works of art, using the antithetical sentence structure.

Example 1: "When you begin to detect the difference between freedom and sloppiness, between serious experimentation and ego therapy, between skill and slickness, between strength and violence, you are on your way to separating the sheep from the goats" (Mannes 182).

Example 2: "So long as our relationship is defined by our differences, we will empower those who sow hatred rather than peace, those who promote conflict rather than cooperation that can help all of our people achieve justice and prosperity" (Obama, June 4, 2009).

At times short pairs of contrasts – another form of antithetical structure – can be quite effective:

Example: "Politics is the art of promise; statesmanship is the art of compromise."

Isocolon

This device consists of using many clauses or phrases (more than two) of approximately the same length in a sentence. The main function of isocolon is to develop a strong rhythm.

Example: "Democracy is a government *of the people, for the people, by the people*" (Abraham Lincoln).

Example: "They were the fathers we never knew, the uncles we never met, the friends who never returned, the heroes we can never repay," said Bill Clinton, gazing out on the rows of still, green graves (*San Francisco Chronicle*, June 7, 1994).

Anaphora

This sentence strategy consists of using many clauses (at least three) that start with the same word/words usually in the same sentence and sometimes in consecutive sentences. Edmund Burke's memorable words from "The Impeachment of Warren Hastings" offer a good example:

Example: "It is a contradiction in terms, it is a blasphemy in religion, it is a wickedness in politics to say that any man can have arbitrary power" (Burke).

It was mentioned earlier that some of the sentence variations overlap. This anaphoric sentence is also a periodic sentence, since the main point is not given until the end – a characteristic of the periodic sentence. Like most repetitions, anaphora functions as a device to create in the reader or listener a compulsion to move forward with the flow of thought.

Parallelism

In its basic variety, parallelism is the method of putting similar thoughts in similar grammatical forms. In the hands of master stylists like Samuel Johnson and Bertrand Russell, parallelism becomes a graceful and impressive means of organizing complex thoughts.

Example from **Johnson**: "We are all prompted by the same motives, all deceived by the same fallacies, all animated by hope, obstructed by danger, entangled by desire, and seduced by pleasure" (Bennett 138).

Example from **Russell**: "From the submission of our desires springs the virtue of resignation; from the freedom of our thoughts springs the whole world of art and philosophy" (Russell in Weaver 189).

Chiasmus

A contrast by reverse parallelism, this variety of sentence structure consists of two parallel structures; the second clause/phrase is an inversion of the content of the first clause/phrase. John F. Kennedy's famous words are an example: "Ask not what your country can do for you; ask what you can do for your country."

Kahlil Gibran's following statement also derives its force from the reversal of ordinary syntax through chiasmus: "Think not you can direct the course of love, for love, if it finds you worthy, directs your course" (Gibran 13).

Another well-known example of chiasmus is Malcolm X's articulation of the African American dilemma: "We [African Americans] did not land on Plymouth Rock; Plymouth Rock landed on us!" Among other easy-to-remember examples of this sentence variation is this popular saying: "The happiest people don't have the best of everything. They just make the best of everything they have." A similar expression is from Dale Carnegie: "Success is getting what you want. Happiness is wanting what you get."

George Bernard Shaw's words are another good example of chiasmus:

"We don't stop playing because we grow old; we grow old because we stop playing."

Combination of Methods

It was noted earlier that isocolon is a part of antithetical and balanced sentences. Sometimes writers combine it with anaphora and periodic structure to achieve powerful rhetorical effect as in the following piece on moral education:

"The central problem of American education is its lack of moral focus. By encouraging mediocrity at the expense of excellence, by promoting, actively or through default, a narrow vocationalism, by transforming colleges and universities into research centers where grantsmanship reigns supreme, by refurbishing the house of intellect with the shoddy merchandise of mass thought, the American university has abandoned all pretense to moral authority. The university has adopted the slogans of the market place. Education is 'big business.' Students are 'consumers.' Professors are 'purveyors'" (*Journal of Thought*, 15:2).

Variety in Paragraph Organization
Deductive, Inductive, and Climactic Arrangement of Details

Two common methods of paragraph organization are *deductive* and *inductive*:

- In a deductively organized paragraph, the topic sentence appears at the beginning or somewhere near the beginning of the paragraph.
- In an inductively organized paragraph, the topic sentence appears at the end of the paragraph.

Thus, in a *deductive* paragraph, the controlling idea (or main point) is presented right at the beginning. Examples, evidence, reasoning, etc., are then used to validate the point.

However, if we anticipate hostility or resistance from the reader or audience, the *inductive* method of organizing details is considered more appropriate and effective. It enables us to present a series of factual, verifiable details, on the basis of which we present our main point. This way the reader is less likely to resist our view because we have stated it *after* presenting verifiable, objective facts. Use of inductive organization of details is, therefore, suggested when we are discussing a controversial point.

Climactic order is the third variety of paragraph organization. According to this method, details, ideas, and arguments are presented in the order of increasing importance.

Other Rhetorical/Stylistic Devices

Solid ideas, adequate vocabulary, appropriate tone, clear organization, and variations in sentence structure and paragraph organization – explained and exemplified in the preceding section – are the required elements in good writing. In addition, there are several stylistic elements that commonly appear in literature and can be effectively replicated in interpretive and analytic essays. Such elements have been explained and exemplified in Chapter Four in the context of discussing style in literature.

Use of figurative language in the form of *simile*, *metaphor*, and *analogy* can transform flat or anemic sentences into lively writing, we can use simile or metaphor. Let us take for an example this statement: *It is important to revise the first drafts.* Here is how Donald Hall makes that statement much more vivid with the help of a *metaphor*: "First drafts . . . are the material that we must shape, a marble block that the critical brain chisels into form" (McCuen and Winkler 604). *Analogy* can be used to clarify a complex idea. The film-maker Jean-Luc Godard used this analogy to point out the close connection between style and content: "style is just the outside of content, and content the inside of style, like the outside and inside of the human body – both go together, they can't be separated" (Williams 1). Similarly, if the context allows, you can empower our writing with other elements of style, such as paradox, verbal irony, understatement, allusion, etc., all of which have been explained and exemplified in Chapter Four.

OPTIONAL REVISION

The compulsory style requirements are met when you have achieved the goals of clarity, brevity, sentence variety, clear organization, authentic voice, suitable diction, and figurative language. If you are so inclined, you can further refine your style by working on other components of good style. To simile, metaphor, analogy, and variety in syntax, rhythm, and paragraph organization (covered in the preceding section on "Compulsory Revision"), you could now add the more challenging elements of personification, allusion, symbol, verbal irony, paradox, understatement, imagery, and other elements available to any writer. Their definitions and examples are in Chapter Four.

Familiarity with these language resources and ability to use them will undoubtedly enlarge your stylistic options and prepare you adequately to experiment with issues of style. On the need to expand our style options, Eastman is persuasive:

"You can't use language without making choices (sometimes unconscious ones) of words, details, sequence, stress, and so forth – and those choices express your values. . . . Again, by expanding your knowledge of possible choices you become aware of more in your experience itself. Your style and your experience build into each other: that is why the development of style belongs near the center of a first-rate education" (Eastman 4).

A word of caution is necessary before launching this conscious effort at style improvement. Initially, some of your attempts may seem awkward. Learning to play an instrument, learning a sport, learning to drive – all seem somewhat awkward in the beginning, but with practice, as artifice leads to nature, they all become natural and an extension of the practitioner's self. Using this self-testing and self-monitoring technique will give you an opportunity to gauge your style improvement and expand your range of expression.

Step-by-Step Method of Style Improvement

When composing your first draft, you do not have to think about the recommended stylistic elements. Some of them you will use without consciously thinking about them. Those suggested elements that are not yet a part of your expression should receive your attention when you are revising to polish your style. A systematic method to expand your range of stylistic options is to use in your papers, especially during revisions, those elements of style that are considered essential to good writing. If you know the effects that are usually associated with specific elements of style, you can use them as needed. Paradox, for example, like an antithetically structured sentence, creates a contrast in which the validity of one point of view is measured against the vitality of its opposite. This interplay between the thesis and its antithesis often leads to a synthesis that partakes of both opposites. This new awareness that transcends the either-or limitation is inherent in the stylistic device called paradox. Irony, through the interaction between the literal and the intended meaning, could also create nuances of perception equally subtle and refreshing. Knowledge of all three aspects of stylistic elements – definitions, examples, and functions/effects usually associated with them – does, indeed, enrich a writer's expression.

The sad fact, however, is that many people cannot even define such simple stylistic elements as simile, metaphor, analogy, personification, etc., let alone use them in their writing. The encouraging prospect is that most of the necessary elements of style can be mastered with the help of a systematic strategy if one has the desire to do so. It is also comforting to know that even established professional authors have to make an effort to come to the right style. The example of Ernest Hemingway, a famous stylist of the twentieth century, illustrates this point. He rewrote the concluding lines of *A Farewell to Arms* thirty-nine times before he was satisfied. When asked by an interviewer from the *Paris Review* if there was some technical problem, Hemingway said, "Getting the words right" was the problem (Trimble 95). Such intensity of style consciousness is uncommon, but all of us can at least revise our first drafts.

When you are unable to use a needed element of style

When uncomfortable with any element of style that you know you need to use, do a preparatory journal exercise (to be kept in your style journal) to show your knowledge of the elusive stylistic element by defining and exemplifying it. Examples of such elements should be, preferably, in your own words. If you cannot create a satisfactory example, the literary work on which you are writing may yield good examples; otherwise you can find examples from any other source and put them in quotation marks and document them. Your journal note to yourself would be an admission that you could not use a difficult but important element of style and a reminder for you to keep trying.

For example, if you are having difficulty using metaphor, your journal entry may read: *I was unable to use a metaphor that I needed to strengthen my expression, but here is its definition, followed by an example*:

Definition: A metaphor is an implied comparison that suggests similarities between dissimilar items.

Example: Hollywood is a dream factory.

This metaphor captures well the mass production aspect of Hollywood film industry, along with connotations of more emphasis on production than the product.

Use this option of borrowing examples of stylistic elements whenever you are unable to create your own. With time, you will master most elements of style through sheer persistence, by increasing your store of ideas, developing your imagination, and reading good writers.

An effective way to expand your range of style is this: When reading literary works or any kind of writing, note down authors' effective uses of elements of style that you would like to use in your own writing. Yet another way to continue style improvement is by including at least one new element in each paper. You can keep using this method until you have mastered major components of style that are considered essential to good writing.

The use of appropriate stylistic elements will make your writing more engaging. At the same time, greater mastery of style will enable you to catch subtleties and finer points in an author's expression and thus improve your reading skills. When you read a literary satire or a humorous essay, for example, your knowledge of the elements of sarcasm, irony, understatement, and paradox would certainly enable you to understand and appreciate it more fully, and, at the same time, bring you a step closer to enrich your own style with those stylistic elements.

It should be apparent from the preceding discussion that the "optional revision" guidelines of this chapter require a higher level of writing competence than compulsory revision. Following the advice relating to compulsory revision will result in good writing, but if your goal is creation of outstanding pieces of prose, then an attempt at optional revision is worth making.

EXAMPLES OF REVISING

First example of revising for brevity and impact

The process of revision and its outcome are demonstrated by the following excerpts from a student's writing. They are taken from the first draft and its final, revised version of Joseph Nugent's essay on James Joyce's short story "Araby." Joseph's complete essay and Joyce's story are in the next chapter.

Here is how Joseph opened his essay in the first draft:

As Stephen Dedalus was famously taken through the long and painful journey from aspiring writer to mature artist, and had his experience telescoped by James Joyce into the one day of Ulysses, *so is the anguished pilgrimage that is the early adolescence of our unnamed young boy concentrated into the evenings of "Araby." About this subject of lost innocence and disappointed expectations, Joyce wove his perennial themes; in his early style of pictorial realism he then addressed these themes; through the quasi-religious device of the epiphany he confronts the first two themes, love and religion, and exposes for us in their conflict, the third and most fundamental – paralysis.*

The entire paragraph consists of two very long sentences. Even though the depth of perception, persuasive interpretation, and command of the language are apparent from this paragraph, improvement in clarity through shorter sentences, clearer arrangement of details, omission of the allusion to the unused novel *Ulysses*, and tense consistency were accomplished through revising the first draft, making it much more readable and clearer:

In "Araby" James Joyce compresses an unnamed adolescent's anguished pilgrimage into one memorable evening. On the subject of lost innocence and disappointed expectations, Joyce weaves his perennial themes. Using the quasi-religious device of the epiphany, he makes us see how the conflict between love and religion results in the third and fundamental topic – that of paralysis.

Also in the first draft, the student's second paragraph had more than necessary details. By keeping only half of the original details and without sacrificing any of the important points, Joseph was able to make this part of his paper much more effective. The student met this challenge very well, as can be seen from these excerpts from the two versions:

First draft

That these themes, so typical of Joyce, should appear in "Araby" is hardly surprising; that they should here fuse with such force is a fact dictated as much by the reality of the intense pain of these early years of awakening as by artistic necessity. It is not necessary, and it would perhaps be unhelpful, to read "Araby" as an autobiographical piece. It can, however, only help our appreciation of the intensity of emotion of the anonymous boy to know that in 1894 the rapidly downwardly mobile John Joyce moved himself and his eleven dependents to an area of Dublin which was on an analogous road into lower middle-class decay. They moved to a blind street named North Richmond Street. And on May 4th of that year there opened, in the better class of neighborhood of Ballsbridge, a "Grand Oriental Fete." It was given by the shrewd promoters, in order to add to the mystique, the exotic title of "Araby." It is further instructive to remind ourselves that one of that unwieldy family, the young James, was just then going through a period of intense piety. It was also a time of the dawning of his sexual feelings. When we consider the possible devastation of such a clash in a boy of exceptional sensitivity – we are speaking here not of the young Joyce but of the younger Stephen, he whom we might call the "pre-Portrait" Stephen – we can see why these themes come together in this story with a force perhaps unequaled in his other writings. Religion and sex meet, clash, and spawn a crisis of conscience which reinforces in a particularly interesting way the other great theme, the overriding theme of all of Dubliners *– paralysis. This theme remains in this story, never overtly stated. It appears only in the dying moments of the tale – and is all the more powerful for that. It is manifested, as we shall see, at the moment of epiphany. But as it is, so to speak, the child of the other two themes, we must first see how they insinuate themselves into the story.*

Revised version

The author was just beginning to go through a period of intense piety, as well as puberty. When we consider the possible devastation of such a clash in a boy of exceptional sensitivity, we can see why these themes come together in this story with a force perhaps unequaled in his other writings. Religion and sex meet, clash, and spawn a crisis of conscience, which reinforces in a particularly interesting way the other great overriding theme of all The Dubliners *stories – paralysis. This theme remains implicit in this story, never overtly stated. It appears only in the dying moments of the tale and is all the more powerful for that reason. It is manifested, as we shall see, at the moment of epiphany. But as it is the child of the other two themes, we must first see how they insinuate themselves into the story.*

There is room for just one more point of comparison between the student's first draft and its transformation through revision. In the middle of the essay, the first draft describes the adolescent protagonist's adoration of the girl whom he knows as "Mangan's sister," in fairly plain language:

First draft

Having found his grail, the young protagonist fully relished the feeling of the invincibility of adolescence when powered by love.

In revising this sentence, the student endows it with sustained metaphoric language that truly captures the magic of adolescent longing.

Revised version

It appears to him that he has indeed found the grail. For who, in their first brush with that great chimera, love, would be convinced that all things are not possible, that all happiness cannot be had, that adulthood will not be one long violet-tinted evening of bliss?

You can enjoy reading Joseph Nugent's complete essay together with Joyce's story in the next chapter. This comparative look at sections of the student's first draft and their polished version was simply meant to demonstrate the vast improvement that can occur with revision.

Second example of revising for correcting the incorrect use of the words *topic,* and *theme*

In her first draft of her journal entry on Leslie Silko's short story "Lullaby," the student Andrea Deyzel did not use the words "topic" and "theme" correctly. Also, the theme did not come out of the topic, resulting in a lack of coherence. She also used specific plot details when stating the topic and the theme, which she was not supposed to do. Taking advantage of my feedback on the first draft, she produced a perfect second draft. The text of the story is in Chapter Ten.

Lullaby Journal
Student author: Andrea Deyzel
First draft

Topic

The topic of "Lullaby" by Leslie Marmon Silko is the mistreatment by the white man. More specifically, it's the mistreatment of a Navajo woman, her husband and family by white men.

My comments on the student's topic

1. A topic should be stated clearly and briefly, for example: The topic of "Lullaby" by Leslie Marmon Silko is the damaging consequences of mistreatment."
2. There should be no specifics in a topic.

Theme

The central theme of the work is loss; the loss of the Ayah's older son Jimmy, her babies to death, her children to social services, her own grandmother from tuberculosis, her home, heritage and eventually the loss of her husband.

My comments on the student's theme

Loss is a topic, not a theme. You have already stated one topic. Stick with it and write a theme that goes with it and also goes with the supporting details.

Support

To support this, Ayah recalls, "A man in a khaki uniform . . . told them that Jimmy was dead." Jimmy essentially died because he was incorporated into the white man's military. She also recalls that "it was the old woman who died in the winter, spitting blood; it was her old grandma who has given the children this disease." Here she's referring to a disease that was brought upon them by the white man. Then when referring to her husband she spoke of finding "him passed out at the bottom of the wooden steps to Azzie's Bar." The white man is again the cause—having introduced alcohol to the American Indians. These relate to the topic of mistreatment by the white man and the theme of loss because the white man is responsible for her misery by bringing these losses down upon her.

Revised version

Topic

The topic of "Lullaby" by Leslie Marmon Silko is continuous loss.

Theme

One culture can irreparably destroy the culture of another, leaving a lasting impact for generations.

Support

Ayah is an old, grey, Navajo woman; we first meet her as she's trudging through the snow, recalling the past. She thinks of her son, Jimmy, as she uses his blanket as a shawl. She tries to dismiss him from her mind but his memory is later brought back into her consciousness. She remembers, "A man in a khaki uniform . . . told them that Jimmy was dead." Jimmy's death was brought about because he was incorporated into the white man's military. For Ayah this is a heavy, personal loss; not just because she lost her son, but also because Jimmy could have helped her in other pressing situations.

Then, when thinking of two of her other children, she recalls that they told her "it was the old woman who died in the winter, spitting blood; it was her old grandma who has given the children this disease." Here she's referring to a disease that was brought upon them by the white man (likely tuberculosis). She doesn't believe that her children are ill, and wants a second, tribal opinion. She is denied that right, and instead her children are taken away from her with little other explanation. She sees her children a few times more, before they hardly recognize her and struggle for the words of their native language. Eventually they are assimilated into the new culture, forever abandoning Ayah and the way of the Navajo.

When referring to her husband she spoke of finding "him passed out at the bottom of the wooden steps to Azzie's Bar." The white man is again the cause—having introduced alcohol to the American Indians. Additionally, it could be supposed that her husband is depressed due to his rejection from the white rancher who evicts them to make way for the new ranch hand. He likely feels betrayed, and has been distanced from his wife, life, and everything—even the culture he was attempting to assimilate into. Although Ayah says, "But she wasn't sorry for him. He should have known all along what would happen." At the end, Ayah is beside her drunken husband, who is curled up in a ball in the snow. She's lost so much, and it seems that she may lose something important yet again.

Third example of revising for improved focus

The student Navneet Kaur's first draft of her journal entry on Leslie Silko's "Lullaby" identifies the story's topic and theme clearly. Her supporting details are perfectly in line with the stated topic and theme until the very last sentence that seems to interject something that was not mentioned in the theme. She was asked to revise the last sentence to reflect the focus of the composition more accurately. The following first draft and its revision show the vast improvement that can be achieved through thoughtful revision.

"Lullaby" by Leslie Silko
Student author: Navneet Kaur

First draft

Topic

The topic of Leslie Silko's short story is memories.

Theme

The short story's theme may be stated in many ways: memories last forever; memories can shape a person's life when they have nothing else but those memories; memories keep a person alive.

Support

"Lullaby" is the story of Ayah, a mother who has lost her children to the forced Native American assimilation process and war. Ayah's life is mostly lived and told through memories of her children. She recalls her life through memories of her children, whom she has lost. Her eldest son, Jimmie, was forcefully recruited by the U.S. army and was killed in war. He sent her a blanket which she keeps with her most of the time. There is reference to Jimmie's blanket throughout the story. Ayah's connection with her son's blanket is deep; by keeping his blanket, she probably feels like he is still with her. She carries a part of Jimmie with her by keeping the blanket as a "memory" of her lost son. Ayah also recalls the lawful abduction of her other two children. They were deceitfully taken from her to be adopted by white Americans, and brought back to visit their biological mother a couple of times. Ayah mentions the slow deterioration of her relationship with her children as they grow older and forget their mother and their Native American heritage. Through the memory of her children, Ayah lives an empty life with her husband.

My comment on the student's concluding sentence:

Your concluding sentence does not do justice to the promise of your statement of theme. It ends too negatively. Your statement of theme shows the strength of memories. You should change the conclusion of your journal entry to reflect your statement of theme accurately.

Student's revised version

The student revised her journal entry in response to this criticism by replacing the concluding sentence of her first draft. Through this revision, she was able to streamline her topic and theme with the supporting details and maintain the correct focus and mood.

Revised version

Although she lives through many tragic events and witnesses the agonizing deterioration of her husband, Chato, Ayah's source of strength is her memories that no one can snatch away from her. Memories help her move on in life. They remind Ayah of her connection with her mother, with her dead son Jimmie, with Mother Nature, and with her Native culture. Her memories enable her to have tranquility in the midst of devastating circumstances.

Fourth example of revising that shows progress from informal journal-like notes to formal writing

America is in the Heart by Carlos Bulosan
Student author: John Starks

First draft: Bulosan takes the reader on a tour through the oppressive quagmire of racism, discriminatory laws, and brutality faced by a Filipino immigrant in the late 40's and 50's. The topic is certainly perseverance. The theme: the fire to create, and the desire to succeed are the driving force behind the immigrants ability to whether the storm of discrimination.

My comment: Your statement of the topic and theme, even though clearly worded, sounds too much like notes and incomplete expression of your ideas.

Revised: Bulosan takes the reader on a tour through the oppressive quagmire of racism, discriminatory laws, and brutality faced by a Filipino immigrant in the late 1940s and 50s. Bulosan's novel treats many important topics; the need and value of perseverance is one of them. In the midst of detailing the numerous hardships that immigrants often experience, Bulosan is able to forcefully affirm the view that the fire to create and the desire to succeed are powerful driving forces behind the immigrant's ability to weather the storm of discrimination.

Checklist of Common Errors: The Final Step in Revising

An important part of the process of revising is making your composition free of grammar and punctuation errors. Some of them are serious enough to get in the way of your communication and considerably weaken your expression of even good ideas. To that end, I have placed on my website a checklist of common errors and an exercise that goes with them. Make it a practice to consult that list whenever you are revising your essays.

Exercises to Test Your Mastery of Chapter Eight

1. The chapter's opening pages contain several experts' views on revising. Whose advice do you find most helpful? Why?

2. What specific steps one must take to transform perfunctory first drafts into polished finished versions?

3. Of the numerous sentence structure variations introduced in the chapter (periodic/suspended, antithetical, balanced, cumulative, etc.), which two come naturally to you? Which two do you have to include in your style with conscious effort? What usual effects upon the reader are associated with the listed elements?

4. What vocabulary-enhancing method would you recommend to someone with a limited range?

5. Style requirements placed in the "Compulsory Revision" category are clarity, brevity, adequate vocabulary, authentic voice, clear focus, variety in sentence structure and paragraph organization. Which three of them would you consider indispensable to good writing? Why?

6. Are there any items under the "compulsory" category that you would rather place under "Optional Revision"? Give supporting reasons for your view.

7. Of the style requirements of simile, metaphor, analogy, verbal irony, paradox, and understatement, which one do you find the hardest to use? Which of these elements would you place under "Compulsory Revision"? Why?

8. Identify this sentence structure variety and comment on its impact: "Vast and primeval, unfathomable, unconquerable, bastion of cottonmouth, rattlesnake and leech, mother of vegetation, father of mosquito, soul of silt, the Okefenokee is the swamp archetypal, the swamp of legend, of racial memory, of Hollywood."

Part Three

Study by Genre

CHAPTER NINE

ESSAYS

Essays are a pleasant means of quick sharing of knowledge and making a point. The range of topics and styles in essays is limitless. Essays are a major part of the genre known as "nonfiction," which spans many kinds of writing, including but not limited to short essays, book-length essays, memoirs, journalism, and literary criticism. This chapter will only cover the essay genre to introduce you to some truly outstanding pieces. Every year, the "Best Essays" series publishes a volume of essays that are rated among the best. You can get that book from any library. College reading textbooks also have outstanding essays on a vast range of topics. They are also easily accessible online.

Since Michel de Montaigne's creation of this literary form in the sixteenth century as a means of personal reflections on topics of interest, the essay has undergone many changes. Montaigne called this kind of writing "essais," the French word for attempts, to emphasize its informal and flexible nature. However, today, essays can be subjective, as they originally were, or they can be objective, keeping the author's personality out of the composition. The following brief listing of essay variations will give you an idea of its multi-faceted nature.

1. Philosophical essays

As their name suggests, such essays take on complex questions that human beings have been called upon to answer through the ages. Even when they do not give any clear-cut answers, the high quality of their analysis and reasoning at least clarifies the issues.

"The Myth of Sisyphus" by Albert Camus (1913-1960) – text included

"A Free Man's Worship" by Bertrand Russell (1872-1970)
Link: http://www.philosophicalsociety.com/archives/a%20free%20man's%20worship.htm

"Reflections on Exile" by Edward Said (1935-2003)
Link: www.dartmouth.edu/~germ43/pdfs/said_reflections.pdf

"Edward Said on Orientalism" by Edward Said
Link: http://www.youtube.comm/watch?v=nOHYX9JvH80

The texts of Russell's and Said's essays could not be included because of the excessively high permissions fees. However, the links provide a convenient access to them.

2. Expository, argumentative essays

The first essay "Between Hell and Reason" by Albert Camus and only a few quotations from his "Letters to a German Friend" are included in this chapter. You can read the rest of the essays online.

Exposition or explanation is an essential part of argumentative, persuasive, analytic, interpretive, subjective, objective, and many other forms of the essay. Examples include:

- "Between Hell and Reason: Thoughts on the Defining Moment of the Twentieth Century" by Albert Camus
- "Letters to a German Friend" by Albert Camus
- Any essay from James Baldwin's *Notes of a Native Son* or *Nobody Knows My Name*
- "In Favor of Capital Punishment" by Jacques Barzun
- "The Real Responsibilities of the Scientist" by Jacob Bronowski
- "Reflections on the Guillotine" by Albert Camus [You can choose an excerpt of this long essay.]
- "Nature Fights Back" from *Silent Spring* by Rachel Carson
- "Why I Am an Agnostic" by Clarence Darrow
- "Instinct and Civilization" from *Civilization and Its Discontents* by Sigmund Freud
- "Work in an Alienated Society" from *The Sane Society* by Erich Fromm
- Any essay from *Charlie Chan Is Dead: An Anthology of Contemporary Asian-American Writing*, ed. Jessica Hagedorn
- "Letter from Birmingham Jail" by Martin Luther King, Jr.
- "Women Students in the Classroom" by Frances Maher
- "How Do You Know It's Good" from *But Will It Sell?* By Marya Mannes
- "Politics and the English Language" by George Orwell
- Any chapter from *The Road Less Travelled: A New Psychology of Love* by M. Scott Peck
- "Man Against Darkness" by W. T. Stace
- "A Modest Proposal" by Jonathan Swift
- "How Should One Read a Book?" from *The Common Reader* by Virginia Woolf
- "College Pressures" by William Zinsser

3. Essays that mix exposition with narration (only the first one is included here)

Narrative essays differ from expository essays in their use of anecdotes, dialogue, a story line, setting, and atmosphere. Here are some notable examples:

- "On Being Crazy" by W.E.B. Du Bois
- Any chapter from *The Heart of a Woman* by Maya Angelou
- "Life in a New Language" from *Lost in Translation* by Eva Hoffman
- "Home Is Every Place" by Pico Iyer
- Any excerpt from *The Woman Warrior* by Maxine Hong Kingston
- "A Hanging," "Marrakech," and "Shooting an Elephant" by George Orwell
- "The Achievement of Desire" from *Hunger of Memory* by Richard Rodriguez
- "Learning to Read" from *Autobiography* and "Letter from Mecca" by Malcolm X
- "America and I" by Anzia Yezierska

4. Humorous essays with strong messages

It is challenging to write a good humorous essay, especially one that makes a strong point in the process of entertaining. The following are a few representative examples:

- "Love Is a Fallacy" by Max Shulman
- "Thinking as a Hobby" by William Golding
- "Courtship Through the Ages" by James Thurber (included in the Humor Chapter Fifteen)

5. Critical essays (literary criticism)

As their name indicates, critical essays engage in analysis and interpretation of literary texts in order to enhance the reader's and one's own understanding of literature. It is this kind of essay that most assignments ask for in a course on literature. In this book, examples are:

- A.C. Bradley's "The Substance of Shakespearean Tragedy"
- Arthur Miller's "Tragedy and the Common Man" (both in the Drama Chapter)
- Numerous essays by the author of this book and by students

6. Descriptive essays

Whereas expository writing explains, descriptive writing, a much more difficult variety of prose to write, is iconic in nature and creates images. Good descriptions creatively stretch the language to its limit, using elements of style that engage not only our intellect but also our senses. A few notable examples, not included in this book but easily available online, are the following:

"The Death of the Moth" by Virginia Woolf

"Once More to the Lake" by E. B. White

"Niagra Falls" by Rupert Brooke

"Total Eclipse" by Annie Dillard

"Flying Over Africa" by Isak Dinesen

"Thoreau's Journal" by Thomas Mallon

"The King of the Birds" by Flannery O'Connor

Ways to read essays

There are many ways to mine the wealth of ideas in essays:

- You can take notes on the essay's major points of focus together with particularly effective supporting details.

- You can compare and/or contrast two essays on the same topic.

- You can write either in support of an essayist's point of view or offer a different perspective on the topic.

- You can imitate the writing and organizational style of a favorite essay.

Of the above-mentioned essay-reading strategies, the first one can be covered using the journaling format that was explained in Chapter Six and is exemplified again in my response to Albert Camus' essay "Between Hell and Reason."

Suggested format for journaling essays

Using the following journal format will help you not only to fully understand the essay that you choose but also enable you to communicate your understanding clearly.

1. Copy the thesis of the essay that you have selected. If the thesis is not stated, formulate it in your own words. The criterion for a good thesis is that it is phrased with care and covers most of the essay's substance. Unlike short stories in which themes are most often implied, not stated, most essays provide a thesis.

2. Copy a few of the topic sentences that develop important aspects or components of the thesis. In some essays that read like narratives, it may not be possible to find formally stated topic sentences, but the topic of the narrative essay will always emerge from the details used by the author. Since informal essays mix narrative and expository modes, they read like stories and sometimes make their major points anecdotally. Make connections between the topic sentences and the thesis. Like the thesis, topic sentences are general statements, free of specific details, such as examples, statistics, facts, etc. These latter go under supporting details.

3. Summarize some of the key supporting, explanatory details and examples used by the author. Link them to the essay's main points. These details are important because without them, thesis statements and topic sentences remain mere unsubstantiated claims.

The above-noted instructions apply not only to formal essays written in the classical style, but also to many of its variations, including your own essays. My journal entry on Albert Camus' passionate political-philosophical essay now follows right after the text of Camus' essay.

Responding to Essays

Albert Camus' editorial from the *Combat* newspaper has appeared in many collections. It was reprinted in a chapter on "Morality and Politics" in *Actuelles*. The importance of the subtitle of Camus' essay – "Thoughts on the Defining Moment of the 20th Century" is not to be overlooked. The dateline given to this piece is August 8, 1945, two days after the bombing of Hiroshima, before the Japanese surrender on August 10th, a day after the Soviet Union declared war on Japan. *Combat*, for which Camus served as editor-in-chief, was an important communications channel for the French Resistance Movement, and printed reports of Nazi atrocities and messages from Charles de Gaulle, leader of the French government-in-exile.

Excerpt from *Between Hell and Reason: Essays from the Resistance Newspaper Combat (1944-1947)*

August 8, 1945

1. The world is what it is, which is to say, nothing much. That is what everyone learned yesterday, thanks to the formidable concert of opinion coming from radios, newspapers, and information agencies. Indeed we are told, in the midst of hundreds of enthusiastic commentaries, that any average city can be wiped out by a bomb the size of a football. American, English, and French newspapers are filled with eloquent essays on the future, the past, the inventors, the cost, the peaceful incentives, the military advantages, and even the life-of-its-own character of the atom bomb.

2. We can sum it up in one sentence: Our technical civilization has just reached its greatest level of savagery. We will have to choose, in the more or less near future, between collective suicide and the intelligent use of our scientific conquests.

3. Meanwhile, we think there is something indecent in celebrating a discovery whose use has caused the most formidable rage of destruction ever known to man. What will it bring to a world already given over to all the convulsions of violence, incapable of any control, indifferent to justice and the simple happiness of men – a world where science devotes itself to organized murder? No one but the most unrelenting idealists would dare to wonder.

4. These discoveries must be reported and given appropriate commentary; they must be announced to the world so that man has an accurate picture of his destiny. But couching these terrible revelations in picturesque or humorous writing is intolerable.

5. Even before the bomb, one did not breathe too easily in this tortured world. Now we are given a new source of anguish; it has all the promise of being our greatest anguish ever. There can be no doubt that humanity is being offered its last chance. Perhaps this is an occasion for the newspapers to print a special edition. More likely, it should be cause for a certain amount of reflection and a great deal of silence.

6. Let us be understood. If the Japanese surrender after the destruction of Hiroshima, having been intimidated, we will rejoice. But we refuse to see anything in such grave news other than the need to argue more energetically in favor of a true international society, in which the great powers will not have superior rights over small and middle-sized nations, where such an ultimate weapon will be controlled by human intelligence rather than by the appetites and doctrines of various states.

7. Before the terrifying prospects now available to humanity, we see even more clearly that peace is the only goal worth struggling for. This is no longer a prayer but a demand to be made by all peoples to their governments – a demand to choose definitively between hell and reason.

Albert Camus (1913-1960)

Journal response by the author of this book

Topic

Abuse of scientific knowledge for "organized murder"

Thesis

"Our technical civilization has just reached its greatest level of savagery. We will have to choose . . . between collective suicide and the intelligent use of our scientific conquests."

Supporting details (with some of Camus' strong topic sentences included)

Camus' essay is even more relevant today than it was when he wrote it on August 8, 1945, two days after the bombing of Hiroshima. In the midst of obscene celebrations of Hiroshima's destruction in Western popular media, Camus interjected a passionate plea for reflection and reason. Humanity, he said, has been blessed with formidable scientific knowledge and technological inventions that should be used for the collective good of the world, not for its destruction, as evidenced in the case of the decimation of Hiroshima.

His own words express his mind forcefully when he reiterates the urgent need of

". . . a true international society, in which the great powers will not have superior rights over small and middle-sized nations, where such an ultimate weapon [the atomic bomb] will be controlled by human intelligence rather than by the appetites and doctrines of various states."

At the time of writing his essay, the death and destruction rained on Nagasaki by a hydrogen bomb, killing thousands more civilians, had not yet occurred.

Fortunately, humanity has been spared another use of the atomic and hydrogen bombs since the tragedies of Hiroshima and Nagasaki, in which more than 100,000 human beings were killed in a matter of minutes and thousands more suffered from the lingering after-effects in the form of excessive, carcinogenic levels of radiation. The United Nations was created as a world forum to discuss and resolve critical international issues. However, Camus' wish for a reasonable balance of power among nations, whereby nations with superior weaponry do not prey upon and exploit the weaker nations remains unfulfilled. The five countries that have the power to veto the proposals of the rest of the world still dominate the United Nations, and conquest and occupation of the weaker nations by stronger nations continues to this day with no sign of abatement.

Camus' parting words in his essay ask for action on our part. It is our collective duty to demand peace of our governments, not as a prayer but as our right. When giving Camus the Nobel Prize in literature in 1957, the Nobel committee cited his ceaseless efforts to "illuminate the problem of the human conscience in our time."

Another of Camus' essays that is thematically linked to "Between Hell and Reason" is his work titled "Letters to a German Friend" that he wrote clandestinely to a German friend during the Nazi occupation of France. The following words from his "Preface" to the letters demand our utmost attention for making peace with whomsoever we regard as the enemy:

"When the author of these letters says "you", he means not "you Germans" but "you Nazis". When he says "we", this signifies not always "we Frenchmen" but sometimes "we free Europeans". I am contrasting two attitudes, not two nations, even if, at a certain moment in history, these two nations personified two enemy attitudes. To repeat a remark that is not mine, I love my country too much to be a nationalist. . . . I loathe none but executioners. Any reader who reads the *Letters to a German Friend* in this perspective – in other words, as a document emerging from the struggle against violence – will see how I can say I don't disown a single word I have written here."

You can read excerpts from his *Letters to a German Friend* by using this link: www.iep.utm.edu/camus/#SH4c. If we pay attention to Camus' honest and very perceptive diagnosis of what ails humanity and act on his advice, we may have a recipe for a better world.

Assignments on Selected Essays

For this exercise, you should choose a well-written and well-organized essay on an important topic. Select an essay that has not been discussed in this book unless you can offer a different interpretation. You may use the journal format or any other method as long as you capture and present the author's ideas in a clear and engaging manner. A very interesting way to enjoy reading essays – an option that is open to you – is by focusing just on one point of interest from an essay, as is demonstrated in the sample journal responses on Edward Said later in this chapter. Provide the essay's text or an accessible link to it with your response if the essay is not in this book.

The following exercises provide you with an opportunity to read four deeply philosophical essays that ponder timeless questions – by Albert Camus, Bertrand Russell, and Edward Said. Included here is also an exercise on Edward Said's famous work *Orientalism*. A link is provided to his video lecture, "Edward Said on Orientalism."

First exercise

Read Albert Camus' famous essay "The Myth of Sisyphus" that appears below. Copy or point out two or three of his statements that urge us to maintain composure even in the worst of circumstances and to celebrate the gift of mental freedom that no chains, no fate, can bind. Explain and support your reasoning with summaries of relevant details from Camus' essay. The following words from Camus' "Preface" to *The Myth of Sisyphus and Other Essays* will orient you to Camus' thinking:

"The fundamental subject of *The Myth of Sisyphus* is this: it is legitimate and necessary to wonder whether life has a meaning; therefore it is legitimate to meet the problem of suicide face to face. The answer, underlying and appearing through the paradoxes which cover it, is this: even if one does not believe in God, suicide is not legitimate. Written in 1940, amid the French and European disaster, this book declares that even within the limits of nihilism it is possible to find the means to proceed beyond nihilism. Although *The Myth of Sisyphus* poses mortal problems, it sums itself up for me as a lucid invitation to live and to create, in the very midst of the desert."

The Myth of Sisyphus

http://www.nyu.edu/classes/keefer/hell/camus.html

The gods had condemned Sisyphus to ceaselessly rolling a rock to the top of a mountain, whence the stone would fall back of its own weight. They had thought with some reason that there is no more dreadful punishment than futile and hopeless labor.

If one believes Homer, Sisyphus was the wisest and most prudent of mortals. According to another tradition, however, he was disposed to practice the profession of highwayman. I see no contradiction in this. Opinions differ as to the reasons why he became the futile laborer of the underworld. To begin with, he is accused of a certain levity in regard to the gods. He stole their secrets. Aegina, the daughter of Aesopus, was carried off by Jupiter. The father was shocked by that disappearance and complained to Sisyphus. He, who knew of the abduction, offered to tell about it on condition that Aesopus would give water to the citadel of Corinth. To the celestial thunderbolts he preferred the benediction of water. He was punished for this in the underworld. Homer tells us also that Sisyphus had put Death in chains. Pluto could not endure the sight of his deserted, silent empire. He dispatched the god of war, who liberated Death from the hands of the conqueror.

It is said also that Sisyphus, being near to death, rashly wanted to test his wife's love. He ordered her to cast his unburied body into the middle of the public square. Sisyphus woke up in the underworld. And there, annoyed by an obedience so contrary to human love, he obtained from Pluto permission to return to earth in order to chastise his wife. But when he had seen again the face of this world, enjoyed water and sun, warm stones and the sea, he no longer wanted to go back to the infernal darkness. Recalls, signs of anger, warnings were of no avail. Many years more he lived facing the curve of the gulf, the sparkling sea, and the smiles of the earth. A decree of the gods was necessary. Mercury came and seized the impudent man by the collar and, snatching him from his joys, led him forcibly back to the underworld, where his rock was ready for him.

You have already grasped that Sisyphus is the absurd hero. He *is* as much through his passions as through his torture. His scorn of the gods, his hatred of death, and his passion for life won him that unspeakable penalty in which the whole being is exerted toward accomplishing nothing. This is the price that must be paid for the passions of this earth. Nothing is told us about Sisyphus in the underworld. Myths are made for the imagination to breathe life into them. As for this myth, one sees merely the whole effort of a body straining to raise the huge stone, to roll it and push it up a slope a hundred times over; one sees the face screwed up, the cheek tight against the stone, the shoulder bracing the clay-covered mass, the foot wedging it, the fresh start with arms outstretched, the wholly human security of two earth-clotted hands. At the very end of his long effort measured by skyless space and time without depth, the purpose is achieved. Then Sisyphus watches the stone rush down in a few moments toward that lower world whence he will have to push it up again toward the summit. He goes back down to the plain. It is during that return, that pause, that Sisyphus interests me. A face that toils so close to stones is already stone itself! I see that man going back down with a heavy yet measured step toward the torment of which he will never know the end. That hour like a breathing-space which returns as surely as his suffering, that is the hour of consciousness. At each of those moments when he leaves the heights and gradually sinks toward the lairs of the gods, he is superior to his fate. He is stronger than his rock.

If this myth is tragic, that is because its hero is conscious. Where would his torture be, indeed, if at every step the hope of succeeding upheld him? The workman of today works every day in his life at the same tasks, and this fate is no less absurd. But it is tragic only at the rare moments when it becomes conscious. Sisyphus, proletarian of the gods, powerless and rebellious, knows the whole extent of his wretched condition: it is what he thinks of during his descent. The lucidity that was to constitute his torture at the same time crowns his victory. There is no fate that cannot be surmounted by scorn.

If the descent is thus sometimes performed in sorrow, it can also take place in joy. This word is not too much. Again I fancy Sisyphus returning toward his rock, and the sorrow was in the beginning. When the images of earth cling too tightly to memory, when the call of happiness becomes too insistent, it happens that melancholy rises in man's heart: this is the rock's victory, this is the rock itself. The boundless grief is too heavy to bear. These are our nights of Gethsemane. But crushing truths perish from being acknowledged. Thus, Oedipus at the outset obeys fate without knowing it. But from the moment he knows, his tragedy begins. Yet at the same time, blind and desperate, he realizes that the only bond linking him to the world is the cool hand of a girl. Then a tremendous remark rings out: "Despite so many ordeals, my advanced age and the nobility of my soul make me conclude that all is well." Sophocles' Oedipus, like Dostoevsky's Kirilov, thus gives the recipe for the absurd victory. Ancient wisdom confirms modern heroism.

One does not discover the absurd without attempting to write a manual of happiness. "What! by such narrow ways--?" There is but one world, however. Happiness and the absurd are two sons of the same earth. They are inseparable. It would be a mistake to say that happiness necessarily springs from the absurd discovery. It happens as well that the feeling of the absurd springs from happiness. "I conclude that all is well," says Oedipus, and that remark is sacred. It echoes in the wild and limited universe of man. It teaches that all is not, has not been, exhausted. It drives out of this world a god who had come into it with dissatisfaction and a preference for futile sufferings. It makes of fate a human matter, which must be settled among men.

All Sisyphus' silent joy is contained therein. His fate belongs to him. His rock is his thing. Likewise, the absurd man, when he contemplates his torment, silences all the idols. In the universe suddenly restored to silence, the myriad wondering little voices of the earth rise up. Unconscious, secret calls, invitations from all the faces, they are the necessary reverse and price of victory. There is no sun without shadow, and it is essential to know the night. The absurd man says yes and his effort will henceforth be unceasing. If there is a personal fate, there is no higher destiny, or at least there is but one which he concludes is inevitable and despicable. For the rest, he knows himself to be the master of his days. At that subtle moment when man glances backward over his life, Sisyphus returning toward his rock, in that silent pivoting he contemplates that series of unrelated actions which becomes his fate, created by him, combined under his memory's eye and soon sealed by his death. Thus, convinced of the wholly human origin of all that is human, a blind man eager to see who knows that the night has no end, he is still on the go. The rock is still rolling.

I leave Sisyphus at the foot of the mountain! One always finds one's burden again. But Sisyphus teaches the higher fidelity that negates the gods and raises rocks. He too concludes that all is well. This universe henceforth without a master seems to him neither sterile nor futile. Each atom of that stone, each mineral flake of that night-filled mountain, in itself forms a world. The struggle itself toward the heights is enough to fill a man's heart. One must imagine Sisyphus happy.

Albert Camus (1913-1960)

Second exercise

When reading Bertrand Russell's essay "A Free Man's Worship" online, keep in mind the following questions. You may make any one or all of these questions the focus of your response or choose yet another approach to this essay that you prefer. You can read the complete essay, using this link: http://www.philosophicalsociety.com/archives/a%20free%20man's%20worship.htm

1. In Mephistopheles' version of the history of the Creation (opening paragraph of Russell's essay), who are the beings whom he [the Creator] tortured and from whom he wanted "undeserved" praise?
2. Identify and comment on the purpose and effectiveness of Russell's use of some of the allusions to mythology, religion, and literature in the essay.
3. We are familiar with love poems and love stories. How could Russell's essay be categorized as an essay about love? What kind of love is celebrated and urged in this essay? What is its therapeutic and bonding value on a universal scale? Pay special attention to the essay's last two paragraphs for relevant information.
4. Compare Russell with Camus in their views of Fate and rebirth as presented in their philosophical essays "A Free Man's Worship" and "The Myth of Sisyphus" respectively. If possible, include a comment on Camus' novel *The Stranger* (discussed at length in the chapter on the novel)In that novel, when nearing his imminent death by execution, the protagonist Meursault feels that he is starting his life all over again (in the novel's last paragraph)Russell mentions rebirth in the fifth paragraph from the end of his essay.
5. What do we learn from these two authors as to how best to live our lives? Can we consider their views spiritual without necessarily being religious in the traditional sense? Demonstrate how their teachings are in full compliance with human ethical values and not very different from the highest values taught by all religions.

Similarities Between Albert Camus and Bertrand Russell
Sample journal by the author of this book

I have used the headings *Topics*, *Thesis*, and *Support* to demonstrate how this essay's structure was conceptualized using the journal format. If I remove these headings, my response reads like a complete essay, not as a journal entry.

Topics

Some similar topics that surface in Camus and Russell concern a heroic sense of rebirth when faced with extinction, human beings as the architects of their own fates, and the unbreakable bond of sympathy and brotherhood between people. They even choose the same words, such as fate, rebirth, blindness, etc.

Thesis

Both Camus and Russell write about the increase in appreciative sympathy for humanity and a truly felt awareness of human brotherhood that people undergo when they actually realize the truth about their own and all other human beings' limited life span. Such awareness could come as a result of an unalterable time limit imposed on someone's life, as in the case of the execution order of Camus' hero Meursault. The dawning of such awareness could also occur when we accept the fact that every human being is living with the news of terminal illness. That terminal illness is life itself that comes with a hidden but certain expiration date.

Support

Camus expresses his above-noted thoughts toward the end of "The Myth of Sisyphus" when the hero, during a momentary pause in his ceaseless labor contemplates that series of unrelated actions which becomes his fate, created by him, combined under his memory's eye and soon sealed by his death. Thus, convinced of the wholly human origin of all that is human, a blind man eager to see who knows that the night has no end, he is still on the go. The rock is still rolling.

Camus' concluding words in this essay are a compelling and inspiring example of creating hope out of despair:

> He [Sisyphus] too concludes that all is well. his universe henceforth without a master seems to him neither sterile nor futile. Each atom of that stone, each mineral flake of that night-filled mountain, in itself forms a world. The struggle itself toward the heights is enough to fill a man's heart. One must imagine Sisyphus happy.

Camus expresses these ideas also in his novel *The Stranger*. Toward the end of the novel, in a sudden epiphany of awareness, Camus' protagonist finally comes to feel (not just know as a concept) that "we're all elected by the same fate" (Camus 121). He then opens himself "for the first time to the gentle indifference of the world. Finding it so much like myself – so like a brother really – I felt that I had been happy and that I was happy again" (Camus 122-123).

In the case of Bertrand Russell, his thoughts, relevant to the above-noted topics, appear in the second-from-last paragraph of "A Free Man's Worship." He writes eloquently about the same dawning of appreciative sympathy and human brotherhood that we noted in Camus. Very much like Camus, Russell expresses beautifully positive feelings that, ironically, are triggered by the negative specter of ubiquitous death:

> United with his fellow-men by the strongest of all ties, the tie of a common doom, the free man finds that a new vision is with him always, shedding over every daily task the light of love. The life of Man is a long march through the night, surrounded by invisible forces, tortured by weariness and pain, towards a goal that few can hope to reach, and where none may tarry long. One by one, as they march, our comrades vanish from our sight, seized by the silent orders of omnipotent Death.

Russell seems to be pleading that we forgive our fellow humans' failings, champion and applaud their achievements, and make it our life's goal to mitigate their suffering and augment their happiness.

"Very brief is the time in which we can help them, in which their happiness or misery is decided. Be it ours to shed sunshine on their path, to lighten their sorrows by the balm of sympathy, to give them the pure joy of a never-tiring affection, to strengthen failing courage, to instill faith in hours of despair. Let us not weigh in grudging scales their merits and demerits, but let us think only of their need -- of the sorrows, the difficulties, perhaps the blindnesses, that make the misery of their lives; let us remember that they are fellow-sufferers in the same darkness, actors in the same tragedy with ourselves. And so, when their day is over, when their good and their evil have become eternal by the immortality of the past, be it ours to feel that, where they suffered, where they failed, no deed of ours was the cause; but wherever a spark of the divine fire kindled in their hearts, we were ready with encouragement, with sympathy, with brave words in which high courage glowed."

Both Camus and Russell tackle some of the most important and elusive problems relating to the nature of human existence, the universe, and human suffering. They also show us ways to make our lives meaningful. They accomplish their objectives by writing in accessible, attractive, and appealing language.

Third exercise

Read Edward Said's essay "Reflections on Exile" by using this link:
www.dartmouth.edu/~germ43/pdfs/said_reflections.pdf

If the link does not work, use a library. One of the many books that have Said's essay in a slightly abbreviated form is *New Worlds of Literature: Writings from America: Many Cultures*. Eds. Jerome Beaty and J. Paul Hunter. New York: Norton, 1994.

Edward Said's essay makes over a dozen statements that combine wisdom, idealism, and fresh insights to solve the problem of intolerance of differences. After a careful reading of the essay, copy a statement that could be used as a basis for acceptance, even celebration, of differences, leading to a harmonious coexistence and a cure for chauvinistic patriotism and confining ties. Explain how your selected quotations from Said would achieve the desired outcome. If you find it difficult to limit yourself to just one statement from the essay, feel free to copy a few concentrated statements that promote acceptance of pluralism and diversity. The length of your response could range from a detailed paragraph to an essay (as is demonstrated by students' sample answers). After reading the samples, you need to select a quotation from Said that has not been covered in any of the sample essays. If you choose a covered quotation, offer an interpretation that is different from the one given in the sample essays.

Readings of Said by several students

To demonstrate the wealth of ideas in Said's essay, I have included several students' responses Some of them select the same exact words from Said's essay, but offer equally illuminating interpretations Their compositions range from just a paragraph to full essays. Essays by Kyle Taylor and Hiromi Ortega Roque are in Chapter-Nine-related material on my website.

Student author: Jovi Bondoc

"Most people are principally aware of one culture, one setting, one home; exiles are aware of at least two, and this plurality of vision gives rise to an awareness of simultaneous dimensions, an awareness that—to borrow a phrase from music—is *contrapuntal*." It can be argued that with the preceding statement, Edward Said endorses acceptance (as opposed to mere tolerance, which would imply indifference rather than enthusiasm) and in turn diversity.

To clarify, the term "contrapuntal" is derived from "counterpoint", referring to two distinct melodic lines or voices that together are polyphonic (or harmonically dependent of one another). In recognizing the definition of such a word, we can gain a better understanding of Said's message. In the struggle for reconciliation and embracing diversity, we should realize that the appreciation of different cultures in the grand scheme of things, as individual as they are in their respective features, can provide a sense of world harmony, not discord or dissonance. This is not to say that we should blindly throw all ways of life into one behemoth of a melting pot and assume every culture falls into a single ambiguous category of the universe; in other words, cultural combination is not the goal. Rather, we should value all aspects of different cultures and, as Ronald Takaki would say, "create a community of a larger memory."

Student author: Maxwell Lynch

As Said quotes Hugo of St. Victor,

> The tender soul has fixed his love on one spot in the world, the strong man has extended his love to all places; the perfect man has extinguished his.

Said quotes Hugo here to make a point about the transitory nature of the concept of home. The first step is to embrace all places with equal respect and vigor, the last seems to reject all concepts of home altogether. In effect, to shed the naivety of bonding with a place, and replace it with the wisdom of bonding with all people equally. If humanism were to truly eclipse nationalism on Earth, it follows that acceptance would replace exclusion – based on the idea of a shared collective fate. Not only would diversity be celebrated, but accepted as an inveterate aspect of human identity: That whatever perceived "sameness" amongst humans is truly illusory – that we are all infinitely unique as individuals.

Student author: Victor Rivas Umana

In Edward Said's essay "Reflection on Exile" we learn about what it means to be an exile. Some of it is negative. Being an exile is never something that happens because of something positive. It is usually a result of negative actions by someone, be it a government, a group within a nation, etc. But Edward Said does not just see it as all negative and full of misery Edward's Said's exile is someone who has a more open-minded view of the world; a different kind of lens to see what surrounds us that is not negative and oppositional. He states that since exiles are not tied to a homeland and are always on the move, they can view history through a different perspective and create a different kind of society. This can be seen when he quotes Hugo of St. Victor who writes about the perfect man. Hugo writes: "It is a source of great virtue for the practiced mind to learn, bit by bit, first to change about invisible and transitory things, so that afterward it may be able to leave them altogether. The man who finds his homeland sweet is still a tender beginner; he to whom every soil is as his native one is already strong; but he is perfect to whom the entire world is as a foreign land. The tender soul has fixed his love on one spot in the world; the strong man has extended his love to all places; the perfect man has extinguished his." This, according to Said, is "the model for anyone wishing to transcend national and provincial limits." He continues by saying that this is the only way historians (but also humanity in general) will be able to "grasp the human experience and its written records in their diversity and particularity; otherwise [we] will remain committed more to the exclusions and reactions of prejudice than to the freedom that accompanies knowledge." To put it simply, we must be like an exile, detached from our "homeland" and constantly crossing borders, in order for us to accept diversity not only in our cultures but also in our histories. This way we avoid jingoistic patriotism as well as negative perspectives like those seen in Orientalism, racism, sexism, etc.

The reason I chose this section of his essay is because it prescribes the solution to pretty much a lot of the problems and conflicts we have in this world: Be it the Israeli-Palestinian conflict, the war on terror, or even domestic problems like those we are facing with racism, sexism, homophobia, etc. If we could detach ourselves from our "homeland," our points of view we learn from being American, or straight or white, or democrats, etc., and then learn to appreciate other points of view and finally, learn to just always be critical of any perspective/history, I think we can learn to be more neutral and see other points of view and appreciate them on face value. Like the exile, detaching ourselves completely from any homeland, we can be critical of negative dichotomies. Only in this way can we change history and reframe it and include other perspectives that are lost in ethnocentric, racist, sexist, homophobic views of history. History and life should not be experienced through one lens; it should not be seen as a constant struggle between ourselves and others around us. It should be more appreciative of those around us who are different but also to acknowledge the similarities that we all may share. You never know you may find someone who is gay or black or Muslim who may enjoy some of the same things you do. Or maybe you will find a culture you once despised and finally learn to appreciate it and incorporate some of its aspects into your life. Edward Said did a great job of analyzing all of this and showing us that our world is constantly changing and is not as static as we make it seem. He advocated a world of inclusion NOT exclusion. Only then can we fully appreciate what is going on around us and learn to incorporate other points of view into our world and find happiness with ourselves and others. We may never reach the status of the perfect man but as long as we are more like the perfect man we can finally start to change the world to a more peaceful and better place.

Student author: Phil Haggerty

"Most people are principally aware of one culture, one setting, one home; exiles are aware of at least two, and this plurality of vision gives rise to an awareness of simultaneous dimensions, an awareness that—to borrow a phrase from music—is contrapuntal."

As well-written as it is interesting, Edward Said's "Reflections on Exile" is a fresh look at the byproducts of exile and some of the positive views and ideas that can come out of such an experience The plight of refugees and exiles has been an important phenomenon in the age of superpowers, military conflicts, occupation, and nationalism Although there is no universal idea or viewpoint that all exiles hold in common, Said points out that there are certain characteristics and life experiences that they do share. These experiences impact their view of life and the world politically, socially, and philosophically. And, exile is a current reality for millions of people on earth.

Nationalism pits human beings against each other based on political boundaries the vast majority of people had no say in determining. Many nationalists believe that our interests are based on borders and that somehow the interests of people in other countries are competitive, different, or less worthy than ours. In the sentence above, Said uses the word *contrapuntal*, which means two or more relatively independent melodies sounded together. Although the melodies are independent, often the most beautiful music is created when two separate melodies blend together in one song. The two melodies still retain their independent identity; and if played without the other, could form their own song. But when they are played together a more beautiful and interesting song is created. This same idea is applicable to our world in which most people are trying to make ends meet, provide for their families, and live happy lives. The people who exploit, torment, and abuse most often in the name of nationalism are in the minority. Plagued by the emphasis on the separate peoples of the world, we have yet to tap well into the human potential of those peoples working together.

We can look to Israel and Palestine as a perfect example. Land is not ethnic or religious; it's just land. The Palestinian whose grandfather's grandfather owned property in Jerusalem is no more entitled to living in the holy land than the Jew whose grandmother immigrated in the 1930s. Jews and non-Jewish

Palestinians were not inevitably doomed to conflict. They lived peacefully together for centuries in a number of areas. It was only when Zionism was introduced, a concept of ethnic nationalism and exclusivity, that the two parties become pitted against each other. One can only imagine the potential of that region without the political division of most Israelis and Palestinians.

Due to deprivation, many exiles are drawn to extremes. But if the exiles can hold on to the multiple-world viewpoints and focus on what we have in common, not solely what we do not, they will not fall victim to nationalism and hatred. I believe that the experience of an exile leads to increased solidarity with other oppressed peoples in the world, Edward Said being a perfect example. I think it is critical that people around the world, exiles or not, create a movement against nationalism, and for international solidarity. We need to take the multicultural view of the exile and apply it to the world. We need to make clear within a progressive movement that true and sustainable progress must be universal and not just national. I look at people that have been through exile with great admiration. They know more than anyone else that we must work together to prevent further tragedies, such as another war and resulting refugee crisis.

Said's sentence above is fairly simple. But I think when taken a step further the multicultural world viewpoint one gains from the experience of exile can be the path to political enlightenment, against nation states but for humanity. We are one people, with many different and beautiful cultures, practices and religions. Our cultures from territory to territory are independent and different from each other, just like those separate melodies. But if we can work together for the sake of humanity and not national gain, we can truly solve some of the world's problems. We have our cultural differences, but ultimately there is no race but the human race.

Fourth exercise

Watch the video essay "Edward Said on Orientalism":
http://www.youtube.comm/watch?v=nOHYX9JvH80. This video lecture consists of four parts of about ten minutes each. If you cannot access this video on YouTube, try finding it on Let Me Watch This. There you would find it in one 40-minute presentation.

Edward Said's video essay is an attempt to present in simplified form his complex ideas from his 1978 book *Orientalism*. In it he describes how we view people of over half the world through the distorting lens of Orientalism. He also laments the fact that the West's knowledge of the East and Middle East is based on a few stereotypes that were gathered by eighteenth-century European historians. He suggests we need new knowledge that is based on facts and not on any colonial agenda designed to subjugate different nations.

In your analysis of Said's views, include his major points from the video, such as the pervasive anti-Arab and anti-Muslim media bias in the United States, and his dismissal of the "clash of civilizations" theory (such as the one presented by Samuel Huntington in his *Clash of Civilizations)*. In your view, how effective could be his concluding suggestion that we should learn to view differences in culture the way we see contrasting notes that lead to harmony in music? Comment also on his suggested recipe that consists of three words: "Coexistence without coercion."

Journaling essays that combine narration with exposition

This essay by W.E.B. Du Bois uses comic dialogue in a dramatic and tense setting to elucidate a very serious subject. We have to understand the author's playful use of several stylistic devices, such as irony, hyperbole, intentional misunderstanding, and understatement to understand the essay's profound message

On Being Crazy

It was one o'clock and I was hungry. I walked into a restaurant, seated myself, and reached for the bill of fare. My table companion rose.

"Sir," said he, "do you wish to force your company on those who do not want you?"

No, said I, I wish to eat.

"Are you aware, sir, that this is social equality?"

Nothing of the sort, sir, it is hunger – and I ate.

The day's work done, I sought the theatre. As I sank into my seat, the lady shrank and squirmed

I beg pardon, I said.

"Do you enjoy being where you are not wanted?" she asked coldly.

Oh no, I said.

"Well you are not wanted here."

I was surprised. I fear you are mistaken, I said, I certainly want the music, and I like to think the music wants me to listen to it.

"Usher," said the lady, "this is social equality."

"No, madam," said the usher, "it is the second movement of Beethoven's Fifth Symphony."

After the theatre, I sought the hotel where I had sent my baggage. The clerk scowled.

"What do you want?"

Rest, I said.

"This is a white hotel," he said.

I looked around. Such a color scheme requires a great deal of cleaning, I said, but I don't know that I object.

"We object," said he.

Then why, I began, but he interrupted.

"We don't keep niggers," he said, "we don't want social equality."

Neither do I, I replied gently, I want a bed.

I walked thoughtfully to the train. I'll take a sleeper through Texas. I'm a little bit dissatisfied with this town.

"Can't sell you one."

I only want to hire it, said I, for a couple of nights. "Can't sell you a sleeper in Texas," he maintained. "They consider that social equality." I consider it barbarism, I said, and I think I'll walk.

Walking, I met another wayfarer, who immediately walked to the other side of the road, where it was muddy. I asked his reason.

"Niggers is dirty," he said.

So is mud, said I. Moreover, I am not as dirty as you – yet.

"But you're a nigger, ain't you?" he asked.

My grandfather was so called.

"Well then!" he answered triumphantly.

Do you live in the South? I persisted, pleasantly.

"Sure," he growled, "and starve there."

I should think you and the Negroes should get together and vote out starvation.

"We don't let them vote."

We? Why not? I said in surprise.

"Niggers is too ignorant to vote."

But, I said, I am not so ignorant as you.

"But you're a nigger."

Yes, I'm certainly what you mean by that.

"Well then!" he returned, with that curiously inconsequential note of triumph. "Moreover," he said, "I don't want my sister to marry a nigger."

I had not seen his sister, so I merely murmured, let her say no.

"By God, you shan't marry her, even if she said yes."

But – but I don't want to marry her, I answered, a little perturbed at the personal turn.

"Why not?" he yelled, angrier than ever. Because I'm already married and I rather like my wife.

"Is she a nigger?" he asked suspiciously.

Well, I said again, her grandmother was called that.

"Well then!" he shouted in that oddly illogical way.

I gave up.

Go on, I said, either you are crazy or I am.

"We both are," he said as he trotted along in the mud.

W.E.B. Du Bois (1868-1963)

Journal response by the author of this book

Topic

Importance of dialogue on explosive issues.

Thesis

Sustained dialogue, patience, and a sense of humor have the power to transform.

Support

Unlike in his earlier confrontations with racists in the essay, in the final encounter the speaker has a much longer and sustained conversation with the racist individual. The speaker remains patient despite several provocations and continues to be rational and reasonable. He counters his racist interlocutor's illogic with cool and comic logic. The result is the racist individual,'s transformation into a new state of awareness: Instead of calling the speaker "crazy," he makes a crucial admission in the dialogue:

"Go on," I said, "either you are crazy or I am."

"We both are," he said, as he trotted along in the mud. The concluding lines of this essay offer the welcome hope that the words of the speaker will reverberate in the racist person's mind and function as a catalyst for change.

Style

In this essay, an outstanding element of DuBois' style is his use of humor-making devices to treat a very serious topic – that of racism.

A racist person objects to the author's sitting at the same table where he is: "Are you aware, sir, that this is social equality [social equality was not yet prevalent]?" The author responds comically with a deliberate misunderstanding: "Nothing of the sort, sir, it is hunger." Later, the author goes to a theater to enjoy a musical performance. As he comfortably sinks into his seat, the lady in the next seat objects to his presence and protests to the usher, "this is social equality," said the lady. "No, madame, it is the second movement of Beethoven's fifth Symphony," replied the usher.

After the theater, the author goes to a hotel, where the clerk tells him, "this is a white hotel." The author once again answers with intentional misunderstanding, refusing to go beyond the literal meaning of "white hotel." "Such a color scheme requires a great deal of cleaning," he said, "but I don't' know that I object." When the clerk says, "We don't keep niggers" because "we don't want social equality," the author gently replies, "Neither do I. I want a bed."

The author's last confrontation in the essay is with a person who insists on denying blacks the right to vote. When the author asks him for the reason for his view, the racist individual says in incorrect English: "Niggers is too ignorant to vote." This simple use of irony effectively and comically shows who really is ignorant. Demonstrating the utter illogicality of prejudice is the same racist person's declaration out of no where: "I don't want my sister to marry a nigger." The author's reassurance "but I don't want to marry her" makes this person angrier, and he yells, "Why not." This white person's anger suggests that he seems to subscribe to the stereotypical notion that all colored people are irresistibly drawn to whites but not vice versa. The illogic of prejudice is such that the author is damned in either case – whether he says yes or not to the question about inter-racial marriage. Like the rest of his stylistic devices, Du Bois' use of comic reduction to absurdity works very well here.

Exercises to test your mastery of Chapter Nine

1. How is the essay form different from short stories and novels?

2. Describe the structure of a typical essay written in a formal style.

3. Describe the structure of a typical informal essay.

4. Read a few of Michel de Montaigne's essays to comment on some of the characteristics of what he termed his "essais" (attempts). Use this link to read his essays, such as "Of Friendship," "Of Cannibals," and "That the Profit of One Man Is the Damage of Another." http://www.gutenberg.org/files/3600/3600-h/3600-h.htm

5. What are some of the features that the essay form has retained over the centuries?

6. Chapter Seven was devoted to teaching you how to write an essay of literary analysis and interpretation. Keeping that knowledge in mind, point out the difference between a literature-based essay and some other nonfiction varieties.

7. From Albert Camus' essay "The Myth of Sisyphus," summarize his major points that support the view that life is worth living despite the worst possible living conditions.

8. What qualities does his hero Sisyphus embody in "The Myth of Sisyphus"?

9. How can Edward Said's essay "Reflections on Exile" be regarded as a crash course on acceptance of diversity and pluralism? Use specific details from his essay.

10. Answer the five questions that are given in the "Second Exercise" of this chapter in the context of reading Bertrand Russell's essay "A Free Man's Worship."

11. Toward the end of Chapter Six, read Albert Camus' essay "Between Hell and Reason" that he wrote at the time of the bombing of Hiroshima during the Second World War. Identify the problems mentioned by Camus that still exist in world politics and pose a threat to human survival.

12. Discuss the importance of Edward Said's video essay on Orientalism in terms of its potential to promote harmony and world peace.

C H A P T E R   T E N

THE SHORT STORY

The short story has surpassed all other literary forms in popularity. The reasons for its appeal are not hard to find. Because of its short length, a story can be finished in one sitting, letting the reader have a complete experience. Since it often presents characters during a moment of crisis, a sense of drama and intensity is guaranteed. While catering to the reader's need for a good story that unfolds its events to satisfy our "What happened next" curiosity, it also becomes a means to raise important social, political, and philosophical questions. In Susan Lohafer's words, this "art form . . . [is] spare and concrete, yet riddled with meaning (Duvall 68). For all these reasons, this latest literary form has also become the most sought after. It shares with the novel the elements of theme, characters, plot, and style (specifically, the narrative point of view, setting, and atmosphere), all of which have already been explained in Chapters One through Four. If you are reading short stories for discussion or for an essay, you will find it helpful to also review the reading advice of Chapter Five, specifically on taking mental and written notes, to keep track of significant topics, themes, supporting details, and stylistic elements. *Also important for this chapter is your use of what you learned in Chapter Seven about the basic structure and organization of an interpretive essay.* Be sure to refer back to the step-by-step instructions and the two sample essays of that chapter whenever you face any difficulty in completing the assignments of this chapter.

Short stories offer many writing options. Some of them are listed below to show how you may enjoy them. Most of the suggested assignments are accompanied by sample essays that demonstrate how you can use the step-by-step instructions and two sample essays of Chapter Seven to follow as well as modify the suggested format when interpreting literary works. My brief explanatory comments introduce the essays.

Options for Writing on Short Stories

If you choose to write on any of the stories on which sample essays have been written, make sure that you offer a different perspective.

1. Using the journaling style as the basis of an essay

This variety of interpretation is a direct extension of the informal journal entry format, which was explained in Chapter Six. If you feel uncomfortable with the restraints of formal writing, at first you may start with this freer format. The only essential requirement is that you include some interpretation, without which your response would be a mere plot summary, not a discussion of the literary work's themes. Noah Reinhertz's essay on the African author Kyalo Mativo's "On the Market Day" shows how this assignment may be completed.

2. Using the formal journal as the basis for an essay with outside research sources

The formal journal format suggested coverage of these items: summary, topic, theme, supporting details, and style. A concluding comment, optional in a journal, will be necessary in an essay. Additional items (recommended but not required) include personal enrichment that the work has brought you, inclusion of a critic's helpful evaluative comment on the work being studied, and insights offered into the culture(s) that the work examines. Linked to a journal response of Chapter Six, the essay on "Odor" in this chapter exemplifies how a journal entry can lead to a research paper.

3. Journaling of short stories with limited time allowed (covered in Chapter Six)

This in-class interpretive writing exercise is students' favorite. The reason may be that you get to read an interesting new story. The instructor chooses the short story; so no time is spent on browsing just to find a story. This assignment does not give us the leisure to procrastinate. Since time is limited, with no room left for extensive daydreaming, your concentration is better. This essay can serve as a first draft for longer papers. At the end of Chapter Six there are several examples of timed responses to short stories: Samantha Gibson on Manto's story "Odor," Serrana Smith on Carson McCuller's "The Sojourner," Jeff Neilson, Renee Rose-Perry, Nick Glasser, Arjuna Sayyed, Lisa Palmer, Davina Fok, Victoria Candau, and Katherine Hijar on Camus' "The Guest."

4. Explicating stories with elusive themes

There are some stories that seem like snapshots with very few explicit clues to themes. Using inferential logic, that is, reading between the lines for implied ideas, you can speculate about significant points in a story. This method is especially suited to stories with elusive themes. Their authors make extensive and effective use of the stylistic element known as the esthetics of omission. This kind of style was discussed at some length in Chapter Four and again in Chapter Eleven in the context of reading Albert Camus' *The Stranger*, E.M. Forster's *The Passage to India*, and F. Scott Fitzgerald's *The Great Gatsby*. In the close reading involved in explication, you make interpretive comments while observing the story's chronology. Cody Corbett's essay on Albert Camus' short story "The Guest" is an example of explication. Another explication sample is my reading of Khushwant Singh's story "The Rape," which you will find on my website. The story is in this chapter under "Stories of Violations of Basic Human Rights and Urgent Social Concern." In this chapter, another story that is well-suited for this type of interpretation is Hemingway's "Hills Like White Elephants," included under "Stories for Further Reading."

5. Stories of hope in the midst of despair

Rising above the tyranny of circumstance, Ernest Gaines' "The Sky Is Gray" is one such story. Thom Lee's essay "Silver Lining in the Gray Sky" on this story exemplifies completion of this writing option.

6. Adding evaluation of an author's style to the discussion of themes

Vincent Largo's essay on the Native American author Leslie Silko's short story "Lullaby" is an example of this option. Silko's story can also be used to show how literature deals with pain to offer consolation and healing.

7. Focusing on just one central topic

Instead of discussing several major themes, you may focus on just one prominent theme or topic, state it clearly, and provide supporting details from the story. Such treatment may not be as comprehensive as the essays that cover several major themes. This is, nevertheless, another valid approach to the study of short stories. In this chapter, Lisa Embry's interpretation of Hemingway's "A Clean, Well-Lighted Place" is an example of concentrating on the story's just one major topic – existentialism.

8. Character analysis leading to a story's world of ideas

A story's themes can be accessed through character analysis. Joseph Nugent's essay "The Road to Araby – An Impossible Journey" explores the stirrings of young love with its ecstasy and heartache in James Joyce's "Araby" to exemplify this form of interpretation.

9. Interpretation through an author's style of writing

Jeffery Tarbell's reading of the story by Hemingway, "The Short Happy Life of Francis Macomber," shows how an author's style becomes a means of theme embodiment.

10. Becoming a collaborator or critic

For this assignment, you may choose the interpretation of any short story either from this book or from another source and become a collaborator with the writer of that essay. You can do so by writing a section on an aspect of the story that the interpreter did not cover. Becoming a sympathetic reader and collaborator is recommended, but if you would rather be critical of the interpreter's reading of the story, that option is also open to you. An example of this exercise is the section on the author's style that I added to Serena Hoe's essay on Chitra Divakaruni's short story "The Word Love."

11. Stories of violations of basic human rights and urgent social concern

The following stories fall in this category: Leslie Marmon Silko's "Lullaby" (also relevant to options 6, 11, and 15), Sherman Alexie's "The Only Traffic Signal on the Reservation Doesn't Flash Red Anymore," Khushwant Singh's "The Rape," Chitra Divakaruni's "The Word Love" (also relevant to option 10), William Faulkner's "A Rose for Emily," Sandra Cisnero's "Woman Hollering Creek," Lu Hsun's "A Little Incident," Amrita Pritam's "The Weed," and Alifa Rifaat's Bahiyya's Eyes," Ghalib Hamzah Abu al-Faraj's "Violets," Augusto Roa Bastos' "The Vacant Lot," Lu Hsun's "A Little Incident," and Rabindranath Tagore's "Samapti." Tagore's story is not in this book, but its film adaptation by Satyajit Ray is discussed at the end of Chapter Six. If you write on a story that is not a part of this book, attach a copy to your essay for your instructor.

12. Probing international conflicts through the clarifying lens of fiction

Kathleen Wong, Dennis Johnson, and Jennifer Hammer have offered a balanced analysis of the tragic conflict between Palestinians and Israelis. They focus on Betty Shamieh's "Tamam" and Alan Kaufman's "The Orchard." Shamieh is an American of Palestinian ancestry, and the Jewish American author Kaufman is an Israeli army veteran. Another student Melanie Tanielian's reading of Saadat Manto's "The Dog of Tithwal" concerns a similar conflict over Kashmir between India and Pakistan. Her interpretation of the story is on my website. Manto's story can be accessed online:
http://www.sikh-history.com/literature/stories/dog.html.

13. Similar themes in works by different authors

Sometimes stories share similar thematic concerns. Their comparative analysis can yield interesting results. Two stories – "Tamam" by Betty Shamieh and "Bahiyyah's Eyes" by Alifa Rifaat" – offer the promise of an interesting paper on the two stories' common theme of the plight of women in societies where women feel oppressed.

14. Probing values and systems that punish the righteous

Many times we witness painful situations in real life and in literary works when someone who does the right thing ethically but ends up in a state of isolation. Tamam in Betty Shamieh's story of the same title and Sarty in William Faulkner's short story "Barn Burning" are just two of many such characters.

15. Stories that deal with pain to offer healing and consolation

There must be a reason why tragedy is considered the highest literary form. Perhaps it is because it probes the sources of human suffering and suggests ways of coping with it. Leslie Marmon Silko's "Lullaby" (discussed under option 6) is such a story.

A note on story selections

All stories in this chapter are very well written and have timeless themes. However, there are many other good stories. After reading this chapter's stories and the sample essays on them, feel free to select stories on your own for the writing assignments of this chapter. You are asked to read some of the stories online to keep the cost of this book affordable. The cost of permission to publish some stories is extremely high. A list of links to many outstanding stories is included at the end of this chapter.

INTRODUCTION TO THE SAMPLE ESSAYS

Sample essays are used throughout this book. They are a priceless source to learn organizing strategies and interpretation techniques through close reading of texts. In the process of learning those skills, you also become familiar with some outstanding works of world literature. A bonus is learning about different cultures through their literature. Most of the papers aim for clarity and readability. The quality of some papers, however, is beyond what is ordinarily expected of students. You may want to use them as samples or as starting points for your own essays to give a different interpretation. The sample essays are also meant to facilitate your completion of various assignments. When you write your own papers after reading so many good essays on outstanding literary works, you will not only have a lot to say but also many ways to express yourself. A brief introduction accompanies every sample essay. Some of the listed assignments do not have sample essays because either they have been covered in another chapter, or they are not too challenging. As stated earlier, because of space limitations, you will need to go to my website: www.professorjabbar.com. Students have devoted a lot of time and energy in crafting their essays. They deserve a caring audience and passionate attention to derive maximum benefit from their labor of love.

Using the journaling style as the basis of an essay (option no. 1)

This chapter's opening story is by the contemporary writer, Kyalo Mativo. A sample essay follows the story.

On the Market Day

Kamali Lango woke up in the midst of the night, long before the village owl. Kokia, his wife, was already up and his food was ready: a maize meal – yesterday's leftovers – which was re-warmed in boiling water, a cup of grade-two hot coffee with a touch of powdered milk, and sour milk. He ate with relish.

He ate to a powerful munching silence. The open-air kerosene can lamp, fondly baptized Shike-n'tandike, flapped its flame noisily as if in a concerted effort to break the uncomfortable silence, and the embers on the hearth cracked in positive response. It was a familiar cracking.

One of the young ones stirred, and the parents froze. The father stopped chewing, and the mother held her breath . . . If only there was a way of destroying that dangerous smell of food . . . But the young one merely turned on his other side and fell back into sleep. That was all.

'Remember, my mother is coming here the day after the day after tomorrow,' Kokia said almost in a whisper. There was no immediate answer; he knew only too well what was on the agenda. But he had to respond in one way or another.

'Yes, I know.'
'What should I do then?'
'I intend to be back by then.'
'And if not?'

The wife was not given to prying. But in trying times vagueness is a crime.

The day after the day after tomorrow is not yet here,' he said defensively. 'There is no cause for hysteria,' he continued. 'We are not yet trashed; so we can still find a way out. Have you joined those hopeless people who go around shouting, "we shall not survive, we shall not survive, this is the end of the tether . . . this is the . . . "?

The words threatened to choke in his throat. And an obstinate sonorous echo continued to ring in his mind like an alarm clock: . . . is the end of the tether . . . the end of the tether . . . end of the tether . . . of the tether. . . .

It was indeed the end of the tether. At least as far as that unpleasant conversation was concerned. So he stood up, picked up his wrapped up blanket, his stick, his small torch, and stepped out into the dark and silent night. From across the Wingoo Valley, the faint and lonely wailing of a dog came riding the air current.

After a reflective interval, the mother lifted up the can-lamp and held it above her head as she bent to survey the young ones. Then she put out the flame and went back to sleep.

All that was routine. Last week she did the same. The week before last, she did the same. Last year, when she had only seven children, it was the same thing. And at the end of the year, when her ninth child begins to walk, she will do it again.

The man was counting his fingers as he groped his way through the dark. Well, he knew his way quite well, he has walked the same path for . . . now let's see . . . three . . . four? No, five years at least. Somehow, even during the darkest of the nights he managed to find his way. 'The sun always rises, even if not always to the Glory of God. That was his magic wand, his consolation. But a consolation.

Last year, he reckoned, he made, ooh, let's see . . . eh . . . about . . . one . . . or . . . . Yes, one hundred shillings net. He lost how many cattle? . . .

The spotted one, the sharp-horned heifer, the brown bull, the white-crowned cow, the black-topped . . . the . . . that's all. Or? Yes, that's all. Nevertheless . . . Nevertheless, the sun always rises 'even if not always to the Glory of God'. This year, if all goes well, 'I mean if the rains fall' . . . he paused for a while to wrestle with an agonizing memory. 'There used to be a thick forest here, saturated with life . . . and now all that remains is a dry whirlwind . . . Anyway this year if the rains come I could make as much as, ooh, two hundred, three hundred . . . ' But he stopped there. There was this disturbing memory, you see, that for the last two years, if he could remember well – and it was a curse to have to remember – there had been no rain, not even an imitation of it. And two or three days ago Radio Wananchi reminded the people that lack of rain, and therefore famine, are natural phenomena against which man is powerless. It added: 'Let that be known to those who are accusing the government of doing nothing; let them know that their rumour-mongering will not be tolerated.'

Kamali Lango had bought himself a transistor radio two . . . three rainy seasons ago to keep abreast with the times. And that night after the message had been relayed to the people, the peasants echoed it back and forth in the usual manner, nodding their heads to the truth of the broadcast and beating their breasts cursing the harsh, invisible and uncontrollable power so magnificently blamed by the broadcast: nature. Naturally it was their fault for failing to come together to gather the necessary money for a water project. Every fool knew it. But one thing was clear: the weather broadcasts had long ceased to bear the summarized forecasts of cold spells and low clouds. They had long turned into out-and-out political commentaries exonerating the government of the people, freely chosen in the most becoming and the latest democratic fashion in the world.

Dawn.

Down the footpath the man had gone quite a distance by now. The first glimmer of light found him still tramping; but not alone. After every other kilometre or so he met a line of villagers from beyond the mountains marching their donkeys in the opposite direction to fetch drinking-water. It was known that these villagers spent four days to accomplish that mission. And the old ones say it was the first time they had known that to happen. Ah well, it was rumour-mongering. But then so what? As the famous broadcast so aptly put it, 'you don't expect things to fall down like manna.'

'Greetings!'
'How do you fare?'
'Well. Only you.'
'And the people.'

The people - Hmm, sorry - the people are well too.

Day-break.

The naked sun rose slowly and surely, an accursed red ball of ill will. For days on end, it had risen in the same manner behind the same mountain. Sure enough, another day-break. And there, all around him, rose a sea of dust, stretching far and beyond the sky-line. It was a familiar sight and the man had long ceased to take note of it. His feet, covered with red soil, carried him triumphantly as they had always done countless times before. He cocked up his head on one side and sent a couple of bullets of spittle hurtling through the air. There was still enough saliva left all right. And when the times are good, a morning like this welcomes him like a ruling monarch; yes, it washes his feet with dew, and the clean air cleanses his foul breath. He shook his head as if to rid himself of an unpleasant thought. It was then, when he lifted his head, that he found out that actually he no longer had the monopoly of the path. He was walking ahead of and behind an ever-growing line of other people, all like him trying to beat the deadline of the tyrannical sun. The line of the people grew longer and longer, and soon there was a steady flow of men and women. Now the path was a sprightly scene of dust from which silence was banished. A spontaneous murmur came into being, changing slowly into a buzz. Jingles joined, and out of this combination a rhythm was born. There was chanting and whistling. The song leader was a fly-whisk-wielding home-made poet in his own right. He marched in the very front of the line and dished out doses of the countryside's pride, and the men joined in at the prescribed intervals while the women provided the chorus. The current song was in praise of a young man who had collected all kinds of degrees from all over the world, but who returned to his native home on foot. White civilisation had failed to annex him. He had come home to serve the people in any capacity they would assign to him The circumstances of this young man's beautiful history were once again unfolded in the song, and all natural elements bore witness to them:

LEADER

When the moon shines
It is because Mbula is out there
Visiting the people;
When the wind blows
It is because Mbula
Is there caring for the sick;
On the market day
When the sun rises

It is because Mbula
Rose up early to attend to the young;
So what do you say?

CHORUS

We have heard his footsteps
Shuffling among the reeds
And on the countryside on rainy days
We have seen his deeds;
And we have felt his tears
Trickling on our cheeks:

ALL

And he will feed the hungry
For he is the son of the country.

It was high season. Everybody knew what that meant. Even Kamali Lango couldn't quite plead innocent of it. Events were galloping to a head in the muddy arena of politics. And so was this procession. And so was the heat of the sun. And shortly they would be there.

Pancreas Mbula was already there. Unlike his opponents, he was the first to arrive. A few other people had already arrived too, but serious business hadn't begun until the group had been reinforced by the new recruits. Then he stood up and spoke about the main points of his programme: free education, free medicine, provision of irrigation projects and establishment of clinics and nursery schools in the villages where the people lived.

'But,' he went on, 'there is no substitute for self-help. We have to start somewhere, and the main force will come from you. On my part, I shall do, as I have always done, what I can to contribute to a fair social set-up. I shall persuade the government to allocate some money to these projects. I pledge myself and promise, as sure as I stand here now, to serve you with all my heart. Indeed I'm aware of what the previous Member of Parliament did during the term of his office; he abused the privilege you bestowed on him, and instead of representing you, he represented himself, his family and his close circle of friends. Ten years ago he entered the Parliament as poor as a butterfly, but ten years later he left it a fat maggot of a millionaire. And that is not all: he has the shamelessness to campaign for another term of office!'

A thunderous applause.

'I say it again as I have done several times before: the real power rests with you. Your votes are too precious to give away to a bloodsucking parasite. Let it be your choice that I be the next MP for Ngangani, and I tell you, before the end of two years, you yourselves will be the witnesses of change. If in two years no changes have occurred, then you have the right to come and say so to my face. I will deserve to be removed without hesitation.'

'What will you do about the lack of rain, son?' the tired voice of a widower demanded from the crowd.

'Well,' he cleared his throat, 'you have all heard the story on the radio about the lack of rain being a natural catastrophe. Right now, we are sitting on a pool of water, and on both sides we are flanked by two perennial rivers. Lift up your eyes,' he said, pointing away, 'do you all see that mountain towering about the clouds with a white cap on top of it? Well, that "cap" is actually a frozen lake whose water melts four times every year and trickles down the mountain-sides right through the thick forest surrounding it, zigzagging its way down the slopes. That melted water is equal to twice as much water again as we receive from natural rain. Indeed with that much water we can turn this semi-desert into a green field all year round. And we have the will and the energy for that . . .'

Another applause went out from the crowd.

'Whoever doubts that, doubts the power of the people . . .'

Another applause.

'. . . And I'm asking only to be blessed with your votes, your valuable votes, in order to make this dream a reality.' The ecstatic crowd broke into the chant:

We have heard his footsteps
Shuffling among the weeds,
And on the countryside on rainy days
We have seen his deeds;
And we have felt his tears
Trickling on our cheeks:
And he will feed the hungry
For he is the son of the country.

For Kamali Lango it was a familiar event processed in a familiar manner. He had seen and heard it all before and, like all others, had waited for the promised changes, and was still waiting. He left the scene of political action and continued on his journey.

It was now midday.

The market place was bursting with pompous peasant pride, a splendid scene of swarming flies, scorching sun, mooing cows and bellowing bulls. And from time to time, in the midst of this motley of noise, a sharp cry of agony would be heard. It was the cry of a baby demanding what in the circumstances was a simple impossibility: food. He walked right through the market from the western to the eastern section of it, until he arrived at the most familiar of all the familiar scenes: the cattle shed.

The auction was already in full swing. The smell of dung, the ceaseless mooing of the cattle, the yelling of the merchants and the boiling earth, all added to the atmosphere of cut-throat competition which brought the men into a beard-to-beard confrontation. And wielding your dagger, you stabbed and got stabbed, for it was the nature of the trade.

'There goes a majestic family bull . . . Look how he strides; what a public show of strength.' It was the auction master announcing the next candidate for raucous bidding.
'Two hundred,' shouted a prospective buyer.
'Two hundred,' repeated the auction master.
'Two hundred and fifty,' came a challenging voice.
'Two hundred and fifty . . . two hundred and fifty . . . '
'Three hundred,' yet another bidder.
'Four hundred.'
'Four hundred . . . four hundred . . . FOUR HUNDRED. The purchase has been made,' concluded the auction master.

Kamali Lango meditated for a while. He wasn't sure any more now whether he could participate in the bidding without running a risk. But then that's exactly what the thing amounted to: risk. Meanwhile another bull was put up.

'. . . A healthy animal of beefy elegance,' the master eulogised.
'Three hundred . . . three hundred . . . '
'Four hundred . . . , four hundred . . . '
'Five hundred . . . , five hundred . . . ; five . . . '

'Six hundred,' a billy-goat-like voice pierced the air with a malicious intent. That was Menge. The audience let out a murmur of indifference. The new bidder was the renowned local cattle-dealer, rumoured to possess the capability to sweep out all the cattle in stock within and outside the community at any given moment. In matters of trade, his word was final. Everybody knew it. But as a matter of formality, the auction master proceeded to make the count-down. And as he did so, a wiry, wind-blown weakling climbed down the buyers' platform and wound his way to the centre of the bargaining shed. Aware of his financial power, Menge began to drive the animal out of the shed long before the count-down was over.

'SEVEN HUNDRED!'

It wasn't just the noise which startled some people, sent others choking with laughter and left others numb. It was simply the unexpected turn of events. It was so devastating that Menge's stick fell down from his hand. He stood still for a moment like one who had been shot in the back with an arrow, then picked up his stick and walked back to the buyers' platform. He needed simply to shout 'one thousand' to silence every prospective challenger. But he wasn't going to accept a challenge from a nondescript peasant. No, he dismissed the challenge with contempt. Meanwhile the auction master had finished the count, and, like a skilful hunter that he felt himself to be at this moment, Kamali Lango stepped down and marched proudly to collect his prey. All watched him walk across the bargaining shed as he drove his new deal out.

Then he went to the cashier's desk and counted seven hundred shillings from his pocket. It was all he had.

Seven hundred shillings was his life-savings, his working capital for five years. Now that it had changed into a four-legged commodity for self-expansion, he ought to get added value of . . . ooh, . . . one . . . two hundred shillings? Who knows? Maybe more, maybe less. But he didn't need to worry about that; it wasn't the first time it had happened to him. Now, as before, there was always the rising sun.

Twilight.

That night, as always, Kamali Lango stayed with a friend of his who lived mid-way between the buying and the selling market. By sunset the next day he would go to the selling market. After selling his bull, he planned to catch a bus leaving for his home that evening. But he would get off at Kaimu market to buy two sacks of maize and then wait for the midnight bus from the coast. He would load his two sacks of maize in it and travel to Kamulamba, the country-bus station nearest to his home where his wife and three other women would be waiting. They would unload the maize, tear the sacks open and transfer the contents to three smaller baskets. They would all carry the maize home. At home his mother-in-law would be waiting. He would give her some of the maize, pay the three women with two cans full of grain each and keep the rest for his family. The supply should keep his family going until the next trip.

It was a familiar pattern. Nothing new, nothing eventful.

Dusk.

His bull behaved well and apparently didn't need a lot to eat. He gave it some grass he had been carrying for the purpose. They walked all day, the man and the animal, until they were both exhausted by the heat. So he decided to stop under a tree for a short rest. He tied the animal to a nearby twig and lay down for a small nap. The quietness of the place lulled him into a deep sleep. How long it had lasted he couldn't quite tell. When he woke up the animal was still there but this time he was also lying down. Well, it was time to go on, so he untethered the animal and patted it on the back.

Hey, up up we go.'

The animal didn't budge. So he hit it slightly with a stick.

'Up, up, I say . . . Get going.'

The animal remained immobile. He hit it harder. Still the animal didn't move. He grabbed its ears and pulled them. That didn't help either. He gave it two or three canes on the back. Then the animal lay on its back and began to kick in the air with froth coming from its mouth.

Kamali Lango dropped his luggage and hurried to open the animal's mouth. That proved to be quite a task. The animal gnashed its teeth and gave a groaning noise. Then there was silence.

It was a long while before the man picked up his remaining property: the stick, the torch, the wrapped-up blanket, and walked away. A battalion of vultures watched him go, and then inched nearer to the scene. They had been waiting impatiently all the while. Unlike the bull, these guardians of the sky had not succumbed yet to an epileptic fit.

Kamali Lango sombrely remembered that at Kamulamba his wife and three other women would be waiting with three baskets. He trudged home in bemused, wobbly steps.

Kyalo Mativo

On the Market Day in Africa
Student author: Noah Reinhertz

In his informal essay on this story by Kyalo Mativo, Noah has mixed plot summary with interpretive comments throughout the essay as some professional critics do. Instead of making thematic statements and then validating them with supporting details from the literary work, Noah has interjected interpretive comments in the midst of plot details.

Subsistence living is a state of survival consistently overlooked by developed countries. The majority of the world's people find their way – day to day – on the barest minimum needed for survival, and often on less. With a long history of exploitation by the West, the African continent is home to none too surprising fruits of imperialism: starvation, corruption, and tragedy. These themes dominate the stories of twenty African writers collected in *The Heinemann Book of Contemporary African Short Stories*. Yet to say that these stories are without hope, beauty and inspiration would be utterly false. One in particular serves to emphasize both the hardships of subsistence level existence, and the joys of a people whose hope is simply to see the next year. Written by Kyalo Mativo, a Kenyan author, "On the Market Day" is an episode of tragedy that shows the simple joys in the deep cycle of poverty and the self-renewing hardships of subsistence living.

Mativo's language is beautiful and sparse. Using images of flame and the sounds of food he opens the day well before dawn as Kamali Lango and his wife prepare for the man's journey to the market. The three opening paragraphs are like quick snap-shots, photographs of many children, and old food; delicious because of its scarcity. The man leaves for market as he has every year, sees the politicians campaigning with promises as they have every year, and buys a bull at auction as he has every year. But as he is returning to his wife where she waits with the other women as they have, year in and year out, the bull dies.

The story's simplicity is the backdrop on which Mativo hangs many images. The family has nine children; the mother, wellspring of life, watches over the ever-increasing number of mouths to feed. Kamali Lango can only earn his bread in the same way he always has, buying cattle and selling them at a higher price to get the grain his family needs to make it through the year. With constant drought, he can farm only the tiniest bit of land, and the government has offered no help, not even simple irrigation. As the man nears the market, he hears the latest ideological political hopeful raising the spirits of the people. He passes on, having heard the speech before, perhaps from a different mouth, but with no more fulfillment of promises than Kamali expects from this man.

Once my high school history teacher brought to class the recordings of a group of anthropologists who had traveled through Africa in search of music. One of the most vigorous rhythms we learned with surprise was actually the sound of many postal workers, singing as they canceled stamps in time with one another. I again saw this ability to hear the music in the mundane in Mativo's story. As Kamali is walking to the market, the sun begins to rise and with it, his spirits. More and more travelers join the path and the sound of their footfalls and the bells of their cattle create the rhythm as the men begin to sing along their trek. The simple joys of the new day and the singing of strangers are without price.

At the cattle auction, however, Kamali's small personal triumph exacts a heavy toll. Kamali rashly outbids the richest man in town for a prize bull. Whether this is a gamble for more profit or simply his need to assert some force in his life is not revealed to the reader, but Kamali swells with pride as he leads the bull away. In the heavy fog of hopelessness, Kamali's brash act shines momentarily like a bright star. His pride, however, is nowhere to be found the next day as he tugs on the rope of the bull, who lies convulsing in the hot sun, struck down by an epileptic fit. In that one moment, Kamali's endless cycle is sent spinning out of control. The women will be waiting as they always have, but he has nothing in his hands as he stumbles toward home.

The risks of gambling with resources are obvious, but was it possible for Kamali to do otherwise? At what point must a human being attempt to break a seemingly endless cycle whose only feeble promise is to see the next day? Mativo's story clearly presents a host of questions, many of which will go unanswered in the wisest of company. For the African continent still struggles for the things many Americans take for granted. Perhaps the power of such authors' writing will serve to call to the minds of the fortunate, questions that, because of their difficulty, are too often pushed aside.

Questions on "On the Market Day"

1. What do we learn about the realities of everyday life in Kenya, and by extension Africa, from this story? Describe some positive and negative aspects.
2. What role does Nature play in this story?
3. How are the political leaders viewed in this story?
4. Comment on the effectiveness of Mativo's descriptive passages and his use of spare, unadorned language.

Using the Formal Journal as the Basis for an Essay
With Outside Research Sources (option no. 2)

Odor
by Saadat Hasan Manto (1912-1955)

The text of Saadat Hasan Manto's story "Odor" is in Chapter Six. Because it is a research paper, it is longer than most essays in this chapter.

This sample essay uses the part-by-part, non-cluster thesis format. It evolved from two students' journal entries on this story in Chapter Six. The headings of "Introduction," "Thesis and support," "Main transition from content to style," and "Conclusion" are to draw your attention to the components of this essay. You should not use them in the final draft of your papers. In a long essay, it is helpful but not required to use thematic subheadings. In this essay I have used the thematic subheadings of "Not Just a Casual Affair," "A Cautionary Tale," "Common Logic versus Uncommon Passion," "Fantasizing the Real," "the Lure of Exoticism," and "the Unanswered Questions" as a focusing device and to facilitate easier reading of the essay. For the title of this essay, I am indebted to my student Cynthia Kwok.

The Primeval Scent: An Interpretation of Saadat Hasan Manto's Controversial Short Story "Bu"
Sample essay by the author of this book

Introduction (with a brief plot summary)

This is one of the stories that triggered charges of obscenity against Manto. The high court ruled in favor of Manto. Defending his writings against such charges, Manto said: "If you find my stories dirty, the society you are living in is dirty. With my stories I only expose the truth." Since so many of Manto's stories are about lives of prostitutes, pimps, and similar so-called "dregs of society," a clarifying comment is in order as to Manto's personal views. In *The Writings of Saadat Hasan Manto*, American scholar Leslie Fleming articulates Manto's position: "Taking a liberal stance, he considers men and their uncontrollable desires as responsible for prostitution and questions the double standard of moral judgment applied to men and women" (JSAL 140). Manto's own words are important here: "My question is: if a woman has honor, is a man devoid of this quality? If a woman can lose her honor, cannot a man? If the answer to these questions is yes, then why are our arrows directed only against women?" (JSAL 140-141).

With these preliminary comments in mind, let us look at Manto's short story that he titled "Bu." Steeped in nostalgia and melancholy, with reminiscence of a monsoon season as its refrain, the story reads like a lament for a lost, irretrievable connection. In Urdu literature, there is a convention known as *noha* that is a form of elegy or lament. Manto's story seems to fall into that category because throughout the entire story, the main male character Randhir's lament over his irretrievable loss seems pervasive. One of Manto's best-written stories, "Bu" is also unique in its subject matter. It is not one of his haunting stories about the Partition of British India. It ventures into the forbidden territory of a frank, honest, and candid treatment of sex. The cast of characters is quite unusual in that the main characters are neither prostitutes nor pimps. Randhir comes from the upper class. The main female character (the Ghatan girl) belongs to a much lower working class, and the woman Randhir ends up marrying comes from the upper class.

Among the challenges that this story offers, its very title "Bu" when translated into English as "Odor," is problematic. Whereas *bu* is neutral, the English word "odor" has a negative connotation. The words *khush* (pleasing) or *bud* (foul) can be added to the root word *bu* to convey the intended meaning. The importance of correct understanding of the meaning of the story's title becomes apparent as we try to arrive at a valid interpretation of the story.

The setting of Manto's "Bu" is colonial India. Randhir, a native Indian, is fascinated by Anglo women and finds them easily accessible. One reason is that in dating these women, there is no danger of crossing the line of Hindu-Muslim taboos. However, the advent of war and admission of whites only into dancing schools puts an end to Randhir's access to Anglo women. He resents this discrimination because he regards himself as handsome, "better educated, more refined, and healthier than the average Tommy." In this period of dejection, he has a brief, passionate, and chance encounter with a laborer from a neighboring factory, simply called the "Ghatan girl" in the story. From his balcony, Randhir sees her under a tamarind tree trying to shelter herself against a monsoon storm. He invites her in just to provide her shelter and offers her dry clothes with no intention of any physical intimacy. However, they end up spending the night together, consensually, with no hint of any coercion or exploitation on Randhir's part. His experience with this woman, whom the story makes into an earth goddess, is so intense that his memory of her becomes an obsession with Randhir. At the end of the story, during another monsoon season, we find Randhir obsessed with the memory of the Ghatan girl just after he is unhappily married to the "heart throb of the college boys" – the rich, fair-skinned daughter of a magistrate.

Thesis and support (part-by-part introduction of the thesis, followed by topic sentences and supporting details)

Manto's poetic, nostalgic, and melancholy tale of an irretrievable passion comes wrapped in an attractive package of consummate story-telling artistry with complex, interconnected themes. A low-key lament opens the story: "It was about this time of year. The monsoons had come and, outside his window, the leaves of the peepal tree danced as the raindrops fell on them. On the mahogany bed . . . a girl lay next to Randhir, their bodies clinging. Outside, in the milky . . . [darkness] of the evening, the leaves of the peepal tree swung in the breeze like a golden ornament on a woman's forehead" (Hasan 69). Taking us into Randhir's state of mind, the story suggests that after experiencing the extraordinary, the ordinary holds little appeal and that the definition of "extraordinary" is deeply personal.

Not just a casual affair

Randhir's experience with the Ghatan girl starts as a casual affair, but with passage of time, in his increasingly obsessive state of mind, it becomes central to his consciousness. The words that describe their union deserve special attention:

"For one night Randhir and the girl had been fused together . . . ; they had merged into each other and slipped down to fathomless depths where they had been transformed into pure ecstasy. . . . They had been like a little bird that soars into the blueness of the sky, higher and higher, until it becomes a motionless dot" (Jalal 46).

The above description raises this tale to the level of a mystical experience. It makes us read into Randhir's struggle a quest for the lost vision and the primeval scent that came to him like a reincarnation from a former life. He held and felt them momentarily but then lost them. In his article on Manto "The Seer of Pakistan," Ali Sethi makes a helpful comment. He sees in the image of the concluding lines of the above quotation

". . . an intimation of divine oneness. . . . From this state there can only be a comedown: Randhir returns to his social reality (does it not feel, after his recent flight, like a socially constructed *unreality*, the very opposite of what is primal and true?) and finds himself trapped in a marriage to a woman of his own class, a carefully chosen, socially coordinated *wife*. In this well-made bed, Randhir is condemned to remember and regret" (Sethi 1).

Sethi's words "an intimation of divine oneness," like the story's narrator, elevate the lower-caste Ghatan girl to the status of an earth goddess. The riveting introduction of this woman into the story and the power of her spell on the upper-class Randhir demonstrate that Manto was unimpressed by man-made social categories. A very helpful analogue, also specific to an Indian setting, is E. M. Forster's divination of a lower-caste character in his famous novel *A Passage to India*. This person is a humble and lowly *punkah* puller whose job is to stir the stagnant air in hot weather by pulling the string of a contraption that is suspended from the ceiling. In Forster's words,

"He had the strength and beauty that sometimes come to flower in Indians of low birth. When that strange race nears the dust and is condemned as untouchable, then nature remembers the physical perfection that she accomplished elsewhere, and throws out a god – not many, but one here and there, to prove to society how little its categories impress her" (Forster 217).

A cautionary tale?

Ethically inclined readers may find "Bu" a cautionary tale directed at two targets: individuals who marry for the wrong reasons and the social pressures that force such unions. The plight of Randhir and his wife at the end of the story shows that they probably paid more attention to social customs and expectations than to their own true feelings. The story gives clear evidence of Randhir's marrying the "heart-throb" of the college boys, but we do not know if she was his heart-throb as well. What he might have considered an enviable feat of "conquest" failed to satisfy his deeper hungers. It seems that feeling pressured by social norms, he blundered into marrying an upper-class woman (the daughter of a magistrate) merely for the sake of image and vanity. As a result, he finds no fulfillment in this union.

The story does not tell us anything about his wife's motivation for marriage to him. We can, however, assume that because the story takes place in India, where customs and conventions play a decisive role in marriage, she might have had little choice. That fact would then point an accusing finger at the tyranny of customs that deny individual freedom in an area as personal and private as marriage. It seems to have been the dictates of customs that, in the first place, would have made it impossible for the upper-class Randhir to think of marrying the lower-class Ghatan girl.

Common logic *versus* uncommon passion

The spell of a powerful memory captures Randhir, but he is not the only one who is ensnared by it. By making the reader feel that logic and reason may be of no help against passion, Manto makes us, at least for a brief duration, Randhir's co-conspirators against the dictates of sensibility and common sense. Those were the standards that Randhir followed when he married the upper-class woman but seems to have rejected them as the story opens. The story, ultimately, becomes an inquiry into the nature of fantasy and obsession. It compels us to consider the human fascination with the exotic – a fascination that may blend with infatuation and obsession to create a state of mind that is fatal to rationality and common sense.

Fantasizing the real

If we succeed in extricating ourselves from the spell of the story, we have to admit that it is one's fantasy that bestows a romantic aura on a person who in someone else's eyes may appear quite ordinary. The Ghatan girl seems to be an ordinary factory laborer, but in Randhir's memory and imagination, she becomes exalted into a superhuman being. If we look into Randhir's mind from a realistic point of view, he might be exaggerating the Ghatan girl's stature because of the spontaneous nature of their sexual encounter brought on by the circumstances. Inflaming Randhir's fantasy and nostalgia, moreover, may be his memory of the naturalness and directness of his union, which is in sharp contrast with the Anglo women's mechanical love-making described in the story: "in bed they were like patent medicines with directions for use" (Jalal 44). They had their naturalness camouflaged and stifled by layers of perfumed veneer.

The lure of exoticism

Relevant to the theme of the exotic are the class and language barriers. Randhir (upper class) and the Ghatan girl (lower class) do not understand each other's language, though they are from the same country. Thus the Ghatan girl is more exotic to Randhir than the Anglo women, many of whom Randhir seems to have known intimately. The strangeness, passion, exoticism, and intensity of a chance encounter like this, however, cannot be institutionalized into marriage or even a long-term relationship. Familiarity undoubtedly would dull the edge of passion. For all these reasons, we cannot see the two characters married to each other. The language and class barriers would make such a union impossible.

All of these rational considerations, however, seem to be far away from Randhir's mind as his alluring fantasy and precious memory take over the mundane reality. This complete surrender to fantasy seems to be ruining his marriage, and we cannot help feeling sympathy not only for him but also for his wife, who seems blameless and happens to walk into the life of this obsessed man.

The unanswered questions

At the end of the story, we are left wondering at several contradictory possibilities: Is Randhir's extraordinary experience with the Ghatan girl making his relationships with other women unsatisfactory, or is there another additional reason for his discontent? Should his pre-marital promiscuity – surely, not conducive to a stable, monogamous marriage – receive some of the blame for his confused state of mind? With the passage of time, will Randhir overcome his passion for the Ghatan girl and find stability in his present marriage, or, on the contrary, will his memory continue to make the acceptance of reality all but impossible? Is it possible that Randhir's memory of his experience with the Ghatan girl may act as his inner voice to extricate him and his new bride from the suffocation of an ill-conceived marriage?

Major transition from content to style

Part of the reason for the appeal of this tale of sensual-mystical passion is Manto's use of primal images of earth and water together with sense-stirring details. The "luminous gray clouds . . . had a strange glow like the one that had lurked in the Ghatan girl's breasts" (Jalal 47). This linking of the forces of nature with human beings is appropriate to depict the working out of instinctive and natural passions. Use of simile, as in the above description, is another of Manto's defining features of style. We have already noted the effective use of simile in the story's opening lines in which he compares the swaying leaves of the peepal tree to a woman's quivering facial ornament. Perhaps the most important use of simile is in the context of defining something that the narrator finds impossible to describe. It is the title word, "Bu" ("odor" in English):

It was like the fresh smell of earth sprinkled with water. . . . It was not an artificial smell like that
of lavender or *attar* [perfume], but something natural and eternal, like the relationship that has
existed between man and woman since the beginning of time (Jalal 46).

It is only through Manto's use of simile -- three of them in this brief quotation – that we come close to understanding the otherwise ineffable and elusive meaning of the story's title and its central thematic role.

Yet another feature of Manto's style is the use of refrain that punctuates the story. References to the rainy season that was the setting of Randhir's encounter with the Ghatan girl appear at the beginning, the middle, and the end of the story. The first time the reference to monsoons provides the physical setting of their meeting. Later references help communicate the passage of time and increasing hold of the elusive woman on Randhir's mind. The words of the refrain thus frame the story and draw us into the images and perceptions that make up the protagonist's consciousness.

Conclusion

Manto treats the complex subjects of sexual passion, obsession, and exoticism with subtlety, suggestiveness, and depth through his eloquent writing. Oddly, some readers still consider his work as bordering on obscenity. A more acceptable view would be to look at his work as frank explorations of the mysteries of passion and obsession. In her book *Another Lonely Voice: The Urdu Short Stories of Saadat Manto*, Leslie A. Flemming makes two illuminating comments, both of which greatly enhance our understanding of Manto's story: She mentions Manto's penchant for "sympathetically portraying characters oppressed by social institutions" (69-70) and she sees in "Bu" the "cosmic meaning of sexual relations, freed from both commercial and social restraints" (p. 116). Other critics think differently. Mahnaz Ispahani, for example, sees in this story not much more than Manto's "languorous, graphic tribute to sex" (186). Regardless of the position one may take, Manto's inimitable style and unusual themes in this story are undeniable. He was fully aware of his artistic genius and the compelling power of his stories, and he was not humble about it, as his self-created epitaph shows:

> Here lies Saadat Hasan Manto and with him lie buried all the secrets and mysteries of the art of short-story writing. . . . Under tons of earth he lies, still wondering who . . . [between] the two is the greater short-story writer: God or he (Hasan: *Bitter Fruit* xxv).

Questions on "Odor"

1. Discuss the scholar Leslie Flemming's view that this story by Manto is about the "cosmic meaning of sexual relations, freed from both commercial and social restraints."

2. Do you find it valid to apply the Greek myth of Pygmalion and Galatea to the two characters, Randhir and the Ghatan girl, in Manto's story? In the Greek myth, the sculptor Pygmalion fashions his ideal woman in Galatea, falls in love with her, and has his prayer granted to transform Galatea's statue into a real woman. To what extent do you see Odor's protagonist Randhir idolizing the Ghatan girl in the story and with what outcome? For more details about the myth, if you are not familiar with it, look it up online or in a book.

3. Discuss the effect of refrain-like repetition of "It was again the monsoon season" at strategic places in the story.

4. How effective is Manto's use of elemental imagery in the story? The images of water, earth, and fire, for example, figure prominently in this story.

5. What evidence is there in the story that the encounter between the protagonist Randhir and the Ghatan girl is something more than sexual? Support your response with arguments based on the text of the story.

6. Create a question based on this story. Your question should draw the reader deeper into the story's substance.

Explicating Stories with Elusive Themes (option no. 4)

The Guest

The schoolmaster was watching the two men climb toward him. One was on horseback, the other on foot. They had not yet tackled the abrupt rise leading to the schoolhouse built on the hillside. They were toiling onward, making slow progress in the snow, among the stones, on the vast expanse of the high, deserted plateau. From time to time the horse stumbled. Without hearing anything yet, he could see the breath issuing from the horse's nostrils. One of the men, at least, knew the region. They were following the trail although it had disappeared days ago under a layer of dirty white snow. The schoolmaster calculated that it would take them half an hour to get onto the hill. It was cold; he went back into the school to get a sweater.

He crossed the empty, frigid classroom. On the blackboard the four rivers of France, drawn with four different colored chalks, had been flowing toward their estuaries for the past three days. Snow had suddenly fallen in mid-October after eight months of drought without the transition of rain, and the twenty pupils, more or less, coming. With fair weather they would return. Daru now heated only the single room that was his lodging, adjoining the classroom and giving also onto the plateau to the east. Like the class windows, his window looked to the south too. On that side the school was a few kilometers from the point where the plateau began to slope toward the south. In clear weather could be seen the purple mass of the mountain range where the gap opened onto the desert.

Somewhat warmed, Daru returned to the window from which he had first seen the two men. They were no longer visible. Hence they must have tackled the rise. The sky was not so dark, for the snow had stopped falling during the night. The morning had opened with a dirty light, which had scarcely become brighter as the ceiling of clouds lifted. At two in the afternoon in seemed as if the day were merely beginning. But still this was better than those three days when the thick snow was falling amidst unbroken darkness with little gusts of wind that rattled the double door of the classroom. Then Daru had spent long hours in his room, leaving it only to go to the shed and feed the chickens or get some coal. Fortunately the delivery truck from Tadjid, the nearest village to the north, had brought his supplies two days before the blizzard. It would return in forty-eight hours.

Besides, he had enough to resist a siege, for the little room was cluttered with bags of wheat that the administration left as a stock to distribute to those of his pupils whose families had suffered from the drought. Actually they had all been victims because they were all poor. Every day Daru would distribute a ration to the children. They had missed it, he knew, during these bad days. Possibly one of the fathers or big brothers would come this afternoon and he could supply them with grain. It was just a matter of carrying them over to the next harvest. Now shiploads of wheat were arriving form France and the worst was over. But it would be hard to forget that poverty, that army of ragged ghosts wandering in the sunlight, the plateaus burned to a cinder month after month, the earth shriveled up little by little, literally scorched, every stone bursting into dust under one's foot. The sheep had died then by thousands and even a few men, here and there, sometimes without anyone's knowing.

In contrast with such poverty, he who lived almost like a monk in his remote schoolhouse, nonetheless satisfied with the little he had and with the rough life, had felt like a lord with his whitewashed walls, his narrow couch, his unpainted shelves, his well, and his weekly provision of water and food and suddenly this snow, without warning, without the foretaste of rain. This is the way the region was cruel to live in, even without men—who don't help matters either. But Daru had been born here. Everywhere else, he felt exiled.

He stepped out onto the terrace in front of the schoolhouse. The two men were now halfway up the slope. He recognized the horseman as Balducci, the old gendarme he had known for a long time. Balducci was holding on the end of a rope an Arab who was walking behind him with hands bound and head lowered. The gendarme waved a greeting to which Daru did no reply lost as he was in contemplation of the Arab dressed in a faded blue jellaba, his feet in sandal but covered with socks of heavy raw wool, his head surmounted by a narrow, short crèche. They were approaching Balducci was holding back his horse in order not to hurt the Arab, and the group was advancing slowly.

Within earshot, Balducci, shouted: "One hour to do the three kilometers from El Ameur!" Daru did not answer. Short and square in his thick sweater, he watched them climb. Not once had the Arab raised his head. "Hello," said Daru when they got up onto the terrace. "Come in and warm up." Balducci painfully got down from his horse without letting go of the rope. From under his bristling mustache he smiled at the schoolmaster. His little dark eyes deep set under a tanned forehead, and his mouth surrounded with wrinkles made him look attentive and studious. Daru took the bridle, led the horse to the shed, and came back to the two men, who were now waiting for him in the school. He led them into his room. "I am going to heat up the classroom," he said. "We'll be more comfortable there." When he entered the room again Balducci was on the couch. He had undone the rope tying him to the Arab who had squatted near the stove. His hands still bound, the cliché pushed back on his head, he was looking toward the window. At first Daru noticed only his huge lips, fat, smooth, almost Negroid; yet his nose was straight, his eyes were dark a full of fever. The cliché revealed an obstinate forehead and, under the weathered skin now rather discolored by the cold, the whole face had a restless and rebellious look that struck Daru when the Arab, turning his face toward him, looked him straight in the eyes. "Go into the other room," said the schoolmaster, "and I'll make you some mint tea." "Thanks," Balducci, said. "What a chore! How I long for retirement." And addressing his prisoner in Arabic: "Come on, you." The Arab got up and, slowly, holding is bound wrists in front of him, went into the classroom.

With the tea, Daru brought a chair. But Balducci was already enthroned on the nearest pupil's desk and the Arab had squatted against the teacher's platform facing the stove, which stood between the desk and the window. When he held out the glass of tea to the prisoner, Daru hesitated at the sight of his bound hands. "He might perhaps be untied." "Sure," said Balducci. "That was for the trip." He started to get to his feet. But Daru, setting the glass on the floor, had knelt beside the Arab. Without saying anything, the Arab watched him with his feverish eyes. Once his hands were free, he rubbed his swollen wrists against each other, took the glass of tea, and sucked p the burning liquid in swift little sips.

"Good," said Daru. "And where are you headed?"

Balducci withdrew his mustache from the tea. "Here, son."

"Odd pupils! And you're spending the night?"

"No, I'm going back to El Ameur. And you will deliver this fellow to Tinguit. He is expected at police headquarters."

Balducci was looking at Daru with a friendly little smile.

"What's this story?" asked the schoolmaster. "Are you pulling my leg?"

"No, son. Those are the orders."

"The orders? I'm not . . ." Daru hesitated, not wanting to hurt the old Corsican. "I mean, that's not my job."

"What! What's the meaning of that? In wartime people do all kinds of jobs."

"Then I'll wait for the declaration of war!"

Balducci nodded.

"O.K. But the orders exist and they concern you too. Things are brewing, it appears. There is task of a forthcoming revolt. We are mobilized, in a way."

Daru still had his obstinate look.

"Listen, son," Balducci said. "I like you and you must understand. There's only a dozen of us at El Ameur to patrol throughout the whole territory of a small department and I must get back in a hurry. I was told to hand this guy over to you and return without delay. He couldn't be kept there. His village was beginning to stir; they wanted to take him back. You must take him to Tinguit tomorrow before the day is over. Twenty Kilometers shouldn't faze a husky fellow like you. After that, all will be over. You'll come back to your pupils and your comfortable life."

Behind the wall the horse could be heard snorting and pawing the earth. Daru was looking out the window. Decidedly, the weather was clearing and the light was increasing over the snowy plateau. When all the snow was melted, the sun would take over again and once more would burn the fields of stone. For days, still, the unchanging sky would shed its dry light on the solitary expanse where nothing had any connections with man.

"After all," he said, turning around toward Balducci, "what did he do?" And, before the gendarme had opened his mouth, he asked: "Does he speak French?"

"No, not a word. We had been looking for him for a month, but they were hiding him. He killed his cousin."

"Is he against us?"

"I don't think so. But you can never be sure."

"Why did he kill?"

"A family squabble, I think. One owed the other grain, it seems. It's not at all clear. In short, he killed his cousin with a billhook. You know, like a sheep, kreezk!"

Balducci made the gesture of drawing a blade across his throat and the Arab, his attention attracted, watched him with a sort of anxiety. Daru felt a sudden wrath against the man, against all men with their rotten spite, their tireless hates, their blood lust.

But the kettle was singing on the stove. He served Balducci more tea, hesitated, then served on the stove. He served Balducci more tea, hesitated, then served the Arab again, who, a second time, drank avidly. His raised arms made the jellaba fall open and the schoolmaster saw his thin, muscular chest.

"Thanks, kid," Balducci said. "And now, I'm off."

He got up and went toward the Arab, taking a small rope from his pocket.

"What are you doing?" Daru asked dryly.

Balducci, disconcerted, showed him the rope.

"Don't bother."

The old gendarme hesitated. "It's up to you. Of course, you are armed?"

"I have my shotgun."

"Where?"

"In the trunk."

"You ought to have it near your bed."

"Why? I have nothing to fear."

"You're crazy, son. If there's an uprising, no one is safe, we're all in the same boat."

"I'll defend myself. I'll have time to see them coming."

Balducci began to laugh, then suddenly the mustache covered the white teeth. "You'll have time? O.K. That's just what I was saying. You have always been a little cracked. That's why I like you, my son was like that."

At the same time he took out his revolver and put in on the desk.

"Keep it; I don't need two weapons from here to El Ameur."

The revolver shone against the black paint of the table. When the gendarme turned toward him, the schoolmaster caught the smell of leather and horseflesh.

"Listen, Balducci," Daru said suddenly, "every bit of this disgusts me, and first of all your fellow here. But I won't hand him over. Fight, yes, if I have to. But not that."

The old gendarme stood in front of him and looked at him severely.

"You're being a fool," he said slowly. "I don't like it either. You don't get used to putting a rope on a man even after years of it, and you're even ashamed—yes, ashamed. But you can't let them have their way."

"I won't hand him over," Daru said again.

"It's an order, son, and I repeat it."

"That's right. Repeat to them what I've said to you: I won't hand him over."

Balducci made a visible effort to reflect. He looked at the Arab and at Daru. At last he decided.

"No, I won't tell them anything. If you want to drop us, go ahead; I'll not denounce you. I have an order to deliver the prisoner and I'm doing so. And now you'll just sign the paper for me."

"There's no need. I'll not deny that you left him with me."

"Don't be mean with me. I know you'll tell the truth. You're from hereabouts and you are a man. But you must sign, that's the rule."

Daru opened his drawer, took out a little square bottle of purple ink, the red wooden penholder with the "sergeant-major" pen he used for making models of penmanship, and signed. The gendarme carefully folded the paper and put it into his wallet. Then he moved toward the door.

"I'll see you off," Daru said.

"No," said Balducci. "There's no use being polite. You insulted me."

He looked at the Arab, motionless in the same spot, sniffed peevishly, and turned away toward the door. "Good-by, son," he said. The door shut behind him. Balducci appeared outside the window and then disappeared. His footsteps were muffled by the snow. The horse stirred on the other side of the wall and several chickens fluttered in fright. A moment later Balducci reappeared outside the window leading the horse by the bridle. He walked toward the little rise without turning around and disappeared from sight with the horse following him. A big stone could be heard bouncing down. Daru walked back toward the prisoner, who, without stirring, never took his eyes off him. "Wait," the schoolmaster said in Arabic and went toward the bedroom. As he was going through the door, he had a second thought, went to the desk, took the revolver, and stuck it in his pocket. Then, without looking back, he went into his room.

For some time he lay on his couch watching the sky gradually close over, listening to the silence. It was this silence that had seemed painful to him during the first days here, after the war. He had requested a post in the little town at the base of the foothills separating the upper plateaus from the desert. There, rocky walls, green and black to the north, pink and lavender to the south, marked the frontier of eternal summer. He had been named to a post farther north, on the plateau itself. In the beginning, the solitude and the silence had been hard for him on these wastelands peopled only by stones. Occasionally, furrows suggested cultivation, but they had been dug to uncover a certain kind of stone good for building. The only plowing here was to harvest rocks. Elsewhere a thin layer of soil accumulated in the hollows would be scarped out to enrich paltry village gardens. This is the way it was: bare rock covered three quarters of the region. Town sprang up, flourished, then disappeared; men came by, loved one another or fought bitterly, then died. No one in this desert, neither he nor his guest, mattered. And yet, outside this desert neither of them, Daru knew, could have really lived.

When he got up, no noise came from the classroom. He was amazed at the unmixed joy he derived from the mere thought that the Arab might have fled and that he would be alone with no decision to make. But prisoner was there. He had merely stretched out between the stove and the desk. With eyes open, he was staring at the ceiling. In that position, his thick lips were particularly noticeable, giving him a pouting look, "Come," said Daru. The Arab got up and followed him. In the bedroom, the schoolmaster pointed to a chair near the table under the window. The Arab sat down without taking his eyes off Daru.

"Are you hungry?"

"Yes," the prisoner said.

Daru set the table for two. He took flour and oil, shaped a cake in a frying pan, and lighted the little stove that functioned on bottled gas. While the cake was cooking, he went out to the shed to get cheese, eggs, dates, and condensed mild. When the cake was done he set it on the window still to cool, heated some condensed milk diluted with water, and beat up the eggs into an omelette. In one of his motions he knocked against the revolver stuck in his right pocket. He set the bowl down, went into the classroom, and put the revolver in his desk drawer. When he came back to the room, night was falling. He put on the light and served the Arab. "Eat," he said. The Arab took a piece of the cake, lifted it eagerly to his mouth, and stopped short.

"And you?" he asked.

"After you. I'll eat too."

The think lips opened slightly. The Arab hesitated, then bit into the cake determinedly.

The meal over, the Arab looked at the schoolmaster.

"Are you the judge?"

"No, I'm simply keeping you until tomorrow."

"Why do you eat with me?"

"I'm hungry."

The Arab fell silent. Daru got up and went out. He brought back a folding bed from the shed, set it up between the table and the stove, perpendicular to his own bed. From a large suitcase which upright in a corner, served as a shelf for papers, he took two blankets and arranged them on the camp bed. Then he stopped, felt useless and sat down on his bed. There was nothing more to do or to get ready. He had to look at this man. He looked at him, therefore, trying to imagine his face bursting with rage. He couldn't do so. He could see nothing but the dark yet shining eyes and the animal mouth.

"Why did you kill him?" he asked in a voice whose hostile tone surprised him.

The Arab looked away. "He ran away. I ran after him."

He raised his eyes to Daru again and they were full of a sort of woeful interrogation. "Now what will they do to me?"

"Are you afraid?"

He stiffened, turning his eyes away.

"Are you sorry?"

The Arab stared at him openmouthed. Obviously he did not understand. Daru's annoyance was growing. At the same time he felt awkward and self-conscious with his big body wedged between the two beds.

"Lie down there," he said impatiently. "That's your bed."

The Arab didn't move. He called to Daru:

"Tell me!"

The schoolmaster looked at him.

"Is the gendarme coming back tomorrow?"

"I don't know."

"Are you coming with us?"

"I don't know. Why?"

The prisoner got up and stretched out on top of the blankets his feet toward the window. The light from the electric bulb shone straight into his eyes and he closed them at once.

"Why?" Daru repeated, standing beside the bed.

The Arab opened his eyes under the blinding light and looked at him, trying not to blink.

"Come with us," he said.

In the middle of the night, Daru was still not asleep. He had gone to bed after undressing completely; he generally slept naked. But when he suddenly realized that he had nothing on, he hesitated. He felt vulnerable and the temptation came to him to put his clothes back on. Then he shrugged his shoulders; after all, he wasn't a child and, if need be, he could break his adversary in two. From his bed he could observe him, lying on his back, still motionless with his eyes closed under the harsh light. When Daru turned out the light, the darkness seemed to coagulate all of a sudden. Little by little, the night came back to life in the window where the starless sky was stirring gently. The schoolmaster soon made out the body lying at his feet. The Arab still did not move, but his eyes seemed open. A faint wind was prowling around the schoolhouse. Perhaps it would drive away the clouds and the sun would reappear.

During the night the wind increased. The hens fluttered a little and then were silent. The Arab turned over on his side with his back to Daru, who thought he heard him moan. Then he listened for his guest's breathing, become heavier and more regular. He listened to that breath so close to him and mused without being able to go to sleep. In this room where he had been sleeping alone for a year, this presence bothered him. But it bothered him also by imposing on him a sort of brotherhood he knew well but refused to accept in the present circumstances. Men who share the same rooms, soldiers or prisoners, develop a strange alliance as if, having cast off their armor with their clothing they fraternized every evening, over and above their differences, in the ancient community of dream and fatigue. But Daru shook himself; he didn't like such musings, and it was essential to sleep.

A little later, however, when the Arab stirred slightly, the schoolmaster was still not asleep. When the prisoner made a second move, he stiffened, on the alert. The Arab was lifting himself slowly on his arms with almost the motion of a sleepwalker. Seated upright in bed, he waited motionless without turning his head toward Daru, as if he were listening attentively. Daru did no stir; it had just occurred to him that the revolver was still in the drawer of his desk. It was better to act at once. Yet he continued to observe the prisoner, who, with the same slithery motion, put his feet on the ground, waited again, then began to stand up slowly. Daru was about to call out to him when the Arab began to walk, in a quite natural but extraordinary silent way. He was heading toward the door at the end of the room that opened into the shed. He lifted the latch with precaution and went out, pushing the door behind him but without shutting it. Daru had not stirred. "He is running away," he merely thought. "Good riddance!" Yet he listened attentively. The hens were not fluttering; the guest must be on the plateau. A faint sound of water reached him, and he didn't know what it was until the Arab came back to bed without a sound. Then Daru turned his back on him and fell asleep. Still later he seemed, from the depths of his sleep, to hear furtive steps around the schoolhouse. "I'm dreaming! I'm dreaming!" he repeated to himself. And he went on sleeping.

When he awoke, the sky was clear; the loose window let in a cold, pure air. The Arab was asleep, hunched up under the blankets now, his mouth open, utterly relaxed. But when Daru shook him, he started dreadfully, staring at Daru with wild eyes as if he had never seen him and such a frightened expression that the schoolmaster stepped back. "Don't be afraid. It's me. You must eat." The Arab nodded his head and said yes. Calm had returned to his face, but his expression was vacant and listless.

The coffee was ready. They drank it seated together on the folding bed as they munched their pieces of the cake. Then Daru led the Arab under the shed and showed him the faucet where he washed. He went back into the room, folded the blankets and the bed, made his own bed and put the room in order. Then he went through the classroom and out onto the terrace. The sun was already rising in the blue sky; a soft, bright light was bathing the deserted plateau. On the ridge the snow was melting in spots. The stones were about to reappear. Crouched on the edge of the plateau, the schoolmaster looked at the deserted expanse. He thought of Balducci. He had hurt him for he had sent him off in a way as if he didn't want to be associated with him. He could still hear the gendarme's farewell and, without knowing

279

why, he felt strangely empty and vulnerable. At that moment, from the other side of the schoolhouse, the prisoner coughed. Daru listened to him almost despite himself and then, furious, threw a pebble that whistled through the air before sinking into the snow. That man's stupid crime revolted him, but to hand him over was contrary to honor. Merely thinking of it made him smart with humiliation. And he cursed at one and the same time his own people who had sent him this Arab and the Arab who had dared to kill and not managed to get away. Daru got up, walked in a circle on the terrace, waited motionless, and then went back into the schoolhouse.

The Arab, leaning over the cement floor of the shed was washing his teeth with two fingers. Daru looked at him and said: "Come." He went back into the room ahead of the prisoner. He slipped a hunting jacket on over his sweater and put on walking shoes. Standing, he waited until the Arab had put on his cleche and sandals. They went into the classroom and the schoolmaster pointed to the exit, saying: "Go ahead." The fellow didn't budge. "I'm coming," said Daru. The Arab went out. Daru went back into the room and made a package of pieces of rusk, dates, and sugar. In the classroom, before going out, he hesitated a second in front of his desk, then crossed the threshold and locked the door. "That's the way," he said. He started toward the east, followed by the prisoner. But, a short distance from the schoolhouse, he thought he heard a slight sound behind them. He retraced his steps and examined the surroundings of the house; there was no one there. The Arab watched him without seeming to understand. "Come on," said Daru.

They walked for an hour and rested beside a sharp peak of limestone. The snow was melting faster and faster and the sun was drinking up the puddles at once, rapidly cleaning the plateau, which gradually dried and vibrated like the air itself. When they resumed walking, the ground rang under their feet. From time to time a bird rent the space in front of them with a joyful cry. Daru breathed in deeply the fresh morning light. He felt a sort of rapture before the vast familiar expanse, now almost entirely yellow under its dome of blue sky. They walked an hour more, descending toward the south. They reached a level height made up of crumbly rocks. From there on, the plateau sloped down, eastward toward a low plain where there were a few spindly trees and, to the south, toward outcroppings of the rock that gave the landscape a chaotic look.

Daru surveyed the two directions. There was nothing but the sky on the horizon. Not a man could be seen. He turned toward the Arab, who was looking at him blankly. Daru held out the package to him. "Take it," he said. "There are dates, bread, and sugar. You can hold out for two days. Here are a thousand francs too." The Arab took the package and the money but kept his full hands at chest level as if he didn't know what to do with what was being given him. "Now look," the schoolmaster said as he pointed in the direction of the east, "there's the way to Tinguit. You have a two-hour walk. At Tinguit you'll find the administration and the police. They are expecting you." The Arab looked toward the east, still holding the package and the money against his chest. Daru took his elbow and turned him rather roughly toward the south. At the foot of the height on which they stood could be seen a faint path. "That's the trail across the plateau. In a day's walk from here you'll find pasturelands and the first nomads. They'll take you in and shelter you according to their law." The Arab had now turned toward Daru and a sort of panic was visible in his expression. "Listen," he said. Daru shook his head: "No, be quiet. Now I'm leaving you," He turned his back on him, took two long steps in the directions of the school, looked hesitantly at the motionless Arab, and started off again. For a few minutes he heard nothing but his own step resounding on the cold ground and did not turn his head. A moment later, however, he turned around. The Arab was still there on the edge of the hill, his arms hanging now, and he was looking at the schoolmaster. Daru felt something rise in his throat. But he swore with impatience, waved vaguely, and started off again. He had already gone some distance when he again stopped and looked. There was no longer anyone on the hill.

Daru hesitated. The sun was now rather high in the sky and was beginning to eat down on his head. The schoolmaster retraced his steps, at first somewhat uncertainly, then with decision. When he reached the little hill, he as bathed in sweat. He climbed it as fast as he could and stopped, out of breath, at the top. The rock fields to the south stood out sharply against the blue sky, but on the plain to the east a steamy heat was already rising. And in that slight haze, Daru, with heavy heart, made out the Arab walking slowly on the road to prison.

A little later, standing before the window of the classroom, the schoolmaster was watching the clear light bathing the whole surface of the plateau, but he hardly saw it. Behind him on the blackboard among the winding French rivers, sprawled the clumsily chalked-up words he had just read: "You handed over our brother. You will pay for this." Daru looked at the sky, the plateau, and, beyond, the invisible lands stretching all the way to the sea. In this vast landscape he had loved so much, he was alone.

Albert Camus (1913-1960)

"The Guest": An Existential Perspective on Life
Student author: Cody Corbett

Cody explicates "The Guest" to trace elements of existentialism in French author Camus' famous story. Even though Camus refused to be called an existentialist and even titled one of his essays, "No I Am Not an Existentialist," there are unmistakable existentialist themes in his work. Such themes were the spirit of the time between the two World Wars and no artist could escape their influence. Among the tenets of existentialist thought, notable are the following:

- *"Existence precedes essence." (Jean-Paul Sartre's words emphasize the necessity of existing, living, and experiencing before one can arrive at his or her own essence.)*

- *Preoccupation with the micro-moments of the fleeting NOW.*

- *Belief in individual integrity.*

- *Leaving out dogma and social rituals that are contrary to an individual's true feelings.*

- *Utmost honesty.*

- *Absurdity – defined by Camus as the clash between these two forces: human longing for clarity and order versus the random nature of the way the world operates.*

- *Inadequacy of reason to explain the complexity of the universe.*

"The Guest" takes place in a desolate area of North Africa involving a French school teacher and an Arab prisoner in custody on charges of murder. The town constable, Balducci, leads the bound prisoner to the house of Daru, the local school master, and hands custody of the Arab over to him for further transport to the neighboring town's jurisdiction. Refusing to do so at first, Daru has no choice but to accept the job in a war-torn world that intrudes into his peaceful sanctuary. What follows is a day-long engagement between the two men and an insight into an important existential perspective on life.

Daru comes to realize that the Arab is a man of honor and integrity and refuses to force him to go to prison, as it would be contrary to his true feelings; his belief in individual integrity outweighs his duty to perform his task, and he gives the Arab a choice between prison and freedom. The story concludes on a shockingly absurd note with the Arab prisoner choosing prison over freedom and Daru receiving a threat of retribution for something he has not done: He did not hand over the Arab prisoner to the authorities but is suspected of doing so by the Arab's friends who do not know the facts.

The story's central theme concerns the complexity of human nature and the difficulty of living according to one's values when they conflict with society's expectations. Truthfulness and an almost apathetic honesty of an existentialist can be one's downfall when operating within the norms of society. The Arab is presented as being incapable of lying or deception. Given that fact, is it possible that he is capable of committing murder? The truth, we learn, is that he did kill his cousin, but the story does not given us any credible reason for the murder. In the absence of any evidence other than the action of the prisoner – going quietly to his sentence as a matter of integrity (much as Meursault goes to his death in *The Stranger*) – the story forces us to ask if a killer and a man of exemplary honor can coexist in the same person? Society rightly demands justice, but is it possible, the story seems to ask, that justice can go awry and may be on the side of the offender (the prosecutors) in this case? Hence the paradox and the tragedy of the situation: On the basis of what Daru has come to know of the Arab during the short time of forced coexistence, he deduces the Arab should go free. At the same time, the unalterable, fatal, and wonderful trait of character that is Daru's honest nature will not allow him to cheat society either. Hence his decision to let the Arab choose his own course.

Camus' second theme that concerns the difficulty of living strictly by one's own values is demonstrated by the fact that Daru does everything to escape violence and conflict. He chooses to live in a desolate area, doing an honorable job of teaching poor Arab pupils. However, life finds him out in his hiding place in the desert-like setting, which he thought would be immune from the violence of the world. He is not only saddled with the unpleasant task of handing over the Arab prisoner to the authorities. He, moreover, receives a threat from the friends of the Arab who mistakenly hold Daru responsible for the Arab prisoner's going into police custody.

Camus chooses a setting that captures the story's mood. The barren plateau acts as a metaphor for the state of mind adopted by the individual existentialist thinker Daru – not exactly lost, but utterly alone. The story's main characters – Daru and the Arab prisoner – are totally apathetic about the world they are placed in. Each is created through Camus' writing to simply exist in the situation, not to change or make sense of it, but to experience it. This, too, is a central credo of the existentialist mind, that one does not experience life depending on the rules of any master plan; one simply is, or is not. Existence is futile; thus apathy follows. Without being an avowed existentialist piece, "The Guest" nevertheless makes some of the elusive elements of existentialism understandable. That philosophy was born as a result of the events of the twentieth century between the two World Wars and remains equally relevant to the events of today.

Questions on "The Guest"

1. Between the host (Daru) and the guest (the Arab prisoner) whom do you consider the story's hero? Can we say that both of them are heroes in their own separate ways?

2. Comment on the haunting stillness of Camus' style in this story. Include an analysis of his use of esthetics of omission and his understated way of presenting intense emotions. Esthetics of omission consists of an author's intentional exclusion of details that are expected and awaited by the reader. If you need help with understanding this stylistic device, Chapters Four and Eleven have that information.

3. The story is unique in that it seems to have two endings – both equally wrenching. Identify each of the two high points of the story. Evaluate Camus' use of the stylistic elements of setting and imagery. How effective are they in reflecting the story's themes?

4. Many statements from the story could be considered thematic. Copy one of them.

5. Why is Daru reluctant to hand over the Arab prisoner to the authorities?

Hope in the Midst of Despair (option no. 5)

The Sky Is Gray
by Ernest Gaines (b. 1933)

Watch the excellent 1980 film adaptation of Gaines' story starring Olivia Cole, preferably as a class. Your instructor can arrange to show this half-hour long film. If you cannot watch the film, you can read the story from a library book. Because of very high permissions cost, the story's text could not be included in this book.

Silver Lining in the Gray Sky
Student author: Thom Lee

After a brief introduction, consisting of a comment on how the title of the story reflects its substance, Thom uses a cluster thesis statement, in which he mentions all three of the major themes. The rest of the essay is an orderly discussion of each theme that he introduces with a suitably worded topic sentence. All relevant supporting details from the story are tied to the topic sentences. The concluding comment emphasizes Ernest Gaines' optimism in spite of the turbulent race relations. The time of the story is during World War II, which explains why James' father had to join the army.

The title of Ernest Gaines' story "The Sky is Gray" prepares the reader for the depressed psychological atmosphere that looms over the lives of Southern Blacks. It also suggests that the human spirit's potential, like the boundless skies, can become limited by the clouds of social injustice. Gray, the mixture of black and white, is symbolic of the delicate balance of relations between the two races. The author employs such imagery to warn of the impending storms of political upheaval that are to occur if social injustice is not rectified.

The major theme of the story is that the innate dignity of the human spirit cannot be debased despite the dehumanizing effects of racism and poverty. Spiritual strength, however, is not gained merely by surviving adverse life conditions. That is why Gaines believes that one must also have the courage to challenge the false values of the status quo; otherwise complacent acceptance can lead to rigidity and submission. The story, moreover, contains a warning that the creation of two parallel societies alienated from one another can make relations between the groups extremely difficult.

Octavia, the mother in this story, clearly personifies the tenacious will of the human spirit to uphold dignity under such oppressive forces as poverty and racism. Her fighting spirit is illustrated in her refusal to surrender to the grief of losing her husband. Rather than wallow in self pity, she redirects her hopes and ambitions towards her son, James. In order to prepare James for the rigors of a harsh reality, Octavia first tells James that he must assume the responsibilities of a man. She constantly reprimands him for crying or showing any other forms of weak and what she considers unmanly behavior. In one scene, She forces him to kill the redbirds he had captured for their dinner. James tearfully resists at first, but finally submits to his mother's goading. The success of her lesson in survival is evident when, at the dinner table, James finally realizes the responsibility he has towards providing for a family. "Suppose she [his mother] had to go away like Daddy went away? Then who'd look after us?" James also concludes that being a man not only entails withstanding pain, but that one must always think of others' welfare and be able to provide for one's family.

Another example of Octavia's determination to temper James' spirit is during their trip into town. As a result of being denied a visit to the dentist, Octavia and James proceed to wander about town trying to pass the time until the dentist is available. Despite the icy and vicious sleet, Octavia speeds along with an obsessive vitality that seems amazing to James. James displays "manly behavior" when despite the hunger pangs, the bone chilling cold, and an aching tooth, he utters not one word of complaint. Octavia's love is reflected in James' awareness that expression of weakness on his part would hurt his mother. He therefore becomes even more determined to bear his discomfort. When they enter the restaurant to eat, James at first refuses the food, lying and saying that he isn't hungry.

James' desire to provide comfort and joy to his mother is shown in his determination to buy her a brand new red coat when he has enough money. After they have traversed the length of town several times, Helena, an old white lady, asks them to come in. Helena sympathizes with James and his mother and, under the pretense of wanting her garbage moved, invites them to share her food. Octavia declares that receiving handouts is beneath her dignity, showing James that despite their impoverished condition, they are not beggars. After James moves the empty garbage cans, they prepare to leave Helena's house. When James automatically turns up his collar to shield himself from the cold, Octavia tells him to turn his collar back down saying, "You not a bum, you a man." This mother-son relationship shows responsible nurturing on the mother's part, and the deep love, respect, and understanding that James has for her. James' self-worth wells up after his mother declared him a man, making him feel that now he is capable of earning a living.

The next notable theme concerning the damaging consequences of complacent acceptance of injustice is illustrated by the debate between the student and the preacher, both of whom are African Americans. The student represents the seed of radical change while the preacher exemplifies the oppressive weight of past traditions. The total lack of respect the student has for past values is the result of his circumstances. Having lost his father and witnessed his mother working herself to death, the student is personally free of past dogmas, yet not ignorant of the abstract forces that oppress him and his people. The fact that he washes dishes to pay his way through college and further his education indicates his intense desire to investigate and communicate the causes of his people's suffering. He links the cause of their oppression to their passivity and silence: "We don't question is exactly our problem. . . ." He also recognizes the difficulty in articulating the causes of their oppression in a language his people can understand and, therefore, encourages them to: ". . . question and question – question everything. Every star, every stripe, every spoken word."

The student's relentless questioning of his people's basic assumptions, from the existence of God to the color of wind, does in fact break the complacent mode of thinking that characterizes other blacks among his audience. The student not only goads them to ponder more deeply the concepts of liberty, freedom, and citizenship rights, but he also becomes a living example of courage and change. He refuses to accept the fate that society has thrust on him by declaring, "Some way or the other I'm going to make it." This is also shown vividly by his audacious questioning of the preacher's most cherished beliefs. After the preacher accuses the student of calling him submissive and ignorant and proceeds to punch him, the student displays great courage and tolerance by offering the other cheek. In this situational irony, the priest is violent whereas the student embodies the virtues of tolerance and self-control.

Gaines uses other ironic examples as well to describe the hypocrisy of the old value system. A woman asks the preacher, "I wonder why the Lord let a child like that suffer?" to which the preacher replies, "Not for us to question." She then comments, "And looks like it's the poor that suffers the most . . ." and the preacher answers back, "Best not even to try, He works in mysterious ways . . ." The dogmas that the preacher reverts back to illustrate how complacent acceptance of one's dishonorable place in society under the guise of "fate" can crush the human spirit and lead to hypocrisy. His answers typify how total submission to an abstract ideal can also ruin one's capacity for independent and critical thinking. The preacher's intolerance and rigidity is shown when he debases himself by twice punching the student. The preacher's protruding belly and dangling gold chain is symbolic of his bondage to a racist value system that keeps him well fed, yet causes his own people to suffer.

How racism creates two parallel societies alienated from one another – the story's third prominent theme – is graphically shown when Octavia and James wander through town. While hunger and cold seem like old companions to James, the white people seem warm and well fed inside their restaurants and boutiques. James is well aware of this duality when he comments to himself, "We pass by another café, but this'n for white people, too, and we can't go in there, either." Clearly, the position that blacks occupy in life seems to be as an outsider looking in. In another example, after the dentist refuses to admit any more patients, a woman comforts Octavia by saying, "Don't feel 'jected, honey. I been around them a long time – they take you when they want to. If you was white, that's something else; but we the wrong color." The fact that whites occupy positions such as dentists and shop owners also indicates the economic privileges whites enjoy solely on the basis of skin color in this story.

The last part of the story portrays how simple human kindness must be disguised in order to bypass the rigid code of behavior inherited from a racist value system. Helena, an old white lady, sympathizes with Octavia and her son when she sees them passing by several times in the freezing cold. But in order to offer them relief from the cold, she pretends that she needs her garbage moved. Helena must impress upon Octavia that this act simply is a business deal and she in no way sympathizes with their condition: "The boy'll have to work for it. It isn't for free. I'm old but I have my pride, too . . ." The fact that the garbage cans were empty and the food plentiful betrays Helena's outward business-like attitude. Octavia must in turn make a pretense at "holding her own," stating, "We don't take no handouts." Later when Octavia purchases twenty five cents worth of salt meat and Helena gives her more than the purchased price, Octavia flatly refuses. Octavia must also show that despite their lowly position, they too have their pride. The elaborate pretenses that people must make in order to express simple human kindness is symptomatic of a segregated and unequal society.

Although the setting of "The Sky is Gray" is the American South it is also descriptive of race relations throughout the world. Gaines neither preaches nor is overtly political; instead he focuses on the psychological effects of racism and poverty. Each character possesses a rich, distinct, and complex psychological make-up. Having journeyed through the internal complexities of each character, one senses in each of them a record and a fear of the terrible storms of racial upheaval that are threatening to burst. The story is not without hope, for James and the student do represent the promise of a courageous new generation of young people who will not only survive the storms, but emerge with the light of understanding and humanity in their eyes.

Questions on "The Sky is Gray"

1. What is the role of the white couple – Helena and Alnest – at the end of the story?

2. Ernest Gaines makes the eight-year boy the narrator of the story. The difficulty of this choice is obvious: The author is limited to the vocabulary and thought processes of a very young boy. What, in your opinion, is the advantage of the author's choice of the narrator? You can look up the part on "Narrative point of view" in Chapter Four if you need help.

3. Why does James' mother treat him with firmness that sometimes borders on harshness? Is her role as a strict disciplinarian necessitated by the story's setting and the family circumstances?

4. What is the role of the preacher and the young student who questions him in the waiting room of the dentist's office?

5. Jordon Pecile has said that "the story is an appeal to the heart at the same time that it is about the suppression of the heart" (Skaggs 452). Apply Pecile's words to the story's content.

Adding Style Evaluation to the Discussion of Themes (option no. 6)

This story by Leslie Silko is eminently suited to analyzing the style-theme connection in a literary work. Student author Vincent Largo's essay demonstrating that connection follows the story.

Lullaby

The sun had gone down but the snow in the wind gave off its own light. It came in thick tufts like new wool-washed before the weaver spins it. Ayah reached out for it like her own babies had, and she smiled when she remembered how she had laughed at them. She was an old woman now, and her life had become memories. She sat down with her back against the wide cottonwood tree, feeling the rough bark on her back bones; she faced east and listened to the wind and snow sing a high-pitched Yeibechei song. Out of the wind she felt warmer, and she could watch the wide fluffy snow fill in her tracks, steadily, until the direction she had come from was gone. By the light of the snow she could see the dark outline of the big arroyo a few feet away. She was sitting on the edge of Cebolleta Creek, where in the springtime the thin cows would graze on grass already chewed flat to the ground. In the wide deep creek bed where only a trickle of water flowed in the summer, the skinny cows would wander, looking for new grass along winding paths splashed with manure.

Ayah pulled the old Army blanket over her head like a shawl. Jimmie's blanket – the one he had sent to her. That was a long time ago and the green wool was faded, and it was unraveling on the edges. She did not want to think about Jimmie. So she thought about the weaving and the way her mother had done it. On the tall wooden loom set into the sand under a tamarack tree for shade. She could see it clearly. She had been only a little girl when her grandma gave her the wooden combs to pull the twigs and burrs from the raw, freshly washed wool. And while she combed the wool, her grandma sat beside her, spinning a silvery strand of yarn around the smooth cedar spindle. Her mother worked at the loom with yarns dyed bright yellow and red and gold. She watched them dye the yarn in boiling black pots full of bee weed petals, juniper berries, and sage. The blankets her mother made were soft and woven so tight that rain rolled off them like birds' feathers. Ayah remembered sleeping warm on cold windy nights, wrapped in her mother's blankets on the hogan's sandy floor.

The snow drifted now, with the northwest wind hurling it in gusts. It drifted up around her black overshoes – old ones with little metal buckles. She smiled at the snow which was trying to cover her little by little. She could remember when they had no black rubber overshoes; only the high buckskin leggings that they wrapped over their elkhide moccasins. If the snow was dry or frozen, a person could walk all day and not get wet; and in the evenings the beams of the ceiling would hang with lengths of pale buckskin leggings, drying out slowly.

She felt peaceful remembering. She didn't feel cold any more. Jimmie's blanket seemed warmer than it had ever been. And she could remember the morning he was born. She could remember whispering to her mother, who was sleeping on the other side of the hogan, to tell her it was time now. She did not want to wake the others. The second time she called to her, her mother stood up and pulled on her shoes; she knew. They walked to the old stone hogan together, Ayah walking a step behind her mother. She waited alone, learning the rhythms of the pains while her mother went to call the old woman to help them. The morning was already warm even before dawn and Ayah smelled the bee flowers blooming and the young willow growing at the springs. She could remember that so cleariy, but his birth merged into the births of the other children and to her it became all the same birth. They named him for the summer morning and in English they called him Jimmie.

It wasn't like Jimmie died. He just never came back, and one day a dark blue sedan with white writing on its doors pulled up in front of the boxcar shack where the rancher let the Indians live. A man in a khaki uniform trimmed in gold gave them a yellow piece of paper and told them that Jimmie was dead. He said the Army would try to get the body back and then it would be shipped to them; but it wasn't likely because the helicopter had burned after it crashed. All of this was told to Chato because he could understand English. She stood inside the doorway holding the baby while Chato listened. Chato spoke English like a white man and he spoke Spanish too. He was taller than the white man and he stood straighter too. Chato didn't explain why; he just told the military man they could keep the body if they found it. The white man looked bewildered; he nodded his head and he left. Then Chato looked at her and shook his head, and then he told her, "Jimmie isn't coming home anymore," and when he spoke, he used the words to speak of the dead. She didn't cry then, but she hurt inside with anger. And she mourned him as the years passed, when a horse fell with Chato and broke his leg, and the white rancher told them he wouldn't pay Chato until he could work again. She mourned Jimmie because he would have worked for his father then; he would have saddled the big bay horse and ridden the fence lines each day, with wire cutters and heavy gloves, fixing the breaks in the barbed wire and putting the stray cattle back inside again.

She mourned him after the white doctors came to take Danny and Ella away. She was at the shack alone that day they came. It was back in the days before they hired Navajo women to go with them as interpreters. She recognized one of the doctors. She had seen him at the children's clinic at Canoncito about a month ago. They were wearing khaki uniforms and they waved papers at her and a black ball-point pen, trying to make her understand their English words. She was frightened by the way they looked at the children, like the lizard watches the fly. Danny was swinging on the tire swing on the elm tree behind the rancher's house, and Ella was toddling around the front door, dragging the broomstick horse Chato made for her. Ayah could see they wanted her to sign the papers, and Chato had taught her to sign her name. It was something she was proud of. She only wanted them to go, and to take their eyes away from her children.

She took the pen from the man without looking at his face and she signed the papers in three different places he pointed to. She stared at the ground by their feet and waited for them to leave. But they stood there and began to point and gesture at the children. Danny stopped swinging. Ayah could see his fear. She moved suddenly and grabbed Ella into her arms; the child squirmed, trying to get back to her toys. Ayah ran with the baby toward Danny; she screamed for him to run and then she grabbed him around his chest and carried him too. She ran south into the foothills of juniper trees and black lava rock. Behind her she heard the doctors running, but they had been taken by surprise, and as the hills became steeper and the cholla cactus were thicker, they stopped. When she reached the top of the hill, she stopped to listen in case they were circling around her. But in a few minutes she heard a car engine start and they drove away. The children had been too surprised to cry while she ran with them. Danny was shaking and Ella's little fingers were gripping Ayah's blouse.

She stayed up in the hills for the rest of the day, sitting on a black lava boulder in the sunshine where she could see for miles all around her. The sky was light blue and cloudless, and it was warm for late April. The sun warmth relaxed her and took the fear and anger away. She lay back on the rock and watched the sky. It seemed to her that she could walk into the sky, stepping through clouds endlessly. Danny played with little pebbles and stones, pretending they were birds eggs and then little rabbits. Ella sat at her feet and dropped fistfuls of dirt into the breeze, watching the dust and particles of sand intently. Ayah watched a hawk soar high above them, dark wings gliding; hunting or only watching, she did not know. The hawk was patient and he circled all afternoon before he disappeared around the high volcanic peak the Mexicans called Guadalupe.

Late in the afternoon, Ayah looked down at the gray boxcar shack with the paint all peeled from the wood; the stove pipe on the roof was rusted and crooked. The fire she had built that morning in the oil drum stove had burned out. Ella was asleep in her lap now and Danny sat close to her, complaining that he was hungry; he asked when they would go to the house. "We will stay up here until your father comes," she told him, "because those white men were chasing us." The boy remembered then and he nodded at her silently.

If Jimmie had been there he could have read those papers and explained to her what they said. Ayah would have known then, never to sign them. The doctors came back the next day and they brought a BIA policeman with them. They told Chato they had her signature and that was all they needed. Except for the kids. She listened I to Chato sullenly; she hated him when he told her it was the old woman who died in the winter, spitting blood; it was her old grandma who had given the children this disease. "They don't spit blood," she said coldly. "The whites lie." She held Ella and Danny close to her, ready to run to the hills again. "I want a medicine man first," she said to Chato, not looking at him. He shook his head. "It's too late now. The policeman is with them. You signed the paper." His voice was gentle.

It was worse than if they had died: to lose the children and to know that somewhere, in a place called Colorado, in a place full of sick and dying strangers, her children were without her. There had been babies that died soon after they were born, and one that died before he could walk. She had carried them herself, up to the boulders and great pieces of the cliff that long ago crashed down from Long Mesa; she laid them in the crevices of sandstone and buried them in fine brown sand with round quartz pebbles that washed down the hills in the rain. She had endured it because they had been with her. But she could not bear this pain. She did not sleep for a long time after they took her children. She stayed on the hill where they had fled the first time, and she slept rolled up in the blanket Jimmie had sent her. She carried the pain in her belly and it was fed by everything she saw: the blue sky of their last day together and the dust and pebbles they played with; the swing in the elm tree and broomstick horse choked life from her. The pain filled her stomach and there was no room for food or for her lungs to fill with air. The air and the food would have been theirs.

She hated Chato, not because he let the policeman and doctors put the screaming children in the government car, but because he had taught her to sign her name. Because it was like the old ones always told her about learning their language or any of their ways: it endangered you. She slept alone on the hill until the middle of November when the first snows came. Then she made a bed for herself where the children had slept. She did not lie down beside Cha to again until many years later, when he was sick and shivering and only her body could keep him warm. The illness came after the white rancher told Chato he was too old to work for him anymore, and Chato and his old woman should be out of the shack by the next afternoon because the rancher had hired new people to work there. That had satisfied her. To see how the white man repaid Chato's years of loyalty and work. All of Chato's fine-sounding English talk didn't change things.

It snowed steadily and the luminous light from the snow gradually diminished into the darkness. Somewhere in Cebolleta a dog barked and other village dogs joined with it. Ayah looked in the direction she had come, from the bar where Chato was buying the wine. Sometimes he told her to go on ahead and wait; and then he never came. And when she finally went back looking for him, she would find him passed out at the bottom of the wooden steps to Azzie's Bar. All the wine would be gone and most of the money too, from the pale blue check that came to them once a month in a government envelope. It was then that she would look at his face and his hands, scarred by ropes and the barbed wire of all those years, and she would think, this man is a stranger; for forty years she had smiled at him and cooked his food, but he remained a stranger. She stood up again, with the snow almost to her knees, and she walked back to find Chato.

It was hard to walk in the deep snow and she felt the air burn in her lungs. She stopped a short distance from the bar to rest and read just the blanket. But this time he wasn't waiting for her on the bottom step with his old Stetson hat pulled down and his shoulders hunched up in his long wool overcoat.

She was careful not to slip on the wooden steps. When she pushed the door open, warm air and cigarette smoke hit her face. She looked around slowly and deliberately, in every corner, in every dark place that the old man might find to sleep. The bar owner didn't like Indians in there, especially Navajos, but he let Chato come in because he could talk Spanish like he was one of them. The men at the bar stared at her, and the bartender saw that she left the door open wide. Snowflakes were flying inside like moths and melting into a puddle on the oiled wood floor. He motioned to her to close the door, but she did not see him. She held herself straight and walked across the room slowly, searching the room with every step. The snow in her hair melted and she could feel it on her forehead. At the far corner of the room, she saw red flames at the mica window of the old stove door; she looked behind the stove just to make sure. The bar got quiet except for the Spanish polka music playing on the jukebox. She stood by the stove and shook the snow from her blanket and held it near the stove to dry. The wet wool smell reminded her of new-born goats in early March, brought inside to warm near the fire. She felt calm.

In past years they would have told her to get out. But her hair was white now and her face was wrinkled. They looked at her like she was a spider crawling slowly across the room. They were afraid; she could feel the fear. She looked at their faces steadily. They reminded her of the first time the white people brought her children back to her that winter. Danny had been shy and hid behind the thin white woman who brought them. And the baby had not known her until Ayah took her into her arms, and then Ella had nuzzled close to her as she had when she was nursing. The blonde woman was nervous and kept looking at a dainty gold watch on her wrist. She sat on the bench near the small window and watched the dark snow clouds gather around the mountains; she was worrying about the unpaved road. She was frightened by what she saw inside too: the strips of venison drying on a rope across the ceiling and the children jabbering excitedly in a language she did not know. So they stayed for only a few hours. Ayah watched the government car disappear down the road and she knew they were already being weaned from these lava hills and from this sky. The last time they came was in early June, and Ella stared at her the way the men in the bar were now staring. Ayah did not try to pick her up; she smiled at her instead and spoke cheerfully to Danny. When he tried to answer her, he could not seem to remember and he spoke English words with the Navajo. But he gave her a scrap of paper that he had found somewhere and carried in his pocket; it was folded in half, and he shyly looked up at her and said it was a bird. She asked Chato if they were home for good this time. He spoke to the white woman and she shook her head. "How much longer?" he asked, and she said she didn't know; but Chato saw how she stared at the boxcar shack. Ayah turned away then. She did not say good-bye.

She felt satisfied that the men in the bar feared her. Maybe it was her face and the way she held her mouth with teeth clenched tight, like there was nothing anyone could do to her now. She walked north down the road, searching for the old man. She did this because she had the blanket, and there would be no place for him except with her and the blanket in the old adobe barn near the arroyo. They always slept there when they came to Cebolleta. If the money and the wine were gone, she would be relieved because then they could go home again; back to the old hogan with a dirt roof and rock walls where she herself had been born. And the next day the old man could go back to the few sheep they still had, to follow along behind them, guiding them, into dry sandy arroyos where sparse grass grew. She knew he did not like walking behind old ewes when for so many years he rode big quarter horses and worked with cattle. But she wasn't sorry for him; he should have known all along what would happen.

There had not been enough rain for their garden in five years; and that was when Chato finally hitched a ride into the town and brought back brown boxes of rice and sugar and big tin cans of welfare peaches. After that, at the first of the month they went to Cebolleta to ask the postmaster for the check; and then Cha to would go to the bar and cash it. They did this as they planted the garden every May, not because anything would survive the summer dust, but be" cause it was time to do this. The journey passed the days that smelled silent and dry like the caves above the canyon with yellow painted buffaloes on their walls.

He was walking along the pavement when she found him. He did not stop or turn around when he heard her behind him. She walked beside him and she noticed how slowly he moved now. He smelled strong of wood smoke and urine. Lately he had been forgetting. Sometimes he called her by his sister's name and she had been gone for a long time. Once she had found him wandering on the road to the white man's ranch, and she asked him why he was going that way; he laughed at her and said, "You know they can't run that ranch without me," and he walked on determined, limping on the leg that had been crushed many years before. Now he looked at her curiously, as if for the first time, but he kept shuffling along, moving slowly along the side of the highway. His gray hair had grown long and spread out on the shoulders of the long overcoat. He wore the old felt hat pulled down over his ears. His boots were worn out at the toes and he had stuffed pieces of an old red shirt in the holes. The rags made his feet look like little animals up to their ears in snow. She laughed at his feet; the snow muffled the sound of her laugh. He stopped and looked at her again. The wind had quit blowing and the snow was falling straight down; the southeast sky was beginning to clear and Ayah could see a star.

"Let's rest awhile," she said to him. They walked away from the road and up the slope to the giant boulders that had tumbled down from the red sand rock mesa throughout the centuries of rainstorms and earth tremors. In a place where the boulders shut out the wind, they sat down with their backs against the rock. She offered half of the blanket to him and they sat wrapped together.

The storm passed swiftly. The clouds moved east. They were massive and full, crowding together across the sky. She watched them with the feeling of horses – steely blue-gray horses startled across the sky. The powerful haunches pushed into the distances and the tail hairs streamed white mist behind them. The sky cleared. Ayah saw that there was nothing between her and the stars. The light was crystalline. There was no shimmer, no distortion through earth haze. She breathed the clarity of the night sky; she smelled the purity of the half moon and the stars. He was lying on his side with his knees pulled up near his belly for warmth. His eyes were closed now, and in the light from the stars and the moon, he looked young again.

She could see it descend out of the night sky: an icy stillness from the edge of the thin moon. She recognized the freezing. It came gradually, sinking snowflake by snowflake until the crust was heavy and deep. It had the strength of the stars in Orion, and its journey was endless. Ayah knew that with the wine he would sleep. He would not feel it. She tucked the blanket around him, remembering how it was when Ella had been with her; and she felt the rush so big inside her heart for the babies. And she sang the only song she knew to sing for babies. She could not remember if she had ever sung it to her children, but she knew that her grandmother had sung it and her mother had sung it:

The earth is your mother,
she holds you.
The sky is your father,
he protects you.
Sleep, sleep.
Rainbow is your sister,
she loves you.
The winds are your brothers,
they sing to you.
Sleep, sleep.
We are together always
We are together always
There never was a time
when this
was not so.

Leslie Marmon Silko (b. 1948)

Means of Survival
Student author: Vincent Largo

For the introductory part of the paper, Vincent gives a brief plot summary. He includes various parts of his thesis in topic sentences to discuss two of the story's major themes relating to the disorienting process of assimilation and the reassuring and healing function of unconditional love. Inclusion of evaluative comments on Silko's style of writing and how it blends with the themes makes this paper a perceptive reading of Silko's moving story.

In the short story "Lullaby," Leslie Marmon Silko writes about the life experiences of Ayah, a Navajo woman, whose family is relocated to Cebolleta, New Mexico. She strongly resents and distrusts the strange environment. Her eldest son dies while serving in the U.S. Army, while the Department of Social Welfare takes away her two younger children, placing them into Colorado homes. Meanwhile, Chato, her husband, tries to conform to the new society by learning to speak English and Spanish and working at a cattle ranch. One day he injures himself and quickly learns the meaning of unemployment. As they barely get by, times become even tougher for them when Chato turns to alcohol in his frustration, carelessly wasting most of the month's allowance. One snowy night, during Ayah's routine search for Chato at the local bar, she finds him shuffling down the highway and joins him. Along the way, they stop to rest and Ayah, with her tenderness, reinstates her love for Chato and family.

One of the major themes in this story is the struggle between assimilation into the dominant culture versus retention of a minority identity. After being taken away by the government, the younger children are brought back in the wintertime to visit Ayah, but Danny is bashful and hides behind the government worker, while Ella does not recognize Ayah until she is taken into her arms. During the last visit, Danny unintentionally mixes "English words with the Navajo," and Ella not only sees her biological mother as unfamiliar, but also frightening. The process of conformity is exemplified through these illustrations; the dominant culture overshadows the minority influence.

In contrast to the assimilation of her family, Ayah maintains her Native American identity by staying connected with the natural environment. She constantly alludes to her harmony with nature. The beginning of the story shows Ayah walking through the snow leaving behind a trail, but the winter storm quickly fills in the gaps to protect her against being pursued. Another depiction occurs on the day of Jimmy's birth when Ayah learns about "the rhythms of the pains. . . [while] the morning was already warm . . . [and smells] the bee flowers blooming and the young willow growing at the springs."

The next illustration takes place when Ayah, with a child in each arm, runs away from the social workers, while "the sun warmth relaxed her and took the fear and anger away." At the end of the story, even though snow is still falling, Ayah decides to rest because the sky is starting to clear. All these examples show Ayah's strong faith in nature as her protector.

Ayah also retains her cultural identity through language. She insists on speaking only Navajo. There is an example of her snubbing Chato for learning to speak another tongue. She reminds him "how the white man repaid Chato's years of loyalty and work. All of Chato's fine-sounding English talk didn't change things."

In addition, Ayah upholds her heritage and minority individuality by means of her thought process. She would reflect upon such things as "weaving and the way her mother had done it" or describe days in relation to canyon caves. In order to stay connected to her native environment, she makes comparisons in terms of different animals: blankets being similar to birds' feathers, social workers regarded as lizards watching flies, likening herself to a spider slowly crossing the room, and Chato's boot rags as little animals' ears in the snow.

Another major theme in this story is that true love is unconditional. When her two younger children come to visit and hardly remember how to relate to her, she accepts it and allows the kids to have a smoother transition into their new lives: "Ayah turned away then. She did not say good-bye." By subduing the desire to have the children remain in her home (a decrepit old shack), she permits them to experience life in a financially secure environment. In addition, after Jimmie (the elder son) leaves the tight-knit family to join the armed forces, Ayah continues to love him. At the end, Chato becomes dejected about his role in life, but Ayah accepts his low spirits and demeanor. She even comforts him in a motherly manner by sheltering him from the cold air, keeping him company through the night, and reassuring him by means of a loving lullaby.

Embedded within the major themes of assimilation versus ethnic identity and unconditional love are the issues of human beings' exploitation and inhumane treatment of one another, intolerance of foreign/minority cultures, rejection of diversity as barbaric and beneath the dominant culture, and loss of humane traditions through rapid modernization heedless of time-honored and tested values.

For this short story, the writer utilizes the stylistic elements of narration (especially in the sense of Native American storytelling), paragraph breaks to signal passage of time, similes (especially in reference to animals), and visual/tactile imagery of the surrounding environment. Many of the sentences are concise, giving the reader a feeling that a tale is being told. The oral-tale tradition emphasizes the importance of the older generations' passing on their knowledge to younger ones. The author also separates some paragraphs from one another in order to indicate that the flashback (or mental digression) is complete, and that she will be returning to the present time. This style captures the attention of the reader and signals that a chronological or topical change is being made.

In the practice of similes involving various creatures, the author further communicates the visual imagery and unique thought process of the individual to the reader. The repetitive exercise of animals as examples is significant because it transmits the closeness of the relationship between the main character and nature, with Ayah being the personification of Nature. The vivid descriptions of the environment awaken the reader's senses to even the most diminutive detail. Notable are her descriptions of "the bee flowers blooming and the young willow growing" as well as the winter storm and the comforting warmth of the sun. Her images entice the reader right into the middle of the story, allowing an intimate association with the main character.

Using the stylistic elements of narration, paragraph separation, animal-related similes, and visual/tactile imagery, Silko is able to masterfully communicate the substance of her story to the reader.

Questions on "Lullaby"

1. How do you interpret the ending of the story? In your view, does either Chato or Ayah or both of them freeze to death? Support your answer with relevant details from the story.

2. Describe some passages that show a strong, spiritual bond between Ayah and Nature. How does that bond sustain and anchor Ayah during her many tragedies?

3. How are the people in power and with authority portrayed in the story?

Writing on Just One Topic from a Story (option no. 7)

A Clean Well-Lighted Place
by Ernest Hemingway

http://www.mrbauld.com/hemclean.html

Read the story online before reading the following essay by Lisa Embry. She chooses to concentrate on just one topic – that of existentialism – as it surfaces in the story. The narrowness of this focus allows an in-depth coverage of this topic in Hemingway's classic. Elements of existentialism are listed in the introduction to the student's essay on Albert Camus' short story, "The Guest," earlier in this chapter.

Existentialism in Hemingway's "A Clean Well-Lighted Place
Student author: Lisa Embry

A clean well-lighted place is a cafe where Hemingway explores how man deals with a sense of nothingness in life. There are three main characters in the story: a young waiter, an older waiter, and an old deaf man who sits alone on the terrace of the cafe enjoying too much brandy.

Through the conversation of the waiters, we learn that the old man has recently tried to kill himself. He is a regular customer who likes to stay until the cafe closes at three in the morning. On this night, he is the only customer left at the cafe before its closing time. The young waiter resents the man for keeping him from leaving work early; eventually, he makes him leave before the scheduled closing time. The older waiter, however, identifies with the old man and understands the importance of the café to him and others like him. He attempts to explain this importance to the young waiter but finds that he is only concerned with his own immediate wants – chiefly, getting home to his wife. After the young waiter has left, the other waiter continues the "conversation with himself," exploring the need that some people have for a clean well-lighted café, and connecting this need to a theory of nothingness.

Here we see how Hemingway has threaded existentialist ideas throughout the story. The waiter says he knows nothingness, and we can gather that the old man lives with it as well. The idea that nothingness is what must be confronted in the absence of a god is made clear when the waiter replaces the key words in the Lord's Prayer with "nada" – nothingness. Moreover, it becomes apparent from the conversation between the two waiters that the old man has plenty of money and that he has tried to kill himself about "Nothing." We come to the understanding that "nothing" is an immense reason for despair and is the reason for the necessity of a clean well-lighted place. The old man's attempted suicide can be looked at as an indication that he did not "fear for his soul," but was without a god and faced nothingness. This notion corresponds with the existentialist idea that a sense of nothingness leads to an awareness of the absurdity of life, and once this absurdity is acknowledged, it may lead to suicide in those who cannot bear a life without a clear purpose and meaning. That is the reason why the café becomes important. Perhaps the old man has not regained the courage to try suicide again. He blots out time as best he can waiting for death, but nothingness is still his unbearable companion, and the cafe helps him fill the void temporarily.

There are several ways in which the cafe accomplishes this purpose. One is that it gives him a dignified place to drink; it is not a typical bar. The older waiter acknowledges the importance of dignity to the old man by pointing out how, even when drunk, he manages to drink from a full glass without spilling and maintains a dignified though unsteady walk. In holding on to dignity, a person claims to be more than an animal; he claims a higher, more meaningful existence and in this way fights nothingness.

Another way in which the cafe fends off nothingness is found in the visual qualities of the atmosphere. The well-lighted cleanliness gives a sense of order to life. All is clear, organized, and has a certain straightforwardness about it that is missing in the old man's life. This order connotes rationality, which goes against the absurdity that arises in the presence of nothingness. Hemingway uses an image of the old man sitting "in the shadow of the leaves of the tree." The repetition of this image three times in the story emphasizes the pervasiveness of the shadows, the antithesis of light with its clarity and order. That the old man sits under the ambiguous, chaotic, ever-changing shadows cast by the blowing leaves could be Hemingway's way of telling us that irrationality is inescapable.

The imagery of the first paragraph of the story effectively conveys the feeling that the cafe triggers in the old man: "In the daytime the street was dusty, but at night the dew settled the dust and the old man liked to sit late because he was deaf and now at night it was quiet and he felt the difference." The paradox of a deaf man feeling quietness and the rarity of this feeling to him makes his soundless world more perceptible to us. We get the feeling that the deaf man is susceptible of a feeling of nothingness to a heightened degree. In giving him the pleasure of this rarely felt sense, the cafe lessens the void made by his deafness and thus lightens the heavy feeling of nothingness.

Though the older waiter also lives with nothingness, he seems capable of embracing existentialism in a different way: He does not seek to end his life. The root of this difference is his acknowledgement of nothingness: "Some lived in it and never felt it but [the waiter] knew it all was nada y pues nada y nada y pues nada." [Nothing and then nothing and nothing and then nothing.] In facing nothingness he is content to live with it. Though both men appreciate the comfort that the cafe gives, the old man needs it but does not know why. However, the waiter understands how a clean well-lighted place softens nothingness and is thus able to appreciate it; he is in control. We see him play with this idea in his response to the barman's "What's yours?" (meaning "What's your drink?"). He answers "Nada."

In the story's last lines, Hemingway delves into the heart of the waiter's character with dramatic irony: "Now, without thinking further," the waiter returns home and is unable to sleep, as usual. He consoles himself with a bit of denial: "After all, he said to himself, it is probably only insomnia. Many must have it." Hemingway seems to say that knowledge of nothingness cannot overcome a basic need for meaning and that confronting nothingness is essential to human life.

Questions on "A Clean Well-Lighted Place"

1. Compare and contrast the characters of the two waiters in this story. How do they view the old man who is a regular customer at this clean and well-lighted cafe? Which of the two has an empathetic understanding of the old man's mental state?

2. Discuss the symbolism of light in this story as a momentary stay against the "nothing" of existential darkness. Include the old waiter's almost blasphemous parody of the opening parts of the Lord's Prayer and of the Ave Maria.

3. Evaluate the effectiveness of Hemingway's characteristic style of understatement throughout this story and especially in the story's concluding lines.

Interpretation through Character Analysis (option no. 8)

James Joyce's story, "Araby," with its two memorable characters, invites character analysis. In the essay that comes after the story, the student author James Nugent traces the story's deeper themes by way of character analysis

This story has been adapted to film. You can find information on this award-winning short film using the link: www.ArabyFilm.com.

Araby

NORTH RICHMOND STREET, being blind, was a quiet street except at the hour when the Christian Brothers' School set the boys free. An uninhabited house of two storeys stood at the blind end, detached from its neighbours in a square ground. The other houses of the street, conscious of decent lives within them, gazed at one another with brown imperturbable faces. The former tenant of our house, a priest, had died in the back drawing-room. Air, musty from having been long enclosed, hung in all the rooms, and the waste room behind the kitchen was littered with old useless papers. Among these I found a few paper-covered books, the pages of which were curled and damp: *The Abbot,* by Walter Scott, *The Devout Communicant* and *The Memoirs of Vidocq.* I liked the last best because its leaves were yellow. The wild garden behind the house contained a central apple-tree and a few straggling bushes under one of which I found the late tenant's rusty bicycle-pump. He had been a very charitable priest; in his will he had left all his money to institutions and the furniture of his house to his sister.

When the short days of winter came dusk fell before we had well eaten our dinners. When we met in the street the houses had grown sombre. The space of sky above us was the colour of ever-changing violet and towards it the lamps of the street lifted their feeble lanterns. The cold air stung us and we played till our bodies glowed. Our shouts echoed in the silent street. The career of our play brought us through the dark muddy lanes behind the houses where we ran the gantlet of the rough tribes from the cottages, to the back doors of the dark dripping gardens where odours arose from the ashpits, to the dark odorous stables where a coachman smoothed and combed the horse or shook music from the buckled harness. When we returned to the street! light from the kitchen windows had filled the areas. If my uncle was seen turning the corner we hid in the shadow until we had seen him safely housed. Or if Mangan's sister came out on the doorstep to call her brother in to his tea we watched her from our shadow peer up and down the street. We waited to see whether she would remain or go in and, if she remained, we left our shadow and walked up to Mangan's steps resignedly. She was waiting for us, her figure defined by the light from the half-opened door. Her brother always teased her before he obeyed and I stood by the railings looking at her. Her dress swung as she moved her body and the soft rope of her hair tossed from side to side.

Every morning I lay on the floor in the front parlour watching her door. The blind was pulled down to within an inch of the sash so that I could not be seen. When she came out on the doorstep my heart leaped. I ran to the hall, seized my books and followed her. I kept her brown figure always in my eye and, when we came near the point at which our ways diverged, I quickened my pace and passed her. This happened morning after morning. I had never spoken to her, except for a few casual words, and yet her name was like a summons to all my foolish blood.

Her image accompanied me even in places the most hostile to romance. On Saturday evenings when my aunt went marketing I had to go to carry some of the parcels. We walked through the flaring streets, jostled by drunken men and bargaining women, amid the curses of labourers, the shrill litanies of shop-boys who stood on guard by the barrels of pigs' cheeks, the nasal chanting of street-singers, who sang a *come-all-you* about O'Donovan Rossa, or a ballad about the troubles in our native land. These noises converged in a single sensation of life for me: I imagined that I bore my chalice safely through a throng of foes. Her name sprang to my lips at moments in strange prayers and praises which I myself did not understand. My eyes were often full of tears (I could not tell why! and at times a flood from my heart seemed to pour itself out into my bosom. I thought little of the future. I did not know whether I would ever speak to her or not or, if I spoke to her, how I could tell her of my confused adoration. But my body was like a harp and her words and gestures were like fingers running upon the wires.

One evening I went into the back drawing-room in which the priest had died. It was a dark rainy evening and there was no sound in the house. Through one of the broken panes I heard the rain impinge upon the earth, the fine incessant needles of water playing in the sodden beds. Some distant lamp or lighted window gleamed below me. I was thankful that I could see so little. All my senses seemed to desire to veil themselves and, feeling that I was about to slip from them, I pressed the palms of my hands together until they trembled, murmuring: O *love!* O *love!* many times.

At last she spoke to me. When she addressed the first words to me I was so confused that I did not know what to answer. She asked me was I going to *Araby*. I forget whether I answered yes or no. It would be a splendid bazaar, she said; she would love to go.

—And why can't you? I asked.

While she spoke she turned a silver bracelet round and round her wrist. She could not go, she said, because there would be a retreat that week in her convent. Her brother and two other boys were fighting for their caps and I was alone at the railings. She held one of the spikes, bowing her head towards me. The light from the lamp opposite our door caught the white curve of her neck, lit up her hair that rested there and, falling, lit up the hand upon the railing. It fell over one side of her dress and caught the white border of a petticoat, just visible as she stood at ease.

—It's well for you, she said.

—If I go, I said, I will bring you something.

What innumerable follies laid waste my waking and sleeping thoughts after that evening! I wished to annihilate the tedious intervening days. I chafed against the work of school. At night in my bedroom and by day in the classroom her image came between me and the page I strove to read. The syllables of the word *Araby* were called to me through the silence in which my soul luxuriated and cast an Eastern enchantment over me. I asked for leave to go to the bazaar on Saturday night. My aunt was surprised and hoped it was not some Freemason affair. I answered few questions in class. I watched my master's face pass from amiability to sternness; he hoped I was not beginning to idle. I could not call my wandering thoughts together. I had hardly any patience with the serious work of life which, now that it stood between me and my desire, seemed to me child's play, ugly monotonous child's play.

On Saturday morning I reminded my uncle that I wished to go to the bazaar in the evening. He was fussing at the hallstand, looking for the hat-brush, and answered me curtly:

—Yes, boy, I know.

As he was in the hall I could not go into the front parlour and lie at the window. I left the house in bad humour and walked slowly towards the school. The air was pitilessly raw and already my heart misgave me.

When I came home to dinner my uncle had not yet been home. Still it was early. I sat staring at the clock for some time and, when its ticking began to irritate me, I left the room. I mounted the staircase and gained the upper part of the house. The high cold empty gloomy rooms liberated me and I went from room to room singing. From the front window I saw my companions playing below in the street.

Their cries reached me weakened and indistinct and, leaning my forehead against the cool glass, I looked over at the dark house where she lived. I may have stood there for an hour, seeing nothing but the brown-clad figure cast by my imagination, touched discreetly by the lamplight at the curved neck, at the hand upon the railings and at the border below the dress.

When I came downstairs again I found Mrs. Mercer sitting at the fire. She was an old garrulous woman, a pawnbroker's widow, who collected used stamps for some pious purpose. I had to endure the gossip of the tea-table. The meal was prolonged beyond an hour and still my uncle did not come. Mrs. Mercer stood up to go: she was sorry she couldn't wait any longer, but it was after eight o'clock and she did not like to be out late, as the night air was bad for her. When she had gone I began to walk up and down the room, clenching my fists. My aunt said:

—I'm afraid you may put off your bazaar for this night of Our Lord.

At nine o'clock I heard my uncle's latchkey in the hall door. I heard him talking to himself and heard the hallstand rocking when it had received the weight of his overcoat. I could interpret these signs. When he was midway through his dinner I asked him to give me the money to go to the bazaar. He had forgotten.

—The people are in bed and after their first sleep now, he said.

I did not smile. My aunt said to him energetically:

—Can't you give him the money and let him go? You've kept him late enough as it is.

My uncle said he was very sorry he had forgotten. He said he believed in the old saying: *All work and no play makes Jack a dull boy.* He asked me where I was going and, when I had told him a second time he asked me did I know *The Arab's Farewell to his Steed.* When I left the kitchen he was about to recite the opening lines of the piece to my aunt.

I held a florin tightly in my hand as I strode down Buckingham Street towards the station. The sight of the streets thronged with buyers and glaring with gas recalled to me the purpose of my journey. I took my seat in a third-class carriage of a deserted train. After an intolerable delay the train moved out of the station slowly. It crept onward among ruinous houses and over the twinkling river. At Westland Row Station a crowd of people pressed to the carriage doors; but the porters moved them back, saying that it was a special train for the bazaar. I remained alone in the bare carriage. In a few minutes the train drew up beside an improvised wooden platform. I passed out on to the road and saw by the lighted dial of a clock that it was ten minutes to ten. In front of me was a large building which displayed the magical name.

I could not find any sixpenny entrance and, fearing that the bazaar would be closed, I passed in quickly through a turnstile, handing a shilling to a weary-looking man. I found myself in a big hall girdled at half its height by a gallery. Nearly all the stalls were closed and the greater part of the hall was in darkness. I recognised a silence like that which pervades a church after a service. I walked into the centre of the bazaar timidly. A few people were gathered about the stalls which were still open. Before a curtain, over which the words *Cafe Chantant* were written in coloured lamps, two men were counting money on a salver. I listened to the fall of the coins.

Remembering with difficulty why I had come I went over to one of the stalls and examined porcelain vases and flowered tea-sets. At the door of the stall a young lady was talking and laughing with two young gentlemen. I remarked their English accents and listened vaguely to their conversation.

—O, I never said such a thing!
—O, but you did!
—O, but I didn't!
—Didn't she say that?
—Yes. I heard her.
—O, there's a . . . fib!

Observing me the young lady came over and asked me did I wish to buy anything. The tone of her voice was not encouraging; she seemed to have spoken to me out of a sense of duty. I looked humbly at the great jars that stood like eastern guards at either side of the dark entrance to the stall and murmured:

—No, thank you.

The young lady changed the position of one of the vases and went back to the two young men. They began to talk of the same subject. Once or twice the young lady glanced at me over her shoulder.

I lingered before her stall, though I knew my stay was useless, to make my interest in her wares seem the more real. Then I turned away slowly and walked down the middle of the bazaar. I allowed the two pennies to fall against the sixpence in my pocket. I heard a voice call from one end of the gallery that the light was out. The upper part of the hall was now completely dark.

Gazing up into the darkness I saw myself as a creature driven and derided by vanity; and my eyes burned with anguish and anger.

James Joyce (1882-1941)

The Road to Araby – An Impossible Journey
Student author: Joseph Nugent

Joseph Nugent's well-written and sensitive reading of James Joyce's "Araby" captures the story's rendition of the adolescent protagonist's rite of passage after what Joseph calls "his first brush with that great chimera, love." The background information that Joseph includes early in the essay and his elucidating comments on Joyce's ways to capture moments of epiphany help us understand the reasons for the story's appeal. The quality of diction, variety in sentence structure, allusions to literary works, and impressive style make this an unusual paper, composed by those who take the time to revise their work carefully.

In "Araby" James Joyce compresses an unnamed adolescent's anguished pilgrimage into one memorable evening. On the subject of lost innocence and disappointed expectations, Joyce weaves his perennial themes. Using the quasi-religious device of the epiphany, he makes us see how the conflict between love and religion results in the third and fundamental topic – that of paralysis.

That these themes, typical of Joyce, should appear in "Araby" is hardly surprising. That they should fuse here with such force is a fact dictated, as much by the reality of the intense pain of these early years of awakening, as by artistic necessity. It is not necessary to read "Araby" as an autobiographical piece. It can, however, only help our appreciation of the intensity of the unnamed boy's emotion to know that in 1894 the downwardly mobile John Joyce (the author's father) moved with his eleven dependents to a dead-end street named North Richmond in a lower middle-class neighborhood. The young James Joyce experienced something similar to the story's main character. A "Grand Oriental Fete" was held in a better class of neighborhood than the young Joyce's. The fair was given the exotic title of "Araby" by shrewd promoters in order to add to the mystique.

The author was just beginning to go through a period of intense piety, as well as puberty. When we consider the possible devastation of such a clash in a boy of exceptional sensitivity, we can see why these themes come together in this story with a force perhaps unequaled in his other writings. Religion and sex meet, clash, and spawn a crisis of conscience, which reinforces in a particularly interesting way the other great overriding theme of all *The Dubliners* stories – paralysis. This theme remains implicit in this story, never overtly stated. It appears only in the dying moments of the tale and is all the more powerful for that reason. It is manifested, as we shall see, at the moment of epiphany. But as it is the child of the other two themes, we must first see how they insinuate themselves into the story.

Religion is apparent immediately in the story. Behind the "brown imperturbable face" of that almost sentient house in which the young protagonist lives, religiousness, but not necessarily holiness, had left its spoor. Its "high cold empty gloomy rooms" had been the haunt of an old priest whose reading matter had been dubious. *The Abbot* by Walter Scott, despite its ostensibly religious title, is actually a historical-romantic tale of deception. The back garden also figures prominently– a place with an apple tree and some bushes under one of which the boy finds a rusty bicycle pump (the snake?) – as alluding to Eden, and as a preparation for the Fall. We already see in these details the hints that all is not as it should be.

Outside the house, by contrast, and affirming the innocence of soon-to-be-lost youth, are the bright, carefree evenings of childhood where, the boy tells us, they played "till (their) bodies glowed." But temptation appears in the form of a girl who comes with no other title than "Mangan's sister." The boy falls for her allure. She becomes for him an "image" to be "adored." Indeed he prostrates himself before her, lying on the floor to watch her comings and going. The weaving of religious and sexual themes is symbolized by the young boy's supplication and worship at this carnal shrine. He guards his imaginary icon of her amid the profane crowds, "through a throng of foes," as a priest would the chalice, as a seeker might the holy grail. The weave of religion and sex finds its culminating expression in an incident in the back drawing room in which the priest had died. This, the sanctum sanctorum, is the scene for a moment of mystical ecstasy in which the boy – feeling, in the intensity of the experience, that he was about to slip from his senses – joins his trembling hands and recites in rhythmic incantation – "O love! O love!"

It appears to him that he has indeed found the grail. For who, in their first brush with that great chimera, love, would be convinced that all things are not possible, that all happiness cannot be had, that adulthood will not be one long violet-tinted evening of bliss? To "annihilate the tedious intervening days," peopled by Christian Brothers and by women with pious purposes, is the dearest wish of the young boy until he can begin the metaphorical journey Eastwards to love, adulthood, the Orient, and the moment of epiphany.

Joyce describes the adolescent protagonist's rite of passage with integrity, refusing to embellish reality. The only tool Joyce will permit himself with which to gild the lily of reality is the lyricism of language. The result is clarity of projection that gives this piece a sparkling pictorial quality. The readers are outsiders looking in. They are not invited to see the world through the eyes of the boy, though it is written in the first person. Only observation is requested – very careful observation of the myriad details – but not empathy. That is until the moment of exposition that is the dramatic heart of the story, comes at the end. It is this delayed sympathy with the main character which gives the moment of epiphany such force for the reader. At this moment we are, for the first time, truly at one with the character, and are, for the first time, invited to see the world through his eyes. Only at this moment, this moment of epiphany, which we shall further explore, do we feel total identification with the character.

Why does it always seem that Joyce builds us up and up with a plethora of minute details only releasing us from tension in the dying moments of his stories? Indeed, release from tension does not always occur in Joyce. His stories often linger long after the book is closed. This curious style is one that few writers would dare because it demands so much from both the author and the reader. There is little drama, little action in these tales. Yet we are left, time and again, stunned, whether by the transforming remorse of Little Chandler in "A Little Cloud," by the devastating inner perception of the newly insightful Gabriel Conroy in "The Dead," or by the anguished and angry vanity of our unnamed boy in "Araby."

These stunning moments of perception come at the end of the story because there is simply nothing more for Joyce to say. It is as if he were telling the reader "Now it's up to you." They are, for us, moments of understanding in which the inner truth of the tale is revealed. They are offered to us by

Joyce primarily as our own (that is, the reader's) moments of grand insight, of an epiphany. They describe, secondly, the epiphany of the character – the recognition, on the part of the hero, of what Joyce called the essential "whatness" of things. They reflect, finally, the occasional realization by the artist of great truths of life which constitute for Joyce the wellspring of art. When these three events are made to coincide in the printed word, the artist, at the interface of the inner and the outer, in that place where the world and the self meet mediated only by language, the complex truth so often manifested in the most seemingly trivial events is exposed. The moment of revelation is, thus, often one of paradoxical banality. It is not a moment of metaphorical understanding; it does not expose something symbolic. It is a moment of actual revelation.

In the case of "Araby" the moment of revelation for the boy takes place at the now deserted bazaar. The lone train journey ends in the darkened show-grounds. The great promise of the gaudily lit hall is fast ebbing. The pervasive silence, like that of a deserted church, is broken first for him by the sounds of coins being counted, as of the temple being blasphemed. And then a conversation overheard –

"O, I never said such a thing!"
"O, but you did!"
"O, but I didn't"
"Didn't she say that?"
"Yes, I heard her."
"O, there's a . . . fib!"

and the awful truth dawns. So this is the reality of love: two English boys and a young assistant, among the porcelain vases and the flowered tea-sets, swap the banal chit-chat of everyday flirtation, and speak of untruths which they dare not even call lies. The truth of his own infatuation, the lie of his so-called love, is now apparent. The grand dreams of love collapse and the imagined chalice of his hope disintegrates in darkness.

The light and dark themes of love and religion now clash in this sacrilegious temple, and the boy looks inward after this moment of terrible enlightenment. The dark pain of disillusionment demands an explanation – there must have been a sin. His examination of conscience duly uncovers one. "I saw myself as a creature driven and derided by vanity; and my eyes burned with anguish and anger." So this, it seems, was the sin. It was not love, of course, that the young boy sought, but sensual gratification. It was "the white curve of her neck," "the white border of a petticoat" he had desired. He had deluded himself by disguising his base mutterings in the enchanting mantra of love. Like so much that the East promises to an active imagination, the image was only that – an image, a mirage. Guilt and disillusionment well up and overflow in his burning eyes; he is now open to the sin he has committed. His journey to the adult world of love has faded to nothing under the gaudy lights of the Café Chantant. He must now go back, to the child's play and the school life which he had so recently derided. He cannot go forward.

Thus, in the terrible clash between vain expectation and reality, the epiphany has spawned that third great theme – paralysis. It is a paralysis produced by the guilt inflicted on him by Jansenistic Catholicism, a doctrinaire religion, which the now angry boy can see as corrupt and deceitful, as much perhaps as the "very charitable" priest whose room had been the scene for the boy's entwining of religious and sexual fantasies.

The truth of the tale, of the metaphorical journey, is now made clear. It has been an impossible journey into nowhere, a journey of disappointment and disillusion, the last act of a Fall from Grace. It began in the blind alley of Richmond Street and it ended in the blind alley of unfulfilled hope. The truth, once realized, was a terrible one. Until the ghostly chains of religious paralysis can be unfettered, there can be no salvation. This would be a tale of unrelieved gloom, but Joyce has offered us some hope. The world can, he insists, be understood. Moments of revelation can happen; our fetters can be broken. We hope the boy can break away as well.

Questions on "Araby"

1. Point out similarities between the story's adolescent protagonist's adoration of Mangan's sister and the way people worship their deities. Is his love for her purely spiritual, or does the story suggest his sexual attraction for her?

2. Discuss the topics of spirituality, sensuality, and materialism as they interact in the protagonist's mind at a subconscious level?

3. What kind of mood does James Joyce evoke in the story's setting in the first two paragraphs? What specific elements trigger that mood?

4. Comment on Joyce's portrayal of the obsessive nature of love. How well is he able to convey the spell of that kind of love? Cite two or three examples from the story.

5. Joyce makes use of allusion several times in the story. For example, his protagonist mentions the books that he had found in "the waste room behind the kitchen." The titles of those books are *The Abbot* by Walter Scott, *The Devout Communicant*, and *The Memoirs of Vidocq*. Later in the story, there is a reference to "The Arab's Farewell to His Steed" (a popular poem of that time). Look up at least one of the allusions to comment on its significance as it relates to the protagonist's experiences in the story. For help with understanding allusions and symbols in the story, read online *via* Google.com <Gray's Notes to Joyce's "Araby" at WWD>.

6. Discuss Joyce's use of symbolism in the story. Of the many symbols, one is "the wild garden behind the house [that] contained a central apple tree." Another is that of the "blind" alley where the protagonist's house is located. What symbolic significance can we attach to these or similar symbols? Support your answer with details from the story.

7. In the story's opening paragraph, Joyce uses personification to describe homes in the protagonist's neighborhood: "The other houses of the street, conscious of decent lives within them, gazed at one another with brown imperturbable faces." In "Stephen Hero," Joyce writes about "those brown brick houses which seem the very incarnation of Irish paralysis." Make a connection between these two descriptions to trace the theme of paralysis and the confining role of conventions in "Araby."

8. Discuss "Araby" as a story about deception, including self-deception.

9. What scene in the story could be called an epiphany – an event that sheds sudden light of unexpected understanding.

10. What is the function of the scene in which a young English saleswoman flirts with two men, all of them blathering about nothing toward the end of the story?

11. There is hardly any conversation between the protagonist and Mangan's sister. What is the impact of this wordlessness between them?

12. Of the total of two lines that he speaks to her, one is this: "If I go, I said, I will bring you something." Discuss the role of this line as the story's plot setter that holds the plot together. Plot-setting devices were explained in Chapter Three.

13. Do you agree with the view that the protagonist judges himself too harshly at the end of the story when he regards himself as someone stricken with vanity?

14. Of the two main characters, which one is more repressed by rigid forms of religion – the protagonist-narrator or Mangan's sister? Give supporting details for your answer.

15. The protagonist is nameless, and the object of his adoration is simply called Mangan's sister. What is gained in the story's impact by not giving her a proper name?

Interpretation through an Author's Style of Writing (option no. 9)

The Short Happy Life of Francis Macomber
by Ernest Hemingway (1899-1961)

The reading of this story online was assigned toward the end of Chapter Four:
http://www.tarleton.edu/Faculty/sword/Short%20Story/The%20Short%20Happy%20Life%20of%20Francis%20Macomber.pdf

Jeffery Tarbell's reading of the story shows how an author's style becomes a means of theme embodiment. He follows the advice of Chapter Seven closely to complete this challenging assignment on style analysis and evaluation. After his observations on the significance of style, he uses the cluster thesis to identify those elements of Hemingway's style that he will discuss along with very brief statements of their functions in the story. He then discusses each element one by one, ending his paper with a comment on Hemingway's accomplishment.

Hemingway's Style in "The Short Happy Life of Francis Macomber"
Student author: Jeffery Tarbell

Style is an author's literary signature. It includes the words s/he chooses as well as how those words are arranged. Style reveals an author's beliefs, values, and views of life. Writing that lacks style soon grows tiresome; we care little for the words we are reading if those words lack the power to ignite our imaginations. Often style is initially noticed only when it is absent; good style is simply enjoyed as great writing and we are carried away to the author's world. Ernest Hemingway is one such author whose masterful style has earned him a place among the world's most popular writers. Reading his works leaves us with the feeling of having spent time with the man himself. And it is his style which brings his works to life.

In the short story "The Short Happy Life of Francis Macomber," Hemingway uses a variety of stylistic devices which not only add color and dimension to the characters but allow him to make his thematic statements more forceful as well. The use of significant character names reinforces our impressions of them in the story. These names serve as an anchor to remind us of the moral underpinnings which each character must live or die by. At the same time, Hemingway's terse, barren, third-person narration and choppy dialogue serve to distance us from the characters and give the reader a certain detached perspective. Through analogy, Hemingway is able to invest the hunting of big game animals on the African plain with the story's larger theme of man's hunt for his own identity, while demonstrating the dangerous consequences of both activities. This use of analogy places everyday events on a higher level where we can then examine actions and reactions from a more understanding perspective.

The names of the three main characters in Hemingway's story are meaningful; each name tells a story. The Francis Macomber of the story's title is a young, rich, handsome coward who has just bolted from his first lion while on safari in Africa. Francis Macomber, one of the "great American boy-men," is given a feminine-sounding name to signify his subservient position and timidity. A man in search of his manhood, he has yet to come to terms with the quiet failures of his life: his wife, his marriage, and his place in the world. Contrast his name and character with that of the professional hunter who leads Macomber and his wife through the jungle: Robert Wilson. That is a name belonging to a man who has long ago conquered his fears and has nothing to prove to himself or others. The fact that Wilson sleeps with Macomber's wife while on the safari shows us that Wilson is basically out for himself and, like Macomber, is also a flawed character, not to be admired. Hemingway seems to be saying that there is not as much distance between these two men's characters as Macomber thinks there is, yet Macomber still wants to be brave, like Wilson. Margot, Macomber's wife, is also a flawed character in that she is only staying with her husband for the sake of his money – not for love. The name Margot has the sound of a rich international jet-setter and this, too, fits in perfectly with Hemingway's sketch of her as a shallow, selfish woman. The characters in the story are revealed by their names as each name resonates with some associated meaning.

Throughout the story, Hemingway's omniscient narration gives the reader the God-like perspective of nature. In the jungle, man is an intruder. Nature is indifferent to the fact that Macomber is a coward, that Margot cheats on him, or that Wilson is a bit of a hypocrite. All that concerns nature, and us, is the actions of the characters. Hemingway describes Macomber's hunt for the lion and the lion's painful ordeal in equal detail. He gives these two events a certain moral equivalence which makes nature come out looking much better than man: animals aren't cowards; they don't have to hunt to prove themselves. This view emerges through Hemingway's style. He often allows us to know what a character is thinking and then adds, "what he said was . . ." This technique gives a reality and extra dimension to the characters that would not be possible if Hemingway had chosen to tell his story from a more confining first person perspective.

The dialogue is sprinkled with short, two- and three-word sentences; his characters don't mince words. They may not always speak their minds but what they do say is concise, important, and totally relevant. For example, when commenting on Macomber's shooting of a buffalo, Wilson tells him, "All right. Nice work. That's three." Hemingway uses this sparse dialogue for two reasons: since we can step into each character's thoughts, dialogue that explains their motives is unnecessary; also, actions are more important than words in Hemingway's world of man and nature and his use of short, punchy sentences accentuates the story's action.

The symbolic hunt for the man in Macomber and the tragic consequence of its discovery constitute the main theme of Hemingway's story. This stylistic device, analogy, allows us to view Macomber's struggle as possibly our own. After Macomber's cowardly behavior in bolting from the lion, his wife sleeps with their guide, Wilson, deepening Macomber's sense of worthlessness. His cowardice allows Margot to maintain control over him; she is confident that his fear of the lion speaks of his fear of her as well. Later, Macomber goes hunting for buffalo. Desperate for another chance to face danger – and thereby redeem himself – he finally breaks through his fear by facing the buffalo head-on and downing them. This facing of danger produces a change in Macomber which threatens Margot's hold over him. "You've gotten awfully brave, awfully suddenly," Margot quips. "You know I have . . . I really have!" Macomber answers, "exploring his new wealth." But as he and Wilson go after one buffalo who had only been wounded, Margot fires at it, hitting her husband instead, killing him. "That was a pretty thing to do," Wilson observes sarcastically, "He would have left you too."

The hunt for self-awareness has tragic consequences for Macomber. But once he had mastered the 'wild animals' of his fears and eliminated his dependence on his wife, he was, for a brief moment, free. By using the analogy of the hunt, Hemingway likens the conquering of our fears to the hunting of ferocious animals which our fears so often resemble. This more universal identity allows us to better understand Macomber and his search; few of us will probably ever hunt lions in Africa but we all have fears, doubts, and limitations which we must try to overcome if we are to grow.

Using the stylistic elements of revealing character names, third person narration combined with choppy dialogue, and analogic illumination of theme, Hemingway has broadened the scope of his work and increased his story's appeal. These elements, and others, combine to enliven his ideas by increasing the surfaces upon which those ideas reflect. By studying these many facets, we may, like Francis Macomber, finally come to understand our place in the world we share.

Annotating an essay

Since a style-based interpretation of a literary work poses special challenges, the following annotation to Jeffery Tarbell's essay on Hemingway's style may help you visualize how each step of this assignment was completed.

Jeffery's introduction consists of a statement about the importance of style in general terms. By the end of the introductory paragraph, he makes a transition to the style of a specific author – the focus of this paper.

The thesis paragraph identifies the elements of Hemingway's style that would be discussed in this essay. A brief comment/claim on the function of each element of style follows.

The first element of style is Hemingway's choice of names for his characters. After identifying this element, Jeffery includes a comment on the function of this element of style. The second element of style – Hemingway's terse, barren narration – is mentioned and its function/effect stated.

Jeffery then names the third and final stylistic element – Hemingway's use of an analogy – along with its function.

At the beginning of the support section (the main body), Jeffery introduces the discussion of the first element of style. Examples of the named element are accompanied by a comment on their effectiveness and function.

Jeffery introduces the discussion of Hemingway's second element of style – that of his choice of the third-person narrative point of view. Some examples from the story are given with comments on their effectiveness.

The last stylistic element – analogy – is discussed in the same manner as the preceding two elements: Jeffery gives examples and then connects this element of style with the story's major theme.

The concluding paragraph sums up Hemingway's stylistic achievement.

Questions on "The Short Happy Life of Francis Macomber"

1. Explain the words "short" and "happy" in the title of Hemingway's story. What part of Francis Macomber's life was short and happy? Why?

2. Give an example of the effectiveness of Hemingway's "less is more" style of writing.

3. What does Hemingway's story gain from using the detached third-person narrative point of view? What would have been lost had he used the first-person point of view, such as telling the story in the voice of one of the characters?

Becoming a Collaborator or Critic (option no. 10)

The sample essay following Chitra Divakaruni's short story was written by student author Serena Hoe in collaboration with this book's author.

The Word Love

YOU PRACTICE THEM OUT LOUD FOR DAYS IN FRONT OF the bathroom mirror, the words with which you'll tell your mother you're living with a man. Sometimes they are words of confession and repentance. Sometimes they are angry, defiant. Sometimes they melt into a single, sighing sound. Love. You let the water run so he won't hear you and ask what those foreign phrases you keep saying mean. You don't want to have to explain, don't want another argument like last time.

"Why are you doing this to yourself?" he'd asked, throwing his books down on the table when he returned from class to find you curled into a corner of the sagging sofa you'd bought together at a Berkeley garage sale. You'd washed your face but he knew right away that you'd been crying. Around you, wads of paper crumpled tight as stones. (This was when you thought writing would be the best way.) "I hate seeing you like this." Then he added, his tone darkening, "You're acting like I was some kind of a criminal."

You'd watched the upside-down titles of his books splaying across the table. Control Systems Engineering. Boiler Operations Guide. Handbook of Shock and Vibration. Cryptic as tarot cards, they seemed to be telling you something. If only you could decipher it.

"It isn't you," you'd said, gathering up the books guiltily, smoothing their covers. Holding them tight against you. "I'd have the same problem no matter who it was."

You tried to tell him about your mother, how she'd seen her husband's face for the first time at her wedding. How, when he died (you were two years old then), she had taken off her jewelry and put on widow's white and dedicated the rest of her life to the business of bringing you up. We only have each other, she often told you.

"So?"

"She lives in a different world. Can't you see that? She's never traveled more than a hundred miles from the village where she was born; she's never touched cigarettes or alcohol; even though she lives in Calcutta, she's never watched a movie."

"Are you serious!"

"I love her, Rex." I will not feel apologetic, you told yourself. You wanted him to know that when you conjured up her face, the stern angles of it softening into a rare smile, the silver at her temples catching the afternoon sun in the backyard under the pomegranate tree, love makes you breathless, as though someone had punched a hole through your chest. But he interrupted.

"So don't tell her," he said, "that you're living in sin. With a foreigner, no less. Someone whose favorite food is sacred cow steak and Budweiser. Who pops a pill now and then when he gets depressed. The shock'll probably do her in."

You hate it when he talks like that, biting off the ends of words and spitting them out. You try to tell yourself that he wants to hurt you only because he's hurting, because he's jealous of how much she means to you. You try to remember the special times. The morning he showed up outside your Shakespeare class with violets the color of his eyes. The evening when the two of you drove up to Grizzly Peak and watched the sunset spreading red over the Bay while he told you of his childhood, years of being shunted between his divorced parents till he was old enough to move out. How you had held him. The night in his apartment (has it only been three months?) when he took your hands in his warm strong ones, asking you to move in with him, please, because he really needed you. You try to shut out the whispery voice that lives behind the ache in your eyes, the one that started when you said yes and he kissed you, hard.

Mistake, says the voice, whispering in your mother's tones.

Sometimes the voice sounds different, not hers. It is a rushed intake of air, as just before someone asks a question that might change your life. You don't want to hear the question, which might be how did you get yourself into this mess, or perhaps why, so you leap in with that magic word. Love, you tell yourself, lovelovelove. But you know, deep down, that words solve nothing.

And so you no longer try to explain to him why you must tell your mother. You just stand in the bathroom in front of the crooked mirror with tarnished edges and practice the words. You try not to notice that the eyes in the mirror are so like her eyes, that same vertical line between the brows. The line of your jaw slants up at the same angle as hers when she would lean forward to kiss you goodbye at the door.

Outside a wino shouts something. Crash of broken glass and, later, police sirens. But you're hearing the street vendor call out momphali, momphali, fresh and hot, and she's smiling, handing you a coin, saying, yes, baby, you can have some. The salty crunch of roasted peanuts fills your mouth, the bathroom water runs and runs, endless as sorrow, the week blurs past, and suddenly it's Saturday morning, the time of her weekly call.

She tells you how Aunt Arati's arthritis isn't getting any better in spite of the turmeric poultices. It's so cold this year in Calcutta, the shiuli flowers have all died. You listen, holding on to the rounded o's, the long liquid e's, the s's that brush against your face soft as night kisses. She's trying to arrange a marriage for cousin Leela who's going to graduate from college next year, remember? She misses you. Do you like your new apartment? How long before you finish the Ph.D. and come home for good? Her voice is small and far, tinny with static, "You're so quiet. . . Are you OK, shona? Is something bothering you?" You want to tell her, but your heart flings itself around in your chest like a netted bird, and the words that you practiced so long are gone.

"I'm fine, Ma," you say. "Everything's all right."

The first thing you did when you moved into his apartment was to put up the batik hanging, deep red flowers winding around a black circle. The late summer sun shone through the open window. Smell of California honeysuckle in the air, a radio next door playing Mozart. He walked in, narrowing his eyes, pausing to watch, You waited, pin in hand, the nubs of the fabric pulsing under your palm, erratic as a heart. "Not bad," he nodded finally, and you let out your breath in a relieved shiver of a laugh.

"My mother gave it to me," you said. "A going-away-to-college gift, a talisman. . . ." You started to tell him how she had bought it at the Maiden fair on a day as beautiful as this one, the buds just coming out on the mango trees, the red breasted bulbuls returning north. But he held up his hand, later. Swung you off the rickety chair and carried you to the bed. Lay on top, pinning you down. His eyes were sapphire stones. His hair caught the light, glinting like warm sandstone. Surge of electric (love or fear?) up your spine, making you shiver, making you forget what you wanted to say.

At night after lovemaking, you lie listening to his sleeping breath. His arms falls across you, warm, protective, you say to yourself. Outside, wind rattles the panes. A dry wind. (There hasn't been rain for a long time.) I am cherished.

But then the memories come.

Once when you were in college you had gone to see a popular Hindi movie with your girlfriends. Secretly, because Mother said movies were frivolous, decadent. But there were no secrets in Calcutta. When you came home from classes the next day, a suitcase full of your clothes was on the doorstep. A note on it, in your mother's hand. Better no daughter than a disobedient one, a shame to the family.

Even now you remember how you felt, the dizzy fear that shriveled the edges of the day, the desperate knocking on the door that left your knuckles raw. You'd sat on the doorstep all afternoon, and passersby had glanced at you curiously. By evening it was cold. The numbness crept up your feet and covered you. When she'd finally opened the door after midnight, for a moment you couldn't stand. She had pulled you up, and you had fallen into her arms, both of you crying. Later she had soaked your feet in hot water with boric soda. You still remember the softness of the towels with which she wiped them.

Why do you always focus on the sad things, you wonder. Is it some flaw in yourself, some cross-connection in the thin silver filaments of your brain? So many good things happened, too. Her sitting in the front row at your high school graduation, face bright as a dahlia above the white of her sari. The two of you going for a bath in the Ganga, the brown tug of the water on your clothes, the warm sleepy sun as you sat on the bank eating curried potatoes wrapped in hot puris. And further back, her teaching you to write, the soft curve of her hand over yours, helping you hold the chalk, the smell of her newly washed hair curling about your face.

But these memories are wary, fugitive. You have to coax them out of their dark recesses. They dissipate, foglike, even as you are looking at them. And suddenly his arm feels terribly heavy. You are suffocating beneath its weight, its muscular, hairy maleness. You slip out and step into the shower. The wind snatches at the straggly nasturtiums you planted on the little strip of balcony. What will you remember of him when it is all over? whispers the papery voice inside your skull. Light from the bathroom slashes the floor while against the dark wall the hanging glows fire-red.

The first month you moved in with him, your head pounded with fear and guilt every time the phone rang. You'd rush across the room to pick it up while he watched you from his tilted-back chair, raising an eyebrow. (You'd made him promise never to pick up the phone.) At night you slept next to the bedside extension. You picked it up on the very first ring, struggling up out of layers of sleep heavy as water to whisper a breathless hello, the next word held in readiness, mother. But it was never her. Sometimes it was a friend of yours from the graduate program. Mostly it was for him. Women. Ex-girl-friends, he would explain with a guileless smile, stressing the ex. Then he would turn toward the window, his voice dropping into a low murmur while you pretended sleep and hated yourself for being jealous.

She always called on Saturday morning, Saturday night back home. The last thing before she went to bed. You picture her sitting on the large mahogany bed where you, too, had slept when you were little. Or when you were sick or scared. Outside, crickets are chanting. The night watchman makes his rounds, calling out the hour. The old ayah (she has been there from before you were born) stands behind her, combing out her long hair which lifts a little in the breeze from the fan, the silver in it glimmering like a smile. It is the most beautiful hair in the world.

And so you grew less careful. Sometimes you'd call out from the shower for him to answer the phone. And he would tease you (you sure now?) before picking it up. At night after the last kiss your body would slide off his damp, glistering one – and you didn't care which side of the bed it was as long as you had him to hold on to. Or was it that you wanted her, somehow, to find out? the voice asks. But you are learning to not pay attention to the voice, to fill your mind with sensations (how the nubs of his elbows fit exactly into your cupped palms, how his sleeping breath stirs the small hairs on your arm) until its echoes dissipate.

So when the phone rang very early that Tuesday morning you thought nothing of it. You pulled sleep like a furry blanket over your head, and even when you half heard his voice, suddenly formal, saying just one moment, please, you didn't get it. Not until he was shaking your shoulder, handing you the phone, mouthing the words silently, your mother.

Later you try to remember what you said to her, but you can't quite get the words right. Something about a wonderful man, getting married soon (although the only time you'd discussed marriage was when he had told you it wasn't for him). She'd called to let you know that cousin Leela's wedding was all arranged—a good Brahmin boy, a rising executive in an accounting firm. Next month in Delhi. The whole family would travel there. She'd bought your ticket already. But now of course you need not come. Her voice had been a spear of ice. Did you cry out, Don't be angry, Mother, please? Did you beg forgiveness? Did you whisper (again that word) love? You do know this: you kept talking, even after the phone went dead. When you finally looked up, he was watching you. His eyes were opaque, like pebbles.

All through the next month you try to reach her. You call. The ayah answers. She sounds frightened when she hears your voice. Memsaab has told her not to speak to you, or else she'll lose her job.

"She had the lawyer over yesterday to change her will. What did you do, Missybaba, that was so bad?"

You hear your mother in the background. "Who are you talking to, Ayah? What? How can it be my daughter? I don't have a daughter. Hang up right now."

"Mother . . ." you cry. The word ricochets through the apartment so that the hanging shivers against the wall. Its black center ripples like a bottomless well. The phone goes dead. You call again. Your fingers are shaking. It's hard to see the digits through the tears. Your knees feel as though they have been broken. The phone buzzes against your ear like a trapped insect. No one picks it up. You keep calling all week. Finally a machine tells you the number has been changed. There is no new number.

Here is a story your mother told you when you were growing up:

There was a girl I used to play with sometimes, whose father was the roof thatcher in your grandfather's village. They lived near the women's lake. She was an only child, pretty in a dark-skinned way, and motherless, so her father spoiled her. He let her run wild, climbing trees, swimming in the river. Let her go to school, even after she reached the age when girls from good families stayed home, waiting to be married. (You know already this is a tale with an unhappy end, a cautionary moral.) He would laugh when the old women of the village warned him that an unmarried girl is like a firebrand in a field of ripe grain. She's a good girl, he'd say. She knows right and wrong. He found her a fine match, a master carpenter from the next village. But a few days before the wedding, her body was discovered in the women's lake. We all thought it was an accident until we heard about the rocks she had tied in her sari. (She stops, waits for the question you do not want to ask but must.) Who knows why? People whispered that she was pregnant, said they'd seen her once or twice with a man, a traveling actor who had come to the village some time back. Her father was heartbroken, his good name ruined. He had to leave the village, all those tongues and eyes. Leave behind the house of his forefathers that he loved so much. No, no one knows what happened to him.

For months afterward, you lie awake at night and think of the abandoned house, mice claws skittering over the floors, the dry papery slither of snakes, bats' wings. When you fall asleep you dream of a beautiful dark girl knotting stones into her palloo and swimming out to the middle of the dark lake. The water is cool on her heavying breasts, her growing belly. It ripples and parts for her. Before she goes under, she turns toward you. Sometimes her face is a blank oval, featureless. Sometimes it is your face.

Things are not going well for you. At school you cannot concentrate on your classes, they seem so disconnected from the rest of your life. Your advisor calls you into her office to talk to you. You stare at the neat rows of books behind her head. She is speaking of missed deadlines, research that lacks innovation. You notice her teeth, large and white and regular, like a horse's. She pauses, asks if you feeling well.

"Oh yes," you say, in the respectful tone you were always taught to use with teachers. "I feel just fine."

But the next day it is too difficult to get up and get dressed for class. What difference would it make if you miss a deconstructionist critique of the Sonnets? you ask yourself. You stay in bed until the postal carrier comes.

You have written a letter to Aunt Arati explaining, asking her to please tell you mother that you're sorry. I'll come home right now if she wants. Every day you check the box for Aunt's reply, but there's nothing. Her arthritis is acting up, you tell yourself. It's the wedding preparations. The letter is lost.

Things are not going well between him and you either. Sometimes when he is talking, the words make no sense. You watch him move his mouth as though he were a character in a foreign film someone has forgotten to dub. He asks you a question. By the raised tone of his voice you know that's what it is, but you have no idea what he wants from you. He asks again, louder.

"What?" you say.

He walks out, slamming the door.

You have written a letter to your mother, too. A registered letter, so it can't get lost. You run outside every day when you hear the mail van. Nothing. You glance at the carrier, a large black woman, suspiciously. "Are you sure?" you ask. You wonder if she put the letter into someone else's box by mistake. After she leaves, you peer into the narrow metal slots of the other mailboxes, trying to see.

At first he was sympathetic. He held you when you lay sleepless at night. "Cry," he said. "Get it out of your system." Then, "It was bound to happen sooner or later. You must have known that. Maybe it's all for the best." Later, "Try to look at the positive side. You had to cut the umbilical cord sometime."

You pulled away when he said things like that. What did he know, you thought, about families, about (yes) love. He'd left home the day he turned eighteen. He only called his mother on Mother's Day and, if he remembered, her birthday. When he told her about you she'd said, "How nice, dear. We really must have you both over to the house for dinner sometime soon."

Lately he has been angry a lot. "You're blaming me for this mess between your mother and yourself," he shouted the other day at dinner although you hadn't said anything. He shook his head. "You're driving yourself crazy. You need a shrink." He shoved back his plate and slammed out of the apartment again. The dry, scratchy voice pushing at your temples reminded you how he'd watched the red-haired waitress at the Mexican restaurant last week, how he was laughing, his hand on her shoulder, when you came out of the rest room. How, recently, there had been more late-night calls.

When he came back, very late, you were still sitting at the table. Staring at the hanging. He took you by the arms and brought his face close to yours.

"Sweetheart," he said, "I want to help you but I don't know how. You've become obsessed with this thing. You're so depressed all the time I hardly know you anymore. So your mother is behaving irrationally. You can't afford to do the same."

You looked past his head. He has a sweet voice, you thought absently. A voice that charms. An actor's voice.

"You're not even listening," he said.

You tried because you knew he was trying, too. But later in bed, even with his lips pressing hot into you, a part of you kept counting the days. How many since you mailed the letter? He pulled away with an angry exclamation and turned the other way. You put out your hand to touch the nubs of his backbone.

I'm sorry. But you went on thinking, something must be wrong. A reply should have reached you by now.

The letter came today. You walked out under a low, graybellied sky and there was the mail- woman, holding it up, smiling – the registered letter to your mother, with a red ink stamp across the address. Not accepted. Return to sender.

Now you are kneeling in the bathroom, rummaging in the cabinet behind the cleaning supplies. When you find the bottles, you line them up along the sink top. You open each one and look at the tablets: red, white, pink. You'd found them one day while cleaning. You remember how shocked you'd been, the argument the two of you'd had. He'd shrugged and spread his hands, palms up. You wish now you'd asked him which ones were the sleeping pills. No matter. You can take them all, if that's what you decide to do.

You'd held the letter in your hand a long time, until it grew weightless, transparent. You could see through it to another letter, one that wasn't written yet. His letter.

You knew what it would say.

Before he left for class this morning he had looked at you still crumpled on the sofa where you'd spent the night. He looked for a long time, as though he'd never really seen you before. Then he said, very softly, "It was never me, was it? Never love. It was always you and her, her and you."

He hadn't waited for an answer.

Wind slams a door somewhere, making you jump. It's raining outside, the first time in years. Big swollen drops, then thick silver sheets of it. You walk out to the balcony. The rain runs down your cheeks, the tears you couldn't shed. The nasturtiums, washed clean, and glowing red. Smell of wet earth. You take a deep breath, decide to go for a long walk.

As you walk you try to figure out what to do. (And maybe the meaning of what you have done.) The pills are there, of course. You picture it: the empty bottles by the bed, your body fallen across it, and hand flung over the side. The note left behind. Will he press repentant kisses on your pale palm? Will she fly across the ocean to wash your stiff eyelids with her tears?

Or – What? what? Surely there's another choice. But you can't find the words to give it shape. When you look dawn the empty street, the bright leaves of the newly-washed maples hurt your eyes.

So you continue to walk. Your shoes darken, grow heavy. Water swirls in the gutters, carrying away months of dust. Coming toward you is a young woman with an umbrella. Shoulders bunched, she tiptoes through puddles, trying hard to stay dry. But a gust snaps the umbrella back and soaks her. She is shocked for a moment, angry. Then she begins to laugh. And you are laughing too, because you know just how it feels. Short, hysterical laugh-bursts, then quieter, drawing the breath deep into yourself. You watch as she stops in the middle of the sidewalk and tosses her ruined umbrella into a garbage can. She spreads her arms and lets the rain take her: hair, paisley blouse, midnight-blue skirt. Thunder and lightning. It's going to be quite a storm. You remember the monsoons of your childhood. There are no people in this memory, only the sky, rippling with exhilarating light.

You know then that when you return to the apartment you will pack your belongings. A few clothes, some music, a favorite book, the hanging. No, not that. You will not need it in your new life, the one you're going to live for yourself.

And a word comes to you out of the opening sky. The word love. You see that you had never understood it before. It is like rain, and when you lift your face to it, like rain it washes away inessentials, leaving you hollow, clean, ready to begin.

Chitra Divakaruni (b. 1956)

The Unbearable Weight of Love
Student author: Serena Hoe

Serena's interpretation captures the story's themes relating to the complex topic of love very well. By adding a section on the author's unique style of writing toward the end of her essay, I become Serena's collaborator.

In the story "The Word Love" by Chitra Divakaruni, the narrator, who is studying for her Ph.D. at University of California, Berkeley, has recently moved into a new apartment with her lover Rex, who is a white American. The narrator's mother, a widow who lives in India, had raised her daughter singlehandedly. She has no knowledge of her daughter's relationship. When the mother calls unexpectedly, the narrator nervously tries to break the news gently and tactfully to her. She knows that telling the truth would hurt her mother, who, coming from a strict upbringing, was unlikely to approve of her daughter's conduct. For that reason, she has been practicing words of "confession and repentance" in front of the bathroom mirror. However, when the mother calls, all the rehearsals are of no avail. The narrator ends up revealing the news of her lover to her mother in a highly unsatisfactory manner. The heartbroken mother responds by disowning the narrator. She does not answer the narrator's calls and letters.

Things are not going well between the narrator and her lover either. Rex, who is not the marrying type and engages in relationships with other women, feels that the narrator loves only her mother. As a result, there are constant arguments about this dysfunctional love triangle. Whenever her "opaque, pebble-eyed" lover talks to her, he is sarcastic and bitter. She tries to tell herself that he wants to hurt her only because he is hurting, because he is jealous of how much her mother means to her. She makes excuses and tries to reconcile by remembering the special times. However, the thoughts of him evaporate like fog, and she only thinks and recollects the memories of her relationship with her mother. As a result, Rex leaves her.

When things are at their worst, the narrator reaches an epiphany while taking a walk during a rainstorm. She realizes that she has been trying to satisfy everyone else's life but her own. She has been carrying an impossible burden on her shoulders. But now it is time to let go and be free. It is time for her to live for herself, to start a new life, and to love herself; the meaning of this love she has never understood before.

The events of this story make us realize that the *word* "love" is simple, but the feeling of love is complicated, so much so that trying to satisfy everyone's expectations of love sometimes becomes an unbearable burden. In the process of grappling with that burden, one becomes aware of the importance of knowing and fulfilling one's own needs and not always sacrificing to please others.

In India, the narrator had an intense mother-daughter relationship. The mother, who became a widow when the narrator was two years old, had "taken off her jewelry and put on widow's white and dedicated the rest of her life to the business of bringing [her] up." She often tells her daughter, "We only have each other." When the narrator had secretly gone to see a popular Hindi movie, which was considered frivolous and decadent by her mother, she was punished, but later they had a very emotional reconciliation.

At the narrator's high school graduation, her mother sat in the front row, "face bright as a dahlia above the white of her sari." The narrator pictures her mother sitting on the large mahogany bed, where she had slept too when she was "sick or scared." It is obvious that this mother-daughter bond shows strong love, but this love comes in many guises. What the narrator and her American boyfriend feel for each other is also categorized as love, but the mother cannot see it as such. She probably would have been happy to arrange a "suitable" match for her daughter. After hearing the shocking news of her daughter's involvement, the mother withdraws the invitation and plane ticket to cousin Leela's wedding and even changes her will. When Ayah (the maid) answers the narrator's calls, the mother, in the background, would say, "Who are you talking to, Ayah? What? How can it be my daughter? I don't have a daughter. Hang up right now." The narrator writes a letter to her mother asking for forgiveness, but the registered letter is returned with a red ink stamp across the address. "Not accepted. Return to sender." Apparently, the mother does not see her daughter as a mature person, capable of good judgment with regard to making decisions concerning her personal life. Having sacrificed her life for her daughter, she expects a similar sacrifice from her.

As if the mother's rejection is not enough, the narrator's lover adds to her misery and burden. Puzzled and dismayed at the situation, he feels slighted by her giving the mother so much importance. He is in constant argument with her. Since he is angry and jealous, he often responds by "biting off the ends of the words and spitting them out." When the narrator is crying, instead of comforting her, he says, "I hate seeing you like this. You're acting like I was some kind of a criminal." When she confides in him that she feels guilty about telling her mother about him, he responds sarcastically:

"So don't tell her that you're living in sin. With a foreigner, no less. Someone whose favorite food is sacred cow steak and Budweiser. Who pops a pill now and then when he gets depressed. The shock'll probably do her in."

Pinning up the batik hanging that she received as a "going-away-to-college gift" from her mother, she nervously awaits his response, but all he says is "Not bad." While she tells him about the Maidan fair in India, he rudely interrupts without a care, carries her to bed, lies on top "pinning . . . her down." At the end, when his anger escalates, he erupts: "You're blaming me for this mess between your mother and yourself. It was never me. Was it? Never love. It was always you and her, her and you."

As a result of the two chaotic and complicated relationships, she finally comes to the realization that she cannot please her mother and her lover if she cannot please herself. She must satisfy herself first.

"You will not need it [the hanging from her mother] in your new life, the one you're going to live for yourself," she tells herself. And with this resolve, she starts a new life.

The following part on Divakaruni's style of writing is an addition by me, the author of this book, to demonstrate collaboration with the student.

Chitra Divakaruni communicates the story's themes with a striking style. The notable elements are the narrative point of view, imagery, and symbolism. The story is told in the second person – a very unusual narrative point of view. The main character is talking to herself throughout, thus telling her story to herself. This unique device appropriately and effectively captures the protagonist's isolation. Having been rejected by both her mother and her American lover, she has no one but herself as an audience.

Among numerous images that make the style vibrant, two stand out. The first is the description of the lover as an "opaque, pebble-eyed" man. The author conveys this man's inaccessibility and lack of tenderness in this telling metaphor. His manner of talking to her – always "biting off the ends of words and spitting them out" – shows the barbed and abrasive nature of his response to her efforts to make him understand her relationship with the mother.

The two prominent symbols in the story are the batik hanging and the rainstorm. The batik, a symbol of the mother-daughter bonding, had controlled her life up to that point. In the story's wrenching last scene, she frees herself from the spell of the past by leaving the batik hanging behind. She must create her own center for her new life. The rainstorm during which she washes herself clean of the two oppressive ties is an appropriate purifying symbol. It is also her baptism and initiation into a new life to be lived on her own terms.

Questions on "The Word Love"

1. In "The Word Love" by Chitra Divakaruni, the main character talks to herself throughout the story. Typically, stories are narrated either from the first-person or third-person point of view. The use of this second-person narrative is an unusual form. What might have necessitated Divakaruni's use of this peculiar style of narration? How effective is it in giving the story an impact?

2. Between the protagonist's mother and her American boyfriend, which of them is less selfish and more concerned about the protagonist? Do they have a genuine grievance about the way they are treated by the protagonist?

3. The story is rich in symbolism – the batik hanging (a gift from the protagonist's mother), rain, and the umbrella that won't hold up against the wind and rain (toward the story's end) are just a few of the symbols. Discuss their effectiveness in expressing the story's themes. Mention and discuss any other use of symbolism by the author.

4. Create a question based on this story. Your question should draw the reader deeper into the story's substance.

Stories of Violations of Basic Human Rights and Urgent Social Concern
(option no. 11)

Stories: "The Only Traffic Signal on the Reservation Doesn't Flash Red
Anymore" by Sherman Alexie
"The Rape" by Khushwant Singh
"Samapti" by Rabindranath Tagore

The Only Traffic Signal on the Reservation Doesn't Flash Red Anymore

"Go ahead," Adrian said. "Pull the trigger." I held a pistol to my temple. I was sober but wished I was drunk enough to pull the trigger.

"Go for it," Adrian said. "You chickenshit."

While I still held that pistol to my temple, I used my other hand to flip Adrian off. Then I made a fist with my third hand to gather a little bit of courage or stupidity, and wiped sweat from my forehead with my fourth hand.

"Here," Adrian said. "Give me the damn thing."

Adrian took the pistol, put the barrel in his mouth, smiled around the metal, and pulled the trigger. Then he cussed wildly, laughed, and spit out the BB.

"Are you dead yet?" I asked.
"Nope," he said. "Not yet. Give me another beer."
"Hey, we don't drink no more, remember? How about a Diet Pepsi?"
"That's right, en it? I forgot. Give me a Pepsi."

Adrian and I sat on the porch and watched the reservation. Nothing happened. From our chairs made rockers by unsteady legs, we could see that the only traffic signal on the reservation had stopped working.

"Hey, Victor," Adrian asked. "Now when did that thing quit flashing?"

"Don't know," I said.

It was summer. Hot. But we kept our shirts on to hide our beer bellies and chicken-pox scars. At least, I wanted to hide my beer belly. I was a former basketball star fallen out of shape. It's always kind of sad when that happens. There's nothing more unattractive than a vain man, and that goes double for an Indian man.

"So," Adrian asked. "What you want to do today?"

"Don't know."

We watched a group of Indian boys walk by. I'd like to think there were ten of them. But there were actually only four or five. They were skinny, darkened by sun, their hair long and wild. None of them looked like they had showered for a week. Their smell made me jealous. They were off to cause trouble somewhere, I'm sure. Little warriors looking for honor in some twentieth-century vandalism. Throw a few rocks through windows, kick a dog, slash a tire. Run like hell when the tribal cops drove slowly by the scene of the crime.

"Hey," Adrian asked. "Isn't that the Windmaker boy?"

"Yeah," 1 said and watched Adrian lean forward to study Julius Windmaker, the best basketball player on the reservation, even though he was only fifteen years old.

"He looks good," Adrian said.
"Yeah, he must not be drinking."
"Yet."
"Yeah, yet."

Julius Windmaker was the latest in a long line of reservation basketball heroes, going all the way back to Aristotle Polatkin, who was shooting jumpshots exactly one year before James Naismith supposedly invented basketball. I'd only seen Julius play a few times, but he had that gift, that grace, those fingers like a goddamn medicine man. One time, when the tribal school traveled to Spokane to play this white high school team, Julius scored sixty-seven points and the Indians won by forty.

"I didn't know they'd be riding horses," I heard the coach of the white team say when I was leaving. I mean, Julius was an artist, moody. A couple times he walked right off the court during the middle of a game because there wasn't enough competition. That's how he was. Julius could throw a crazy pass, surprise us all, and send it out of bounds. But nobody called it a turnover because we all knew that one of his teammates should've been there to catch the pass. We loved him.

"Hey, Julius," Adrian yelled from the porch. "You ain't shit."

Julius and his friends laughed, flipped us off, and shook their tail feathers a little as they kept walking down the road. They all knew Julius was the best ballplayer on the reservation these days, maybe the best ever, and they knew Adrian was just confirming that fact.

It was easier for Adrian to tease Julius because he never really played basketball. He was more detached about the whole thing. But I used to be quite a ballplayer. Maybe not as good as some, certainly not as good as Julius, but I still felt that ache in my bones, that need to be better than everyone else. It's that need to be the best, that feeling of immortality, that drives a ballplayer. And when it disappears, for whatever reason, that ballplayer is never the same person, on or off the court. I know when I lost it, that edge. During my senior year in high school we made it to the state finals. I'd been playing like crazy, hitting everything. It was like throwing rocks into the ocean from a little rowboat. I couldn't miss. Then, right before the championship game, we had our pregame meeting in the first-aid room of the college where the tournament was held every year.

It took a while for our coach to show up so we spent the time looking at these first-aid manuals. These books had all kinds of horrible injuries. Hands and feet smashed flat in printing presses, torn apart by lawnmowers, burned and dismembered. Faces that had gone through windshields, dragged over gravel, split open by garden tools. The stuff was disgusting, but we kept looking, flipping through photograph after photograph, trading books, until we all wanted to throw up. While I looked at those close-ups of death and destruction, I lost it. I think everybody in that room, everybody on the team, lost that feeling of immortality. We went out and lost the championship game by twenty points. I missed every shot I took. I missed everything.

"So," I asked Adrian. "You think Julius will make it all the way?"

"Maybe, maybe."

There's a definite history of reservation heroes who never finish high school, who never finish basketball seasons. Hell, there's been one or two guys who played just a few minutes of one game, just enough to show what they could have been. And there's the famous case of Silas Sirius, who made one move and scored one basket in his entire basketball career. People still talk about it.

"Hey," I asked Adrian. "Remember Silas Sirius?"

"Hell," Adrian said. "Do I remember? I was there when he grabbed that defensive rebound, took a step, and flew the length of the court, did a full spin in midair, and then dunked that fucking ball. And I don't mean it looked like he flew, or it was so beautiful it was almost like he flew. I mean, he flew, period."

I laughed, slapped my legs, and knew that I believed Adrian's story more as it sounded less true.

"Shit," he continued. "And he didn't grow no wings. He just kicked his legs a little. Held that ball like a baby in his hand. And he was smiling. Really. Smiling when he flew. Smiling when he dunked it, smiling when he walked off the court and never came back. Hell, he was still smiling ten years after that."

I laughed some more, quit for a second, then laughed a little longer because it was the right thing to do.

"Yeah," I said, "Silas was a ballplayer."

"Real ballplayer," Adrian agreed.

In the outside world, a person can be a hero one second and a nobody the next. Think about it. Do white people remember the names of those guys who dove into that icy river to rescue passengers from that plane wreck a few years back? Hell, white people don't even remember the names of the dogs who save entire families from burning up in house fires by barking. And, to be honest, I don't remember none of those names either, but a reservation hero is remembered. A reservation hero is a hero forever. In fact, their status grows over the years as the stories are told and retold.

"Yeah," Adrian said. "It's too bad that damn diabetes got him. Silas was always talking about a comeback."

"Too bad, too bad."

We both leaned further back into our chairs. Silence. We watched the grass grow, the rivers flow, the winds blow.

"Damn," Adrian asked. "When did that fucking traffic signal quit working?"
"Don't know."
"Shit, they better fix it. Might cause an accident."

We both looked at each other, looked at the traffic signal, knew that about only one car an hour passed by, and laughed our asses off. Laughed so hard that when we tried to rearrange ourselves, Adrian ended up with my ass and I ended up with his. That looked so funny that we laughed them off again and it took us most of an hour to get them back right again. Then we heard glass breaking in the distance.

"Sounds like beer bottles," Adrian said.
"Yeah, Coors Light, I think."
"Bottled 1988."

We started to laugh, but a tribal cop drove by and cruised down the road where Julius and his friends had walked earlier.

"Think they'll catch them?" I asked Adrian.

"Always do."

After a few minutes, the tribal cop drove by again, with Julius in the backseat and his friends running behind.

"Hey," Adrian asked. "What did he do?"
"Threw a brick through a BIA pickup's windshield," One of the Indian boys yelled back.
"Told you it sounded like a pickup window," I said.
"Yeah, yeah, a 1982 Chevy."
"With red paint."
"No, blue."

We laughed for just a second. Then Adrian sighed long and deep. He rubbed his head, ran his fingers through his hair, scratched his scalp hard.

"I think Julius is going to go bad," he said.
"No way," I said. "He's just horsing around."
"Maybe, maybe."

It's hard to be optimistic on the reservation. When a glass sits on a table here, people don't wonder if it's half filled or half empty. They just hope it's good beer. Still, Indians have a way of surviving. But it's almost like Indians can easily survive the big stuff. Mass murder, loss of language and land rights. It's the small things that hurt the most. The white waitress who wouldn't take an order, Tonto, the Washington Redskins. And, just like everybody else, Indians need heroes to help them learn how to survive. But what happens when our heroes don't even know how to pay their bills?

"Shit, Adrian," I said. "He's just a kid."
"Ain't no children on a reservation."
"Yeah, yeah, I've heard that before. Well," I said. "I guess that Julius is pretty good in school, too."
"And?"
"And he wants to maybe go to college."
"Really?"
"Really," I said and laughed. And I laughed because half of me was happy and half of me wasn't sure what else to do.

A year later, Adrian and I sat on the same porch in the same chairs. We'd done things in between, like ate and slept and read the newspaper. It was another hot summer. Then again, summer is supposed to be hot.

"I'm thirsty," Adrian said. "Give me a beer."
"How many times do 1 have to tell you? We don't drink anymore."
"Shit," Adrian said. "I keep forgetting. Give me a god-damn Pepsi."
"That's a whole case for you today already."
"Yeah, yeah, fuck these substitute addictions."

We sat there for a few minutes, hours, and then Julius Windmaker staggered down the road.

"Oh, look at that," Adrian said. "Not even two in the afternoon and he's drunk as a skunk."
"Don't he have a game tonight?"
"Yeah, he does."
"Well, I hope he sobers up in time."
"Me, too."

I'd only played one game drunk and it was in an all-Indian basketball tournament after I got out of high school. I'd been drinking the night before and woke up feeling kind of sick, so I got drunk again. Then I went out and played a game. I felt disconnected the whole time. Nothing seemed to fit right. Even my shoes, which had fit perfectly before, felt too big for my feet. I couldn't even see the basketball or basket clearly. They were more like ideas. I mean, I knew where they were generally supposed to be, so I guessed at where I should be. Somehow or another, I scored ten points.

"He's been drinking quite a bit, enit?" Adrian asked.
"Yeah, I hear he's even been drinking Sterno."
"Shit, that'll kill his brain quicker than shit."

Adrian and I left the porch that night and went to the tribal school to watch Julius play. He still looked good in his uniform, although he was a little puffy around the edges. But he just wasn't the ballplayer we all remembered or expected. He missed shots, traveled, threw dumb passes that we all knew were dumb passes. By the fourth quarter, Julius sat at the end of the bench, hanging his head, and the crowd filed out, all talking about which of the younger players looked good. We talked about some kid named Lucy in the third grade who already had a nice move or two.

Everybody told their favorite Julius Windmaker stories, too. Times like that, on a reservation, a basketball game felt like a funeral and wake all rolled up together. Back at home, on the porch, Adrian and I sat wrapped in shawls because the evening was kind of cold.

"It's too bad, too bad," I said. "I thought Julius might be the one to make it all the way."
"I told you he wouldn't. I told you so."
"Yeah, yeah. Don't rub it in."

We sat there in silence and remembered all of our heroes, ballplayers from seven generations, all the way back. It hurts to lose any of them because Indians kind of see ballplayers as saviors. I mean, if basketball would have been around, I'm sure Jesus Christ would've been the best point guard in Nazareth. Probably the best player in the entire world. And in the beyond. I just can't explain how much losing Julius Windmaker hurt us all.

"Well," Adrian asked. "What do you want to do tomorrow?"
"Don't know."
"Shit, that damn traffic signal is still broken. Look."

Adrian pointed down the road and he was right. But what's the point of fixing it in a place where the STOP signs are just suggestions?

"What time is it?" Adrian asked.
"I don't know. Ten, I think."
"Let's go somewhere."
"Where?"
"I don't know, Spokane, anywhere. Let's just go."

"Okay," I said, and we both walked inside the house, shut the door, and locked it tight. No. We left it open just a little bit in case some crazy Indian needed a place to sleep. And in the morning we found crazy Julius passed out on the living room carpet.

"Hey, you bum," Adrian yelled. "Get off my floor."

"This is my house, Adrian," I said.

"That's right. I forgot. Hey, you bum, get your ass off Victor's floor." Julius groaned and farted but he didn't wake up. It really didn't bother Adrian that Julius was on the floor, so he threw an old blanket on top of him. Adrian and I grabbed our morning coffee and went back out to sit on the porch. We had both just about finished our cups when a group of Indian kids walked by, all holding basketballs of various shapes and conditions.

"Hey, look," Adrian said. "Ain't that the Lucy girl?"

I saw that it was, a little brown girl with scarred knees, wearing her daddy's shirt.

"Yeah, that's her," I said.
"I heard she's so good that she plays for the sixth grade boys team."
"Really? She's only in third grade herself, isn't she?"
"Yeah, yeah, she's a little warrior."

Adrian and I watched those Indian children walk down the road, walking toward another basketball game.

"God, I hope she makes it all the way," I said.

"Yeah, yeah," Adrian said, stared into the bottom of his cup, and then threw it across the yard. And we both watched it with all of our eyes, while the sun rose straight up above us and settled down behind the house, watched that cup revolve, revolve, until it came down whole to the ground.

Sherman Alexie (b. 1966)

Balancing Hope Against Despair in Sherman Alexie
Student author: Jarrod Roland

Jarrod uses a modified journal format for this interpretation of Sherman Alexie's story. He supports his reading of the story with valid reasoning and character analysis. He shows the connection between the story's theme and Alexie's choice of symbols, pointing out also the author's irrepressible sense of humor. Another student Jack Murray's essay on the same story is on my website.

Sherman Alexie's short story "The Only Traffic Signal on the Reservation Doesn't Flash Red Anymore" is about two Native American men named Victor and Adrian. They sit on their porch everyday and drink Diet Pepsi. The narrator of the story is Victor, who describes his feelings on seeing Julius Windmaker, the latest reservation basketball hero. Victor and Adrian discuss the fact that Julius has not started drinking alcohol, both agreeing that it would only be a matter of time. Victor talks about the days when he was a reservation basketball hero, and how important having heroes is on the reservation. Victor and Adrian reminisce about heroes from the past until they hear some glass breaking in the distance. They see that the trouble was caused by Julius Windmaker, whose actions support their thoughts of his going bad. Victor goes on to talk about the pessimism that exists on the reservation and how there is little hope for Native Americans.

This story flashes forward one year to Victor and Adrian still sitting on their front porch, drinking Diet Pepsi, and the two seeing Julius Windmaker walking down the street drunk at about two in the afternoon. Victor tells his story about getting drunk before one of his final games and just how disconnected he felt throughout it. After going out to one of Julius' games, Victor and Adrian talk about their sadness and disappointment on seeing their latest basketball prodigy fall short of their expectations. The two go to sleep and leave the front door open for any "crazy Indians needing a place to sleep." When they wake up, they find none other than Julius Windmaker passed out on the floor. Victor and Adrian assume their positions on the porch and begin talking about a third-grade girl named Lucy, a rising star on the basketball court. They speculate that she may make it all the way.

Sherman Alexie's story is about tenacity of hope in the Native American culture. Even when everything in life points to the negative, one can still choose to focus on the positive. Victor and Adrian seem to have given up on themselves as being heroes, but they have quite a bit of hope invested in Julius Windmaker. Victor talks about all of the negative aspects of living on the reservation – alcoholism, poverty, poor diet, and racism – but he still hopes that some of the Native American youth can overcome these obstacles and become heroes. They tell stories over and over about what certain Indians like Silas Sirius have accomplished to keep their hope alive. The title of the story –"The Only Traffic Signal on the Reservation Doesn't Flash Red Anymore – implies that no one would bother to stop and worry about the people on the reservation. Native Americans keep getting addicted to alcohol and die from diabetes because of a poor diet. In spite of all these negative indicators, Sherman Alexie points toward hope for the survival of Native Americans.

To convey a sense of stubborn hope that characterizes the story's two spokesmen for Native Americans, Sherman Alexie uses complex symbolism. The stoplight represents success of the Native American culture in the "White World"; but just because success is not prominent for them does not mean that they have to give up hope. The basketball heroes, besides being real heroes on the reservation, represent hope that the culture and the people who live on these poverty-stricken and alcohol-afflicted reservations will survive.

Strong characterization is another element that is notable in Alexie's style of writing. He develops Victor and Adrian's characters to give the reader a real glimpse into what it would be like to see the world through their eyes, off the porch, in between cans of Diet Pepsi. Appropriate language is another feature of Alexie's style that gives the reader a feeling of being a part of the story. The word "enit," used by Victor and Adrian to agree with each other, is an expression mostly used on Native American reservations. The most striking element of Alexie's style, however, is humor. Even though some of the material he writes about is not meant to be funny, he still has the ability to make us laugh while pondering the painful implications of his story.

Questions on "The Only Traffic Signal . . ."

1. Explain the meaning of the title of Sherman Alexie's short story "The Only Traffic Signal on the Reservation Doesn't Flash Red Anymore."

2. Does the story offer any hope that the Native Americans living on that reservation can get past the problem of alcoholism and government neglect? Support your answer with details from the story.

3. The story attempts to create mythic figures. Identify one or two of them and write their character analysis. What is their role in the story?

1. While waiting for the coach in the first-aid room of the college, the basketball players happen to look at the first-aid manuals. They see pictures of mangled bodies and all kinds of horrible injuries. They feel nauseated at "those close-ups of death and destruction." Alexie's narrator says: "I think everybody in that room, everybody on the team, lost that feeling of immortality. We went out and lost the championship game by twenty points. I missed every shot I took. I missed everything." Make a connection between what the players saw in the first-aid manuals and their miserable performance in the game and their dramatically altered view of immortality.

2. Create a question based on this story. Your question should draw the reader deeper into the story's substance.

The Rape

Khushwant Singh's short story "The Rape" provokes diametrically opposed responses as to the position that the story takes on the two characters' responsibility in the rape and on the definitions of the term "rape." Perhaps the most controversial part of the story is its ending. This story is one of the best examples of what is known in literary style as the esthetics of omission that consists of intentionally withholding information that readers expect. As a result, the characters' motives for their actions remain a mystery to the readers. A careful reading of the culture-related clues in the story is essential to valid interpretations. My sample essay on this story tries to shed light on questions of cultural relevance. Read this story on your own. It could not be included in this book because of problems with copyright permissions. Even if you are unable to read the story, my following essay on this story gives sufficient plot summary to make it easy for you to understand my interpretation and the story's themes.

An explication of the story by this book's author

Using the note-taking method introduced in Chapter Five to interpret complex works

This story concerns an important societal issue. However, it offers several challenges of interpretation. In some works the motives of characters and the author's position are so inscrutable that a definitive explication is difficult. "The Rape" is such a story. Using the note-taking system, suggested in Chapter Five and especially helpful when reading complex works, I put dots in the margins of those passages that carried important plot and thematic details. In the process of converting dots into numbers for content, I focused on those sections that hinted at the mutual attraction of the story's two young protagonists despite their families' mutual animosity. The scene on the roof tops of the adjoining homes of the two protagonists carries this hint. The two characters' actions suggest that they are almost sleepwalking through life. They seem to feel more at home in their reveries and dreams than in the harsh reality and their routine duties. In fact, the climactic moment of the rape scene has the character of a dream. I made a marginal note of the hot weather and the soft breeze, symbolic of the stirrings of their passion. Since Bindo's response to the rape is very significant, it receives three dots in the margin and eventual conversion to a major support for my interpretation of the story's enigmatic ending. My explication of the story now follows.

The setting of this controversial story is an extremely hot, humid and still night in an Indian Punjabi village. The oppressive heat and invading mosquitoes stretch Dalip Singh's patience to the limit. However, a torture that is even more unbearable than the weather is Dalip's passion for Bindo, his cousin, whom he espies on the adjoining rooftop. Since Bindo's father, Banta Singh, murdered his brother (that is, Dalip's father), the relations between the families have been strained. As a soft breeze begins to blow, Bindo stands up beside her bed.

> "She picked up her skirt from the two corners which fell just above her knees and held it across her face with both hands, baring herself from the waist to her neck, letting the cool breeze envelop her flat belly and her youthful bust. Then someone said something in an angry whisper [perhaps telling her that someone was watching her from the adjoining rooftop] and Bindo let down her shirt. She dropped on her charpoy [cot] and was lost in the confused outlines of her pillow."

Dalip is haunted in his dreams by Bindo's figure that starlight had revealed to him. His shut eyes "opened into another world where Bindo lived and loved, naked, unashamed and beautiful." Awakened in early hours before the dawn by his mother, Dalip goes through the routine of ploughing his fields – all the time thinking about Bindo. As the day disappears into night, Dalip goes out to his fields to clear the water channels for irrigation. Having done his work, Dalip "stretched himself on the cool grassy bank [of a stream]. . . Then the world relapsed into a moonlit silence."

The sound of splashing water jolts Dalip out of his reverie. He notices Bindo washing herself by the stream. "She rinsed her mouth and threw handfuls of water over her face. Then she stood up leaving her baggy trousers lying at her feet. She picked up her shirt from the front and bent down to wipe her face with it." At this point Dalip's "assault" on Bindo begins. His frenzy hurls him on her. He "smothered her face with passionate kisses and stifled her frightened cry by gluing his mouth to hers." Bindo resists but is soon exhausted and gives up. Later, Bindo's tearful eyes cause remorse in Dalip because he "had never intended hurting her. . . . Bindo opened her large black eyes and stared at him blankly. There was no hate in them, nor any love." Bindo's companions have been calling out for her, but she remains quiet. One of her friends discovers what has happened and calls for help as Dalip disappears into the dark.

Bindo's wealthy father, Banta Singh, bribes the officials so that there is no delay in the administration of justice, and all is set for Dalip to be sent to jail when Dalip persuades the magistrate to ask Bindo whether she had gone to him of her own free will. "Through the many folds of the shawl muffling her face Bindo answered 'Yes' " to the magistrate's question, and the story ends there.

This surprise ending leaves many questions unanswered: Is this story about the rape of Bindo, or is it about Bindo's clever seduction of Dalip? Is Dalip more "sinned against" than a sinner, to use a phrase from Shakespeare's *King Lear*? Does Bindo resort to her strategy of enticing Dalip because she wants to marry him in opposition to her family's plans? Since Dalip's passion for Bindo is genuine and sincere and since he never intends to hurt her, would it be valid to infer that public knowledge of consummation of his passion would inevitably lead to marriage – to the mutual happiness of both of them? In view of the prevailing cultural values that emphasize the woman's purity, are we to assume that, as a rape victim, she would become undesirable to another man, thus nullifying her family's plans of marrying her off to someone else? Such plans are not stated in the story, but since Bindo's father murdered Dalip's father, the hostility between the two families is apparent and would make the marriage of the two youngsters impossible. Viewed from this perspective, Bindo could be regarded as the architect of her own fate. After her rape, Bindo was faced with this predicament – loss of Dalip to a jail term and disgrace in the eyes of everyone. By telling the magistrate that she went to Dalip by choice, she might have made the best of the situation.

There is little doubt that Bindo's pursuing Dalip into the fields was a daring act, but she had followed him to be loved, not raped. Having been put into a very undesirable situation, she used her intelligence in the court scene to come up with an idea that might save her from ruin. All these questions are hard to avoid as well as to answer. However, by raising the necessary questions – even when they cannot be answered conclusively – an explication can bring us closer to the story's meanings. The challenge of such works is that the reader has to fill in the missing details of the story, in which what is excluded from the narration is as important as what is included.

Questions on "The Rape"

1. Some readers have read this story as Bindo's clever seduction of Dalip. In their view, Dalip is more "sinned against" than a sinner, to use a phrase from Shakespeare's *King Lear*. Do you agree with this interpretation of the story?

2. Is Dalip's love for Bindo genuine and sincere?

3. Is there any evidence in the story that Bindo is attracted to Dalip?

4. What are presented in the story as some of the cultural impediments to Dalip's dream of being with Bindo and their possible marriage?

5. Public knowledge of her rape would considerably reduce Bindo's chances of marriage in a culture where purity in a bride is expected. In view of the unfortunate situation in which Bindo is placed, what do you see as her options?

6. Just as his sentencing was about to be announced, why do you think Dalip insisted that the magistrate ask Bindo if she went to him willingly?

7. The hardest question to answer in this story is Bindo's word that ends the story. Why does she say "Yes" to the magistrate's question asking her if she went to Dalip of her own accord?

Samapti (Conclusion)

This story by Rabindranath Tagore is not in this book, but you can read the plot summary in the sample journal entry on its film adaptation by Satyajit Ray. Here we have the ideal combination of a brilliant filmmaker and a consummate author. Presenting universal themes with optimism, the story and the move reaffirm the power of love and kindness in resolving human conflicts. The story also demonstrates that it takes a person of extraordinary courage and intelligence to challenge entrenched traditions that deprive women of their power to choose in as vital an area as marriage. The only reason the story has a happy ending is because of the protagonist Amulya's tenderness and understanding in handling his new bride's finding herself in a marriage that was imposed on her by her family mainly for economic reasons. Veena Parekh's well-crafted essay captures the movie's emotional depth and illuminates its thematic richness.

The Triumph of Kindness and Love
Student author: Veena Parekh

"The Conclusion" is a touching love story. It weaves themes of kindness and growing up into a fascinating commentary on the long-held Indian tradition of arranged marriage. This story also illuminates the deep and intricate relationship between mother and son in Indian culture. It begins when the son, Amulya, comes home from college after his final exams and his mother starts pressuring him to get married. She has already picked the perfect girl; she can cook, sew, sing, and is an adequate housekeeper. What more could any man want in a woman? She's reasonably pretty too.

Amulya doesn't want a wife for only those reasons. He has a mind of his own and he wants something more in a woman. He becomes enamored of a beautiful, entirely un-womanly girl whom the townspeople refer to as Puglee the tomboy. Puglee is bright and mischievous, displays no social manners, climbs trees, and plays on the swings like a boy. Against all social reasoning, the mother finally gives her consent to the marriage. Puglee's family agrees, shocked at Puglee's good luck at being accepted into a family with such a good reputation.

But Puglee doesn't want to be married. She is not ready to give up either her freedom or her childhood ways. She is stubborn and headstrong, with a mind of her own. She tries to cut off her hair but is caught in the act and is beaten by her mother. The story draws to a climax on their wedding night, when the newly wed couple is alone in Amulya's room. In her bridal finery, Puglee stands in the corner and refuses to budge.

Amulya asks her, perplexed, "Why do you resent me so? Tell me."

"Why did you marry me?" she answers quietly.

After much thought he replies, "Because I wanted to I suppose. Is that so wrong?"

"Doesn't what I want matter?"

"Is it marriage you object to, or being married to me?"

"Why was I forced into it? Am I a child?"

This dialogue gives voice to the confusion and anger Puglee feels at not being consulted in the crucial matter of her marriage. The marriage was a good match for her in a logical sense. She could not have hoped to have married any better. Puglee, not emotionally ready, was too independent-minded to submit to what others thought to be best for her.

On the wedding night, after Amulya falls asleep, Puglee sneaks out of the window and runs away. She is found the next morning, asleep on a swing and is taken back to her new home. Her mother-in-law's eyes are filled with anger and gross public shame. She orders the girl upstairs and locks her in a room. Amulya is deeply distressed. In the meantime, Puglee begins smashing everything she can find. As Amulya heads toward the door of the room his mother shouts, ". . . and don't be gentle with her! She needs a good lesson."

Amulya does not beat her but says that he will go away to Calcutta and she may go back and live at her old house again. He will not return to her until she writes to him, as a wife to a husband, asking him to come back. The kindness Amulya displays is touching, as one is almost positive that she will be beaten. He is true to his word and does not come back for a long time. Puglee falls into a deep depression and for several months eats very little and does not leave the house. She realizes her immaturity and her husband's kindness and feels immeasurably remorseful. She writes Amulya asking him to come home and the story ends with an implied "happily ever after".

Besides conjugal love, other notable issues raised in the story are the clash between the old and the new and the strong bond between the mother and son. Amulya, being highly educated and exposed to Western culture in the big city, does not want the traditional stereotype of a wife. He wants something more. He wants the "right" woman, not just an adequate one. He is attracted to Puglee for her individuality and spunkiness. Under most circumstances his wishes would be overridden by conventional wisdom and his parents would choose a girl whom they deemed fit. Because of the close bond between mother and son and the absence of a father, he is allowed to have his way.

The relationship between the doting mother and the devoted son — portrayed so often in Indian literature — has become archetypal. Their bond is deep and the mother is utterly and completely devoted to "her treasure" (in her own words). When he first arrives home, she sits on the floor fanning him as he eats his meal. When he goes to Calcutta after the wedding, she begins to miss him. He refuses to come when she asks him to visit her. She then sends him a postcard saying that she is desperately ill and he must come right away. He does of course come directly and is very angry upon finding that she had lied to him about her illness. His anger softens as he realizes that she played the trick of feigned illness because she loves him and missed him so much that she could hardly stand it.

In The Conclusion Tagore has created a beautiful drama illustrating some of the difficult issues facing the tradition of arranged marriage. He gives the viewer a peek into the daily Indian life and social values. The author enables us to see how kindness and tenderness can facilitate the growth of people. It leaves us with the hope that kindness has the power to change our lives for the better. The Conclusion is a story that is at the same time enriching and thoroughly enjoyable, leaving one uplifted and in tears.

Questions on "Samapti"

1. Compare the protagonist Dalip of Singh's story "The Rape" with Amulya, the protagonist of "Samapti." How do they handle the situation in which they find themselves?

2. Compare and contrast the main female characters Bindo and Puglee from the above mentioned two stories. How do they cope with their dilemmas?

Confronting International Conflicts through the Clarifying Lens of Fiction (option no. 12)

Students Kathleen Wong, Dennis Johnson, and Jennifer Hammer have written short essays on "Tamam" by Betty Shamieh and "The Orchard" by Alan Kaufman. Melanie Tanielian's longer essay on "The Dog of Tithwal" by Saadat Manto is on my website: <www.professorjabbar.com>.

Tamam

My name is Tamam. It means enough. I was called that because my family wanted no more daughters. I am the last of seven sisters, good luck for the family. After me there were two brothers and now there is only one. Why do we rejoice when a boy is born? Because we from Gaza understand the power of might. The strong make the rules, name the cities, and decide who live in them, or so they think. We know what it means to be weak, to cement a settlement of resentment, brick by brick, in our own ravaged hearts and shell-shocked minds, with every comet littered with bullets, tear gas canisters, that say "Made in Pennsylvania" on them.

Times like these call for soldiers. The ones we had have fallen. A birth of a girl is different from a boy. A girl is a gift that's too precious, a reminder that soft things don't last long in our world. Parents here fool themselves, thinking a boy child has at least almost a fighting chance. I want to talk about something smaller than me that became bigger. I want to talk about my brother. Don't believe the stories you've heard. I was far more religious than he. I never had the heart to wake him to pray. He was hoping to study medicine in Iraq while building Israeli settlements in Gaza so we could eat. I let him sleep through the call. He was caught with a rock in his hand and a curse on his lips. I went to the jail to visit my brother. Most of my people looked at the Israeli guards with every ounce of hatred a human heart can hold, their faces twisted not like they tasted something bitter, like something bitter was forced down their throats. I was smarter than that. I knew I must navigate through the maze of might, and did my best to be kindly, polite, hoping perhaps that I would remind them of a Rachel or Sarah or Ruth that they knew or would have liked to know. So when they beat my brother, that thing that started out smaller than me and got bigger, they would lighten their touch.

I am a pretty woman. It's not a compliment; it's not a boast. It's a fact. Looks are a commodity, an asset, a possession I happen to possess. It's why my grandmother said no, when my brother-in-law asked for my hand. The family that was good enough for my plain sister wasn't good enough for me. I'm a pretty woman. It's not a boast. It's a fact. I smiled my best smile when the soldiers opened that gate for me. Weighed down with baskets of food, I brought extra hoping to create the illusion that the dirty jail was one place where there was enough and extra for all the guards to eat twice. Otherwise, my brother would get none, unless there was enough and extra. They thanked me for the food and they raped me right in front of him, forcing my brother's eyes open so he had to watch. They wanted to know something that he preferred not to tell them. They skewered the support for their argument into my flesh. I'm told that their torture specialists who study the "Arab" mind, realized rape would enrage our men. Enraging a man is the first step on the stairway that gets him to a place where he becomes impotent, helpless. They not only refer to us as the cockroaches, they examine us, experiment upon us, as if we were that predictable, that much the same, that easy to eradicate. Their studies show that Arab men value the virtue of their womenfolk. Their studies show something within me was supposed to be inviolate.

Say what you want about Arab men and women and how we love one another. There is one thing that's for certain. There are real repercussions for hurting a woman in my society. There are repercussions. When the first hand was laid upon me, we both screamed. The evolutionary function of a scream is a cry for help. They tied down the only one who could so I silenced myself. That was the only way to tell my brother I didn't want him to tell. I flinched when I had to. But I kept my breath regular. My brother tried to look every other way. But I realized I needed him to look me in the eyes and understand. They thought making us face one another in our misery would break us. But we were used to misery. It's like anything else. You can build up a tolerance for it.

Someone else told them what they wanted to know, so they released my brother two weeks later. That's when he built something more intricate than the human heart, hugged it to his chest, and boarded a bus that was going nowhere and everywhere. The day he did it, he told me over breakfast that "oppression is like a coin maker. You put in human beings, press the right buttons and watch them get squeezed, shrunk, flattened till they take the slim shape of a two-faced coin. One side is a martyr, the other a traitor. All the possibilities of a life get reduced to those paltry two. The coin is tossed in the air; it spins once for circumstance, twice for luck, and a third time for predilection before it lands flat. The face that points down towards hell determines not only who you are, but how you will become that way." What he was really saying was goodbye. Had I known, I would have said something more than "It's interesting you think oppression makes us turn into a form of money, a currency, how odd."

Listen, I don't agree with killing innocent people under any circumstances ever. The irony is there were Palestinians who were Israeli citizens on that bus too. My brother wasn't counting on that. No one was counting on that. I want to feel sorry when anyone is suffering, no matter who they are or what their people have done to mine. No one's life should be snuffed out. I'm the kind of human being who refuses to get high on the drug of hate. In my opinion, that's the only kind of human being there is. In other words, no one is going to reduce me to a coin. There are no absolutes, it's wrong to kill, period. And since the Israelis have killed five times the number of my people as we have killed theirs, I think they are five times as wrong. It's hard to feel sad for them sometimes, but I swear to you that I try my best. But it's not easy. They complain they can't go to a pizza parlor while they bomb us in our homes. I should have known what my brother was bound to do. I could have stopped him. I said every time he went out to face their guns with rocks "don't go, let's achieve peace by peaceful means. Let's use non-violence. Don't be a pawn. What kind of fool would face a gun with a rock. Let others risk their lives. They can never truly win. They could kill every Palestinian and the wind would howl our names and the rocks will rise up and throw themselves." I'd always say, "Don't go." But I didn't say, "you are the most precious thing in the world to me. The fact that you exist makes the earth spin on its axis; it is rolling for joy because you are here. The sun shows up to see you, and the moon chases the sun off to be in your sky and none of them love you like I do brother not even close. There is no goal, no political means worth wrenching your life from mine. If Palestine is Utopia, Palestine is already here. Palestine is my brother being by my side and screaming for joy when I have my firstborn and living long and laughing loud with me over hot tea and warm bread each morning which is all we can afford, but if you are by my side, is more than enough. If you think this is a gift for me, the box will be empty brother. How can it not be? Everything will be empty, if you're not here. Don't hurt yourself and others in my name or for my sake. I will not forgive you if you leave me. I will not be comforted. I will not be." Instead I said, "don't go" and I didn't say it loud. They bulldozed our house because you blew up that bus. In all this, I didn't realize what true fear, true dread, was till I watched our younger brother watching them destroy our home witnessing each swoop and scoop with more anger in his eyes than I had ever seen in yours.

I was engaged to be married to the love of my life and the richest man in Gaza. My father went to his house and told his father what had happened to me. He didn't want scandal if we went ahead and married and it was found I was not . . . as I was before. My love left me because of his father's insistence. His mother, who never liked me anyway, took him and married him to a girl from her town. He moved to London with her and I haven't seen him since. I try to convince myself that I wouldn't want to be married to a man who could ever betray me. I try to convince myself I'm better off without him. Try is the operative word. His cowardice was a violence that hurts and haunts me more than what the guards did to me. Because I have no one to blame but my own people, which is as hard to do as blaming yourself. I married my brother-in-law, who was made aware that I was not . . . as I was before. My youngest brother went to Iraq the week before my first child was born. He went to study engineering. I'm worried about him. Our friends there say he disappears for months at a time. He never tells me where he goes or when he'll return. I'm worried about him.

My husband and I understand each other, which is not exactly a good thing. My husband never lets me live it down that my family once rejected him. He calls me a whore when he is angry and stuck up when he is not. He gets angry often, especially when I tell him he is worthless and not a man when he can't find enough food. It's the only way to make him steal it. Like I said before, we understand one another. I think of my first love who deserted me. Every day I visualize a new way I'd tell him what a traitor he was to leave me, in case I happen to ever see him again. It makes me sad that though he wronged me in more ways than one, he'll only have ears to listen to the first words I say. You only get one chance to tell people they are wrong. You get that chance because it takes people a minute or two to realize you're telling them stuff they don't want to hear. Then they shut you out, though they might be still standing before you, smiling, they make sure the door between the ear and the heart is locked and they forever take away your key. Because they know if they keep listening they might not change, but it will be a little harder to stay the same. If I saw him today, I would tell him: "You should have married me. I was still a virgin, even after what the Israeli soldiers did to me. I was still a virgin, because I don't consider the men who raped me human, and if you had any inkling of what a true man was or how to be one, neither would you." My name is Tamam. It means enough.

Betty Shamieh

The Orchard

That morning, when it was done, when we were sickened unto death, and curfew reigned, we tore our helmets off and sped through the riot streets of shattered glass over blood spattered flagstones. Past bullet-punched walls we flew. The boiling black smoke pillars of burning tires stalked us like the desert God. Our wheels scattered spent shells, crimson rocks. Here and there, one of our "cousins," as we called the locals, curled in a doorway, defiant, weeping with rage, his kaffiyeh clenched in his teeth.

The air reeked of camel shit and dread. My sleepless eyes drifted shut: on their side six shot, no telling how many dead, and from our end two wounded, bad, and one, curly-headed Reuvi, the newlywed, bagged for a grave. Only twenty-four he was, the boy. A mob-tossed hand grenade mangled his guts. A bad scene. My mouth yawned wide to gulp the morning air, and my filthy fingers pried my eyes apart. I was no boy and needed strong mud coffee. But we did not stop. We could not. Neither did we take the patrol route back to base: we fled town. Good riddance. Fuck them all!

The blurred green-black road trembled, the sun risen over us with an ill-sounding birdsong. Sometimes a song can sound diseased. We stopped our ears. I put my fists to mine. I shook. Then the armored car swerved sharply and Brandt shouted something indecipherable and we rumbled through a vineyard into a clearing. At the end of the road it was, in a grove of olive trees. Right there, we pulled off the red clay and onto thick brown grass and stopped. Brandt and Uri jumped out, dropped their guns to the ground, shrugged off their gear, threw themselves down, and passed out, clutching the grass like a woman's hair. Groggily, I followed suit.

The last thing I saw before sleep was a giant black fly stropping its legs on my hand.

I was the first who awakened to see the old Arab squatting there beside our guns. A Palestinian. My eyes snapped from him to the weapons and back. He held out apples, said whatever: I didn't care to know. Climbing casually to my feet I walked with a fiercely pounding heart to the guns, shouldered mine, and, collecting the others', deposited them next to my sleeping comrades, whom I brought awake with sharp kicks. The Arab took in all this.

When Uri talked to him in perfect Arabic, the old man listened carefully, his black clotted eyes mucal with age. His thin frowning face had a prominent square jaw, covered with gray thistles. His apricot-colored skin was mapped with a thousand prehistoric wadis. An aura of bandoliers and virgin brides hung about him, and scores of grandchildren playing in his ravines. He wore a white kaffiyeh with a black agal, the traditional head dress; a long white Shillahat robe with billowing sleeves and turquoise sirwal pants. He was a ragged old rake. He had rope sandals on his thickly callused feet. In his worn leather belt was that short Bedouin knife they use to cut the throats of game birds. When a breeze stirred the kaffiyeh, it revealed large sculpted ears delicately inlaid with fine white hairs. Finally, Uri finished and the old man thought.

Then he spoke, his hands gesturing with strong, graceful motions that trembled for age. When he finished, he looked around at us and nodded to each emphatically, slapping the back of one hand against the palm of the other, again and again.

"He says," Uri began, "that his name is Jamal Abu-Da'ud.

That we are guests on his farm. That we are in an orchard here, planted by his own hands with the help of three sons and ten grandchildren. His wife is dead. His daughters all married. He has lived here since infancy. Wants we should eat his fruit. Ours to eat, he says. Says that we have nothing to fear."

Uri paused. Then: "And he says that he knows that our peoples are at war. That he has seen what his own people do and he knows the war they make is cruel. And he has also seen Israeli soldiers like us come and go and what we do. He thinks that everyone has gone very crazy. But that is out there, he says, beyond the orchard, and not here. And yes, if they ask him to, he will join them to fight, because he is a patriot. Then, yes, he too will make war on us. But not here, he says. Here we are not Arab or Jew, but only men eating fruit. He encourages us to eat our fill before we go. He wishes us a good rest. There is no rush. He'll bring water to refresh ourselves with." And with that, Uri nodded and the old man rose and walked off.

"Eat up quick, and let's get the fuck out of here before he returns with 'friends,'" said Brandt. He spit in the dust. And added: "Murdering old son of a bitch!"

Hurriedly we filled our helmets with apples, jumped aboard the armored car, and roared off. They all had guns hidden some place. Even an old man like that. "How good is your Arabic?" Brandt snarled at Uri, whom we knew to be a real peacenik. "I think you made up that old shit's speech!"

We laughed, Uri too. We were so dead tired. True or not about Uri's little speech, we all feared our return to the city of graves, where more rioting loomed. But even as we laughed in despair, we peered back hard at the old man's groves. We no longer searched for his gun's muzzle flash, but watched his trees recede, growing smaller and smaller, his world disappearing, and even now, long after it has vanished altogether, still we glance back to there, or what we think is there, so far away. We look with a sense of longing and regret, though that too is fast fading.

Alan Kaufman

Four Essays by Student Authors

"Tamam" and "The Orchard" concern the conflict between Israelis and Palestinians. "The Dog of Tithwal" is about the conflict between India and Pakistan over Kashmir. In causes, duration, and as a grave threat to world peace, the two conflicts bear striking resemblances.

Bridging the Divide Between Palestinians and Israelis
Student author: Kathleen Wong

Americans are bombarded with a myriad of violent images of the Palestinian/Israeli conflict through the media. I believe that the prevailing sentiment is that everyone wants to see an end to this war and the achievement of some form of peaceful co-existence. In both stories, "Tamam" by Betty Shamieh and "The Orchard" by Alan Kaufman, the authors seem to be advocating for an end to the violence and a greater respect for humanity.

In Shamieh's story, Tamam, the narrator, explains how her brother is put in prison for throwing rocks and she is raped by Israeli soldiers when she visits him. She explains the logic of the other side in regards to the litany of atrocities against her and her Palestinian people. Yet, she is asking her people to transcend the anger and desire for revenge and to build a tolerance for this misery. At the same time, she sees the wrong in the actions of her own people as well. In spite of all that has happened, Taman wants to see all people as human beings. She says "you only get one chance to tell people they are wrong. You get that chance because it takes people a minute or two to realize you're telling them stuff

334

they don't want to hear. Then they shut you out – because if they keep listening, they might not change, but it will be harder to stay the same." The importance of people listening to what each other is saying and simply having a dialog is an important message in this story.

There is a similar message in "The Orchard." The soldier who is called "the peacenik" by the other Israeli soldiers is translating the words of the old Arab. The old man knows they are fighting a war against each other, but he wants them to know that his orchard is a safe haven where they can rest, refresh themselves and enjoy his apples without fear. As in the previous story, the idea of human beings relating to other human beings, surfaces. In his orchard, the old man says, "Here we are not Arab or Jew, but only men eating fruit." The generations of violence and war, staunch nationalism, and perception of the other as the eternal enemy make it difficult to hear the Arab's words. It is the same shutting out that Taman speaks of in Shamieh's story. One of the soldiers comments to the "peacenik" soldier that he thinks he "made up that old shit's speech!" As the soldiers leave, they "look back with a sense of longing and regret, though that too is fast fading." These soldiers haven't changed, but something in them may not be the same. Kaufman hints at the way this human dialog has had some kind of effect on these men, but they remain too afraid and suspicious for it to make a dramatic change in their perspective.

The tone of these stories should have favorable appeal to fellow citizens of these authors because they both point to the narrow nationalism and senseless violence of both the Palestinians and Israelis. The suspicion and mistrust for the enemy is so embedded in the psyche of both the Palestinians and Israelis that having any genuine dialog as human beings relating to other human beings almost seems unfathomable. However, this dialog of compassion and understanding for the other is exactly what Shamieh and Kaufman are advocating in the telling of these stories. As Taman says at the end of Shamieh's story, "My name is Taman. It means enough."

There Must Be a Better Way
Student author: Dennis Johnson

Both Betty Shamieh and Alan Kaufman appeal to universal qualities in the human spirit. Even though one is a Palestinian-American and the other a pro-Israel Jewish American, the fact that their stories are so universal makes them appealing to the readers.

Shamieh writes about the horrors that her family has experienced at the hands of the Israelis. She tells of her own rape by Israeli soldiers with her brother forced to watch. Any woman will sympathize with her unnerving story. We can begin to understand why her brothers became radicalized and how one of them became a suicide bomber. We can even imagine that we ourselves might respond in the same way if we had experienced what she and her family went through. At the end, she says "My name is Tamam. It means enough." Her readers will agree that the kind of terror she has experienced has to stop.

Kaufman writes of the horror of war and of finding an island of peace in the midst of enemy territory. The soldiers are fighting the hated Palestinians when they come across Jamal Abu-Da'ud, an old Palestinian man who lives in a quiet orchard. He is alone on the land, on which he has planted the trees with his own hands. In spite of the enmity between the Palestinians and the Israelis, he invites the men to put down their weapons and enjoy his apples. He says "Here we are not Arab or Jew, but only men eating fruit." The soldiers take the fruit but decide not to wait for the old man to bring them water, fearing that he will return with a gun and shoot them. In the end, the soldiers speed away, but as they go, they look back and fantasize about a world at peace, where people can sit down together as brothers.

Both stories contain elements of longing and regret — longing for a world of peace and regret for the circumstances that have brought us to war and distrust. In both cases, the reader is left feeling "Enough." There must be a better way.

Prospects for Peace between Israel and Palestine
Student author: Jennifer Hammer

In "Tamam," Betty Shamieh is appealing to the world and the American people in particular by exposing the horrors that Israelis are perpetrating on Palestinians in Gaza (the rape of Tamam, for example). She is also exposing America's complicity in these horrors, in the corners littered with bullets, in the shell-shockedness, in the tear gas canisters that say "Made in Pennsylvania" on them. Shamieh also explains the anger behind some of the Palestinians' actions, like blowing up a bus, without condoning the action, and she puts a human face on a suicide bomber: he was Tamam's little brother, he was going to study medicine in Iraq. Even after being raped and losing her brother, Tamam refuses to get "high on the drug of hate." She firmly believes that "no one's life should be snuffed out."

Very poignantly, Shamieh shows the tragic irony of life in Palestine. Her brother was building Israeli settlements in Gaza in order to feed the family. Because of American support of and bias toward Israel, Shamieh's story is important and moving in that it exposes "the other side", a side we often do not see or hear about in the American media or governmental positions.

In "The Orchard" by Alan Kaufman, the writer is showing that "peaceniks" have been drafted into the Israeli army; not everyone in Israel, even those who are performing the actions, agrees with Israel's military actions. The scenes are horrific, and the Israeli soldiers are "sickened unto death". As they drive along, the narrator of the story states: "We did not stop. We could not. Neither did we take the patrol route back to base: we fled town. Good riddance. Fuck them all."

Contrasting with this hatred, the soldiers are treated to the apples in an orchard of an old Arab. They are wary of him even though he'd told them they were guests. The old Arab describes the war and says, "Everyone has gone very crazy, but that is out there [outside the orchard]. . . . Here we are not Arab or Jew, but only men eating fruit."

One soldier, however (Brandt) is suspicious and still wary. He doesn't believe what the Arab said, and even while gathering up the apples, the narrator states "They all had guns hidden someplace. Even an old man like that." But as the tired soldiers leave to go back to the city of graves and riot patrol, they "no longer searched for his gun's muzzle flash" (meaning they were no longer wary of the old Arab; they took him for his word). Perhaps if they were not so afraid and suspicious, they would not have to look back at the orchard with longing – for the peace they experienced for a moment – and regret. "Perhaps if our peoples were not at war . . ."

Questions on "Tamam" and "The Orchard"

1. In the story by Betty Shamieh, Tamam points out the double standards in her culture that demand chastity from women but not from men. How does Tamam become a victim of this aspect of her culture?

2. What is Tamam's position on suicide bombing?

3. How does Tamam view the U.S. role in the conflict between Israel and Palestine?

4. In the story by Alan Kaufman, discuss the apples and the orchard as symbolic of the Garden of Eden.

5. Kaufman fought on Israel's side against the Arabs in the 1967 war. There seems to be a desperate attempt on his narrator's part to create hope for peace between the two enemies. Give a few examples to support that view.

The Dog of Tithwal
by Saadat Manto

Read this story online http://www.sikh-history.com/literature/stories/dog.html
Read Melanie Talienian's essay on this story on my website in papers linked to Chapter Ten.

Questions on "The Dog of Tithwal"

1. In Manto's "The Dog of Tithwal," discuss the dog as symbolic of the people of Kashmir, who are caught between the two warring countries – India and Pakistan. Support your answer with details from the story, using relevant historical and political facts pertinent to this conflict.

2. The author seems to be drawing a contrast between Nature and human actions. Discuss the different ends to which Nature and human beings seem driven. In Chapter Five, Henry Reed's poem "Naming of Parts" makes a similar contrast between Nature and human beings.

3. What is the author's tone, that is, his attitude toward the dog and toward the story's human characters?

Similar Themes in Works by Different Authors (option no. 13)

The stories relevant to this topic are Betty Shamieh's "Tamam" and Alifa Rifaat's "Bahiyya's Eyes." They concern the common theme of women's plight in cultures where some customs prevail that could be viewed as oppressive to women. Both stories are included in this chapter. Another pair of stories with a common theme (also included in this chapter) are Chitra Divakaruni's "The Word Love" and Amrita Pritam's "The Weed." They treat the topic of love and arranged marriage as it impacts women's lives. Both are by feminist authors – one an Indian American (Divakaruni) and the other an Indian (Pritam). Compare the main characters of these stories to determine their very different coping strategies in their difficult situations. Which of them faces a harder challenge? How? Another story relevant to the theme of arranged marriage, in which the woman has little choice, is Rabindranath Tagore's story "Samapti." That story is not in this book, but its film adaptation is discussed at the end of Chapter Six.

You can find many more stories with shared themes on your own.

The Price of Right Conduct in the Wrong Environment (option no. 14)

For this exercise, you may choose any two fictional characters who act responsibly and ethically but find themselves isolated as a result. Describe their actions, settings/contexts, and the systemic defects that create such dilemmas for caring and sensitive individuals. You may consider, for example, the protagonist Tamam in Betty Shamieh's story of the same title and Sarty in William Faulkner's short story "Barn Burning." You can read Faulkner's story online or in a library book, or watch its excellent film adaptation (40 minutes), directed by Peter Werner.

Stories that Deal with Pain to Offer Healing and Consolation
(option no. 15)

Besides "Lullaby" by Leslie Silko that fits both option No. 6 and this option, you can find several other stories in this book that relate to this topic, such as "The Man from Kabul" by Rabindranath Tagore in Chapter One and "The Other Side of the Hedge" by E. M. Forster in Chapter Two. You can also access on your own several relevant stories, such as "The Sword of Shiva" by Khawaja Ghulam Abbas and "In the Ruins" by Bei Dao.

Sherman Alexie's story "This is What it Means to Say Phoenix, Arizona" also fits this category. Student author Sydney McIver's journal entry on this story succinctly demonstrates this option.

This is What it Means to Say Phoenix, Arizona
by Sherman Alexie (b. 1966)

You can read Sherman Alexie's short story, "This is What it Means to Say Phoenix, Arizona" online: *http://courses.csusm.edu/ltwr325bc/phoenix.html*.

Student author: Sydney McIver

Topic
Tradition

Theme
Modern life can cause one to reject old traditions, but when great challenges arise it is what one needs the most to overcome those obstacles.

Support
Since Thomas upheld the tradition of story telling, he was rejected by the other boys on the reservation. But when his cousin Victor needed help retrieving and mourning his father, Thomas and his belief in tradition were there for Victor to fall back on. Thomas was there for Victor because his own faith and Victor's father's faith in the old traditions brought them together, and reminded them both of the need to "Take care of each other."

STORIES FOR FURTHER READING

Hills Like White Elephants

by Ernest Hemingway (1899-1961)

Read this story online, using this link: http://flightline.highline.edu/tkim/Files/Lit100_SS2.pdf

Questions on "Hills Like White Elephants"

1. Analyze Hemingway's style of writing in "Hills Like White Elephants," focusing on the setting and compressed time, symbolism, and characterization.

2. Identify some prominent symbols in the story and comment on their impact in embodying the author's theme.

3. The story is mostly a dialogue between a young man and a woman with nothing that could be called authorial or narrative intrusion. What is the young couple talking about? What are their varying positions on how they should resolve the problem at hand?

4. Picking up on any clues in the story, such as the title of the story, which of the two characters seems to get the author's/narrator's support? Or do you think the author/narrator takes no sides whatsoever? Support your answer with relevant details.

5. Create a question based on this story. Your question should draw the reader deeper into the story's substance.

A Little Incident

Six years have slipped by since I came from the country to the capital. During that time I have seen and heard quite enough of so-called affairs of state; but none of them made much impression on me. If asked to define their influence, I can only say they aggravated my ill temper and made me, frankly speaking, more and more misanthropic.

One incident, however, struck me as significant, and aroused me from my ill temper, so that even now I cannot forget it. It happened during the winter of 1917. A bitter north wind was blowing, but, to make a living, I had to be up and out early. I met scarcely a soul on the road, and had great difficulty in hiring a rickshaw to take me to S—— Gate. Presently the wind dropped a little. By now the loose dust had all been blown away, leaving the roadway clean, and the rickshaw man quickened his pace. We were just approaching S—— Gate when someone crossing the road was entangled in our rickshaw and slowly fell.

It was a woman, with streaks of white in her hair, wearing ragged clothes. She had left the pavement without warning to cut across in front of us, and although the rickshaw man had made way, her tattered jacket, unbuttoned and fluttering in the wind, had caught on the shaft. Luckily the rickshaw man pulled up quickly, otherwise she would certainly have had a bad fall and been seriously injured.

She lay there on the ground, and the rickshaw man stopped. I did not think the old woman was hurt, and there had been no witnesses to what had happened, so I resented this officiousness which might land him in trouble and hold me up.

"It's all right," I said. "Go on."

He paid no attention, however—perhaps he had not heard—for he set down the shafts, and gently helped the old woman to get up. Supporting her by one arm, he asked:

"Are you all right?"

"I'm hurt."

I had seen how slowly she fell, and was sure she could not be hurt. She must be pretending, which was disgusting. The rickshaw man had asked for trouble, and now he had it. He would have to find his own way out. But the rickshaw man did not hesitate for a minute after the old woman said she was injured. Still holding her arm, he helped her slowly forward. I was surprised. When I looked ahead, I saw a police station. Because of the high wind, there was no one outside, so the rickshaw man helped the old woman towards the gate.

Suddenly I had a strange feeling. His dusty, retreating figure seemed larger at that instant. Indeed, the further he walked the larger he loomed, until I had to look up to him. At the same time he seemed gradually to be exerting a pressure on me, which threatened to overpower the small self under my fur-lined gown. My vitality seemed sapped as I sat there motionless, my mind a blank, until a policeman came out. Then I got down from the rickshaw.

The policeman came up to me, and said, "Get another rickshaw. He can't pull you anymore."

Without thinking, I pulled a handful of coppers from my coat pocket and handed them to the policeman. "Please give him these," I said.

The wind had dropped completely, but the road was still quiet. I walked along thinking, but I was almost afraid to turn my thoughts on myself. Setting aside what had happened earlier, what had I meant by that handful of coppers? Was it a reward? Who was I to judge the rickshaw man? I could not answer myself.

Even now, this remains fresh in my memory. It often causes me distress, and makes me try to think about myself. The military and political affairs of those years I have forgotten as completely as the classics I read in my childhood. Yet this incident keeps coming back to me, often more vivid than in actual life, teaching me shame, urging me to reform, and giving me fresh courage and hope.

Lu Hsun (1881-1936)

Questions on "A Little Incident"

1. Does the narrator like what he calls the "affairs of state"?

2. What formative influence did his six years in the capital have on the narrator's attitude toward the big-city people in general?

3. The "little incident" in this story played a big role in raising the narrator's awareness of important human obligations. Describe the incident in a few sentences; then summarize the process that sensitized the narrator toward a more humane perspective on life.

4. Who, in your opinion, is the hero in this story – the narrator or the rickshaw puller? Support your answer with details from the story.

5. Create a question based on this story. Your question should draw the reader deeper into the story's substance.

Early Autumn

When Bill was very young, they had been in love. Many nights they had spent walking, talking together. Then something not very important had come between them, and they didn't speak. Impulsively, she had married a man she thought she loved. Bill went away, bitter about women.

Yesterday, walking across Washington Square, she saw him for the first time in years.

"Bill Walker," she said.

He stopped. At first he did not recognize her, to him she looked so old.

"Mary! Where did you come from? "

Unconsciously, she lifted her face as though wanting a kiss, but he held out his hand. She took it.

"I live in New York now," she said. "Oh," he said, smiling politely. Then a little frown came quickly between his eyes.

"Always wondered what happened to you, Bill. "
"I'm a lawyer. Nice firm, way downtown. "
"Married yet?"
"Sure. Two kids. "
"Oh," she said.

A great many people went past them through the park. People they didn't know. It was late afternoon, nearly sunset. Cold.

"And your husband? " he asked her.
"We have three children. I work in the bursar's office at Columbia. "
"You're looking very well," he said (he wanted to say old). She understood.

Under the trees in Washington Square, she found herself desperately reaching back into the past. She had been older than he then in Ohio. Now she was not young at all. Bill was still young.

"We live on Central Park West," she said. "Come and see us sometime "

"Sure," he replied. "You and your husband must have dinner with my family some night. Any night. Lucille and I'd love to have you. "

The leaves fell slowly from the trees in the Square. Fell without wind. Autumn dusk. She felt a little sick.

"We'd love it," she answered. "You ought to see my kids." He grinned.

Suddenly the lights came on up the whole length of Fifth Avenue, chains of misty brilliance in the blue air.

"There's my bus," she said. He held out his hand "Good-bye. "

"When . . ." she wanted to say, but the bus was ready to pull off. The lights on the avenue blurred, twinkled, blurred. And she was afraid to open her mouth as she entered the bus. Afraid it would be impossible to utter a word.

Suddenly she shrieked very loudly "Good-bye!" But the bus door had closed. The bus started. People came between them outside, people crossing the street, people they didn't know. Space and people.

She lost sight of Bill. Then she remembered she had forgotten to give him her address – or to ask him for his – or tell him that her youngest boy was named Bill too.

Langston Hughes (1902-1967)

Questions on "Early Autumn"

1. Langston Hughes' story uses minimum words to carry maximum meanings. State the story's theme to capture some of its meaning.

2. Comment on Hughes' writing style, specifically, the lines that describe the setting and the way Hughes expresses the characters' strong feelings and elicits the reader's involvement.

3. Which of the two characters in the story – the male or the female – seems to show stronger emotion about their past intimate relations? Give supporting details.

4. Which of the two characters seems to have aged more quickly than the other?

5. Create a question based on this story. Your question should draw the reader deeper into the story's substance.

Bahiyya's Eyes[1]

We praise Him and thank Him for His favour for whatever He decides. Here I am, daughter, alive and well, still like a cat with seven lives. Forgive me if I worried you by getting our neighbor to write you a letter asking you to come and stay with me for a while so that my eyes could take their fill of you. You see, a few days ago I decided to take myself off to the government hospital. I washed my *galabia* and my head-veil overnight so I'd be nice and clean for the doctor. I got fed up telling people to take me to the doctor's whenever someone passed by me. They kept saying to me: 'Ma, just wait till we find you a donkey to take you there – it's too far for you.' And then they'd just put it out of their minds. Anyway, that's life for you, and everyone's got his excuse. So, I'm telling you, I got myself up early and put on my *galabia* which still wasn't all that dry except I told myself it would dry out on the way. I took up the palm branch stick I use for chasing up my chickens and put myself into Allah's hands. Off I walked and eventually I got there. The nurse, Allah keep her safe, said to me: 'Mother, support yourself on my arm and never mind that stick of yours,' and straight away she took me in to see the doctor. Directly he saw me he said: 'Bahiyya, sit down on the chair in front of me.' I said to him: 'Your Honour, excuse me but it wouldn't be right - can the eye rise higher than the eyebrow?' He laughed and said: 'Sit down, Bahiyya, so I can examine you.' So, my dear, I sat myself down and he put on an electric light and with his own hand he took off my head-veil and went on peering for a while into one eye and then into the other, while I was so embarrassed I didn't know what to say. Then he asked me: 'Tell me, Bahiyya, about your eyes and what you feel.' So I said to him: 'May the Lord light your path and protect your sight, my eyes used to be beautiful and round as saucers and I used to be able to spot someone walking as far away as the other side of the canal and be able to tell you who it was.' He said to me: 'These eyes of yours must have been troubling you for a long time. Can you tell me when they first started hurting you?' I said to

---

1. There is a traditional song of this title which tells of the beauty of the eyes of a peasant girl called Bahiyya.

him: 'May the good Lord never bring you any harm, sir, I'm a poor woman and all on my own, you see my husband died long ago and left me with the children to bring up as best I could and all I could think about is how I'd get tomorrow's bread. By the precious life of Your Honour, I can't remember when they first started closing up and filling with stuff. After a little while they'd get better and I'd put kohl on them and they'd be fine. But a couple of years ago I found the light draining out of them bit by bit like water from a cracked pitcher. I told myself I was getting old – and old age holds its warnings. But for some time now I've been finding tears flowing from them, you'd think it was rain. So I told myself it was high time I went to be examined by the doctor – our Lord is forgiving and merciful.' Then, daughter, he told me I'd made a big mistake and that I should have gone to him ages ago, and that it was all caused by the flies and the dirt. Anyway, he wrote me out a piece of paper and told me it was for some drops that would do me good. You ask me how often I use them? I tell you I didn't even trouble to get them though they told me they were for free. No, my child, I know and the doctor knows that there's no hospital has any drops that will bring back my sight. As I left I said to the nurse: 'Dear, hand me the stick 'cos it seems I'll be holding it all the time from now on.' Bless them, they did what they could, but cure lies in the hands of Allah alone. Daughter, it's all written on the forehead and there's not a doctor alive or dead can change fate. And what was all that he was saying about flies? Perhaps in his books they tell him it's from flies, but I know better. It all comes from the tears I shed since my mother first bore me and they held me up by the leg and found I was a girl. The whole of my life I went on crying and how often my mother'd tell me not to but it wasn't any use. My mother, Allah have mercy on her, was good and kind to us, she'd take us one by one every night and wash our faces and put us down to sleep alongside each other on the bench above the stove, while she, Awwad and my father'd sleep to one side. Three of us girls and a boy were the ones that lived: your Uncle Awwad was the one I came directly after – he was just ahead of me – and then there was your Aunt Nazeera and your Aunt Fadeela, Allah have mercy on her. Daughter, it's all a question of fate and destiny and it's that that made me write to you and ask you to come right away so I could take a good long look at you before my sight goes and I'm not able to tell white from black. My mother was always saying about me that I took things too much to heart as though I was always looking for something to cry about. And what good did it do me except that I ruined my eyes? My poor sister Fadeela had more reason to cry than me. How she suffered and didn't see a day's happiness in her life! When the bit of glass got into her foot and it swelled up, she went on screaming with the pain day and night, poor thing, before she died and she was still only a child. After she died I and your Aunt Nazeera were left, also your Uncle Awwad. As he grew up he became worse and worse with us, always pinching us and hitting us. It was as if he enjoyed hearing us scream. When we complained to my mother, Allah have mercy upon her, she'd tell us 'When your father's gone he'll be the man in the family and what he says goes so you'd better get used to it. Whenever she used to go off to the field with my father she'd always take Awwad along with them and she'd lock up us girls at home. When we grew up a bit they'd get us to go out in the lanes to collect up the dung for my mother to sell as fuel to the man who owned the bakery. Nazeera and I would each make a heap of cowpats on the roof and mine was always more than twice as large as hers. The fact is I was clever and bright and full of energy. I was also the best looking of us sisters and so the evil eye was on me. While we were spending the whole day collecting up the dung, Awwad would be playing in the water channel or romping round the fields, and when he came home he'd expect us to serve him like my mother served my father. He'd just sit back and think up things for us to do and find fault with us so he could give us a clout over the ear. Of course our life was the same as that of all the other girls, but it seems they were able to take it and not care a hang and just laugh it off. But my nature wasn't the same and the tears were always running down my cheeks. It was like my eyes were preparing themselves for what was to come, because it's not as if life got any easier as I grew up. Just the opposite. The fact is there's no joy for a girl in growing up, it's just one disaster after another till you end up an old woman who's good for nothing and who's real lucky if she finds someone to feel sorry for her. No, daughter, don't say it's not so. You tell me, then, what use I am. It's not every daughter who's kind enough to trail all the way from the town to our village just to visit her mother. Allah bless you through the glory of the Prophet. I'm sorry, daughter, if I've not stopped talking from the moment you arrived. It's because no one comes and sees me these days. Can you believe it that I sometimes find no one to talk to so I find myself chatting away to my chickens just in case I forget how to talk? Anyway, when I began to grow up my eyes opened to the world more and I understood its ways and how the Lord had ordered His creation. On certain days my father would take us to the field, and he and Awwad would put the seeds in the furrow and Nazeera and I would cover them over with earth afterwards. Through the power of the Lord, with water and sun, the little seeds would with the days break through the earth and become all sorts and kinds of blessings, some beans, some maize, some I-don't-know-what. I also noticed that the cats and the dogs, and the donkeys and the rabbits and the goats would jump onto each other and have children. Bit by bit I was able to understand how the same thing went on between men and women, and that those of their children who died died by Allah's will, and those of their children who lived by Allah's will, and that, in His wisdom, for everyone that died there was always another one to take his place. I realized that Allah the Sublime had in this manner given the female the task of continuing His creation. Isn't that so? Isn't it we who are pregnant for nine months and give suck to the child and worry about it till it grows strong, while the man's part in the whole affair is just one night of fun? When I'd understood these things I'd stay awake at night and listen to my mother and father may Allah forgive me. Of course the whole of life wasn't all misery and not having enough to eat and being beaten. There were times when I enjoyed myself, specially when I'd steal off on my own among the fields and sit down and play alongside the water channel and make things out of mud and leave them in the sun to dry. At first I made little pots and pans and water jars, and then I tried to make cats and dogs and birds. One day I said to myself 'Why don't I make my mother and father.' I made both of them with arms and legs and a head and then I put a thing like a cat's tail on my father. I didn't know what to put for my mother, so I lifted my *galabia* and didn't find anything there except for something lying there between two leaves, all hidden away inside, something like a sort of mulberry. Then early one day as I was about to go out to have a look at my mud things and see whether or not they'd dried yet in the sun, I found the women coming in and gathering round, and then they took hold of me and forced my legs open and cut away the mulberry with a razor. They left me with a wound in my body and another wound deep inside me, a feeling that a wrong had been done to me, a wrong that could never be undone. And so the tears welled up in my eyes once again. When the wound in my body healed my mother said to me that the time had come for me to go to the Quranic school so as to learn about my religion. I was happy about this and thought I'd just play around a bit, but the Sheikh we had used to beat us on the soles of our feet whenever one of us made a mistake in a single word and would shout at us: 'Girl, pronounce it right - this is the Qur'an not just any old words. If you don't you'll go to Hell.' Then one day I suddenly found the wound was bleeding again, so I ran to my mother and told her: 'See what you've done to me!' She told me this was the period and that I was now all ready to be a bride. She took hold of me and tied a belt round my middle and a piece of old cloth between my legs and said to me that from now on I had to be careful and keep away from boys. So I began putting kohl on my eyes and tying the kerchief over my head at a jaunty angle and making a noise with my anklets as I walked along in my coloured sandals. By this time I'd found my breasts had swollen and become like pomegranates and when I walked they'd bounce about and there was no controlling them. I swear to you the boys went crazy when they used to see me. But it was Hamdan who really loved me. He used to sit under the sycamore tree in front of our house and sing the *mawwap*[2] about Bahiyya's eyes so that the whole village came to know he was singing it to me. Of course I'd known him from when I was young and often we'd played together, but when we grew up we looked at one another with different eyes. He would follow me about wherever I went, keeping at a distance, and we never had the courage to speak to each other. Only the way he looked at me told me of his love for me. And what nights I spent dreaming of him and telling myself that this was the man who'd make me feel glad I was born a woman! These were the happiest days I passed in my whole life, for there's no happier time for a girl than when her heart's still green and full of hopes. Then suddenly all these hopes were shattered when my father came in one day and said to me: 'Congratulations, Bahiyya, we've read the Fatiha[3] for you with Dahshan.' What a black day that was! I just sat where I was and cried. I didn't dare say I wanted to marry Hamdan or even to look up at my father. I was an ignorant girl and who was I to say I wanted this man and not that one? He'd have cut my throat for me. So I told myself that my destiny was with Dahshan and that was that. And what shall I tell you, daughter, about my life with him, and he your father who was taken from me and passed away when you were still a child at my breast? I wasn't all that happy with him, perhaps because of the bilharzia that was eating away at his strength, or perhaps the reason was what those women did to me with the razor when I was a young girl. After he died I found myself in a different position. All my life I'd been ruled by a man, first my father and then my husband. I thought when he died I'd be free and on my own and would do as I liked. The trouble was though that I'd still got some life in me and was still young and I didn't find a hand stretched out to me as I struggled to bring you up, especially as your Uncle Awwad had travelled abroad and your Aunt Nazeera had married and gone off to another village so that I was like a branch that has been lopped off a tree, all alone and like a stranger in my own village. At that time I felt that a woman without a man was like a fish out of water among people, and the women would look at her as a danger to their men and you'd find them keeping away from her as though she were a dog with the mange. But what's the point, daughter, of going on talking? A man's still a man and a woman will remain a woman whatever she does. Anyway, here you are, daughter mine, and Allah willing you'll be staying with me for a few days. Just let's hope the good Lord allows me to end my days before I become completely blind and helpless and a burden to my children. Daughter, I'm not crying now because I'm fed up or regret that the Lord created me a woman. No, it's not that. It's just that I'm sad about my life and my youth that have come and gone without my knowing how to live them really and truly as a woman.

Alifa Rifaat (1930-1996)

---

2. A mawwap is a poem in the colloquial language.

3. The Fatiha, or first short chapter of the Qur'an, is read when a marriage contract is made.

Questions on "Bahiyya's Eyes"

1. Alifa Rifaat's short story "Bahiyya's Eyes" treats the topic of suppression of women's freedom, including female genital mutilation that is practiced in several African and other cultures. How effectively does the author make the reader aware of the seriousness and widespread nature of the problem?

2. Research the topic of female genital mutilation to identify the countries where this problem exists. How are the feminist movements in those countries and elsewhere making people aware of the existence of the problem? Trace the origins and causes of this practice.

3. Write a character analysis of Bahiyya, focusing on her courage and endurance in the worst of circumstances. What are the sources of her strength? What values does she seem to cherish?

4. Bahiyya is a fatalist. Ordinarily fatalism is not regarded positively, but in her case, does fatalism bring her some relief? Support your answer with details from the story.

5. What does Bahiyya have to say about the life of a girl in her society? Does her daughter have the same view?

6. What evidence is there in the story to reveal the extent of Bahiyya's loneliness?

7. What is the reason for Bahiyya's daughter's visit to see her mother?

8. In your view, why has the author used no paragraph divisions in this narrative? Is there a thematic or stylistic reason for it?

9. Create a question based on this story. Your question should draw the reader deeper into the story's substance.

The Weed

Angoori was the new bride of the old servant of my neighbour's neighbour's neighbour. Every bride is new, for that matter; but she was new in a different way: the second wife of her husband who could not be called new because he had already drunk once at the conjugal well. As such, the prerogatives of being new went to Angoori only. This realization was further accentuated when one considered the five years that passed before they could consummate their union.

About six years ago Prabhati had gone home to cremate his first wife. When this was done, Angoori's father approached him and took his wet towel, wringing it dry, a symbolic gesture of wiping away the tears of grief that had wet the towel. There never was a man, though, who cried enough to wet a yard-and-a-half of calico. It had got wet only after Prabhati's bath. The simple act of drying the tear-stained towel on the part of a person with a nubile daughter was as much as to say, 'I give you my daughter to take the place of the one who died. Don't cry anymore. I've even dried your wet towel'.

This is how Angoori married Prabhati. However, their union was postponed for five years, for two reasons: her tender age, and her mother's paralytic attack. When, at last, Prabhati was invited to take his bride away, it seemed he would not be able to, for his employer was reluctant to feed another mouth from his kitchen. But when Prabhati told him that his new wife could keep her own house, the employer agreed.

At first, Angoori kept *purdah* from both men and women. But the veil soon started to shrink until it covered only her hair, as was becoming to an orthodox Hindu woman. She was a delight to both ear and eye. A laughter in the tinkling of her hundred ankle-bells, and a thousand bells in her laughter.

'What are you wearing, Angoori?'
'An anklet. Isn't it pretty?'
'And what's on your toe?'
'A ring.'
'And on your arm?'
'A bracelet.'
'What do they call what's on your forehead?'
'They call it *aliband.*'
'Nothing on your waist today, Angoori?'

'It's too heavy. Tomorrow I'll wear it. Today, no necklace either. See! The clasp is broken. Tomorrow I'll go to the city to get a new clasp . . . and buy a nose-pin. I had a big nose-ring. But my mother-in-law kept it.'

Angoori was very proud of her silver jewellery, elated by the mere touch of her trinkets. Everything she did seemed to set them off to maximum effect.

The weather became hot with the turn of the season. Angoori too must have felt it in her hut where she passed a good part of the day, for now she stayed out more. There were a few huge *neem* trees in front of my house; underneath them an old well that nobody used except an occasional construction worker. The spilt water made several puddles, keeping the atmosphere around the well cool. She often sat near the well to relax.

'What are you reading, *bibi*?' Angoori asked me one day when I sat under a *neem* tree reading.

'Want to read it?'
'I don't know reading.'
'Want to learn?'
'Oh, no!'
'Why not? What's wrong with it?'
'It's a sin for women to read!'
'And what about men?'
'For them, it's not a sin'.
'Who told you this nonsense?
''I just know it.'
'I read. I must be sinning.'
'For city women, it's no sin. It is for village women.'

We both laughed at this remark. She had not learned to question all that she was told to believe. I thought that if she found peace in her convictions, who was I to question them?

Her body redeemed her dark complexion, an intense sense of ecstasy always radiating from it, a resilient sweetness. They say a woman's body is like a lump of dough, some women have the looseness of under-kneaded dough while others have the clinging plasticity of leavened dough. Rarely does a woman have a body that can be equated to rightly-kneaded dough, a baker's pride. Angoori's body belonged to this category, her rippling muscles impregnated with the metallic resilience of a coiled spring. I felt her face, arms, breasts, legs with my eyes and experienced a profound languor. I thought of Prabhati : old, short, loose-jawed, a man whose stature and angularity would be the death of Euclid. Suddenly a funny idea struck me: Angoori was the dough covered by Prabhati. He was her napkin, not her taster. I felt a laugh welling up inside me, but I checked it for fear that Angoori would sense what I was laughing about. I asked her how marriages are arranged where she came from.

'A girl, when she's five or six, adores someone's feet. He is the husband.'
'How does she know it?'
'Her father takes money and flowers and puts them at his feet.'
'That's the father adoring, not the girl.'
'He does it for the girl. So it's the girl herself.'
'But the girl has never seen him before!'
'Yes, girls don't see.'
'Not a single girl ever sees her future husband!'
'No. . .' she hesitated. After a long, pensive pause, she added, 'Those in love. . . . they see them.'
'Do girls in your village have love-affairs?' 'A few'.
'Those in love, they don't sin?' I remembered her observation regarding education for women.
'They don't. See, what happens is that a man makes the girl eat the weed and then she starts loving him.'
'Which weed?'
'The wild one.'
'Doesn't the girl know that she has been given the weed?'
'No, he gives it to her in a *paan*. After that, nothing satisfies her but to be with him, her man. I know. I've seen it with my own eyes.'
'Whom did you see?'
'A friend; she was older than me.'
'And what happened?'
'She went crazy. Ran away with him to the city.'
'How do you know it was because of the weed?'
'What else could it be? Why would she leave her parents. He brought her many things from the city: clothes, trinkets, sweets.'
'Where does this weed come in?'
'In the sweets : otherwise how could she love him?'
'Love can come in other ways. No other way here?'
'No other way. What her parents hated was that she was that way.'
'Have you seen the weed?'
'No, they bring it from a far country. My mother warned me not to take *paan* or sweets from anyone. Men put the weed in them.'
'You were very wise. How come your friend ate it?'
'To make herself suffer,' she said sternly. The next moment her face clouded, perhaps in remembering her friend. 'Crazy. She went crazy, the poor thing,' she said sadly. 'Never combed her hair, singing all night. . . .'
'What did she sing?'
'I don't know. They all sing when they eat the weed. Cry too.'

The conversation was becoming a little too much to take, so I retired.

I found her sitting under the neem tree one day in a profoundly abstracted mood. Usually one could hear Angoori coming to the well; her ankle-bells would announce her approach. They were silent that day.

'What's the matter, Angoori?'

She gave me a blank look and then, recovering a little, said, 'Teach me reading, *bibi*.'
'What has happened?'
'Teach me to write my name.'
'Why do you want to write? To write letters? To whom?'

She did not answer, but was once again lost in her thoughts. 'Won't you be sinning?' I asked, trying to draw her out of her mood. She would not respond. I went in for an afternoon nap. When I came out again in the evening, she was still there singing sadly to herself. When she heard me approaching, she turned around and stopped abruptly. She sat with hunched shoulders because of the chill in the evening breeze.

'You sing well, Angoori'. I watched her great effort to turn back the tears and spread a pale smile across her lips.

'I don't know singing'.
'But you do, Angoori!'
'This was the . . .'
'The song your friend used to sing.' I completed the sentence for her.
'I heard it from her.'
'Sing it for me.'

She started to recite the words. 'Oh, it's just about the time of year for change. Four months winter, four months summer, four months rain! . . .'

'Not like that. Sing it for me,' I asked. She wouldn't, but continued with the words :

Four months of winter reign in my heart;
My heart shivers, O my love.
Four months of summer, wind shimmers in the sun.
Four months come the rains; clouds tremble in the sky.

'Angoori!' I said loudly. She looked as if in a trance, as if she had eaten the weed. I felt like shaking her by the shoulders. Instead, I took her by the shoulders and asked if she had been eating regularly. She had not; she cooked for herself only, since Prabhati ate at his master's. 'Did you cook today?' I asked.

'Not yet.'
'Did you have tea in the morning?'
'Tea? No milk today.'
'Why no milk today?'
'I didn't get any. Ram Tara . . .'
'Fetches the milk for you?' I added. She nodded.

Ram Tara was the night-watchman. Before Angoori married Prabhati, Ram Tara used to get a cup of tea at our place at the end of his watch before retiring on his cot near the well. After Angoori's arrival, he made his tea at Prabhati's. He, Angoori and Prabhati would all have tea together sitting around the fire. Three days ago Ram Tara went to his village for a visit.

'You haven't had tea for three days?' I asked. She nodded again. 'And you haven't eaten, I suppose?' She did not speak. Apparently, if she had been eating, it was as good as not eating at all.

I remembered Ram Tara : good-looking, quick-limbed, full of jokes. He had a way of talking with smiles trembling faintly at the corner of his lips.

'Angoori?'
'Yes, bibi'.
'Could it be weed?'

Tears flowed down her face in two rivulets, gathering into two tiny puddles at the corners of her mouth.

'Curse on me!' she started in a voice trembling with tears, 'I never took sweets from him... not a betel even . . . but tea . . .' She could not finish. Her words were drowned in a fast stream of tears.

Amrita Pritam (1919-2005)

Questions on "The Weed"

1. Explain the cultural taboo against romantic love in the story.

2. Is the narrator sympathetic to or critical of Angoori's attraction to Ram Tara, the young night watchman?

3. How does the narrator feel about Angoori's belief that if one is fed "the weed," one is drawn helplessly toward the person who feeds the weed? In the village setting that Angoori comes from, could this belief be considered a rationalization to justify the otherwise forbidden romantic love?

4. When Angoori says that it is a sin for women to learn reading, the narrator tells us that Angoori "had not learned to question all that she was told to believe." She then adds: "I thought that if she found peace in her convictions, who was I to question them?" Do you approve of the narrator's attitude and policy?

5. Is there a change in Angoori's thinking at any point in the story? If you find there is a change, mention what triggers it. If you find no change, support your answer.

6. Create a question based on this story. Your question should draw the reader deeper into the story's substance.

For the remaining stories in this chapter, write in any way that you like – an informal essay, a formal essay, or an informal or structured journal response. The only requirement is that your writing should be an interpretation, not just summarizing.

The Gift of the Magi

One dollar and eighty-seven cents. That was all. And sixty cents of it was in pennies. Pennies saved one and two at a time by bulldozing the grocer and the vegetable man and the butcher until one's cheeks burned with the silent imputation of parsimony that such close dealing implied. Three times Della counted it. One dollar and eighty- seven cents. And the next day would be Christmas.

There was clearly nothing to do but flop down on the shabby little couch and howl. So Della did it. Which instigates the moral reflection that life is made up of sobs, sniffles, and smiles, with sniffles predominating.

While the mistress of the home is gradually subsiding from the first stage to the second, take a look at the home. A furnished flat at $8 per week. It did not exactly beggar description, but it certainly had that word on the lookout for the mendicancy squad.

In the vestibule below was a letter-box into which no letter would go, and an electric button from which no mortal finger could coax a ring. Also appertaining thereunto was a card bearing the name "Mr. James Dillingham Young."

The "Dillingham" had been flung to the breeze during a former period of prosperity when its possessor was being paid $30 per week. Now, when the income was shrunk to $20, though, they were thinking seriously of contracting to a modest and unassuming D. But whenever Mr. James Dillingham Young came home and reached his flat above he was called "Jim" and greatly hugged by Mrs. James Dillingham Young, already introduced to you as Della. Which is all very good.

Della finished her cry and attended to her cheeks with the powder rag. She stood by the window and looked out dully at a gray cat walking a gray fence in a gray backyard. Tomorrow would be Christmas Day, and she had only $1.87 with which to buy Jim a present. She had been saving every penny she could for months, with this result. Twenty dollars a week doesn't go far. Expenses had been greater than she had calculated. They always are. Only $1.87 to buy a present for Jim. Her Jim. Many a happy hour she had spent planning for something nice for him. Something fine and rare and sterling--something just a little bit near to being worthy of the honor of being owned by Jim.

There was a pier-glass between the windows of the room. Perhaps you have seen a pier-glass in an $8 flat. A very thin and very agile person may, by observing his reflection in a rapid sequence of longitudinal strips, obtain a fairly accurate conception of his looks. Della, being slender, had mastered the art.

Suddenly she whirled from the window and stood before the glass. her eyes were shining brilliantly, but her face had lost its color within twenty seconds. Rapidly she pulled down her hair and let it fall to its full length.

Now, there were two possessions of the James Dillingham Youngs in which they both took a mighty pride. One was Jim's gold watch that had been his father's and his grandfather's. The other was Della's hair. Had the queen of Sheba lived in the flat across the airshaft, Della would have let her hair hang out the window some day to dry just to depreciate Her Majesty's jewels and gifts. Had King Solomon been the janitor, with all his treasures piled up in the basement, Jim would have pulled out his watch every time he passed, just to see him pluck at his beard from envy.

So now Della's beautiful hair fell about her rippling and shining like a cascade of brown waters. It reached below her knee and made itself almost a garment for her. And then she did it up again nervously and quickly. Once she faltered for a minute and stood still while a tear or two splashed on the worn red carpet.

On went her old brown jacket; on went her old brown hat. With a whirl of skirts and with the brilliant sparkle still in her eyes, she fluttered out the door and down the stairs to the street.

Where she stopped the sign read: "Mne. Sofronie. Hair Goods of All Kinds." One flight up Della ran, and collected herself, panting. Madame, large, too white, chilly, hardly looked the "Sofronie."

"Will you buy my hair?" asked Della.

"I buy hair," said Madame. "Take yer hat off and let's have a sight at the looks of it."

Down rippled the brown cascade.

"Twenty dollars," said Madame, lifting the mass with a practised hand.

"Give it to me quick," said Della.

Oh, and the next two hours tripped by on rosy wings. Forget the hashed metaphor. She was ransacking the stores for Jim's present.

She found it at last. It surely had been made for Jim and no one else. There was no other like it in any of the stores, and she had turned all of them inside out. It was a platinum fob chain simple and chaste in design, properly proclaiming its value by substance alone and not by meretricious ornamentation--as all good things should do. It was even worthy of The Watch. As soon as she saw it she knew that it must be Jim's. It was like him. Quietness and value--the description applied to both. Twenty-one dollars they took from her for it, and she hurried home with the 87 cents. With that chain on his watch Jim might be properly anxious about the time in any company. Grand as the watch was, he sometimes looked at it on the sly on account of the old leather strap that he used in place of a chain.

When Della reached home her intoxication gave way a little to prudence and reason. She got out her curling irons and lighted the gas and went to work repairing the ravages made by generosity added to love. Which is always a tremendous task, dear friends--a mammoth task.

Within forty minutes her head was covered with tiny, close-lying curls that made her look wonderfully like a <u>truant</u> schoolboy. She looked at her reflection in the mirror long, carefully, and critically.

"If Jim doesn't kill me," she said to herself, "before he takes a second look at me, he'll say I look like a Coney Island chorus girl. But what could I do--oh! what could I do with a dollar and eighty- seven cents?"

At 7 o'clock the coffee was made and the frying-pan was on the back of the stove hot and ready to cook the chops.

Jim was never late. Della doubled the fob chain in her hand and sat on the corner of the table near the door that he always entered. Then she heard his step on the stair away down on the first flight, and she turned white for just a moment. She had a habit for saying little silent prayer about the simplest everyday things, and now she whispered: "Please God, make him think I am still pretty."

The door opened and Jim stepped in and closed it. He looked thin and very serious. Poor fellow, he was only twenty-two--and to be burdened with a family! He needed a new overcoat and he was without gloves.

Jim stopped inside the door, as immovable as a setter at the scent of quail. His eyes were fixed upon Della, and there was an expression in them that she could not read, and it terrified her. It was not anger, nor surprise, nor disapproval, nor horror, nor any of the sentiments that she had been prepared for. He simply stared at her fixedly with that peculiar expression on his face.

Della wriggled off the table and went for him.

"Jim, darling," she cried, "don't look at me that way. I had my hair cut off and sold because I couldn't have lived through Christmas without giving you a present. It'll grow out again--you won't mind, will you? I just had to do it. My hair grows awfully fast. Say `Merry Christmas!' Jim, and let's be happy. You don't know what a nice-- what a beautiful, nice gift I've got for you."

"You've cut off your hair?" asked Jim, laboriously, as if he had not arrived at that patent fact yet even after the hardest mental labor.

"Cut it off and sold it," said Della. "Don't you like me just as well, anyhow? I'm me without my hair, ain't I?"

Jim looked about the room curiously.

"You say your hair is gone?" he said, with an air almost of idiocy.

"You needn't look for it," said Della. "It's sold, I tell you--sold and gone, too. It's Christmas Eve, boy. Be good to me, for it went for you. Maybe the hairs of my head were numbered," she went on with sudden serious sweetness, "but nobody could ever count my love for you. Shall I put the chops on, Jim?"

Out of his trance Jim seemed quickly to wake. He enfolded his Della. For ten seconds let us regard with discreet scrutiny some inconsequential object in the other direction. Eight dollars a week or a million a year--what is the difference? A mathematician or a wit would give you the wrong answer. The magi brought valuable gifts, but that was not among them. This dark assertion will be illuminated later on.

Jim drew a package from his overcoat pocket and threw it upon the table.

"Don't make any mistake, Dell," he said, "about me. I don't think there's anything in the way of a haircut or a shave or a shampoo that could make me like my girl any less. But if you'll unwrap that package you may see why you had me going a while at first."

White fingers and nimble tore at the string and paper. And then an ecstatic scream of joy; and then, alas! a quick feminine change to hysterical tears and wails, necessitating the immediate employment of all the comforting powers of the lord of the flat.

For there lay The Combs--the set of combs, side and back, that Della had worshipped long in a Broadway window. Beautiful combs, pure tortoise shell, with jewelled rims--just the shade to wear in the beautiful vanished hair. They were expensive combs, she knew, and her heart had simply craved and yearned over them without the least hope of possession. And now, they were hers, but the tresses that should have adorned the coveted adornments were gone.

But she hugged them to her bosom, and at length she was able to look up with dim eyes and a smile and say: "My hair grows so fast, Jim!"

And them Della leaped up like a little singed cat and cried, "Oh, oh!"

Jim had not yet seen his beautiful present. She held it out to him eagerly upon her open palm. The dull precious metal seemed to flash with a reflection of her bright and ardent spirit.

"Isn't it a dandy, Jim? I hunted all over town to find it. You'll have to look at the time a hundred times a day now. Give me your watch. I want to see how it looks on it."

Instead of obeying, Jim tumbled down on the couch and put his hands under the back of his head and smiled.

"Dell," said he, "let's put our Christmas presents away and keep 'em a while. They're too nice to use just at present. I sold the watch to get the money to buy your combs. And now suppose you put the chops on."

O. Henry (William Sydney Porter, 1862-1910)

Las Papas

He turned on the faucet of the kitchen sink and washed off the knife. As he felt the splashing water, he looked up through the front window and saw the September wind shaking the tender shoots of the trees on his street, the first hint of fall.

He quickly washed the potatoes one by one. Although their coloring was light and serene, they were large and heavy. When he started to peel them, slowly, using the knife precisely and carefully, the child came into the kitchen.

"What are you going to cook?" he asked. He stood there waiting for an answer.

"Chicken cacciatore," the man answered, but the child didn't believe him. He was only six, but he seemed capable of objectively discerning between one chicken recipe and another.

"Wait and see," he promised.
"Is it going to have onions in it?" asked the child.
"Very few," he said.

The child left the kitchen unconvinced. He finished peeling the potatoes and started to slice them. Through the window he saw the growing brightness of midday. That strong light seemed to paralyze the brilliant foliage on the trees. The inside of the potatoes had the same clean whiteness, and the knife penetrated it, as if slicing through soft clay.

Then he rinsed the onions and cut into them, chopping them up. He glanced at the recipe again and looked for seasonings in the pantry. The child came back in.

"Chicken is really boring," the child said, almost in protest.
"Not this recipe," he said. "It'll be great. You'll see."
"Put a lot of stuff in it, "the child recommended.
"It's going to have oregano, pepper, and even some sugar," he said.

The child smiled, approvingly.

He dried the potato slices. The pulp was crisp, almost too white, more like an apple, perhaps. Where did these potatoes come from? Wyoming or Idaho, probably. The potatoes from his country, on the other hand, were grittier, with a heavy flavor of the land. There were dark ones, almost royal purple like fruit, and delicate yellow ones, like the yolk of an egg. They say there used to be more than a thousand varieties of potato. Many of them have disappeared forever.

The ones that were lost, had they been less firmly rooted in the soil? Were they more delicate varieties? Maybe they disappeared when control of the cultivated lands was deteriorating. Some people say, and it's probably true, that the loss of even one domesticated plant makes the world a little poorer, as does the destruction of a work of art in a city plundered by invaders. If a history of the lost varieties were written it might prove that no one would ever have gone hungry.

Boiled, baked, fried, or stewed: the ways of cooking potatoes were a long story in themselves. He remembered what his mother had told him as a child: at harvest time, the largest potatoes would be roasted for everybody, and, in the fire, they would open up—just like flowers. That potato was probably one of the lost varieties, the kind that turned into flowers in the flames.

Are potatoes harvested at night in the moonlight? He was surprised how little he knew about something that came from his own country. As he thought about it, he believed *harvest* wasn't even the correct term. *Gathering? Digging?* What do you call this harvest from under the earth?

For a long time he had avoided eating them. Even their name seemed unpleasant to him, *papas*. A sign of the provinces, one more shred of evidence of the meager resources, of underdevelopment—a potato lacked protein and was loaded with carbohydrates. French-fried potatoes seemed more tolerable to him: they were, somehow, in a more neutralized condition.

At first, when he began to care for the child all by himself, he tried to simplify the ordeal of meals by going out to the corner restaurant. But he soon found that if he tried to cook something it passed the time, and he also amused himself with the child's curiosity.

He picked up the cut slices. There wasn't much more to discover in them. It wasn't necessary to expect anything more of them than the density they already possessed, a crude cleanliness that was the earth's flavor. But that same sense transformed them right there in his hands, a secret flowering, uncovered by him in the kitchen. It was as if he discovered one of the lost varieties of the Andean potato: the one that belonged to him, wondering, at noon.

When the chicken began to fry in the skillet, the boy returned, attracted by its aroma. The man was in the midst of making the salad.

"Where's this food come from?" the child asked, realizing it was a different recipe.
"Peru," he replied.
"Not Italy?" said the child, surprised.
"I'm cooking another recipe now," he explained. "Potatoes come from Peru. You know that, right?"
"Yeah, but I forgot it."
"They're really good, and there are all kinds and flavors. Remember mangoes? You really used to like them when we went to see your grandparents."
"I don't remember them either. I only remember the lion in the zoo."
"You don't remember the tree in Olivar Park?"
"Uh-huh. I remember that."
"We're going back there next summer, to visit the whole family."
"What if there's an earthquake?"

The boy went for his Spanish reader and sat down at the kitchen table. He read the resonant names out loud, names that were also like an unfinished history, and the man had to go over to him every once in a while to help explain one thing or another.

He tasted the sauce for the amount of salt, then added a bit of tarragon, whose intense perfume was delightful, and a bit of marjoram, a sweeter aroma.

He noticed how, outside, the light trapped by a tree slipped out from the blackened greenness of the leaves, now spilling onto the grass on the hill where their apartment house stood. The grass, all lit up, became an oblique field, a slope of tame fire seen from the window.

He looked at the child, stuck on a page in his book; he looked at the calm, repeated blue of the sky; and he looked at the leaves of lettuce in his hands, leaves that crackled as they broke off and opened up like tender shoots, beside the faucet of running water.

As if it suddenly came back to him, he understood that he must have been six or seven when his father, probably forty years old, as he was now, used to cook at home on Sundays. His father was always in a good mood as he cooked, boasting beforehand about how good the Chinese recipes were that he had learned in a remote hacienda in Peru. Maybe his father had made these meals for him, in this always incomplete past, to celebrate the meeting of father and son.

Unfamiliar anxiety, like a question without a subject, grew in him as he understood that he had never properly acknowledged his father's gesture; he hadn't even understood it. Actually, he had rejected his father's cooking one time, saying that it was too spicy. He must have been about fifteen then, a recent convert devoutly practicing the religion of natural foods, when he left the table with the plate of fish in his hands. He went out to the kitchen to turn on the faucet and quickly washed away the flesh boiled in soy sauce and ginger. His mother came to the kitchen and scolded him for what he had just done, a seemingly harmless act, but from then on an irreparable one. He returned to the table in silence, sullen, but his father didn't appear to be offended. Or did he suspect that one day his son's meal would be refused by his own son when he served it?

The emotion could still wound him, but it could also make him laugh. There was a kind of irony in this repeating to a large extent his father's gestures as he concocted an unusual flavor in the kitchen. However, like a sigh that only acquires some meaning by turning upon itself, he discovered a symmetry in the repetitions, a symmetry that revealed the agony of emotions not easily understood.

Just like animals that feed their young, we feed ourselves with a promise that food will taste good, he said to himself. We prepare a recipe with painstaking detail so that our children will recognize us in a complete history of flavor.

He must have muttered this out loud because the child looked up.

"What?" he said. "Italian?"
"Peruvian," he corrected. "With a taste of the mountains, a mixture of Indian, Chinese, and Spanish."

The child laughed, as if he'd heard a private joke in the sound of the words.

"When we go to Lima, I'll take you around to the restaurants," he promised.

The child broke into laughter again.

"It tastes good," said the child.
"It tastes better than yesterday's," the man said.

He poured some orange juice. The boy kneeled in the chair and ate a bit of everything. He ate more out of curiosity than appetite.

He felt once again that brief defenselessness that accompanies the act of eating one's own cooking. Behind that flavor, he knew, lurked the raw materials, the separate foods cooked to render them neutral, a secret known only to the cook, who combined ingredients and proportions until something different was presented to eyes and mouth. This culinary act could be an adventure, a hunting foray. And the pleasure of creating a transformation must be shared, a kind of brief festival as the eaters decipher the flavors, knowing that an illusion has taken place.

Later, he looked for a potato in the pantry and he held it up against the unfiltered light in the window. It was large, and it fit perfectly in his barely closed hand. He was not surprised that the misshapen form of this swollen tuber adapted to the contour of his hand; he knew the potato adapted to different lands, true to its own internal form, as if it occupied stolen space. The entire history of his people was here, he said to himself, surviving in a territory overrun and pillaged several times, growing in marginal spaces, under siege and waiting.

He left the apartment, went down the stairs and over to the tree on the hillock. It was a perfect day, as if the entire history of daytime were before him. The grass was ablaze, standing for all the grass he had ever seen. With both hands, he dug, and the earth opened up to him, cold. He placed the potato there, and he covered it up quickly. Feeling slightly embarrassed, he looked around. He went back up the stairs, wiping his hands, almost running.

The boy was standing at the balcony, waiting for him; he had seen it all.

"A tree's going to grow there!" said the boy, alarmed.
"No," he said soothingly, "potatoes aren't trees. If it grows, it will grow under the ground."

The child didn't seem to understand everything, but then suddenly he laughed.

"Nobody will even know it's there," he said, excited by such complicity with his father.

Julio Ortega (b. 1942)
(translated by Regina Harrison)

One of These Days

Monday dawned warm and rainless. Aurelio Escovar, a dentist without a degree, and a very early riser, opened his office at six. He took some false teeth, still mounted in their plaster mold, out of the glass case and put on the table a fistful of instruments which he arranged in size order, as if they were on display. He wore a collarless striped shirt, closed at the neck with a golden stud, and pants held up by suspenders. He was erect and skinny, with a look that rarely corresponded to the situation, the way deaf people have of looking.

When he had things arranged on the table, he pulled the drill toward the dental chair and sat down to polish the false teeth. He seemed not to be thinking about what he was doing, but worked steadily, pumping the drill with his feet, even when he didn't need it.

After eight he stopped for a while to look at the sky through the window, and he saw two pensive buzzards who were drying themselves in the sun on the ridgepole of the house next door. He went on working with the idea that before lunch it would rain again. The shrill voice of his eleven-year-old son interrupted his concentration.

"Papa."

"What?"

"The Mayor wants to know if you'll pull his tooth."

"Tell him I'm not here."

He was polishing a gold tooth. He held it at arm's length, and examined it with his eyes half closed. His son shouted again from the little waiting room.

"He says you are, too, because he can hear you."

The dentist kept examining the gold tooth. Only when he had put it on the table with the finished work did he say:

"So much the better."

He operated the drill again. He took several pieces of a bridge out of a cardboard box where he kept the things he still had to do and began to polish the gold.

"Papa."

"What?"

He still hadn't changed his expression.

"He says if you don't take out his tooth, he'll shoot you."

Without hurrying, with an extremely tranquil movement, he stopped pedaling the drill, pushed it away from the chair, and pulled the lower drawer of the table all the way out. There was a revolver.

"O.K.," he said. "Tell him to come and shoot me."

He rolled the chair over opposite the door, his hand resting on the edge of the drawer. The Mayor appeared at the door. He had shaved the left side of his face, but the other side, swollen and in pain, had a five-day-old beard. The dentist saw many nights of desperation in his dull eyes. He closed the drawer with his fingertips and said softly:

"Sit down."

"Good morning," said the Mayor.

"Morning," said the dentist.

While the instruments were boiling, the Mayor leaned his skull on the headrest of the chair and felt better. His breath was icy. It was a poor office: an old wooden chair, the pedal drill, a glass case with ceramic bottles. Opposite the chair was a window with a shoulder-high cloth curtain. When he felt the dentist approach, the Mayor braced his heels and opened his mouth.

Aurelio Escovar turned his head toward the light. After inspecting the infected tooth, he closed the Mayor's jaw with a cautious pressure of his fingers.

"It has to be without anesthesia," he said.

"Why?"

Because you have an abscess."

The Mayor looked him in the eye. "All right," he said, and tried to smile. The dentist did not return the smile. He brought the basin of sterilized instruments to the worktable and took them out of the water with a pair of cold tweezers, still without hurrying. Then he pushed the spittoon with the tip of his shoe, and went to wash his hands in the washbasin. He did all this without looking at the Mayor. But the Mayor didn't take his eyes off him.

It was a lower wisdom tooth. The dentist spread his feet and grasped the tooth with the hot forceps. The Mayor seized the arms of the chair, braced his feet with all his strength, and felt an icy void in his kidneys, but didn't make a sound. The dentist moved only his wrist. Without rancor, rather with a bitter tenderness, he said:

"Now you'll pay for our twenty dead men."*

The Mayor felt the crunch of bones in his jaw, and his eyes filled with tears. But he didn't breathe until he felt the tooth come out. Then he saw it through his tears. It seemed so foreign to his pain that he failed to understand his torture of the five previous nights.

Bent over the spittoon, sweating, panting, he unbuttoned his tunic and reached for the handkerchief in his pants pocket. The dentist gave him a clean cloth.

"Dry your tears," he said.

The Mayor did. He was trembling. While the dentist washed his hands, he saw the crumbling ceiling and a dusty spider web with spider's eggs and dead insects. The dentist returned, drying his hands.

"Go to bed," he said, "and gargle with salt water."

The Mayor stood up, said goodbye with a casual military salute, and walked toward the door, stretching his legs, without buttoning up his tunic.

"Send the bill," he said.

"To you or the town?"

The Mayor didn't look at him. He closed the door and said through the screen:

"It's the same damn thing."

Gabriel Garcia Marquez (b. 1927)

Homecoming

The road ahead of him was long, dull, winding and pocked with holes scoured by the rain that decayed the mud walls of the houses that had once been beautiful. Its face was rutted like an old man's face, and time had left upon it all its dusty memories. How dear to him this road was, how many dreams and secrets he had told it!

Ahmed's heart leaped in his chest like a caged wild bird. He felt like a knight returning home from the long wars with the sweat of life dried on his face, returning victorious. Yet he felt a strangeness in his excitement, too, something unfamiliar and unexpected. Perhaps he had suffered too much to fulfill his dreams.

Actually, his dreams had never exceeded marrying Khalidah, his childhood neighbor and his love. Would he find her as he had dreamed of her these eight years? Her soft body would have filled out. Her smile would still lighten not only the darkness of his soul, but the whole universe. She was the full moon showing herself from behind the black clouds.

She used to wait for him, each morning, as he left his home. She would sit behind the door, and peep around it to give him her beautiful smile. He loved her golden hair in its two pony tails tied with red yarn, her beautiful dark eyes that looked at him in tender love covered with shyness. When he returned her gaze with his thirst for love, she would run to hide. During his days he would find excuses, errands, that would take him home to see if she were there, hoping for another of those loving smiles, which became a necessity of life itself.

No one in the village could afford her dowry. She was the daughter of Abu Surayh, who would set a high bride-price in his pride, especially since his son Masud had gone away to the oil fields and become rich.

How would he find his father? Would he still walk with his thick cane, making the stones jump to the sides of the path as he struck the earth with every step on his way to the bazaar? Did he remember how that stick had bruised and cut his son's flesh? Ahmed remembered those blows as if they were engraved on his legs. In those days his name was only "Ox" or "Donkey" in his father's mouth. But in the last few years he had become "My dear son Ahmed" in his father's letters. Had this ox or donkey suddenly become dear to his father, or was it the money he sent home? Or – may Allah forgive you, Father – had his father been mellowed by some suffering or crisis?

Would he find his aunt sitting on the old mat, with her big smile of tender love? Had eight years further sharpened her long tongue that so often boiled her brother whenever she defied him? How he loved this spinster aunt – for without her, how could he have lived with his father after his mother's death? He wished he could remember his mother's features. But why did he let his thoughts mar his return? Let yourself be content with your aunt, he told himself, and thank Allah who provided you with this other mother who waited on you with love.

She had often defied his father on his behalf. Whenever his father mentioned his desire to remarry, too, she had defied him: "You should live for your child only!" (What child? The donkey?) Was it not expected of his aunt to let him marry, as any man would? But she would not have it so. Maybe now he could understand their conflict, could help resolve it, could repay her a bit.

Once, the donkey had summoned the courage to ask the question that overwhelmed him.

"Father . . . " But his tongue could not finish.

"What do you want?"

Then he had blushed and bowed his head, burning a hole in the carpet with his lost look, and said whisperingly: "My father . . . I want . . . I want to marry."

His father's loud laugh had shaken him and his legs trembled. "Marry, then!" his father had taunted. "But where will you get the money? Or do you want me to buy you a wife and support your wife and children all my life, you . . . ox?" Even in his terror and shame, Ahmed had smiled bitterly at his father's hesitation between "donkey" and "ox." Yet it was normal enough for a father to help his son get married – for any father.

"No, my father, I was planning to work, to travel. I want to go to the Eastern District. Abu Surayh let Masud go . . ." He was about to add that he wanted to marry Abu Surayh's daughter, but he could not find the courage to express his desire. Too well he knew the results of his tongue's mistakes. There would be a better time.

He had retreated, carrying his failure with him, and his father's taunt: "Show me, then, what a donkey can do!"

Eight years. Another world, a new world he had never dreamed of, nor would anyone in his village believe what he could tell. What if he told of thousands of foreign women walking naked but for transparent dresses, showing more than they hid of beautiful legs, broad backs, ivory breasts, walking through the city streets exhibiting their femininity that blew fire in men thirsty like himself? Who would believe the buildings that touched the sky, the meat and vegetables in sealed metal cans, the television and movie screens on which the strangenesses of life, the secrets of the universe, appeared? If he described such things, he would not be safe to live in his old home. Eight years!

Khalidah. What a big name; he even enviedhis lips their utterance of that beautiful name. His loving heart moved like a six-month baby in its mother's belly. His thoughts flew like ghosts leaving their lamps, to imagine their wedding night. How he had wanted to return home sooner, so that his bird love would not be hunted by someone else! But he had to build the stage for their future, for the morning smiles in each other's arms, not just around a door.

Eight years. He remembered the train wreck that almost took his life, and the fire that had blown the oil well as they were repairing the pump, spraying them with oil that attracted fire as flame attracts moths. These accidents had happened in the beginning, when he was still green. He thought of the communities of work: the friendships with men of many tribes and backgrounds, quickly developed through share work and risk, and firm as lifetime village friendships – as long as the work community lasted – and then as quickly forgotten when someone moved away. He hadn't even see Masud for a year.

Later he had been transferred to the mechanic shop, where he had shown talent and dependability that his superiors valued in the shape of certificates and increased salaries. He was proud of that. In the oil fields men took more pride in their skills than their tribes – a different kind of dignity.

The 5,000 Riyals he had sent to his father might have eased the conflict between his father and his aunt. He hoped so. Perhaps his father was even saving some of it for Ahmed's marriage. And now he felt no fear of announcing his desire to marry Khalidah.

"Who is knocking?"

"I'm . . . Ahmed!"

The door opened a little way, revealing a face that looked familiar. He should know her . . .I she resembled Khalidah . . . Oh! Oh, God! He cried inwardly, may Allah curse my fossilized memory! No, it was impossible. Where was the glowing smile? Where was the beauty? The slenderness?

"How are you . . . Khalidah?" He could hardly say her name.

"Thanks be to Allah, I'm fine. Welcome, Ahmed . . ." She opened the door and gestured. Oh! God, what were these new changes that had blown up her waist and filled her face with sadness? Did she know that he had left for her alone, and come back for her alone? Could she have forgotten the agreement, the promise, that he and she had signed with their eyes?

"Is my father here?"

"No . . . There's no one but me in the house."

God's curse on the devil! Why was she in his house alone? Or had he missed the way?

"But tell me – is this not my father's home?"

"Yes, but he isn't here. You may come in."

Alone by herself? What a strange puzzle! "Where is my aunt?"

"Your aunt is angry with your father, and is now at a relative's house."

"And you!" he shouted. "What are you doing here alone?"

"I'm in my home," she said. "In my husband's home."

Ahmed's feet moved to the road that had moments before witnessed his memories dancing before his eyes. It was long, dull, winding, dusty, and pocked with holes.

Ibrahim An-Nasir (b. 1932)

A Fairy Tale

I ran into her on the beach at Sidi Bishr, exactly where I had met her 12 years ago. I was then 17 years old; she was 2 years younger. We had then begun to inhabit a story which lasted 30 days, whose first word we inscribed in blood.

I do not exaggerate when I say 'blood.' She was a girl who spent her days immersed in books of fairy tales and who wished to make a fairy tale out of her love. She suggested I cut my finger so that she could suck the blood from it; she would cut her finger too so I could do the same. We did so. My blood then coursed through her veings as did her through mine – and we fancied that we were henceforth bound together for all eternity.

But eternity only lasted 30 days. We separated after that to meet intermittently over the years through swiftly exchanged, silent glances interrupted by an esteemed spouse, her spouse, and children like delicate blossoms, her three children. Never did I once meet her without feeling her blood in my veins and feeling its taste and its warmth – the taste of blood and its warmth – between my lips and on the tip of my tongue. I felt as if I were propelled towards her by a force unknown to me and she was a part of me that had broken away and then become lost; and that, indeed, I have the right to reclaim her and restore her to her place in my arms. It even seemed to me that whenever I saw her I could observe my blood in her veins and sense that this blood was trying to break free and return to its master and keeper.

I believe she shared the same sentiments. The languor that would appear on her face whenever she glanced at me and the weakness that would overcome her so that she had to hold on to her husband's arm and cling to him hard, as if afraid to take flight from his side and crash between my arms; the light that would glimmer in her eyes as if it were a reflection of the flames of the fire that had suddenly flared up in her veins – all this led me to believe that the tale, the fairy-tale of blood we had once believed in, continues to live on in our hearts and has taken control of our nerves. It continues to sound in the depths of our beings like the chanting of a priest among worshippers of magic, invoking demons.

Whenever our paths crossed for those fleeting moments, I would live with her for days in a web of fantasy, a fantasy in which the past, the present, and the future all became intertwined.

The past – when she would leap out of the window of her house to meet me in the desert of Sidi Bishr. She was well able to leave through the door, but she always preferred to leave through the window – for that is how it was in the stories she read.

The past – when she would close her eyes, lean against my chest and whisper tenderly to me, "O my beloved 'Braudelian'!"

I would attempt to protest, but she would place her delicate finger on my lips and say, "Shush! Don't try to remind me that your name is Fathi!"

The past – when she came to me in terror and surprised me by asking, "How much money do you have with you?"

I said, "I have twenty piasters."

She said, "And I have fifty. That should be enough."

I inquired, "Enough for what?"

She said, "For running away."

She related to me that her family had discovered her relationship with me and that she had confessed to them that she loved me and wished to marry me. They tried to convince her that I was not suitable for marriage, that I had no grand station in life, and that I was not an heir and not likely to inherit anything. Moreover, I was still a secondary school student and it mattered that I was a good-for-nothing lout. She objected to their low opinion of me and said that she liked me just as I was and that I tried to appear lowly but that I was not! Then she leaped out of her window as was her custom and came to run away with me.

I agreed to flee with her – but our flight lasted for only a day. We spent all the money we had on a single meal at the Shatbi café. Then she went back home and I went back to mine. However, we made a pact to steal whatever fell into our hands, then run away again. But she did not steal anything, for her family packed her off to Cairo. Next, they took her to their country home, from which she emerged only to marry a young physician – and what a fine specimen of a husband he was!

That is the past – in its madness, its youthfulness, and its splendor. The past was a day when she and I lived in the sky and viewed the world through the eyes of our imagination and we lived in it as we willed, not as it willed for us.

The present. She is a happily married woman and I am a happily married man. But we have tumbled down from the sky to dwell on earth and we have grown to believe in reality, not in fantasy. We devote ourselves to our needs, but not to our souls. Sometimes she wishes to return to me, sometimes I wish to return to her. But neither of us returns – for we disbelieved in the fairy-tales, even though they reside in our blood, and we only believed in the fleeting day, even though it is not a part of us.

The future. It holds nothing for us – except that she pray for me and I for her!

Ihsan Abd al-Quddus (1919-1991)
(Trans. Asma Afsaruddin)

Child's Paradise

"Daddy."

"Yes."

"My friend Nadia and I are always together. . . ."

"Of course, darling; she's your friend."

"In class, on walks, at meal times. . . ."

"That's marvelous. She is a pretty girl with good manners."

"But when the religion lesson comes, I go into one room, and she goes into another. Why is that?"

He looked at her mother and saw that she was smiling though she was busy embroidering.

"That's only for the religion lesson. . . ." he replied with a smile.

"Why, Daddy?"

"Because you belong to one religion, and she belongs to another."

"How is that, Daddy?"

"You are a Muslim and she is Christian."

"Why, Daddy?"

"You're very young. You will learn later on."

"I'm a big girl, Daddy."

"No, you're not; you're a little girl, my darling."

"Why am I a Muslim?"

He had to be patient and cautious; he shouldn't give up the principles of modern education at first attempt.

"Daddy is a Muslim and Mummy is a Muslim," he replied, "and so you're a Muslim too."

"And Nadia?"

"Her father's a Christian and her mother is too, and so she is a Christian."

"Is it because her father wears glasses?"

"No, no. It's got nothing to do with wearing glasses. It's because her grandfather was a Christian as well. . . ."

He decided to continue the chain of ancestors all the way to infinity so that she would get bored and change the subject. But instead she asked, "Which is better?"

He thought for a moment. "Being a Muslim girl is good," he said, "and so is being a Christian girl. . . ."

"Mustn't one be better than the other?"

"One is good and so is the other."

"Shall I be made into a Christian so that we can always be together?"

"No, no, darling; that's impossible. Every little girl stays just like her Daddy and Mummy. . . ."

"But why?"

This modern education was really tough! "Won't you wait till you grow up?" he asked her.

"No, Daddy. . . ."

"All right. You know all about fashion; some people like one style and others prefer another. Your being a Muslim is the latest fashion, and so you must stay a Muslim. . . ."

"You mean, Nadia is old-fashioned?"

Blast you and Nadia, both of you! It was obvious that, in spite of all the care he had taken he had made a mistake and was being driven mercilessly into a bottle neck. "It's a question of taste," he replied "But every little girl must stay like her Daddy and Mummy. . . ."

"Shall I tell her that she's old fashioned and that I'm up-to-date?"

"Every religion is good," he replied quickly. "Muslim girls worship God, and so do Christians. . . ."

"Why does she worship Him in one room and I in another?"

"In one room, they worship Him in one way, and in the other room, in another way. . . ."

"What's the difference, Daddy?"

"You will learn about it in the coming year or else the year after that. For the moment, it's enough for you to know that a Muslim little girl worships God and a Christian little girl does too."

"Who is god, Daddy?"

He had been caught. He thought for a while. "What did teacher say at school?" he asked to get a bit of leeway.

"She reads the chapter from the Qur'an and teaches us prayers, but I don't know. Who is God, Daddy?"

He thought for a while. "He is the Creator of the whole world," he replied with an enigmatic smile.

"All of it?"

"What does Creator mean, Daddy?"

"It means that he makes everything."

"How, Daddy?"

"With a might power."

"Where does he live?"

"In the whole world."

"What about the time before the world?"

"He lived up there. . . ."

"In Heaven?"

"Yes."

"I want to see Him."

"Impossible."

"Not even on television?"

"That's impossible too."

"Can't anyone see Him?"

"No."

"How do you know that He's up there?"

"That's the way He is."

"Who knows He's up there?"

"The prophets."

"The prophets?"

"Yes, like our lord Muhammad."

"How, Daddy?"

"Through a special power he had."

"Has he got powerful eyes?"

"Yes."

"Why. Daddy?"

"That's how God created him."

"Why, Daddy?"

"He is free to do what He wishes," he replied, controlling has flagging patience.

"And how does he see Him?"

"Very mighty, very powerful, capable of doing anything."

"Like you, Daddy?"

"There is no one like Him," he replied, suppressing a laugh.

"Why does He live up there?"

"The earth is not big enough for Him, but He sees everything."

For a moment she was distracted. "But Nadia told me that He lived on the earth," she said.

"Because He sees everywhere, it seems as if He is living everywhere."

"She said that people killed Him!?"

"But He is alive, He doesn't die."

"Nadia said they killed Him. . . ."

"No, no, my darling. They thought they killed Him, but He's alive, He doesn't die."

"Is my grandfather alive too?"

"No, he is dead."

"Did people kill him?"

"No, he died of his own accord. . . ."

"How?"

"He was ill, then he died. . . ."

"Will my sister die because she is ill?" He frowned a little, noticing a gesture of protest coming from her mother's direction.

"No, no, she will get better, God willing."

"Why did my grandfather die?"

"He was an old man when he fell ill. . . ."

"You fell ill and you're old. Why didn't you die?" Her mother scolded her. The little girl looked at the two of them in bewilderment.

"We all die when God wishes it," her father replied.

"Why does God want us to die?"

"He is free to do what He wishes."

"Is death nice?"

"No, my sweet. . . ."

"Why does God want something which isn't nice?"

"It is nice as long as God wants it for us."

"But you said it wasn't nice."

"I was wrong, darling. . . ."

"Why was Mummy angry when I said you would die?"

"Because God doesn't want that yet."

"Why does He want it, Daddy?"

"He brings us here, and then takes us away."

"Why, Daddy?"

"So that we can do nice things here before we leave."

"Why don't we stay?"

"The world wouldn't be large enough for everyone if they all stayed."

"And do we leave the nice things behind?"

"We will be going on to much nicer things than them."

"Where?"

"Up there."

"Where God is?"

"Yes."

"Will we see Him?"

"Yes."

"Is that nice?"

"Of course."

"Do we have to go then?"

"We haven't done any nice things yet."

"Did my grandfather do some nice things?"

"Yes. . . ."

"What did he do?"

"He built a house and grew plants in a garden. . . ."

"What did my cousin Toto do?"

He frowned for a moment, then glanced sympathetically at her mother. "He built a little house too before he went. . . ." he continued.

"But our neighbor Lu'lu hits me and never does anything nice."

"He's a naughty boy."

"But he will never die!"

"Only when God wishes it. . . .I"

"Even though he never does anything nice?"

"Everyone dies. Those who do good things go to God, and those who do bad things go to Hell. . . ."

She sighed and then was silent. He was well aware of how much pressure he was under, and didn't know how much of what he had said was right and how much was wrong. The stream of questions had aroused question marks deep down inside him.

"I want to stay with Nadia all the time," the little girl shouted after a little while.

He looked at her in curiosity.

"Even in the religion lesson!" she continued. He laughed loudly, and so did her mother. "I don't think it's possible to discuss these questions on that level!" he said with a yawn.

"One day she will grow up," his wife said, "and then you'll be able to offer her all these facts you sseem to know!!!"

He turned angrily in her direction to see whether she really meant what she said, or was just being sarcastic. He found her engrossed once again in her embroidery.

Naguib Mahfouz (1911-2006)

Violets

The violets were wilting under the hot August rays. It seemed a more severe August than last year's. Only the tall palms in the garden kept their greenness despite the heavy heat.

He was waiting impatiently among the trees for the return or" his daughter. Soha, or Doctor Soha as he liked to call her, had given herself totally to her work since she had earned her M.D. and her specialization. She was a gynecologist at the University Medical Hospital in Jeddah.

He always had worried when she was late, but in the years since his wife's death he had become even more afraid when she was delayed. It was not just because she was his only child, but also because she exerted so much effort for her patients. Such a gentle lady was not supposed to be able to do that.

When he heard the bell he rushed to open the door, not waiting for his servant, to meet her with a smile.

"What are you doing here, Daddy?" she asked him.

"Waiting for your return, as usual."

"But I am twenty-four! You should be confident of my well-being. Often my work keeps me there late."
"Even so, I still will wait, until that day when Samir comes back from his studies and makes you his wife."

Soha took his hand and entered the hallway of the villa. "Believe me, my father, my heart is telling me that I will not be married to that cousin."

Surprised, he turned toward her and asked, "Why do you say that?"

My heart tells me so. Especially since I was granted my degrees while he failed his studies."

"But he loves you."

"He might love me, but I know Samir better than you do. Even if he is my cousin, he is selfish in his thinking and looks at life only through his own perspective."

"But how do you know that?"

"He has shown me himself. He tried many times to talk me out of continuing my studies. We talked a lot about that. He doesn't want an educated wife, a wife with a profession or a dedication outside the home. I told him that I'd wait for him, to fulfill my mother's promise, for you know how much Mother loved his mother. But I also told him that he did not have to keep the promise if he found somebody more suitable for him. Or found himself unable to continue his studies. And now five years have passed and he is still in America, and still doesn't have his M.S. in engineering, and all his friends have come back successfully."

Then she was silent. "And what else?" he asked softly.

"There is another thing that I did not want to mention, but I will. When Thurayya came back from visiting her brother in Houston, she told me that she learned a lot of things about Samir. He became friends with a Swedish student, and everybody there knew their love story. How many months have passed since lor you received any letters from him? Isn't that proof that he has forgotten, or is trying to forget? I'm as loyal as I must be to the promise my mother made to her sister, but I just wish he would get his degree and come back. Alone or with her. I'm not afraid of being at a loss."

"Would you agree if he asked your hand?"

"No," she said emphatically, "not willingly. But we have to put our hearts aside sometimes. At least our society believes in getting used to each other as the way to love. We're not like the Americans and Europeans who choose their own. So I don't worry about Samir. If I worry, it is only about my patients."

She went to her room and he returned to the garden, where the violets were wilting in the sun.

When would his heart be able to relax? He treasured every memory of his years with his daughter, who so reminded him of his wife; he treasured every day of her life in his home now; yet he wanted her to marry. He wanted the promise fulfilled. Yet Samir . . . Ah, but man's life is like a book of blank pages written by the pen of fate in a strangely perfect way that surprises even those who have experienced many years.

His memories gathered in front of him. He tried to get a sense of his place in this world after his wife's death left him with their daughter whose childhood filled his life as he tried to make her happy. He had helped her to fulfill her goals.

Allah had given him money, a special status that made it his duty to give. Though he had lost the gentle companionship of his wife, he still felt her presence. Her soul lived with him. He had not seen her before their wedding, for tradition did not allow such a premature meeting, but from the moment he saw her he loved her. Everything came according to his desire. He compared the days of his marriage to the present time, when it had become the right of the bride and groom to see each other before the wedding-and even before consenting to marriage. In his day, the mere request was an unforgivable insult to one's parents, to the girl's family, to all involved in making the match, to all propriety.

His brother's marriage to his wife's sister became the crown of their family happiness through which the family lived its most beautiful years, until that time when his wife began to lose her strength and wilt like the violets under the hot August sun. He had tried every way to save her. That last night she had opened her eyes with a smile and begun to talk about her life with him. She spoke of her happiest memories, and of their daughter Soha. She asked him what he would do for her.

"Cherish her. Care for her in every way."

"I'll not ask you not to remarry, for I know that it would be unfair to ask that," she said. "Remarry if you wish, after Soha is old enough to marry. She shouldn't have to suffer a stepmother."

He promised. That was twelve years ago, and he was still at his daughter's side taking loving care of her. He knew that Soha felt the sacrifice of his singleminded devotion to her.

Everybody in the family knew that Soha was for Samir, as they watched them grow up together.

But Soha was very different from Samir. She was brilliant, and a hard worker. She would be one of the great future physicians in Jeddah. Soha was right: Samir was an indifferent student, satisfied to take his time in his studies and to depend on his father's income. He might never be able to take care of a family responsibly. He might never learn to cherish Soha's competence.

If the ideas of the young and the old are always different, he thought, it is not because the facts of life differ from one generation to another, but because of the way the generations view them. Soha looked gentle and spoke gently, but she had a determined mind that knew how to plan her future independently. She had decided not to tie herself to Samir. That was her opinion, and he knew that what Soha decided was not something that could be negotiated. Though she was her father's only child, and perhaps a bit spoiled, she still had an excellent mind that enabled her to differentiate between what was good ·and what was bad.' She had judgment.

When would serenity come? They said that fathers must live always under tension, always looking for rest. His rest would be in seeing his daughter married, settled. But was there a man who deserved her?

"Of course, Daddy."

He turned and saw Soha standing behind him. "Are you reading my mind?" he asked gently.

Soha laughed and said, "I've been watching you for the last ten minutes, observing your worry and reading every word you whispered to yourself. Many strings draw me toward you. Your thoughts were flying over more than one garden until you arrived to your question. There are many who deserve Soha, and whom she deserves. Your daughter is one who knows how to choose, when she sees that the time is right to choose. So do not be sad, Daddy. Look at my face and realize how good I am! After all, I'm the daughter of a noble man who knows how to plant virtues in his daughter!

She was silent, and her hands reached out to surround him in an embrace that reminded him of his wife, whenever he surprised her with a gift or a compliment. He smiled delightedly and began to sing a children's song, as if Soha were still a baby. Soha played the role of child with him willingly. Then he looked into her face and said, "I think you want to say things that you have not yet said."

She nodded. "It is not yet time to tell you all I want to say, but be sure I will listen to your opinion when it is time. As you know, I am waiting for him whom my mother chose with my consent. When he returns, I shall find myself free of her promise, because I'm sure he won't return alone."

"But how sure are you of what you're saying?"

"Do you know, my father, that I have been happier since I thought I might be released from my mother's promise to her sister. My cousin gave me that happiness without realizing it."

"Is there somebody else, then?"

"Not yet. I'm very busy in my work, and that's the truth. Still, I'm waiting for the knight of my dreams. Do not worry! He will appear at the right time, and the criteria for 'marriageable age' and 'spinster' are changing. I don't have to hurry. I won't stay unmarried forever."

They laughed, and she went to her room to prepare herself to visit a friend. He stared at the horizon. It was true that Soha had achieved her professional position, but all professional positions were very small in his eyes. He saw her in her white wedding dress walking among the women guests, and saw a smile of satisfaction appear on her mother's radiant face.

Pity those parents who think that when their children are grown they can relax! he thought. They are very much mistaken, for the problems with one's children only grow bigger as the children grow.

He went to his room and examined his face in the mirror. Wrinkles around his eyes pointed to his years. He sighed and thought deeply of the future. He longed to see grandchildren playing in front of his eyes as Soha had played.

The telephone rang. It was his brother's voice, in tones of chagrin.

"Do you believe it? The traitor has come back!"

"Who?"

"My son and yours," his brother said.

"That is happy news! He has returned after a long absence!"

"I wish he hadn't."

"Why?"

"He didn't come alone."

"Who is with him?"

"A woman from America whom he calls his wife-and two children."

"But be happy, Brother!"

"What about the promise between our wives?"

"It is no longer binding, so do not worry."

His brother was very surprised. "Are you not angry, as I am, then?"

"No, and neither is Soha. She already knows everything."

"But why did you and she not tell me?"

"We left that for the right day, and it is today. And now you know everything, so receive your son in joy, and your daughter, and your grandchildren. But tell·me . . ."

"What?"

"The most important thing. Did he finish his studies?"

"He says he wants to go on to his Ph.D.," his brother said. "Of that I'm proud."

"Oh. I see that a little differently. One who has taken all these years for the M.S. might not yet be worthy to pursue the Ph.D. without working for a while. But I'm sure you will know what's best."

"Soha and you, will you come over to see us?"

"We shall, but Soha is out right now. When she comes back, we will agree on a time."

"Until then, then!"

He put the receiver down quietly and stared at the horizon. Soha was now free of her mother's promise. She had not insisted on freeing herself, though she did not want to marry him. Fate gives both what one craves and what one dreads; Soha was both wise and fortunate.

He looked at the violets and found that in the evening's cool sea breeze their wilted leaves were reviving.

Ghalib Hamzah Abu al-Faraj (b. 1932)

Black Night at Miawaddy

**According to folklore,
if people had to throw their bag of troubles
into a common pot and then choose one bag,
they would select their own.**

HE had been careful throughout the trip to avoid recognition. Once over the top of the hill, a towering stronghold of a hill that made another world of that section of the borderland, the bus plunged down steeply past slopes where the pine-trees grew in thick clusters. The sun which had been hovering over the treetops dipped behind the branches, flashing dazzling beams into the passengers' eyes. Sometimes the bus would turn onto the unfinished road which, when completed, would be the Asian Highway linking Thailand with Burma, and then it had to turn back onto the Old road, leaving a trail of dust clouds high against the green foliage. At last the bus bumped its way out of the mountains and approached Mae Sod.

Mae Sod to the uninitiated would seem like any other average-sized village, a knot of scattered dwellings. But its market-place was crowded, the houses and stores were thronged with people, a hive of unexpected activity. It certainly was not the quiet little border town it appeared to be at the first, casual glance.

The bus stopped at the market-place and Korn drew a sharp breath of relief. The irksome journey was over at last. He had been worried on the bus, not so much fearing that at any minute it might run off the treacherous road and plunge into the chasm, but that someone might already be on his trail. At the last checkpoint before Mae Sod he had almost panicked when the bus was halted for inspection even though the police were interested in the merchandise it carried and cast only a cursory glance at the human cargo.

Before Korn stepped off the bus he asked the driver to direct him to the Mae Mei Hotel. That was where he had arranged to meet Ong Tone, his Burmese contact. Humping his bag, he hailed a samlor and made it to the hotel in under five minutes.

He paid off the samlor, went into the hotel and set down his bag on a table. A middle-aged man, sitting behind the counter busy with accounts, came out.

"Are you wanting a room, sir?" Korn did not answer but countered with another question. "Has a man called Ong Tone, a Burmese from the other side, been around here making inquiries?"

"Oh, yes, about two days ago. He left a message. If anyone came to inquire after him, he would be waiting at the usual place." He gave Korn another look. "That's yourself, of course?"

The young man nodded.

"Thank you. Please give me a room. One bed only . . ."

"Right, sir. Please step this way, upstairs."

Korn was shown into a room on the right-hand side. It was just like any other provincial hotel room. The wash-basin, the bathroom, and the bed were none too clean. Attempts had been rnade to maintain cleanliness but dust and dirt had managed to emerge triumphant.

"Will you be staying long, sir?" the manager asked.

371

"I don't know yet," Korn said. "I'll tell you later."

"Please ring if you need anything. At your service," said the manager before he went downstairs.

Korn closed the door, undressed, and scooped water over his shoulders from the stone jar in the bathroom. He dressed quickly afterwards and left the hotel.

He headed straight for the Mei River, which formed the natural border between Thailand and Burma.

It was about six kilometres from the market to the Mei River. By then it was quite dark. Korn walked steadily along the road which took him past the Border Patrol Police camp and the airfield. The night belonged to the waxing moon, rising over the tree-tops in glowing loveliness. At the bank of the river, Korn could make out the Burmese Miawaddy check-point etched in darkness on the far bank. Behind it loomed the roundness of a temple chedi, catching splinters of silver from the new moon.

Ever since the Burmese had closed the border, communication between the villagers who lived on different sides of the river had to be stealthy. Both river banks lay quiet and desolate.

Korn·chose a place where the water was at its shallowest, and waded out towards the Miawaddy bank. The Mei is a strange river. It does not run southward like other rivers, but flows steadily northward, perhaps because of the high plateau. In the dry season, when the river was shallow, the sandy bank of the Miawaddy ran out almost exactly half-way across. But on the Thai side, the Miawaddy ran deep.

In midstream, Korn froze. Something or someone was moving on the opposite bank. He stood still for a moment, and saw a figure start out across the river.

When the figure came nearer, Kom saw that it was a girl. She stopped with a quick glance at him, then waded on. She was Burmese, and beautiful, but Korn gave her no more than a brief glance as soon as he saw that she was not Ong Tone, the Burmese who had promised to help him defect to Burma. When he reached the Miawaddy bank, Korn waited, his anxiety mounting.

An hour passed, and more, without a sign of Ong Tone.

He passed the time watching the Burmese girl. She was hovering around a deserted building that had once been a riverside bar, gone out of business when the border was closed. She seemed to be waiting too.

Korn looked at his watch. It was almost nine.

It was not like Ong Tone to break his word. There must have been a hitch.

When another half hour had passed, Korn decided to cross back to the Thai bank. Once again, he passed the Burmese girl in midstream. She was going back to Miawaddy.

Korn stood around awhile on the sandy bank then he strolled casually towards the closed bar, and border check-point. When he was still some distance from it the moonlit idyll was shattered.

A voice from a bush in front of him rapped out his name. "Nai Korn! Stay where you are. This is the police. We call on you to surrender. Do not resist."

The voice rooted him to the spot as two or three armed men in police uniform jumped out and blocked his way menacingly. Korn seemed to freeze for a breath, his thoughts racing desperately. Suddenly he knew what he had to do. He did not waste a moment.

He struck out for the river bank and dropped into the long grass, rolling as he struck the ground. He had no thought but flight.

He heard bursts of gun-fire behind him as he fled along the bank. He rounded a bend and reached a thick grove, scrambled up the bank and ran on, relying on the trees for cover. He fled swiftly on, amazed at his own speed and the amount of ground he had covered. He fancied the gun-fire was echoed from the distant Miawaddy bank. Could the Burmese police have been alerted to co-operate with the Thais? Korn rushed on in panic ignoring the stinging thorns and twigs that lashed his hurtling body. He kept on running until he could no longer hear the guns. Feeling out of danger, if only temporarily, Korn stopped, gasping air into his tortured lungs. He was at the edge of a small wood close to the river.

He had not expected violence so near the border. Someone must have tipped the police off so they could ambush him.

"I'll never find Ong Tone now," he thought, still panting. He was filled with a sudden great weariness. Now he had missed the rendezvous, he had little hope of being able to join his comrades in Burma and help them organize an effective force. Right here, on the banks of the Mei River, all he had worked for had come to nothing.

He heard a sound behind him, and crouched hastily against a tree trunk. A figure emerged from the other side of the wood and came towards his hiding-place.

One of its hands was clutching an arm and it was moaning as it ran, as if in pain. Korn watched, silently, until the fugitive fell to the ground. Only then did he move, going swiftly over to have a look.

It was the girl. She looked up, as surprised as Korn himself, and gasped. "I'm hit." Her Thai had a strange, heavy accent.

"Hit?"

"The Burmese police. The bullet grazed my arm, but it's not too bad." He bent down to look at her right arm, grasped tight in her left hand. The dark blood was already spreading over her clothes. "Is the pain bad?" he asked. He did not dare to touch her. He could only look.

She smiled, and he realized again that she was beautiful. But this was not the time . . . The first thing was to attend to her wound.

"It's all right. I can bear it," said the Burmese girl. Then she asked him, "What are you doing here, anyway?"

"I was on the run from the police too," he sighed harshly.

"Running from the police?" she repeated, opening her eyes wide. "Oh, the other shots! I heard them but I did not think that it was you . . ." She sat up. "I'm a student from Rangoon. You can call me Mayin Nu."

"Mayin Nu," Korn repeated her name. "I am Korn Pakdithai. I'm a student from Bangkok."

The Burmese girl looked at the Thai man.

"That's strange," she said. "I have a feeling we have something in common."

"I feel the same," he nodded, looking excitedly into her eyes. He would have liked to ask her more, but there was no time to waste on personal exchanges. The police might be hot on the trail that would lead them straight to their hiding-place.

"Let's get away from here," he urged. "It is not safe to stay still too long. Can you go on, Mayin Nu?" For the first time he called her by name.

"Yes, Korn, I can go on."

They looked at each other, eyes steady.

Korn Pakdithai tore a strip off his shirt and dressed the wound on the arm of the girl from Rangoon. Then they moved off together along the river bank. -In the deep silence of the night, the jungle made their footfalls sound unnaturally loud. The night and the silence deepened. The sound of dew dropping onto the leaves punctuated the continuous fluttering of the wings of small insects. The two fugitives kept walking doggedly when the moon was directly above their heads and even when it began to sink towards the western horizon. Finally, it slipped past the tree-tops, down out of sight, leaving the jungle to the horrors of darkness. The young man and the girl, fleeing to seek their freedom like two birds who desired only to fly beneath the high, wide uncluttered sky, stopped for a moment to draw breath.

"Does it hurt?" asked Korn, helping the girl to rest against a tree trunk. She looked tired and helpless, he saw with compassion. He himself was so exhausted he could scarcely walk, and he was a strong man, while she was a girl, and wounded.

Mayin Nu smiled at him.

"Don't worry, please. The wound is not deep. Anyway, we have to run, don't we?" She looked deep into his eyes, grateful for his concern, this young man from Thailand, with whom she had had such an unexpected encounter. If he had not been there to help her, she would never have escaped.

"What about you, Korn, aren't you tired?"

He smiled at her.

"Never mind me. I am a man." He looked around. "We have come far. I think we are safe enough now."

"Thank you for your help," said Mayin Nu.

"We are human beings, and fated to suffer so we must help each other when we can," he replied smiling towards the indistinct paleness that was her face in the trees' shadow. "Whatever did you do to get the police after you like that?"

The Burmese girl sighed.

"Well, it's politics."

"Politics," he repeated incredulously, his eyes on her face.

"That's right," nodded Mayin Nu. "I am a known sympathizer with the other side."

"So you are in sympathy with the democratic doctrines?"

"Yes, I reject the socialist regime. Socialism deprives the people of all authority. Absolute power rests with a handful of administrators. We want democracy, with recognition of the rights and freedom of the people. I am determined to cross the border and organize a strong party in Thailand. I have been in touch with Voramit, a Thai I knew, and he was to meet me at the border. But the police found me first." Mayin Nu was quiet for a moment. "And then I was shot and had to run away."

Korn rose, stunned by the Burmese girl's words. He was at a loss, unable to think clearly. What had seemed so right and beautiful was beginning to lose its lustre.

Mayin Nu was still speaking.

"Once, long ago, my country suffered under the heel of a colonial power. Today, we are at the mercy of neo-colonialism. We are terribly unfortunate. My friends and I reject all colonialists and their running dogs. We want to live in freedom under a democratic regime."

"So? Yet I have heard socialists branding all democratic regimes as colonialism."

"Oh, that was in the bad old days when Great Powers were snapping up countries for colonization," she explained. "The socialism I am running from is a form of neo-colonialism where countries are snapped up for ideological indoctrination."

The jungle rang with the musical crowing of the cocks. The sky began to lighten. The girl student from Rangoon was curled up at the foot of a tree, covered by Korn's shirt. She stirred, opening her eyes, then sat up and looked around. She smiled when she caught sight of Korn, sitting on a felled tree a short distance away, enjoying a quiet smoke. He was wearing only his undershirt. He had taken his shirt off to cover the sleeping Mayin Nu as dawn approached.

"Have you been awake long?" she asked. The pain of her arm made her wince a little but the wound had stopped bleeding.

"I did not sleep all night," he answered, coming over to join her.

"Why ever not?" asked Mayin Nu with raised eyebrows.

"I could not sleep, so I went and sat over there." He pointed at the log then reached for his shirt and shrugged it on. "How's the wound?" he asked, bending to look at the dressing on her arm.

"Better, thank you," she said. "We may find some village nearby where I can ask for some sort of ointment to put on it."

"It is not so bad," Korn agreed, lifting the crude dressing to look. "Last night, in the dark, I thought it was much worse."

"It is not bad," said Mayin Nu. She changed the subject. "Where are we heading today? We have to keep on running, I suppose."

The student from Bangkok stood still for a moment before speaking.

"There's no real use running," he said. "I was thinking about it all night. I came to the conclusion that we ought to stop running, once and for all."

The Burmese girl looked at him as if she could not believe her ears.

"What do you mean?"

He shook his head slowly from side to side.

"Everywhere in the world it is the same," he said. "There is always more than one school of thought, more than one faction. Even if you attain the things you really believe in, you'll always run into other people whose beliefs conflict with your own. The opposition, the unconverted. I see it as clear as I see you right now. It's like looking at a picture postcard and seeing only the breath-taking beauty of the view. In reality, everything has a good side and a bad one, so one thing is as good as another."

Mayin Nu looked puzzled.

"What is it you are trying to say?"

"I am trying to tell you something important. Stop trying to reach out after what you think you want. Once you have it safely in your grasp, you will want something else and try to reach for that too. The quest is never-ending."

Mayin Nu was speechless.

"Please believe me, don't go on," he said earnestly. "People are strange. They find something good and at once they want something better. We are always eager to believe that the grass grows greener in other pastures. We always want things different from what they are. Mayin Nu, give up your plan to get into my country. Once you are in Thailand you will find you face the same problems that drove you from Burma. I had a plan, too. I wanted to defect to your country, as you wanted to run away to mine."

"Korn, can it be true that you wished for socialism?" Mayin Nu asked, her eyes wide.

"I did not really know what I wanted," he shook his head, "until I met you. Now I know. I want to stay in my own home, not live among strangers."

Soon the sky lightened into morning. The runaways, their races different, but their dreams not so very different, walked back together to the river.

"There is no place like home," said Korn, looking at the river and the pale threads of mist curling lazily upwards. "Go back and live happily among your countrymen in your own land!"

"I will," said Mayin Nu resignedly. "If what I want really does not exist anywhere, I suppose I shall just have to go home." Korn took a deep lungful of the clean morning air. For the first time in a long while, he felt wonderfully at peace. "We have survived our black night. Let's hope we shall never have to go through another one."

The morning grew brighter and brighter, until it exploded into sunrise; rays groped across the face of the lapping water that idled between the towering jungle banks. Birds were leaving their nests, calling to each other. The dark jungle behind the Mei River was abruptly wakened from the sleep of night. At the river, which formed the natural border between Thailand and Burma, the young Thai and the girl from Burma parted to go their separate ways.

"Goodbye, Mayin Nu." "Goodbye, friend. Let's hope we'll never meet again, like this anyway."

Their eyes held each other with the special friendship that comes from a danger shared, and with a pledge not to forget their black night at Miawaddy. Then they turned, each taking the path which would lead them home to the country they had tried to leave.

Paradon Sakda

SHORT STORIES ONLINE

There are many short story classics that could not be included in this book to keep the cost affordable. However, you can enjoy reading them online or on our own. Here are the links to some of them:

The Tangerines by Ryunosuke Akutagawa
ecmd.nju.edu.cn›tangerine.doc

In a Grove by Ryunosuke Akutagawa
home.roadrunner.com/~jhartzog/inagrove.html

The Spider's Thread by Ryunosuke Akutagawa
http://tonygonz.blogspot.com/2006/05/spiders-thread-akutagawa-ryunosuke.html

This is What it Means to Say Phoenix, Arizona by Sherman Alexie
http://courses.csusm.edu/ltwr325bc/phoenix.html

Woman Hollering Creek by Sandra Cisneros
http://www.docstoc.com/docs/14721279/Woman-Hollering-Creek

The Boy Who Painted Christ Black by John Henrik Clarke
This is not available online at the present time. If you can't find it online, you can read it on your own. It has also been made into a short film.

Hope Deferred by Alice Dunbar-Nelson
http://classiclit.about.com/library/bl-etexts/adunbar/bladunbar-hope.htm

A Rose for Emily by William Faulkner
http://flightline.highline.edu/tkim/Files/Lit100_SS2.pdf

Barn Burning by William Faulkner
http://lssc.edu/faculty/holly_larson/Shared%20Documents/Barn%20Burning%20by%20William%20Faulkner.pdf

The Last of the Belles by F. Scott Fitzgerald
http://gutenberg.net.au/fsf/THE-LAST-OF-THE-BELLES.html

The Circuit by Francisco Jimenez
http://www.nexuslearning.net/books/holt-eol2/collection%208/circuitpg1.htm

Show and Tell by Andrew Lam
http://www.terrain.org/fiction/2/lam.htm

Those Who Walk Away from Omelas by Ursula K. LeGuin
http://www-rohan.sdsu.edu/faculty/dunnweb/rprnts.omelas.pdf

Half a Day by Naguib Mahfouz
http://heep.fltrp.com/cce/images/jd2xs.pdf

Exercises to Test Your Mastery of Chapter Ten

In the beginning of this chapter, 15 options were listed on short-story related topics. Write on the topics that appeal to you or are assigned. Do not write on a story that has been discussed in any of the sample essays unless your reading of the story is very different. In the remaining questions in this exercise, there may be a slight repetition from items that are listed as writing topics at the beginning of this chapter. This repetition is intentional.

1. Select a story that has not been discussed in this chapter to demonstrate how literature deals with pain to offer consolation and healing. In this chapter "Lullaby" by Leslie Silko comes close to serving this healing function. You can choose a relevant story from any source. See Option No. 15 in the list of topics at the start of this chapter.

2. Evaluate an author's two or three prominent elements of style in a story of your choice. Name each element that you are discussing, give an example, and comment on its function. Jeffery Tarbell's essay on Hemingway's style in "The Short Happy Life of Francis Macomber" shows how this assignment may be completed. If you like, you may write about two or three salient features of Albert Camus' style of writing in "The Guest." Camus' style is considered eminently discussable. Feel free to write on any author of your choice.

3. Write on a story that depicts a distant culture to capture its unique features. The stories about outside cultures that are discussed in this chapter are "On the Market Day" by Kyalo Mativo," "The Rape" by Khushwant Singh, "The Guest" by Albert Camus, "A Little Incident" by Lu Hsun, "The Weed" by Amrita Pritam, "Bahiyya's Eyes" by Alifa Rifaat, "Tamam" by Betty Shamieh, "The Orchard" by Alan Kaufman, "Odor" by Saadat Manto, "Las Papas" by Julio Ortega, "One of These Days" by Gabriel Garcia Marquez, "Homecoming" by Ibrahim An-Nasir, "A Fairy Tale" by Ihsan Abd al-Quddus, "Child's Paradise" by Nagib Mahfuz, "Violets" by Ghalib Hamzah Abu al-Faraj, and "Black Night at Miawaddy" by Paradon Sakda.

4. Another story from a different culture is "In the Ruins" by Bei Dao. It is an exceptionally moving story about the Chinese Cultural Revolution. If you write about it, place it in that context and trace its central message. The main character is a Chinese intellectual facing death sentence by the government. A little girl plays a pivotal role in the outcome of this story. You can read this story either online or from a library book. The book title is *Waves.* Because of its very high permissions cost, I could not include it in the book.

5. "The Circuit" by Francisco Jimenez is an exceptionally good story about the hard life of migrant workers in the United States. It could not be included in the chapter because of very high permissions cost. You can read it online, using this link: http://www.nexuslearning.net/books/holt-eol2/collection%208/circuitpg1.htm. A student Ineca Quiteno's essay on this story is on my website in the section connected to Chapter Ten. Choose for analysis any aspect of this story that you find most appealing. It could be a major theme, a feature of the author's style, or any other topic that interests you.

6. "Show and Tell" by Andrew Lam is a serio-comic story about a Vietnamese boy whose family had to flee their native country. He is harrassed by a school bully, but with the help of his teacher and a fellow student is able to prove his racist accuser wrong. It is a very entertaining story for you to explore. Here is the link to this story: http://www.terrain.org/fiction/2/lam.htm

7. Themes of some stories are not evident. They require reading between the lines for implied ideas. Hemingway's short story "Hills Like White Elephants" (included under "Stories for Further Reading" in this chapter) is well-suited for this type of interpretation. Since there is no sample essay on this story, you can write on it. However, you are not limited to the stories in this chapter. The only requirement is that the story you choose should have a theme that is not evident. If the story that you choose is not in the book, attach it to your paper for the convenience of your instructor.

8. "A classic is classic not because it conforms to certain structural rules, or fits certain definitions . . . It is classic because of a certain eternal and irrepressible freshness." Apply Ezra Pound's criterion to analyze a short story classic of your choice. If your selected story is not in the book, attach it to your paper.

9. Use either an informal or formal journal entry of yours as a basis for a 750-word paper on a short story. The journal format was explained in Chapter Six.

10. Which one of this chapter's writing assignment topics did you find most appealing? Why? Add a new assignment to this chapter's offerings.

11. Write a one-page annotation of an essay on a challenging assignment to delineate each of its major parts and to show how the process leads to the product. My annotation of Jeffery Tarbell's essay on Hemingway's style in this chapter is a sample.

12. Hemingway's 1936 story "The Short Happy Life of Francis Macomber" was filmed in 1947 as "The Macomber Affair," starring Gregory Peck and Joan Bennett. Compare the film version with Hemingway's story to point out significant changes that the film director made. Discuss the effects of those changes.

13. Log on to "Timeless Hemingway," a website devoted to Ernest Hemingway. http://www.timelesshemingway.com. Read the webmaster Josh Silverstein's interpretation of the ending of Hemingway's story "The Short Happy Life of Francis Macomber." How does it differ from the interpretation included in Chapter Four of this book. Which interpretation do you find more persuasive?

14. The student Lisa Embry has written an essay on the topic of existentialism in Hemingway's short story "A Clean, Well-Lighted Place." Use the following link to read the online essay and compare it with Lisa's reading of the same story. Which interpretation is more appealing to you? Why? http://www.novelguide.com/acleanwelllightedplace/themeanalysis.html

15. Write on a short story that concerns a pressing racial, cultural, political, economic, or social issue. Evaluate the author's handling of the topic. Read Susan Glaspell's story "A Jury of Her Peers" online and answer the reading questions: http://www.wwnorton.com/college/english/litweb05/workshops/fiction/glaspell1.asp
Another relevant story is Faulkner's "A Rose for Emily" which you can find online at: http://flightline.highline.edu/tkim/Files/Lit100_SS2.pdf

16. Type "short stories with analysis" in Google search. Choose an analysis of a story of your choice, summarize it, and add your own interpretation.

17. Compare Tagore's short story "Samapti" with its film adaptation by Satyajit Ray. A review of the movie is in Chapter Six and an essay on the story is in this chapter. Comment on what is lost and what is gained by this story-to-movie translation.

18. In Dennis Courtney's award-winning film adaptation of James Joyce's short story "Araby" compare and contrast character and theme development in the two media's handling of this classic.

CHAPTER ELEVEN

THE NOVEL

The novel, in its modern form, emerges in the eighteenth century. It was a refinement of two earlier forms – the fourteenth-century Italian novella (such as Boccaccio's *Decameron*) and the sixteenth-century narrative that was loosely organized and known as the Spanish picaresque. Unlike drama that required a theater and a group of actors, the novel could be enjoyed in one's quiet privacy. The scope of the novel is also vaster than that of any other literary form. Drama is restricted in its coverage because of the conventions of keeping the plot action within credible limits. In the strict classical tradition, it meant that the action portrayed on the stage should concern events that occur within 24 hours. The short story and most forms of poetry are also limited by their very size. The comparative vastness of coverage is liberating for novelists, who can give freer rein to their imagination.

Evolution of the Novel

What helped popularize the novel was the ease with which hand-written manuscripts could be quickly turned into printed books for mass consumption by an eager reading public. The German printer Johann Gutenberg's much earlier revolutionary invention of printing with movable type thus became an important ally in the spread of the novel.

Miguel de Cervantes' great work, *Don Quixote* (1605), which is a chivalric romance on the subject of illusion *versus* reality, is often regarded as the forerunner of the modern novel. Since its origins, the novel has assumed many forms – romantic, realistic, historical, philosophical, didactic, political, and psychological, to name just a few. Writers have also been experimenting with various narrative styles and plot variations. Today's novel has evolved into one of the most popular forms of writing.

Definitions

We have readily available sets of definitions of other forms of literature, but, curiously, there has been a reluctance to give the novel a definitive definition. In his classic work on the craft of fiction – *Aspects of the Novel* – E. M. Forster ventured a definition that may seem arbitrary today in matters of length: "Any fictitious prose work over 50,000 words" may be classified as a novel (p. 6). It is in the process of explaining his inability to come up with a precise definition that he succeeds in capturing an important aspect of fiction:

"Principles and systems may suit other forms of art, but they cannot be applicable here – or if applied their results must be subjected to re-examination. And who is the re-examiner? Well, I am afraid it will be the human heart. . . . The final test of a novel will be our affection for it, as it is the test of our friends, and of anything else which we cannot define" (23).

There are other attempts to define the novel. Cynthia Ozick, for example, says: "In fiction, things should not be said, they should be felt. The two are very, very different because fiction comes out of experience and imagination" (Benson E-1). In the introduction to *The Best American Short Stories 2004*, the writer and professor Lorrie Moore acknowledges the much bigger challenge that the novel poses in comparison with the short story: "the novel arrives to reader and writer alike, baggy, ad hoc, bitter with ambition, already half ruined." By contrast, a story's "very shortness ensures its largeness of accomplishment, its selfhood and purity . . . a story lies less. It sings and informs and blurts. It has nothing to lose." In *How Fiction Works*, James Wood enumerates qualities of good fiction: It

". . . favors the telling and brilliant detail; . . . it privileges a high degree of visual noticing [and] maintains an unsentimental composure and knows to withdraw, like a good valet, from superfluous commentary; . . . it judges good and bad neutrally; . . . it seeks out the truth, even at the cost of repelling us; and . . . the author's fingerprints on all this are, paradoxically, traceable but not visible" (39).

Differing Views

Drawing on her vast knowledge of the craft of fiction, Zadie Smith, one of today's outstanding novelists, offers several helpful insights. While respecting diverse views and practices, such as those of Jane Austen, Henry James, and others, she uses, for her initial motto, Thomas Pynchon's following words from his novel *Gravity's Rainbow* – words that she had pinned on her door for five years while writing her first two novels:

"We have to find meters whose scales are unknown in the world, draw our own schematics, getting feedback, making connections, reducing the error, trying to learn the real function . . . zeroing in on what incalculable plot?" (*The Guardian*, November 1, 2003).

In the process of composing her manifesto about the new novel, Zadie Smith sums up the theory of fiction that remained prevalent for a long time. The prestigious critic F. R. Leavis, author of *The Great Tradition*, was its proponent.

"We recall the strategies by which F. R Leavis secured the novel's status within the academy, treating the novel with circumspection; as if it were not quite a novel, but rather a piece of social history, or an example of moral philosophy, or a mission statement, or a piece of public policy. It did not matter, really, as long as the novel was seen to be treated rigorously and made relevant. Like Leavis, we are not quite sure that the novel as novel will do. An admission of love, in this context, would only be seen as weakness. And certainly, as an undergraduate, I was suspicious of the subjective affective response."

There were authors like Roland Barthes who tried to offer a different view of the novel but initially met with limited success. He suggested that the then prevailing theories were not sacrosanct and that there was room for new ideas about the craft of fiction. But established traditions are hard to shake, and the new generation of readers, while looking for freer responses to the experience of reading fiction were still kept confined to a narrow view of fiction. Smith describes the predicament of the seekers of new theories:

"At Cambridge at least, Roland Barthes did not fully convince my generation of readers that the text is a pleasure. We rejected the very idea that novels could either make us feel good or do us good, and along with this bathwater we threw out the baby who wailed that the ethical discussion has any relationship to the literary discussion. Our interest was analytical, not ethical. But I think now that there was, in fact, a sneaky, submerged ethic in our disdain for the novels that made us feel good, which seemed too simple and therefore (we believed) produced too much pleasure. Nietzsche would have considered us pathologically Christian in our literary habits. Oh yes, my generation liked to be in some pain when they read. The harder it was, the more good we believed it was doing us" (Zadie Smith, *The Guardian*, Saturday, 1 Nov. 2003).

Smith's emphasis on the validity of subjective, emotive response to fiction takes us back to E. M. Forster, whom she admires. As quoted earlier, Forster declared the human heart to be the ultimate judge of the quality of fiction: "The final test of a novel will be our affection for it."

Something for Every Taste

When coming to a literary form that has been around as long as the novel, we have to accept the fact that there are many varieties of novels and novelists and many valid theories and practices. Some of us may prefer the sureness of touch of Jane Austen's comic novels. Others may be drawn to the consummate craft with which F. Scott Fitzgerald delineates romance and the American dream. Some may be captivated by the minimalism with which Albert Camus is able to open the floodgates of our emotions; others may be partial to the deliberate imperfections of style (as in some of Forster's novels) to reflect the character flaws and the flawed human condition. Still others may welcome the current theories, such as those espoused by Zadie Smith, that embrace emotive, affective responses to fiction. With infinite variety of novelists, such as Charles Dickens, George Eliot, Emily Bronte, Charlotte Bronte, Gustav Flaubert, Thomas Hardy, D. H. Lawrence, Virginia Woolf, James Joyce, Mark Twain, Willa Cather, William Faulkner, Ernest Hemingway, F. Scott Fitzgerald, Richard Wright, Maya Angelou, Albert Camus, Jean-Paul Sartre, Herman Hesse, Toni Morrison, Alice Walker, Philip Roth, and Zadie Smith, to name just a few, both in form and substance the novel offers something for every taste and preference.

READING THE NOVEL

To develop the skill of sustained interpretation, the novel, like drama, offers an ideal opportunity by virtue of its length. At the same time, it also poses a special challenge because we have to keep the entire literary work in mind when venturing an interpretation. We have to check the validity of our assertions against a much larger volume of details than in a short story or poem. The chances of writing something that contradicts a detail in the work being interpreted increase in proportion to the length of that work.

Using the Skills Learned in Earlier Chapters

Since both the novel and short story are forms of fiction, to write on novel-based topics, you can use, to some extent, the same guidelines that were offered in Seven when discussing short stories. That advice, together with methods of note taking and the clues to recognizing themes in literature and film, given in Chapter Five, can be used to interpret any form of literature with minor adjustments necessitated by the nature of each genre. To begin with interpretation skills that you learned in Chapters Seven and Nine, you can enjoy the world of ideas, feelings, and interaction among characters of any novel just as you did with the short stories.

In comparison with other literary works, the novel, because of its length, offers many more topics for discussion and opportunities to pick up structural devices, some of which are listed below. Such elements often connect the reader with a wealth of implied content as this chapter's discussion of four classics of fiction – *Pride and Prejudice*, *The Stranger*, *The Great Gatsby*, and *A Passage to India* – and the review of Mary Shelley's *Frankenstein* at the end of the chapter will demonstrate.

Note taking

Taking notes according to any method of annotation (one was suggested in Chapter Five) is essential to keeping control over the spread of the novel. Since there are so many kinds of novels – historical, impressionistic, psychological, and naturalistic, to name just a few varieties – it is difficult to offer reading advice that would cover all forms. However, there are certain patterns that do emerge as we read fiction, and there are conventions that novelists either observe or choose to ignore. An understanding of those patterns and conventions can give us reliable means to enhance our comprehension of novels. We have to keep in mind that sometime honored conventions may no longer be observed. An example is the classical emphasis on a neat resolution at the end of a serious literary work. In John Milton's often-quoted words, echoing Aristotle, a work should end "in the calm of mind, all passion spent." In our study of modern fiction and drama, we may discover that authors strive for effects that are contrary to tradition. Instead of offering a neat resolution, they may leave the conflict unresolved. Taking notes on the types of patterns and practices listed in the following section will keep you anchored in the flow of the novel.

What to Look for When Reading Novels

Direct statements of themes

Make a note of any direct statements of themes by narrators and characters. Such overt statements of themes function as topic sentences to control a large volume of plot details. Sometimes such statements embody universal truths, but we should be aware of the possibility of their ironic implications and presence of contrasting themes in the novel. For example, Elizabeth Bennett (the heroine) and Charlotte Lucas make important but contrasting statements on the topic of marriage in Jane Austen's *Pride and Prejudice*, a novel that we will discuss in this chapter.

Link between cause and effect

Draw a cause-and-effect relationship between the actions of characters and their state of being at the end of the story. In some instances, characters get what they deserve. This kind of distribution of reward and punishment on the author's part is known as poetic justice. However, some authors, including Shakespeare, do not subscribe to this view for the simple reason that it is not realistic. In real life, many times scoundrels prosper whereas good people come to grief. Whichever approach an author takes, readers can arrive at their independent interpretations by tracing a connection or a disconnect between causes and effects. We can even make inferences about the author's worldview, based on such analysis.

Style-theme connection

Analyze various stylistic devices that authors use to embody themes. Subtly suggested themes, often embedded in deeper layers of works, can be accessed through an author's use of elements of style, such as imagery, coincidence, symbols, patterns, parallel sets of characters, settings, allusions, language, and narrative style. It is the suggested ideas, the implicit details, that engage our interpretive skills, since interpretation essentially is reading between the lines. By inviting us to go beyond the obvious, this kind of reading urges us to pause and reflect whenever we come across theme-embodying sections. If a scene, for example, seems to be inconclusive and fragmentary, we should try to see a connection between the fragmented style and the author's thematic concern. Similarly, we should be vigilant about any features of style that stand out as potential theme-bearers.

Analogues

Think of familiar literary works that stirred feelings similar to those created by the work you are studying. Such analogues are often variations on the same theme. Your prior experiences of works with similar thematic concerns or styles can furnish some valid points of departure.

The esthetics of omission

Pay attention to the esthetics of omission. Unexpected omissions in statements, events, and responses can be meaningful in creating themes and impressions. A substantial part of this chapter is devoted to the discussion of this important literary device in *The Great Gatsby*, *A Passage to India*, and *The Stranger*.

Don't overlook to enjoy the obvious

By way of further reading advice, it may be noted that as with other literary works, when we read a novel, we should pay attention to and enjoy those aspects that give instant, effortless gratification. Notable among those elements are the story line, well-written descriptive and reflective passages, characters' actions, their reactions, sequence of events, their consequences, outcomes of characters' struggles, their rewards and punishments, and their conduct during critical moments. All of these aspects are often the immediate reasons why we read novels.

THE NOVEL'S ARCHITECTURE

To understand structural design in novels, let us see how some of the above-noted literary devices apply to four novels known for their consummate artistry and enduring themes: *Pride and Prejudice* by Jane Austen, *The Stranger* by Albert Camus, *The Great Gatsby* by F. Scott Fitzgerald, and *A Passage to India* by E. M. Forster. Authors use various means to organize their plots, develop characters, and embody themes to maximize readers' engagement. Each novel is different in its use of available building blocks, but the methods and principles elucidated in this chapter are applicable to most works of fiction. Having understood how prominent elements shape themes, conflicts, resolutions, and meanings in fiction, you will be able to apply that knowledge to most novels that you read and to your own writing of novels.

Pride and Prejudice by Jane Austen (1775-1817)

http://www.pemberley.com/janeinfo/pridprej.html#voli

English author Jane Austen's eighteenth-century masterpiece offers a good opportunity to review not only the five just-noted literary devices but also revisit the skill-oriented aspects of reading a novel, most of which were introduced in Chapter Three ("Plot"):

- Identifying the novel's plot-setting device
- Grasping the author's way of developing characters
- Understanding how the author develops topics into recognizable themes
- Appreciating the author's crafting of credible scenes, including exposition, distribution of flat and round characters, climax, and denouement.

Demonstrating qualities that we traditionally expect of great fiction, Jane Austen's novel treats timeless themes, is clearly written, has an interesting story, build-up, and resolution, together with a diverse cast of characters and a strong heroine in Elizabeth Bennet. Characterization is one of Austen's strong points. In *How Fiction Works*, James Wood points out that most of Austen's minor characters are flat and "belong to a certain stage of theatrical satire." Playing a necessary, complementing role, they move with the currents and remain unchallenged by forces faced by the protagonists. Austen's heroines, on the other hand, are round characters who "possess the secret of consciousness" and "belong to the newly emergent, newly complex form of the novel" (131).

The author treats some of the universal topics, such as love and marriage, classism, fallibility of our initial judgments, the process of acquiring self-knowledge, appearance *versus* reality, and the importance of balance and restraint in passion. Austen also adds something new to the conventional comedy of manners genre: Her crisp dialogue brings the novel closer to drama in that she allows the characters to reveal themselves through dialogue and through character interaction. The novel's most celebrated scenes are created with the device of repartee – a witty exchange of words in dialogue. Among those scenes are what the critic Tony Tanner has called "conversational fencing matches" between Darcy and Elizabeth and a thrilling scene in which Elizabeth holds her own against the arrogant Lady Catherine de Bourg (Darcy's aristocratic aunt).

Essential Plot Structure

A very brief plot summary of the novel's major details will help place Austen's above-noted accomplishments in context. The novel was originally called "First Impressions," pointing to the importance but also the unreliability of first impressions in formulating judgments. On the surface, pride and arrogance characterize the main male character Darcy's conduct. At the dance where he meets Elizabeth for the first time, he conspicuously refuses to ask her for a dance. Elizabeth hears him say that he was in no mood to attend to women slighted by other men. He acts what he is – wealthy and aristocratic – which Elizabeth is not. To prove to him that he has met his match, Elizabeth avenges that affront by refusing to dance with him in a later scene. This initial antagonism between the two major characters sets up the classical element of conflict. At this point, Darcy has no idea of Elizabeth's qualities of self-esteem, brilliance, and candor. In essence, the scene of this conflict between Elizabeth and Darcy is the novel's plot-setting device that reverberates throughout the story.

Typical of the social mores of the time, the Bennet sisters (and especially the mother) had started building up expectations of matrimonial possibilities with the aristocratic Bingleys' move into their neighborhood. The arrogant behavior of Mr. Bingley's friend Darcy had soured that expectation. From that point on, the novel brings into play some other sources of conflict. Elizabeth's sister Lydia elopes with Wickham, an apparently dashing army officer who is the godson of Darcy's father. Misunderstandings are created by Wickham's lies about Darcy that Elizabeth accepts as truth. These problems are eventually resolved to give the novel a happy ending that is artistically satisfying.

Interpretation Skills Reviewed

Before looking at major themes of this novel, let us review the interpretation skills that have been taught in the earlier chapters. Having interpreted several short stories in the preceding chapter as well as in Chapters Six and Seven, you know by now that there is no mystery to finding and discussing themes in a literary work. First, you find the topic. Next you see how the topic is introduced and developed. In the process, you analyze the characters that embody the topic and events that carry it forward. You also notice, if applicable, any theme-generating or theme-reinforcing elements of style. Finally, to complete your interpretation, you state the novel's or, if possible, the author's position on the topic. The topics that we have mentioned so far relate to *marriage and love, appearance* versus *reality, fallibility of our* initial judgments, the process of acquiring self-knowledge, and *the importance of balance and restraint in passion.* Let us see how Jane Austen introduces some of these topics and develops them into themes.

Major Themes in *Pride and Prejudice*

Love and Marriage

The novel wastes no time to announce one of its major topics. The famous opening sentence states: "It is a truth universally acknowledged, that a single man in possession of a good fortune, must be in want of a wife." The story then immediately introduces Mrs. Bennet's hope that Mr. Bingley, the rich eligible bachelor who is moving into the neighborhood, will marry one of her daughters.

On the topic of marriage, another overt thematic statement is made by Charlotte Lucas: "Happiness in marriage is entirely a matter of chance" (69). Such statements, however, are not to be accepted as themes, that is, the novel's ultimate position on marriage. They are rather a drama-like presentation of contrary views to lead us to real themes, such as those embodied in Elizabeth Bennet's views and actions. In this scene, for example, Charlotte agrees to marry Mr. Collins without knowing much about him other than the fact that he is a man of means and that she, being a woman, must get married to complete her womanhood. Elizabeth, who has rejected Collins' marriage proposal, politely criticizes Charlotte's thoughtless submission to a prescriptive view of marriage. Charlotte's response is worth noting. Some may see a point to her thinking, but most readers would pity her desperation to become a wife. This is how she has persuaded herself, not unlike many of her peers:

"If the dispositions of the parties are ever so well known to each other, or ever so similar before-hand, it does not advance their felicity in the least. They always continue to grow sufficiently unlike afterwards to have their share of vexation."

So far Charlotte's views are quite valid. However, it is what she says next that is problematic: "and it is better to know as little as possible of the defects of the person with whom you are to pass your life" (69-70). To her, marriage is essentially a "preservative from want," and the state of being married is far more important than the person she is married to.

Tony Tanner's words from his introduction to Austen's novel sum up Charlotte's predicament: "In such a society, the need for an 'establishment' is a very real one, and in putting prudence before passion, Charlotte is only doing what the economic realities of her society . . . all but force her to do" (37-38). It is this kind of desperation under social pressures of the times that most likely drew Mr. and Mrs. Bennet, paragon of incompatibility, into bonds of matrimony. And it is such thinking that pushes Lydia and Wickham into an inevitable but questionable marriage after their elopement. Passion like theirs is equated with folly in Jane Austen's novels.

The words "connubial bliss" are used only to describe Elizabeth's union with Darcy. Jane Austen's world, like the world of her fiction, was material and secular. It is, therefore, tempting to see what view of love among its many variations, prevails in the novel. Interestingly, it is Elizabeth who brings up the question of "the difference in matrimonial affairs, between the mercenary motive and the prudent motive." We may think that our world today is different from Jane Austen's world in terms of matrimonial bonding, but that may not be entirely true. The matrimonial landscape today is also littered with mismatches like those of Mr. and Mrs. Bennet, Charlotte and Collins, Lydia and Wickham. Elizabeth Bennet and, we may assume, Jane Austen are surprisingly modern in their suspicion of misunderstood sexual attraction. Our social mores today also emphasize the getting-to-know part of relationships before commitment and caution against being swept away by passion. Moreover, the necessity of comfortable means of livelihood also plays an important part in matrimonial considerations even today.

Tony Tanner is persuasive in exploring the topics of love and marriage in *Pride and Prejudice*:

"And one of the things the book sets out to do is to define a rationally based 'mode of attachment' – something between the exclusively sexual and the entirely mercenary. Thus words like 'gratitude' and 'esteem' are used to describe Elizabeth's growing feeling for Darcy. She comes to feel that their union would have been 'to the advantage of both: by her ease and liveliness, his mind might have softened, his manners improved; and from his judgment, information, and knowledge of the world, she must have received benefit of greater importance' . . . . What differentiates Elizabeth's choice from Charlotte's . . . is the fact that it is a free choice . . . based on more awareness, knowledge, and intelligence than Charlotte brings to her cool but instant capitulation. Elizabeth loves for the best reasons, and there are always reasons for loving in Jane Austen's world" (38).

The Elizabeth-Darcy pairing thus demonstrates the possibility and desirability of harmonious blending of freedom and boundaries, of passion and reason.

Performance *versus* Reflection; Appearance *versus* Reality

As was just demonstrated in treating the topic of marriage and love, several other thematic layers in the novel can be accessed through careful interpretation of plot details. One way to initiate a meaningful inquiry into any novel is a look at the story line itself. As Tony Tanner has pointed out, the movement of *Pride and Prejudice* is away from performance of the initial scenes toward reflection of the novel's later scenes. "Jane Austen's book is, most importantly, about pre-judging and rejudging. It is a drama of recognition – re-cognition" (8). At first, all important players in the novel are caught up in performing as if they are on stage. Even Elizabeth's ample energies are preoccupied with reacting to Darcy's overheard negative reason why he does not ask her for a dance as she sits alone without a partner. For a fuller development of Elizabeth's character, this reactionary and performance stage has a purpose: It shows the heroine's vivacity, wit, candor, and personal magnetism. On the negative side, she hastily forms an inaccurate impression of Darcy, primarily because she is misinformed about him by the novel's villain, Wickham, whose appearance and social charm initially impresses her favorably. However, as her maturing judgment becomes her guide, she moves away from meretricious appearances to substance and reality. The proof of her dawning awareness is her words to her sister Jane, comparing Darcy with Wickham: "There certainly was some great mismanagement in the education of these two young men. One has got all the goodness, and the other all the appearance of it."

Fallible Judgments

Associational logic often leads us to interconnected themes. Closely tied to the theme of appearance *versus* reality is that of the fallibility of our judgments. When Elizabeth and others have formed a negative view of Darcy, it is Elizabeth's idealistic sister Jane who "pleaded for allowances, and urged the possibility of mistakes." Soon the judgments are reversed. Wickham falls while Darcy rises in Elizabeth's esteem, especially when Darcy is able to use his influence to change Lydia's elopement with Wickham into marriage. Even before that scene, while visiting Darcy's estate of Pembroke in the company of her aunt in Darcy's absence, Elizabeth comes to have a positive view of Darcy. The house keeper describes him as "the best landlord, and the best master."

Standing before Darcy's portrait "in earnest contemplation," Elizabeth thinks about the wrongness of making a snap judgment about Darcy, based on one evening's interaction. From "the proudest, most disagreeable man in the world," he now became the object of her longing and regret for having turned down his marriage proposal:

"She began now to comprehend that he was exactly the man who, in disposition and talents, would most suit her. . . . It was a union that must have been to the advantage of both. . . . But no such happy marriage could now teach the admiring multitude what connubial felicity really was."

Process of Self-Knowledge

The dawning of major characters' self-knowledge is an integral part of classical literature. The novel's movement from performance to reflection has already been mentioned. A major catalyst for that change in Elizabeth is Darcy's letter to her in which he answers Wickham's wrong accusations against him. Making a significant part of the novel's narrative are 44 letters. They add a note of self-reflection. Written in the privacy of self-possession, not in response to the rush of social interaction, letters like the one from Darcy to Elizabeth introduce reflective self-analysis and move characters to self-knowledge. Jane Austen's choice of the stylistic device of letters for character development is strikingly effective.

The end result of thoughtful self-analysis is the emergence of a new woman in Elizabeth, who is not afraid to admit her guilt: "How despicably have I acted! . . . I, who have prided myself on my discernment! . . . Till this moment I never knew myself." Whereas Elizabeth learns to shed her prejudice, the formerly arrogant Darcy is made to learn humility. He tells Elizabeth, "By you I was properly humbled."

Since *Pride and Prejudice* is a comedy, self-knowledge leads to self-fulfillment, not to tragedy. In Tony Tanner's apt summation, "this is a happy book and we are not shown the wilting of playfulness under the force of regulation, but rather a felicitous 'uniting' of both" (Tanner 42).

THREE MODERN NOVELS

After studying Jane Austen's comic classic, *Pride and Prejudice*, the three novels that we are going to study next are considered major works of modern fiction – *The Stranger* by Albert Camus, *The Great Gatsby* by F. Scott Fitzgerald, and *A Passage to India* by E. M. Forster. All three of them share qualities of superior plots that were mentioned in Chapter Three on "Plot." Those qualities are very briefly listed below:

- All details are interconnected and have cause-and-effect linkage.
- All events, actions, and characters serve a purpose and contribute to the plot's unity.
- Using the esthetics of omission, a plot may communicate many ideas through *implication* rather than statement.
- For deeper engagement of readers' interest, an effective plot uses elements of mystery and suspense, which are often achieved through manipulation of chronology, point of view, flashback, premonition (flash forward), suspension of logic, parallelism, coincidence, and similar strategies.
- In good plots, events, settings, moods, and questions reverberate in the reader's imagination long after the book is finished. In E. M. Forster's words, expansion "is the idea the novelist [or any literary artist] must cling to. Not completion. Not rounding off but opening out" (Forster 169).

Let us apply these criteria to the three novels one by one to see how they measure up to them.

The Stranger by Albert Camus (1913-1960)

This novel can be read online: http://www.macobo.com/essays/epdf/CAMUS,%20Albert%20-%20The%20Stranger.pdf or

http://www.amazon.com/Stranger-Albert-Camus/dp/0679720200/ref=sr_1_1?s=books&ie=UTF8&qid=1373228927&sr=1-1&keywords=camus+the+stranger#reader_0679720200

Compared to Jane Austen's innovative classic of conventional fiction, French author Albert Camus' *The Stranger* uses many elements that are considered central to modern fiction. A close reading of this work will elucidate novel-related concepts, conventions, and strategies of interpretation similar to as well as additional to those observed in Austen's *Pride and Prejudice.* Camus' novel is ideally suited to understanding and appreciating the challenges experienced in reading a complex work of fiction. An analysis of this novel will show how modern authors use various elements to organize their plots, develop characters, and embody themes to maximize the reader's engagement.

An important reason for focusing on *The Stranger* is the fact that it was misread by so many famous people of the author's time, such as Wyndham Lewis, Father Troisfontaines, Pierre Lafue, and Aime Patri, that Camus had to defend his hero in a "Preface." The misinterpretation of the novel and the author's correction of that misreading should alert us to similar challenges in our own readings. Modern novelists' preference for suggestion rather than statement demands a high degree of mental alertness from the reader. Camus' following words about the style of certain "great novelists" also reveals his own subtly suggestive method that invites and urges interpretation:

"The fact that certain great novelists have chosen to write in terms of images rather than of arguments reveals a great deal about a certain kind of thinking common to them all, a conviction about the futility of all explanatory principles, and of the instructive message of sensory impression" (Camus, *Sisyphus*).

Camus' words should not be misread to mean that literary works cannot have themes. He is rightly stating that ordinary language cannot express the quandaries and mysteries of life. Therefore authors have to rely on images. The words "instructive message" in Camus' quotation suggest that literature has messages and that "sensory impressions" can absorb those messages. Camus' words also hint at the human capacity for intuition. It is this source that the act of interpretation draws on to capture the "instructive message" of a literary work. In *The Stranger*, Camus used this oblique narrative style to suggest the theme that a society can be self-righteously obtuse and inflexible when someone's honesty challenges its questionable biases that are disguised as values.

Steps in Reading Modern Novels

The section on "Interpretation Skills Reviewed" in the context of reading Jane Austen's *Pride and Prejudice* demonstrated how the skill of interpretation works in novels that adhere to conventions of classical fiction. The following points of reading advice, tied to Albert Camus' *The Stranger*, will greatly facilitate an in-depth reading of modern fiction.

Pay Close Attention to the Text

When it comes to interpretation, there is no substitute for close textual study, and there is no better novel than *The Stranger* to learn that skill. When the novel was first published in 1942, many readers, including some prominent people of that time (mentioned by Camus in his "Preface" after the novel's publication) misread the novel. The misinterpretation was so egregious that Camus had to correct serious misunderstandings by writing his "Preface." To avoid any such misreadings, careful attention to the text is the most important pre-requisite. Still your interpretation may be only just one of the several valid readings when it comes to a complex novel like *The Stranger*.

What causes questionable interpretations

The main reason for drawing incorrect inferences about Camus' novel, especially about his protagonist, has been the readers' failure to pay adequate attention to certain details in the novel. There is no problem with a novel's highly visible and telling details. They command the reader's attention. The problem occurs with those details that are mixed with understated data. We should remain alert to the statements that are dropped in casually but carry the core of a character's being and can serve to validate our interpretations of elusive topics. One such topic concerns innocence and guilt in *The Stranger*. Meursault is condemned to death for two reasons.

Two charges against Meursault

The first charge is that he did not observe the socially required rituals of mourning. This failure on his part led to the false assumption that he did not care for his mother. The second reason for his punishment was his failure to show proper remorse for his murder of the Arab. Close attention to key details relevant to these two charges is critical to accurate interpretation.

Examining the first charge

Looking at the first charge against Meursault, several of his casual statements need to be considered. One of them is a profoundly optimistic and consoling idea: "You can always find something to be happy about" (Camus) He received this idea from his mother. Struggling to cope with gross miscarriage of justice, he taps into the reservoir of his sources and finds support in his mother's words. The readers who thought that Meursault did not care for his mother and was, therefore, a monster must have overlooked important clues in these lines:

"At the time, I often thought that if I had had to live in the trunk of a dead tree, with nothing to do but look up at the sky flowering overhead, little by little I would have gotten used to it. I would have waited for birds to fly by or clouds to mingle, just as here I waited to see my lawyer's ties and just as, in another world, I used to wait patiently until Saturday to hold Marie's body in my arms. Now, as I think back on it, I wasn't in a hollow tree trunk. There were others worse off than me. Anyway, it was one of Maman's ideas, and she often repeated it, that *after a while you could get used to anything*" (77, italics added for emphasis).

The italicized words in the above quotation carry an important theme, casually introduced by Meursault almost as an after-thought. We can see his acknowledgment of help from his mother not only at this difficult time but also later at the critical moment when he has to face his own death:

"For the first time in a long time I thought about Maman. I felt as if I understood why at the end of her life she had taken a 'fiancé,' why she had played at beginning again. Even there, in that home where lives were fading out, evening was a kind of wistful respite. So close to death, Maman must have felt free then and ready to live it all again. Nobody, nobody had the right to cry over her. And I felt ready to live it all again too" (122)

It is at this moment that Meursault finally makes his peace with life and gets ready to face death.

From close attention to the selected key details, it becomes apparent that at critical moments in his life, it is Meursault's recollection of his mother's wisdom and courage that sustains him and gives him strength. The readers who overlook Meursault's seemingly random but deeply significant statements about his mother are likely to miss the important intellectual and emotional link of Meursault with his mother.

Examining the second charge

To take a reasonable position on the second charge against Meursault, the one about his lack of remorse, a careful interpretation of his words is necessary. He states clearly, "I never intended to kill the Arab" (102). In reply, the judge asks him to "state precisely the motives for . . . [his] act" (103). The judge's demand is absurd because Meursault has already stated that he never intended to kill the Arab. His words, if heard, should have made it clear to the judge that he had no motive for murder. From this scene, an alert reader can draw two possible conclusions: Either the judge is not listening to Meursault, or the outcome of his trial has already been pre-determined. Camus thus makes the trial scene little more than a charade.

The question whether Meursault felt any remorse or not also requires meticulous grasp of relevant details to arrive at a valid interpretation. Is "remorse" the right word for the situation? Wouldn't "remorse" imply preceding guilt. One may ask that if Meursault thinks that he is innocent of any intent to murder, why should he be expected to feel remorse? He explains to the prosecutor "cordially, almost affectionately, that I had never been able to feel remorse for anything. My mind was always on what was coming next, today or tomorrow" (100). Is that an adequate answer on Meursault's part, or is he incriminating himself with his candor about his philosophical position on remorse. In an earlier scene the examining magistrate, who called Meursault "Monsieur Antichrist," asks him if he was sorry for what he had done. Meursault answered "that more than sorry I felt kind of annoyed." He then adds that he "got the impression he [the magistrate] didn't understand" (70). How should one interpret Meursault's words? His answer states that he feels more annoyed than sorry. That does not mean that he is not sorry. His answer could be interpreted to mean that he feels sorry, but his dominant feeling about the incident is that of annoyance. To arrive at an accurate interpretation, we have to read the exchange between the judge and Meursault and between the examining magistrate and Meursault very carefully. On our understanding of those exchanges hinges the validity of our conclusions.

Look for Other, More Visible Structural Devices

Besides the use of details that require close textual study for interpretation and theme formulation, novelists also draw on several other means to construct and enrich their narratives. We now turn to some of those devices.

Look for major divisions by themes

Novelists find it helpful to organize their plots in thematically significant sections. Camus divides the book in two parts of almost equal length. Part One contains lived moments free of any thought content and free of any attempt to make cause-and-effect connections. Each sentence stands alone like the isolated and unique moments of pure existence unalloyed by reflection. However, in Part Two, circumstances force Meursault, the protagonist, to evaluate his life and prepare himself for death. It is in the second part that we see Meursault's potential for deep thinking. Jean-Paul Sartre expressed one of existentialist philosophy's core principles: "Existence precedes essence." Even though Camus refused to be categorized as an existentialist, the two parts of his novel are a perfect illustration of the two phases: Part One is existence; Part Two is essence. Not every novel will have such clear plot divisions, but when this pattern exists in a novel, it greatly helps our comprehension.

Look for sustained and systematic use of imagery

Another visible structural device besides thematically significant plot divisions is imagery. In *The Stranger*, Camus uses images of light, dark, and heat to organize various parts of his novel. Patterns of images of light and heat become associated with painful, unpleasant feelings. Through a similar pattern, darkness and coolness are linked with positive feelings of peace and contentment. The vigil on his mother's death, with which the novel opens, was marked by irritating dazzling lights that were kept on all night, making Meursault extremely uncomfortable. It was also under the influence of the blinding, eye-stabbing light of the sun that Meursault had fired at the man who had earlier stabbed Raymond.

"My eyes were blinded. . . All I could feel were the cymbals of sunlight crashing on my forehead and, indistinctly, the dazzling spear flying up from the knife in front of me. The scorching blade slashed at my eyelashes and stabbed at my stinging eyes. That's when everything began to reel. My whole being tensed and I squeezed my hand around the revolver. The trigger gave."(59)

His trial opens "with the sun glaring outside" (82). In the prison scene, just before Meursault tells us that he "was feeling a little sick," we find this sentence: "Outside, the light seemed to surge up over the bay window." (p.75) In his mind, the association of hot weather with something unpleasant is evident from his words: "And I knew as soon as the weather turned hot that something new was in store for me" (82).

Through another pattern, evenings, night, and coolness signal comfort, peace, and contentment for Camus' protagonist. Swimming brings immense pleasure to Meursault and respite from oppressive heat. Meursault recalls early evenings as his favorite time of day. When leaving the courthouse in the "darkness of my mobile prison" (the police van) he "recognized . . . the smell and color of the summer evening . . . all the familiar sounds of a town I loved and of a certain time of day when I used to feel happy. . . . Yes, it was the hour when, a long time ago, I was perfectly content." (p.97) It is also under the night sky that Meursault finally makes his peace with life and with death:

"I woke up with the stars in my face. . . . Smells of night, earth, and salt air were cooling my temples. The wondrous peace of that sleeping summer flowed through me like a tide . . . ; for the first time, in that night alive with signs and stars, I opened myself to the gentle indifference of the world. Finding it so much like myself – so like a brother, really – I felt that I had been happy and that I was happy again" (122-123).

After we have noted the patterns of light and dark imagery and their association with distress and peace respectively, we still feel compelled to complete our interpretation by trying to find some *meaning* behind the contrasting imagery in the novel. The novel does not give us any explanation as to why Camus overturns the traditional symbolism that associates light with reason (reassurance) and dark with its opposite. The reader has to rely on inferential logic, intuition, and, in Camus' own words, on the instructive "sensory impressions."

Safe and valid interpretation of light and dark imagery

Interpretations of imagery, in fact of any element of style, range from valid to questionable. Let us begin with a relatively non-controversial reading of Camus' use of imagery. Meursault wants to feel that he is a part of Nature. He also feels that all of humanity is united in at least one respect: Everyone has to meet the same end – death. He even thinks – in a rare repetition on his part – that he "was like everybody else, just like everybody else" (66). The first time when he is made to feel like an outsider in the trial scene, he "had this stupid urge to cry, because I could feel how much all these people hated me" (p.90). The night and the dark suggest Meursault's ideal of unity. Unlike light that separates objects and makes them stand out, night blurs objects and distance into an impression of unity and thus projects a feeling of harmony. Meursault wants to perceive the world in terms of togetherness, not separateness. For this reason, the night/evening is Meursault's favorite time and the dark his desired image. The harsh light of daytime shatters the semblance of unity by separating things into different entities. If we develop our discussion along these lines, we would be on firm ground as to the validity of our interpretation.

Questionable but interesting interpretation of light and dark imagery

We may be tempted to venture beyond "safe" reading and thus come up with the following kind of interesting but risky interpretation of this novel. Camus' peculiar use of the imagery of dark and light reinforces the disturbing feeling that the novel evokes: thousands of years of cultivation of reason (represented by light in the novel) have not brought us anywhere close to accepting each person's uniqueness and individuality. A true civilization should prepare us not only to tolerate each other's uniqueness but to celebrate diversity. Obviously, we are nowhere near that goal in spite of our show of upholding reason and logic as the ultimate arbiters. Camus' own words from his "Preface to *The Stranger*" confirm this collective failure of humanity to live up to the vaunted ideal of reason.

"The hero of the book is condemned because he does not play the game. . . He says what he is, he refuses to hide his feelings, and immediately society feels threatened. . . . One would not be much mistaken to read *The Stranger* as the story of a man who, without any heroics, agrees to die for the truth." (Camus, *Essays* 336-337)

By revealing society's hypocrisy, Camus is suggesting that true Reason which illuminates is absent in our dealings. What we have in its place is a perverse form of logic, reduced by Camus to absurdity as in the prosecutor's totally unreasonable argument in asking for capital punishment for Meursault:

". . . in this court the wholly negative virtue of tolerance must give way to the sterner but loftier virtue of justice. Especially when the emptiness of a man's heart becomes, as we find it has in this man, an abyss threatening to swallow up society. . . . Tomorrow, gentlemen, this same court is to sit in judgment of the most monstrous of crimes: the murder of a father. . . . I am convinced, gentlemen, that you will not think it too bold of me if I suggest to you that the man who is seated in the dock [that is Meursault] is also guilty of the murder to be tried in this court tomorrow. . . . I ask you for this man's head" (101-102).

The prosecutor's absolutely nonsensical argument is that because Meursault's crime preceded the other man's crime of parricide, Meursault, by his example, "foreshadowed and even legitimized" this other man's crime. Light, in this novel, is a symbol of this kind of travesty of reason and logic.

Interpreting the "dark"

Unraveling the light symbolism completes only half of our job. There is the other half – the darkness – that urges us to explore its depths. Why does Meursault find darkness comforting? No philosophy has been able to solve the enigma of life and death to Meursault's content. He, therefore, creates his own philosophical consolation through contemplation of the "dark wind":

"Throughout the whole absurd life I've lived, a dark wind had been rising toward me from somewhere deep in my future, across years that were still to come, and as it passed, this wind leveled whatever was offered to me at the time. . . . What did other people's deaths or a mother's love matter to me; what did his [the chaplain's] God or the lives people choose or the fate they think they elect matter to me when we're all elected by the same fate" (121).

Meursault's important self-debate is a process of detachment from life so that his approaching death can be bearable. The simple realization dawns on him that all people are like his brothers because the inevitable mystery of death – the "dark wind" – that comes to every single person unites them in this universal fate. Death or the "dark wind" is inevitable though the time of its visit is unpredictable. If one has lived a full life, then he or she has a right to feel content with life's end, even if it happens sooner than one would expect or hope for. Such is Meursault's attempt at coming to a sense of acquiescence in life's unalterable end. An understanding and acceptance of the "dark wind" of fate can be comforting.

When confronted with the challenge of interpreting a difficult topic, we can also reach for a familiar analogue. In his meditation on death in the essay, "Free Man's Worship," Bertrand Russell, much like Meursault, offers a stoic way to face death, and Russell's following words have an uncanny, striking similarity to Meursault's words (quoted earlier):

"Brief and powerless is Man's life; on him and all his race the slow, sure doom falls pitiless and dark. Blind to good and evil, reckless of destruction, omnipotent matter rolls on its relentless way; for Man, condemned today to lose his dearest, tomorrow himself to pass through the gate of darkness, it remains only to cherish . . . the lofty thoughts that ennoble his little day (Russell 56-57).

Even though Russell's view is not the same as Meursault's, the two are close enough to bring us nearer to an understanding of Meursault's thoughts about the "dark wind" of fate.

At the end of our analysis of Camus' unconventional attribution of values to the symbols of light and dark, it is evident that he is subverting a manipulative and crafty kind of reason, symbolized by light in this novel, and upholding the need to understand the dark, mysterious forces in the world as well as in the human consciousness. In brief, it is a plea to re-think some of our values and embrace the comforting truth about the pockets of darkness in human nature.

Look for omissions of the expected details

A highly effective strategy is authors' use of the device known as the esthetics of omission, whereby they tell the story through deliberate omission of the expected details. As we will see, two other novelists featured in this Chapter besides Camus – F. Scott Fitzgerald and E. M. Forster – also subscribe to this methodology. Commenting with approval on Emily Bronte's *Wuthering* Heights, Forster said, "What is implied is more important to her than what is said" (Forster 145-146). About meaningful omissions in *The Great Gatsby*, Fitzgerald said that what he took out of the novel would make another book. Using this strategy, an author maintains a delicate balance between the inclusion and exclusion of details. What is omitted is sometimes more important than what is included. Such noticeable withholding becomes an effective tool to point to important themes.

In Meursault's first-person memoir, Camus uses a style that encourages misperception of the real feelings of his protagonist if we go by the surface meaning of his words. However, the alert reader, by reading between the lines, can correctly perceive what Camus would really like us to think of his hero. The real reason why Meursault is condemned to death is not his unpremeditated and random murder of an Arab (left nameless in the novel). He is punished because he sent his mother to a home for the elderly to be cared for and because, at her funeral, he did not express sadness in the socially approved manner. He is unreasonably judged as an unfeeling brute. However, using his style of omission, explained earlier, Camus is able to give much more information by not saying anything as in the scene at the end of Chapter Four, Part One.

When the dog of Meursault's elderly neighbor Salamano runs away, he hears the old man crying at night. The relationship between the man and his dog had been one of constant struggle, but still the man is stricken with grief upon losing his dog. Meursault had been respectful to his mother, but because of the demands of his work, he could not spend enough time with her and therefore sent her to a home for the elderly where she presumably found good companionship with people of her own age. Instead of explaining these details, Camus indirectly offers us a glimpse into Meursault's feelings, using this man-dog relationship as a parallel to Meursault's connection with his mother. On hearing Salamano's whimpering, Meursault says:

"For some reason I thought of Maman. But I had to get up early the next morning. I wasn't hungry and I went to bed without any dinner" (Camus 39).

Here Camus makes Meursault show his grief by hiding it. Had he said he missed his mother too much to eat his dinner, the effect would not be the same. His friend Marie is able to understand Meursault's unexpressed feelings, for she tells him he had a "funeral face" (p.47). Another character, Raymond, also perceives Meursault's inner feelings of sadness. This is how Meursault describes Raymond's perceptiveness:

"I must have looked tired, because Raymond told me not to let things get to me. At first I didn't understand. Then he explained that he'd heard about Maman's death but that it was one of those things that was bound to happen sooner or later. I thought so too." (33)

With the exception of the few friends that understand Meursault, the society, the judge, jurors, and especially the prosecutor, do not understand him, causing him to feel estranged from life.

Books like Camus' *The Stranger* challenge facile interpretations. When reading books that shun explanations and overt statements of themes, thus posing a risk of misinterpretation, we should ask ourselves this question: Even though the book carries no clearly stated didactic message and relies on what Camus called the "instructive message of sensory perceptions," does the book imply, through stylistic elements, a view of the world and of human nature beneath the surface of the narrative. The validity of our interpretation of the book will greatly depend on our ability to answer this question.

So far we have looked at the use of understated but significant details, visible structural devices, sustained imagery, and omission of the expected details. With the help of Camus' novel, let us look at some other elements that also serve as novelists' tools of organization and readers' aids to interpretation.

Look for parallel sets of characters

Novelists often use parallel sets of characters to organize thematically significant plot details. Camus uses this device in the prison scene when he introduces the mother-son pair. An old woman comes to visit her son, and they have a very touching, silent communication with their eyes and gestures. This is how Meursault describes the scene: The young man "wasn't saying anything. I noticed that he was across from the little old lady and that they were staring intently at each other." During this scene, many visitors, including Meursault's friend Marie, come to see the prisoners. All of them have to speak louder and louder in order to be heard. In fact Meursault uses the word "shout" to describe how Marie had to speak. In the midst of all this noise, "the only oasis of silence," in Meursault's own words, is the wordless communication between the mother and her son. As the visitors are asked to leave, "The little woman moved closer to the bars, and at the same moment a guard motioned to her son. He said, 'Goodbye Maman,' and she reached between the two bars to give him a long, slow little wave" (76).

This scene serves two purposes. Firstly, Meursault finds in this pair a reflection of his own relationship with his mother. Secondly, it shows how wrong everyone has been in assuming that Meursault has no feelings for his mother. A perceptive reader would be able to connect Meursault with the young prisoner and Meursault's mother with the young prisoner's mother.

Another parallel set of characters that Camus uses to link plot details was discussed in the immediately preceding section under "Telling the story through deliberate omission of expected details." This parallel involves old Salamano's relationship with his dog to mirror Meursault's similar connection with his mother. When the dog is around, the old man does not appreciate it, but when it runs away, the loss leaves a huge void in Salamano's life. Similarly, after his mother's death, Meursault also begins to realize how much she had meant to him and to what extent she had shaped his thinking.

Look for contrasting characters and topics that carry contrasting themes

The word "foil" is used to describe a contrasting character who may espouse values that are the opposite of the protagonist's. A thematic contrast in the novel is between the mechanical *versus* the natural. The robot woman in the novel represents the mechanical, whereas Meursault stands for the natural. The nameless robot woman goes through life like an automaton. Contrasting Meursault, who lives for and in the current moment, she lives for the future, passing the present moments on marking those radio programs that she plans to watch in the future. Even before she starts her meal, she adds up the exact amount of the bill plus tip and sets it down on the table for the waiter. Instead of enjoying the food, she "meticulously continued this task [of marking up radio programs] throughout the meal" (43). Meursault is so fascinated by this woman that when she exits the restaurant, he follows her for some distance but loses her as she disappears "with incredible speed and assurance, never once swerving or looking around" (43).

This robot-like human being, through associational logic, brings to mind a piece of actual machinery that engages Meursault's considerable time and energy. It is the guillotine. While awaiting execution but still hoping for the impossible acquittal, he relishes momentarily the possibility of "escaping the *machinery of justice*" (108; italics added). He would like to make up new laws that gave the condemned person a chance even if in a one to ten ratio. The condemned, for example, could be given a mixture of chemicals that "would kill him nine times out of ten." "The trouble with the guillotine was that you had no chance at all, absolutely none" (111). In addition to the actual machine of execution, mechanical systems (like the rigid legal procedures) and mechanical people (such as the robot woman) as well as the uniformly mechanical customs are viewed negatively in the novel.

All of the preceding structural devices that we have discussed enable authors to embed their themes in plot details, and our grasp of such indirect communication of themes brings us a step closer to understanding those themes.

Pay attention to the role of coincidence and chance

Random events and chance are a real part of life. When used judiciously on a limited basis, occurrence of chance can enhance realism and impact of a literary work. However, overuse of chance weakens the essential component of plot design – the link between cause and effect. As readers we have to determine if an author's use of coincidence and chance is artistically defensible. An example of the use of coincidence in *The Stranger* is Meursault's chance encounter with the Arab that tragically ends in the completely unintended murder by Meursault. The reader of the novel knows that all Meursault wanted was the embrace of the sea to find relief from the suffocating heat. When asked during the trial why he went to the same spot where the Arab had earlier stabbed his friend Raymond, Meursault spoke the truth that it was purely by chance. When asked why he was armed when he went to the spot where he encountered the Arab, his answer once again was absolutely true: "it just happened that way" (p. 88). He had no intention of using the gun. We remember that when earlier he found Raymond exploding with anger, he took away the gun from him to prevent murder. Who was to know that Meursault himself would end up using that gun? However, for the judge, the prosecutor, and the jury, who were predisposed to find him guilty – primarily because of his unconforming ways – the two examples of chance looked like premeditation.

Formulate a theme to capture the significance of coincidence and chance

By using the device of coincidence, Camus is able to deepen the mystery and convey an important theme that we cannot free our lives of random events that have no recognizable causes and that logic is not adequate to explain some of life's mysteries. There are occurrences in life for which we have developed no tools of comprehension. Meursault's words in this scene sound irrational even though he speaks the truth, and the members of the legal machinery are wrong in their judgment of Meursault even though supposedly they have logic on their side. Reason is not allied with truth in this court scene. Like the sun in this novel, reason befuddles.

This view is compatible with the popular existential belief that irrational forces in the universe cannot be explained away. It is the same view that Shakespeare articulated so well through Hamlet: "There are more things in heaven and earth, . . . Than are dreamt of in your philosophy" (I, v, 166-167). By using the element of chance so well, Camus alerts us to the possibility of other ways of thinking and being than those that prevail.

Analyze analogues

Analogues are valuable tools both as a structural device for authors and as an aid to interpretation for the reader. If we have read a work or seen a movie that evoked in us a feeling similar to the one created by the new work being interpreted, our prior experience can serve us well. Let us apply this method of analogy to interpret Camus' elusive set of symbolism in *The Stranger* – the sun, sand, and the sea. According to one possible interpretation, the sun in this novel represents death; the sea represents life, and sand is symbolic of time. What greatly helps us in arriving at this interpretation is this sonnet by Shakespeare:

That Time of Year

That time of year thou mayst in me behold
When yellow leaves, or none, or few, do hang
Upon those boughs which shake against the cold,
Bare ruined choirs where late the sweet birds sang.
In me thou see'st the twilight of such day
As after sunset fadeth in the west,
Which by and by black night doth take away,
Death's second self, that seals up all in rest.
In me thou see'st the glowing of such fire,
That on the ashes of his youth doth lie
As the deathbed whereon it must expire,
Consumed with that which it was nourished by.
This thou perceivest, which makes thy love more strong,
To love that well which thou must leave ere long.

Shakespeare (1564-1616)

Shakespeare's sonnet is an urgent invitation to life. He depicts the gradual decline through the aging process that inevitably leads to death. Shakespeare uses the images of autumn (first quatrain), twilight fading into "black night" (second quatrain), and dying fire (third quatrain). Having sketched the stages of life – actual rendition of old age together with flashes of memories of past youth in twelve lines – Shakespeare delivers the poem's message in unequivocal terms in the concluding couplet:

This thou perceivest, which makes thy love more strong,
To love that well which thou must leave ere long.

In this couplet, the first "This" refers to the ephemeral nature of life described in the preceding twelve lines. In the last line the pronoun "that" stands for life. The speaker tells the person addressed that the fact of death should make one's love for life stronger. The ever-present phenomenon of death lends intensity to life. Similarly, in Camus' novel the unpleasant sun (death) drives Meursault towards the sea

401

(life). In both of these works the authors' use of paradox is effective in attributing a life-affirming function to death. Our familiarity with Shakespeare's sonnet makes our interpretation of Camus' symbolism easier.

Camus' theme that even when living "in the trunk of a dead tree," *we can transform nothingness into something positive* has its analogue: Our familiarity with Omar Khayyam's famous quatrain would tell us that Meursault's affirmation of life is a variation on a theme also touched on by earlier authors:

> Khayyam, if you are drunk with wine, be happy;
> If you sit with a beautiful one for a moment, be happy;
> The end of all worldly existence is nothingness;
> *Think of nothingness as being*, be happy. (Italics added for emphasis)

Camus' novel has offered us an opportunity to analyze some of the important elements that engage our skills of interpretation. We were also able to look at safe *versus* risky interpretation. Having seen how Camus has used visible structural devices, thematically significant imagery, omission of expected details, casually introduced thematic statements, parallel sets of characters, and analogues, you can apply that knowledge to your study of any novel. Let us trace some of these elements in the design of *The Great Gatsby* and *A Passage to India.*

Plot Structuring Devices in *The Great Gatsby* and *A Passage to India*

Two other important novels of the twentieth century – *The Great Gatsby* by American F. Scott Fitzgerald (1896-1940) and *A Passage to India* by English author E. M. Forster (1879-1970) – share with *The Stranger* certain attributes that are considered hallmarks of modern fiction. They have suspense, mystery, suggestiveness, and interconnectedness of all details in an intricately patterned plot, with endings that implement Forster's view of good endings: They suggest not "rounding off but opening out (Forster 169). All three novels make effective use of similar structural means to carry their narratives. Since the plot of a novel is only a shell unless it is energized and animated with appropriate content and methods of organization, we need to examine how each author meets this challenge.

The Esthetics of Deliberate Omission in *The Great Gatsby* and *A Passage to India*

Offering for our contemplation far too many questions than answers, *The Great Gatsby* and *A Passage to India* share with *The Stranger* the theme of impossibility of ever knowing the truth in important matters. To draw up a plot's architectural plan for a novel with this kind of theme, an author's reliance on the strategy of the esthetics of omission seems a natural choice. This device enables them to communicate important ideas by withholding rather than giving information. It also calls for a special creativity not only on the author's part but also a similar creative effort by the reader to appreciate this device. It is not surprising, therefore, that all three authors make use of it effectively. We have already noted Camus' use of this strategy in *The Stranger*. Let us see how the same strategy drives the narratives of *The Great Gatsby* and *A Passage to India*.

Omissions of thematic importance in *The Great Gatsby*

In *The Great Gatsby*, for example, we never know why the narrator Nick Carraway did not confront Tom Buchanan (Daisy's husband) with the truth that it was Daisy who was driving Gatsby's car when she ran over and killed Tom's mistress Myrtle Wilson. Gatsby was merely a passenger. Myrtle's husband George wrongly assumes that since it was Gatsby's car that killed Myrtle, the culprit must have been the owner of that car. Tom did nothing to dispel that misunderstanding when George, in a distraught state of mind, came to see him with the resolve to kill Gatsby.

Toward the end of the novel when Tom tells Nick the lie that Gatsby "ran over Myrtle like you'd run over a dog and never even stopped his car," why didn't Nick confront Tom with the truth? Holding back the key details that the reader expects, all that Fitzgerald allows Nick to say is this: "There was nothing that I could say, except the one *unutterable* fact that it wasn't true" (Italics for emphasis; p. 187). Why is the truth "unutterable"? Does it mean that Nick did not even try to tell the truth? Wasn't it Nick's duty to set the record straight so that his friend Gatsby's name is not tarnished with such a huge and wrongful accusation? Fitzgerald's oblique style forces us to answer this question in many different ways. Had Nick given up – like Meursault in *The Stranger* and Mrs. Moore in *A Passage to India* – on the possibility of ever convincing anyone about the truth? Did he think that Tom already knew the truth from his wife Daisy but was going to deny it? Is it possible that in not declaring the truth, Nick was doing what Gatsby would have liked him to do and what Gatsby himself might have done – that is, never implicate Daisy in any kind of danger and take all the blame on himself?

By giving Nick the above-quoted line about the "unutterable fact" at the end, Fitzgerald makes the novel endlessly suggestive. There is one more notable example of artistic and deliberate omission of expected and needed details that evokes suspense and suggestion. It concerns the otherwise articulate Nick's speechlessness when he wants to tell Gatsby something important:

"Through all he said, even through his appalling sentimentality, I was reminded of something – an elusive rhythm, a fragment of lost words, that I had heard somewhere a long time ago. For a moment a phrase tried to take shape in my mouth and my lips parted like a dumb man's, as though there was more struggling upon them than a wisp of startled air. But they made no sound and what I had almost remembered was uncommunicable forever" (118).

As mentioned earlier in this chapter, the importance of what the plot includes in the novel or excludes from it was noted by Fitzgerald himself in his "Preface" to the Modern Library edition: "What I cut out of it both physically and emotionally would make another novel."

In this novel, Fitzgerald did achieve his ideal: "I want to write something *new* – something extraordinary and beautiful and simple and intricately patterned" (Bruccoli vii). It is not surprising that in a letter to Fitzgerald, T. S. Eliot, one of the most influential critics of the twentieth century, called the novel "The first step American fiction has taken since Henry James" (Reprinted in *The Crack-Up*).

Omissions of thematic importance in *A Passage to India*

Later in this chapter, you will read a complete essay on this novel.

E.M. Forster uses the esthetics of omission in a crucial part of the plot: We are never told who attempted to rape Adela Quested. She first wrongly accuses the innocent Dr. Aziz but takes back her charge during the trial. Nevertheless, we do not know the real culprit, nor do we know with certainty that such an attempt was in fact ever made. There is a hint that Adela might have suffered a hallucination. Another mystery in the novel concerns the meaning of the shattering echo in the Marabar Caves. All we know is that hearing the echo is an unnerving and jolting experience for some (such as Mrs. Moore and Adela) and totally harmless to others, such as the native Indians. The meaning of the echo, however, eludes us. In the narrator's words, there are

"some exquisite echoes in India [but]. . . the echo in a Marabar cave is not like these, it is utterly devoid of distinction. Whatever is said, the same monotonous noise replies, and quivers up and down the walls until it is absorbed into the roof. 'Boum' is the sound as far as the human alphabet can express it, or 'bou-oum' or 'ou-boum'."

As for the effect of the echo on Mrs. Moore, ". . . the echo began in some indiscernible way to undermine her hold on life...it had managed to murmur. . . 'Everything exists, nothing has value'." (149) However, to the native Indians, the echo conveys no such shattering message. Making an ancient Marabar cave the setting for this echo adds to its intensification and symbolic richness, because a cave suggests the inner reaches of the unconscious, and the two English women's experiences in the cave reflect their hidden states of mind. It is important to note that by leaving the meaning of the echo unfixed, Forster is able to leave open the possibility of numerous interpretations. This is how Wilfred Stone, for example, interprets the echo:

"We are in fact one. . . . Not only are we related, each to each, as persons, but we partake also of the earth, sky, and water; of mud, temples . . . crystals, and birds – and the unseen as well. . . .Without preaching, the novel asks us to be responsible, to integrate ourselves, to link reason and instinct, to base our civilized arrangements on what the human race has in common instead of on what rivets it into races, classes, religions, sexes, and divided personalities (Stone 339-340).

Among other prominent interpretations of the echo, two more deserve a mention. To Ahmed Ali, Mrs. Moore's experience in the Marabar Caves symbolizes

"the incapacity of the soul to embrace a new spiritual world so near to and yet so far away from the awakening heart. The hope and vision of the Christian 'Let there be Light' fails because it does not absorb the Hindu evanescence of all that man perceives" (Natwar-Singh 34).

Austin Warren talks about Mrs. Moore's "skeptical blight":

"It is the . . . desolating skepticism which insinuates that human values have no basis in the nature of things; that our moral distinctions are factitious; that the universe mocks sinner and saint alike; that both our aspirations and our intellects are folly in the presence of the blind if not malevolent destiny" (Warren, 247-248).

Forster's use of the device of artistic omission invites numerous such provocative readings. Like Camus and Fitzgerald, Forster also purposely leaves out information to make us hunger for it all the more and to effectively communicate the theme of the elusive nature of truth.

Other Plot-Structuring Devices in *The Great Gatsby* and *A Passage to India*

Besides the deliberate exclusion of expected details to achieve multiple meanings for complex questions, there are other devices that authors use in their plot construction. We have already discussed Camus' use of parallelism, suspension of logic, symbolism, imagery, and coincidence. Let us now turn to some of the same and some different devices in *The Great Gatsby* and *A Passage to India*. The goal is to familiarize you with the commonly used fiction-making devices so that you can apply most of that knowledge to interpret any novel.

The Great Gatsby

In *The Great Gatsby*, the easily identifiable elements of plot construction are parallelism, flashback, flash forward, and use of symbolism to tie in various parts.

Parallelism

Parallelism is a device that novelists use frequently. It is noticeable in the numerous parties which Fitzgerald uses to introduce various characters and organize details of their actions and values. It seems that the entire novel is organized around parties that were thrown in the short span of a summer. In Chapter One, the first party at Tom and Daisy's mansion, where Nick meets Jordan Baker, is followed by the party at Tom's mistress Myrtle Wilson's apartment. That party introduced the streak of violence that is to explode later. In that party, Tom breaks Myrtle's nose. The Third Chapter describes one of Gatsby's parties, to which people flock just to have a good time. Most of the so-called guests don't even know Gatsby. Chapter Six mentions a party at Gatsby's, to which Daisy brings Tom. It is here that Tom, who suspects intimacy between his wife and Gatsby, develops a strong dislike for his rival. In the climactic next chapter (Seven) is another party, this one at Tom and Daisy's. We remember that Chapter One was organized around a party at their mansion. Fitzgerald uses the telephone to link the two chapters. What also connects the two chapters is this ironic reversal: Tom was cuckolding George Wilson in Chapter One, but here he is being cuckolded by Gatsby.

Flashback and flash forward

Besides parallelism, Fitzgerald uses contrast in narrative styles. He uses a series of flashbacks in a non-chronological order to tell the story of Gatsby's life. Using several narrators, he brings in Jordan Baker to tell the story of Daisy and Gatsby's past relationship. Mr. Wolfsheim offers his version of Gatsby's story, calling him "a perfect gentleman" as well as an "Oggsford man" (p.76). Gatsby's father also becomes a narrator after his son's death, to reveal, through dramatic irony, that Gatsby's tragedy remains misunderstood by all except Nick. This complicated style of organizing Gatsby's mysterious story through a series of flashbacks is appropriate and artistically compelling.

But Fitzgerald does not have to rely on foreshadowing alone to create suspense. He makes effective use of the device of flash forward. At one point he tells us exactly what is going to happen but in such a way that it creates almost unbearable moments of suspense. Before we know anything about the fatal car accident, for example, Fitzgerald has Nick tell us: "So we [Tom, Daisy, Jordan, and Nick] drove on toward death through the cooling twilight" (143). This sudden statement is followed by a major transition that Fitzgerald indicates by using blank space. Suddenly, dramatically, we are told of the inquest, but whose death is being examined we do not know for a few paragraphs of wrenching suspense. This is a masterpiece of arrangement of details for maximum impact.

Symbols

Symbols serve as objects to hold and solidify the shifting plot details. At the same time, they stand for ideas. Good symbols are integrated into plot; they often blend with plot, characters, and main ideas. In *The Great Gatsby*, just as in *The Stranger* and *A Passage to India*, symbols are an important source of grouping thematic details.

Machines

In *The Great Gatsby*, the telephone functions as a negative symbol because it intrudes to disrupt relationships. In Chapter One, during a gathering at Tom and Daisy's house, Tom's adultery was revealed to us through his phone conversation with his mistress that spoiled the cordial mood of that gathering. In Chapter Seven, during another party at Tom and Daisy's, we are told that "Through the hall of the Buchanans' house blew a faint wind, carrying the sound of the telephone bell out to Gatsby and me as we waited at the door" (121). Jordan Baker whispers, "The rumor is that that's Tom's girl on the telephone" (122).

Besides the telephone, there are other machines that play a negative role in the novel. Automobiles are given negative connotations and are even associated with death. A line of "grey cars crawls along an invisible track" in the valley of ashes. A "dust-covered wreck of a Ford . . . crouched in a dim corner" in Wilson's garage, and Gatsby's car that killed Myrtle is called "the death car." The automobile accident of Chapter Three after one of Gatsby's parties foreshadows the accident that kills Myrtle. In Chapter Four, Nick and Gatsby see a hearse as they drive into New York, thus raising the number of death cars to two. The hearse they see is also a premonition of the three deaths that later occur in the story, just as the mournful foghorn that opens Chapter Eight prefigures Gatsby's death.

Another negative image of machinery is that of the juicer in Gatsby's kitchen that squeezes life out of "crates of oranges and lemons," reducing them to "a pyramid of pulpless halves." It is notable that Fitzgerald gives this convenience item clearly negative connotations. There is also an implied analogy between the processing of fruit and a similar processing of people at Gatsby's parties.

Dust and ashes

Dust and ashes – a hallmark of mechanical civilization – crop up everywhere in the novel. The opening of Chapter Two contains a famous passage that describes the desolate "valley of ashes." It is "a fantastic farm where ashes grow like wheat into ridges and hills and grotesque gardens, where ashes take the forms of houses and chimneys and rising smoke and finally, with a transcendent effort, of men who move dimly and already crumbling through the powdery air. Occasionally a line of grey cars crawls along an invisible track, gives out a ghastly creak and comes to rest, and immediately the ash-grey men swarm up with leaden spades and stir up an impenetrable cloud which screens their obscure operations from your sight" (27).

Instead of nourishing and vitalizing human life, the abused land is able to create only "ash-grey men" carrying on their "obscure operations" (27). Dust and ashes are symbolic of industrialization of farming land, the consequent decimation of nature, and disintegration of the American dream. Brooding over the "solemn dumping ground" that is "bounded on one side by a small foul river" are the gigantic eyes of the ophthalmologist Dr. T.J. Eckleburg, whose abandoned billboard advertisement itself has decayed. George Wilson, who owns an automobile service facility in what may be called the epitome of industrialism's wasteland, mistakes the eyes on the billboard for the eyes of God – an instance of misplaced faith in the culture of materialism and advertisement – the new icons in the American pantheon.

The wind song

No discussion of symbolism in *The Great Gatsby* would be complete without an interpretive look at the wind that is mentioned at least ten times in the novel to connect themes and details. In importance, the wind symbolism of *Gatsby* is comparable to the "dark wind" of the concluding section of Camus' *The Stranger*. Nick tells us he had a "short affair with a girl . . . but her brother began throwing mean looks in my direction, so when she went on her vacation in July I *let it blow quietly away*" (61; italicized for emphasis). Here is a suggestion that the wind is symbolic of all shifting and ephemeral relationships in the story -- a fact that is also emphasized in a subtly related symbolism of Nick's writing the names of Gatsby's guests on a railway timetable. The fact that the schedule is effective July 5, 1922, suggests that the 4th of July celebrations are over and one is left facing the anticlimax of the aftermath. Another wind image underscores casual contact and temporary ties: ". . . the *air* is alive with chatter and laughter and casual innuendo and introductions forgotten on the spot, and enthusiastic meetings between women who never knew each other's names" (44). Still another wind-swept sentence echoes the flirtatious, ever-changing connections: The "wind in the trees . . . blew the wires and made the lights go off and on again as if the house had winked into the darkness," (86)

The wind images are too many to discuss in their entirety, but deserving of attention are two more descriptions of the wind that combine and connect the theme of finality in one case and a dramatic turn in the other. The first image makes the wind draw to a close the cycle of Gatsby's life:

"With little ripples that were hardly the shadows of waves, the laden mattress [carrying Gatsby's body] moved irregularly down the pool. A small gust of wind that scarcely corrugated the surface was enough to disturb its accidental course with its accidental burden. The touch of a cluster of cleaves revolved it slowly, tracing, like the leg of a compass, a thin red circle in the water" (170).

It is as if the wind is composing Gatsby's requiem, using a cluster of autumn leaves "like the leg of a compass" and Gatsby's blood for ink.

The very last image of wind in the novel is also of the nature of a requiem, this one meant for the end of Nick's experience of the East: "After Gatsby's death the East was haunted for me like that, distorted beyond my eyes' power of correction. So when the blue smoke of brittle leaves was in the air and the wind blew the wet laundry stiff on the line I decided to come back home" (185).

Echoes of hope and longing

In the midst of the novel's negative symbols and imagery, echoes of Nick's nostalgic longings for an Edenic, pre-lapsarian past are heard when he imagines New York as "the city seen for the first time, in its wild promise of all the mystery and the beauty in the world" (73). Feeding this nostalgia and also a lament on the death of a dream are Nick's words that Fitzgerald puts towards the end of the novel. They describe America's magic through Dutch sailors' eyes as they happened to come upon " a fresh green breast of the new world" to dream "the last and greatest of all human dreams" (p.189). Showing how symbols link plot details and exemplifying Fitzgerald's intricate plotting patterns, the "green breast" of this description connects the book's ending with the green light on Daisy's dock that was mentioned at the end of Chapter One. It was toward this light that Gatsby had "stretched out his arms" in "trembling" adoration (25-26).

Other Structural Devices Besides the Esthetics of Deliberate Omission in *A Passage to India*

We have already seen E. M. Forster's superb use of the esthetics of omission to communicate his meaning not through words but through wordlessness, not through statement but through silence. Let us now assess his use of some other notable devices in *A Passage to India*. Forster is not only a novelist but also author of a classic study of the craft of fiction – *Aspects of the Novel*. From that book, several important quotations were used in the chapter on plot (Chapter Three). One would, therefore, expect a consummate plot structure from this author.

Three-part structure of the novel

Starting with a few questions is one way to bring ourselves closer to an understanding of Forster's structural design. Why, for example, does he divide his novel into three parts? Why does he name those parts "Mosque," "Caves," and "Temple"? Why is the part on "Caves" so much longer than the other two parts? Why does Forster put "Caves" in the middle of the novel between "Mosque" and "Temple"? These questions have to do with style, but they also have a bearing on plot, form, and content. By pondering these questions on the novel's visible form, we are drawn to its deeper structure, where content and form blend perfectly.

In the novel's probing of the complexity of human relations and the presence of undeniable supra-rational forces in the universe, Forster's choice of the novel's divisions makes sense. Mosques are associated with Islam, and temples with Hinduism. Caves, in the novel, are symbolic of the supra-rational mysteries which reason and rationalism cannot explain. Christianity is briefly introduced in this chapter through Mrs. Moore, who finds it ineffectual in grappling with the irrational forces in the universe:

". . . Religion appeared, poor little talkative Christianity, and she knew that all its divine words from 'Let there be Light' to 'It is finished' only amounted to 'boum'. Then she was terrified over an area larger than usual; the universe, never comprehensible to her intellect, offered no repose to her soul, the mood of the last two months took definite form at last, and she realized that she did not want to communicate with anyone, not even with God" (150).

In view of this thematic outline of Forster's rich narrative, we may see in "Mosque" and "Temple" puny but very important human attempts to make some sense of life's mysteries (subject of the sprawling middle section "Caves") and bend them to a semblance of order. Christianity's brief appearance in "Caves" serves the same purpose. The greater length of the middle section suggests that much more still remains to be mapped and charted than what is so far understood by human beings. Everything that happens in a plot of this nature has a purpose, and the novel invites the reader to arrive at an understanding of that purpose.

Recurring images

Besides the three-part division of the novel discussed above, Forster uses image repetition. Authors of well-crafted novels use patterns of images that organize a lot of plot details and build up the reader's anticipation and expectation. Once you have understood the process, you can apply that knowledge to the interpretation of any novel. Among prominent recurrent images in Forster's novel are those of heat and coolness. Much like Fitzgerald in *The Great Gatsby* and Albert Camus in *The Stranger*, Forster uses hot weather as the setting for ominous events and the coolness to usher in auspicious happenings. The sun is a harsh image. The caves are described as the "flesh of the sun," having been ripped from the sun during the birth of the solar system. They are the starkest images in the novel.

Hot weather spells trouble. During their first meeting, Dr. Aziz warns Mrs. Moore that she has chosen the wrong time to visit India when the hot weather is starting. Mrs. Moore and Adela hear the shattering echo of Marabar Caves during moments of oppressive and baffling heat. Conversely, rain imagery brings coolness and is associated with peace. The novel's major reconciliations and unions take place during the coolness of rainy season. It is as if rain softens the sharp angularity of the harsh sun. Examples are an end to estrangement between Dr. Aziz and Fielding and between Dr. Aziz and Adela. Forster uses the Monsoon season of rains as a setting for the novel's conclusive and joyous festival of the birth of the Hindu god of love – Krishna. It is in this setting that we have a momentary glimpse of humanity's potential for love and understanding. Here we are brought a step closer to Mrs. Moore's ideal of "God is Love." Even the Hindu Prof. Godbole and the Muslim Dr. Aziz make an effort to drown their differences.

Symbolism of the mechanization of civilization

Lastly, *A Passage to India* shares with *The Great Gatsby* and *The Stranger* an anti-machine view that appears several times in the novel to organize contrasting details. An understanding of this process is useful in approaching those novels that ponder mechanization of life negatively, positively, or with ambivalence. Of the notable examples in Forster's novel, the first one describes the daily intrusion of civilization in the form of a train into the heart of mysterious Marabars:

"In the twilight, all resembled corpses, and the train itself seemed dead though it moved – a coffin from the scientific north which troubled the scenery four times a day. As it left the Marabars, their nasty little cosmos disappeared, and gave place to the Marabars seen from a distance, finite and rather romantic" (161).

The second example equates Western control of India to a machine that is triumphant only momentarily and is destined to succumb to and mingle with the enduring forces of Nature: "The triumphant machine of civilization may suddenly hitch and be immobilized into a car of stone, and at such moments the destiny of the English [in colonial India] seems to resemble their predecessors', who also entered the country with intent to refashion it, but were in the end worked into its pattern and covered with its dust" (211).

These quotations serve not only to organize sets of contrasting details but also as thematic load-bearing pillars in the novel's architecture.

ENHANCED UNDERSTANDING WITH CRITICS' HELP

After reading a literary work on your own and taking journal notes along the lines suggested in Chapter Six, the next step for deeper appreciation of any work is seeking help from critics. To exemplify this point is this summary of the novelist and critic Zadie Smith's comparison between Jane Austen and E. M. Forster – two novelists with whom you have become familiar through this chapter. My sample essay on Camus at the end of this chapter also seeks help from a prominent critic Germaine Bree to understand a difficult issue in *The Stranger.*

Zadie Smith (b. 1975) on Jane Austen and E. M. Forster

http://www.guardian.co.uk/books/2003/nov/01/classics.zadiesmith

Zadie Smith traces the humane basis of the English comic novel in the work of Jane Austen:

"All of Austen's positivist protagonists read situations, refine them, strip the irrelevant information from the significant, and proceed accordingly. They are good readers and as such . . . they encourage good reading from others" (*The Guardian*).

Smith devotes a major part of her discussion to E. M. Forster. She defends his so-called muddled plots, characters, and style because they are emblems of the similarly flawed human condition and human relations:

". . . it is Forster's fiction that goes further in showing us how very difficult an educated heart is to achieve. It is Forster who shows us how hard it is to will oneself into a meaningful relationship with the world; it is Forster who lends his empathy to those who fail to do so. And it is Forster who, in his empathic efforts, will allow his books to get all bent out of shape – *The Longest Journey*, an infamous melodrama to some, was the novel the author loved best."

Smith's comment on Forster's style brings to mind Virginia Woolf's similar observation on the effect of oppressive conditions on Charlotte Bronte's style in *Jane Eyre*: "we constantly feel an acidity which is the result of oppression, a buried suffering smouldering beneath her passion, a rancour which contracts those books, splendid as they are, with a spasm of pain" (Woolf 76). Woolf makes another probing comment, this one showing preference for a style that appears imperfect because of its vulnerability to the pain of its content. Comparing the perfectly controlled style of Max Beerbohm with that of Charles Lamb, she said that Lamb's essays were "superior . . . because of that wild flash of imagination, that lightning crack of genius in the middle of them which leaves them flawed and imperfect, but starred with poetry" (Woolf 6-7).

Zadie Smith extols Forster's innovation – something that she embraces in her own art:

"He allowed the English comic novel the possibility of a spiritual and bodily life, not simply to exist as an exquisitely worked game of social ethics but as a messy human concoction. He expanded the comic novel's ethical space (while unbalancing its moral certainties) simply by letting more of life in. Austen asks for toleration from her readers. Forster demands something far stickier, more shameful: love."

Ushering in a new era for the English comic novel, enriched by Sigmund Freud's discoveries about the human mind, Forster accepts the possibility that our very consciousnesses might be "faulty and fearful, uncertain and mysterious," suggesting "that the great majority of us are not like an Austen protagonist." Similarly, in Zadie Smith's view, "what Forster's muddled style has to tell us is that there are some goods in the world that cannot be purely pursued rationally, we must also feel our way through them."

Expanding her points of comparison between the two great English novelists – Jane Austen and E. M. Forster, Smith points out:

"He famously championed intimacy over sociality, friendship over country. In his novels, he can never completely condemn his conscientious abstainers – he has a soft spot for them. His empathic instincts and enthusiasm rest always on those exiled from a societal network, a concept Austen only obliquely and tragically refers to in the 'fallen' state of unfortunate girls."

WRITING A REVIEW OF A LITERARY WORK OR MOVIE

This exercise involves interpretation and analytical thinking skills that are central to good reading, writing, and viewing. Interpretation of literature and film requires similar skills. In both media, themes (the emotional and intellectual content) are grasped by analyzing events, physical details, characters' deeds, and stylistic features. "Style" in literature is somewhat like cinematography, technical elements, and special effects in movies.

Weak reviews are little more than plot summaries. Summarizing, no doubt, is essential, but a reviewer is also obligated to grapple with the elusive questions of theme and style of the work being reviewed. Reviews can be infinitely varied. Some give out just enough information to rouse the reader's interest, while others are comprehensive in their treatment of the plot, characters, themes, and stylistic features. The instructions and format offered here are for a comprehensive review. Feel free to modify the suggested format to suit your way of organizing details, but try to cover the work's topic, themes, plot summary, and some notable stylistic/technical features.

Before You Write/View

Taking some preparatory steps would help in comprehending the work's focus. As you read a book or watch a movie, keep in mind questions like the following:

What kind of world (peaceful or war-torn, affluent or impoverished, offering hope or despair) is presented in the work? What is the setting? What are the values, aspirations, fears, and motives of prominent characters? What are the characters' significant deeds, and what happens to them as a result of their values, attitudes, and actions? What appears to be the work's central topic and the author's/director's position on that topic? Such questions should lead to impressions that will later help you formulate the major themes.

Note any significant order of scenes, flashbacks, flash forwards, imagery, symbolism, and allusion. In the case of movies, also note lighting, colors, costumes, camera angles, close-ups, and music. Be attentive to the use of dramatic as well as verbal irony, understatement, paradox, repartee, sarcasm, and other humor-making devices in the dialogue. Attention to such aspects will enable you to appreciate the contribution that technical and stylistic features make in developing a theme, guiding the reader/viewer, and adding to the entertainment value of art.

Organization and Format for the Review
(suggested length: 750 words)

These instructions can be used to write a review of a movie or a literary work – collections of poems, collections of short stories, a novel, or a play. With slight modifications, these instructions are also applicable to reviewing a book of nonfiction.

Try to cover the following points in your review:

- If you are reviewing a book, give the author's name, book title, place of publication, publisher, year, number of pages, and price (if known).

- If the book you are reviewing is a classic, mention the reasons for its fame and point out the book's most appealing features. If you choose a new book that, in your opinion, is destined to become a classic, enumerate some of its outstanding qualities. Mention any cultural and historical forces that might have influenced the composition of the work.

- When interpreting a complex topic, try to make it accessible by relating it to another well-known work with a similar theme.

- Analyze the important characters and identify the values that they represent.

- Mention some of the major events in the work. Keep a balance between summarizing them and analyzing their significance through interpretation.

- Capture and communicate the work's comment on the human condition. You can answer this question in the form of statements of major themes.

- Analyze and evaluate some of the outstanding elements of style in the work (technical elements in film).

- Mention some of the outstanding aspects of the work. Include your judgment as to the kind of audience that would find it appealing.

Format

Since the main purpose of a review is to put the reader/viewer in touch with the emotional and intellectual content of the work and convey a sense of its stylistic/technical artistry, the assignment calls for coverage of **plot summary**, formulation of **central themes**, discussion of the **technical/stylistic aspects**, and a **concluding comment**. Completion of these requirements could take the following form:

> **I.** A suitable **title**
>
> **II.** Discussion of the novel, play, book, or movie's **content**
>
> > A. Open with a brief plot **summary** (about 150 words).
> >
> > B. Grasping the work's **central theme**(s)/emphasis (about 400 words)
>
> **III.** Discussion of the **technical and stylistic elements** (150-200 words)
>
> **IV.** Concluding statement (50 to 100 words)

I: Creating a Good Title

Ideally, a title should suggest the content of your review and establish its scope. It should lead naturally to the next component of the review. As was explained in Chapter Seven, the title that you choose will direct your thesis, which, in turn will control your entire composition.

II: A. Advice on Summarizing

The purpose of a summary is to introduce the reader to the setting, plot, major characters and events. End this section with a clear identification of the major **topics** without stating the themes.

II: B. Help with Formulating the Central Theme (about 400 words)

A distinction is to be made between handling works of imaginative literature (fiction, drama, poetry) and film on the one hand and works of nonfiction on the other.

For imaginative literature

After making a transition from the summary, formulate the theme(s) by identifying the work's stand or position on the topic(s) that you mentioned at the end of the summary. Statements of themes are often based on the work's theme-bearing events, characters, deeds, conflicts, outcomes, and resolutions, if any. For subtlety of style, it is preferable to initially mention the important topics, followed by supporting details, before narrowing the topics down to clear statements of themes.

Usually, authors communicate their central themes through words spoken by their characters, including narrators ("voice over" in movies). Don't forget to analyze characters and their values that help to illustrate a theme.

When well-stated, themes are the distillation of hundreds of images in a movie. They are the movie's emotional and intellectual content and their inclusion is required in an interpretation. The total length of this entire part should not exceed 150 words in a 750-word essay.

If you experience difficulty in formulating the theme, review the questions that were listed under "Before You Write/View" earlier in this chapter. Answering those questions should lead you to impressions that you can phrase as major themes. If you need further help, concentrated information on this topic appears at the end of Chapter Five. Since formulating the central theme is an important part of this assignment, you should select a work that has a recognizable and supportable theme.

For books of nonfiction

After a transitional statement following the summary, copy the book's thesis if it has been stated by the author. If the thesis is stated in several parts, introduce it in the author's own words as much as possible, quoting the most condensed statements that cover and control most of the book. The thesis in a book of nonfiction is often restated several times and consists of the author's interpretation of the details and material used in the book. If the thesis has not been stated explicitly, you should formulate the book's thesis on the basis of implicit comments and evidence in the work.

After identifying or formulating the thesis, select from the book's main body a few of the best thought clusters (at least three in a 750-word review), which introduce and develop important parts of the thesis. Copy the key words from these clusters, often written in the form of supporting, clarifying, and explanatory details to show how the author has developed the controlling ideas. Mix your own summarizing words with those of the author, especially with the author's well-written words and phrases. Include some of the concrete details and examples that the author has used to develop the major points.

This process is to be repeated to capture the depth of each selected thought cluster (a concentrated statement of ideas).

III. Discussion of the Technical and Stylistic Elements (150 to 200 words)

This part should be about one-fourth of the total length of your essay. Without sounding repetitious, restate the book's/movie's theme in one or two sentences before starting the discussion of its technical aspects. In a transitional statement, introduce no more than three stylistic elements (technical features in a movie) that you are going to discuss. (Example: The author/director intensifies the plot with appropriate images, dramatic scenes, and crisp dialogue.) Since a review should give the reader a taste of the author's style and the director's technical achievement, one interesting way to do so would be selecting three outstanding elements, citing their examples, and commenting on their effectiveness in enhancing the work's appeal. You should try to connect at least one technical/stylistic element with the work's theme or main topic, if you have not done so earlier. The other devices can be discussed in the context in which they appear, such as mood creation, suspense, humor, characterization, etc.

IV. Concluding Statement (50 to 100 words)

Your concluding statement may include an observation on the awareness the reviewed work has brought to you through answering or at least raising some of the enduring questions.

SAMPLE ESSAYS

Writing on a Single Topic from a Novel, Combining Plot, Character, and Theme

The Awakening of Meursault in Camus' *The Stranger* by the author of this book

Set in Algeria, Albert Camus' famous novel *The Stranger* is the story of an ordinary man named Meursault, to whom extraordinary things happen. His mother dies in a home for the elderly, where she has been living for some time. On receiving the telegram about her death, Meursault travels to Marengo, keeps the customary vigil, attends the funeral, and returns to his clerical job and mundane existence, which, in his case, is characterized by living from moment to moment. During the funeral, Meursault's conduct is conspicuous owing to his unconventionality in smoking cigarettes and accepting coffee during the vigil. Another peculiarity of his conduct during the funeral is his failure to show any grief in the socially expected and approved manner. Right after he returns from the funeral, he starts an intimate relationship with Marie Cardona, with whom he had been previously acquainted. They go to see a popular comic film, and Marie spends the night with him.

Meursault befriends Raymond, who is rumored to be a pimp. He helps him when he gets into trouble with the police as a result of a fight with his mistress. On the day when Raymond, Meursault and Marie, along with Masson and his wife arrange a seaside picnic, some Arab relations of Raymond's mistress confront Raymond. One of the Arabs stabs Raymond. Sensing Raymond's anger, Meursault takes away Raymond's revolver, saying that he would use the weapon if anyone attacked Raymond. Meursault's real intent is to prevent Raymond from using the revolver.

As the absurdities begin to compound, Meursault ends up killing one of the unnamed Arabs with Raymond's revolver. This single unintended action brings to an abrupt halt his life of primitive, elemental, unthinking and sensual joys that he had so far taken for granted. Camus uses the rest of the story – a major portion of Part Two of the novel – to satirize and ridicule the injustices of the legal system that attaches more importance to the irrelevant issues of personal background and religious beliefs of the accused and loses sight of the actual offense for which the accused is prosecuted.

The second part of the novel is also a record of Meursault's transformation from a man steeped in the life of the senses to a man who tries to make some sense of his life and of life in general. In this way Camus' novel becomes a perfect illustration of Sartre's phrasing of a central principle of existentialism: "Existence precedes essence." Part One of the novel deals with existence as Meursault is shown living from moment to moment, too busy to analyze any of his actions and values. In Part Two, he attempts to arrive at the essence of what his life has amounted to, and what all lives add up to.

He realizes, at the unconscious level, how much he has been in love with the life that is being snatched away from him. He is able to appreciate the wise belief of his mother: Sooner or later one gets used to everything. This awareness dawns on him when he learns to appreciate life even in the confines of a prison cell. In the concluding pages of the novel, he can understand his mother's heroic gesture in her taking on a "fiancé" (Perez) as death begins to stalk her. This is perhaps the famous revolt of the absurd man against death. Instead of accepting death with resignation, the absurd man endeavors to make a fresh start as life nears its end, thus packing his life to the fullest with lived moments as opposed to mere existence.

It is reasonable to conclude that the entire novel presents not a completed action but a continuous process of Meursault's gradual awakening to the affirmation of his values. Camus himself had this to say about his protagonist:

"For me, therefore Meursault is not a piece of social wreckage, but a poor and naked man enamored of a sun that leaves no shadows. Far from being bereft of all feeling, he is animated by a passion that is deep because it is stubborn, a passion for the absolute and for truth. This truth is still a negative one, the truth of what we are and what we feel, but without it no conquest of ourselves or of the world will ever be possible.

"One would therefore not be much mistaken to read *The Stranger* as the story of a man who, without any heroics, agrees to die for the truth" (Camus, Essays 336-337).

True to the spirit of Camus' view is Germaine Bree's moving summation of Meursault's end as "an apotheosis." In the earlier part of the novel Meursault's concern is with time as fragmented moments of being. Toward the end, however, he is able to perceive "an inner coherence, an affirmation of the supreme value of life. His end is an apotheosis – a descent into the sea and sun, a reintegration into the cosmos" (Bree 116). What Bree describes is a very unusual apotheosis, but it is the only kind possible for someone who rejects the conventional consolations of religion without rejecting spiritualism.

The novel's ending is anything but clear as to Meursault's motive for his concluding sentence: "For everything to be consummated, for me to feel less alone, I had only to wish that there'd be a large crowd of spectators on the day of my execution and that they greet me with cries of hate." In his classic work *Aspects of the Novel,* E.M. Forster writes about the superior novel endings that do not close in but open out. *The Stranger* exemplifies that ending because it leaves the reader wondering about the meaning of the novel's last sentence.

One can speculate that Meursault has finally become aware of the horrible break in the chain of human brotherhood that his unintentional murder of the Arab caused and he needs to be cleansed of his unexpressed guilt. He does speak of the sense of brotherhood with the world that he feels in his last moments. Before then, he had felt at peace with himself in his conduct. As he had told the judge, he had no intention of killing the Arab. We also know that he rightly felt that way because he had taken his companion Raymond's revolver from him, fearing that in a fit of rage, Raymond might end up killing the Arab. He must have utterly puzzled how he himself ended up using that same weapon to commit the horrible murder. He does say that he was blinded by the sun's reflection off the Arab's knife: "the dazzling spear flying up from the knife in front of me." He might have felt that he was about to be attacked when the trigger pulled itself. Notice that his description does not say that he pulled the trigger. The words are: "The trigger gave." The novel's concluding sentence suggests that Meursault might have started to feel differently about his murder. His desire for hate of a large crowd of people at his execution might indicate that change. However, that is pure speculation.

On the topic of Meursault's innocence and guilt, his answer to the judge's question, asking him if he felt sorry for his crime, is misunderstood by the judge and by most readers. His answer is that more than sorry he felt annoyance. That answer clearly implies that he did feel sorry but more than that he felt annoyed that it happened. The nature of the words Camus has given to Meursault is such that their meaning will be debated endlessly. We need to include the novel's concluding sentence in that debate.

In Defense of Meursault
Student author: Joanne Rotella

Joanne's creative piece demonstrates how an otherwise ordinary topic can be transformed into a gripping argumentative paper. Close attention to the novel's details makes it a persuasive argument.

When I first began reading *The Stranger*, I very much disliked Meursault. As some others in class, I felt he was base, unfeeling and an annoyingly unsympathetic character. That is definitely how I felt at the end of Chapter 1.

I can't say that my impression changed much in the first part of Chapter 2, but I found myself drawn into the simplicity of Meursault's thoughts, the pleasure he derived from remembering the little details of his life – the smells, sights and sounds. I also developed a great dislike for the prosecutor and many of the other officials Meursault was exposed to during his trial and imprisonment, and that made me shift a bit to his side.

Nevertheless, I was surprised to find myself in tears as the prosecutor asked the jury for Meursault's head. The agony of seeing him through to his end was heart-wrenching. I have always thought that if I was a lawyer (and thank heavens I'm not), it would be difficult for me to defend someone who I knew was guilty. It is because of all these conflicting feelings that I chose to write an argument in defense of Meursault. And it is causing me to examine once again my feelings about capital punishment.

My argument assumes that, as Meursault's defending attorney, I would have been able to question witnesses differently in order to bring to light some of the facts I, as a reader, came to know about Meursault.

Closing statement for the defense of Meursault

Gentlemen of the jury, the defendant has admitted that he killed a man. I will not insult you by asking you to find him innocent. But what kind of man is it that committed this crime, under what circumstances and how should he pay for his actions?

The prosecutor would have you believe that the defendant is a monster, a man without morals or a soul. He has even gone so far as to suggest that the defendant is guilty of another completely separate murder, in no way related to him, which is to be tried in this court tomorrow. And he has asked the jury for his head. This is absurd – and it is an outrage.

Let me re-introduce you to the defendant by giving you an honest appraisal of the young man we met during the course of this trial. A young man whose very life you hold in your hands.

The defendant has been accused of being unfeeling towards his mother in life and in death. I don't see it that way. Certainly he could not be considered a doting son. But I am sure his feelings and actions are no different than those of many other young men.

The defendant has been criticized for putting his mother in a nursing home. But the home's director has testified that, in fact, the defendant did the right thing by bringing his mother there because he wasn't able to care for her properly. She needed someone to look after her. The director even stated that Madam Meursault was happier there at the home than she was living with her son. At the home, she had friends her own age. She even had an admirer in Mr. Perez. In the end, she would have been very upset if the defendant had taken her out of the home. She had gotten used to it.

When informed of his mother's death and funeral the next day, the defendant immediately made arrangements to leave work and then traveled two hours to the home where his mother had been living. He walked over two kilometers from the village to the home. He wanted to see his mother right away but the caretaker told him he had to see the director first.

Much has also been made of the defendant's behavior at his mother's visitation and funeral. I believe this is much ado about nothing. The caretaker offered coffee with milk to a son who had lost his mother. Was it wrong for the caretaker to offer him some comfort, and for the son to accept that comfort? All who were there drank coffee together. And yes, the defendant had a cigarette. But he hesitated, because he innocently did not know if he could do so with his mother right there. Is it a crime not to know the rules of etiquette for being in the presence of a deceased person? Maybe it shows ignorance or a lack of sensitivity, but it is certainly not a crime. May I remind you that the caretaker joined him. If it was such an offense, shouldn't the caretaker have gently, kindly, suggested that such an action might not be appropriate?

Later, when the defendant went to the church for the funeral, he noticed right away that the screws had been tightened on the casket. This was a young man realizing the definitive end of his mother. She was being permanently taken from this life. Unscrewing the casket to let him have a glimpse of her dead body would not change anything. That final vision and realization affected him profoundly, even more than he himself realized.

Gentlemen, let me re-introduce you not to a monster, but rather, to a somewhat tragic young man who has learned to relate to his feelings in a purely physical way. Is it his fault that he is emotionally closed off? The prosecutor has accused the defendant of being "morally guilty of killing his mother." It appears, however, that she did not nurture in him the emotional awareness and social sensibilities necessary to win the approval of the 'prosecutors' of this world.

And yet, this same, supposedly unfeeling young man, hearing his neighbor crying over his lost dog, thought about his mother. Clearly, he was crying inside, experiencing the loss of his mother. He lost his appetite and went to bed without dinner.

It is true, the defendant entered into a liaison with a young woman the day after his mother's funeral. Perhaps it was an ill-timed affair. But after losing his mother, the first human being he connected with, what action could be more life-affirming than to feel a real connection with another human being, another woman? Perhaps, if you give him the chance to marry this same woman, in time she will be able to touch his soul, transform him – allow him to connect emotionally, not just physically, with this world.

The defendant clearly showed poor judgment in becoming a party to the schemes of a dubious character such as his friend, Raymond, the alleged procurer. He is guilty of participating in the letter-writing scheme, for not intervening when his friend was hurting his mistress and for defending his friend at the police station. He is paying dearly for those mistakes.

In an ironic twist of fate, by trying to prevent his friend from shooting the Arab, who was clearly looking for revenge, the defendant took the gun from him. And it is by having this gun in his pocket that he himself ended up committing the very crime he tried to prevent. He traded fates with his friend, and in this way saved him. Despite this tragedy, he has not once blamed his friend for what has happened to him.

Let us look again at that fateful day when the defendant pulled the trigger. I have said that he has learned to react physically. Imagine him tormented by the blinding sun and extreme heat, his head pounding, his eyes pierced with the glare from the ocean and sand. In front of him is the man who attacked his friend. I truly believe the defendant momentarily lost his mind, fear took over and his body reacted physically – the one way he knows how to react – and he pulled the trigger, then pulled it three more times, in a surreal drama happening somehow outside of himself.

Let me re-introduce you to the defendant. No matter how under attack the young man has been during this trial, how hated and accused by the prosecution, in many ways, he has displayed some of the most honest traits of anyone I have encountered. He has _individual_ integrity. *He does not subscribe to dogma or social rituals which are contrary to his own true feelings.* He has responded throughout this ordeal with the *utmost honesty* – even when he must have realized that these responses were incriminating to him.

The defendant is not an entirely likable young man. But he is certainly no "monster." He is too flat. He lacks the emotional intensity or viciousness necessary to be a monster. Nothing affects him in such a way as to cause him to act in a monstrous way. Not one of his actions was premeditated. They really did "just happen." *Sometimes reason is simply inadequate to explain the universe.*

Gentlemen of the jury, I appeal to your human hearts, with the words of the esteemed Albert Camus: "Every time you have decided to consider a man as an enemy, you make him abstract. You set him at a distance; you don't want to know that he has a hearty laugh. He has become a silhouette."

And as spoken of in Dostoevsky's masterpiece, *The Brothers Karamazov*, everyone is responsible for everything before everybody. That applies to you as a jury as well as to the defendant. As you judge the defendant for taking a man's life, do not cause yourself to be guilty of the same crime, by asking for the defendant's life.

Find the defendant guilty. But spare his life. Let him serve his time in prison, growing in appreciation for the life you have granted him, until one day, he can be released to the embrace of the sun and sea, to live a changed life.

Perils of the American Dream
Student author: Paul Brandt

F. Scott Fitzgerald's *The Great Gatsby* is a novel inspired by the rapidly changing ideals and social norms of the Twenties, the post-industrialization era in the United States. During this time, a sort of post-adolescent period in the development of American culture, with the advent of so much new technology, a prosperous economy, and the overseas success of the first World War, there was a widespread sense of exhilaration and a desire to let loose and enjoy the moment. This attitude, which discards the more traditional values of family and community for self-indulgence and materialism, is displayed in the lifestyles of Daisy, Tom, Jordan, Myrtle, and the countless extras that flock to Gatsby's parties. Nick and Gatsby, however, are not as easily understood. Both characters are somewhat of a paradox; at times they seem to be just as shallow and self-serving as the rest of the characters but occasionally they reveal a deeper, more complex side of themselves. It is through the complexity of these characters that Fitzgerald is ultimately able to make his statement, his response to the materialistic, superficial values that were rapidly being woven into the fabric of American society.

The character of Gatsby, contemptible for the unscrupulous means he has apparently used to acquire his wealth and for the blatant lies with which he tries to manufacture himself an estimable past, somehow exudes a dignified, endearing quality. In his essay "Scott Fitzgerald's Criticism of America," Marius Bewley explains:

"Gatsby, the 'mythic' embodiment of the American dream, is shown to us in all his immature romanticism. His insecure grasp of social and human values, . . . his blindness to the pitfalls that surround him in American society . . . are realized in the text with rare assurance and understanding. And yet the very grounding of these deficiencies is Gatsby's goodness and faith in life, his compelling desire to realize all the possibilities of existence. . . . A great part of Fitzgerald's achievement is that he suggests effectively that these terrifying deficiencies are not so much the private deficiencies of Gatsby, but are the deficiencies inherent in contemporary manifestations of the American vision itself (Bewley 140-1)."

Gatsby is a product of the same social and economic conditions that inspired the American dream; he is an artifact of the pioneering spirit that parlayed equal opportunity into capitalistic exploitation. However, Gatsby's dream is not material success. Though the achievement of wealth and status is integral to his vision, it is only because Daisy is herself inseparable from such things. Striving to free himself from his humble beginnings, ambitiously trying to rekindle his youthful romance, Gatsby has acquired an immense fortune, not for the wealth itself, but because its lack is the one thing that stands between him and Daisy. Though racketeering is the source of his sustenance, his true livelihood is hope.

Gatsby's determination to return to Daisy, to their immature, short-lived relationship, with time becomes an obsession. But what he is entranced with is the idea of Daisy, the idea that he could be a part of her seemingly idyllic world. Their relationship, which never had a chance to mature or develop past its initial stage of bliss, cut-short by circumstances, leaves Gatsby with the sincere, but naive, belief that Daisy is the one thing that will make him complete, that his happiness is somehow dependent on her. In his essay "The Great Gatsby: Thirty-Six Years After," A. E. Dyson explains that

"the romantic promise which in Daisy herself was the merest facade became, for him, an ideal, an absolute reality. He built around her the dreams and fervors of his youth: adolescent, self-centered, fantastic, yet also untroubled by doubt, and therefore strong" (Dyson 118).

Fitzgerald uses Gatsby's unrealistic fixation on achieving something that is essentially superficial as a metaphor for the American dream and thereby illustrates the ridiculous irrationality of such "vision."

Certainly though, as Gatsby is a product of the culture and social environment of his time, so also are the other characters. Both outsiders to the social world that surrounds them, Nick recognizes in Gatsby something that he himself lacks: a "heightened sensitivity to the promises of life , , , [and] an extraordinary gift for hope" (Fitzgerald 6). Yet despite the yearning that he seems to have for such a hopeful, romantic disposition, Nick has lost faith in society. "As narrator in Gatsby," John F. Callahan explains, "Nick comes to see the collective 'we' of America damned from the start" (Callahan 33). Though he may desire for the world to be "in uniform and at a sort of moral attention forever" (Fitzgerald 6), he realizes the futility of such a desire. When he encounters Tom on the street after the turn of events whereby Gatsby finds his end, with the opportunity to reveal the truth of what really happened the night Myrtle was killed, Nick says nothing. Whether Nick feels an obligation to Gatsby, to not tarnish Daisy's name, or whether it is simply intimidation that causes Nick to give in to taciturnity, it is clear that he sees the truth is unimportant in what Fitzgerald illustrates is a world of superficial ideals.

Fitzgerald's contention becomes clear as Nick considers the lengths to which Gatsby's vision had taken him: "his dream must have seemed so close that he could hardly fail to grasp it. He did not know that it was already behind him" (Fitzgerald 189). There is tragic irony in the truth that Gatsby may have "turned out all right at the end" (6). Freed of having to bear the realization that what he had been living for was just an illusion, that it would never have materialized, Gatsby was spared the realization of his purposelessness.

Fitzgerald points out that though admirable to dream of success, to dream of a better life, to dream of fulfillment, there is inevitable tragedy in resting one's hopes and efforts on a single end – particularly if that end is based on material success. He illustrates in The Great Gatsby that the American dream has become an illusion, that its deceptive, entrancing promise cultivates within individuals the desire to pursue empty, superficial dreams.

Sample essay by the author of this book

For maximum clarity in handling the complex novel Passage to India, *I have used the straightforward journal format that was introduced in Chapter Six. This format consists of summary, topics, themes, support, and style evaluation. To make it a formal essay, all that needs to be done is remove the headings. I have kept those headings in only to show how a structured journal entry becomes a formal essay.*

Summary

Forster's novel records interactions among six major characters, representing different racial and religious groups. Mrs. Moore, who seeks universal brotherhood and believes that "God is Love," comes to India with her would-be daughter-in-law, Adela Quested, with the intention of seeing her married to Ronny Heaslop (Mrs. Moore's son from a previous marriage). Adela espouses the admirable value of utmost honesty but suffers from inadequate capacity to feel, thus embodying one of Forster's recurring themes some readers have called the problem of an underdeveloped heart. Heaslop holds the position of a city magistrate in India. Both women are disappointed at the inhumanity of the English toward the Indians.

Besides these three characters, there is the enlightened Englishman, Cyril Fielding. An educator by profession, he takes on the challenge of viewing human beings as individuals. Fielding's unflinching support of Dr. Aziz (the Muslim Indian doctor) causes his rejection and persecution by other English people. His morally upright stand to help Adela during her crisis — when she first accuses and then retracts her charge of attempted assault against Aziz — temporarily costs him his friendship with Dr. Aziz. In the novel, Aziz is a character who stands for "secret understanding of the heart." The sixth major character in the novel is the Indian Hindu mystic, Professor Godbole, through whom Forster introduces the theme of humanity's collective responsibility for all that happens. The book shows us a way to overcome narrow-mindedness and stereotyping. It teaches us the necessity of respecting cultures other than one's own.

Topics

Forster's complex novel deals with many topics. Notable among them relate to the barriers between people, their causes, and ways to overcome them. Roles of love, emotion, intuitive understanding, collective human responsibility for the state of the world, necessity of utmost honesty.. Forster, moreover, points to the limitations of reason to fathom the mysterious side of life.

Since this novel has many topics, for this essay, I had to limit my discussion to only two of them – those that concern barriers and life's mysteries.

Themes

E. M. Forster warns us that prejudice, which is the basis of negative stereotyping, is the cause of barriers between people. His vision of global unity and reconciliation is attainable through "culture, [emotional] intelligence, and goodwill." However, despite humanity's scientific advancement, there are inexplicable and incomprehensible aspects of life.

Support

Forster has woven his themes of estrangement and reconciliation, using major characters as theme-bearers. Ronny Heaslop, McBryde, and their circle dramatize the theme of barriers. Ronny, the city magistrate, shamelessly declares that he is in India to "hold this wretched country by force. . . . We're not pleasant in India, and we don't intend to be pleasant. We have something more important to do" (Forster 50). His mother, Mrs. Moore, however, thinks otherwise. She introduces the idea of the divine nature and necessity of love, as the uniting principle. She believes that "God is love." Dr. Aziz brings in his heart-based relationships, especially between members of different cultures; as in his espousal of the "secret understanding of the heart." Professor Godbole, the Hindu mystic, makes us aware that all of us are collectively responsible for all good and bad that happens in the world. Adela Quested's recipe for peace is utmost honesty. She asks Mrs. Moore, "If one isn't absolutely honest, what is the use of existing?" (98) Lastly, the English educator, Cyril Fielding, who is supposed to represent the author, articulates the novel's central message: "The world, he believed, is a globe of men who are trying to reach one another and can best do so by the help of good will plus culture and intelligence" (Forster 62).

The theme of the damaging consequences of letting oneself be led by stereotypes rather than respecting individual variables receives special attention of the author. He dramatizes the widespread incidence of stereotyping by showing this weakness in many prominent characters and situations. First, there is the English practice of stereotyping all Indians as being alike and not worth helping. When Adela expresses her desire to meet Indians, an English woman exclaims, "Wanting to see Indians! How new that sounds!" Another English woman, who has been a nurse, speaks with authority about Indians: "A most unsuitable position for any Englishwoman – I was a nurse in a Native State. One's only hope was to hold sternly aloof." When Mrs. Moore asks her, "Even from one's patients?" Mrs. Callendar joins in with a shocking answer: "Why, the kindest thing one can do to a native is to let him die." Mrs. Callendar's sweeping generalization reduces all Indians to a less than human state.

Two more examples of stereotyping in the novel are the assumed connection between climatic zones and human conduct, and the equally questionable assumption that dark races are attracted to light races but not *vice versa*. When Aziz is wrongly accused of an attempted assault on Adela Quested, the narrator gives us a startling theory put forth by Mr. McBryde, the District Superintendent of Police, who is, ironically, described as "the most reflective and best educated of the Chandrapore officials":

"Mr. McBryde was shocked at his [Aziz's] downfall, but no Indian ever surprised him, because he had a theory about climatic zones. The theory ran: 'All unfortunate natives are criminals at heart, for the simple reason that they live south of latitude 30. They are not to blame, they have not a dog's chance – we should be like them if we settled here'" (Forster 166-167).

Later in the novel, McBryde himself was caught in an illicit affair with an English woman, which caused his downfall. Undoubtedly, he would have explained away his conduct as a consequence of his living in India. During the trial of Aziz, McBryde cannot resist expounding his favorite theme concerning "Oriental Pathology":

"Taking off his spectacles, as was his habit before enunciating a general truth, he looked into them sadly, and remarked that the darker races are physically attracted by the fairer, but not *vice versa* – not a matter for bitterness this, not a matter for abuse, but just a fact which any scientific observer will confirm" (Forster 218-219).

It would, however, be a mistake to think that the tendency to stereotype and fallaciously generalize is confined only to the British in India. When the Indians interact with each other, they are also unable to free themselves of their ingrained prejudices: In his mind, Aziz associates Hindus with cow-dung, and the Hindu magistrate Das, associates Muslims with violence. Forster's narrator, thus, allows us a frightening look into the problem of barriers between people.

The movement of the novel, however, is toward reconciliation and transcendence; even Hindus and Muslims learn to respect each other and rise above their differences. After his trial, when Aziz feels he must leave Chandrapore to start a new life away from British control, Godbole, at that time the Hindu Minister of Education at Mau, helps him get a position. Even though Godbole himself is not free of certain prejudices, it is with his help that Aziz becomes the personal physician of the Hindu Rajah of Mau. When Colonel Maggs, the British Political Agent for the area, cautions the old Rajah against "permitting a Moslem doctor to approach his sacred person," the Rajah tells him that Hindus are "less exclusive than formerly . . . and he felt it his duty to move with the times."

An especially heartening gesture of reconciliation occurs toward the end of the novel in the form of Dr. Aziz's letter to Adela: "Through you I am happy here with my children instead of in a prison, of that I make no doubt. My children shall be taught to speak of you with the greatest affection and respect. . . . For my own part, I shall henceforth connect you with a name that is very sacred in my mind, namely, Mrs. Moore" (Forster 317, 320).

Style

Forster has embodied his themes with a highly effective style. An outstanding feature of his style is symbolism. For his major organizing principle, he divides the book into three parts – Mosque, Caves and Temple. The opening and concluding parts are shorter than the longest middle section on "Caves." "Mosque" and "Temple" are named after Muslim and Hindu places of worship. Thus, in the context of the novel, they symbolize seemingly ineffectual human attempts to make some sense of the all-too-powerful and elusive challenges of "Caves," the book's sprawling middle part, which Forster's narrator makes into a catalyst to demolish the cultural and religious barriers that humanity has so diligently constructed. Only after such forced renunciation of comfortably self-deluding values can one begin the difficult but necessary task of reconciliation.

In their role of stripping away the veneer of civilization to restore humanity to fundamentals, caves also represent the mysterious, enduring primeval forces that render ineffective all man-made means to fathom the mysterious cosmic rhythm of creation and destruction:

"The triumphant machine of civilization may suddenly hitch and be immobilized into a cart of stone, and at such moments the destiny of the English seems to resemble their predecessors', who also entered the country with intent to re-fashion it but were in the end worked into its pattern and covered with its dust" (Forster 211).

A critic, Denis Godfrey, in *E .M. Forster's Other Kingdom*, has interpreted the caves as "primeval nothingness." In *The Cave and the Mountain*, another critic, Wilfred Stone sees in these caves a symbol of the collective unconscious, with which we must integrate ourselves in order to achieve unity and be at peace with life. The novel's Marabar caves can thus be seen as emblematic of both a negative and a positive force. The negative impact of the caves is that their echo reduces everything to nothingness and robs us of our comfortable certitudes and dependence on fixed values, however flawed their foundation may be. On the positive side, the equalizing effect of the caves' echo levels down all false hierarchies and forces us to rethink our systems of values and base them on egalitarianism.

Another example of highly effective use of symbolism, haunting in its impact, occurs in the opening chapter of "Caves." The narrator describes the typical visitor's experience of these caves. As the visitor strikes a match,

"another flame rises in the depths of the [shiny] rock and moves towards the surface like an imprisoned spirit. The two flames approach and strive to unite, but cannot, because one of them breathes air, the other stone. . . the flames touch one another, kiss, expire."

In spite of their desire and attempt to unite, the flame and its reflection (like Aziz and Fielding) Indians and the English cannot unite. This symbolism reinforces the theme of barriers between people. The author's skillful use of symbolism bestows his narrative with infinite suggestions for interpretation.

SAMPLE BOOK REVIEW

Frankenstein
by Mary Shelley (1797-1851)
http://www.literature.org/authors/shelley-mary/frankenstein/

Student author: Eithne Doorley

Of all the monsters to come to life in the pages of literature, there are few, if any, with such a hold on the popular imagination as the grotesque creation in English author Mary Shelley's *Frankenstein*. Through this monster and his creator, Victor Frankenstein, Mary Shelley examines the wisdom of man's burgeoning quest to "penetrate the secrets of nature" (35), the responsibilities of a creator to his creation and society, the question of how man becomes aware of his world, and the influences which form a character for good or evil. Frankenstein, a wealthy young man blessed with a loving family and lively intellect, becomes totally possessed by a desire to "unfold to the world the deepest mysteries of creation" (92). After years of obsessive study, he pieces together a body from various corpses and "on a dreary night of November – infuses a spark of being into the lifeless thing" (101). Frankenstein is overcome by horror at the hideousness of the animate monster he has created, and flees leaving the enormous, deformed "newborn" to fend for itself. The monster, intelligent and sensitive, is initially full of goodwill towards man; all he desires is a reciprocation of the "love and fellowship" (259) he has to offer, but his appearance excites such revulsion and terror that this proves impossible. Embittered and frustrated by the desertion of his creator and the rejection of society, the monster becomes evil and vengeful; he determines that Frankenstein should also experience the utter misery of despair before he lures him to his death. This done, the monster prepares for his own end, since, "polluted by crimes and torn by bitterest remorse," (260) he can only find rest in death.

The pitiful life and death of the monster is a powerful argument against the irresponsible scientific pursuit of the secrets of life. Frankenstein thinks only of discovering and creating; he never considers the reality of the being he is going to bring to life until it is too late. His vainglorious dreams conjure up "a new species [that] would bless me as its creator and source" and "many happy and excellent natures [who] would owe their being to me" (97). However, when the animated creature fails to match up to expectations, Frankenstein, instead of accepting his responsibility for, and to, the creature, runs away, hoping that the spark of life will extinguish itself. Frankenstein's reaction is that of a child, who, overwhelmed by the enormity of what he has done and feeling helpless to rectify it simply hopes it will disappear like a bad dream.

Mary Shelley has great misgivings about the wisdom of meddling with the mysterious power that creates life, and the ability of those who pursue it to deal with the consequences of their discoveries. Frankenstein's father is an interesting contrast to his obsessive and secretive son; he is a man of great integrity, prepared to shoulder public and private responsibility, possessed of an unusual degree of compassion for the less fortunate and deeply suspicious of anything which disturbs the mind's tranquility. He is the balanced and socially responsible ideal, who would never have strayed so far into the recesses of life, but, who, if faced with the reality of the creature, would presumably accept his responsibility and treat him with compassion and understanding.

Unfortunately, it is not the father, but the son, who first encounters the monster and promptly deserts him, fervently desiring his death. Despite these inauspicious beginnings, the monster, full of goodwill, makes a valiant attempt to understand the world and find his place in it. However, his best efforts fail, and he repeatedly meets with violent rejection. Finally, in a moment of despairing anger, he kills Frankenstein's young brother and finds pleasure in the idea that he "too can create desolation" (183); he too can inflict pain and torment on his creator, who abandoned him so cruelly. The creator bears a responsibility to its creation, and to the society the creation will inhabit. To the former he owes the possibility of a meaningful existence and the latter deserves to have its peace and security preserved; the monster displays his awareness that his creator has denied him the possibility of a meaningful existence, and consequently created a threat to his society, when he compares his predicament to that of the first man:

"Like Adam, I was apparently united by no link to any other being in existence; but his state was very different from mine in every other respect. He had come forth from the hands of God a perfect creature, happy and prosperous, guarded by the especial care of his Creator; he was allowed to converse with and acquire knowledge from beings of a superior nature, but I was wretched, helpless, and alone. Many times I considered Satan as the fitter emblem of my condition, for often, like him, when I viewed the bliss of my protectors, the bitter gall of envy rose within me" (171).

In the monster we see the pity of abandoned humanity, the waste and perversion of all the inherently noble instincts of man when he is denied the benefits of society and education. Man apprehends the world through his senses and uses his rational faculty to understand it; but he cannot lead a fruitful existence alone and despised: he is a product of his environment; nurture him and he will repay you in kind, despise him and he will pay you in spite.

Mary Shelley relates the story through three speakers. Walton, an explorer driven by the same urge for discovery as Frankenstein, approximates the reader's reaction and serves to complete the story. Frankenstein and the monster also speak, revealing their innermost thoughts and feelings. Thus the monster, who could easily deteriorate into a ghoul, arouses pity and understanding as well as terror.

Mary Shelley dramatizes and heightens the terror and emotion of the story by using and describing landscape in the expressive style of the Romantics. To accentuate the theme of creation, she sets the major encounters between the two protagonists at the wild and untamed boundaries of the known world: this impresses us with the sense of man alone with his creator at the beginning of the world, and conveys something of the awesome might that is nature. Man is truly insignificant in the face of such power, and we are warned that we should not try to harness it until we can properly understand its full implications.

FIVE MORE NOVELS INTRODUCED WITH STUDENTS' SAMPLE JOURNAL ENTRIES AND AN ESSAY

Besides the four classics that have been discussed in depth, five more major novels are briefly introduced through students' writings to expand this book's coverage of fiction. Journal entries on Wright, Bulosan, Thomas, and Tan are followed by an essay on Andre Dubus' novel House of Sand and Fog. *The journaling technique that you learned in Chapter Six once again shows its attractive informality and potential to help you toward a fuller appreciation of novels. The student authors focused on just one prominent topic from each novel listed below. You can read additional essays by students on my website.*

"The Library Card" from *Black Boy* by Richard Wright
America is in the Heart: A Personal History by Carlos Bulosan
Down These Mean Streets by Piri Thomas
"A Pair of Tickets" from *The Joy Luck Club* by Amy Tan
House of Sand and Fog by Andre Dubus III

"The Library Card" from *Black Boy*
by Richard Wright (1908-1960)
http://www.is.wayne.edu/mnissani/Fall2003/library.HTM

Student authors Jovi Bondoc and Max Lynch respond to Richard Wright's "The Library Card" *from his novel* Black Boy.

Student author: Jovi Bondoc

Topic
Richard Wright's nameless narrator demonstrates the power of discourse.

Theme
Words can either be empowering, or even weakening, because knowledge is power.

Support
In other words, it is important to make the distinction that although reading and learning can be engrossing in a positive sense, it could conversely be detrimental to one's psyche because, depending on the content being perused, the acquisition of new and intriguing information could actually drive one to wish they had not come across such information in the first place.

The protagonist of "The Library Card" evidently digested this food for thought, beginning with a broadened understanding of the "American type" and a newfound fervor for change in his circumstances after discovering the eloquence of Sinclair Lewis and (perhaps more meaningfully, at least to him) H.L. Mencken. Clearly, he had been initially fascinated with and influenced by Mencken's way of "fighting with words … Then, maybe perhaps, I could use them as a weapon? No. It frightened me … what amazed me was not what he said, but how on earth anybody had the courage to say it." In

430

proceeding to read the works of other authors, however, his anxious yet enthusiastic admiration transitioned into a quiet acceptance of his present conditions, for "in buoying me up, reading also cast me down, made me see what was possible, what I had missed." Though his family had begun to make small strides in their lives, the narrator nonetheless came to recognize that history continued to set parameters on how he could live life: not completely submitting, but not entirely overcoming either.

Student author: Maxwell Lynch

In "The Library Card" Richard Wright weaves a story that describes obstacles to enlightenment - specifically, that oppressive parties will seek to prevent the social mobility of a particular group by preventing their access to the tools of intellectualism and therefore, enlightenment. He shows the obstacles to the acquisition of knowledge a young black man faces in the pre-civil rights southern United States. Specifically, Wright symbolizes the library card as a tool of enlightenment itself - a symbol of the freedom to explore oneself and the world without fear of retribution. The boy, of course, is "not allowed to patronize [the library's] shelves any more than the parks and playgrounds" (Wright 117).

Being tempted by a magazine article, the boy seeks to clandestinely obtain the objects of such intellectual treasure through a somewhat less-persecuted Irish Catholic workmate. Wright portrays his pursuit of books in a surreptitious manner to highlight the clear obstacles whites have placed between him and intellectual growth. He shows that the boy has been long deprived of self-realization, enlightenment and thus, the inevitable social mobility that follows. Furthering his belief that words are knowledge and therefore, power, Wright says "this man was fighting, fighting with words. He was using words as a weapon . . . perhaps, I could use them as a weapon? No. It just frightened me" (Wright 120). The more he reads, the more isolated and uncomfortable he feels, as the truth distances himself further from both whites and his black peers. Now that he sees his condition as a black American more lucidly, he feels an even deeper sense of mistrust and hopelessness. Ultimately, Wright seems to be saying that any people long stifled by a suffocating blanket of repression are further frustrated when the self-actualization their intellectual revolution promises is delayed by a reflexive fear of consequences and the unknown.

Excerpts from *America is in the Heart: A Personal History*
by Carlos Bulosan

Besides Fitzgerald's classic The Great Gatsby, *Carlos Bulosan's* America is in the Heart *is another variation on the theme of the American Dream. You can start by reading the following excerpts from Bulosan's novel. You can read more about Carlos Bulosan online:* http://www.answers.com/topic/carlos-bulosan#ixzz2BxIYfopy *and also listen to a reading of an excerpt from America is in the Heart on YouTube:* http://www.youtube.com/watch?v=kkA-pt8dJTQ.

It is but fair to say that America is not a land of one race or one class of men. We are all Americans that have toiled and suffered and known oppression and defeat, from the first Indian that offered peace in Manhattan to the last Filipino pea pickers. America is not bound by geographical latitudes. America is not merely a land or an institution. America is in the hearts of men that died for freedom; it is also in the eyes of men that are building a new world. America is a prophecy of a new society of men: of a system that knows no sorrow or strife or suffering. America is a warning to those who would try to falsify the ideas of free men.

America is also the nameless foreigner, the homeless refugee, the hungry boy begging for a job and the black body dangling from a tree. America is the illiterate immigrant who is ashamed that the world of books and intellectual opportunities is closed to him. We are that nameless foreigner, that homeless refugee, that hungry boy, that illiterate immigrant and that lynched black body. All of us, from the first Adams to the last Filipino, native born or alien, educated or illiterate -- We are America! * * *

The old world is dying, but a new world is being born. It generates inspiration from the chaos that beats upon us all. The false grandeur and security, the unfulfilled promises and illusory power, the number of the dead and those about to die, will charge the forces of our courage and determination. The old world will die so that the new world will be born with less sacrifice and agony on the living . . .

We in America understand the many imperfections of democracy and the malignant disease corroding its very heart. We must be united in the effort to make an America in which our people can find happiness. It is a great wrong that anyone in America, whether he be brown or white, should be illiterate or hungry or miserable.

Carlos Bulosan (1913-1956)

You can read more selections from Bulosan's novel on my website.

Student author: John Starks

Bulosan takes the reader on a tour through the oppressive quagmire of racism, discriminatory laws, and brutality faced by a Filipino immigrant in the late 1940s and 50s. Bulosan's novel treats many important topics; the need and value of perseverance is one of them. In the midst of detailing the numerous hardships that immigrants often experience, Bulosan is able to forcefully affirm the view that the fire to create and the desire to succeed are the driving forces behind the immigrant's ability to weather the storm of discrimination.

Bulosan describes the difficulty he and his brother faced finding housing in America. Mostly they were steered away from decent neighborhoods. Other times they were met with outright hostility. It was this poverty and isolation that first gave Bulosan the desire to find an escape in books. We see Bulosan's desire to write and the inspiration he drew from other immigrant writers. "I found Younghill Kang . . . an immigrant from Korea . . . it was his indomitable courage that rekindled in me a fire of hope." Young

Bulosan goes on to describe how he developed a voracious appetite for Asian Immigrant writers and used them as intellectual guides to his own creative outlet, poetry.

For his brothers, the desire to carve out a path in the hostile times would lead them to serve in the armed forces. Even with the racist policies toward immigrants, they were still willing to serve in the armed forces in order to secure their places in America. In the end we know that Bulosan, though alone and poor, will be okay. He has the pull of his art and the legacy of the thousands who came before him to bolster his courage and resolve.

Down These Mean Streets
by Piri Thomas (1928-2011)

Student authors Sydney McIver and Andrea Deyzel write on the novel Down These Mean Streets *by Piri Thomas.* Available online are his *"Foreword" to the book*: http://cheverote.com/texts/foreword1.html *and his 1997 "Afterword" to the thirtieth anniversary edition*: http://www.cheverote.com/texts/30thed.html. *You can read the entire novel on your own.*

Student author: Sydney McIver

Topic
Personal growth

Theme
Those who triumph over their past mistakes, learn from them, are able to move forward, and experience positive personal growth.

Support
Piri was given a chance to turn his life around, once he recovered from his drug addiction during six years in prison. His time in prison gave him time to reflect on the downfalls of his past and he figured out how he would make his future better. His only regression early in the story showed that what he learned from his time in prison helped him become a better person. Instead of falling back into his old pattern, which felt easy and comfortable, he felt horrible remorse for his actions, and the small taste of his old life scared him. If anything, that regression proved an opportunity for even further growth, and put his past that much farther behind him. Suffering the consequences of a drug addict's lifestyle by spending six years in prison, Piri learned the value of staying sober.

At the end of the story Piri sat with an old friend Carlito as Carlito injected himself with drugs. Piri had a moment of temptation and overwhelming desire to join Carlito. But as Carlito started to ramble about how he was going to stop doing drugs soon, Piri saw how pathetic and desperate Carlito's choices had made him. This was a chance for Piri to evaluate how far he had come in his recovery and in the building of a new and better life for himself. There is a scene where Piri went to visit an old girlfriend and her family, and he is disappointed that she didn't instantly want him back. But this experience showed him that there was never any going back to the way things used to be, for anyone; and ultimately, he didn't want to go back in time. By the end of the story Piri reached peace with his new life, a sign of great personal growth, and he was able to start letting go of his past.

Chapters from Down These Mean Streets *covered in this journal entry: "Hey Barrio—I'm home" and "I Swear to God and the Virgin"*

Student author: Andrea Deyzel

Topic

The topic of the excerpts from *Down These Mean Streets* by Piri Thomas is: A second chance can be cause for change.

Theme

The theme of the work is: The meaning of true freedom is known best to those who have been bound.

Support

Piri expects to be tossed in jail, and hopes for a less severe six-year sentence. However, Piri is shocked by a lenient district attorney, and a judgment that gives him probation instead. He says "This shook me up inside, but my face stood still" (p. 175). When finally outside and free, he writes, "Inside, the dizziness of being free was like a night that changed into day; all the shadows became daylight sharp" (p. 175). His perspective changed, and he was sure he would do anything to maintain his freedom. He quickly does as required of him; he finds work and stays clean for quite some time before he relapses. After his relapse he sees himself in the mirror and is shameful. He says "[I] hid myself in the friendly darkness" (p. 177). He vows to put himself back on the right track, and does.

Piri knows what it is like to be shackled into something. He understands the binds of both his physical prison and also those of drug abuse. He realizes that he wants "to be somebody." He says, "I want to laugh clean. I want to smile for real, not because I have to . . ." (p. 177). He's learned to appreciate his freedom because he's had it taken away from him. The leniency of the district attorney and the consequent judgment of probation aids in a transformation within him; Piri is free from prison and drug abuse because of it.

"A Pair of Tickets"
excerpted from The Joy Luck Club
by Amy Tan (b. 1952)

Student authors Maxwell Lynch and Andrea Deyzel respond to an excerpt "A Pair of Tickets" from Amy Tan's novel, The Joy Luck Club. *Maxwell chose not to use the headings "topic," "theme," and "support" in his informal journaling style. You may read this novel on your own. Excerpts from the movie are available on YouTube: http://www.youtube.com/watch?v=U4wOlEdl9IM.*

Student author: Maxwell Lynch

In this excerpt, "A Pair of Tickets," Tan explores the fragmented personal identity of immigrants. More specifically, that despite inevitable rifts in language and culture, the ethnic identity of an immigrant is innate and may be rediscovered. Jing-Mei admits denying her Chinese identity as a youth, as she struggled for acceptance as all youths do. But along the way, the once far-fetched sounding words of her mother gradually became true - "Someday you will see…it's in your blood, waiting to be let go." The key to Jing-Mei's rediscovery lies in the enigma that is her family, and thus she must make a conscious effort to engage them - hence her journey to China.

The loss of her mother, as sad as it is for her, seems almost a necessary, precipitating event for her journey of self-discovery. In fact, her mother symbolizes the "pure Chinese" in Jing-Mei, the part of her that she has shied away from, at times been afraid of, but ultimately lacking a thorough understanding. She regrets not knowing this part of herself as intimately while her mother was alive, which at least partly propels her quest.

Though some immigrant families are so tragically torn apart (by war, especially) that there is little hope for a "regrouping" of sorts, Jing-Meh's family, somewhat miraculously, is able to come together, even though it takes many years. For her, this togetherness is the catalyst for the rediscovery and reconciliation of her ethnic identity, as Tan puts it "I also see what part of me is Chinese…It is my family. It is in our blood."

Student author: Andrea Deyzel

Topic

Endless hope in Amy Tan's *Joy Luck Club.*

Theme

Dreams can be so powerful that they transcend death.

Support

Both tragic and inspiring, this story is about three sisters brought together by their deceased mother's endless hope. Suyuan's older twin daughters were "little babies she was forced to abandon on a road as she was fleeing Kweilin for Chung-king in 1944. She later re-marries and has another daughter, who is the story's narrator. After searching for them for many years, Suyuan ceases to talk about her twins. Her second husband assumes she has come to terms with their loss and was too ashamed of her actions. However, he later tells his daughter that "Suyuan didn't tell me she was trying all these years to find her daughters . . . Naturally I didn't discuss her daughters with her. I thought she was ashamed she had left them behind." She had an endless hope that they were alive and that she would find them. "When letters could be openly exchanged between China and the United States, she wrote immediately to old friends in Shanghai and Kweilin. It is a few months after her death that one of her old school friends eventually meets the twins by chance.

Suyuan's youngest daughter, Jing-mei, fulfills her mother's dream of finding her daughters. She is saddened that her mother can't be there to see them, "If only, I think, if only my mother had lived long enough to be the one walking toward them." Jing-mei's father wonders if it was her "mother's dead spirit who guided her Shanghai schoolmate to find her daughters." In the end the three are re-united and Jing-mei feels that they have fulfilled their mother's "long-cherished wish."

House of Sand and Fog
by Andre Dubus III (b. 1959)

This novel focuses on the sinister aspect of the American dream. Andrew Keller's essay treats this topic, with focus on plot, character, and historical allusion. If you don't have time to read the novel you can watch its film adaptation by director Vadim Perlman. A trailer of this movie is online at http://www.moviefone.com/movie/house-of-sand-and-fog/16395/trailers.

The Sinister Side of the American Dream
Student author: Andrew Keller

The Academy Award winning film *House of Sand and Fog* based on this masterpiece changes the way we see ourselves as Americans. It is the story of two parties who clash at the success and collapse of their dreams. Kathy Nicolo is evicted from the house that she inherited from her father, and it is auctioned by the local government. Massoud Amir Behrani, an exiled colonel from the Iranian military, buys the house in hopes of re-selling it in order to improve the financial situation of his family. The pursuit of their dreams leads both characters and their loved ones into a conflict of hostility that ultimately ends in tragedy for all.

The story begins with the eviction of Kathy from her house, and her introduction to Deputy Sheriff Lester Burden, whose name ironically depicts his role in the movie. It is clear that Kathy is not at her peak in terms of success. Her husband broke up with her eight months prior, her house is very messy despite the fact that her profession is house cleaning, and she is struggling with addiction to cigarettes and alcohol. Kathy's situation is seen as a common downfall in American culture, and she is perceived as an average Jane whose life is on the rocks.

Forced to leave their country, the Behrani family seeks what many American immigrants dream of: to live successful, comfortable lives while maintaining the culture of their homeland. With the introduction of Mr. Behrani, it is clear that although he is a construction worker and a clerk at a liquor store, he was once a prominent military figure in his home country of Iran. When Col. Behrani sees the ad for the seized home being auctioned at a below-market price, he decides that he will buy, renovate, and re-sell it in order to make enough money to send his son to a good university. Neither he nor his wife expresses joy about being in America. Both long to be home, but know they cannot go back for their lives will be at stake presumably because of their close ties with the now deposed Shah of Iran. The colonel's struggle is that of the American immigrant of past and present, because often when a person immigrates, their past experiences, titles, and sometimes even education mean very little here. In America, respect is not about who you were somewhere else, or even who you are here; it's simply about how much money you have. This definitely served as great motivation for buying the house as the profit margin would allow him to find other sources of income and create a new life.

In contrast, their son, Ishmael, has adjusted to the American lifestyle very well. He is an average American teenager who skateboards and plays video games. He contributes hugely to Behrani's will to succeed, in that Ishmael's future is his father's motivation, which is why he can't sell the "investment home" back to the city so that it can be returned to Kathy. This is where the Behrani's dreams of success clash with Kathy's hope for an easy and comfortable life to which she feels this house entitles her.

Kathy and Behrani's conflicting claims of legitimacy of rights lead to a tragic crisis. Although both sides are unfair to each other, Kathy and Lester do more damage to the Behranis than one would believe possible. After all, it was Kathy who did not pay her taxes and therefore lost her house. However, she had to pursue the Behranis physically and walk on their dreams of living peacefully. They could have achieved their dream of success by implementing their perfectly legal plan to sell the house. To Kathy's credit, however, it must be added that she uses nonviolent means to try to convince the Behranis that she is the rightful owner, while Lester, never with Kathy's full knowledge of his intentions, uses threats and force to try to achieve his goals.

Deputy Sheriff Lester Burden seems to invest his entire being in Kathy when he leaves his wife and children for her, then continues to go to great lengths, all of which are illegal, in an attempt to get her house returned to her. First, he uses his status as a police officer to threaten Col. Behrani with deportation to prevent him from selling the house. After holding the Behranis hostage, Lester forces the colonel and his son to come to the city and sign the house to Kathy. Tragically, on this trip, Ishmael is shot dead by police officers, which leads to Behrani's poisoning of his wife, and killing himself.

House of Sand and Fog is an amazing novel in which we discover who we are, both the American and the immigrant parts of us. A devastating tale and one with an ending that will leave you breathless; it is a tragedy of the American dream.

To read additional essays on novels go to my website: <Professorjabbar.com>

Exercises to Test Your Mastery of Chapter Eleven

Engaging your critical thinking and interpretation skills, the questions in these exercises will lead to interesting discussions. Some items are of general relevance to all novels, while others are specific to the novels discussed in this chapter: Jane Austen's *Pride and* Prejudice, Albert Camus' *The Stranger*, F. Scott Fitzgerald's *The Great Gatsby*, E. M. Forster's *A Passage to India,* Richard Wright's "Library Card" from his novel *Black Boy,* Carlos Bulosan's *America Is in the Heart,* Piri Thomas's *Down These Mean Streets,* Amy Tan's "A Pair of Tickets" from her novel *The Joy Luck Club*, and Andre Dubus' *House of Sand and Fog.* By using these questions as samples, you can also formulate similar questions of your own on any novel. Since only a limited number of novels could be covered in one chapter, I have added some questions as a means to expand the chapter contents and as learning resources. The number of novels students read in a semester, quarter, or summer session depends on the nature of the course. Whatever kind of course you are taking, answering these questions will add to your enjoyment and deeper understanding of fiction.

Questions on the novel in general

1. Combine plot summary with character analysis to formulate and discuss an important theme in a novel of your choice.

2. Choose just *one* significant chapter from a novel to write an essay on one or two major themes in the chapter, thus treating the chapter like a complete story. For a slightly different and more challenging assignment, do everything as explained for this assignment and add an additional section to trace your selected chapter's connection with two other chapters. To do so, connect one of the chapter's themes to two other chapters. Include supporting details.

3. Focus on a major topic and trace its development throughout a novel of your choice. A sample is the student Paul Brandt's essay "Perils of the American Dream" on *The Great Gatsby.*

4. A novel with a single major character can generate an interesting discussion if our focus on the novel's protagonist yields an understanding of her/his values and dilemmas while, at the same time, offering us a glimpse into the author's mind. Trace the protagonist's path along the lines of this question in a novel of your choice.

5. Choose a topic that figures prominently in a novel and discuss it with reference to character, plot, and theme. The sample essay "The Awakening of Meursault in Camus' *The Stranger* is an example.

6. Using instruction No. 3 of the "Step-by-Step Instructions" for "Writing on Themes of a Literary Work" (Chapter Seven), write a thesis paragraph of no more than 100 words for an essay on any novel's two or three prominent themes. (Time limit: 30 minutes). This exercise is to be completed after you have finished a careful reading of the novel. You are being asked to write only a thesis paragraph, not an essay.

7. Expand the thesis paragraph of No. 6 above into an essay of about 750 words. Use the sample essay on Kate Chopin's "The Story of an Hour" in Chapter Seven for help.

8. This question on style is for advanced students. You can come back to this question later if you are not quite ready for it now. Answer both parts (i) and (ii). Both of them concern authors' styles of

writing. If you like, you may write on any author's style in a novel that has been discussed in this chapter, but you should not repeat what has already been said. Limit your discussion to any two or three relevant stylistic elements.

(i) Using instruction No. III of the "Step-by-Step Instructions" for "Writing on an Author's Style" (Chapter Seven), write a thesis paragraph of no more than 100 words for an essay on any novelist's style of writing. (

ii) Discuss effective use of the element of style known as the esthetics of omission in any novel. Authors often use it to denote and handle the inexplicable.

9. (For advanced students) Expand the thesis paragraph of No. 8 (i) into an essay of about 750 words. One easy way to complete this task is this: After completing the thesis, introduce one best example of the first element of style, followed by a comment on its function and effectiveness. Do the same with the other elements of style. Use the sample essay on Alberto Moravia's style in Chapter Seven for help.

10. Enumerating qualities of good fiction in *How Fiction Works*, James Wood says "that it favors the telling and brilliant detail; that it privileges a high degree of visual noticing; that it maintains an unsentimental composure and knows to withdraw, like a good valet, from superfluous commentary; that it judges good and bad neutrally; that it seeks out the truth, even at the cost of repelling us; and that the author's fingerprints on all this are, paradoxically, traceable but not visible" (39). Identify and analyze any two of these qualities in any novelist of your choice.

11. The following four questions are based on film adaptations of novels:

A. Bernard Dick has defined voice-over as the "off-camera narration or commentary" (Dick 57). Do you find this voice-over device in film as effective as a narrator's words in literature? Give a reasoned response.

B. Do you agree with the film critic Mick LaSalle's view that the film adaptation of Michael Cunningham's Pulitzer Prize-winning novel *The Hours* is in many ways an improvement over the book? "The cinematic form is well suited to the novel's aim to show parallel movements in the lives of three women in different eras. Meryl Streep and Julianne Moore are fine, but Nicole Kidman takes acting honors for her transformation into an utterly convincing Virginia Woolf." (M. LaSalle, *San Francisco Chronicle*, July 11, 2003, page D-14). Support your answer with specific details from the movie and the novel.

C. *Elegy* is a movie with a rich literary script. It is based on Philip Roth's novella *The Dying Animal*. Directed by the Spanish director Isabel Coixet, it stars Ben Kingsley and Penelope Cruz. Assess the gain and loss to the book in this book-to-movie transition.

D. *Rashomon* is another movie that is based on rich literary text of two stories – "Rashomon" and "In a Grove" – by Ryunosuke Akutagawa. Directed by Akira Kurosawa, the movie stars Toshiro Mifune. Write a comparative analysis of the movie and the short stories.

Questions on Jane Austen's *Pride and Prejudice*

12. Of the various themes from Jane Austen's *Pride and Prejudice*, which one seems most important to you. Why? If you choose a theme that has already been discussed in this chapter, add to the supporting details a few paragraphs of details not already mentioned in this chapter.

13. Discuss the novel's theme concerning the importance of balance and restraint in passion. This theme was mentioned but not discussed in the chapter.

14. Mr. Collins' proposal of marriage to Elizabeth in Chapter 19 (p. 146 of Penguin edn., 1985) is a masterpiece of comedy. Compare his proposal with that of Darcy in Chapter 34 for character analysis.

15. Jane Austen wished her readers to enjoy her epigrammatic style of writing. One example has already been cited in this Chapter when Elizabeth compares Darcy with Wickham when talking to her sister Jane: "There certainly was some great mismanagement in the education of these two young men. One has got all the goodness [referring to Darcy], and the other all the appearance of it [referring to Wickham]." Another example is Mr. Bennet's words to Elizabeth that her mother will never forgive her if she didn't marry Collins and he (Mr. Bennet) will never forgive her if she did. The novel is full of such witty and pithy remarks. Point out a few of them and comment on their effectiveness for humor, character revelation, theme development or any other function.

16. One of the numerous scenes sparkling with wit and humor is in Chapter 56 when the arrogant Lady Catherine de Bourg tries to prevent Elizabeth from accepting her nephew Darcy's marriage proposal because he is supposed to marry Lady Catherine's daughter. Choose this or any other scene for a critical appreciation of its power to make us laugh while at the same time moving forward the story's thematic design.

17. What is the function of Elizabeth's visit to Darcy's estate at Pemberley?

18. Charlotte Bronte, a contemporary of Jane Austen and author of the famous novel *Jane Eyre*, made this negative comment about *Pride and Prejudice* in a letter to H. G. Lewes: "a carefully fenced, highly cultivated garden, with neat borders and delicate flowers . . . no open country, no fresh air, no blue hill . . . I should hardly like to live with her ladies and gentlemen, in their elegant but confined houses" (Tanner 7). To what extent do you agree with Charlotte Bronte's criticism of the novel? Optional part of the question: Compare and contrast Jane Austen's novel with *Jane Eyre* by Charlotte Bronte. If you don't have time to read Bronte's novel, you can watch its film adaptation.

19. Another famous contemporary of Jane Austen was Charlotte's sister Emily Bronte, whose novel *Wuthering Heights* has become a classic of romantic fiction. You may either read Bronte's novel or watch its film adaptation to compare and contrast how the two novels treat the topics of love and marriage or any other topic. The film version with Lawrence Olivier is a faithful rendition of the novel.

20. One common comment on Austen is that her novels have very little overt action. In Tony Tanner's words, "during a decade in which Napoleon was . . . transforming Europe, Jane Austen composed a novel in which the most important events are the fact that a man changes his manners and a young lady changes her mind" (Tanner 7). Is this lack of action a weakness or strength in Austen's work? When answering this question, keep in mind Jane Austen's following words to her nephew Edward that describe her work as "that little bit (two inches wide) of ivory, in which I work with so fine a brush as produces little effect after much labour" (Tanner iii).

Questions on F. Scott Fitzgerald's *The Great Gatsby*

21. Compare or contrast the characters of Jay Gatsby (in F. Scott Fitzgerald's novel) and Walter Younger (in Lorraine Hansberry's play *A Raisin in the Sun*). By identifying their respective dreams, the

impediments to their goals, the means they employ, and the outcome of their pursuits, you can generate an interesting character-based interpretation of the topic of the American dream. Alternatively, you can compare/contrast any two fictional characters to write on the concept of the American dream.

22. In his "Preface" to *The Great Gatsby*, Matthew Bruccoli cites Fitzgerald's own words about his idea of a great novel: "I want to write something new – something extraordinary and beautiful and simple + intricately patterned" (vii). Did Fitzgerald succeed in reaching his goal in *The Great Gatsby*? How?

23. Referring to the love that might have existed between Tom and Daisy, Gatsby dismissed it as "just personal" (p. 160). What does Gatsby mean?

24. The wind appears as a recurring image/symbol in *The Great Gatsby*. Identify some of its occurrences and explain their function. This chapter has discussed a few wind images.

25. Fitzgerald's novel is rich in gestures that act like the "esthetics of omission" or wordless communication. Mention any two of the gestures and explain their effectiveness.

26. Apply Arthur Miller's words on the morality and lesson of tragedy (in his essay "Tragedy and the Common Man," included in Chapter Twelve) to analyze the character of Gatsby. Do you consider Gatsby a tragic hero? Note that the reader does not know what Gatsby is really thinking about in his final moments. Instead, our sense of Gatsby's last moments, like much of our understanding of Gatsby, is derived through Nick (Gatsby's friend and the narrator). Do you agree with Nick that Gatsby "himself didn't believe it would come [Daisy's call] and perhaps he no longer cared" (p. 169)? Would knowing more about Gatsby's final moments change your opinion of whether or not Gatsby is a tragic hero?

27. A. Explain the symbolism of the billboard with the eyes of Dr. T. J. Eckleburg that brood over the wasteland of *The Great Gatsby*. What symbolic meaning does the "valley of ashes" represent?

    B. Discuss any two image clusters and any two symbols from *The Great Gatsby*. Connect them to any relevant theme or topic from the novel.

28. Briefly explain how Fitzgerald, through the narrator Nick's musings, reveals his feelings about America. Toward the end of the novel after the murder of Gatsby, Nick's words are charged with symbolic meanings as he tries to find peace in Nature before leaving the East for his hometown in the Midwest:

    "Then I wandered down to the beach and sprawled out on the sand. . . . And as the moon rose higher the inessential houses began to melt away until gradually I became aware of the old island here that flowered once for Dutch sailors' eyes – a fresh, green breast of the new world. Its vanished trees, the trees that had made way for Gatsby's house, had once pandered in whispers to the last and greatest of all human dreams; for a transitory enchanted moment man must have held his breath in the presence of this continent, compelled into an aesthetic contemplation he neither understood nor desired, face to face for the last time in history with something commensurate to his capacity for wonder"(189).

29. Fitzgerald's narrative technique consists of

    a. frequent shifts not only from past to present, but also changes in perspective (for example, the opening lines of Chapter Nine of the novel)

b. use of two narrators – Nick Carraway (the main narrator) and Jordan Baker, who takes over the narrator's role for a short time in Chapter Four of the novel.

What is the impact of this technique? How is this style more effective than a straightforward, chronological narration by the same narrator?

30. A. Interpretation question: Write an interpretation of a complex passage from the novel, such as the opening of Chapter 2, the second-from-last paragraph of Chapter 8, or the novel's last three paragraphs.

B. Write an interpretation of Nick's dream that he describes toward the end of the novel. This dream is mentioned in the paragraph that starts with "Even when the East excited me most . . ." (page 184). Your interpretation should help the reader understand important events, themes, and characters in *The Great Gatsby*.

C. Fitzgerald has the reputation of handling romantic love and nostalgia particularly well. Point out and analyze from *The Great Gatsby* a few passages in which this talent of the author shows at its best.

31. In the 2013 film adaptation of the novel directed by Baz Luhrmann and starring Leonardo DiCaprio, the character of Gatsby's father is left out. What is gained or lost by that omission?

32. At the end of the same movie Nick gives the title of "Gatsby" to the story that he has told in the novel. Then, as an afterthought, he adds the words "The Great" before "Gatsby." What is significant about this modification of title as an afterthought?

Questions on Albert Camus' *The Stranger*

33. What is the function of the "robot woman" and the story of the Czech? Do they serve any thematic purpose in the novel? If you can perceive Camus' use of parallel sets of characters for comparison or contrast (discussed in this chapter), you can analyze that element of style to answer this question.

34. Camus' language on pp. 57-59 makes us feel that Meursault is fighting something. What is he fighting? How? Your answer should not be too literal. For example, do not say Meursault was fighting the sun unless you also explain what the sun symbolizes in the novel.

35. In Part One of his narrative, Meursault gives everything equal weight, not discriminating between what seems to us more important and less important details. Moreover, he does not establish connections between events in terms of any rational causality. Most of the time the sentences stand alone, unassisted by connecting, coordinating, or subordinating conjunctions such as "and," "because," "therefore," etc. What theme or idea could be connected with these elements in Camus' style?

36. In *Albert Camus and the Literature of Revolt*, John Cruickshank describes Camus' novel as a "complicated attempt to appear uncomplicated." Cite a few examples of Camus' above-mentioned method and show how your examples support Cruickshank's view. You may include in your discussion Camus' use of such artistic devices as narrative point of view, vocabulary, time, and tense. After citing each example, relate Camus' technique to the ends he wishes to achieve.

37. Write an interpretation of Camus' novel in the light of Jean-Paul Sartre's following words, often cited as an important belief in existentialism: "Existence precedes essence." If it is compatible with your thinking, you may interpret the novel along the following lines:

Part One of the novel is primarily descriptive. Meursault is busy living his life without reflecting on the significance or meaning of anything. His consciousness has to catch up with events. He is preoccupied with each passing moment, unconcerned with the past or the future. In this way the first half of the novel goes with the word "Existence" in Sartre's quotation. In Part Two, Meursault tries to make some sense of his life and of life in general. The novel's second part, thus, is evaluative in nature and corresponds to the word "essence" in Sartre's quotation. Give details from the novel to support this interpretation, or write your own analysis of the novel's structure.

38. At one point in Meursault's trial, his attorney says, "everything is true and nothing is true!" (p.91). Interpret this statement as it relates to the novel.

39. Toward the end of the novel, Meursault says: "The little robot woman was just as guilty as the Parisian woman Masson married, or as Marie, who had wanted me to marry her" (p.121). What are these women "guilty" of? For this question, you may seek help from the passage that starts with these words: "Throughout the whole absurd life I'd lived, a dark wind had been rising toward me from somewhere deep in my future." (121)

40. Demonstrate how Meursault's story describes a process of integration, estrangement, and reintegration. You may consider points such as these for inclusion in your interpretation: Up until the trial scene, Meursault feels integrated with life around him; he thinks he is just like everybody. However, the truth – in the form of people's response in the courtroom – makes him feel like crying. After this estrangement that is forced upon him, he makes an attempt at reintegration at the end of his narrative. Does he succeed? With what forces does he seek integration? With impersonal Nature and universe? With the society that has condemned him? Or with both? In his final attempt to reintegrate, Meurault, "for the first time," opened himself to the "gentle indifference of the world," and found it "so much like myself – so like a brother." This realization makes him feel "that I had been happy and that I was happy again." However, the very next sentence – the novel's last sentence – is enigmatic and defies facile interpretation: "For everything to be consummated, for me to feel less alone, I had only to wish that there be a large crowd of spectators the day of my execution and that they greet me with cries of hate." After persuading himself to feel a fraternal bond with all people, why does he wish to hear "cries of hate" from them?

41. In the light of E. M. Forster's view of novels' superior endings that open out instead of closing in, do you think that *The Stranger* fits that criterion? Do you think the novel's ending is an opening out or closing in?

42. Capturing the essence of Camus' view of Meursault (expressed by Camus in his "Preface" to *The Stranger*), Germaine Bree concludes that Meursault's end is an apotheosis – "a descent into the sea and the sun, a reintegration into the cosmos (Bree 116). In the light of this remark, evaluate Meursault as a different kind of tragic hero. Usually, the word "apotheosis" is used to describe the hero's ascent toward a higher form life after his or her death. How is "descent" an appropriate word to describe Meursault's transformation?

43. Relate the following remark to a scene or a character from *The Stranger*: "The illogic of life is such that it must be lived forward but understood backward."

44. To the following list, add a few more examples from the novel to demonstrate Camus' "less is more" stylistic trait.

A. **"The days had been long since she stopped writing"** (p. 115). These words suggest Meursault's depth of feeling for Marie, expressed in an understated manner.

B. **"No one can imagine what nights in prison are like"** (p. 81). That is all Meursault says about his nights in prison. He leaves the rest to our imagination. **This style is also known as showing by hiding.**

45. Had you been in Meursault's place, what would you have said in your defense in the trial scene without compromising any of his principles?

46. A. Camus writes about his hero Sisyphus's plan to escape death in *The Myth of Sisyphus*. In *The Stranger* (pages 108-109) Meursault thinks of escaping the guillotine." Draw a parallel between these two protagonists' state of mind as they face their unacceptable punishment. The text of "The Myth of Sisyphus" is in Chapter Nine.

B. Compare Meursault's thoughts in the scene described above with Peyton Farquhar's thoughts at the moment just before his execution. Farquhar is a character in Ambrose Bierce's short story "An Occurrence at the Owl Creek Bridge," which you can read online. A film version of the story is also available.

47. Interpret Meursault's following words carefully to arrive at a conclusion as to whether he feels any remorse at taking the life of a human being: "He [the judge] simply asked me in the same weary tone, if I was sorry for what I had done. I thought about it for a minute and said that more than sorry I felt kind of annoyed" (p. 70).

48. Write an interpretation of the novel's last three sentences:

"As if that blind rage had washed me clean, rid me of hope; for the first time, in that night alive with signs and stars, I opened myself to the gentle indifference of the world. Finding it so much like myself – so like a brother, really – I felt that I had been happy and that I was happy again. For everything to be consummated, for me to feel less alone, I had only to wish that there be a large crowd of spectators the day of my execution and that they greet me with cries of hate."

49. "Rational explanations are mere rationalizations; the truth escapes us." Give two examples from *The Stranger* to support this statement by the critic Victor Brombert.

50. In the voice of Marie (that is, imagining yourself as Marie) write a letter to Meursault, expressing Marie's innermost feelings for him and about life in general. Try to capture Marie's values and outlook on life. This letter need not be limited to but should include your inference as to the final stage of their relationship. What you write is imaginary but should reflect the two characters' personalities and values as revealed to us by Camus in the novel.

51. Point out a few similarities between Meursault and the two main characters (Daru and the unnamed Arab) in Camus' short story "The Guest" (Chapters Six and Ten). Whom does Meursault resemble more – Daru or the Arab? Support your analysis with relevant plot details.

52. Mention any three salient principles of existentialism. Relate them to characters, situations, and themes in Camus' novel.

53. Comparing *The Great Gatsby* and *The Stranger*:

A. Compare/contrast the use of the wind as a symbol in *The Great Gatsby* (pp. 12, 25, 86, 61, 114, 121, 159, 167, 170, and 185) with Camus' use of the "dark wind" (p. 121) in his novel.

B. Both Gatsby and Meursault **are stubborn** in their own ways. What are they stubborn about? How do you react to and judge this trait in them? Give supporting details from the two books.

Questions on E. M. Forster's *A Passage to India*

54. Had Mrs. Moore been at the trial of Dr. Aziz, what would she have said with regard to Adela's charge against Aziz? What would have been the effect of her testimony?

55. What is the meaning of the echo? How is it interpreted by various characters?

56. Do most of the characters ever find their way out of the challenging situation described by the narrator as the "muddle"?

57. Why did Adela accuse Dr. Aziz of assaulting her in the cave if she never really saw the attacker clearly?

58. Our lives seem to be ruled by random occurrences, but at times we can perceive the presence of a design behind them. Give relevant details from the novel to support these assertions.

59. Forster divides the novel in three parts – "Mosque," "Caves," and "Temple." What is their symbolic significance? How do these headings reflect the contents of those sections? Do they contribute toward the novel's thematic unity?

60. Irony and symbolism are considered Forster's notable stylistic traits. Give a few examples of them from the novel and comment on their effectiveness.

61. Read Pauline Kael's 1985 review of *A Passage to India*: www.npr.org/…/atc/…/kael/010904.**kael**.html. What part of her review do you find most helpful in furthering your understanding of Forster's novel?

Questions on book reviews

62. Using the book review instructions from this chapter, review a novel or a book of nonfiction of your choice. The opening pages of this chapter addressed the range and variety of fiction. You may be drawn to a novel because of its themes or because of the author's style of writing. The presence of both of these qualities is ideal. You will find many thoughtful and well-crafted works on almost every topic. To make your selection of novels, read book reviews in journals and newspapers.

Some books become instant classics in their genre. Among political novels, for example, *The Reluctant Fundamentalist* by Mohsin Hamid, *The Sorrow of War* by Bao Ninh, *Men in the Sun* by Ghassan Kanafani, and *What's the What* and *Zeitoun* by Dave Eggers gained immediate and immense popularity. When looking for a book of nonfiction, you can look at the list of best sellers maintained by prominent newspapers. For example, *Three Cups of Tea* by Greg Mortenson and David Relin was No. 1 on *New York Times'* best sellers' list for over 100 weeks. *Best Books of the Year* series is also a useful source for book selection. You may also wish to consult the 100-plus titles on Francine Prose's list of "Books to Be Read Immediately" in *Reading Like a Writer*.

Questions on essays based on research

63. Use a critic's words on any novel as a basis for your essay of about 500 words. You may either agree or disagree with the critic. If you agree, add your own views to strengthen the critic's position. If you

disagree, offer your dissenting opinion with supporting details. Use Gale Literature Resource Center to find an article of literary criticism.
http://www.pulaskitech.edu/library/content/DB_Search_Tips_Literature_Resource_Center.pdf.

64. You can use the web site <novelguide.com> to read about novels, plays, and short stories. You can select from these six items: summary, character profiles, metaphor analysis, theme analysis, top ten quotes, and biography.

     After reading the theme analysis of *The Great Gatsby,* add one or two important points to the novel's discussion in this chapter.
     http://www.novelguide.com/thegreatgatsby/themeanalysis.html.

65. Using the same web source, read the theme analysis of *Pride and Prejudice.* Select one or two points from this source to add to the novel's discussion of themes in this chapter.

66. On the same web site, read the summary and theme analysis of Toni Morrison's novel *Beloved.* Connect any of the novel's themes to any other literary work or movie.

67. Read online Herman Melville's short novel *Bartleby, the Scrivener*: http://www.bartleby.com/129/ The text is also available via this link: http://www.enotes.com/bartleby-scrivener-text/bartleby-scrivener-1. After reading the novel, watch the film adaptation of this work featuring Crispin Glover. Point out the differences between the movie and the novel to discuss what is gained and what lost in the novel-to-film transition.

68. Read either online or from a library book the chapter titled "A Pair of Tickets" from Amy Tan's novel *The Joy Luck Club* and demonstrate how this excerpt from Tan's novel can be viewed as reconciliation with a painful past to find peace. There are some journal essays on this selection in this chapter.

69. Explain the meaning of the title of Carlos Bulosan's novel *America Is in the Heart.*

70. Some of the scenes in this novel are quite wrenching and pull at the reader's heartstrings. Describe any two or three such scenes.

71. Point out a few scenes of blatant racism from the novel.

72. In Piri Thomas's novel *Down These Mean Streets,* the adolescent narrator, who is about to be sent to prison for a drug-related crime, is let go by the judge very unexpectedly. What is the effect on the narrator of this kind gesture on the judge's part?

73. Discuss Piri Thomas's novel as a chronicle of pain, redemption, and altruism.

74. In Richard Wright's "Library Card" (which is a chapter from his novel *Black Boy*), the young narrator has to borrow someone's library card to read books because at that time blacks were not allowed privileges, such as the library use. Why does the narrator choose an Irish Catholic to lend him the library card?

75. What is the impact of reading books on the narrator's mind? Does it make him happy or restless?

76. Identify the most suspenseful moment in "Library Card."

CHAPTER TWELVE

DRAMA

Required Background Knowledge: A Quick Overview

Compared to reading fiction and viewing movies, watching a play is a different experience. When reading fiction, we have the narrator's assistance to understand and interpret plot details, and we can read a work of fiction at our own pace. Neither the narrator's help nor the choice relating to pace is available to us when we are watching a live performance on stage or a movie in a theater. Plays are different from movies in that the scenes in movies are the result of many re-takes and directorial editing. What we see is the finished product. A play, on the other hand, in spite of repeated rehearsals, carries with it the risk of mistakes in a live performance, thus making it unique in this respect.

Like poetry, drama is also an ancient and complex form of literature. Dramatic works, such as tragedy, comedy, and tragicomedy follow certain conventions and patterns, familiarity with which is necessary to appreciate them. In the place of a narrator in fiction and a speaker in poetry, a play has only stage directions. Thornton Wilder, author of the classic play *Our Town,* noted that the action on stage occurs "in a perpetual present time. . . . In the theater, we are not aware of the intervening storyteller. The speeches arise from the characters in an apparently pure spontaneity. A play is what takes place. A novel is what one person tells us took place" (Barnet 9-10). Absence of the narrative voice makes extra demands on the reader and viewer. A brief overview of relevant background information is necessary to understand various aspects of drama. A more in-depth discussion of drama follows this brief survey. The discussion of various plays in this chapter contains enough plot details to make the points understandable even to those who are not familiar with those works.

Navigation Chart for this Chapter

In view of the vast scope and complex nature of the subject, use this navigation chart if you are unable to read the chapter from start to finish.

1. Use most of the background information and discussions of various theories of drama on an as-needed basis.

2. Be sure to fully understand the listed 15 elements that are considered central to the study of serious drama. This information appears early in the chapter.

3. Be able to distinguish between various forms of drama: tragedy, comedy, tragicomedy, absurdist plays, and other innovations.

4. Read the sample essays, including those on my website. They appear toward the end of the chapter, but you do not need to postpone reading them until then. After you have read item 2, read a tragic play, such as *Hamlet,* and then read a sample essay on it. In conjunction with item 3, read a comedy, tragicomedy, an absurdist play, or any other contemporary innovative play. Then read a sample essay. If time permits, try to read or watch at least one play from each era: classical Greek,[1] Shakespearean, and modern.

5. If a play assigned by your instructor is not discussed in the chapter, you can still apply this chapter's relevant content to that play. Theoretical principles are applicable to most plays, even when individual playwrights intentionally deviate from those principles. Since Shakespeare's *Hamlet* is the most discussed play, besides being a masterpiece of dramatic art, it receives its well-deserved attention in this chapter. Other plays discussed in this chapter are George Bernard Shaw's *Pygmalion*, Eugene O'Neill's one-act play *Before Breakfast*, his comedy *Ah Wilderness*, his tragic play *Long Day's Journey into Night*, Susan Glaspell's *Trifles*, Samuel Beckett's *Waiting for Godot*, Lorraine Hansberry's *A Raisin in the Sun*, Caryl Churchill's very brief play *Seven Jewish Children – A Play for Gaza*, and Wajahat Ali's *Domestic Crusaders*. Most dramatic works are stage plays with film adaptations. You can easily access them on the internet.

6. Master these three sources of theories of drama: Hamlet's words on drama, A. C. Bradley's chapter on "The Substance of Shakespearean Tragedy," and Arthur Miller's essay "Tragedy and the Common Man." Answer the questions that are based on them.

7. Besides the sources listed in item 6, familiarize yourself with views and practices of prominent playwrights, such as Eugene O'Neill, Tennessee Williams, Harold Pinter, Bertolt Brecht, and others.

8. When writing a paper, pay attention to the wording of the assignment.

---

[1] You may read the entire Greek play *Oedipus the King* by Sophocles online: http://classes.mit.edu/Sophocles/oedipus.pl.txt as well as a summary and analysis: http://sparknotes.com/drama/Oedipus/

Brief History of Drama

Greek Drama

Basic background information on Greek drama is readily available in numerous books. A succinct presentation is in Michael Meyer's excellent anthology *Bedford Introduction to Literature*, to which I am indebted for some of the information on Greek origins of drama. The word *drama* comes from the Greek word that means "to perform" or "to do." Herein lies drama's chief distinction from other forms of literature: even though a play can be read as a book, it is primarily written for performance with the help of actors.

Origins

Fifth century B.C. was the high point of Greek drama, which originated in religious festivals in the honor of Dionysus, the god of wine and fertility. It included dancing and singing to celebrate Dionysian legends. Plays by Aeschylus, Sophocles, and Euripides were performed in contests at the festivals. Only a few plays have survived from this over 500-year time span. The importance of plays to Greek society is obvious from the fact that the state contributed to their funding. Amphitheaters were built into hillsides to create raised rows to accommodate more than fourteen thousand people. An *orchestra* or "dancing place" was in the middle, where the *chorus* (about 12 men) sang and danced. The chorus commented on the characters' actions and thus molded the audience response. The poet Thespis added an actor who was not part of choral singing and dancing. Aeschylus added a second actor and Sophocles a third. These additions made it possible for drama to stage conflicts and complex relationships. The two or three male actors played all the roles. Sometimes equivalent of divine intervention was used in the form of godly figures that were lowered onto the stage with the help of mechanical devices to resolve complicated situations. The Latin phrase *deus ex machina* (god out of the machine) describes any implausible and thus artistically inferior, forced resolution in a story.

Enormous distance between the audience and actors might have necessitated large masks, padded costumes, and elevator shoes, which made the actors larger than life. A typical Greek play consisted of five parts: (1) The *prologue* was an opening speech or dialogue to set the stage for the play's action. (2) In *Parodos*, the chorus gave its perspective on the prologue. (3) The play's main body consisted of several episodes (*episodia*) to dramatize through dialogue the play's conflicts. (4) Each episode was followed by a choral ode (*stasimon*) that interpreted the preceding dialogue. (5) The *exodus* offered the resolution, following the final episode and *stasimon*.

Period between Classical Greek and Shakespearean Drama

With minor differences in matters of form, the Romans continued to adhere to the classical Greek idea of drama. However, drama declined in Europe after the fall of Rome during 5th and 6th centuries. In the years 400 to 900 A.D. there were no dramatic productions. Only minstrels and other itinerant entertainers like acrobats and jugglers kept the art of performance alive. The excesses of Roman productions prompted the Catholic Church to suppress drama. In the absence of state sponsorship, there were no festivals to bring people together as had been the case in Greek and earlier Roman times.

The tenth century witnessed the revival of theater by the Church. Parts of the Gospels were incorporated into the Mass as dialogue, resulting in mystery plays, miracle plays, and morality plays. The emphasis in these plays was on religious instruction rather than entertainment. Mystery plays were dramatizations of Biblical stories, such as *The Second Shepherd's Play* (c. 1400-1450) which concerns Christ's nativity. Saints' lives became the source of miracle plays, for example, *Saint Mary Magdalene* (first printed in 1566)

Morality plays were allegories with virtues and vices as characters to show the way to salvation as in *Everyman* (fifteenth century). During the middle ages, an important change occurred when trade guilds replaced members of the clergy as performers outside the church, thus leading to the secularization of drama.

Shakespearean Drama (Late 16th to early 17th centuries)

During Shakespeare's time, neither the church nor trade guilds in England patronized the theater. It was, therefore, necessary to have an enclosed space with controlled entrance to charge an admission fee. Playwrights and actors had to be on their toes to attract people. Elizabethan theatres could accommodate up to 2500 people. Sources of this information are drawings, building contracts, and stage directions. People of all tastes and classes came to these plays. Some went for intellectual stimulation while others went in search of adventure. Such gatherings sometimes became dens of illegal activity, violence, gambling, and prostitution. Strict laws forced some theaters to locate themselves outside the city's jurisdiction. The Globe (associated with Shakespeare), for instance, was built on the south bank of the Thames River.

Tragic and Serious Drama

There is nothing esoteric about tragic drama. Anyone who has felt that life can sometimes run counter to one's desires can relate to this literary form. Enhanced awareness of life's mysteries and spiritual enlightenment are among its educational elements. Characters in a tragedy face suffering and death with dignity. Since these two facts are the unavoidable lot of every human being, the therapeutic value of tragic drama is self-evident. Because education, growth, and final recognition of some of the mystical elements of life are important elements of tragedy, sudden death in auto accidents, plane crashes, fires, shootings, etc., are not suitable subjects for literary tragedy, howsoever painful such events may be.

There is an abundance of literature on this subject. To begin with, it is helpful to know a few of the prevailing concepts of tragedy, which has been regarded as the highest form of literature over the centuries, even though different eras have given different meanings to tragic drama. To Aristotle, tragedy meant serious drama with a heavy moral and ethical emphasis without necessarily involving the death of the protagonist. Most discussions of tragedy begin with Aristotle's famous definition: "Tragedy is a representation of an action, which is serious, complete in itself, and of a certain length; it is expressed in speech made beautiful in different ways in different parts of the play; it is acted, not narrated; and by exciting pity and fear it gives a healthy relief to such emotions" (Lucas 25). Aristotle gives us not only a definition and function of tragedy but also tells us what form and linguistic style it bears and how it communicates its themes. In the Middle Ages, tragedy meant any story with an unhappy ending, usually in the form of a narrative. Thus in the Middle Ages, tragedy's connection with drama was forgotten. Aristotle had mentioned in his famous definition of tragedy that tragic action has to be represented in a dramatic, not a narrative form. During Shakespeare's time and since then, tragic drama has often involved the death of the protagonist.

By writing his masterpiece of tragic drama, *Death of a Salesman*, and its accompanying essay "Tragedy and the Common Man," Arthur Miller eloquently and convincingly demonstrated that the highly placed individuals, such as kings, queens, princes, and generals do not have a monopoly on heroism. Common people can also meet the qualifications of a tragic hero. Amazingly, it took humanity over 2000 years to come up with this idea, and the credit for this achievement clearly goes to Miller. As you will see when you read his brief essay "Tragedy and the Common Man," with the exception of this view relating to the stature of the hero, Miller retained all other essential principles of classical and Shakespearean traditions – a tribute to the enduring nature and relevance of the classical theory of drama.

Elements Central to Tragic Drama

After an overview of the origins and evolution of theories relating to serious drama, the next important requirement is an understanding of the elements that are central to tragic drama.

1. In the classical tradition, which Shakespeare also follows, the **tragic hero/heroine** is a highly placed individual because the impact of the fall of an important person is felt far and wide.

2. The hero/heroine has a **flaw** (Greek word: *hamartia*). Aristotle describes the protagonist as someone "not pre-eminently virtuous or just, whose misfortune, however, is brought upon him not by vice or depravity, but by some error of judgment" (Leech 1-2). The phrase "error of judgment" seems to make the flaw entirely character-related. However, in many instances, the surrounding events and circumstances equally contribute to the disaster in which the protagonist perishes. No matter what action the hero takes, the tragic outcome seems inescapable – as in *Oedipus the King* and to some extent in *Hamlet*. Therefore, a definition of *hamartia* that links the hero's failing with the circumstances and with misunderstanding of some kind would be reasonable. Shakespeare adds something to the theory of tragedy in this respect, for in Shakespeare the tragic flaw sometimes is a virtue carried to excess. An instance is Hamlet's perfectionism.

3. **Conflict** between the protagonist and the antagonist is the essence of drama. In *Hamlet*, for example, the conflict is between Hamlet and Claudius, who usurps the throne by secretly killing Hamlet's father.

4. **Resistance** on the part of the hero against overwhelming odds is essential to the spirit of tragedy. Even when the odds are impossible, the hero has to continue his or her struggle. In most tragic plays, the hope of the hero's victory is kept alive almost until the inevitable end. When viewing or

reading *Hamlet* and *Oedipus*, the audience never rules out the hero's victory until the end. Such hope keeps the audience's interest level high.

5. **Reversal** (Greek word: *peripeteia*) which is an important source of the tragic feeling, means an unexpected turn in the hero's fortunes. The character's actions end up having an effect that is the opposite of what was intended. Hamlet thinks he has everything under control for his just revenge and drives his sword through the curtain to kill Claudius, but ends up murdering Polonious, the king's spy, who had been hiding behind the arras in the Queen's bed chamber. After this unintended murder, Hamlet is entirely at the mercy of Claudius. Similarly, Oedipus thinks that he is running away from his dreadful fate, whereas, it turns out that he has been galloping toward it. Both Hamlet and Oedipus end up in situations that they had never expected.

6. The hero in Shakespeare's plays is fated to die, which is not always the case with Greek tragedy. When it does happen, death leads to the hero's **apotheosis** in classical tragedy. In Shakespeare, there is a feeling that the hero's spirit returns to the exalted ultimate power that rules the world of tragedy and that uses the hero as an instrument of its moral design.

7. At the end of a tragic play, the audience/reader experiences a **cleansing** (Greek word: *catharsis*) of the turmoil caused by the spectacle and action of tragedy. In Aristotle's *Poetics*, two emotions – pity and fear – are regarded as characteristic of a tragic play. We feel pity for the hero's suffering, which often seems excessive and disproportionate to his/her flaw. The feeling of fear is both for the hero and for ourselves (the audience), because the same afflictions that descend upon the hero could be our fate. To these two emotions we can add admiration and compassion for the hero.

8. The feeling of peace and acquiescence, which is connected to catharsis, results from the **affirmation of human values** in the characters' dignified stance and fearless pursuit of truth, as happens not just in *Hamlet* and *Oedipus* but in all great tragedies.

9. In the classical tradition, **fate** plays a crucial part. In Sophocles' *Oedipus the King*, an oracle prophesies to Oedipus that he is destined to kill his father and marry his mother. Oedipus does everything possible to run away from that fate, even leaving Corinth and his royal family. However, through inscrutable happenings, he ends up doing exactly what he thought he had been running away from. In Shakespeare, fate also plays a significant role, but the cause of tragedy is traceable to the character's personality to a much larger extent than in classical Greek drama. In Shakespeare, **character** *is* sometimes destiny.

10. Feeling of **a sense of waste** of great potential exists simultaneously with a sense of elation at the strength of the human spirit in a tragic play. In "The Substance of Shakespearean Tragedy," included later in this chapter, A. C. Bradley discusses this topic at some length.

11. **Discovery or recognition** is an important part of the conclusion. It refers to the moment when the protagonist finally understands an elusive, painful mystery and accepts the inevitable with admirable courage. Hamlet eventually realizes that "There's a divinity that shapes our ends,/Rough-hew them how we will" (V, ii, 10-11). And Oedipus finally accepts the painfully mysterious unfolding

and coming true of the dreadful prophesy about him. Both *Oedipus the King* and *Hamlet*, besides numerous other tragic plays, are good examples of this discovery.

12. Tragedy serves a **therapeutic function** as well: It provides a socially acceptable release of sadness, fear, and similar emotions. Moreover, watching the gigantic suffering of tragic characters dwarfs our personal, hopefully smaller, tragedies.

13. The classical tradition gives primary importance to **plot** as the main ingredient of tragedy. In Shakespeare, however, **characters** tend to assume the chief significance.

14. **The three unities** – of action, time and place – are observed in the classical tradition. The unity of action means that the play's action should move in a straight line without distracting subplots. This convention also disallows mixture of tragedy and comedy. The concept of the unity of time has differing interpretations. To some critics it means that the duration of time represented on stage through plot should not exceed 24 hours, whereas others playwrights, would like to limit it to as few as three hours – same as the approximate length of the performance. The unity of place advises against too many changes of scenes. Needless imitation of these classical unities makes little sense. However, their judicious observance does contribute to a play's cohesiveness and intensity. Shakespeare and many modern dramatists, however, often refuse to observe these unities. And for a good reason: their observance puts too much restraint on the creative imagination and limits the play's scope into extremely narrow confines of space and time. Shakespeare observes these unities perfectly in *The Tempest*, which shows that he could follow the tradition if he wanted. Prominent American playwrights, such as Arthur Miller, Eugene O'Neill, and Tennessee Williams appear more classical Greek than Shakespearean in their observance of the three unities.

15. An important element in tragedy is the **unity of impression**, which Allardyce Nicoll explains in *The Theory of Drama*: ". . . every great drama shows a subordination of the particular elements of which it is composed to some central spirit by which it is inspired . . . [;] any drama which admits emotion not so in subordination to the main spirit of the play will thereby be blemished" (Nicoll 57).

Other Important Discussions of Tragic Drama

1. Shakespeare's own words from *Hamlet*, Act III, scene ii, lines 1-47, included in this chapter.
2. "The Substance of Shakespearean Tragedy" from A. C. Bradley's influential book, *Shakespearean Tragedy*, discussed in this chapter and available on my website.
3. Joseph Wood Krutch: "The Tragic Fallacy" from *The Modern Temper*, discussed in this chapter.
4. Arthur Miller's short essay, "Tragedy and the Common Man" (also included in this chapter).

Answering the questions given in the "Test on Theories of Tragedy" later in this chapter will enable you to check your familiarity with the preceding information. Moreover, listening to audio lectures and viewing videotapes such as the following will vastly increase your ability to evaluate and enjoy plays:

1. *Shakespearean Tragedy* (Films for the Humanities production): This lucid introduction to tragedy in the form of a video lecture goes well with A.C. Bradley's already mentioned chapter on "The Substance of Shakespearean Tragedy."

2. C. B. Purdom: " Shakespeare and the Fundamental Law of Drama." Purdom's lecture is a good introduction to the theory of tragedy. It includes a discussion of Aristotle's definition of tragedy as well as recognition of Shakespeare's contributions to the theory of drama.

3. Maynard Mack's four video lectures (1/2 hour each) on the Elizabethan world and *Hamlet*.

4. Moelwyn Merchant and Terence Hawkes: "*Hamlet* as a Play of Revenge" (audio lecture).

5. *The Great Hamlets*, Programs 1 and 2 (Films for the Humanities and Sciences production). In these two programs, famous actors interpret major scenes of the play.

6. There are some good audio lectures on practically every major play.[2]

Comedy

The word *comedy* is reserved for plays that have a happy ending. Movement from unhappiness to happiness is characteristic of comedy. In the "Structure of Comedy," Northrop Frye points out that happy endings in comedies do not impress us as true, but as desirable, and they are brought about by manipulation" (Barnet 79). Christopher Fry expresses a similar view: "Comedy is an escape, not from truth but from despair: a narrow escape into faith. It believes in a universal cause of delight" (Barnet 68). Comic drama lacks the high seriousness of tragedy but brings to dramatic art the medicine of laughter and the scalpel of satire, wit, and irony. Comedy presents life not as it might be but as it often is.

Shunning idealism, comic characters often subscribe to the credo declared in Moliere's *Amphitryon*: "I prefer a convenient vice to a tiresome virtue." Louis Kronenberger sums up this essential difference between the two forms of drama: "Tragedy is always lamenting the Achilles tendon, the destructive flaw in man; but comedy, in a sense, is always looking for it. . . . In tragedy men aspire to more than they can achieve; in comedy, they pretend no more" (Kronenberger 4-5).

In keeping with its comic intentions, comedy may use any devices that provoke laughter: sarcasm, understatement, paradox, irony, caricature, parody, burlesque, repartee, humorous juxtaposition, etc. Susanne Langer defines comedy as "an art form that arises naturally wherever people are gathered to celebrate life, in spring festivals, triumphs, birthdays, weddings, or initiations. . . . the rhythm of sheer vitality makes comedy happy" (Langer in Felheim 244).

At their best, comic plays, like those of Shakespeare and George Bernard Shaw, always go beyond laughter. After initial distancing devices to make the audience feel detached from and superior to the characters, such writers often introduce a sudden and dramatic identification between the audience and character to make the former realize they have been laughing at themselves. Foibles of humanity are thus exposed and ridiculed while serious philosophical questions emerge from the plays simultaneously.

---

[2]At this point in the chapter, you should either read or watch a play that embodies some of the principles of tragic drama.

Shaw, whom Northrop Frye calls "the greatest comic dramatist of the age" (Frye 138), explains this mixture of instruction with laughter:

"If I make you laugh at yourself, remember that my business as a classic writer of comedies is to 'chasten morals with ridicule'; and if I sometimes make you feel like a fool, remember that I have by the same action cured your folly" (Shaw iv).

In distinguishing comedy from tragedy, Horace Walpole's words are still illuminating: "This world is a comedy to those that think, a tragedy to those that feel." Detached thinking, both the dramatist's and the audience's, is the way of comedy. In the words of Henri Bergson, "The comic demands something like a momentary anesthesia of the heart" (Felheim 215). Tragedy, however, engages the feelings and demands an involvement and identification between the audience and the protagonist. Whereas tragedy leads to an awareness of the protagonist's isolation, comedy points to the individual's connection with the mainstream of humanity. Northrop Frye perceptively observed that the "resolution of comedy comes . . . from the audience's side of the stage; in a tragedy, it comes from some mysterious world on the opposite side" (Frye in Felheim 72). The two forms of drama also differ in characterization: "Comedy, unlike tragedy, seems to move logically up toward the final curtain call in which all the characters are equally applauded" (Frye 139). Yet another distinction between the two forms of drama, noted by Bergson, is that "every comic character is a *type*" unlike the highly individualized characters in tragedy. Bergson claims that "there could be no better definition of comedy" (Felheim 229).

In *Anatomy of Criticism*, Northrop Frye has noted a recurrent feature of Shakespeare's romantic comedies: the play's action moves from the ordinary world of discord to "the green world" – the Forest of Arden in *As You Like It*, Windsor Forest in *The Merry Wives of Windsor*, and the pastoral, mythical world of Bohemia in *The Winter's Tale*. Among the plays that use magic and enchantment, the action in *The Tempest* moves forcefully to a magical island, on which the unpleasant past is rectified, and in *A Midsummer Night's Dream*, the setting for most of the action is the fairyland itself. The movement from the "world of experience into the ideal world of innocence and romance" (Frye, *Anatomy* 182) culminates in the metamorphosis of the comic resolution and the final return to the normal world. The basis of a typical comic plot thus turns out to be "an erotic intrigue blocked by some opposition and resolved by a twist in the plot known as "discovery" or recognition. . . . In Shakespeare . . . the comic context is usually presented as a collision of two societies" (Frye in Weil 140).

Tracing Shakespearean romantic comedy's origin to the tradition of the seasonal ritual play, Frye sees in such plays the celebration of the victory of summer over winter. He regards such plays not as escapist but as an embodiment of deep human longing for a better life:

"Thus Shakespearean comedy illustrates, as clearly as any *mythos* we have, the archetypal function of literature in visualizing the world of desire, not as an escape from 'reality' but as the genuine form of the world that human life tries to imitate" (Frye 184).

In essence, Frye's words about Shakespeare's romantic comedy are also applicable to other Shakespearean works that go by the name of "dark comedies" or "problem plays" but have a happy ending. In *Measure for Measure*, for example, the world of magic, enchantment, and pastoral peace is conspicuously absent. The action of the play transpires in a city that is marked by lawlessness and violation of sexual ethics. In the conflict between virtue and vice, between love and lust, it is the former that comes out victorious. However, the transgressors are not destroyed; they are saved and reformed. It seems that Shakespeare has secularized and urbanized the pastoral impulse in *Measure for Measure*, for the action does not move away from Vienna; rather Vienna itself is transformed into a better place with the good-hearted Duke assuming godlike powers of omnipresence and omnipotence – powers that he needs to create happiness out of potential disaster.[3]

Tragicomedy

As its name suggests, tragicomedy is a hybrid form of drama, combining elements of tragedy with comedy and allowing the dramatist greater freedom than either of the other two varieties. With a few exceptions, the works of most contemporary authors, such as Samuel Beckett, Eugene Ionesco, Harold Pinter, and Luigi Pirandello, can be classified as tragicomedies. Some plays are more accurately described as "problem plays" because they deal with a serious problem and maintain a delicate balance between comedy and potential tragedy. Lorraine Hansberry's popular play *A Raisin in the Sun*, discussed at some length below, exemplifies this variety of drama.

It should be noted that tragicomedy is not a new form. Shakespeare wrote many plays that are tragicomedies – plays that have serious thought content but end happily. However, as the following discussion will show, differences between Shakespearean tragicomedy and modern seriocomic plays are striking. *The Tempest* and *Measure for Measure* are two prominent examples of Shakespearean tragicomedy. Both plays maintain a delicate balance between tragedy and comedy. Both have the potential for tragedy but end happily. In *The Tempest*, the rightful Duke of Milan (Prospero) and his daughter (Miranda) are set adrift on the sea in a rickety boat by Prospero's brother, who usurps the throne. Prospero and Miranda are expected to drown soon. However, as it often happens in comedy, Nature intervenes favorably for the protagonist: a storm carries Prospero and his daughter to an enchanted island, on which new bonds are established (as between Miranda and Ferdinand) and old, broken ties (as between Prospero and his brother) are mended to make reconciliations possible.

In *Measure for Measure*, young Claudio almost loses his life for getting his betrothed Julia pregnant before their marriage. In fact the stern deputy – Angelo – to whom the Duke of Vienna entrusts the affairs of the state during the Duke's supposed visit abroad, orders Claudio's execution. However, the Duke does not leave Vienna. Disguised as a friar, he oversees the conduct of his deputy and his people. With help from Isabella (one of Shakespeare's strongest and brightest female characters), he saves the play from becoming a tragedy, intervening at the right time to save several lives. At the end he shows merciful justice to people who have transgressed the harsh laws of the state. Both plays by Shakespeare end with wedding bells.

---

3. At this point in the chapter, you should either watch or read a comedy.

The following distinction between Shakespearean and contemporary tragicomedy appropriately sums up this topic:

"From tragedy . . . tragicomedy takes the movement but not the disturbance of the feelings, the pleasure and not the sadness, the danger but not the death. From comedy, it takes laughter that is not excessive, modest amusement, feigned difficulty, happy reversal, and above all, the comic order. Speaking of the style proper to tragicomedy . . . its norm [is] combined not with the grave as in a tragedy, but with the polished" (Nagarajan xxxi).

Other Forms of Modern Drama

In addition to tragicomedy, modern drama assumes several other forms that are discussed in this section. Exercises at the end of this chapter ask you to apply theoretical knowledge of modern drama to specific plays. After completing a few of those exercises, you will have a better grasp of the general principles that are now introduced.

Dialectical Theater

The German playwright Bertolt Brecht's dialectic theater made a clean break with conventional drama in many significant ways. This is how the drama critic John Lahr describes Brecht's approach:

"It was a theater that aspired to go beyond tragedy to action. Brecht wanted a theatrical event that did not dramatize Man as powerless in the vise of Fate; but manipulated by society yet capable of mastering it. . . . [The] actor in a Brecht play must not lose himself in his role. His actions must shade in the character while never allowing the audience to forget that theater is artificial" (Lahr xi).

Brecht's anti-illusionist theater stressed that the audience is not to be spellbound and that empathetic identification with characters is not the goal; rather the goal is detachment so that dialectical exchange can occur. "Through every facet of stagecraft, Brecht was trying to build up the public's intellectual muscle to understand and sustain the Marxist revolution" (Lahr xi).

Absurdist Drama

Another popular new form is the absurdist drama. *Waiting for Godot* by Irish dramatist Samuel Beckett (1906-1989) discussed below at some length, is a good example. In Arnold Hinchliffe's view, this play, first produced in 1955, heralds the beginning of the new theater and firmly established the theater of the absurd. It influenced almost all succeeding playwrights. Harold Pinter, the Nobel laureate of 2005, admired Beckett and admitted to his influence.

Existential Plays

The French playwright and philosopher Jean Paul Sartre (1905-1980) is the chief proponent of existentialism. In *Existentialism*, William Kauffman links the existentialist authors only in terms of refusal:

"The refusal to belong to any school of thought; the repudiation of the adequacy of any body of beliefs whatever, and especially of systems; and a marked dissatisfaction with traditional philosophy as superficial, academic, and remote from life – that is the heart of Existentialism" (Kauffman in Hinchliffe 27).

The Angry Theater

In any discussion of the new theater, the "Angry" theater and the theater of "Cruelty" deserve at least a brief mention. Tracing the origins of these movements in drama, Hinchliffe tells us that the "Angry" dramatists were as angry with what the theater was doing as with life around them. Their importance is in their social concerns – the Bomb, the Cold War, and global starvation, in particular. In *Anger and After*, John Russell Taylor regards John Osborne's *Look Back in Anger* (1956) as the central work of the "Angry" theater genre. This is how he sums up the play's conclusion:

"Faced at last with a really effective example of his own handiwork, Jimmy quails, and at last he and Alison are united again in their own idyllic world of bears and squirrels, content, perhaps, never to make it as human beings in the real world around" (Taylor 115).

The Theater of Cruelty

The theater of "Cruelty," another new-genre variety with Antonin Artaud as its central practitioner reflects, in Hinchliffe's words, "the condition of man faced with the unrelenting malignancy of the incomprehensible cosmic powers that govern him" (Hinchliffe 26).

More on the Theater of the Absurd

Since the theater of the absurd has come to dominate the modern scene, it deserves a more detailed treatment. In his influential work *The Theater of the Absurd*, Martin Esslin captures the essence of this school of drama:

"The Theater of the Absurd . . . bravely faces up to the fact that for those to whom the world has lost its central explanation and meaning, it is no longer possible to accept art forms still based on the continuation of standards and concepts that have lost their validity; that is, the possibility of knowing laws of conduct and ultimate values, as deducible from a firm foundation of revealed certainty about the purpose of man in the universe" (Esslin cited in Hinchliffe 29-30).

Notable is this succinct summation of an important feature of the theater of the absurd by Hinchliffe: "Life is not so much absurd as it is a game that can be sinister, savage, pathetic, compassionate, and comic. . . . Contemporary drama is a kind of comedy that teases and troubles the audience while it makes it laugh" (33).

Samuel Beckett's *Waiting for Godot*

Act I: http://samuel-beckett.net/Waiting_for_Godot_Part1.html
Act II: http://samuel-beckett.net/Waiting_for_Godot_Part2.html

Because of its pivotal position in the new theater, Irish playwright Samuel Beckett's *Waiting for Godot* merits a closer look. Its plot details are basic and simple. The two main characters, Vladimir and Estragon, live out their sterile existence from day to day, contemplating suicide and waiting for Godot, who might never come and of whom – should he ever come – the two tramps don't know what they would ask. As is often the case in absurdist drama, the godlike faculty of reason, instead of bringing enlightenment, leads to confusion and obfuscation. An important character, Lucky's long speech, which is supposed to symbolize the breakdown of logic, is a classic demonstration of the inadequacy of reason to explain the human condition and human destiny.

In such plays human beings are, indeed, reduced to the level of animal existence: Vladimir and Estragon live on carrots and turnips in a desert-like place (a desolate country road) stripped of all veneer of civilization. However, the characters in the play do not have the luxury of animal freedom to live an instinctual life. Something has destroyed their capacity to feel anything but pain and despair. Estragon receives beatings daily from the anonymous crowd referred to as "they" in the play. Both characters move in circles. They have made no progress by the end of the play. They say the same mechanical lines, do the same mechanical chores, and sometimes even complete and anticipate each other's lines, indicating that they have been doing this routine for a very long time and will probably go on with it forever.

The torture that Estragon's boots (symbolic of man-made civilization) inflict on his feet strengthens the feeling that civilization's restrictions have become painful for individuals, but simple return to nature is not possible: Estragon cannot discard the boots even though they cause him great pain.

Such plays raise profound questions about the place of human beings in the universe, about their responsibility, and about their desperate need to create hope. Existential nothingness is a central issue in contemporary absurdist drama, and in Beckett's play, Vladimir and Estragon are humanity stripped of its material comforts that cover up its essential nothingness. In the words of Eugene Ionesco, a prominent writer of the drama of the absurd, "cut off from his religious, metaphysical, and transcendental roots, man is lost; all his actions become senseless, absurd, useless" (Ionesco 257). Bereft of the faith in divine grace, the characters in contemporary plays can rely only on their own inner strength and give their lives their own meaning and purpose. Such plays, in this way, maintain a delicate balance between hope and despair.

To grasp yet another essential feature of contemporary absurdist tragicomedy, we have Ionesco's own words used in the context of discussing his play, *The Chairs*:

> I have tried to deal . . . with emptiness, with frustration, with this world, at once fleeting and crushing. The characters I have used are not fully conscious of their spiritual rootlessness, but they feel it instinctively and emotionally (N. Y. Times, 6-1-58).

An In-Depth Look at Theories and Practices of Serious Drama

For easier understanding of the evolving concepts of drama, it would be helpful to either read or watch a tragicomedy, an absurdist play, or any other modern play.

After a quick survey of drama since its inception to the present, the next step is to study the sources that are considered central to various theories of drama. Three essential sources are discussed in this order:

1. Shakespeare's own words,
2. British literary scholar A. C. Bradley's articulation of Shakespeare's theory of tragedy, and
3. American playwright Arthur Miller's "Tragedy and the Common Man."

Shakespeare's and Miller's views come in small packages; however, Bradley's chapter on "The Substance of Shakespearean" is longer but equally important.

First Source of Theories of Serious Drama: Hamlet's Words

In a rare and precious scene, Shakespeare seems to be expressing his own theory of drama through Hamlet's words to the players in Act III, scene ii, lines 1-47. Hamlet's words relate both to dramatic acting and to writing plays. Our focus here is on the words relating to the style/technique of writing and to the purpose of drama. Here are the relevant lines from the play:

[Scene II. The castle] Enter Hamlet and three of the Players.

Hamlet. Speak the speech, I pray you, as I pronounced it to you, trippingly on the tongue. But if you mouth it, as many of our players do, I had as lief the town crier spoke my lines. Nor do not saw the air too much with your hand, thus, but use all gently, for in the very torrent, tempest, and (as I may say) whirlwind of your passion, you must acquire and beget a temperance that may give it smoothness. O, it offends me to the soul to hear a robustious periwig-pated fellow tear a passion to tatters, to very rags, to split the ears of the groundlings, who for the most part are capable of nothing but inexplicable dumb shows and noise. I would have such a fellow whipped for o'erdoing Termagant. It out-herods Herod. Pray you avoid it.

Player. I warrant your honor.

Hamlet. Be not too tame neither, but let your own discretion be your tutor. Suit the action to the word, the word to the action, with this special observance, that you o'erstep not the modesty of nature. For anything so o'erdone is from the purpose of playing, whose end, both at the first and now, was and is, to hold, as 'twere, the mirror up to nature; to show virtue her own feature, scorn her own image, and the very age and body of the time his form and pressure.

Now, this overdone, or come tardy off, though it makes the unskillful laugh, cannot but make the judicious grieve, the censure of the which one must in your allowance o'erweigh a whole theater of others. O, there be players that I have seen play, and heard others praise, and that highly (not to speak it profanely), that neither having th' accent of Christians, nor the gait of Christian, pagan, nor man, have so strutted and bellowed that I have thought some of Nature's journeymen had made men, and not made them well, they imitated humanity so abominably.

Player. I hope we have reformed that indifferently with us, sir.

Hamlet. O, reform it altogether! And let those that play your clowns speak no more than is set down for them, for there be of them that will themselves laugh, to set on some quantity of barren spectators to laugh too, though in the meantime some necessary question of the play be then to be considered. That's villainous and shows a most pitiful ambition in the fool that uses it. Go make you ready. [*Exit Players*]

Interpreting Hamlet's Words

1. Emphasis on "temperance" in the midst of "whirlwind" of passion is the equivalent of understatement – something that modern authors value greatly. According to Hamlet, a style that is ostentatious (loud and noisy) can "tear a passion to tatters."

2. Style and substance, form and content should complement each other: "Suit the action to the word, the word to the action."

3. In emphatic words, Hamlet states the purpose of drama for all time: " to hold, as 'twere, the mirror up to nature." Plays should be realistic in addressing contemporary "pressures."

4. Drama should cater to the "judicious" and not lower itself just to make "the unskillful laugh."

5. The role of jesters and clowns should be carefully monitored so that they don't drown out "some necessary question of the play" in their eagerness to please "barren spectators."

Second Source of Theories of Serious Drama: "The Substance of Shakespearean Tragedy" by A. C. Bradley

As you read Bradley's chapter on my website, take notes on the topics and questions listed below.

What, according to Bradley, is the substance of Shakespearean tragedy? Your answer to this question should be in the form of brief summaries of the following points from Bradley's chapter. One condensed paragraph for each item would be sufficient for numbers 2 through 5. Numbers l, 6, and 7 may require longer answers. Use a combination of quotations from Bradley and summation in your own words. Cite those sentences that are especially well written to capture the major points.

You may answer the following items (1 through 7) either separately or in the form of an essay, numbering your paragraphs to go with each item. The essay format would require transitions between paragraphs when necessary. Your response to item l could be your introduction and thesis for the remaining items 2 through 7.

1. Definition of Shakespearean tragedy and its essential features. Include what Bradley considers to be two necessary statements about the "tragic fact" as Shakespeare represents it.

2. Shakespeare's use of the supernatural, of abnormal mental conditions (for example, insanity in Hamlet), and of chance.

3. Fundamental tragic traits of the protagonist.

4. "Impression of waste": its definition and source.

5. What is poetic justice? Does Shakespeare observe it in his plays? What reasons does Bradley give for Shakespeare's practice?

6. The "ultimate power" that rules the world of tragedy: Can this "ultimate power" be called "fate"? Is this ultimate power totally indifferent to good and evil, right and wrong? Does it suggest a moral order and a moral necessity for what happens? Finally, is this ultimate power inanimate, or is it capable of feeling?

7. It has been said that in Shakespeare's tragic plays "character is destiny." What does this expression mean? How does Shakespeare emphasize the importance of characters' deeds without discounting the contribution of circumstances?

Outstanding quotations from Bradley's lecture

You should read Bradley's "The Substance of Shakespearean Tragedy" on my website. Here are just a few quotations from his lecture to give you an idea of its pivotal importance in Shakespeare scholarship..

1. Shakespearean "tragedy brings before us a considerable number of persons (many more than the persons in a Greek play, unless the members of the Chorus are reckoned among them); but it is pre-eminently the story of one person, the 'hero,' or at most of two, the 'hero' and 'heroine'."

2. "The story . . . leads up to, and includes, the *death* of the hero. . . . [No] play at the end of which the hero remains alive is, in the full Shakespearean sense, a tragedy. . . . [The] story depicts also the troubled part of the hero's life which precedes and leads up to his death; and an instantaneous death occurring by "accident" in the midst of prosperity would not suffice for it. It is, in fact, essentially a tale of suffering and calamity conducting to death."

3. "The suffering and calamity are, moreover, exceptional. They befall a conspicuous person. . . . They are also, as a rule, unexpected, and contrasted with previous happiness or glory. A tale, for example, of a man slowly worn to death by disease, poverty, little cares, sordid vices, petty persecutions, however piteous or dreadful it may be, would not be tragic in the Shakespearean sense."

4. "No amount of calamity which merely befall a man, descending from the clouds like lightning . . . could alone provide the substance of its story. . . . The calamities of tragedy do not simply happen, nor are they sent; they proceed mainly from actions, and those the actions of men."

5. "What we do feel strongly, as a tragedy advances to its close, is that the calamities and catastrophe follow inevitably from the deeds of men, and that the main source of these deeds is character. The dictum that, with Shakespeare, 'character is destiny' is no doubt an exaggeration . . . but it is the exaggeration of a vital truth."

6. "Shakespeare, occasionally . . . represents abnormal conditions of mind; insanity, for example, somnambulism, hallucinations. . . . but these abnormal conditions are never introduced as the origin of deeds of any dramatic moment. Lady Macbeth's sleepwalking has no influence whatever on the events that follow it. Macbeth did not murder Duncan because he saw a dagger in the air: he saw the dagger because he was about to murder Duncan. Lear's insanity is not the cause of a tragic

conflict any more than Ophelia's; it is, like Ophelia's, the result of a conflict: and in both cases the effect is mainly pathetic. If Lear were really mad when he divided his kingdom, if Hamlet were really mad at any time in the story, they would cease to be tragic characters."

7. "Shakespeare also introduces the supernatural into some of his tragedies; he introduces ghosts, and witches who have supernatural knowledge. This supernatural element certainly cannot in most cases, if in any, be explained away as an illusion in the mind of one of the characters. And further, it does contribute to the action, and is in more than one instance an indispensable part of it: so that to describe human character, with circumstances, as always the *sole* motive force in this action would be a serious error. But the supernatural is always placed in the closest relation with character. It gives a confirmation and a distinct form to inward movements already present and exerting an influence: to the sense of failure in Brutus, to the stifled workings of conscience in Richard, to the half-formed thought or the horrified memory of guilt in Macbeth, to suspicion in Hamlet. Moreover, its influence is never of a compulsive kind. It forms no more than an element, however important, in the problem which the hero has to face; and we are never allowed to feel that it has removed his capacity or responsibility for dealing with this problem."

8. "Shakespeare . . . in most of his tragedies allows to 'chance' or 'accident' an appreciable influence at some point in the action. Chance or accident here will be found, I think, to mean any occurrence (not supernatural, of course) which enters the dramatic sequence neither from the agency of a character, nor from the obvious surrounding circumstances. It may be called an accident, in this sense, that Romeo never got the Friar's message about the potion, and that Juliet did not awake from her long sleep a minute sooner; an accident that Edgar arrived at the prison just too late to save Cordelia's life; an accident that Desdemona dropped her handkerchief at the most fatal of moments; an accident that the pirate ship attacked Hamlet's ship, so that he was able to return forthwith to Denmark. Now this operation of accident is a fact, and a prominent fact, of human life. To exclude it *wholly* from tragedy, therefore, would be, we may say, to fail in truth. . . . On the other hand, any *large* admission of chance into the tragic sequence would certainly weaken, and might destroy, the sense of the casual connection of character, deed, and catastrophe. And Shakespeare really uses it very sparingly. . . . and some things which look like accidents have really a connection with character, and are therefore not in the full sense accidents. Finally. . . almost all the prominent accidents occur when the action is well advanced and the impression of the casual sequence is too firmly fixed to be impaired."

9. The "ultimate power in the tragic world . . . appears to be a mythological expression for the whole system or order, of which the individual characters form an inconsiderable and feeble part; which seems to determine, far more than they, their native dispositions and their circumstances, and, through these, their action; which is so vast and complex that they can scarcely at all understand it or control its workings; and which has a nature so definite and fixed that whatever changes take place in it produce other changes inevitably and without regard to men's desires and regrets. . . . [This] order shows characteristics . . . which would lead us to describe it as a moral order and its necessity as a moral necessity. . . . The rigor of its justice is terrible, no doubt, for a tragedy is a terrible story; but, in spite of fear and pity, we acquiesce, because our sense of justice is satisfied."

10. "The . . . order against which the individual part shows itself powerless seems to be animated by a passion for perfection. . . . Yet it appears to engender this evil within itself, and in its effort to overcome and expel it it is agonized with pain, and driven to mutilate its own substance and to lose not only evil but priceless good. [Tragedy] "would not be tragedy if it were not a painful mystery. . . .

We remain confronted with the inexplicable fact, or the no less inexplicable appearance, of a world travailing for perfection, but bringing to birth, together with glorious good, an evil which it is able to overcome only by self-torture and self-waste. And this fact or appearance is tragedy."

Third Source of Theories of Serious Drama: Essay by Arthur Miller, "Tragedy and the Common Man"

As you read Miller's essay, take notes on the following points:

Parts 1 and 2 require longer answers. Questions 3 through 8 can be answered in a sentence or two for each item. Mix your own words with Miller's in answering items 1 and 2, but answer items 3 through 7 almost entirely in Miller's own words, which are so well written that any substitution is likely to be unsatisfactory.

1. Mention three of the strongest points Miller presents in support of his thesis that the common man is a suitable subject for tragedy.

2. When we are watching a tragedy, exactly what evokes the tragic feeling in us? On this topic, how similar is Miller's view to that of Shakespeare as stated by Bradley?

3. For what goal does the tragic hero/heroine struggle?

4. How does Miller define the "tragic flaw"?

5. What, according to Miller, is the morality and lesson of tragedy?

6. From what source does the audience feel exaltation? And what causes the feeling of awe in the audience?

7. What forces are ripe for attack and examination in tragedy?

8. Which form of drama – tragedy or comedy – shows more optimism and suggests a belief in the perfectibility of man? How?

Tragedy and the Common Man

In this age few tragedies are written. It has often been held that the lack is due to a paucity of heroes among us, or else that modern man has had the blood drawn out of his organs of belief by the skepticism of science, and the heroic attack on life cannot feed on an attitude of reserve and circumspection. For one reason or another, we are often held to be below tragedy – or tragedy above us. The inevitable conclusion is, of course, that the tragic mode is archaic, fit only for the very highly placed, the kings or the kingly, and where this admission is not made in so many words it is most often implied.

I believe that the common man is as apt a subject for tragedy in its highest sense as kings were. On the face of it this ought to be obvious in the light of modern psychiatry, which bases its analysis upon classic formulations, such as the Oedipus and Orestes complexes, for instances, which were enacted by royal beings, but which apply to everyone in similar emotional situations.

More simply, when the question of tragedy in art is not at issue, we never hesitate to attribute to the well-placed and the exalted the very same mental processes as the lowly. And finally, if the exaltation of tragic action were truly a property of the high-bred character alone, it is inconceivable that the mass of mankind should cherish tragedy above all other forms, let alone be capable of understanding it.

As a general rule, to which there may be exceptions unknown to me, I think the tragic feeling is evoked in us when we are in the presence of a character who is ready to lay down his life, if need be, to secure one thing – his sense of personal dignity. From Orestes to Hamlet, Medea to Macbeth, the underlying struggle is that of the individual attempting to gain his "rightful" position in his society.

Sometimes he is one who has been displaced from it, sometimes one who seeks to attain it for the first time, but the fateful wound from which the inevitable events spiral is the wound of indignity, and its dominant force is indignation. Tragedy, then, is the consequence of a man's total compulsion to evaluate himself justly.

In the sense of having been initiated by the hero himself, the tale always reveals what has been called his "tragic flaw," a failing that is not peculiar to grand or elevated characters. Nor is it necessarily a weakness. The flaw, or crack in the character, is really nothing – and need be nothing, but his inherent unwillingness to remain passive in the face of what he conceives to be a challenge to his dignity, his image of his rightful status. Only the passive, only those who accept their lot without active retaliation, are "flawless." Most of us are in that category.

But there are among us today, as there always have been, those who act against the scheme of things that degrades them, and in the process of action everything we have accepted out of fear or insensitivity or ignorance is shaken before us and examined, and from this total onslaught by an individual against the seemingly stable cosmos surrounding us – from this total examination of the "unchangeable" environment – comes the terror and the fear that is classically associated with tragedy.

More important, from this total questioning of what has previously been unquestioned, we learn. And such a process is not beyond the common man. In revolutions around the world, these past thirty years, he has demonstrated again and again this inner dynamic of all tragedy.

Insistence upon the rank of the tragic hero, or the so-called nobility of his character, is really but a clinging to the outward forms of tragedy. If rank or nobility of character was indispensable, then it would follow that the problems of those with rank were the particular problems of tragedy. But surely the right of one monarch to capture the domain from another no longer raises our passions, nor are our concepts of justice what they were to the mind of an Elizabethan king.

The quality in such plays that does shake us, however, derives from the underlying fear of being displaced, the disaster inherent in being torn away from our chosen image of what and who we are in this world. Among us today this fear is as strong and perhaps stronger, than it ever was. In fact, it is the common man who knows this fear best.

Now, if it is true that tragedy is the consequence of a man's total compulsion to evaluate himself justly, his destruction in the attempt posits a wrong or an evil in his environment. And this is precisely the morality of tragedy and its lesson. The discovery of the moral law, which is what the enlightenment of tragedy consists of, is not the discovery of some abstract or metaphysical quantity.

The tragic right is a condition of life, a condition in which the human personality is able to flower and realize itself. The wrong is the condition which suppresses man, perverts the flowing out of his love and creative instinct. Tragedy enlightens – and it must, in that it points the heroic finger at the enemy of man's freedom. The thrust for freedom is the quality in tragedy which exalts. The revolutionary questioning of the stable environment is what terrifies. In no way is the common man debarred from such thoughts or such actions.

Seen in this light, our lack of tragedy may be partially accounted for by the turn which modem literature has taken toward the purely psychiatric view of life, or the purely sociological. If all our miseries, our indignities, are born and bred within our minds, then all action, let alone the heroic action, is obviously impossible.

And if society alone is responsible for the cramping of our lives, then the protagonist must needs be so pure and faultless as to force us to deny his validity as a character. From neither of these views can tragedy derive, simply because neither represents a balanced concept of life. Above all else, tragedy requires the finest appreciation by the writer of cause and effect.

No tragedy can therefore come about when its author fears to question absolutely everything, when he regards any institution, habit or custom as being either everlasting, immutable or inevitable. In the tragic view the need of man to wholly realize himself is the only fixed star, and whatever it is that hedges his nature and lowers it is ripe for attack and examination. Which is not to say that tragedy must preach revolution.

The Greeks could probe the very heavenly origin of their ways and return to confirm the rightness of laws. And Job could face God in anger, demanding his right and end in submission. But for a moment everything is in suspension, nothing is accepted, and in this stretching and tearing apart of the cosmos, in the very action of so doing, the character gains "size," the tragic stature which is spuriously attached to the royal or the highborn in our minds. The commonest of men may take on that stature to the extent of his willingness to throw all he has into the contest, the battle to secure his rightful place in his world.

There is a misconception of tragedy with which I have been struck in review after review, and in many conversations with writers and readers alike. It is the idea that tragedy is of necessity allied to pessimism, Even the dictionary says nothing more about the word than that it means a story with a sad or unhappy ending. This impression is so firmly fixed that I almost hesitate to claim that in truth tragedy implies more optimism in its author than does comedy, and that its final result ought to be the reinforcement of the onlooker's brightest opinions of the human animal.

For, if it is time to say that in essence the tragic hero is intent upon claiming his whole due as a personality, and if this struggle must be total and without reservation, then it automatically demonstrates the indestructible will of man to achieve his humanity.

The possibility of victory must be there in tragedy. Where pathos rules, where pathos is finally derived, a character has fought a battle he could not possibly have won. The pathetic is achieved when the protagonist is, by virtue of his witlessness, his insensitivity or the very air he gives off, incapable of grappling with a much superior force.

Pathos truly is the mode for the pessimist. But tragedy requires a nicer balance between what is possible and what is impossible. And it is curious, although edifying, that the plays we revere, century after century, are the tragedies. In them, and in them alone, lies the belief – optimistic, if you will, in the perfectibility of man.

It is time, I think, that we who are without kings, took up this bright thread of our history and followed it to the only place it can possibly lead in our time – the heart and spirit of the average man.

Arthur Miller (1915-2005)

Testing your understanding of Miller's theory and practice of tragic drama

Watch any video recording of Miller's play *Death of a Salesman* (one with Lee J. Cobb and the other with Dustin Hoffman stand out). You can watch the Hoffman version online at
http://www.hulu.com/#!watch/355302.

Determine the extent to which Miller observes his own theory of tragedy that he articulated so eloquently in his essay "Tragedy and the Common Man." To enhance your understanding of the play, read online Joyce Carol Oates' article "Arthur Miller's *Death of a Salesman*: *A Celebration*, which was originally published in *Michigan Quarterly Review*, Fall 1998. http://www.usfca.edu/jco/arthurmiller/.

Among other numerous cost-free online sources of help are
http://www.novelguide.com/deathofasalesman/index.html
http://www.cliffsnotes.com/WileyCDA/LitNote/Death-of-a-Salesman.id-73.html

Debate on Classical *versus* Modern Tragedy
Is Modern Tragedy a Misnomer?

Joseph Wood Krutch had argued in "The Tragic Fallacy," a chapter in his book *The Modern Temper* (1929), that modern "tragedies" are a misnomer because they produce in the reader

> a sense of depression which is the exact opposite of that elation generated when the spirit of a Shakespeare rises joyously superior to the outward calamities which he recounts and celebrates the greatness of the human spirit whose travail he describes (Krutch 118).

Tragedy, in the classical and Shakespearean sense, was "essentially an expression, not of despair, but of the triumph over despair and of confidence in the value of human life" (Krutch 123). Even in the darkest of his plays, for example, Shakespeare was able to create "the elemental grandeur of Othello and the pensive majesty of Hamlet" (Krutch 123). Among the reasons given to account for the demise of truly tragic drama one often-quoted has been the enfeeblement of the human spirit, which, in turn, comes from the belief that the divine spark no longer animates the human soul and passion.

Whatever the reasons for this change in tragic drama of the great classical tradition, we have to acknowledge the new form of tragedy, as practiced by prominent playwrights like Arthur Miller, Tennessee Williams, Eugene O'Neill, and others as truly expressive of modern temper and genius, however "non-heroic" in the traditional sense. We may argue that calling their plays tragic is not, therefore, a misnomer. Major modern plays, such as Arthur Miller's *Death of a Salesman*, Eugene O'Neill's *The Long Day's Journey into the Night,* and Tennessee Williams' *The Night of the Iguana* offer a much more nuanced view of tragic drama than just an exaltation of the human spirit. They also dramatize pitiful shrinking of man's stature, moral ambivalence, demise of a value system, lack of certitude in every area from religion to politics, and anti-heroic stance in the face of devaluation of heroic action. Classical plays of the past and modern tragic drama may not be as far apart as we sometimes tend to think. One helpful explanation can be found in Tennessee Williams' following words from his "Preface" to *Sweet Bird of Youth*:

"[I]f there is any truth in the Aristotelian idea that violence is purged by its poetic representation on a stage, then it may be that my cycle of violent plays have had a moral justification after all. I know that I have felt it. I have always felt a release from the sense of meaninglessness and death when a work of tragic intention has seemed to me to have achieved that intention, even if only approximately, nearly.

"I would say that there is something much bigger in life and death than we have become aware of (or adequately recorded) in our living and dying. And, further, to compound this shameless romanticism, I would say that our serious theater is a search for that something that is not yet successful but is still going on" (xi).

In *The Broken World of Tennessee Williams*, Esther Jackson further expands on Williams' views:

"Apparently shocked and frightened by the growing threat of human annihilation, he [Williams] suggests that the theatre cannot afford to exalt man, to praise and to commend his nature. He insists that the proper function of the modern drama is to expose man's hidden nature, to search out his motives, to discover his limits, and, ultimately, to help him to find a mode of salvation. . . . He concludes that the only hope for man is compassion" (87).

Is tragic drama optimistic or pessimistic?

Another topic hotly debated among scholars and playwrights relates to the question whether tragic drama is optimistic or pessimistic. In "Tragedy and the Common Man," we have already read Arthur Miller's strident assertion that tragedy implies more optimism and belief in the perfectibility of man than comedy. Eugene O'Neill, the only American playwright to win the Nobel Prize for literature, has expressed the same view eloquently:

"I have been accused of unmitigated gloom. Is this a pessimistic view of life? There is a skin deep optimism and another higher optimism, not skin deep, which is usually confounded with pessimism. To me, the tragic alone has that significant beauty which is truth. It is the meaning of life – and the hope. The noblest is eternally the most tragic. The people who succeed and do not push on to a greater failure are the spiritual middle classers. Their stopping at success is the proof of their compromising insignificance. How petty their dreams must have been! The man who pursues the mere attainable should be sentenced to get it – and keep it. Let him rest on his laurels and enthrone him in a Morris chair, in which laurels and hero may wither away together. Only through the unattainable does man achieve a hope worth living and dying for – and so attain himself. He with the spiritual guerdon of a hope in hopelessness, is nearest to the stars and the rainbow's foot" (Caputi 447).

O'Neill ends his critique with this memorable paradox: "Damn the optimist anyway! They make life so damned hopeless!" (Caputi 449).

After reading Arthur Miller's, Tennessee Williams', and Eugene O'Neill's spirited defense of their view of tragedy, do we feel that questions like those raised by Krutch have been answered adequately? Both contrary views seem to have merit and deserve recognition and respectful audience. As Krutch himself stated, "A tragic writer does not have to believe in God, but he must believe in man" (127). In their works, Miller, Williams, O'Neill, and other modern dramatists prove that they believe in their protagonists even though they are, in some ways, different from classical or Shakespearean models.

To appreciate and understand the differences and similarities among classical, Shakespearean, and modern tragic plays, you need to read or watch at least one play from each era. Constraints of space have permitted fuller discussion of *Hamlet* only in the form of discussion questions and sample essays, coupled with brief references to Sophocles' *Oedipus the King*. My website has many more sample essays. After reading Arthur Miller's essay "Tragedy and the Common Man" and applying the principles of that important work to his play *Death of a Salesman*, you should now apply Tennessee Williams' and Eugene O'Neill's concepts of drama to their plays, such as Williams' *The Glass Menagerie* and *A Streetcar Named Desire*, and Eugene O'Neill's *The Long Day's Journey into Night* and *Desire Under the Elms*. Watching or reading any of their plays in the light of theoretical knowledge that you have gained from their own and other prominent critics' words can only be enlightening and enjoyable. There are many links to films of some of the major plays by these authors and their reviews online -- *The Night of the Iguana, The Sweet Bird of Youth, The Glass Menagerie, A Streetcar Named Desire, A Long Day's Journey into Night,* and *Desire Under the Elms,* to name a few.

One-Act Plays

In recent years, one-act plays have been gaining in popularity. They are to drama what short stories are to novels. Their appeal is understandable in view of shorter amount of time it takes to read or watch them. A well-composed one-act play can pack a lot of subject matter in a little time and space. There are numerous collections of such plays. One among them is titled *One Act: Eleven short plays of the modern theatre*, edited by Samuel Moon. It has plays by prominent dramatists, such as August Strindberg, William Butler Yeats, Luigi Pirandello, Thornton Wilder, William Saroyan, Tennessee Williams, Sean O'Casey, Jean Anouilh, Archibald MacLeish, Arthur Miller, and Eugene Ionesco. In one small volume, you can enjoy the craft of eleven authors. Live viewings of short plays and their video recordings are available without much effort, and you can read and watch one-act plays online free of cost. Constraints of space will allow us to look at only a brief sampling of such plays.

Before Breakfast by Eugene O'Neill (1888-1953)

Read the play online at: http://www.eoneill.com/texts/bb/contents.htm
You can also watch a reading of the play: http://www.youtube.com/watch?v=dMvTql-65lA

This play, one of American dramatist Eugene O'Neill's earlier works, is ideal for understanding how authors handle point of view, conflict, characterization, and setting in a short play. The entire play is a dramatic monologue, in which the wife (Mrs. Rowland) berates her off-stage husband Alfred for nearly 20 minutes until the horrifying conclusion. Even though the wife comes across as a spiteful person and Alfred as a sensitive, failed artist, there is enough in the plot to suggest that he has contributed to their domestic crisis, making it a genuine conflict. She does try to clean up after Alfred: "Look at the mess you've made of this floor – cigarette butts and ashes all over the place. Why can't you put them on a plate? No, you wouldn't be considerate enough to do that. You never think of me." Throughout the play, Mrs. Rowland is "viciously" sweeping and cleaning the apartment. She does seem to have a point when she says, "All your friends know about your unhappy marriage. I know they pity you, but they don't know my side of it. They'd talk different if they did." The irony is that she does tell her side of their story, for it is only her point of view that is presented in the play. O'Neill's use of dramatic irony is effective in her characterization.

In the stage directions, she is described to be in "her early twenties but looks much older." At one point she says: "Heaven knows I do my part – and more – going out to sew every day while you play the gentleman and loaf around bar rooms with the good-for-nothing lot of artists from the Square." It doesn't take long to know that Alfred married her out of guilt after making her pregnant: "I suppose you thought I'd ought to be glad you were *honorable* enough to marry me – after getting me into trouble."

They come from widely divergent backgrounds and have incompatible temperaments and goals in life: "You were ashamed of me with your fine friends because my father's only a grocer." "All you do is moon around all day writing silly poetry and stories that no one will buy – and no wonder they won't." The couple has known domestic tragedy in the birth of a stillborn child: "It's lucky the poor thing was born dead, after all. What a father you'd have been!"

They have serious financial problems to the point that Alfred has to pawn his watch to bring in the much-needed money. His gesture was not appreciated: "It's been nothing but pawn, pawn, pawn, with you – anything to put off getting a job, anything to get out of going to work like a man." To make matters worse, both of them seem to have a drinking problem. "What was the use pawning your watch if all you wanted with the money was to waste it in buying drink?" She defends her own drinking: "You know how sick I've been this last year; and yet you object when I take a little something to keep up my spirits."

The conflict intensifies when Mrs. Rowland finds in Alfred's pocket a note from Helen, a woman she thinks he is involved with and has impregnated. She vows never to divorce Alfred to give Helen the satisfaction of marrying him. She goes through painful self-analysis at this point only to deny any wrongdoing whatsoever: "No one can say *I've* done anything wrong."

Besides characterization, point of view, and conflict, O'Neill's use of setting and stage directions is also superb. The opening scene describes several potted plants that "are dying of neglect." As the plot unfolds, we realize that it is not only the plants that are dying in that house. In the middle of her furious sweeping, the stage direction says: *"From the inner room comes the sound of a razor being stropped."* When the stage direction reveals that she hears *"a sharp exclamation of pain from the next room,"* she responds with "There! I knew you'd cut yourself." She taunts Alfred for his shaky hands and warns him: "One of these mornings you'll give yourself a serious cut [while shaving]." Her warning foreshadows what is to come and creates suspense. The last we hear of Alfred is in the form of a stage direction: *"There is a stifled groan of pain from the next room."* Because of the masterly use of stage directions, the suspense about his cutting himself continues to build up until the end.

Internet sources on this and other plays and literary works

There are numerous discussions of O'Neill's play. You can start with this link and then browse on your own. http://www.provincetownplayhouse.com/beforebreakfast.html

This article, like several others through Google, can be accessed free of cost, but for Gale Literature Resource Center and Questia, you need membership. Most college and public libraries subscribe to these online resources.

Gale Literature Resource Center: http://www.gale.cengage.com
Questia, The Online Library of Books and Journals: http://www.questia.com

Notable Features of Contemporary Plays

Most Greek, Shakespearean, and other classics were based on well-known stories that were modified by dramatists to suit their thematic and artistic aims. People who went to watch those plays already knew the essential plot details. That, however, is not the case with contemporary plays. For that reason, the audience can expect surprises as the unknown plot unfolds before them.

An instructive example would be a typical play by a prominent contemporary British playwright Harold Pinter. Awarding him the 2005 Nobel Prize for Literature, the Nobel Committee recognized the British playwright for his role in restoring theater "to its basic elements: an enclosed space and unpredictable dialogue, where people are at the mercy of each other and pretense crumbles. With a minimum of plot, drama emerges from the power struggle and hide-and-seek of interlocution" (Winn A-2).

Other notable features of Pinter's plays, noted by Steven Winn, are their "corrosive humor," "unnerving silences," "minutely observed reality," "keenly pruned detail, jolting surprises, sinister hilarity, and pitiless scrutiny of behavior and buried motivations. . . . Images rather than ideas . . . ignite his plays" (Winn A-2). Pinter's reliance on images rather than ideas is also recognized by another critic Arnold Hinchliffe:

"However natural his dialogue, however naturalistic some of the situations . . . Pinter's plays are also basically images, almost allegories, of the human condition" (Hinchliffe 34).

A defining Pinteresque trait is that "all his plays take place in a kind of eternal present tense. . . . He never relies on exposition. He never believes that the past is verifiable. Nothing exists until the actors step out on the stage" (Perloff in Winn A-2). To the attributes of Pinter's plays mentioned by Winn and Hinchliffe, we may add the deception of memory and unreliability of knowledge.

Pinter is sometimes placed among comic ironists. According to J. L. Styan, the playwrights of this school "practice a new illogicality, yet one pregnant with the logic of feeling that belongs to a subconscious world of tragicomedy. As in the novels of Franz Kafka and William Golding, the normal world of ordinary human relationships can suddenly become quick and sinister and even violent" (Styan 234-35).

As in the case of classical, Shakespearean, and modern tragic drama, you will acquire a fuller understanding of contemporary plays when you apply theoretical concepts that you have learned in this chapter to specific plays. Several helpful questions and topics are included on contemporary authors in the exercises at the end of this chapter. [4]

---

[4] At this point in the chapter, depending on your course requirements, you should read a play either by Harold Pinter or any contemporary playwright. *The Birthday Party* and *The Homecoming* are among Pinter's most popular plays. The full text of *The Birthday Party* is at http://www.slideshare.net/Johof/the-birthday-party-full-text-2073679#btnNext.

Plays on Pressing Current Issues

Trifles
by Susan Glaspell (1876-1948)

Read this play online using the link: http://etext.virginia.edu/etcbin/toccer-new2?id=GlaTrif.sgm&images=images/modeng&data=/texts/english/modeng/parsed&tag=public&part=1&division=div1

Read online Suzy Clarkson Holstein's article "Silent Justice in a Different Key: Glaspell's *Trifles.*" The Midwest Quarterly 44 (2003): 282-290. *Here is the link:* http://www.articlemyriad.com/trifles.htm

Also read "A Literary Analysis of Glaspell's Drama *Trifles*" by Metropolis Flower: http://www.associatedcontent.com/article/186744/a_literary_analysis_of_glaspells_drama_pg3_pg3.html?cat=38

Susan Glaspell's murder mystery is usually seen as criticism of the typical male view expressed by Mr. Hale that "women are used to worrying about trifles." In this play, however, what men consider trivial turns out to be crucial to finding a motive for Minnie's murder of her husband, Mr. John Wright. The play offers two divergent points of view – one male, the other female. The men are only interested in finding a motive why Mrs. Wright killed her husband.

They focus on what they regard as legally significant aspects of the case. The women, on the other hand, have a much more profound pursuit: Not just the motive but, more importantly, the reason for a motive – what drives someone to a motive for murder?

In Mrs. Wright's case, the two women find out what the sheriff, the country attorney, and the neighbor Mr. Hale could not: the immediate reason for her crime was the husband's act of killing her songbird by wringing its neck. However, the two women went much deeper. Using two clues, they successfully traced the stages that built up Minnie's misery to the point of explosion. The first clue was when they noticed an irregularity in Minnie's stitching pattern, suggesting a distraught mind.

"Here, this is the one she was working on, and look at the sewing! All the rest of it has   been so nice and even. And look at this! It's all over the place! Why, it looks as if she didn't know what she was about!"

The second clue, a decisive one, was their discovery of the dead bird. Minnie had put the dead bird in a box, probably to bury it later.

You may watch a production of *The Birthday Party* starring Pinter on YouTube at http://www.youtube.com/watch?v=0vbXyXeEDhU and read an online review of *Homecoming*: http://theater2.nytimes.com/2007/12/17/theater/reviews/17home.html.

The two women go through an ethical dilemma: Should they reveal the incriminating evidence or withhold it. As they summon up their memories of youthful and lively Minnie's singing at the choir and her post-marriage cheerless existence, they conclude that Mr. Wright had not only killed the song bird but also Minnie's spirit. Mrs. Hale adds that John Wright was "a hard man. . . . Just to pass the time of day with him . . . [was] like a raw wind that gets to the bone." They decide to hide the evidence. The women's sense of camaraderie with Minnie was established early in the play. When men were complaining too much about the dirty kitchen towels, Mrs. Hale answered: "Those towels get dirty awful quick. Men's hands aren't always as clean as they might be." There is a double meaning of men's hands not being clean, implying that the murdered Mr. Wright might have contributed to his demise. The country attorney understands the two women's defense of Minnie and comments: "Ah, loyal to your sex, I see." This casual remark could be taken as foreshadowing of the women's later resolve to support Minnie.

At the end, when the country attorney derisively asks the two women whether Mrs. Wright was going to quilt it or knot it, Mrs. Hale responds triumphantly: "We call it – knot it, Mr. Henderson." It is a perfect ending for this play, which opened with the men's teasing women about their preoccupation with "trifles," such as whether Minnie was going to quilt it or knot it. The words "knot it" have a double meaning – one referring to Minnie's knitting, and the other to the knot that Minnie made with a rope around her husband's neck. Since the so-called trifling details turn out to be the most significant ones in this play, we can make several inferences about the wrongness of demeaning women's contributions. The play was written at the beginning of the twentieth century, and our notions of gender-specific roles have changed considerably, but underestimating the value of women's work continues to this day.

Besides this obvious theme of culturally driven questionable value attached to male and female roles and work, another important theme in the play is often overlooked. The catalyst for this theme is Mrs. Hale's confession:

"I could've come. I stayed away because it weren't cheerful – and that's why I ought to have come. I – I've never liked this place . . . it's a lonesome place and always was. I wish I had come over to see Minnie Foster sometimes. I can see now – "

Later in the play, Mrs. Hale considers her not visiting Minnie once in a while a crime:

"Oh, I wish I'd come over here once in a while. That was a crime! That was a crime! Who's going to punish that?"

The theme that emerges from this serious hand wringing is that one should not avoid cheerless people because they may need help.

In spite of the somber mood and a gloomy, frigid setting, reflecting the cheerless marriage of John and Minnie Wright, the play is not without humor. The sheriff ridicules the two women's preoccupation with what he and other men consider "trifles": "They [the women] wonder if she [Minnie] was going to quilt it or just knot it." Mrs. Peters responds: "Of course they've got awful important things on their minds." This exchange of words is ironic because the evidence of motive is in the so-called unimportant things.

All of the women's important discoveries take place in the kitchen while men spend their time upstairs in a fruitless search of some big evidence of motive. After all, trifles turn out to be the most significant details. The humor is inherent in this situational irony.

In addition to the sarcastic, humorous exchanges between men and women about the relative merits of their respective pursuits, there is a scene full of grim humor. It is also where John Wright's death is revealed in a dramatically understated way. When the neighbor Mr. Hale comes to see John Wright, he finds Mrs. Wright in a distraught state of mind:

"She didn't ask me to come up to the stove, or to set down, but just sat there, not even looking at me, so I said, 'I want to see John.' And then she – laughed . . . 'Ain't he home,' says I. 'Yes,' says she, 'he's home.' 'Then why can't I see him?' . . . 'Cause he's dead,' says she." When Hale asked her' 'what did he die of?' she answered: 'He died of a rope round his neck'."

Glaspell's play deserves its rank as a classic because of its subtle characterization, control of point of view, dramatic scenes, suspenseful build-up and denouement as well as the timeless nature of its themes.

Seven Jewish Children – a play for Gaza
Performance:
http://www.guardian.co.uk/stage/2009/feb/26/caryl-churchill-seven-jewish-children-play-gaza.

One recent play that made instant headlines is "Seven Jewish Children – a play for Gaza" by Caryl Churchill. You can read it here and also watch it performed online. A playlet only six pages long, with a 10-minute total performance time needed for the seven brief scenes, it compresses over 80 years of Jewish history from the Holocaust to the creation of the state of Israel, ending with the invasion of Gaza in December 2008 through January 2009. The entire play consists of a conversation among adult family members about what to tell Jewish children and what not to tell them about the Jews' being victims and victimizers. The Guardian's Michael Billington called it a "heartfelt lamentation." If you are not familiar with the tragic Israeli-Palestinian conflict, research the topic so that you can understand the historical allusions in this play.

Complete text of the play

[Playwright introduction]: No children appear in the play. The speakers are adults, the parents and if you like other relations of the children. The lines can be shared out in any way you like among those characters. The characters are different in each small scene as the time and child are different.

1
Tell her it's a game
Tell her it's serious
But don't frighten her
Dont tell her they'll kill her
Tell her it's important to be quiet

Tell her she'll have cake if she's good
Tell her to curl up as if she's in bed
But not to sing.
Tell her not to come out
Tell her not to come out even if she hears shouting
Dont frighten her
Tell her not to come out even if she hears nothing for a long time
Tell her we'll come and find her
Tell her we'll be here all the time.
Tell her something about the men
Tell her they're bad in the game
Tell her it's a story
Tell her they'll go away
Tell her she can make them go away if she keeps still
By magic
But not to sing.

2

Tell her this is a photograph of her grandmother, her uncles and me
Tell her her uncles died
Dont tell her they were killed
Tell her they were killed
Dont frighten her.
Tell her her grandmother was clever
Dont tell her what they did
Tell her she was brave
Tell her she taught me how to make cakes
Dont tell her what they did
Tell her something
Tell her more when she's older.
Tell her there were people who hated jews
Dont tell her
Tell her it's over now
Tell her there are still people who hate jews
Tell her there are people who love jews
Dont tell her to think jews or not jews
Tell her more when she's older
Tell her how many when she's older
Tell her it was before she was born and she's not in danger
Dont tell her there's any question of danger.
Tell her we love her
Tell her dead or alive her family all love her
Tell her her grandmother would be proud of her.

3

Dont tell her we're going forever

Tell her she can write to her friends, tell her her friends can maybe come and visit
Tell her it's sunny there
Tell her we're going home
Tell her it's the land God gave us
Dont tell her religion
Tell her her great great great great lots of greats grandad lived there
Dont tell her he was driven out
Tell her, of course tell her, tell her everyone was driven out and the country is waiting for us to come home
Dont tell her she doesnt belong here
Tell her of course she likes it here but she'll like it there even more.
Tell her it's an adventure
Tell her no one will tease her
Tell her she'll have new friends
Tell her she can take her toys
Dont tell her she can take all her toys
Tell her she's a special girl
Tell her about Jerusalem.

4
Dont tell her who they are
Tell her something
Tell her they're bedouin, they travel about
Tell her about camels in the desert and dates
Tell her they live in tents
Tell her this wasnt their home
Dont tell her home, not home, tell her they're going away
Dont tell her they dont like her
Tell her to be careful.
Dont tell her who used to live in this house
No but dont tell her her great great grandfather used to live in this house
No but dont tell her Arabs used to sleep in her bedroom.
Tell her not to be rude to them
Tell her not to be frightened
Dont tell her she cant play with the children
Dont tell her she can have them in the house.
Tell her they have plenty of friends and family
Tell her for miles and miles all round they have lands of their own
Tell her again this is our promised land.
Dont tell her they said it was a land without people
Dont tell her I wouldnt have come if I'd known.
Tell her maybe we can share.
Dont tell her that.

5

Tell her we won
Tell her her brother's a hero
Tell her how big their armies are
Tell her we turned them back
Tell her we're fighters
Tell her we've got new land.

6

Dont tell her
Dont tell her the trouble about the swimming pool
Tell her it's our water, we have the right
Tell her it's not the water for their fields
Dont tell her anything about water.
Dont tell her about the bulldozer
Dont tell her not to look at the bulldozer
Dont tell her it was knocking the house down
Tell her it's a building site
Dont tell her anything about bulldozers.
Dont tell her about the queues at the checkpoint
Tell her we'll be there in no time
Dont tell her anything she doesnt ask
Dont tell her the boy was shot
Dont tell her anything.
Tell her we're making new farms in the desert
Dont tell her about the olive trees
Tell her we're building new towns in the wilderness.
Dont tell her they throw stones
Tell her they're not much good against tanks
Dont tell her that.
Dont tell her they set off bombs in cafes
Tell her, tell her they set off bombs in cafes
Tell her to be careful
Dont frighten her.
Tell her we need the wall to keep us safe
Tell her they want to drive us into the sea
Tell her they dont
Tell her they want to drive us into the sea.
Tell her we kill far more of them
Dont tell her that
Tell her that
Tell her we're stronger
Tell her we're entitled
Tell her they dont understand anything except violence
Tell her we want peace
Tell her we're going swimming.

7

Tell her she cant watch the news

Tell her she can watch cartoons

Tell her she can stay up late and watch Friends.

Tell her they're attacking with rockets

Dont frighten her

Tell her only a few of us have been killed

Tell her the army has come to our defence

Dont tell her her cousin refused to serve in the army.

Dont tell her how many of them have been killed

Tell her the Hamas fighters have been killed

Tell her they're terrorists

Tell her they're filth

Dont

Dont tell her about the family of dead girls

Tell her you can't believe what you see on television

Tell her we killed the babies by mistake

Dont tell her anything about the army

Tell her, tell her about the army, tell her to be proud of the army. Tell her about the family of dead girls, tell her their names why not, tell her the whole world knows why shouldn't she know? tell her there's dead babies, did she see babies? Tell her she's got nothing to be ashamed of. Tell her they did it to themselves. tell her they want their children killed to make people sorry for them, tell her I'm not sorry for them, tell her not to be sorry for them, tell her we're the ones to be sorry for, tell her they can't talk suffering to us. tell her we're the iron fist now, tell her it's the fog of war, tell her we wont stop killing them till we're safe, tell her I laughed when I saw the dead policemen, tell her they're animals living in rubble now, tell her I wouldn't care if we wiped them out, the world would hate us is the only thing, tell her I don't care if the world hates us, tell her we're better haters, tell her we're chosen people, tell her I look at one of their children covered in blood and what do I feel? tell her all I feel is happy it's not her.

Dont tell her that.

Tell her we love her.

Dont frighten her.

Caryl Churchill (b. 1938)

Note from the play's author: Please feel free to download the play. This play can be read or performed anywhere by any number of people. Should you wish to apply for rights, please contact ruth@casarotto.co.uk, who will license the performances free of charge provided that no admission fee is charged and that a collection is taken at each performance for Medical Aid for Palestinians (MAP), 33a Islington Park Street, London N1 1 QB. Tel: 020-7226 4114. Website: map-uk.org. Email: info@map-uk.org]

Comments by the author of this book

In Churchill's play, all characters are parents and relatives of the children. They are talking to one another about what to tell their children about the Israeli-Palestinian conflict. Children will receive this information about their ancestral history and present dilemmas according to their ages and situations. A part of the play relates to the time before the families moved to Israel. Other parts concern their lives after their move.

Every line in this short piece is replete with decades of history, and the play can be considered a brief introduction to the history and politics of the Israeli-Palestinian conflict, in which the United States has played a major role. Since the play makes extensive use of historical allusions and specifics of the present on-going conflict, students not familiar with it need to look up relevant facts on their own. The following brief section-by-section commentary is meant to explain some of the references.

1. The characters hope that the problem is only a passing nightmare from which their children should be protected.

2. They don't know what to tell their children:

    "Don't tell her they [relatives] were killed
    Tell her they were killed."

    They are not sure whether they should tell their children about the lingering anti-Semitism:

    "Tell her there are still people who hate jews
    Tell her there are people who love jews."

3. They are not sure whether they should mention to their children the threat to their survival in Israel. At the time of moving to Israel, what should parents tell their children about their move?

    "Don't tell her we're going forever . . . .
    Tell her we're going home
    Tell her it's the land God gave us."

4. Jewish children are to be told that Palestinians live in tents and "travel about," implying that they have no fixed abodes.

    "Dont tell her they said it was a land without people."
    "Dont tell her I wouldn't have come if I'd known."
    "Tell her maybe we can share."
    "Dont tell her that."

    The characters are having trouble with falsification of the truth: Palestine was *not* a land without people when Zionists decided to create a state there. The area had been home to Palestinians for thousands of years. It is like saying that the United States was a land without people before the Europeans came here. Does the speaker feel cheated into being brought to Palestine on the basis of false information?

    The last three lines are packed with regret ("Don't tell her I wouldn't have come if I'd known"), hope ("Tell her maybe we can share"), and painful doubt about success ("Don.t tell her that"). The elders want to seek reconciliation and peace but, fearful of alienating their children, find it difficult to tell the unpleasant truth.

5. Jewish children are to be told that the Israelis defeated the Arab armies decisively.

6. This section pertains to the most sensitive and controversial issue of settlements – a term used to describe illegally taking over of Palestinian land to build Jewish homes. In those settlements occupying Israelis live in the luxury of abundance. They have swimming pools when Palestinians don't even have enough drinking water, nor water to irrigate their crops.

Another issue this section raises pertains to bulldozing of Palestinian homes. Collective punishment is imposed on the entire family if any family member is arrested carrying out anti-Israel activities. Sometimes just throwing stones at the Israeli soldiers results in this kind of collective punishment. A young 23-year-old American peace activist, Rachel Corrie, was bulldozed to death while protesting the bulldozing of a Palestinian home. The documentary "Occupation 101" mentions this tragic incident. On this topic, there is also a play, "My Name Is Rachel Corrie," and Leslie Simon, an author and professor at City College of San Francisco has written a poem "Driving Under the Influence," which you can read in Chapter Thirteen under poems for further reading. The parents seem particularly concerned that they should hide such bitter facts from their children. Hence their caution:

"Don't tell her anything about bulldozing."

All of these issues are covered well in the documentary "Occupation 101."

This section also brings up the problem of Israeli check points all over occupied Palestine. A journey that ordinarily would be completed in half an hour could take up to six hours or more because of those check points, making it impossible for Palestinians to reach their schools, places of work, and businesses in a timely manner. The documentary that covers this topic well is Anne Baltzer's "Life in Occupied Palestine."

The children are also to be protected from information about the killing of Palestinian boys by the Israeli army. The reason for these killings is that the Palestinian boys throw stones at Israeli soldiers. The parents have to struggle with their conscience here:

"Tell her they [stones] are not much good against tanks."
"Don't tell her that."

Parents feel that in order to save their youth from terrorist attacks by Palestinians, they have to be warned of such dangers. At the same time, they feel their children should not have to live in constant fear:

"Don't tell her they set off bombs in cafes
Tell her, tell her they set off bombs in cafes."

The parents also mention the Israeli wall between occupied West Bank and Israel), which has been declared illegal by the International Court of Justice. The children are to be told:

"We need the wall to keep us safe.
Tell her they want to drive us into the sea."

After mentioning the last detail, parents seem stricken by their conscience at the untruthfulness of that information. According to the information in former U.S. President Jimmy Carter's book *Palestine Peace Not Apartheid*, it was the Zionists who invented this threat that Palestinians want to drive the Israelis into the sea. Palestinians did not invent that slogan. After the only one-time mention of Israelis wanting peace, this section ends the way it started – with swimming pools.

7. In the play's final section, the parents seem to have given up on hiding facts from their children in their attempt to mold their thinking because the whole world knows those facts. From trying to feed their children only selected information in a subtle way, one parent now assumes an aggressive posture, refusing to care if the world hates them for what they are doing to Palestinians. Now Israeli children will be told unequivocally that Palestinians are the enemy:

481

". . . I wouldn't care if we wiped them out."

Even the families of dead Palestinian girls don't receive any sympathy now:

"Tell her they want their children killed to make people sorry for them."

Unlike the play's earlier sections that are arranged with symmetrical line breaks, a part of the last section (no. 7) abandons any pretense to order. This style gives the impression that in the course of processing their painful history and thinking up specious strategies, they have become disoriented. The play, however, ends on a note of full disclosure to face facts as they are. Depending on one's perspective, this ending may be viewed as optimistic. As pointed out in my comments on section 4, there are glimpses of hope. It seems that the elders do want to seek reconciliation and peace but, fearful of alienating or frightening their children, find it difficult to tell the unpleasant truth. The tragic Israeli-Palestinian conflict has taken too many precious lives in its long history. Churchill is to be commended for the world's attention to it in an incredibly brief and cryptic manner.

The Domestic Crusaders
by Wajahat Ali

You can use these links to access the play. The Kennedy Center performance:
http://www.kennedy-center.org/explorer/artists/?entity_id=66901&source_type=B

A brief interview with the author and video clips from the play on the NBC Weekend Today Show with Pat Battle on YouTube: http://www.time.com/time/video/player/0,32068,27017677001_0,00.html
The New York Times review:
http://theater.nytimes.com/2009/09/09/theater/09domestic.html?_r=0&adxnnl=1&adxnnlx=1355246682-XWvzfd33V+QC21FlFV0JzA

Essay by the author of this book

Pakistani-American author Wajahat Ali's play is about the post-9-11 life of Muslims in America. It depicts the tensions and divisions within a contemporary Pakistani-American Muslim family. The author traces the genesis of the play to 9-11-2001 when he was a student at University of California, Berkeley, taking a class with Prof. Ishmael Reed. Prof. Reed asked Wajahat Ali to write a play about Muslim Americans because he was tired of seeing them portrayed as caricatures. That assignment eventually resulted in this play.

We can trace the inter-generational conflicts among the family members to two sources. First, the rival pulls of modernity and tradition, and, secondly, Islamophobia and the consequent intolerance that characterizes many segments of the American society. The tensions of the larger society seep into the lives of characters in this play. The famous physicist Stephen Hawkins said, "The greatest enemy of knowledge is not ignorance. It is the illusion of knowledge." When these two ills of ignorance and the illusion of knowledge combine, the result is a deadly mixture. The ignorant do not feel the need to seek knowledge and the problem of misinformation continues to hurt the society. Even though all "crusaders" seem adamant about the rightness of their conflicting views, the play does offer a glimpse into their underlying unity.

Pulitzer Prize nominated author Mitch Berman, who calls Ali "a major new voice in American literature," compared Ali's play to Lorraine Hansberry's A Raisin in the Sun: Ali's play "is to Muslim American theater what A Raisin in the Sun is to African American theater." Commenting on the play's thrust toward inculcating acceptance and tolerance of diversity, Emma Thompson, Academy Award winning actress and screenwriter, said: "The Domestic Crusaders is exactly the sort of theater we need today. The gulf that separates cultures must be bridged and Art is one of our best hopes."

In Ali's own words from his interview with Pat Battle of the NBC Weekend Today Show, "art can heal and art can be a bridge that brings cultures together." Commenting on his characters, he said that he portrays people as they really are: complex, messy, funny, blunt, a bit hypocritical, and unpredictable. By the end of the play, "we learn something not only about Muslim Americans but also about ourselves."

Study Questions to Prepare for
A Timed Test on Theories of Serious Drama

Answering the following questions will add theoretical depth to your discussion of plays. Prepare all of these questions thoroughly for self-testing. Your instructor may also ask you to answer just a few of these questions depending on the time constraints and class assignments. All of these questions have been answered in the preceding parts of this chapter.

1. This chapter has given you background information on classical, Shakespearean, and modern concepts of tragedy. Add two elements to the 15 items listed in the beginning of this chapter. Use any points from your reading of A. C. Bradley, Arthur Miller, and any other sources, mentioned earlier in this chapter under the heading of "Other famous discussions of tragic drama."

    When answering this question, avoid details that you are using to answer other parts of this test. Also avoid repeating elements that I have already included in the list of fifteen items in the beginning of the chapter.

2. Theory of drama according to Hamlet: In my interpretation of Hamlet's speech, I listed 5 points that Hamlet presents on the nature and function of drama. Add a new point on your own based on the same speech by Hamlet.

3. Theory of Shakespearean tragedy according to A. C. Bradley: Be prepared to answer any of the seven items that go with Bradley's chapter. Add a new item not covered by me.

4. Arthur Miller's view of tragedy in his essay "Tragedy and the Common Man": You should be able to answer all eight items that are designed to help your mastery of Miller's essay. Apply Miller's theory of tragedy to his play *Death of a Salesman* or any other modern play by another dramatist.

WRITING ESSAYS ON TOPICS FROM PLAYS

Having been introduced to classical as well as modern and contemporary concepts of tragedy, comedy, tragicomedy, absurdist plays, and other innovations, you have sufficient preparation to write about any play that you watch or read. As you prepare to write this assignment, keep John Lahr's following words in mind: "Through the grab bag of set, costume, language, gesture, and sound, theater stimulates feeling and makes ideas irresistible. . . . theater acts out problems and celebrates discovery. It demands imagination, not gullibility" (Lahr 9).

Assignment and Instructions

Write an essay of 750 to 1000 words on a major topic from any play. A list of topics on Shakespeare's *Hamlet* and prompts for writing on contemporary drama are given at the end of these instructions. That list is to show how a topic is selected and narrowed to manageable scope. Once understood, this skill of topic formulation can be applied to any play.

When completing this assignment, adjust the scope of the topic to suit the nature of the assignment. If a topic is too broad, the result will be a superficial discussion, and a topic that is too narrow leads to unreasonable stretching and over interpretation.

To discover a suitable topic, compile as a part of your reading and prewriting a list of topics that seem important to you. It does not have to be a long list. For most plays, four or five topics will suffice, out of which you may make your final selection. Since *Hamlet* is a complex play, it offers an abundance of discussable topics.

Among other points to remember, one is that in the kind of essay that this assignment calls for – and this is true of all literature-based essays – use supporting details from the plays in the form of a mixture of direct quotations and summary of relevant facts in your own words. You may refer to other literary works, theories, and to any historical or contemporary events to clarify and develop your points, but most of the supporting details have to come from the literary work on which you are writing. When summarizing plot details, be sure to include some analytic comments to connect your support with the main point that you are making.

Another important guideline to keep in mind is that somewhere in the paper you should write clearly what you infer to be the author's or the play's stand on the topic. As was explained in Chapter One, this stand is also called a *theme.* The statement of such a theme – sometimes quite hard to determine in plays – is essentially an exercise in literary interpretation, reasoned analysis, and thoughtfulness as opposed to a purely subjective, emotional response. As was mentioned earlier in this chapter, Allardyce Nicoll calls this kind of theme the "central spirit" by which the play is inspired and which gives the play unity of impression. Augustus W. Schlegel's following interpretation of *Hamlet* is a good example of such a thematic statement:

"*Hamlet* is . . . a tragedy of thought inspired by continual and never-satisfied meditation on human destiny and the dark perplexity of the events of this world, and calculated to call forth the very same meditation in the minds of the spectators" (Schlegel 404).

In many complex plays – indeed in any form of artistic expression – the author may not take a clear position. Writing on such works, you should acknowledge the author's ambivalence or refusal to take a clear stand and rely for your inferences on the impressions created by the play's totality – its events, characters, their deeds and key statements, along with various other details of the subject matter. Because of their complexity, such plays offer an ideal opportunity to develop interpretive skills. The format for interpretive essays was explained in Chapter Seven, which you can adapt as necessary to suit your style.

Optional (for extra credit or bonus points)

Using verbal irony, understatement, and paradox

The elements of style that you may use in this paper to continue expanding your range of expression and creative uses of language are verbal irony, understatement, and paradox. Use these elements when you are revising your paper for effectiveness. Remember that the first draft is for simply putting down your thoughts on paper, the second for clarity, and the third and subsequent drafts for effect. Footnote or endnote their use to draw the reader's attention to your attempt at style improvement. As was the case with earlier assignments, ideally these elements of style should be your own creation, but if you are unable to use any or all of the suggested elements, you still have these two options: (1) include in your sentences examples of someone else's use of the suggested stylistic elements and acknowledge the source or (2) in a note at the end of the paper, give a definition and an example of the element(s) you are unable to use. The second option is not useless because by exercising it, you will become more familiar with the yet-to-be mastered stylistic element.

Topics for Discussion and Writing on *Hamlet*

Since *Hamlet* is one of Shakespeare's most popular plays, and also the most discussed, it can serve as a basis to demonstrate the process of creating good discussion topics on any play. Experiencing a play with the selected topics in mind should result in a deeper understanding of the play. The merit of topics is judged by that criterion. The following are some of the possible topics for writing on Shakespeare's complex play. When the meaning of a topic is not self-evident, an explanation is included.

1. If you were compiling a book of profound observations on life, which three statements from *Hamlet* would you include? Why? The direct quotations that you choose should be of general relevance and understandable even to someone unfamiliar with the play.

2. Perfection in an imperfect world: virtue becoming a tragic flaw:

   Hamlet's conscientious and cautious approach in refusing to act against Claudius without conclusive proof of Claudius' guilt contributes to Hamlet's death. Moreover, Hamlets' virtue of being "Most generous and free from all contriving" makes him the victim of the Claudius-Laertes conspiracy (IV, vii, 134-139).

3. Fate of innocence in a corrupt environment: virtue becoming a tragic flaw:

   Ophelia is a loving daughter and sincere in her love for Hamlet. Still she is dragged into the quicksand of corruption and intrigue that proves fatal to her.

4. Vicious cycle of revenge—its ultimate futility. In ultimate terms, revenge brings no personal satisfaction to Hamlet and Laertes, who seek and wreak revenge in the play; Fortinbras, who overcomes his desire for revenge on Denmark, eventually becomes the King of Denmark.

5. Difficulty of acting against the grain (against one's essential nature):

   Hamlet drops his guard many times because he cannot go on pretending. An important instance is in Act III, scene I, lines 149-151, when, sensing Claudius' and Polonius' presence behind the arras, Hamlet tells Ophelia, "I say we will have no more marriage. Those that are married already – all but one – shall live. The rest shall keep as they are." In saying "all but one" shall live, Hamlet is literally saying that he will kill Claudius. Another example of Hamlet's dropping his guard is his frank revelation to Claudius' spies, Rosencrantz and Guildenstern, that he (Hamlet) is not really insane: "I am but mad northwest: when the wind is southerly I know a hawk from a handsaw" (II, ii, 387-388).

   After Hamlet has worked so hard to put on the mask of insanity to protect himself from Claudius and to be left alone to plot his revenge against the murderer of his father, Hamlet's sudden dropping of guard suggests the difficulty of acting against one's grain. Being an honest, straightforward person, Hamlet hates playing games and finds his own game playing –albeit necessitated by the circumstances – unbearable. Through Hamlet's unwise dropping of his guard, Claudius realizes Hamlet's threat and decides to get rid of him under the pretext of sending him to England (III, i, 165-173).

6. Interpretation of a specific scene, a speech, or a specific soliloquy – its connection with the play's larger theme(s) mentioned elsewhere in the play.

   Examples:

   A. the play within the play (III, ii, 141-276)
   B. the duel scene toward the end of the play (V, ii, 227-332)

C. any ONE of Hamlet's or Claudius' soliloquies

D. Ophelia's so-called "insane" speeches in IV, v, 23-73

E. the speech by Gertrude in which she describes Ophelia's death by drowning (IV, vii, 166-183)

F. Hamlet's speech about the inevitability of death and being ready for it (V, ii, 220-224):

The key words in this speech are "There is special providence in the fall of a sparrow" and "The readiness is all." This speech by Hamlet represents an important theme. Develop your essay by analyzing relevant supporting details and quotations from the play. Feel free to briefly mention any philosophical and religious ideas that support this important theme.

G. Hamlet's forceful words to Horatio: (V, ii, 343-349). With these words the dying Hamlet prevents Horatio from following him in death by gulping down the remnants of the poisoned drink. Hamlet's words invite us to look upon death in a different than usual way: Death could be "felicity" (bliss) whereas life, with its "slings and arrows" could be a painful state of being. You can develop your own independent analysis of Hamlet's words with an eye on the context in which the words appear to avoid invalid generalizations. There are numerous other statements in Hamlet that invite analysis, such as "Brevity is the soul of wit," "Madness in great ones must not unwatched go," and many more. You can choose an appealing statement from any play by any author to analyze it in its context.

7. Hamlet's (possibly Shakespeare's) attitude toward self-serving politicians: Hamlet talks about "a certain convocation of politic worms" (IV, iii, 22-23), among other jabs at corrupt politicians.

8. Hamlet -- the potential philosopher king, a corrective to corrupt politics: Hamlet is considered an extraordinary human being by his friends and foes alike.

9. Inconstancy of human beings: Gertrude marries Claudius soon after her first husband's death; people who made faces at Claudius when King Hamlet was alive now purchase Claudius' miniature portraits (II, ii, 371-376). The Player-King tells the Player-Queen in the play within the play,

"The great man down, you mark his favorite flies; The poor advanced makes friends of enemies" (III, ii, 210-211).

10. Inconstancy of human passions: Besides the example of Gertrude's inconstancy, the Player-King's words are important on this.

Purpose is but the slave to memory,
Of violent birth, but poor validity. . . .
What to ourselves in passion we propose,
The passion ending, doth the purpose lose.
The violence of either grief or joy
Their own enactures with themselves destroy."

(III, ii, 194-195, 200-203)

11. Paradoxical elements in human nature: An important speech on this topic is by Hamlet as he talks to Rosencrantz and Guilderstern about "What a piece of work is a man."(II, ii, 312-319).

12. Consequences of unjust ambition: The main focus would be King Claudius, but other characters, such as Polonius, Rosencranz, and Guildenstern, are also relevant.

13. Theory of drama as expressed by Hamlet in III, ii, 1-47

14. Consequences of crime: The main focus would be on the deeds and fate of Claudius, but Hamlet's accidental murder of Polonius would also be relevant.

15. Humor in *Hamlet*: More than just comic relief.

    Use of humor in tragic plays makes them more realistic, because tears and laughter often coexist in real life. Shakespeare's tragic plays contain humor, unlike classical Greek plays that were either pure tragedies or pure comedies, no intermixture. Almost every scene with Hamlet in it has some humor in the form of sarcasm, wit, and puns, especially when he is talking to Polonius, the King, Rosencrantz and Guildenstern. The entire scene with Osric in Act V, scene ii, is a masterpiece of comedy.

16. The Ghost's role in *Hamlet*

    When writing on this topic, address the often-asked question: Why can't Gertrude see the Ghost when Hamlet can see him in the Queen's closet? In that second appearance to Hamlet, is the Ghost only an extension of Hamlet's unconscious, reminding him of his still unfinished duty of avenging his father's murder? Why is the ghost in a military uniform when he is seen in the play the first time but wears plain clothes when he appears to Hamlet in the Queen's bedroom?

17. Women in *Hamlet*: Of the only two women in the play, Ophelia is usually regarded as a weak person who cannot think for herself, but the character of Gertrude is quite complex. (See item No. 23.)

18. A character's role in the play, for example, the grave-diggers in *Hamlet*, (V, i, 1-184) and Osric in Act V, scene ii.

19. Constant flicker of hope in *Hamlet*:

    A. Hope associated with the character of Horatio: Of all characters in the play, Horatio receives the highest compliments from Hamlet. His wisdom and level-headedness is always a source of hope that somehow he will come up with a solution to even the most intractable problems.

    B. Hope associated with Hamlet's cautious nature: His habit of carefully weighing every move that he makes and his commitment to doing the right thing create hopefulness.

    C. Hope associated with the nature of human conscience: The fact that even the most inveterate villain like Claudius has a conscience and shows vulnerability to qualms in the prayer scene in Act IV is a cause for hope. Martin Luther King, Jr.'s words are relevant to this topic: "The arc of moral compass is long, but it inevitably bends toward justice."

    D. Reason for hope in Hamlet – Evil's finite reign: In spite of his power and privilege, Claudius' reign of evil comes to an end. You can also relate this topic to A. C. Bradley's view, expressed in his chapter on "The Substance of Shakespearean Tragedy" (included earlier in this chapter), that at the end of a tragic play, there is a suggestion that evil eventually is purged and the order restored.

20. Limitless range of ideas in *Hamlet*: Of special relevance are Hamlet's words to Horatio,

    "There are more things in heaven and earth, Horatio, Than are dreamt of in your philosophy" (I, v, 166-167).

21. Hamlet – the reluctant hero: Even though Hamlet faces every challenge with utmost heroism, he seeks no heroics, does not think of himself as a great hero, but is pulled into a vortex over which he has no control. Evidence for this view is in Hamlet's speech right after he learns (from the Ghost of

his dead father) about the circumstances of King Hamlet's murder by Claudius and the possible guilt of his mother (Gertrude):

"The time is out of joint. O cursed spite that ever I was born to set it right!" (I, v, 188-189)

Hamlet's words clearly show that he does not wish to be the moral rectifier of such a corrupt world. He is pushed into this not only unpleasant but seemingly impossible role. You may wish to speculate as to what Hamlet *really* wanted to do as opposed to what he ended up doing. Support each claim and inference with evidence from the play.

22. "Frailty, thy name is woman": Gertrude – a slut or an exploited woman? Writing on a character requires careful analysis of the character's deeds, values, and fate, along with the author's tone and prominent characters' opinions of the character you are writing about. You can formulate a well-reasoned opinion about any character. About Gertrude, some possible positions, defensible on the basis of evidence from the play, are the following.

  A. Gertrude as a weak woman who yields too soon to Claudius, disregarding her son's feelings of hurt and betrayal

  B. Gertrude as a decent woman with normal needs and desires, living as a pawn in a male-dominated world.

  C. Gertrude as a loving mother, a perceptive, intelligent woman, espousing values far ahead of her time.

23. Seeking Inspiration from a critic's Interpretation:

  We can generate an interesting discussion by using a critic's words as the starting point. When responding to a critic's view, we may agree with it and offer evidence and arguments in support, or we may disagree and refute the critic's opinion with valid reasoning. Still another option we have is agreeing with only a part of the critic's judgment. Throughout this chapter, there are many statements by critics that could inspire a worthy response.

24. Shakespeare's craft: You may choose to discuss any one or more of the elements that belong under the broad topic of craft or style. These terms are explained in item No. 6 in the next section "Topics Relevant to Drama in General." Since evaluating a playwright's craft is a challenging aspect of drama, an example or two of its usages from film may help facilitate its comprehension in drama. Use of symbolism provides a good example.

  Symbolism. When discussing symbolism in *Hamlet* you may learn from the example of the Russian version of Shakespeare's *Hamlet*, directed by Grigori Kozintsev. In this production the courtiers are shown moving in a clockwise circle, while the isolated and alienated hero Hamlet moves counterclockwise. Hamlet's movement is symbolic of his going against the current of contemporary affairs and values, which, in his view, are filled with vice and corruption. He is at cross purposes with everyone around him with the exception of Horatio. The symbol of the clockwise and counterclockwise movements appears as a reinforcement of Hamlet's famous words that conclude the play's first act:

  > The time is out of joint. O cursed spite,
  > That ever I was born to set it right! (I: v, 204-205)

  As we can see, like the playwrights, directors also rely on the suggestive power of symbolism to enrich the plays' contents. Once we are sensitized to the use of symbolism in film, we can apply that approach to the play's stage version. Do we see any recurring symbols or images that set Hamlet apart from members of King Claudius' circle? "A congregation of politic worms" is how Hamlet describes the King's courtiers. It is a strong image that gets reinforced by symbols of the "unweeded garden that grows to seed" – Hamlet's description of the Danish court's corrupt environment. Hamlet's use of the words "mildewed ear blasting his wholesome brother" describe parasites that destroy healthy crops, and, by implication, Claudius' murder of his brother King Hamlet. Understanding how dramatists craft the content of their plays enriches the plays' meanings.

The point of comparing drama with film is that since cinematography (style) in film is more visible and more easily noticeable than literary style, we can use style in film to understand style in literature.

Topics Relevant to Drama in General

As you have seen from the list of topics on *Hamlet*, plays offer an abundance of writing material. A few more items that relate to drama in general are mentioned below to continue refining the process and skill of topic generation and to give you opportunities to enhance your knowledge.

1. Imagine that you are compiling a book of profound observations on human existence. Which three statements from a play of your choice would you include? After writing each statement, explain in a sentence what makes your selected statement profound.

   The statements you choose should be in the form of direct quotations from the play. They should be of general relevance, not applicable only to a specific character in a specific situation. Such theme-like quotations should exemplify profound wisdom and understanding of human nature. Here are a few examples from three of Shakespeare's popular plays – *Hamlet*, *King Lear*, and *Macbeth*. When analyzing such statements, you should be mindful of ironic implications because they may not necessarily express the author's views. They may express a character's view in a specific situation but may have the potential of general relevance.

   A. Hamlet to Rosencrantz: ". . . there is nothing either good or bad but thinking makes it so." (II, ii, 253-254)

   B. Hamlet utters this startling truth to his mother: "For use almost can change   the stamp of nature." (III, iv, 169)

   C. Polonius' advice to his son Laertes: "Neither a borrower nor a lender be,/For loan oft loses both itself and friend." (I, iii, 75-76)

   D. Lear to Gloucester on seeing a constable lashing a prostitute:

      Through tatter'd clothes small vices do appear;
      Robes and furr'd gowns hide all. Plate sin with gold,
      And the strong lance of justice hurtless breaks;
      Arm it in rags, a pigmy's straw doth pierce it. (IV, vi, 164-167)

   E. Gloucester on seeing a mad beggar:

      As flies to wanton boys, are we to the gods
      They kill us for their sport. (IV, I, 86-87)

   F. Edgar to Gloucester, a statement that echoes Hamlet's "The readiness is all":

> Men must endure
> Their going hence, even as their coming hither:
> Ripeness is all. (V, ii, 9-11)

G. Macbeth's musings on life:

> Tomorrow, and tomorrow, and tomorrow
> Creeps in this petty pace from day to day
> To the last syllable of recorded time;
> And all our yesterdays have lighted fools
> The way to dusty death. Out, out, brief candle!
> Life's but a walking shadow, a poor player
> That struts and frets his hour upon the stag
> And then is heard no more. It is a tale
> Told by an idiot, full of sound and fury
> Signifying nothing. (V, v, 19-28)

2. If you were to introduce a play by Shakespeare or by any other author to today's audience, which play would you choose? Write an introductory essay to make the play appealing and relevant. You should include observations on the play's content (which consists of themes, events, characters, etc.) and also comment on the outstanding features of the author's craft. (See item No. 6 for help with craft.)

   Summarize parts of the play to support your points but do not allot too much space to unstructured summarizing of the play's events. Include analytical and critical comments which should control your summaries. In a proper place, cite from the play some statements that could be regarded as proof of the author's depth of perception.

3. Choose any topic from any play. In your introductory thesis paragraph, convert the topic into a succinctly worded statement of what you consider to be an important theme, that is, the play's position on that topic, often expressed by implication rather than by statement. Cite evidence from the play in the form of a mixture of direct quotations and summary of relevant details in your own words to support each major point.

4. Write a self-analysis of a literary character in his or her own voice, taking on the character's persona.

5. Analyze a literary character by writing him or her a letter, alerting them to potential problems in their thinking and suggesting ways to improve.

6. Evaluating a playwright's craft: You may choose to discuss any one or more of the following elements that belong under the broad topic of craft or style:

   - stage directions
   - dialogue
   - variety in language and speech rhythm to distinguish characters from one another
   - crafting the opening and closing scenes of a play to maximize effect
   - arrangement and order of scenes
   - pacing
   - foreshadowing
   - suspense
   - use of setting to create appropriate moods and to suggest themes

- means of character development
- use of symbolism, allusion, irony, paradox, understatement, analogy, figurative language, and imagery
- effectiveness of the plot-structuring devices such as an event or a statement somewhere near the play's opening, to which everything that follows is connected (somewhat like a thesis statement in an essay).

Analysis of some of the stylistic elements leads to the discovery of themes in plays as in other forms of literature. This style-theme connection has been fully explained in Chapter Four.

7. You may make your essay a research paper by including two or three critics' opinions and documenting them properly.

8. Write an interpretation of a specific scene, a dramatic monologue, or a soliloquy. A dramatic monologue is a speech in which there are listeners but no dialogue, whereas a soliloquy is a speech in which a character thinks aloud, no other character listening.

9. Plot construction strategies

Evaluate the effectiveness of an author's primary and secondary plot-structuring devices which were fully discussed in Chapter Three. Very briefly, a primary plotting device is the use of an event that becomes pivotal to the story, such as the Ghost's appearance in *Hamlet*'s Act I, the eagerly awaited insurance check in *A Raisin in the Sun*, and the wager, in George Bernard Shaw's *Pygmalion*, between Henry Higgins and Colonel Pickering that Higgins would transform the flower girl Eliza's uneducated speech into polished speech of a duchess within three months. Among the secondary plot-structuring devices, notable are the author's use of parallelism, sequencing of events, pacing, arrangement of scenes, and attention-getting, attention-retaining, and suspense-creating devices.

10. Compare Shakespeare's view of tragedy with that of any of the twentieth-century dramatists, such as Tennessee Williams, Eugene O'Neill, and Arthur Miller with reference to any play by them. For comparison and contrast, apply to your selected play the following two comments by A. C. Bradley, taken from his chapter on "Substance of Shakespearean Tragedy." Bradley's complete lecture is on my website. A few outstanding quotations from that lecture are included in this chapter.

    i. "Two statements . . . may at once be made regarding the tragic fact as he [Shakespeare] represents it: one, that it is and remains to us something piteous, fearful and mysterious; the other, that the representation of it does not leave us crushed, rebellious or desperate."

    ii. "And why is it that a man's virtues help to destroy him, and that his weakness or defect is so intertwined with everything that is admirable in him that we can hardly separate them even in imagination?"

    Do Bradley's statements about "the tragic fact" and about virtues in a person becoming a source of his or her destruction apply to the works of Williams, O'Neill, or Miller that you select to discuss? Support your analysis with relevant details from the play.

11. Reviewing a contemporary play

Besides making classical plays accessible, the knowledge of fundamental principles of dramatic art offered in this chapter has also prepared you to enjoy new, unfamiliar plays that treat important daily occurrences in our lives. As you approach these plays, apply to them those theoretic underpinnings that you have learned.

The variety and scope of contemporary plays – both in matters of style and substance – would become apparent from a glance at the number of theatrical performances and professional reviews listed in local news. As a part of your preparation to write about current theater and as a sample for this exercise, read the theater critic Robert Hurwitt's review of *Gibraltar* (included under "Sample Essays" later in this chapter). Hurwitt comments on "the emotional depth, sensual poetry, flesh-and-blood characters and gracefully intricate structure of the play." The themes noted by the reviewer relate to interconnections of dreams, fantasy, and reality.

For your review, select a play that has thematic depth, intricately layered plot (structure), engaging language, and interesting characters. The literary elements of themes, characters, plot, and style were covered in Chapters One through Four of this book.

12. Writing a critique of a review. Another interesting review-related assignment is becoming a critic or collaborator of a reviewer. You may add a section to an existing review to cover an area overlooked by the reviewer, or you may choose to write a different interpretation of the play.

SAMPLE ESSAYS

Plays are full of fascinating characters and themes that invite interaction and analysis. The sample essays that follow analyze just a few plays. You will find many more reviews on my website connected to this book. These essays elucidate some of the principles of drama that we have been discussing in this chapter. They provide engaging and concrete contexts for them.

Hamlet's Enduring Appeal
An essay by the author of this book

Is *Hamlet* a murder mystery, a detective story, a revenge play, or philosophy of life disguised as drama? The prevalent view is that this play combines all these elements and, thus, like Shakespeare's most other plays, has something for every taste. His ability to feel the pulse of his audience made Shakespeare the most popular dramatist of his day. It would, however, be wrong to say that popularity was his chief goal. He had a clear conception of the role of the dramatist as someone who, while providing entertainment, would not overlook the moral and philosophical aspects of drama.

Shakespeare's view of drama

Fortunately, the play itself contains a clear and concentrated statement of Shakespeare's view of drama presented to us in Hamlet's words in Act III, Scene ii, lines 1-47.[5] Here Hamlet is advising the actors about acting and about his concept of drama. His words on acting can be applied with equal validity to the writing of plays. Hamlet emphasizes the following points:

1. Use restraint (understatement) in expressing passion so that we don't tear it to tatters: ". . . in the very torrent, tempest, and . . . whirlwind of your passion, you must acquire and beget a temperance that may give it smoothness" (III,ii,5-8).

---

5 *Shakespeare: Complete Plays and Poems.* (New York: Houghton Mifflin & Company, 1942)

2. Make the style and substance complement each other: "Suit the action to the word, the word to the action" (lines 18-19).

3. Represent the universal in human nature as well as the particular in the dramatist's time and place:

   ". . . the purpose of playing . . . both at the first and now, was and is, to hold, as 'twere, the mirror up to nature; to show virtue her own feature, scorn her own image, and the very age and body of the time , , , [its] form and pressure" (lines 21-25).

4. Maintain a clear sense of audience. Entertaining the unskillful is less important than pleasing the judicious viewer/reader. What makes the "unskillful laugh" may make "the judicious grieve, the censure of the which one must in your allowance o'erweigh a whole theater of others" (lines 27-30).

5. Represent human nature realistically; some writers and actors portray humanity "so abominably" that it seems "some of Nature's journeymen had made men, and not made them well" (lines 35-36).

6. Limit the role of clowns so that they serve, not disrupt the play's important questions:

   "And let those that play your clowns speak no more than is set down for them, for there be of them that will themselves laugh, to set on some quantity of barren spectators to laugh too, though in the meantime some necessary question of the play be then to be considered. That's villainous and shows a most pitiful ambition in the fool that uses it" (lines 40-47).

This scene shows that Shakespeare (using Hamlet as his spokesman) felt writers should address important questions.

Earlier Hamlet had commented on a play that was not well received by the masses, yet he thought it to be a good play because it was free of trendy ostentation and affectation:

"I heard thee speak me a speech once, but it was never acted, or if it was, not above once, for the play, I remember, pleased not the million; 'twas caviary to the general, but it was (as I received it, and others, whose judgments in such matters cried in the top of mine) an excellent play, well digested in the scenes, set down with as much modesty as cunning [;] . . . there were no sallets in the lines to make the matter savory; nor no matter in the phrase that might indict the author of affectation" (II,ii,44-454).

With Shakespeare's aforementioned criteria of great plays in mind, let us look at *Hamlet* as a play that combines the elements of murder mystery, detective story, revenge play, and philosophy.

Hamlet as a murder mystery

In the play's opening, jittery lines we learn from the sentinels that an apparition, resembling the late King of Denmark, has been haunting the platform of the royal castle at Elsinor. Later in Act 1 (scene v), the Ghost reveals to Prince Hamlet that the prince's uncle and the present King Claudius is the one who had murdered his own brother – King Hamlet. The "official" reason for King Hamlet's death had been given out to be a snake bite. Now the Ghost tells Hamlet that the snake that bit him wears his crown.

This is all quite confusing to Hamlet, who intuitively feels the Ghost's words to be true, but being a just, honorable, and conscientious man, he wants to be sure of Claudius' crime before taking revenge.

Hamlet's confusion is evident in these lines:

The spirit that I have seen/May be a devil; and the devil hath power/T'assume a pleasing shape; yea, and perhaps/Out of my weakness and my melancholy/ . . . Abuses me to damn me. I'll have grounds/More relative than this (II,ii,606-616).

Hamlet as a detective story

To test the Ghost's veracity, Hamlet must become a detective, and here the murder mystery becomes a detective play. There are, of course, other detectives in the play. They are Hamlet's former friends Rosencrantz and Guildenstern, whose services the King engages to spy on Hamlet. And then there is Polonius, the chief spy in the court of Elsinor. However, our concern is primarily with Hamlet as a detective. When some actors come to Elsinor, Hamlet devises a plan. He will ask the visiting actors to act out on stage the circumstances and manner of King Hamlet's murder by Claudius as reported to Hamlet by the Ghost. If Claudius reveals his guilt when watching this mirror image of his crime, Hamlet would be sure of Claudius's crime and then would know his course. Hamlet is here expressing an artist's faith in the power of drama:

I have heard that guilty creatures sitting at a play have by the very cunning of the scene been struck so to the soul that presently they have proclaimed their malefactions. For murder, though it have no tongue, will speak with most miraculous organ. I'll have these players play something like the murder of my father before mine uncle. . . . The play's the thing wherein I'll catch the conscience of the King (II,ii,601-617).

Since the life of King Claudius is at stake, Hamlet does not want to be the sole judge lest he should make an error of Judgment. To make certain that his own eyes do not deceive him, Hamlet asks his wise friend Horatio to observe Claudius's response to the murder scene in the play-within-the-play.

Hamlet as a revenge play

When Claudius reveals his guilt, the detective component in the story of Hamlet comes to an end and the revenge component begins. Now Hamlet knows his course, but the first decisive step that he takes is the accidental murder of Polonius, who had been hiding "behind the arras" to listen in on the conversation between Hamlet and his mother. Hamlet mistook Polonius for Claudius; what business, after all, did Polonius have in the Queen's bedroom? This unintended murder of Polonius complicates the plot and Hamlet's situation. Claudius uses Hamlet's act as an excuse to get rid of him under the pretext of sending him to England. Escorted by Rosencrantz and Guildenstern, Hamlet is to be put to death immediately on reaching England. That is Claudius's secret command to the king of England. Thus, potentially, Claudius is already guilty of at least two murders.

Looking at *Hamlet* as a revenge play, we find that revenge is an important topic in the play. In fact, the Ghost's call for revenge on Claudius is the plot-setting device that controls the play's movement. Even though *Hamlet* includes many elements of the popular tradition of the revenge play, Shakespeare adds a philosophical dimension to the typical, action-oriented drama.

Hamlet as a philosophy of life

A poignant reminder of the ultimate futility of the vicious cycle of revenge is that when vengeance is finally carried out, it is not in the form we had hoped for, nor does it bring the expected satisfaction. Along with Claudius die the Queen, Laertes, and Hamlet. Revenge brings no personal satisfaction to Hamlet and Laertes, who seek and wreak revenge in the play. On the other hand, Fortinbras, who overcomes his desire for revenge on Denmark, eventually becomes the king of Denmark.

This philosophical reflection on the futility of revenge is but one of the numerous great ideas Shakespeare has enshrined in stunning and memorable language. Some will undoubtedly and persuasively maintain that the play's philosophical component is its most enduring quality. In fact if there ever were to be composed one single book of profound observations about human existence, *Hamlet* would, undoubtedly, be a prominent source.

Some other philosophical reflections in *Hamlet*

The following random thoughts in response to just a few of the memorable passages from *Hamlet* by no means cover the wealth of great ideas in this play.

Scruples of conscience and how they bind a thinking man, sometimes to the point of paralysis of will: "Thus conscience does make cowards of us all, and thus the native hue of resolution is sicklied o'er with the pale cast of thought" (III,I,83-88). Conscience, Hamlet comes to know, is the ultimate controller of a thoughtful man's actions.

On the question of how to live one's life, unsurpassed are Shakespeare's following words – ironically uttered by Polonius, who can give great advice but fails to practice it: ". . . . Give each man thine ear, but few they voice; take each man's censure, but reserve thy judgment. . . . Neither a borrower nor a lender be, for loan oft loses both itself and friend, ... This above all, to thine own self be true, and it must follow, as the night the day, thou canst not then be false to any man (I,iii,61-80).

Validity of our statements in the heat of passion: What credibility do our words carry in such a state of heightened emotions? Once again, Polonius' words furnish the answer: "When the blood burns, how prodigal the soul lends the tongue vows" (I,iii,116-117).

The paradoxical elements in human nature -- our zenith as well as our nadir: "I have of late, but wherefore I know not, lost all my mirth, . . . this goodly frame, the earth, seems to me a sterile promontory; . . . it appeareth nothing to me but a foul and pestilent congregation of vapors. What a piece of work is a man, how noble in reason, . . . in apprehension how like a god: the beauty of the world, the paragon of animals; and yet to me, what is this quintessence of dust? . . . (II,ii,303-318).

Ideal temperament and desirable attitude in adversity: For guidance we need to look at Horatio, who embodies these enviable qualities:

"A man that Fortune's buffets and rewards hast ta'en with equal thanks; and blest are those whose blood and judgment are so well comeddled that they are not a pipe for Fortune's finger to sound what stop she please. Give me that man that is not passion's slave, . . ." (III,ii,68-76).

Whereas Hamlet sees himself as passion's slave and as such an easy instrument to be exploited by fate, Horatio's stoical nature enables him to rise above life's fever and fret.

Desirable conduct – the importance of kindness in human dealings: In response to Polonius's plan to treat the players "according to their desert," Hamlet urges him to treat them "much better": "Use every man after his desert, and who should scape whipping? Use them after your own honor and dignity. The less they deserve, the more merit is in your bounty" (II,ii,540-543).

Random distribution of sorrows: When Claudius's crafty schemes backfire, he learns the bitter truth expressed in a way that lifts the cliché-like "When it rains it pours" to new heights of artistic expression: "When sorrows come, they come not single spies, but in battalions" (IV,v,78-79).

Backfiring designs: It has been long known that those who lay traps for others may themselves fall into them, and at the end of the play, Horatio talks about "purposes mistook/Fall'n on th' inventors' heads" (V,ii,385-386). However, this wisdom has never been expressed so eloquently as in these words of Hamlet: "For 'tis the sport to have the enginer/Hoist with his own petar" (III,iv.207-208).

The inconstancy of human beings: Of other universal truths, the Player-King has chronicled for all time the truth about the inconstancy of human passions: " . . . . What to ourselves in passion we propose, the passion ending, doth the purpose lose" (III, ii, 192-209). This theme of inconstancy of human beings comes up many times in the play. Gertrude marries Claudius soon after her husband's death. What is surprising is the fact that the love between King Hamlet and Gertrude was so special that it seemed to grow continuously. It is precisely because theirs seemed to be a perfect match that Gertrude's marriage to Claudius soon after her husband's death puzzles Hamlet: ". . . That it should come to this: But two months dead . . . frailty, thy name is woman – a little month, or ere those shoes were old with which she followed my poor father's body like Niobe, all tears, why she, even she – O God, a beast that wants discourse of reason would have mourned longer – married with my uncle" (I,ii,137-151). In fact, Hamlet's mind is so tainted by his mother's conduct that he starts seeing her in every woman. When Ophelia comments on the brevity of the prologue to the play being performed, Hamlet retorts that the prologue is brief like "woman's love" (III,ii,159).

Hamlet notices inconstancy of human beings in yet another respect – the nature of public memory. People who made faces at Claudius when King Hamlet was alive now purchase Claudius's miniature portraits (II,ii,371-376). The Player-King, too alludes to this phenomenon: "the great man down, you mark his favorite flies; the poor advanced makes friends of enemies (III,ii,210-219).

Hamlet would like to understand the reasons for these defects in human nature, and he counts on philosophy to furnish an answer, but he finds philosophy very limited in explaining the mystery of human nature and existence. Hence Hamlet's famous words to Horatio: "There are more things in heaven and earth, Horatio, than are dreamt of in your philosophy" (I,v,166-67).

The inevitability of death and the importance of readiness: As to the ultimate philosophical question that brings us face to face with the oblivion of inevitable, ever-approaching death, what can surpass Hamlet's words that culminate in the famous "readiness is all" attitude: "There is special providence in the fall of a sparrow. If it be now, 'tis not to come; if it be not to come, it will be now; if it be not now, yet it will come. The readiness is all. Since no man of aught he leaves knows, what is't to leave betimes? Let it be" (V,ii,220-225). Some things are simply beyond our control and the best we can do is submit to the inevitable.

Ironic tricks of fate: Hamlet has been dying to tell the truth about Claudius's crime of fratricide and his other evil acts. Finally, when the right moment offers itself, Hamlet's voice is silenced by death. Instead of a harmonious speech tying all loose ends, as Hamlet plunges into Claudius the same envenomed weapon that has mortally hurt him and Laertes and as he forces the remainder of the poisoned drink down Claudius's throat, he expends the last ounce of his energy and the last seconds of his time. All that he can tell the dumbfounded courtiers is this: "You that look pale and tremble at this chance, had I but time (as this fell sergeant, Death, is strict in his arrest) O, I could tell you – but let it be. Horatio, I am dead; . . . report me and my cause aright to the unsatisfied" (V,ii,335-341). Hamlet's speech captures the pathos of human helplessness and fate's capriciousness.

Horatio is left to tell his friend's story – a story that the whole play has not been able to tell. Thus, in one of the most perfect finishes in drama, the story is both ending and beginning – ending of Hamlet's story as the play attempted to tell it and the beginning of Hamlet's story as his friend Horatio would tell it.

The list of great ideas from the play could continue indefinitely because *Hamlet* remains Shakespeare's longest, most discussed, and most complex play. It bristles with probing questions and profound observations on the human condition. The deeply meditative and riddlesome nature of the play was captured by A.W. Schlegel nearly 150 years ago:

"Hamlet is singular in its kind: a tragedy of thought inspired by continual and never-satisfied meditation on human destiny and the dark perplexity of the events of this world, and calculated to call forth the very same meditation in the minds of the spectators. This enigmatical work resembles those irrational equations in which a fraction of unknown magnitude always remains, that will in no way admit of solution" (Schlegel 404).

For a list of themes and topics please read the following section on Topics for Discussion and Writing in Hamlet. *Details from the play supporting topics and themes are included with the topics.*

Play discussed: Shakespeare's *Hamlet*

Using Chapter Two's advice on writing a character analysis, Stella Carey's interpretation of Horatio's role in Shakespeare's "Hamlet" is lucid and persuasive. Especially welcome is her finding in Horatio a source of hope. Re-read the plot analysis of this play in Chapter Three. If you have not yet read the play, at least watch any of its many film adaptations. Sir Lawrence Olivier's is one of the best.

Horatio: A Source of Hope in *Hamlet*
Student author: Stella Carey

Critics frequently dismiss Horatio as a minor character in Shakespeare's *Hamlet*. He is often viewed as little more than a foil for Hamlet or a reflection of the prince's conscience. However, deeper consideration of Horatio's function in the play reveals a much more significant role. Horatio is the only character Hamlet trusts, and as such he is a true friend and the sole confidant of the prince. He also brings a sense of balance and stability to the play by virtue of his calm and rational nature. Finally, Horatio provides an outside perspective which serves to validate the audience's point of view. Horatio is essential to understanding Hamlet's personality and the tragic events that come to pass in the play.

Perhaps the most important of Horatio's functions in the play is his role as Hamlet's ally and confidant. There is a strong bond of friendship between Hamlet and Horatio, and this connection offers unique insight into Hamlet's personality and character. Only in his interactions with Horatio can the prince completely be himself, free from pretense, feigned madness, or bitterness and disdain that dominate his exchanges with most other characters in the play. Hamlet seems to truly enjoy Horatio's company, and at times the two friends exchange jokes and lighthearted banter, such as in the graveyard scene (Act 5, Scene 1) or the dialogue with Osric (Act 5, Scene 2). These are some of the few moments during the play when Hamlet seems happy. Interactions between Hamlet and Horatio provide the only glimpse into Hamlet's true self, as he was before the tragic events surrounding his father's death began to unfold.

Horatio is the only character, aside from Hamlet's own late father, that the prince respects and reveres. In Act 3, Scene 2, before confiding his plans to entrap Claudius, Hamlet lavishes his friend with praise:

> Since my dear soul was mistress of her choice
> And could of men distinguish her election,
> S'hath seal'd thee for herself, for thou hast been
> As one, in suff'ring all, that suffers nothing,
> A man that Fortune's buffets and rewards
> Has ta'en with equal thanks; and blest are those
> Whose blood and judgment are so well comeddled
> That they are not a pipe for Fortune's finger
> To sound what stop she please. Give me that man
> That is not passion's slave, and I will wear him
> In my heart's core, ay, in my heart of heart,
> As do I thee. (III, ii, 65-76)

Hamlet sees in Horatio qualities that he finds enviable. The prince admires his friend's equanimity, integrity, and even temperament. Horatio is sensitive, but not ruled by emotion; he is not "passion's slave." As Hamlet struggles with his own emotional distress, he recognizes the value of Horatio's strong character.

It is this strength of character that enables Horatio to provide a sense of stability and equilibrium to other characters in the play. In the first scene the sentinels turn to him for guidance in dealing with the ghost. "Thou art a scholar," (1.1.42) Marcello remarks, and urges him to confront the apparition. True to his rational nature, Horatio questions the ghost without fear, and then determines that Hamlet should be informed about the ghost. It is the same lucidity and resolve that later prompts hamlet, as he is dying at the end of the play, to entrust Horatio to tell his story.

Another vital role Horatio fulfills in the play is to provide the audience with an outside perspective that validates their point of view. Because Horatio is a sound and sensible person, he lends credibility to aspects of the play that may otherwise be questionable. Horatio sees and believes the ghost, so the audience can be confident that it is not a figment of Hamlet's troubled mind. Horatio also helps to confirm Hamlet's sanity by providing an outlet for the prince to let down his guise of madness when he is talking to Horatio. Without the counterpoint that Horatio provides, the audience would be in doubt as to Hamlet's true mental state.

The character of Horatio is vital to *Hamlet* in a number of ways. And Shakespeare was no doubt cognizant of the character's importance, for the playwright emphasizes Horatio by featuring him prominently in both the opening and closing scenes of the play. Horatio's constancy of presence and of character throughout the play provides crucial insight into the mind of the prince and the events that transpire. Thus Horatio helps the audience better understand and appreciate the story and meaning of Hamlet's life.

Play discussed: *Pygmalion* by George Bernard Shaw (1856-1950)

This review is based on the Irish playwright's written text, not on a performance.

Either read the play or watch any of its film adaptations, preferably before reading this review. You can read the play online at: http://www.bartleby.com/138/. The 1938 film version with Leslie Howard and Wendy Hiller is excellent and faithful to the text and you can watch it on YouTube: http://www.youtube.com/watch?v=tmdPj_XbF30. The film musical of 1962, based on this play, was called "My Fair Lady," and starred Rex Harrison and Audrey Hepburn. It won eight Oscars, including best picture. You can view it on YouTube: http://www.youtube.com/watch?v=da5Md6OzUPo

Education and Class in Shaw's *Pygmalion*: A Review
by the author of this book

The Plot-setting Bet

The plot of Shaw's popular romantic comedy revolves around a bet between two scholars of phonetics—Henry Higgins and Colonel Pickering. The play's main male character claims that he can transform the unschooled flower girl Eliza Dolittle (the play's heroine) into a speaker of perfect, upper class English in just three months. The unbelieving Colonel Pickering offers to bear all costs of this experiment. The success or failure of the project is to be tested at an ambassador's garden party, where Eliza is to pass off as a duchess. The experiment is a huge success owing to a number of reasons: Eliza has a great desire to learn to speak "proper" English; she is intelligent; she has the benefit of good instruction, and she works hard at picking up the rhythm, intonation, and diction of educated speech.

Eliza's Incredible Success

In a few months, wearing a fancy dress and the right accent, she is able to pass off as a duchess at an ambassador's party. Everyone at the party is captivated by her charms and wants to know more about her background which she has to struggle to conceal, rightly afraid that if the truth about her background is found out, she would not only be thrown out but punished for her impudence. She wins Higgins' bet. However, Eliza herself is not happy with her transformation because she has to be constantly on guard to hide her "low" origin in order to mix with the people whose language she has learned after hard work. What she tells Higgins and Pickering during the party expresses her feelings: "I don't think I can bear much more . . . nothing can make me the same as these people" (Shaw 95). She is also disappointed that Higgins regards her no more than a subject in a successful experiment.

The Turning Point

At the end of the party at which Eliza passes off as a duchess, Higgins fails to acknowledge Eliza's achievements in his conversation with Pickering, overheard by Eliza: "Thank God it's over! . . . It was interesting enough at first, while we were at the phonetics; but after that I got deadly sick of it . . . It was a silly notion: the whole thing has been a bore . . . The dinner was worse . . . with nobody but a damned fool of a fashionable woman to talk to! I tell you, Pickering, never again for me. No more artificial duchesses. The whole thing has been simple purgatory" (98-99). No wonder she throws Higgins' slippers at him when he asks for them.

Eliza's Dilemma

Eliza is left to ponder her predicament all alone. She describes her current *versus* former situations eloquently, "I sold flowers. I didn't sell myself. Now you've made a lady of me I'm not fit to sell anything else. I wish you'd left me where you found me" (103). As a flower girl she made her living by selling flowers, but now she has to sell her integrity to be a part of the elite. At the party where she is surrounded by all the admiring aristocracy, deep inside she feels miserable because she does not like being with those people. What is to become of her now? In the class-ridden society, mastering the language of the upper class has given her the opportunity to enter the privileged group without the means to stay there and be a part of it. Her dilemma is that she cannot go back to her former occupation of selling flowers. The education she has received makes it impossible for her to relapse into a "guttersnipe". In Shaw's own words from the postscript to the play, Eliza has become "disclassed."

The Play's Themes

Shaw's object of attack is the rigid social stratification that makes movement across the established lines impossible. Higgins tells us how this class system makes people desperate to learn the elite lingo when they run into money and want to be a part of the upper class: When Pickering, who is returning from India, asks Higgins if there is a living in phonetics, Higgins answers: "Oh, yes. Quite a fat one. This is an age of upstarts. Men begin in Kentish Town with £80 a year, and end up in Park Lane with a hundred thousand. Now I can teach them" (27).

He is also suggesting that decent education is the right of everyone, that given an opportunity, everyone can benefit from it, and that depriving people of this birthright fosters the social evil of creating "the haves" and "have nots." However, the problem gets even more complicated when we realize that to enjoy respect in a class-ridden society, only education is not enough. Money is also a necessity. Those like the family of Clara and Freddy, who have the status without the money, are also miserable in that system. In his postscript to the play, imagining the lives of his characters after the play is over, Shaw explains that to maintain the "air of gentility," Freddy's mother discourages him from accepting a clerical job or opening a flower shop with Eliza because it will "damage her [Clara's] matrimonial chances." The Eysford-Hill family has been "clinging for so many years to that step of the social ladder on which retail trade is impossible (141).

For the same snobbish reason, Clara does not work, even though the family needs the money desperately. Eventually, in Shaw's postscript, she is forced by the circumstances to sell for a lady of a furniture shop, resulting in two huge gains: First, since Clara has accepted a sales position, there can be no opposition to Eliza and Freddy's opening a flower shop. Secondly, Clara enjoys the thrill of freedom in her ability to earn her living:

"It exasperated her to think that the dungeon in which she had languished for so many unhappy years had been unlocked all the time, and the impulses she had so carefully struggled with and stifled for the sake of keeping well with society, were precisely those by which alone she could have come into any sort of sincere human contact" (143-144).

Character-Theme Connections

Shaw used Higgins to satirize the upper class. To expose the sham of the so-called middle class respectability, he uses Alfred Dolittle, who is pushed into the middle class from his carefree disclassed poverty as a result of Higgins' silly joke in telling an American philanthropist Ezra Wannafeller that "the most original moralist in England . . . was Alfred Dolittle, a common dustman" (115). Wannafeller's bequest leaves Dolittle £3000 a year on the condition that he lecture for the Wannafeller Moral Reform World League up to six times a year. Dolittle points out the self-imposed fetters of the middle class that force them "to live for others" and not for themselves (116). On this transformation, Dolittle laments, "I was happy. I was free. I touched pretty nigh everybody for money when I wanted it . . . Now I am worrited [sic]; tied neck and heels; and everybody touches me for money . . . I'll have to learn to speak middle class language from you, instead of speaking proper English." (116) When Mr. Higgins reminds Dolittle that he does not have to accept the bequest, he explains his predicament: Since he has been an "undeserving poor" unable to "put by a bit", he has no choice but to accept the offer: "They've got you every way you turn: it's a choice between the Skilly [sic] of the workhouse and the Char Bydis [sic] of the middle class. [Dolittle is referring to the myth about the monster Scylla and the dangerous whirlpool Charybidis]. The proverb for this situation is to be caught between the devil and the deep blue sea.

Higgins is evidently the title's Pygmalion, but in Shaw's adaptation of this famous myth, Eliza is not inert material waiting to be shaped into form by Pygmalion. She has a mind of her own as is evident in her spirited and defiant response to Higgins' bullying. She tells him that she can be better at teaching people phonetics because besides having a quick mind and a good ear, she is also better than Higgins at human relationships. She tells Higgins all she has to do is advertise that she was a cockney flower girl who learned to speak like a duchess in six months and could pass on the same skill to anyone interested for a thousand guineas. She goes on to declare her independence: "I can do without you: don't think I can't." (127) Eliza's assertiveness jolts Higgins out of his usual smugness and elicits this surprising response from him: "You never asked yourself, I suppose, whether *I* could do without you" (127). Higgins does admit—although grudgingly—that he has learned something from Eliza: "I have learnt something from your idiotic notions: I confess that humbly and gratefully" (127). Therefore, the play should not be regarded only as the education of Eliza by Higgins, but also the education of Higgins by Eliza. By the end of the play Eliza is able to have her desire for respect fulfilled. She has earned a place of equality with Higgins and Pickering as the transformed Higgins admits:

"Five minutes ago you were like a millstone round my neck. Now you're a tower of strength: a consort battleship. You and I and Pickering will be three old bachelors instead of only two men and a silly girl" (132).

Shaw's Effective Comic Devices

All of the aforementioned serious issues are introduced without sacrificing any chance to interject laughter, which makes this comedy especially enjoyable. Shaw effectively employs the frequently used comic devices of repartee, hyperbole, and dramatic irony along with suspenseful moments. The witty verbal exchanges of repartee are used in most of the dialogue. Eliza's screams as she is subjected to the rigors of a proper bath by Higgins' housekeeper Mrs. Pearce is just one of the examples of hyperbole. A masterpiece of dramatic irony is the introduction of Neppomuck, who is called the "hairy-faced Dick." He claims to be an expert in language and phonetics, but can't even use basic grammar correctly. Among the play's gripping moments of suspense, notable is the scene when Eliza is playing the part of a duchess and is in danger of being found out. Another scene that keeps the audience guessing is the play's ending. We don't know until the very end as to what will happen to the deep bond that gets established between Higgins and Eliza during the few months they have been together as teacher and student. We are not sure whether Eliza will stay with the emotionally indifferent Higgins or go with the passionately avid young admirer Freddy until the very end when she declares her intention to marry Freddy.

Questions on Pygmalion

1. Why did Shaw call his play "Pygmalion"? There is no character by that name, and there is no reference to Pygmalion in the play. Comment on Shaw's use of the ancient myth of Pygmalion and Galatea. Who were they in Greek mythology? Explain how Shaw changes the original story to suit his purposes.

2. Cite an example of dramatic, verbal, and situational irony from the play. Comment on their function either by relating them to themes and topics or by pointing out their effectiveness in any other way.

3. What theme can you relate to the character of Eliza's father Alfred Doolitle in *Pygmalion*? How? Shaw was very fond of this character.

4. *Pygmalion* is ostensibly about the flower girl Eliza's education by the professor of phonetics Henry Higgins. Demonstrate how the play is also about the education of Higgins by Eliza. What does he learn from her?

5. Comment on the realism and effectiveness of the play's ending.

6. What role does Freddy Eynsford-Hill play? Can he be considered a foil to Henry Higgins?

7. Discuss the play as a criticism of the British class system.

8. The critic Stanley Weintraub has said that Shaw was the "enemy of whatever represented the Establishment." Where in *Pygmalion* do you detect this tendency in Shaw? Which characters embody it? You may include comments on any or all of the following: Shaw's characterization, themes, topics, significant events, statements, etc. that show his being anti-establishment.

9. What is the plot-structuring device that holds the play together?

10. Read the comparison between Shaw's *Pygmalion* and Shakespeare's *The Taming of the Shrew* in the following article. In "Shakespeare's *Taming of the Shrew* vs. Shaw's *Pygmalion:* Male chauvinism vs. Women's Lib, Lise Pederson, for example, associates Shaw's play with women's liberation and Shakespeare's play with male chauvinism. Which of the critics do you find persuasive? *www.archive.org/stream/.../gbshawacollectio000699mbp_djvu.txt -*

Play Discussed: Eugene O'Neill's *Long Day's Journey into Night*

A New Direction in the American Drama
by the author of this book

To read my essay on this play, go to Chapter Twelve-related material on my website.

Play discussed: *Ah, Wilderness* by Eugene O'Neill

This play was made into a movie of the same title in 1935, directed by Clarence Brown. You can read the play's synopsis using this link: www.bard.org/education/studyguides/wilderness/wilderness.html

A 1945 reading of this play is online: http://www.eoneill.com/artifacts/flash/awr/awr.htm

What follows is a brief introduction to Eugene O'Neill's romantic comedy.

O'Neill's Rare Romantic Comedy
by the author of this book

This play is a delightful romantic comedy and a rare detour for O'Neill into light entertainment. The play is about the 17-year old Richard's initiation into adulthood. It was inspired by Omar Khayyam's famous quatrain No. XI:

> Here with a Loaf of Bread beneath the Bough,
> A Flask of Wine, a Book of Verse – and Thou
> Beside me singing in the Wilderness –
> And Wilderness is Paradise enow.

Muhammad Iqbal, the famous philosopher-poet of India and Pakistan, said that poets not only give words that live but also words to live by. The protagonist Richard seems to be living his life by the words of Omar Khayyam, the twelfth-century astronomer, poet, and philosopher. The books of verse that he has been reading are those by Swinburne, Oscar Wilde, and similar poets, who, in Richard's mother's view, are corrupting her son's mind. The "Thou" of Khayyam's quatrain is Richard's girlfriend Muriel, whose father is irate at the influence Richard is exerting on her daughter and tries to break up the relationship, producing a letter from Muriel to that effect. It becomes apparent that Muriel has been forced to write that letter because she sets up a tryst with Richard that night.

It would be hard to imagine an O'Neill play without a drunk. Richard's gentle uncle Sid fits well into that role. There is even a scene in which the reluctant and naïve Richard finds himself in the company of a young prostitute as a result of a double date soon after being handed Muriel's letter terminating their relationship. When Richard returns home late and drunk, it is Sid who, being well-versed in such matters, takes care of him. The parents plan to punish Richard for his conduct.

The young lovers are briefly thwarted, but love eventually wins out, and the play ends happily. The play's conclusion shows not only Richard and Muriel's bond established but also Richard's parents kissing.

Play discussed: *A Raisin in the Sun*
by Lorraine Hansberry (1930-1965)

Before reading the following analysis of Lorraine Hansberry's play, Raisin in the Sun, *read the play or watch any of its film adaptations. One version is at* http://www.youtube.com/watch?v=5xgxLmnzURc *and there are scenes from another film featuring Danny Glover and Esther Rolle at* http://www.youtube.com/watch?v=ybffbxq5Jag.

A Perfect Plot Design for American Dreams and Nightmares
by the author of this book

To see how Hansberry's play exemplifies tragicomedy, let us look at its content and form. In terms of thematic substance, it addresses many important issues, such as race relations, classism, sexism, family relations, and the American dream. The sample essays will explore some of these topics. The focus here in this discussion is on the play's form, specifically its meticulous handling of all plot components. Having created a mood of tension, struggle, and weariness through her precise opening stage directions, which the director has to transfer to either the stage or the screen, Lorraine Hansberry quickly introduces the entire Younger family – Ruth, Walter, Travis (their son), Beneatha (Walter's sister), and Lena Younger (Mama) in the *exposition* part.

The plot structuring device

The play's primary *plot-structuring device* is the insurance check for ten thousand dollars, which is expected to arrive soon. The play does not tell us, but we can assume that this amount is the life insurance on the deceased Walter Younger, Sr. We do not know how recent the family's bereavement is, nor do we know any clear cause of Younger, Sr.'s death. Later in the play Lena refers to her husband's great love for his children and suggests that he might have pushed himself toward death through the exhaustion of overwork after their baby died. In Lena's words, "I guess that's how come that man finally worked his self to death like he done. Like he was fighting his own war with this here world that took his baby from him" (Hansberry 45). We are not told how the world caused the baby's death. These ambiguities, the result of the esthetics of omission, have an enriching effect on the play's content. They are among the mystifying details, but the source of *conflict* in the family is delineated clearly.

Internal family conflict

Walter would like to invest the money in a liquor business to break out of the crushing cycle of demeaning jobs he, his wife, and mother have to perform to survive in a ghetto. Mama is opposed to Walter's idea. She and Walter's wife Ruth would like to use the money to make down payment on a home after Mama makes sure that part of the money is set aside to help her daughter Beneatha with her medical school expenses.

Escalation of this conflict forms the play's *rising action*, which contains some wrenching scenes between Walter and Ruth, Walter and Mama, and Walter and Beneatha. There are some moments of excruciating suspense after Mama declares that she has spent the money to buy a home. Walter accuses her of butchering his dream. Fearing her son's collapse, Lena reveals a few weeks after the fact what she has actually done with the insurance money. She has put $3500 down toward the purchase of a house. The rest of the money she hands over to the unbelieving and ecstatic Walter, who is to take charge from then on and do whatever he thinks fit with the money after putting $3000 in a savings account for Beneatha's education. This phase of the play closes with Walter's famous words to his son Travis: "Son . . . I hand you the world" (Hansberry 109).

The play's climax

However, a critical test of the family's moral strength, courage, and solidarity has yet to come in the play's *climax*. Just as Walter begins celebrating his good fortune, Karl Lindner shows up with a "generous offer" to the Youngers if they would change their mind about moving into a white neighborhood. Then soon after Lindner's racist offer is rejected and he is asked to leave, the crushing news arrives that Willie Harris has run away with the entire amount of $6500. In the hope of making a big profit, Walter had chosen not to set aside $3000 for Beneatha's education.

Falling action

The play's *falling action* takes the Younger family to the point of utter hopelessness, so much so that Walter declares he will call Lindner and accept his demeaning offer. He does call Lindner, but by the time the representative of the exclusively white neighborhood arrives, Walter has been shamed by Mama into having second thoughts.

Resolution

The *resolution* is uplifting because Walter and the family decide to move into their new home and leave the miserable ghetto life behind. Through collective hard work, they vow to finally make their dream come true and not let it dry up like a raisin in the sun.

Problematic conclusion

The play's conclusion may seem to be a happy one, but it is not without some sinister possibilities. It perfectly illustrates E. M. Forster's idea of a superior conclusion: Expansion "is the idea . . . [the author] must cling to. Not completion. Not rounding off but opening out" (Forster 169). In view of the information we have in the play that homes of minorities have been firebombed, we cannot think of the play as having a purely happy ending. Lorraine Hansberry's own words help us understand the conclusion's complexity. Referring to a reviewer, she said, "If he thinks that's a happy ending, I invite him to come live in one of the communities where the Youngers are going" (Hansberry xv). We are tempted to agree with Robert Nemiroff that the play's ending "leaves the Youngers on the brink of what will surely be, in their new home, at best a nightmare of uncertainty" (Hansberry xiv). As we can see, Lorraine Hansberry has skillfully woven the play's themes into a perfect plot design.

Chris Finn explores the theme of the American dream in Hansberry's play. Through character analysis, specifically making connections between characters and themes, he focuses on the Younger family's courage in facing oppression and standing up for their rights.

True to Your Dreams
Student author: Chris Finn

Lorraine Hansberry's play, *A Raisin in the Sun,* is a powerful look at many of the issues surrounding an African American family's life in an oppressive white-dominated society. Some of the issues include gender dynamics, living with a low income, and generational differences, and the husband and wife relationship; but all of these issues are secondary to the greater, more important issue of the oppression that affects every part of their life. The greatest effect the oppression has in the play is seen in how it affects the dreams of the family. The author shows that there is a choice to advance by conforming to the oppressive culture, but the purest most pride-worthy response is to challenge the oppression and stay true to your values and dreams. The main characters in the play are Lena Younger, the mother of the family in her sixties, Walter and Beneatha, her son and daughter, and Ruth and Travis, Walter's wife and son. They all live together in a small two-bedroom apartment in a black section of Chicago's south side with the dream of someday moving out.

Acceptance of oppression

Mrs. Johnson, the Youngers' neighbor, is an example of the type of person who accepts oppression. She has accepted a position in life that does not conflict with the oppressive society and actively discourages other African Americans who try to challenge oppression. She appears in the play while the Youngers are packing up for their move to a new house that happens to be in a white neighborhood. She claims to have come to help, but has brought along a copy of the latest paper with an article about the latest black family to be bombed out of their house in a white neighborhood. She pretends to be positive, but slips in a comment that next month's paper will probably have the Youngers' name all over it with the headline, " NEGROES INVADE CLYBOURNE PARK – BOMBED!" (102).

Her negative attitude applies to any attempt on the part of the Youngers to improve things for themselves. She also has a problem with African Americans getting an education, claiming that they get too pruned if they're educated and even refers to a quote that she attributes to Booker T. Washington – "Education has spoiled many a good plow hand" (103). She feels that servant work is fine for blacks and that even though Walter is not satisfied as a chauffeur, there is nothing wrong with being a chauffeur. Mrs. Johnson takes offense that the Youngers have too much pride to be content as servants and that they want to improve things for themselves.

Denying one's roots

George Murchison, a rich black man whom Beneatha is dating, is an example of the type of person who chooses to advance by conforming to the oppressive culture. At one point, she refers to him as an assimilationist Negro which she defines as "someone who is willing to give up his own culture and submerge himself completely in the dominant, and in this case *oppressive* culture!"(81). He doesn't support Walter or Beneatha's celebration of their identity as blacks or as African Americans and puts them down in their attempts to do so. One time as Walter greeted him as "Black Brother!", George's response was, "Black Brother, hell!"(79). His response to Beneatha when he found out that she was going to wear her hair natural and nappy had the same tone; to be natural meant to be eccentric to him and that was nothing to be proud of (80). He also distanced himself from his heritage "as nothing but a bunch of raggedy-assed spirituals and some grass huts!" (81).

Oppression by the unknowing oppressed

George has adopted not only the customs of the white culture but also the value systems of the oppressive culture. He applies this same oppressive behavior to Beneatha by telling her that he's not interested in what she wants, and that what she wants is actually interfering with her being successful with men. He wants her to present herself as men want her to be and wants to accept her on his terms without having to hear her thoughts and feelings. He states that her thoughts as an individual don't matter "because the world will go on thinking what it thinks regardless"(97). This statement shows his belief that the world is unchangeable and that the world's thoughts matter more than any thoughts an individual may have.

His oppression of Beneatha parallels the oppression that they are all subjected to by the white culture. His statement that the purpose of an education is to advance in the system and get a degree and not to learn new thoughts (97) shows that he sacrifices his own thoughts to get by easier in life. Now he wants Beneatha to do the same for him. He doesn't want her to be natural or eccentric, or to express herself; he wants her to conform to his way just as he has conformed to the powerful, rich, white culture. Beneatha refuses to compromise her values because her drive to be in touch with her identity and to fully express herself is too strong.

Betrayal for financial gain

Willy Harris is similar to George in that he has shown that he is willing to turn his back on members of his race if it means personal gain for him. Willy is someone who Walter thought was a friend and with whom he invested the family savings to make Walter's dream come true. Willy abandoned Walter and ran off with the money, taking all of the Younger family's money along with Walter's dream of owning his own business and Beneatha's dream of becoming a doctor. Even before this happens, Walter describes himself as a volcano; he's that full of bitterness at seeing other people rich while his family barely has enough and of seeing stars that he can't reach out and grab (85).

Walter's momentary, frightful surrender

After Willy has taken the money, Walter starts to think that maybe his values aren't the right ones and maybe Willy has it right. He tells his family that he's figured it out and that right and wrong aren't what matter because life is divided up "between the takers and the 'tooken'"(141). He claims that they have been wasting time always worrying about what's right and wrong while the takers are out there taking (142). He decides that that is the value system that he will live by and tries to convince himself that his pride doesn't matter. In the last scene of the play, he is prepared to sell out his family's dreams by going against everything his family stands for and has worked for. He calls Lindner, a man from the white neighborhood where the Youngers are supposed to move, with the intention of agreeing to accept Lindner's offer of money not to move into their neighborhood.

Walter's awakening

This last scene is actually a definitive one for showing the differences between those who would compromise their values and those who are too proud of their identity and their heritage to compromise either their values or their dreams. Throughout the play, the Younger family's pride is evident and their dreams and values as individuals and as a family are described. Beneatha's dream is to be a doctor; Walter's dream is to move up in the world by owning his own business; and Mama and Ruth dream of moving out of their apartment to a better place. Some of their values can be seen by the way that they support each other in the face of outside pressure. In private, Walter tells Beneatha that she should just be a nurse, but when he is talking to Lindner, he stresses the pride that the family has and makes note of the fact that someday Beneatha will be a doctor.

In another example, when Beneatha is ready to stop supporting her brother, Mama reminds her that the time to love someone most is not when they made things easy for everybody, but "when he's at his lowest and can't believe in his self 'cause the world done whipped him so!"(145). Other values can be seen in how the family interacts with Mrs. Johnson, George Murchison, and Asagai an African friend of Beneatha's, or even Lindner the first time he comes to the house. The Youngers are polite but firm in who they are and what they represent. They respect life and they value their dreams and they compromise neither their dreams nor their values. These are the reasons that the last scene is so intense. Lindner is there to make the deal and the whole Younger family is there to watch Walter's expected handing over their dignity and all that they stand for. The climax comes when Walter realizes that he can't accept the idea that his family is not just as deserving as any other family and further that his family will not abandon their dreams or their dignity no matter what the consequences may be. He stays true to his family's values and dreams and exhibits all the pride of the family as he tells Lindner his father earned that house brick by brick and that the family will not be accepting the offer; they are moving in.

Suspenseful Conclusion

The last scene is interesting because in a way it is positive, but it is far from being a happy ending. The reason it is climactic is because Walter is on the verge of throwing away five generations of struggle, and he fights through everything that brought him to that point to say that he won't give up. This means that the family keeps their dignity, but that they will continue to have to struggle and that now the struggle will be even more difficult; it will literally be life-threatening. The play in itself shows the ugliness of oppression and the fact that it can be apparent in every aspect of people's lives, especially in the lives of women and people of color. The play also shows the extreme strength and courage demonstrated by those who face oppression every day of their lives.

Questions on *A Raisin in the Sun*

1. In writing *A Raisin in the Sun*, what were two of the major challenges and difficulties encountered by Lorrain Hansberry? Demonstrate how she overcame them.

2. In his 1989 review article, "*A Raisin in the Sun*: The Uncut Version," the critic Dean Peerman pointed out the viewers' misunderstanding of Hansberry's play:

   "[A]udiences and reviewers alike seemed to pass over what to Hansberry were some of the play's more pertinent themes; indeed, America seemed to be embracing the play without fully understanding it – or perhaps without wanting to understand it. And although Hansberry was gratified by the acclaim and the attention that were coming her way, she was increasingly disturbed by what some of the critics were saying – including some of those who were giving the play high praise."

   In developing a short essay response (about 150 words), identify which of the play's more pertinent themes have the potential of being passed over by the critics and the audience?

3. Which of the African-American characters in the play can be called an assimilationist? Give a reason for your answer.

4. Do you think the play has a happy ending? Before answering this question, keep in mind the following points without necessarily agreeing with them: Hansberry's husband and author Robert Nemiroff felt that the ending was "at best a nightmare of uncertainty."[6] Lorraine Hansberry herself said, "If he [the viewer] thinks that's a happy ending, I invite him to come to live in one of the communities where the Youngers are going."[7]

5. Discuss the themes of inequities of race, class, and gender in the play.

6. What is the main plot-structuring device – an event or a fact that drives the plot action and holds the play together?

---

7. Lorraine Hansberry. *A Raisin in the Sun*, introduction by Robert Nemiroff. New York: New American Library, 1986

8. "Make New Sounds: Studs Terkel Interviews Lorraine Hansberry," *American Theater*, November 1984.

Play discussed: *Gibraltar* by Octavio Solis (b. 1962)

http://www.desdemona.org/blog/?portfolio_item=gibraltar

You can use this review of Mexican-American playwright Octavio Solis's play "Gibraltar" by Robert Hurwitt, "San Francisco Chronicle" Theater Critic, as a sample to write your own review of a contemporary play of your choice. For more guidance, please re-read item 11 (Reviewing a contemporary play) under "Topics Relevant to Drama in General" from an earlier part of this chapter.

Solis' *Gibraltar* Drills the Depths of Love and Loss
A review by Robert Hurwitt

"Love is love is," a character says with simple, weary finality. The line reverberates with intimations of Gertrude Stein-like profundity. But playwright Octavio Solis earns its every conceivable nuance, and overcomes any allusion-driven doubts, with the emotional depth, sensual poetry, flesh-and-blood characters and gracefully intricate structure of *Gibraltar* . . . at the Oregon Shakespeare Festival's New Theatre.

Stories nestle within stories, like lovers in each other's arms, echoing or altering each other in the embrace. Love is passion, comfort, grief, jealous rage, sudden lust, suicidal despair, the unexpected immediacy of a memory of who one's lover once was. Written with soul-searching honesty and breathtaking mastery, exceptionally well performed and staged (by Liz Diamond) with painterly precision, the world premiere of *Gibraltar* was the luminous highlight of six generally strong productions seen by this critic at the festival in Ashland last week. . . .

The 70-year-old Tony Award-winning festival is one of the largest regional repertory companies in the country, employing some 450 theater artists on a budget of almost $21 million. The sizable Bay Area portion of its audience will feel right at home at *Gibraltar*. And not just because the play is set in San Francisco (where Solis lives), with the large, multi-paned window at the center of Richard Hay's set affording a view of the lights of Berkeley beyond the "deep, perfect, unanswerable black" of the bay. *Gibraltar*, though developed in Ashland – in part, from improvisations with festival actors – reflects the vibrant immediacy of life, love and loss in a poetically enhanced and concentrated multicultural Bay Area.

The themes are so universal, though, and the characters so truthfully drawn, that its appeal should be widespread. Solis gives us four stories of love and loss wrapped within a battle between two storytellers, a kind of mortal combat between equally wounded and fundamentally opposed emotional worldviews.

Amy, in a searingly and exhilaratingly honest portrait by Vilma Silva, is a painter whose husband has fallen – or jumped – from his sailboat (named after her) outside the Golden Gate. With his body still not found, Amy is a stunning image of depression, consumed with her loss and her fear of losing the intensity of her grief. She can't paint. She can't go into her bedroom. She can scarcely move from the mattress on the floor in the middle of a sinuously snaking black floor that takes up most of the set, alternately lit by Chris Parry as a river, an ocean shoreline or a road (its liquidness enhanced by Jeremy J. Lee's sound design). From her one trip to the supermarket – the Marina Safeway, no less – Amy has brought home a Mexican drifter. Unless he's a figment of her overheated imagination. Palo (a sensual and ominously feral Rene Millan), so-called because he's thin as a stick, is jealous violence wrapped in self-flagellating remorse. He insists on calling Amy "Lila," the name of the wife he brutally beat after seeing her kiss another man.

She left and he's been following her footprints in the sands of beaches ever since, north from their Baja home.

From there, *Gibraltar* (the subject of Amy's painting no longer in progress) spirals ever deeper in a struggle to separate love from death and passion from violence. Palo, who sees Amy as a Latina divorced from her cultural heritage, tells stories to illustrate those violent connections. Amy intervenes in the telling to interpose more hopeful outcomes. A gently strong, deeply torn Kevin Kenerly is riveting as a young, black dockworker still mourning the father who killed himself for love of a white woman in Alabama, and Dee Maaske is quietly, affectingly focused as the older white artist who confronts the chaos of his passion.

U. Jonathan Toppo is a remarkably collected human time bomb as a by-the-book cop consumed with murderous and/or suicidal rage when his wife (a bright, tense Julie Oda) leaves him for a woman. The superb Bill Geisslinger and Judith-Marie Bergan are heartbreaking as an older man who gazes at his brain-damaged wife and still sees his young bride.

Amy's own story is among those told, in the full complexity of her feelings of guilt, betrayal, anger and complicity. Diamond skillfully orchestrates the heartfelt performances to bring out the muscularity of Solis' poetic language and the rich dramatic tension between the undertow of violence and surging tides of sensuality in his script. Amy and Palo's stories converge and separate, as the solidity of the eponymous Gibraltar gives way to the liquid interface between dreams, fantasy and reality.

The deeper Solis plunges into the multiple facets of love, the more his *Gibraltar* echoes not only the allusive poetics of Stein and flowing imagery of Garcia Lorca, but something of the wisdom of Solomon's "Many waters cannot quench love, neither can the floods drown it." As Amy struggles valiantly back toward the surface from the depths of her depression, *Gibraltar* grapples boldly, beautifully and honestly with the question of whether love really "is strong as death" (*San Francisco Chronicle*, July 11, 2005, p. C-1).

Exercises to Test Your Mastery of Chapter Twelve

In addition to the exercises to test your mastery of the chapter, some topics are also added to expand the chapter contents. Answering these questions will bring you closer to understanding, enjoying, and discussing dramatic art. The number of plays students read in a semester, quarter, or summer session depends on the nature of the course. Whatever kind of course you are taking, you will find these questions helpful. Some of them are of a general nature; they are required work. Questions that relate to specific plays can be tailored to the focus of your course.

1. Write extended definitions of tragedy, comedy, and tragicomedy, mentioning their distinguishing characteristics and evolution. The first part of this chapter addressed these topics.

2. Write a 250-word synopsis of C. B. Purdom's audio lecture on "Shakespeare and the Fundamental Law of Drama."

3. Summarize in about 250 words the audio lecture on "Hamlet as a Play of Revenge" by Moelwyn Merchant and Terence Hawkes.

4. How does Shakespearean drama differ from the classical Greek and modern plays? Refer to specific details from relevant plays to support your points.

5. Evaluate a character of your choice as a tragic hero, keeping in mind the elements that are considered central to tragic drama. Fifteen of such elements are listed near the beginning of this Chapter.

6. This chapter has given you some background information on classical, Shakespearean, and modern concepts of tragedy. **Add two elements to the list of 15 items** that were mentioned under "Elements central to tragic drama" near the beginning of this chapter. Use any points from your reading of A. C. Bradley's "The Substance of Shakespearean Tragedy," Arthur Miller's essay "Tragedy and the Common Man" (both included in this Chapter), and this chapter's discussion of "The Tragic Fallacy" by Joseph Wood Krutch, Richard Sewall's *The Vision of Tragedy*, and any other sources, such as these:

A. "Shakespeare and the Fundamental Law of Drama" by C. B. Purdom (an audio lecture)
B. "Hamlet as a Play of Revenge" by Moelwyn Merchant and Terence Hawkes (an audio lecture)
C. *Shakespearean Tragedy* (Films for the Humanities production)

When answering this question that asks you to add two elements of tragedy on your own, avoid repeating elements that I have already included in the list of fifteen items.

7. The absence of a narrator makes theme formulations from plays more difficult than is the case with fiction. Themes in drama have to be extracted mainly from dialogue and soliloquies. Answering questions like the following would, therefore, prove rewarding in your training to discover and formulate themes from plays.

A. What theme can you formulate from the following dialogue between Isabella and Angelo in Shakespeare's *Measure for Measure*. You don't have to be familiar with the play to answer this question.

> Isabella: I will proclaim thee, Angelo; look for 't:
> Sign me a present pardon for my brother,

> Or with an outstretched throat I'll tell the world aloud
>
> What man thou art.

Angelo: Who will believe thee, Isabella?

> My unsoiled name, the austereness of my life,
>
> . . . and my place in the state,
>
> Will so your accusation outweigh,
>
> That you shall stifle in our own report
>
> And smell of calumny.

This exchange occurs between the two characters when Angelo asks Isabella to have sex with him to save her brother from execution. When formulating the statement of theme based on the quoted lines, remember that a good statement of theme covers most of the material on which it is based.

B. In the closing lines of Shakespeare's *Hamlet*, Fortinbras orders four captains to

> Bear Hamlet like a soldier to the stage
> For he was likely, had he been put on,
> To have proved most royal; and for his passage
> The soldier's music and the rite of war
> Speak loudly for him.

Fortinbras is just returning from his Polish adventure; he is, therefore, not likely to know   what has happened in Denmark by way of conspiracies. How is it that he chooses only Hamlet for special honor in the above-quoted lines and disregards the reigning monarch and Queen Gertrude?

Formulate a theme to cover the already-quoted lines from Fortinbras' speech and to satisfy the question I have raised.

C. What do we learn about the values embraced by Hamlet and Polonius from the following exchange between them?

Polonius: My lord, I will use them [the players] according to their desert.

Hamlet: God's bodkin, man, much better: use every man after his desert, and who shall 'scape whipping? Use them after your own honor and dignity. The less they deserve, the more merit is in your bounty. (II, ii, 538-543)

8.   Interpretation of a play: You can choose either an informal or formal style.

Informal
After reading a play of your choice, formulate a few statements of theme that you think are central to understanding the play. Include specific details from the play to support each theme.

Formal
Use either a cluster thesis or a part-by-part thesis format for this interpretation exercise. When introducing supporting details from the play, you will need well-written topic sentences. If you need help with this exercise, use instruction No. 3 ("Thesis") of Chapter Seven's first assignment "Writing on Themes of a Literary Work." Advice for creating good topic sentences was given in item No. 4 ("Support") of the "Step-by-Step Instructions" in Chapter Seven.

9.   In a play of your choice, analyze the dramatist's style. Select two or three of the following elements that constitute style in a play:

- stage directions (in the written version of a play)

- setting and atmosphere (mood)

- dialogue: repartee (quick, witty, entertaining exchange of words between characters)

- verbal irony (saying one thing but meaning the opposite, often with humorous effects)

- understatement (saying much less than is expected by the reader or audience) for impact, sometime for humor

- dramatic irony (a character says something without understanding its full meaning, which the audience and the author know)

- situational irony (what happens is the opposite of what was expected)

- characterization (including the way of introducing and developing a variety of characters)

- pacing of events

- use of symbols, allusions, understatement, recurrent images, and any similar elements. When discussing symbolism identify the symbols, explain what they symbolize, insure their effectiveness as a means of intensifying, compressing, and enriching the play's emotional and/or intellectual content.

- use of lighting, music, colors, etc., to enhance a point (especially when evaluating a live performance)

- use of gestures

- motifs. For help, use instruction No. III and its sample on "Writing on an Author's Style (the last part of Chapter Seven).

10. Comment with examples on the special relevance of dramatic and situational irony to both tragedy and comedy.

11. An important theme in Lorraine Hansberry's A Raisin in the Sun, expressed with brilliant use of verbal irony, is that racism can take on an innocent and rational appearance. Karl Lindner is the character that embodies that theme. Point out the author's use of verbal irony in Lindner's speech. State another theme, expressed with the help of verbal irony, either from this or any other play and identify the character that carries it. To familiarize yourself with Hansberry's play, read the discussion of its plot in this chapter.

12. The plot-structuring device in Bernard Shaw's popular play Pygmalion is the wager between Henry Higgins and Colonel Pickering. The bet is that Higgins, a famous phonetician, will transform the cockney flower girl Eliza to speak like a duchess in three months. To demonstrate that the story revolves around this detail, give relevant supporting details from the play.

13. Provide evidence from *Pygmalion* for Shaw's feminist perspective in the play.

14. Write a 250-word obituary of a character from any play.

15. Write a 750-word essay on the thematic and dramatic functions of any important scene from a play. Show how the scene fits in with the author's arrangement – of the immediately preceding and following scenes. Remember to keep your focus on the subject scene when you refer to other scenes. You may point out any of these elements:

- the scene's mood-creating effect

- dramatic necessity of the scene for change of pace, eliciting a desired audience response, character revelation, theme development, etc.

- significant topics that surface in the scene to link the preceding and following events and ideas

16. Creating a missing scene and changing a play's ending. This skill was introduced at the end of Chapter Three under "Experimenting with Plot Design." Try completing the following two exercises or create your own assignment relating to a play of your choice to appreciate the complexities of plot design.

    A. Claudius instructs Rosencrantz and Guildenstern to escort Hamlet to England. They carry Claudius' written command to the British sovereign for Hamlet's immediate death as soon as the Prince arrives in England. We do not know with certainty whether Rosencrantz and Guildenstern know the contents of the warrant. However, we are disposed to dislike their fawning behavior, their playing into Claudius' hands, and their becoming Claudius' spies, thus betraying their friendship with Hamlet. As we know from the play, Hamlet discovers the plot on his life, writes a new death warrant with the names of Rosencrantz and Guildenstern on it, seals the warrant and puts it in the place of the original warrant in the belongings of Rosencrantz and Guildenstern. At the end of the play, ambassadors from England come to Denmark to report that Claudius's command to kill Rosencrantz and Guildenstern has been carried out.

       With this background information in mind, create a scene of about 20 lines, in which Rosencrantz and Guildenstern plead in vain with the King of England that some mistake has been made in the warrant and that they are loyal servants of Claudius and deserve reward, not death. Write in verse, prose, or their mixture in Shakespearean language or your own.

    B. In the closing scene of *Hamlet*, Fortinbras, the ambassadors from England, and the aristocracy of Denmark are gathered to hear Horatio's speech about "carnal, bloody, and unnatural acts;/Of accidental judgements, casual slaughters,/Of deaths put on by cunning and forced cause,/And, in this upshot, purposes mistook/Fall'n on th' inventors' heads" (V,ii,394-398). Since sudden death allowed Hamlet no time to explain how and why the play's mysterious events came about, Horatio honors his friend's dying wish in assuming the responsibility of telling the world Hamlet's story.

       Shakespeare leaves out Horatio's speech from the play because it would have sounded repetitive to the audience who have seen everything. However, the mere inclusion of the fact that Horatio will set the record right and clear up Hamlet's name lifts the gloom of futility from the play's ending. We now have a right to believe that the deaths in *Hamlet* will not be in vain and that the world will know Hamlet's story as he himself would have told it had "the fell sergeant, Death," not been so "strict in his arrest" (V,ii,343-344). Knowing how fair and thorough Horatio is, we are certain that no loose ends, no muddle, will remain and that Horatio will report Hamlet and Hamlet's cause "aright to the unsatisfied" (V, ii, 346-347). Horatio's task, however, is very difficult. He has to tell virtually the whole story right from the play's eerie opening to its tragic end.

       Having read these preparatory comments, write Horatio's speech as you imagine it to be. Write it either in prose or blank verse or a combination of them but do not exceed 50 lines.

17. Read on the internet <SFGate.com> Jan Hoffman's newspaper article "To Be or Not to Be Guilty? Legal Scholars Consider the Case of the Prince of Denmark." Take the position either of Hamlet's defense attorney or the prosecutor and add your own arguments to those of the defense or opposition as presented in the article. In this mock trial, legal experts and Shakespeare scholars gathered at the City Bar Association in Manhattan, New York, to present their arguments on "People

vs. Hamlet." In this trial Hamlet is accused of the deaths of Polonius, Ophelia, Rosencrantz, Guildenstern, Laertes, and Claudius.

18. Some syndromes are associated with or named after famous literary characters – the Oedipus complex and the Hamlet syndrome being prominent among them. Oedipus complex is the term Sigmund Freud invented to describe the disorder of obsessive attachment to one's mother while harboring extreme hostility toward the father. The Hamlet syndrome may be defined as the predicament of overthinking underachievers. Similarly, we may name a syndrome after Hamlet's beloved Ophelia. This condition is characterized by a young woman's submission to the contrary pulls of male authority figures at a tragic cost to her own feelings and mental well-being. In Ophelia's case, the male figures are her father (Polonius), her brother (Laertes), and her lover (Hamlet).

Along these lines, identify and analyze a literary or film character that deserves to be linked to a new syndrome that is coined by you. Use internet <SFGate.com> to read the newspaper article on "The Hamlet Syndrome" to gather ideas for this writing exercise.

19. If you were the editor of a play of your choice, what would you write in your introductory essay to make the play appealing and relevant to your peers. You should include observations on the play's general subject, themes, characters, and events, along with a brief discussion of the dramatist's craft. You will have to summarize parts of the play to support your points, but you should not allot too much space to mere summarizing of the play's events. Include appropriate analytical and critical comments, which should control the plot summaries. In a suitable place in the essay, cite from the play at least three profound observations which could be regarded as representative of the dramatist's wisdom and insight.

20. Near the start of this chapter, the unity of impression was mentioned as an important element of tragic drama (item 15) under "Elements Central to Tragic Drama." Re-read that item before answering this question: In *The Theory of Drama*, Allardyce Nicoll mentions a "central spirit" by which every play is inspired. He adds: "any drama which admits emotion not so in subordination to the main spirit of the play will thereby be blemished" (Nicoll 57). Assuming Nicoll's "central spirit" to mean an overarching theme, demonstrate how that theme inspires any play of your choice.

21. After reading this chapter's discussion of modern tragicomedy, existential absurdist drama, the angry theater, theater of cruelty, and the bare-bones plays of Harold Pinter, select a play from any of the above forms of drama to write a comprehensive review. For review instructions, read the relevant part toward the end of Chapter Ten. For a sample essay, read Robert Hurwitt's review of Octavio Solis's play *Gibraltar* in this chapter.

22. Apply some of the major points about tragic drama from Arthur Miller's essay "Tragedy and the Common Man" (included in this chapter) to his play *Death of a Salesman*. Include a comparison of Miller's views of the tragic hero and the tragic feeling with those of Shakespearean practice as summed up by A.C. Bradley. Bradley's chapter on "The Substance of Shakespearean Tragedy" is included in this chapter.

Contemporary Drama

23. Analyze the quality of dialogue in any of Pinter's plays to verify the claim that "beneath the faithful reproduction of the banality of average conversation, we catch unexpected resonances that give the talk weight and depth" (Hinchliffe 165).

24. Evaluate Pinter's craftsmanship in sculpting any one of his plays with his following words in mind: "I am very concerned with the shape and consistency of mood of my plays. I cannot write anything that appears to me to be loose and unfinished. I like the feeling of order in what I write" (Pinter 8-10).

25. Robert Hurwitt's review of Caryl Churchill's play *Owners* ends with this statement of theme: "At the heart of its plentiful humor . . . *Owners* puts all forms of ownership on trial." Give plot details from the play to support this theme. Hurwitt's review can be accessed through the internet.

26. Commenting on Churchill's use of appropriate stylistic elements to communicate the play's main theme, Hurwitt makes this observation:

    "The brilliantly convoluted plot centers on Marion's efforts to control people the way she buys and sells buildings, but it's also not nearly so simple as that. Churchill cleverly sidles into the theme in short, crisp, vigorously written scenes. She sets us up to be sympathetic to Marion before we meet her, as the object of the murderous musings of her sanctimoniously sexist butcher husband Clegg . . . and the unstinting admiration of her assistant Worsley."

    Cite and interpret two other scenes from the play to demonstrate the interconnectedness of style with plot, character, and theme.

27. The British playwright Caryl Churchill wrote her play *Seven Jewish Children* after Israel's invasion of Gaza in December 2008 that killed 1300 Palestinians (most of them civilians). Thirteen Israelis were also killed. Write a research paper to document the causes of this conflict. Choose sources from both sides and arrive at your own independent conclusion. Suggest a solution to this conflict that has been going on since 1948 when Palestine was partitioned to make room for the new state of Israel. In answering this question, show your knowledge of Churchill's play.

28. During the month of November, 2012, Israel again invaded Gaza, this time killing over 170 Palestinians, mostly civilians, 34 of them children and many women. Six Israelis (two of them soldiers) were also killed in this 8-day invasion by Israel. If you were in the playwright Churchill's place, what would you have liked to add to her play to bring it uptodate?

29. Explain and analyze three or four major historical allusions in Churchill's play.

30. What does Churchill seem to be aiming for in writing this short play? Why did she call this monologue a play? Why did she treat a vast topic so briefly?

31. Relate Churchill's play and her defense of the play (that you can read online) to any aspects of "Tamam" and "The Orchard" – two of the stories that you read in Chapter Nine.

32. Comment on the appropriateness of the use of the word "crusaders" in the playwright Wajahat Ali's title of his play *The Domestic Crusaders*.

33. The theme of the cross-generational conflict remains unchanged because it is timeless. In addition the play also brings up the topic of Islamophobia in the wake of 9-11 attacks on the U.S. Discuss Ali's treatment of that topic in the play. Do you see any difference in the incidence of Islamophobia soon after 9-11 and today? Support your answer with facts.

34. Scott Kaiser based his play *Splittin' the Raft* (2005) on Mark Twain's novel *Adventures of Huckleberry Finn*. Compare and contrast the two works with emphasis on what is gained and what is lost in this novel-to-play transformation. Do an internet search to find a review of Kaiser's play. If you are not familiar with Twain's classic, you can get it from any library or watch a film adaptation of the novel. You can read a review of Kaiser's play on the internet.

35. Trace the source of the title of Heather Raffo's play *Nine Parts of Desire* and explain how it relates to the play's major theme. Read Victoria Linchon's review of the play on Google. Among several themes in the play, one is how art can remake the world. Trace that theme in the play's content. The play presents nine Iraqi women's perspectives. Raffo is one of the six participating writers for the play *The Middle East, in Pieces*. It addresses current developments in the Middle East, focusing on the conflicts in Israel, Iraq, and Lebanon.

36. *In Darfur* by Winter Miller is a play about the ongoing genocide in Darfur. This play is based on the reports of genocide survivors who were interviewed at the Sudan border by Miller and Nicholas Kristoff. Apply to this play A.C. Bradley's words that are quoted in Question 38.

37. From Craig Wright's play *The Pavilion*, find supporting details for the theme of human longing to recapture the past and the outcome of this struggle. Charles Isherwood finds this theme at the center of the play. Here is the link to Isherwood's review of the play:

   http://theater2.nytimes.com/2005/09/21/theater/reviews/21pavi.html

38. Relate A. C. Bradley's following words to any current play that addresses a tragic condition. These words come from "The Substance of Shakespearean Tragedy," included in this chapter:

   Everywhere, from the crushed rocks beneath our feet to the soul of man, we see power, intelligence, life and glory, which astound us and seem to call for our worship. And everywhere we see them perishing, devouring one another and destroying themselves, often with dreadful pain, as though they came into being for no other end. Tragedy is the typical form of this mystery, because that greatness of soul which it exhibits oppressed, conflicting and destroyed, is the highest existence in our view.

39. Type "plays with analysis" in Google search. Choose an analysis of a play of your choice, summarize it, and add your own interpretation.

40. Read or watch Margaret Edson's Pulitzer Prize winning drama *Wit* on your own. The play chronicles the last two hours in the life of an English professor dying of cancer. In spite of the grim subject, the protagonist's death-defying, brilliant wit does not allow even one dull moment in the entire play.

   Comment on Edson's effective use of witty and metaphoric language to deflate the play's painful content. The following internet sources are helpful:

   A. "Death Be Not Proud: An Analysis of Margaret Edson's *Wit*" by Madeline M. Keaveney; *Women and Language*, vol. 27, 2004

      www.questia.com/PM.qst?a+o&se=gglsc&d=5008326873

   B. Read this review by Sarah Lyall:

      "Television/Radio; For 'Wit' a Star Who Supplies a Wit of Her Own"

      http://www. Nytimes.com/2001/03/18/arts/television-radio-for-wit-a-star

   C. Wit summary and study guide – Margaret Edson – eNotes.com

41. Write a character analysis of any of your favorite protagonists. Include your response to what Richard Sewall calls "the main sources and locus of tragic man's suffering" in his book The Vision of Tragedy:

   "He [or she] suffers because he is more than usually sensitive to the 'terrible disrelations' he sees about him and experiences in himself. He is more than usually aware of the mighty opposites in the universe and in man, of the gulf between desire and fulfillment, between what is and what should be. This kind of suffering is suffering on a high level, beyond the reach of the immature or brutish, and forever closed to the extreme optimist, the extreme pessimist, or the merely indifferent" (353-354).

36. Compare Ruben Santiago-Hudson's one-man memory play *Lackawanna Blues* with its adaptation for the screen. What is gained and/or lost by this play-to-film creation? Read on the internet Ruthe Stein's movie review titled "Dancing is steamy, sorrow's intense, love is abundant in *Lackawanna Blues*." Log on to SFGate.com for *San Francisco Chronicle*. The date of the article was February 12, 2005.

37. The problem in adapting a great play to the screen is that "the verbal metaphors are stronger than the visual accompaniments." Discuss this problem of screen adaptation of any great play that you have read. Demonstrate how the director transfers the play's verbal metaphors to the screen, keeping in mind Thomas Sobchak's words "that a good film's images do not merely duplicate the verbal metaphors; rather . . . the images match the metaphor" (Sobchack 319).

38. This question concerns casting. Each one of us has an idea as to what a character from a play should be like on the stage or on the screen. Some literary classics have offered this seemingly insurmountable difficulty: the casting director's choice seems to conflict not only with the viewer's concept of a character but runs counter also to the author's own vision. You may discuss any play whose casting left you dissatisfied. Give reasons for your discontent.

39. Some critics have noted the problem with film when it comes to portraying literary symbolism.

Thomas and Vivian Sobchack, for example, have analyzed this problem persuasively:
"Film literalizes what may function symbolically in literature; it robs the symbol of its mystery. Unless the filmmaker is able to recharge the image with some cinematically communicated richness . . . to recharge the literal with its own mystery and symbolism . . . that literary symbol will not function successfully on the screen. . . . Because film is necessarily representational, it is extremely difficult for objects to accumulate symbolic meanings. . . . But because it is difficult does not mean that it can't or hasn't been done. . . . [The director has] to compensate for the photographic image's reductive concreteness (325-327)."

CHAPTER THIRTEEN

POETRY

Use of Poetry in a Reading and Writing Development Program

In a reading and writing development program, inclusion of poetry is a means to bring in the excitement of emotion, the pleasure of musical sound, a swift expansion of vocabulary, and a rich harvest of interesting topics for discussion. However, poetry, like drama, poses a great challenge to undergraduate students. The reason is students' lack of preparation in these two areas of literary studies. In view of this need, the chapters on these two genres have provided more background information than on other genres – the short story, novel, and film – forms with which students are more familiar. Knowledge of various aspects, varieties, and concepts of poetry will make your access to poetry easier and smoother and enable you to write about it with greater confidence. First of all, however, it should be understood that poetry "is essentially a game, with artificial rules, and it takes two – a writer and a reader – to play it. If the reader is reluctant, the game will not work" (Scholes 423).

Introduction to Some Forms of Poetry

Poetry is the oldest form of literature. Springing to life with the dawn of humanity, poetry has always been a medium of expressing emotion – both sacred and secular – in almost every culture. The defining characteristic of poetry is the harmony of its rhythm and sound. As you start to feel comfortable with poetry, you should become familiar with its various forms, with stylistic elements central to poetry, and with poetic meter and rhythm. Meter consists of groups of stressed and unstressed syllables arranged according to a pattern. The groups or units of syllables are called feet. You will find books like Charles Barber's *Poetry in English: An Introduction*, M.H. Abrams' *A Glossary of Literary Terms*, and *Handbook of Literary Terms* by X. J. Kennedy, Dana Gioia, and Mark Bauerlein helpful to understand various poetic terms.

Many unique features of poetry go with its various forms. Grandeur of style and substance marks the *epic* form of poetry. *The Epic of Gilgamesh* from Mesopotamia – the first written literary work – was composed in the form of poetry around 3000 B.C., and oral poetry dates farther back in time by thousands of years.

Extreme compression of meaning in the limited space of fourteen lines, strict rhyme requirements (sometimes not observed by contemporary poets), and introduction, development and resolution of a complex topic are the outstanding features of the **sonnet.** The Italian or Petrarchan sonnet had a two-part structure. The first eight lines, called the octave, introduced and developed the central topic. The last six lines, called the sestet, offered the resolution. In Shakespearean variety of the sonnet, we have three quatrains that accomplish the task of the classical octave. They introduce, develop, and complicate the topic. The concluding couplet offers the resolution. In this chapter, John Keats's "Bright Star" mixes the classical with Shakespearean model in that it has a two-part structure of the octave and sestet but ends with a couplet. Shelley's "Ozymandias" is an example of the classical, Italian sonnet, whereas Robert Hayden's "Those Winter Sundays" exemplifies its modern variation. Absence of rhyme makes Hayden's sonnet unconventional only in that respect; it observes all other requirements of this poetic form.

Seriousness of tone, meditative mood, lofty subject matter, elaborate stanzaic structure, and movement of thought through complex stages toward an attempted resolution are some of the outstanding features of the **ode.** In this chapter, Keats's "Ode to a Nightingale" and "To Autumn" are two well-known examples of the ode.

A **ballad** is a song that tells a story in an easy-flowing, conversational style reminiscent of its oral tradition. The narrator relates the dramatic incidents in an impersonal manner, often starting with the climactic scene and relying mainly on dialogue and action to move the narrative along. The ballad, thus, becomes the equivalent of our folk song. As an example, you can read "Ballad of Birmingham" by Dudley Randall on the internet. http://www.poetryfoundation.org/poem/175900.

Sestina is an elaborately structured poetic form, in which six end words (that take the place of the end rhyme) are repeated in the first 36 lines (sometimes divided into six stanzas of six lines each). The poem concludes with a three-line *envoi*, in which the six words are repeated. Obviously this form seems complicated, but if you read a good sestina, like Alberto Rios' "Nani," you will find the poet's artistry in meeting the challenge of this form exciting. To read Rios' poem on the internet, use this link:
http://www.asu.edu/research/reserchmagazine/1997Summer/Sum97p38-40.pdf

The **limerick** is yet another form of poetry, which is used strictly in humorous verse. It consists of five lines using anapestic meter (that is, a sequence of two unstressed syllables followed by a stressed syllable). The first, second, and fifth lines have three accents and rhyme with one another; lines three and four have two accents and rhyme with each other. "A monkey sprang down from a tree" and "Two brothers devised what a sight" (both limericks by Laurence Perrine included in Chapter Fifteen) will make you laugh.

A poetic form of French origin – **villanelle** – has nineteen lines divided into six stanzas. The first five stanzas consist of three lines each, and the final stanza has four lines. The villanelle resembles the sonnet in its brevity. However, while the sonnet uses many rhymes, the villanelle has only two rhymes according to a fixed pattern. It also uses a refrain. Dylan Thomas's poem, "Do Not Go Gentle into That Good Night" is considered a masterpiece of this form of poetry. To read the poem on the internet use this link: http://www.poemhunter.com/poem/do-not-go-gentle-into-that-good-night/.

The short **lyric** has been the most popular form of poetry. Originally, a lyric was a poem written to be set to music. It is in this sense that we use this word today when we evaluate the lyrics (words) of a songwriter. At first the lyric was a non-narrative form, essentially an expression of a mood or an emotion with very little intellectual weight. Over the years since the sixteenth century, the lyric has become disconnected with the song but has retained some of its original features. It still exalts the personal feeling over the impersonal idea. After having been divorced from poetry for centuries, the song has made a comeback in poetry today. The sonnet and the ode, discussed earlier, are often regarded as two of the lyric's sub-categories.

Reasons for the Difficulty of Some Modern Poetry

Both in comprehending its themes and appreciating its style, poetry offers a far greater challenge than any other form of literature. The difficulty of poetry is the result of compression of feelings and thoughts into minimum words and omission of usual connecting devices. Looking at modern poetry, one reason for its difficulty is that many modern poets deny the reader certain pleasures that have been traditionally associated with and expected of poetry.

By refusing to use rhyme, modern poets fail to create pleasant repetition of expected yet surprising harmony of sound; by creating characters who are difficult to empathize with, the poets create a feeling of distance; by adopting a tone of detachment, they place too tight a hold on emotion, and even in their choice of subjects – alienation, threat of uncontrolled industrialization and urbanization, inability to feel strong emotions of a positive nature, loss of faith in religious and spiritual values – many contemporary poets offer the reader a bill of fare that is wholesome but not easy to digest. Admitting poetry's challenges for the uninitiated reader while emphasizing its importance, David Kirby diagnoses some of the problems that can be solved with more frequent and guided exposure to poetry: "With its allusiveness, its rarefied vocabulary and its preference for image over statement, poetry doesn't seem to be all that interested in addressing us directly. Yet it shouldn't be ignored" (Kirby 4).

Virginia Woolf's comparison of the new with the old poetry and her reasons for the difficulty of modern poetry are instructive:

"The very reason why the [earlier] poetry excites one to such abandonment, such rapture, is that it celebrates some feeling that one used to have (. . . before the war perhaps), so that one responds easily, familiarly, without troubling to check the feeling, or to compare it with any that one has now. But the living poets express a feeling that is actually being made and torn out of us at the moment. One does not recognize it in the first place; often for some reason one fears it; one watches it with keenness and compares it jealously and suspiciously with the old feeling that one knew. Hence the difficulty of modern poetry; and it is because of this difficulty that one cannot remember more than two consecutive lines of any good modern poet" (Woolf 14-15).

Another reason for the obscurity of so much of modern poetry may be that today's poets shun the direct statement of theme, which characterized the poetry of earlier eras. However, one may find exceptions among modern poets such as the Imagists Hilda Doolittle, Amy Lowell, Marianne Moore, Richard Aldington, and William Carlos Williams, who are relatively accessible.

Whether one is reading older or modern poetry, R. P. Blackmur's following words are always helpful: "Poetry may have three meanings: what is immediate, what comes by study, and what only gradually reveals itself." Blackmur's principle of gradual revelation of a complex poem's meaning applies to most great poems. Knowing this, we should not be impatient with them.

Some Definitions of Poetry

Study of a few well-known definitions of poetry is an interesting way to introduce you to various views and to help you discover for yourself what kind of poetry you favor. For a meaningful interaction between theory and practice, try to apply the definitions that interest you to specific poems that, in your view, exemplify those definitions.

On the importance of passion in poetry, Samuel Taylor Coleridge remarks in *Biographia Literaria* that images, which constitute the chief ingredient of poetry, "become proofs of genius only so far as they are modified by a predominant passion, or by associated thoughts or images awakened by that passion." He also defines poetry as the best words in their best order.

Another prominent poet of the nineteenth-century English Romantic Movement, William Wordsworth, defined poetry as "a spontaneous overflow of powerful feelings." This "overflow" occurs during the poet's tranquil recollection of emotion. Wordsworth's view of poetry, thus, represents a synthesis of passion and tranquillity.

John Keats's definition emphasizes the spontaneous quality of poetry: " . . . if poetry comes not as naturally as the leaves to a tree it had better not come at all" (Keats 545). Keats's simile also underscores the lifelike, organic interconnectedness of the various parts of a poem.

Ezra Pound and T.S. Eliot have been two key figures who place emotion at the center of poetic creation. In Pound's words, "only emotion endures" and "nothing counts save the quality of the emotion." Pound also upholds the idea of the richness of the poetic language, which is charged with meaning. To him poetry is a repository of the wealth of different cultures. Pound's cosmopolitan outlook freed poetry from dull parochialism and restored to poetry its high place. T.S. Eliot's theory and practice have touched all poets who came after him. Some have abided by his precepts while others have rejected him. An understanding of his poetics can bring us closer to grasping much of modern poetry. In spite of the highly intellectual content of many of his poems, Eliot, too declares the sovereignty of emotion in poetry: "The poet who 'thinks' is merely the poet who can express the emotional equivalent of thought." In his view, poets should be able to "feel their thought as immediately as the odor of a rose." He admires poetry in which thought has the definiteness and palpability of feeling. In *The Use of Poetry and the Use of Criticism*, he observes that memories mixed with deep feelings often constitute the poetic image. On the function of poetry, Eliot said that poetry "makes us . . . a little more aware of the deeper unnamed feelings which form the substratum of our being, to which we rarely penetrate; for our lives are mostly a constant evasion of ourselves." Eliot's words provide a direct access to an important aspect of his famous poem "Love Song of J. Alfred Prufrock," which you will read later in this chapter.

Among poets of more recent years, Robert Bly has written eloquently about his concept of poetry in "A Wrong Turning in American Poetry." According to him, "a poem is something that penetrates for an instant into the unconscious." In "What the Image Can Do," Bly sets down the following powers or "energy sources" that make up a good poem: image; spoken language free from archaisms and with a variety of pitches; psychic weight that comes from opening the body to grief; sound; the drum beat; and the tale.

Among other poets who have theorized about poetry, Robert Creeley, Louis Zukofsky, Tess Gallagher, David Budbil, and Lawrence Ferlinghetti are noteworthy. Emphasizing the kinetic nature of poetry, Creeley thinks of it as energy which the poet gathers from some source and passes on to the reader by way of the poem. Louis Zukofsky's concept of poetry in *A Test of Poetry* centers around "the range of pleasure it offers as sight, sound, and intellection." Tess Gallagher includes the reader of poetry as its co-maker with the poet:

" . . . the reader is also the maker of the poem as it lives again in his consciousness, his needs, his reception, and even his denials. The poem is in a state of perpetual formation and disintegration. It is not at the mercy of pure subjectivity, but, as Ortega y Gasset would say, it is 'intersection of the different points of view.' This, then, brings about a succession of interpretations of which no single one, even that of the poet, is the definitive one. In this way, the poem enters and *becomes* time" (Gallagher 93).

David Budbil's definition emphasizes poetry's transforming and healing aspect through rendition of feeling:

"Poetry is about feeling, about being healed through feeling. Poetry is not about language. Language is a tool, a means to an end, and that end is vivid pictures, powerful emotion, musical expression – in short, cathartic emotional experience. Poetry, for me, like music, is a path to the emotional articulation of the joys and sorrows of this life, and when that articulation is good we are somehow, mysteriously, if only for a moment, transformed and healed."

Lawrence Ferlinghetti ascribes to poetry the role of a savior. In *Poetry as Insurgent Art*, he declares: "Poetry can save the world by transforming consciousness." He cautions that "poems must be more than want ads for broken hearts." Affirming poetry's unifying role, he says that "poetry is the shortest distance between two humans." Another among prominent poets of today is Adrienne Rich. In her poem "Poetry: I" the speaker is a young person who finds "our glosses [on poems] wanting" and who is disappointed at the overemphasis on the non-alive jargon, such as "*modernism, trope, vatic, text.*" This angry youth longs for the time when "the poets taught how to live."

As we can see, most definitions of poetry share the view that poetry is made of emotion, which is intensely felt and harmoniously transmitted in various forms.

Befriending Poetry

To enhance your understanding and appreciation of poetry, it will be helpful to devise a system like the simple format suggested below. With the help of your notes taken according to these instructions, you can quickly start feeling at home with poetry, not to mention doing very well on any tests on the assigned poems.

I. For Every Assigned Poem

1. Write down the topic of each assigned poem. You can identify the topic in one word or a phrase.

2. Note the poet's words (or at least the line numbers) that illustrate or embody that topic. If a supporting quotation from the poem is too long, you may copy only the opening and closing words of that quotation with line numbers for easy identification and reference.

This exercise is to be completed on each assigned poem **before** the poem is discussed in class. In other words, you have to identify the assigned poem's topic **on your own**, even if you are dissatisfied with your formulation of the poem's topic. **This is the first essential step that you** add to your notes any interpretations that appeal to you. Through such revisions, you will be able to refine and improve your evaluations of poems. Occasionally, the instructor may ask you to read from your notes so you can share your interpretations with the class. It does not matter if your reading of a poem is wrong. **The only requirement is that you make an honest attempt.**

II. For selected poems

Use the following journal format that was introduced in Chapter Six.

1. **Summarize** the poem's significant details in about fifty words.

2. Identify the poem's **main topic(s).**

3. State in one or two sentences what you perceive to be the poet's **major theme or themes**. Your statement of theme can be completed in your own words, or you may mix your words with some key words from the poem; such borrowed words should be placed in quotation marks.

4. Write two or three sentences of relevant details, mixing words from the poem with yours to **support the theme** formulated by you in item 3 above.

5. Include a comment on the effectiveness of the poet's **style**. As you must have noticed by now, becoming comfortable with this aspect of literature takes time.

Writing on a Poem's Themes
Supported by the poem's content and style

Using poetry to develop the skills of critical analysis and interpretation, let us re-read Robert Hayden's sonnet "Those Winter Sundays" that was explicated in Chapter Six. You may want to read that explication also to better appreciate how this essay evolved from it. *The text of the poem is in Chapter Six.*

Taking the (by now) well-worn path of journal to essay, we can give our interpretation of Hayden's poem the following form.

Introduction

The speaker, now an adult, is reminiscing about his childhood. He blames his lack of knowledge and perception ("What did I know, what did I know") for his failure to understand and appreciate the love his father offered, not through soft words but through his actions, such as getting up early even on Sundays to light a fire to drive out the cold, polishing the speaker's shoes, and doing extremely hard manual work (his "cracked hands . . . ached from labor") to provide for the family.

Statement of the poem's first theme

From Robert Hayden's poem we learn that love can be offered in many different ways, but if it is not shown in a way the recipient understands, it is not going to be seen as love. Caring acts when carried out in a routine and undemonstrative manner can be mistaken for duties and obligations, performance of which is a thankless job, often taken for granted by those whom those acts are meant to serve. When such love is not understood, it cannot be appreciated and leads to frustration and loneliness on both sides.

After stating the theme, you will need to quote and summarize relevant details in support of the theme without repeating the words from your introduction as much as possible.

Supporting details
Using relevant statements from the poem to support the theme

The love offered by the father is described as having been of an "austere" kind, which might consist of withholding rather than bestowing much affection, perhaps to prepare the narrator for the harsh world of reality. The necessity of such austere conduct seems to have caused the father great pain because the narrator finally perceives "love's austere and lonely offices," but by then it is too late.

As a child, the poem's speaker saw no love – only resentful performance of duties and "chronic angers" in his/her father's daily acts of concern and sacrifice. The father's alienation is conveyed by the words, "No one ever thanked him." The implication is that there were others in the house beside the father and the speaker, but no one appreciated the father's sacrifices. The poem thus becomes a lament for missed opportunities for closeness between a father and son/daughter.

Statement of the poem's second theme

Hayden's poem is also a moving reminder that we should communicate our feelings before time takes away the opportunity.

Supporting details

The speaker regrets too late, "What did I know, what did I know/Of love's austere and lonely offices." The father, whom the speaker would like to thank, is most likely dead by the time the speaker thinks of showing his/her appreciation. As a child the speaker noticed the sullen atmosphere – "the chronic angers of the house" – but failed to perceive love in the father's daily acts of self-sacrifice. The child neither understood nor appreciated what the father did for the family. Now as an adult the speaker can finally understand the father's acts of sacrifice as love.

Use of the poet's style to support the theme

The paradox in the concluding lines effectively captures the paradoxical nature of such love that consists of withholding rather than giving and which, instead of curing loneliness, leads to loneliness. The paradox is inherent in the fact that ordinarily we associate love with giving, not with holding back, and we think of love as a cure for, not a cause of loneliness. However, in the context and circumstances of the poem, true love is displayed through small everyday actions, through holding back emotion (exercising austerity in displaying emotion), and through suffering from isolation as a result of finding no appreciation for this kind of love, especially when this is the only form of love that might best prepare the child for real life.

This example continues the method that you have learned from other chapters to use summary of relevant statements and details to support a theme. You can also see in this example how an author's style supports a theme.

A concluding comment on Hayden's poem can be made as follows or in any other way to suit your emphasis.

Conclusion

In fourteen lines, using language charged with emotion that is held just below the exploding point, Robert Hayden has taken us through a person's memories of childhood, his/her failure to appreciate the father's sacrifices for the family, and eventual enlightenment about the father's difficult role. The poem thus becomes a memorial, a monument to the spiritual bond that overrides parents' and children's imperfect ways to express it.

Interpretation of a Complex Poem

Robert Hayden's poem that we just discussed is written in a style of simple elegance. There is another variety that is characterized by studied grace and lofty expression. Keats's famous "Ode to a Nightingale" is such a poem. After reading the poem, complete the following two-step exercise before looking at this interpretation:

1. Write down three themes that you consider prominent in the poem.
2. Then write just one sentence of supporting details from the poem for each theme.

Remember to review the clues to recognizing themes in literature if you need help. Those clues, given at the end of Chapter Five, can help you grasp themes in any form of literature and film.

After independently arriving at the poem's three significant themes and supporting them with details from the poem according to the two-step exercise, compare your interpretation of the poem with mine that follows, remembering that we may have reached different but equally valid and equally supportable themes. **This fact of the validity of different interpretations, as long as they are supported by the poem's content, should never be overlooked.**

Organization

In organizing the paper, follow the same principles that you have been using throughout the earlier chapters. First mentioned at the end of Chapter One and fully explained and exemplified in Chapter Seven, they are only briefly listed here:

1. A clear title
2. An inviting introduction and a supportable thesis
3. Topic sentences for each separate section
4. Conclusion

Maintaining correct focus

Since maintaining correct focus and style evaluation tend to be the problem areas, the relevant guidelines are briefly reviewed here. In essays written in response to literature and film, the most recurrent weakness occurs in the main body in the form of incorrect focus. Writing starts to sound like a summary, not an essay, the moment we allow the focus to deteriorate. To solve this problem, keep all specific details from the poem subordinate to topic sentences. Secondly, place key words of your thesis in topic sentences. This strategy will link the main body with your thesis and title.

Review the sample essay on Hayden's poem (earlier in this chapter) to see how the introduction, thesis, supporting details, and conclusion are written on just one theme from the poem. This current sample essay is on three themes from Keats's "Ode to a Nightingale" and, therefore, offers more of a challenge in organization and focus.

Style evaluation

Besides weak focus, another common problem occurs during style evaluation. If you need help, look up the coverage of style in the following parts of the book:

1. The entire Chapter Four relates to style. The section that is of special relevance here is the one on "Style in Poetry."
2. Chapter Six also gives brief guidelines for style evaluation in the context of explaining the journal format.
3. The second part of Chapter Seven gives a clear format as well as a sample essay on an author's style of writing in prose fiction.

The basic guidelines that you need to observe are the following:

1. Analysis of an author's style becomes meaningful if we can demonstrate its connection with themes and characters.
2. Style evaluation consists of three steps: (a) identifying an element of style, (b) giving an example, and (c) determining its function or effectiveness in communicating a theme, developing a character, etching a scene, creating a mood, engaging the senses, etc.

The sample essay that follows the complex poem "Ode to a Nightingale" by John Keats demonstrates how the above-mentioned steps are to be implemented.

Ode to a Nightingale

I.

My heart aches, and a drowsy numbness pains
My sense, as though of hemlock I had drunk,
Or emptied some dull opiate to the drains
One minute past, and Lethe-wards had sunk:
'T is not through envy or thy happy lot,
But being too happy in thine happiness,--
That thou, light-winged Dryad of the trees
In some melodious plot
or beechen green. and shadows numberless,
Singest of summer in full-throated ease.

II.

O , for a draught of vintage! that hath been
Cool'd a long age in the deep-delved earth,
Tasting of Flora and the country green,
Dance, and Provencal song, and sunbunt mirth!
0 for a beaker full of the warm South,
Full of the true, the blushful Hippocrene,
With beaded bubbles winking at the brim,

And purple-stained mouth:
That I might drink, and leave the world unseen,
And with thee fade away into the forest dim:

III.

Fade far away, dissolve, and quite forget
What thou among the leaves hast never known,
The weariness, the fever, and the fret
Here, where men sit and hear each other groan:
Where palsy shakes a few, sad, last gray hairs,
Where youth grows pale. and spectre-thin, and dies;
Where but to think is to be full of sorrow
And lead en-eyed despairs,
Where Beauty cannot keep her lustrous eyes.
Or new Love pine at them beyond to-morrow.

IV.

Away! away! for I will fly to thee,
Not charioted by Bacchus and his pards.
But on the viewless wings of Poesy,
Though the dull brain perplexes and retards:
Already with thee! tender is the night,
And haply the Queen-Moon is on her throne,
Cluster'd around by all her starry Fays:
But here there is no light,
Save what from heaven is with the breezes blown
Through verdurous glooms and winding mossy ways.

V.

I cannot see what flowers are at my feet,
Nor what soft incense hangs upon the boughs.
But, in embalmed darkness, guess each sweet
Wherewith the seasonable month endows
the grass, the thicket, and the fruit-tree wild :
White hawthorn, and the pastoral eglantine:
Fast fading violets cover'd up in leaves:
And mid-May's eldest child,
The coming musk-rose, full of dewy wine,
The murmurous haunt of flies on summer eves.

VI.

Darkling I listen: and, for many a time
I have been half in love with easeful Death,
Call'd him soft names in many a mused rhyme,
To take into the air my quiet breath:
Now more than ever seems it rich to die,
To cease upon the midnight with no pain,
While thou art pouring forth thy soul abroad

In such an ecstasy!
Still wouldst thou sing, and I have ears in vain--
To thy high requiem become a sod .

VII.

Thou wast not born for death, immortal Bird!
No hungry generations tread thee down:
The voice I hear this passing night was heard
In ancient days by emperor and clown:
Perhaps the self-same song that found a path
Through the sad heart of Ruth, when, sick for home,
She stood in tears amid the alien corn:
The same that oft-times hath
Charm'd magic casements, opening on the foam
Of perilous seas, in faery lands forlorn.

VIII.

Forlorn! the very word is like a bell
To toll me back from thee to my sole self
Adieu! the fancy cannot cheat so well
As she is fam'd to do, deceiving elf.
Adieu! adieu! thy plaintive anthem fades
Past the near meadows, over the still stream,
Up the hill-side: and now 'tis buried deep
In the next valley-glades:
Was it a vision, or a waking dream?
Fled is that music: -- Do I wake or sleep?

John Keats (1795-1821)

What Does the Nightingale Really Say?
A reading of Keats's "Ode to a Nightingale"
by the author of this book

Introduction

Keats's poem is about the feelings the song of a nightingale evokes in the speaker. The range of his feelings covers many subjects. The poem opens with the speaker's discontentment with human life, which leads to his longing to escape into an idealized world of beauty, harmony, and permanence, symbolized by the song of the nightingale. The speaker wishes to reach that coveted world with the help of human imagination – "on the viewless wings of Poesy" (line 33). He rejects wine and other intoxicants as a means to his imaginative leap. He refuses to be "charioted by Bacchus [the god of wine] and his pards [leopards]" (line 32). Burdened with unbearable pain, he longs for the luxury of "easeful death" but soon rejects the death wish, realizing that in death the speaker will lose not only his pain but also his consciousness of beauty. The speaker becomes aware at the subconscious level that it is the healing power and timelessness of the song of the nightingale that makes the bird immortal. The poem implies an analogy between the role of the artist and that of the nightingale, ending with return to reality and acceptance of, even respect for, the unalterable laws of nature.

It is apparent from this short summary that Keats's poem is rich in ideas and feelings. From the wealth of topics, we need to select a few significant ones and narrow them down to specific statements of themes for this exercise in interpretive writing.

First theme (part of the thesis)

The thought content of Keats's famous poem can be expressed in simple words: When reality becomes oppressive, the flight of imagination ("the viewless wings of Poesy") can enable us to escape into a better world. Such imaginative experiences have a therapeutic effect, for they relieve some of our suffering, and when the inevitable return to reality occurs, we are better prepared to face it.

Second theme (part of the thesis)

Another theme from Keats's poem is in the form of a paradox that is inherent in human consciousness: The price of being human is painful awareness; a feeling of regret at the transience of beauty and youth coexists with joy at the gift of awareness, which brings both pleasure and pain. In another of his famous poems, "Ode on Melancholy," Keats has used the phrase "wakeful anguish of the soul" to describe this trait of human sensibility.

Third theme (part of the thesis)

Several significant details in Keats's poem generate still another important theme: A true work of art enjoys the same immortality that the song of a nightingale does. Like the song of the nightingale in Keats's poem, an artistic creation becomes a source of healing, consolation, and renewal for people of all ages, cultures, and classes.

Topic sentence followed by supporting details for the first theme (first section of support)

The theme of therapeutic effects of imaginative experiences is apparent from the change in the speaker's mood and attitude. Earlier, the speaker had been feeling imprisoned in a world

> Where but to think is to be full of sorrow
> And leaden-eyed despairs,
> Where Beauty cannot keep her lustrous eyes,
> Or new Love pine at them beyond tomorrow. (lines 27-30)

After his experience of the ideal world with the help of his imagination, he progresses to an acceptance of reality. He refuses to linger in the world of dreams too long – just long enough for a momentary escape from the burdensome consciousness of human misery:

> Adieu! The fancy cannot cheat so well
> As she is famed to do, deceiving elf. (lines 73-74)

The speaker succeeds in rallying to his support the ultimate resource that he can always count on – his "sole self":

> Forlorn! the very word is like a bell
> To toll me back from thee to my sole self! (lines 71-72)

However, this is not the grieving, anguished self of the opening lines; it is now a resilient self able to assume control of his runaway fantasy and be successful in harnessing the power of imagination for renewal of spirit, not for a permanent escape into the dream world.

Topic sentence followed by support for the second theme
(second section of support)

Keats expresses the theme of paradoxical simultaneity of beauty and pain in human consciousness most clearly in those lines where the speaker first expresses and then, immediately thereafter, rejects his death wish:

> Now more than ever seems it rich to die,
> To cease upon the midnight with no pain
> While thou art pouring forth thy soul abroad
>
> In such an ecstasy!
> Still wouldst thou sing, and I have ears in vain –
> To thy high requiem become a sod. (lines 55-60)

He realizes that it is only the living human being – alive in a deeper sense than mere breathing (that is, gifted with great sensitivity) – who can experience beauty, which is inseparable from pain, for the beautiful evokes in us the desire to perpetuate beauty, and we know the painful fact that this desire is in vain. Rather than "become a sod," the speaker chooses acute awareness, however painful, for that is at once the great reward and the inescapable price of being human. The very source of the speaker's intense awareness of the beauty of the nightingale's idealized world has been the human imagination, which cannot exist except as a part of human consciousness – that paradoxical mixture of ecstasy and pain.

Topic sentence followed by support for the third theme
(third and last section of support)

The preceding juxtaposition of pain and ecstasy leads naturally and immediately (in the very next stanza) to the poem's third significant theme that, by implication, claims the same timeless, healing, consoling, and inspirational power in an artist's creation that exists in the song of the nightingale:

> Thou wast not born for death, immortal Bird!
> No hungry generations tread thee down;
> The voice I hear this passing night was heard
> In ancient days by emperor and clown:
> Perhaps the self-same song that found a path
> Through the sad heart of Ruth, when, sick for home,
> She stood in tears amid the alien corn;
> The same that oft-times hath
> Charmed magic casements, opening on the foam
> Of perilous seas, in faery lands forlorn. (lines 61-70)

This theme is subtle but unmistakable, and the awareness that it brings is the means of transition from despair at the human lot of the poem's earlier part to the poem's concluding triumphant affirmation of human life with all its paradoxes of pain and pleasure in beauty.

Conclusion

The poem has a trance-like effect on the reader. It opens with "drowsy numbness," takes the reader through an intense imaginative experience, and ends in the same deeply meditative state between wakefulness and sleep that characterizes the poem's opening. If the song of a poet could accomplish what the song of the nightingale has achieved in this poem, it should be cause for elation for any artist.

Complex Poems and Conflicting Interpretations: T. S. Eliot's "The Love Song of J. Alfred Prufrock"

The third poem selected for interpretation – T. S. Eliot's "The Love Song of J. Alfred Prufrock" – is one of the most difficult yet popular poems of the twentieth century. Being even more complex than Keats's "Ode to a Nightingale," it makes greater demands on the reader. Some readers view Prufrock as a pathetic, spineless character who himself is to blame for his predicament. Others have seen in him a heroic character whose creativity and courage have been suffocated by his social milieu. Readers also differ sharply about the meaning of the word "love" in the poem's title: How is it a love poem? Who is the lover? And who is the object of his desire? One of the more accepted interpretations has been that even though there is the presence of a woman in the poem, whose braceleted arms seem to fascinate Prufrock, ultimately the poem is the poet's love song for humanity. However, as a reader you have to come to your own conclusion.

Before reading my interpretation, read the poem and complete the same two-step exercise that you did in the case of Keats's "Ode to a Nightingale." That exercise asked you to (1) formulate formal statements of three major themes from the poem and (2) give one sentence of supporting details for each theme. After completing this reading and writing exercise, you can proceed with the poem's interpretation.

The Love Song of J. Alfred Prufrock

S'io credesse che mia risposta fosse
A *persona che mai* tornasse *aJ mondo,*
Questa fiamma staria *senza piu* scosse.
Ma *perciocche giammai di questo fondo*
Non tome vivo alcun, sTado il vero,
Senza tema *d'infamia* ti *rispondo.*

Let us go then, you and I,
When the evening is spread out against the sky
Like a patient etherised upon a table;
Let us go, through certain half-deserted streets,
The muttering retreats
Of restless nights in one-night cheap hotels
And sawdust restaurants with oyster-shells:
Streets that follow like a tedious argument
Of insidious intent
To lead you to an overwhelming question . . .   10
Oh, do not ask, "What is it"
Let us go and make our visit.

In the room the women come and go
Talking of Michelangelo.

The yellow fog that rubs its back upon the window-panes,
The yellow smoke that rubs its muzzle on the window-panes
Licked its tongue into the corners of the evening,
lingered upon the pools that stand in drains,
Let fall upon its back the soot that falls from chimneys,
Slipped by the terrace, made a sudden leap,   20
And seeing that it was a soft October night,
Curled once about the house, and fell asleep.
And indeed there will be time
For the yellow smoke that slides along the street,
Rubbing its back upon the window-panes;
There will be time, there will be time
To prepare a face to meet the faces that you meet;
There will be time to murder and create,
And time for all the works and days of hands
That lift and drop a question on your plate;   30
Time for you and time for me,
And time yet for a hundred indecisions,
And for a hundred visions and revisions,
Before the taking of a toast and tea.

In the room the women come and go
Talking of Michelangelo.

And indeed there will be time
To wonder, "Do I dare" and, "Do I dare?"
Time to turn back and descend the stair,
With a bald spot in the middle of my hair –   40
(They will say: "How his hair is growing thin!")
My morning coat, my collar mounting firmly to the chin,
My necktie rich and modest, but asserted by a simple pin –
(They will say: "But how his arms and legs are thin!")
Do I dare
Disturb the universe?
In a minute there is time
For decisions and revisions which a minute will reverse.

For I have known them all already, known them all :
Have known the evenings, mornings, afternoons,   50
I have measured out my life with coffee spoons;
I know the voices dying with a dying fall
Beneath the music from a farther room.
So how should I presume?

And I have known the eyes already, known them all
The eyes that fix you in a formulated phrase,
And when I am formulated, sprawling on a pin,
When I am pinned and wriggling on the wall,
Then how should I begin
To spit out all the butt-ends of my days and ways?   60
And how should I presume?

And I have known the arms already, known them all
Arms that are braceleted and white and bare
(But in the lamplight, downed with light brown hair!)
Is it perfume from a dress
That makes me so digress?
Arms that lie along a table, or wrap about a shawl.
And should I then presume? And how should I begin?

          *   *   *

Shall I say, I have gone at dusk through narrow streets   70
And watched the smoke that rises from the pipes
Of lonely men in shirt-sleeves, leaning out of windows?. . .

I should have been a pair of ragged claws
Scuttling across the floors of silent seas.

          *   *   *

And the afternoon, the evening, sleeps so peacefully
Smoothed by long fingers,
Asleep . . . tired . . . or it malingers,
Stretched on the floor, here beside you and me.
Should I, after tea and cakes and ices,
Have the strength to force the moment to its crisis?   80
But though I have wept and fasted, wept and prayed,
Though I have seen my head (grown slightly bald)
Brought in upon a platter,
I am no prophet – and here's no great matter;
I have seen the moment of my greatness flicker,
And I have seen the eternal Footman hold my coat, and snicker,
And in short, I was afraid.

And would it have been worth it, after all,
After the cups, the marmalade, the tea,
Among the porcelain, among some talk of you and me,
Would it have been worth while,   90
To have bitten off the matter with a smile,
To have squeezed the universe into a ball
To roll it toward some overwhelming question,
To say: "I am Lazarus, come from the dead,
Come back to tell you all, I shall tell you all " –
If one, settling a pillow by her head,

Should say: "That is not what I meant at all.
That is not it, at all. "

And would it have been worth it, after all,
Would it have been worth while,   100
After the sunsets and the dooryards and the sprinkled streets,
After the novels, after the teacups, after the skirts that trail along the floor
And this, and so much more? —
It is impossible to say just what I mean
But as if a magic lantern threw the nerves in patterns on a screen:
Would it have been worth while
If one, settling a pillow or throwing off a shawl,
And turning toward the window, should say:
"That is not it at all,
That is not what I meant, at all."   110

          *   *   *

No! I am not Prince Hamlet, nor was meant to be;
Am an attendant lord, one that will do
To swell a progress, start a scene or two,
Advise the prince; no doubt, an easy tool,
Deferential, glad to be of use,
Politic, cautious, and meticulous;
Full of high sentence, but a bit obtuse;
At times, indeed, almost ridiculous
Almost, at times, the Fool.

I grow old . . . I grow old . . .   120
I shall wear the bottoms of my trousers rolled.

Shall I part my hair behind? Do I dare to eat a peach?
I shall wear white flannel trousers, and walk upon the beach.
I have heard the mermaids singing, each to each.

I do not think that they will sing to me.

I have seen them riding seaward on the waves
Combing the white hair of the waves blown back
When the wind blows the water white and black.

We have lingered in the chambers of the sea
By sea-girls wreathed with seaweed red and brown   130
Till human voices wake us, and we drown.

                         T.S. Eliot (1888-1965)

Interpretation of Eliot's poem

As we have done in writing on the themes of Robert Hayden's and Keats's poems, we can introduce our interpretation of T. S. Eliot's poem by summarizing its events, the main character's state of mind, and the subject matter.

Introduction

Prufrock (the speaker in this poem) is talking either to himself or to someone else about going to a social gathering. He imagines the people who would be there at the tea party and what they would think of him and of his ideas. He fears that they will dismiss as irrelevant his humanitarian concern about bringing comfort to lonely people and overcoming the abject fear of aging and death. He anticipates only rejection of his other universally important but unstated ideas. His fear of the disapproving and hostile world paralyzes him to the point that he does not even go to the party mentioned earlier in the poem. Eliot ends this poem with Prufrock's indulgence in the beautifully perfect world of his dreams which, however, now seems threatened by the encroaching demands of reality's human voices.

Interpretation in the form of succinct statements of the poem's major themes

In spite of its seductively languorous and deliciously indolent images, Eliot's poem is a warning that the world of fantasy, however rich, beautiful, and comforting it may be, has its perils, for overindulgence in it can render the dreamer incapable of facing reality. Dramatizing a cause-and-effect sequence in the poem, Eliot also reveals how fear of disapproval can paralyze and force a person into a state of withdrawal. An individual afflicted with such paralysis of will becomes prey to imaginary fears and fearful of contact with the real world, which seems so hostile that it even threatens to take away the security of one's dreams. Still another of the poet's themes is that the potential of good ideas is wasted when they remain locked inside the thinker's mind either because the world, on account of its narrow-mindedness, becomes unworthy of benefiting from a great thinker's ideas or because the thinker is too afraid to take the risk of exposing his thoughts.

Supporting details

An exercise at the end of this chapter asks you to provide supporting details for this poem's three themes stated above. The exercise also asks you to formulate another theme that you perceive as important to the poem. Your theme is to be supported with details from the poem. As you know by now, once you have formulated the themes of a literary work, offering supporting evidence from the text is quite easy. To complete your interpretation of the poem, all you need after the thesis is adding relevant supporting details from the poem in the organized manner of the preceding two sample essays on "Winter Sundays" and "Ode to a Nightingale."

Evaluation of Style in Poetry
A challenging but essential assignment

Style evaluation continues to be a challenging assignment. Considering the benefits, acquisition of this skill is worth striving for. Becoming style-conscious makes one a better reader and a better communicator. Of all literary genres, style is most visible in poetry. Reading poetry is like taking a crash course in style awareness and style improvement. In fact, throughout the ages, poetry has been a source of renewal of language. Richard Lanham remarks that "poetry, by putting language under pressure in new verbal environments, creates it anew, refreshes it, invents new metaphors or . . . galvanizes the clichés with irony" (Lanham 81). C. Day Lewis also emphasizes poetry's revolutionizing, invigorating, and vitalizing impact on language:

"If you are at the beach, and you take an old, dull, brown penny and rub it hard for a minute or two with handfuls of wet sand (dry sand is no good), the penny will come out a bright gold color, looking as clean and new as the day it was minted. Now poetry has the same effect on words as wet sand on pennies. In what seems an almost miraculous way, it brightens up words that looked dull and ordinary. Thus, poetry is perpetually re-creating languages. It does this in several ways" (Day-Lewis 8)

The steps and methods involved in appreciating a poet's style are similar to those observed in writing about an author's style in prose fiction in Chapter Seven. As was explained in Chapter Four on "Style," some stylistic elements, such as symbol, imagery, allusion, and figurative language, are common to all genres, yet poetry has its own unique style, as will become apparent in the process of analyzing poetic style in this chapter.

Assignment

For this critical appreciation of a poet's style, choose from poems that are complex and have stylistic elements that you can discuss. Focus on two or three outstanding stylistic devices. Connect one of them to a theme or topic by showing how that particular element expresses or reinforces the poem's theme/topic. You may discuss the remaining elements of style without necessarily connecting them to a theme or topic. If necessary, review the advice on style evaluation given in Chapters Four, Six, and Seven.

Work that precedes the discussion of a poet's style

Reviewing once again the guidelines for style evaluation, as a general rule, it is always helpful to first recognize the poem's major theme or topic. This step may be either in the form of a mental note, or you may write it down in one or two sentences as a part of your yet-to-be refined notes. As your next step, make a list of those stylistic elements that stand out. After this preliminary preparation, you should read the poem with the identified theme/topic in mind and note any stylistic elements that embody or enhance that theme. Style serves many other functions besides reinforcing themes, such as creating a mood and surprising the reader with unusual combination of words and pleasing sounds. Here,

543

however, we are primarily concerned with those elements in a poet's style that are, in some way, connected with the poem's theme or topic.

Reading the poet e. e. cummings' poem "the greedy the people" with these general guidelines in mind, one is surprised that such a short and simply written poem has so much style in it. Asking some probing questions can lead us in the right direction.

1. What statement does the poem make about the greedy people?
2. Why does the poet end every stanza with a capitalized word?
3. Is that word a symbol?
4. Is there another word (not capitalized) in the stanza that contrasts with the capitalized word?
5. What do the two contrasting words represent?
6. Why does cummings take liberties with the rules of grammar, using conjunctions like "when" and "how" as verbs?
7. Why does he put certain words in parentheses?

As the next step, we can narrow the focus to these four items:

- What is cummings' major theme?

- Identify the symbols (one in each stanza) used by cummings. Then connect those symbols to the poem's topic or theme.

- The last word of each stanza contrasts with another word in the stanza. Identify the contrasting words, connecting this use of contrast to the poem's theme.

- Identify another different element of cummings' style, exemplify it (giving one or two examples), and comment on its function in the poem.

The outcome of these preliminary notes is the following style-based interpretation of cummings' poem "the greedy the people."[1]

---

[1] The poet does not use a capital "C" in the first letter of his name.

the greedy the people

the greedy the people
(as if as can yes)
they steal and they buy
and they die for because
though the bell in the steeple
says Why

the chary and wary
(as all as can each)
they don't and they do
and they turn to a which
though the moon in her glory
says Who

the busy the millions
(as you're as can i'm)
they flock and they flee
through a thunder of seem
though the stars in their silence
say Be

the cunning the craven
(as think as can feel)
they when and they how
and they live for until
though the sun in his heaven
says Now

the timid the tender
(as doubt as can trust)
they work and they pray
and they bow to a must
though the earth in her splendor
says May

e. e. cummings (1894-1962)

Evaluation of e. e. cummings' Style in "the greedy the people" by the author of this book

Since cummings has a reputation for being an innovator of new forms and styles to express his ideas, an analysis of one of his poems can illuminate the style-theme connection. Although one may not go so far as to say with Marshall McLuhan that the medium is the message, it is undeniable that the styles poets choose to express their ideas are not the result of a chance happening. Good artists select means that are best suited to the expression of their feelings.

Before starting a systematic analysis of cummings' poem, a brief statement of the poem's subject is necessary. The object of cummings' attack and pity is the kind of people who spend their lives mainly in the pursuit of material gain. The poet's feeling seems to be that such people's greed for wealth and an unhealthy neglect of everyday opportunities for pleasure make them blind conformists to rigid systems that dehumanize them and cause them to live fragmented and incomplete lives. Nature's good intentions and cautions are disregarded by such people in their obsessive concern for accumulation of material wealth. In this short poem, cummings even suggests a cure for this malaise – a cure that is embodied in the poet's style and is surprisingly simple.

The meaning of cummings' poem is conveyed by its form and by the various stylistic devices that the poet has used, such as the poem's structural pattern, cummings' playful manipulation of the various parts of speech, and suitable word choice, especially use of contrasting words to emphasize his points.

To begin with form, cummings' poem is so structured that it seems like a design of interlocking patterns. Of course, the poem flows from one line to the next as good poems do. But there is a unique feature that shows in the arrangement of lines: the first line of each stanza can be read together with its counterparts in the remaining stanzas; similarly, the second, third, fourth, fifth, and sixth lines of each stanza can be read together with their counterparts in other stanzas.

One has to wonder why cummings used such a tightly structured pattern for the form of his poem. Cummings' strict design serves the same function as the various symbols of universal significance which appear in every stanza to invite people to live their lives as free individuals and not as prisoners of their self-imposed chains. These symbols are "the bell in the steeple,' "the moon," "the stars," "the sun," and "the earth." It is paradoxical that the poet has used a tightly controlled and an unfree form to extend an invitation of freedom, but this stylistic device works well in the poem.

This organizational plan shows by example that freedom is not synonymous with anarchy, absence of principle, or lack of discipline. Quite to the contrary. Just as within the limits of the self-imposed and strict discipline of this poem, the poet attains freedom from the requirements of the usually overemphasized rules of grammar and punctuation and is able to move with freedom and grace, similarly people can also live freely and fully within certain healthy limits. Perhaps in writing this poem with its emphasis on freedom, cummings did not want to be misunderstood as recommending anarchy or irresponsibility; therefore, he chose a structured form through which he expressed his meaning fully and gracefully, thus showing by practice and example that attainment of freedom is possible even within limitations.

Along with the form of the poem, the poet's choice of words reinforces his meaning. One device is his use of conjunctions/adverbs in the place of verbs, as in line 21: "they *when* and they *how*." Ordinarily, the verb is regarded as a very important part of the sentence, without which a sentence is incomplete, whereas the conjunction is a relatively less important part of the sentence. Also, a verb, by definition, expresses an action or a state of being. Cummings must have felt that the activities of the people in this poem – limited to selling, buying, flocking, and fleeing – did not deserve the name of action. Nor could their lives be regarded as appropriate states of being. Therefore, he avoided using verbs in strategic places and substituted conjunctions for them. This simple rhetorical device is very effective in conveying incompleteness and emptiness in the lives of the people who are the subject of this poem.

Cummings uses another effective device in contrasting the last word of line 4 with the last word of line 6 in every stanza: *because* is contrasted with *Why* which with *who*, *seem* with *Be*, *until* with *Now*, and *must* with *May*. The latter of these pairs of words in each group is desirable to the poet and receives obvious emphasis through capitalization. As we analyze these words, their use by the poet begins to assume significance. People

> die for because
> though the bell in the steeple
> says Why

The capitalized and thus emphasized word *Why* is a contrast to *because*. Dying for a cause can be meaningful and sometimes even admirable, but dying for because suggests throwing away the precious gift of life without even knowing what for. Death, indeed, seems as pointless as the life that preceded it.

In stanza 2, cummings says that people

> turn to a which
> though the moon in her glory
> says Who

Both *which* and *Who* are relative pronouns, the only difference being that which is used mostly for inanimate objects, whereas Who is reserved for living beings. Cummings' simple device of using these two contrasting pronoun forms suggests the possibility that people are drawn to material, non-living objects, instead of being attracted to living and life-giving phenomena.

Stanza 3, through a contrast of *seems* and *Be*, serves a similar function. The greedy people ("the flock"), their activities ("fleeing"), and their fleeting, noisy existence ("through a thunder of seem") are here contrasted with the *Being* – loftiness, serenity, and permanence – of the stars.

Stanza 4 contrasts *until* (or some unknown future for which people sacrifice their immediate pleasures) with *Now*, celebration of which is the sun's exhortation, disregarded of course by the greedy people.

The last stanza of the poem makes use of this same stylistic device of contrasting word choice (between must and *May*) for the desired effect:

> And they bow to a must
> Though the earth in her splendor
> says May

The word *must* has obvious negative connotations of absence of choice. Having been led or rather misled into the belief that the lifestyle they have is the only way of life, these people fail to exercise their choice by the word May. They fail to break away from the confinement of their sterile existence.

There are some other stylistic devices used by cummings, which do not stand out as having a great deal of significance, but are still noticeable in the poem. Three of these devices are (1) skillful arrangement of the sound pattern; (2) length of lines; and (3) use of parentheses. Cummings uses alliteration, assonance and rhyme to emphasize the key words. Alliteration is used in lines 15,16,17,19, and 25, whereas assonance is used in the first line. The first line rhymes with the fifth line in each stanza to make the connection between these lines and to point out the contrast of their contents. Internal rhyme is used in "sun" and "heaven" (line23), And in "bell" and "steeple" (line 5), again to show the connection between these words.

Another device, that of long and short lines, is noticeable in this poem. The last line of each stanza is the shortest, consisting of just two words which exemplify the right kind of attitude or the right way of being. Cummings' choice of the shortest line in this context suggests that the answer to the problem is so simple and brief that it is almost ridiculous for us to miss it.

As for cummings' use of parentheses, each stanza contains a line which is enclosed in parentheses. This particular line juxtaposes what is, with what could be, for example, "(as think as can feel)" (line 20) and "(as doubt as can trust)" (line26). Cummings might have placed these lines in parentheses to show that people only think, but they can also feel; people only doubt, but they can also trust. Thus the possibilities for a better life are there, although the good qualities are trapped with the bad ones, imprisoned within the symbols of parentheses.

Through this analysis of cummings' style, we can see the close connection between style and theme. We can also see how a poet's choice of style has crucial impact on the poem's content.

OPTIONS FOR WRITING ABOUT POETRY

After reading this chapter's introduction to poetry and demonstration of interpretation skills, the next step for you is writing about poetry. To help you with choice of topics, numerous options are listed below. After reading all samples included here, you can choose the option that appeals to you. Reading of the sample essays is not just to provide you with an assignment topic. It is also meant to give you an opportunity to enjoy literary essays created by your peers.

Since through this exercise (suggested length 750 – 1000 words), you are learning how to interpret poetry, choose from poems that have appealing complexity and promise an interesting discussion. Keep in mind T.S. Eliot's view that even the most complex of poems communicates its feeling to the reader instantly at the level of intuition long before the reader understands its discursive meaning. *Transforming that intuitive, subjective understanding into a logically supported and valid interpretation is the challenge of this assignment.* Because of space restraints, samples could not be provided for every single option listed below.

1. Many poems have been written about the art of poetry. Discuss any two poems that, in your view, illuminate the nature and function of poetry. The student Margaret Ghuman's analysis of Linda Pastan's "Ars Poetica" and Archibald MacLeish's poem of the same title serves as a good sample.

2. Explicate a complex poem. Student Ayana Summer explicated William Blake's "London" in Chapter Five.

3. Select for discussion a poem that dramatizes the all-consuming nature of love. Student Mariana Maguire's "Rejection of Immorality" in John Keats's poem "Bright Star" offers a good example.

4. Write on two or three prominent themes from a poem. Support your interpretation with relevant details from the poem. My essay on Keats's "Ode to a Nightingale" may be used as a sample.

5. Write on a poet's theme(s) and style in any one poem of your choice. At least one-third of the paper should be on style. You may discuss one or more prominent themes from the poem and comment on two or more stylistic elements. Student Greg Hamaguchi's essay on Janice Mirikitani's "Insect Collection" is an example of how this assignment may be completed.

6. Write on two or three stylistic elements in a poem, connecting at least one element of style to a prominent theme in the poem. You may connect all stylistic devices to the poem's theme(s) if it is possible to do so. If an element of style does not have a directly theme-bearing role, comment on its effectiveness in creating mood, revealing character, or generating anticipation and excitement through suspense. A sample is my analysis of e. e. cummings' style in "The greedy the people."

7. Write on just one outstanding stylistic feature of a poem, making the style-theme connection. No sample.

8. Compare and/or contrast the themes and stylistic features of two poems either by the same poet or by two different poets. You may, for example, choose two poems on any topic and show the differences in the two poets' views. Include a comparison/contrast of the poets' styles. Student Nicky Newton's essay that compares Robert Frost's "Design" with Emily Dickinson's "Apparently with no surprise" shows how this exercise may be completed.

9. Write on four or five poems by any one poet and trace the poet's development of thought and style from one poem to the next. No sample.

10. Write a paper to introduce a reluctant reader of poetry to four or five poems that are outstanding in some respect and have the potential to convert haters into lovers of poetry. Include a brief interpretation and evaluation of each selected poem. Student Martin Spence's essay "Pheasant Hunting" exemplifies completion of this assignment.

11. Compare the thematic substance of a poem with that of a novel, a short story, a movie, or a play. Point out striking similarities. Student Carolyn Nash covers this topic in her paper "Big Fish Stories" that compares Elizabeth Bishop's poem "The Fish" with Ernest Hemingway's novella *The Old Man and the Sea*. The second sample essay on this option by the author of this book compares the movie *Hiroshima Mon Amour* with the poem "Vergissmeinnicht."

12. Select one or two poems to demonstrate how literature deals with pain to offer consolation and healing. Pablo Neruda's poem "If I die" (included in this chapter) is an excellent poem on this topic. "The Letter" by Jane Kenyon and "Out, Out" by Robert Frost (that you can read on the internet) are also many of other choices that you have.

13. Write an interpretation of a complex poem primarily through character analysis. Student Joseph Nugent's reading of T. S. Eliot's famous poem "The Love Song of J. Alfred Prufrock" shows how this assignment may be completed.

14. Write on one or two poems that connect the mystery of life with the magic of art. Kirsten Schneider's comparison of John Keats's "Ode to a Nightingale" with William Butler Yeats's "The Wild Swans at Coole" covers this option.

15. Major events of the 1960s made Herb Caen reminisce about Matthew Arnold's famous poem "Dover Beach." Using Caen's article as your guide, connect a great poem from the past with a significant event of today.

16. Write a review of a movie that concerns the life and work of any prominent poet. Some examples are *Sylvia* (based on Sylvia Plath's life), *Tom and Viv* (concerning T. S. Eliot and his wife Vivian), *Postman* (inspired by Pablo Neruda's life and work), and *Bright Star* (about John Keats). Relate some relevant poems by the subject poet to details from the film. Question No. 10 in "Exercises" at the end of this chapter gives you further helpful information on how to complete this assignment.

17. Write on a poem with a significant historical, cultural, social, or political theme. Lawrence Ferlinghetti's "The History of the Airplane," Suheir Hammad's "First Writing Since," and Joseph Bruchac's "Ellis Island" are among poems of this nature. Read student Jennifer Hammer's comparison of Ferlinghetti's poem with the one by Hammad for an example.

18. Write on one or two poems that handle emotional pain with aesthetic beauty, illustrating the concept that art has the power to beautify tragedy and pain. Two samples are papers by students Erin Kehoe and Indigo Wilmann. The two poems selected for this exercise are "Getting Out" by Cleopatra Mathis and "Getting Through" by Deborah Pope.

19. Include at least two sources from literary criticism in your interpretation. Student Scott Roland, for example, uses some critics' opinions in his essay to contrast Emily Dickinson's rational skepticism in "These are the days" with John Keats's sensuous optimism in "To Autumn." Both poems are inspired by an autumn day.

Optional stylistic elements that you use in your own writing

If you would like to make your writing impressive rather than just expressive, your use of a few optional stylistic elements is recommended. Based on your instructor's discretion, this effort at style improvement may also earn you some bonus points. To expand your range of expression and vary your style, try using in your own writing as many of the following elements as possible: **simile, metaphor, analogy, semicolon, colon, and explanatory dash.** In the end notes, draw the reader's attention to your best use of each element only once. You may use a stylistic element several times in the paper, but endnote it only *once*. These style notes should preferably appear in any of your pre-final drafts, not in the final version. These notes are meant to sensitize you to the intricacies of style and to enable you to compare your use of the selected elements with those that empower the writing of good professional authors. Using this method, you can systematically refine and polish your style. The important condition is that none of the elements used by you should sound forced.

If your use of a suggested element sounds forced, omit it. In its place, include its definition and an example at the end of your pre-final draft on a separate page. The example should preferably be your own, but if you cannot create one, copy it from any source and acknowledge it. In this way, you will be at least looking at some good examples to advance yourself from the position of a mere admirer to that of a practitioner of good writing.

SAMPLE ESSAYS

As in earlier cases, the sample essays appear after the poems. Many of the sample essays are by students.

Analyzing poems on poetry
(option no. 1)

Poems: "Ars Poetica" by Archibald MacLeish and "Ars Poetica" by Linda Pastan

Ars Poetica

A poem should be palpable and mute
As a globed fruit,
Dumb
As old medallions to the thumb,
Silent as the sleeve-worn stone   5
Of casement ledges where the moss has grown —
A poem should be wordless
As the flight of birds.
                          *

A poem should be motionless in time
As the moon climbs,   10
Leaving, as the moon releases
Twig by twig the night-entangled trees,
Leaving, as the moon behind the winter leaves,
Memory by memory the mind —
A poem should be motionless in time   15
As the moon climbs.
                          *

A poem should be equal to:
Not true.
For all the history of grief
An empty doorway and a maple leaf.   20
For love
The leaning grasses and two lights above the sea —
A poem should not mean
But be.

Archibald MacLeish (1892-1982)

Ars Poetica

1. THE MUSE

You may catch
a butterfly
in a net
if you are swift enough
or if you keep
perfectly still
perhaps it will land
on your shoulder.
Often
it is just
a moth.

2. WRITING

In the battle
between the typewriter
and the blank page
a certain rhythm evolves,
not unlike the hoofbeats
of a horse groomed for war
who would rather be
head down, grazing.

3. REJECTION SLIP

Darling, though you know
I admire your many
fine qualities
you don't fill all my needs
just now, and besides
there's a backlog
waiting to fit
in my bed.

4. REVISION

The tree has been green
all summer, but now
it tries red ... copper ...
even gold. Soon
leaf after leaf
will be discarded,
there will be nothing
but bare tree, soon
it will be almost time
to start over again

5. ARS POETICA

Escape from the poem
by bus, by streetcar any
way you can,
dragging a suitcase
tied together with twine
in which you've stuffed
all your singular belongings.
Leave behind
a room
washed by sun
or moonlight.
There should be a chair
on which you've draped a coat
that will fit anyone.

Linda Pastan (b. 1932)

The Art of Poetry According to Archibald MacLeish
and Linda Pastan
Student author: Margaret Ghuman

Ars Poetica by Archiblad MacLeish and *Ars Poetica* by Linda Pastan share the same title, but the similarity ends there. MacLeish attempts to define the essence of poetry by emphatically telling the reader what a poem should or should not be. His definition proposes that poetry merely exists as a part of Nature, transcending meaning or truth.

Pastan is more concerned with the mechanics of creating poetry. Her poem moves deliberately, step-by-step, through the creative process from the elusive inspiration to the challenge of writing, the setback of rejection, the catharsis of revisions, to its eventual completion.

MacLeish states that the art of poetry is timeless and equal to all of life's experiences. Lines 17-18 support this belief, which is re-emphasized in lines 23-24:

> A poem should be equal to:
> Not true.
> A poem should not mean
> But be.

Pastan, on the other hand, sees poetry as having a universal appeal, a meaning for every reader. Her analogy in lines 48-50 supports this belief:

> There should be a chair
> on which you've draped a coat
> that will fit anyone.

Both poets use appropriate stylistic elements to make their points. MacLeish's poem is composed almost entirely of similes. His language is spare but descriptive. Poetry is presented as a solitary, uncommunicative art with the words "mute," "dumb," "silent," and "wordless," reinforcing the separateness of poems from the rest of life. His metaphor for the mind releasing memories — "as the moon releases twig by twig the night-entangled trees" (lines II-12)--is very powerful. Lines 9-10—

> A poem should be motionless in time
> As the moon climbs

appear to be a paradox as "motionless" seems to contradict "climbs." "An empty doorway" (line 20) is an effective metaphor for the void created by grief. And the enduring quality of love is beautifully expressed in lines 21-22: "For love, the leaning grasses and two lights above the sea." MacLeish's philosophical tone in the first sixteen lines turns assertive in the remaining eight as he resounds his theme.

The form of Pastan's poem is one of progression, with each section building on the last. She has divided the poem into five parts, each having a distinct mood. The first part, "The Muse," has a romantic tone with a touch of reality: "You may catch a butterfly" (line I) but "Often it is just a moth" (lines 9-11). The second part, "Writing," captures the tense feelings of struggle and resistance with its description of the "battle between the typewriter and the blank page" (lines 13-14). Part three," Rejection Slip," introduces a new voice from the harsh world of publishing with the superficial "darling" (line 20). In "Revision" (the last part), the speaker assumes a philosophical tone with the beautiful analogy between a poet trying words only to discard them, and a tree approaching winter:

> it tries red . . . copper . . .
> even gold. Soon
> leaf after leaf
> will be discarded,
> there will be nothing
> but bare tree. (Lines 30-35)

In "Ars Poetica," Pastan creates a desperate feeling in the first stanza as she urgently encourages the poet to "escape" from her creation "any way you can." Her haste is aptly expressed as she describes the suitcase "stuffed" and "tied together with twine." Her tone changes dramatically in the second stanza as she serenely describes "a room washed by sun or moonlight" containing the "coat" that will fit anyone.

Although the two poems express very different ideas about the art of poetry, they do seem to agree that poetry is a powerful art capable of encompassing all of life's experiences.

After comparing these two poems, I wondered if the poets were possibly inspired by one of Keats' axioms about poetry:

> It is easier to think what Poetry should be than to write it.

Poems that dramatize the all-consuming nature of love
(option no. 3)

Bright Star

Bright star, would I were stedfast as thou art –
Not in lone splendour hung aloft the night
And watching, with eternal lids part,
Like nature's patient, sleepless Eremite,
The moving waters at their priestlike task   5
Of pure ablution round earth's human shores,
Or gazing on the new soft fallen mask
Of snow upon the mountains and the moors –
No – yet still steadfast, still unchangeable,
Pillow'd upon my fair love's ripening breast,   10
To feel for ever its soft fall and swell,
Awake for ever in a sweet unrest,
Still, still to hear her tender-taken breath,
And so live ever – or else swoon to death.

John Keats (1795-1821)

Rejection of Immortality in Keats's "Bright Star"
Student author: Mariana Maguire

The speaker in this poem is talking about the loneliness he feels apart from his lover, and his desire for an intimate, tangible relationship. By comparing himself to a star, he discusses what he does not like about a removed and distant, though perhaps immortal life of a star. If asked to choose between the star-like detached permanence and the intimate, time-bound embrace of his beloved, he would prefer the latter because not having intimacy with her would be like death to him.

Keats constructs a richly figurative poem to reject immortality and accept life's passing sensual beauty and transitory sensory experience for the sake of love. The speaker begins by establishing a dialogue with the star, at first expressing his desire to be like it. Yet he soon finds qualities that do not appeal to him, qualities he does not want to imitate. Most importantly, he does not wish to be "in lone splendor hung aloft the night," alone in the vast emptiness "like nature's patient, sleepless Eremite," observing the passage of life from a removed and lonely distance. This line (4) implies that the star is indeed at the mercy of nature and very much alone, like a hermit, withdrawn from the rest of the world. Line 3 identifies the star as a distant observer, and 5 through 8 go on to describe the view from its solitary post.

The "moving waters at their priest-like task of pure ablution round the earth's human shores" allude to the oceans, constantly churning with currents, waves washing onto man's dry domain, sweeping away anything in their path like baptismal waters rinsing away sin. Similarly the star gazes "on the new soft fallen mask of snow upon the mountains and the moors" signifying that the star watches unaccompanied as time passes. Both images connote a view of the world from a very distant point high above it, as is the view one might imagine from the surface of a star.

Line 9 begins with a simple but adamant response to lines 2 through 8. The "No," set apart by dashes, is a final negation of those celestial attributes the speaker is not interested in. He then continues with an explanation of those stellar qualities that he does welcome, such as its "steadfast" and "unchangeable" nature that initially caught his interest. The speaker wishes to be permanently "pillowed" upon his "fair love's ripening breast," embraced and held by her, and drawn into her softness. Her breast's "fall and swell" parallels with ocean tides previously described. Therefore, the speaker implies that he wants to be drawn into the ocean, which in turn implies tangible incorporation into the world rather than distance from it.

He wants to "awake forever in a sweet unrest" in line 12, again indicating direct and sensual interaction with the world, and specifically with his love. The concept of "sweet unrest" establishes a paradox that implies sexual desire. Yet he is not interested in contact with his lover solely for sexual purposes either. In lines 13 and 14 he expresses his ultimate joy: to "hear her tender-taken breath" which in turn breathes life into him as he is happy just to be near his love.

Somewhat as an aside he mentions at the end of the last line that if he were to be just a removed spectator, not an intimate part of her world, he would collapse and perish. He would like to endure forever, like the star, but not at the cost of intimacy with his lover, for without her he could not endure.

To express this unique idea, Keats employs effective metaphors, comparison, and image parallels. The star itself is a metaphor, as well as an independent character; the star is personified through the dialogue Keats establishes between it and the speaker and again as the "sleepless Eremite" in line 4. The description of the star's view of earth is a rich metaphor in itself, connoting the passage of time and the smallness of humanity, thereby reinforcing the idea of the star's immortality.

In line 11 he draws a parallel between the rise and fall of the woman's breast due to her breathing and the rise and fall of the oceans. This comparison simultaneously sets her on a grander scale, and turns the vastness of the oceans into a more personal, welcoming force. An important paradox is introduced in line 12 relating to the heat of passion and sexual desire that is not merely physical but emotional as well; it is a welcome distress. Keats' use of dashes is also very important, as it sets the two parts of the poem apart, effectively dividing the imagery as well as the tone. The imagery throughout is nonetheless sweet and pleasant. The tone is calm and contemplative, as if the speaker is at peace and simply reflecting upon his feelings in light of the universe before him.

Poems that blend theme and style in a unique manner
(option no. 5)

Insect Collection

I collected insects
for my biology class
beetles,
crickets,
butterflies,
dropped them into a bottle
of cyanide fumes
and quickly stilled
those beating wings.
He locked me
In an airless vault of shame,
The darkness of closets, barns,
And muffled bedrooms.
Kept me in a jar
Of silence,
The poisons of threat:
"If you speak of this,
you will kill our mother."
I pinned dead insects
neatly on paraffin with gleaming
Silver straight needles.
I think I hear
butterflies
scream.
He peeled back my skin,
Pierced my flesh
With the dull blades
Of his hands,
Slowly pulled off my wings,
Impaled me, writhing.
Without swift mercy
Of insecticide
I suffocated slowly,
Swallowing bits of my tongue.
My body,
Hollow
As the mute row
of corpses
pinned
to paraffin.

Janice Mirikitani (b. 1941)

Silenced Pain: Evaluation of Mirikitani's Theme and Style in "Insect Collection"

Student author: Greg Hamaguchi

The horror and shame that a victim of child abuse must contend with might not be comprehendible to the average person who has fortunately been spared the experience. Janice Mirikitani's poem, "Insect Collection," is about child abuse, perpetrated by a parent, and the anguish that it causes. This short poem pulls the reader into the speaker's world to offer a glimpse of her pain, both mental and physical. It begins with the preparation of insects for mounting in a biology class and progresses quickly into the story of the speaker's victimization. The back-and-forth shift from insect to human victim indicates that the two may share many similarities.

The silence of the victim of molestation is expressed as a major theme in Mirikitani's poem. The poet impresses upon the reader the victim's painful silence by using words and phrases that are either synonymous or associated with noiselessness: "airless vault", "muffled bedrooms," and "mute row of corpses." Particularly effective is the image of the speaker "swallowing bits" of her tongue, figuratively keeping silent about her victimization.

In form, the poet makes a distinction between the experiences of the insect, and the experiences of the speaker by shifting the stanzas revolving around the act of molestation to the right. The speaker's preparation of the insects in a biology class becomes the act that triggers memories of the speaker's traumatic experiences at home. These shifted stanzas are "flashbacks." In stanzas 1-2, the insect and human experiences, though similar in action, are kept separate by form. In stanza 4, these two experiences begin to merge, when the poet writes, "I think I hear butterflies scream." By the final stanza, the link between the biology class and the trauma at home are not implied, but clearly stated. This form leads the reader along a disturbing road, to a final destination, as the speaker realizes the similarity between herself and the insect also "pinned" and silenced.

In comparing the elements involved in mounting insects to the act of molestation, metaphor and simile are the poet's most prominent elements of style. The speaker is the metaphorical insect; she is collected, impaled, and her beating wings are "stilled". The insect is silenced ("dropped them into a bottle/ of cyanide fumes/ and quickly stilled/ those beating wings."), as is the speaker ("the poisons of threat: 'If you speak of this,/ you will kill your mother'.")

The simile in "My body, hollow as the mute row of corpses pinned to paraffin" communicates not only the theme of her silence (through the use of the word "mute"), but includes another important theme. The speaker also compares herself to the dead, or that she might as well be. She likens herself to one of the "corpses pinned to paraffin". Mirikitani alternates between the insect and the victim throughout the poem, effectively convincing the reader to equate "typical" qualities of insects (small, powerless and voiceless) to those of the molested child.

In comparing the insect to the molested victim, the poet does not just stress similarities. She also seems to say that, in some ways, the insect is better off than the child. "I pinned dead insects neatly on paraffin

559

with gleaming silver straight needles." In contrast: "He peeled back my skin,/ Pierced my flesh/ With the dull blades/ Of his hands,/ Slowly impaled me, writhing./ Without swift mercy/ Of insecticide I suffocated slowly."

Mirikitani's poem is a vivid portrayal of child abuse through the eyes of the victim. It offers insights into the heart, and thought process of the speaker and effectively captures the monstrosity of such cruel acts. The victim, like the insect, is helpless and, most notably, silent, "poisoned" by threat and left to feel that she is worth as much as dead insect, pinned to paraffin.

Poems with contrasting views on the same topic
(option no. 8)

Poems: "Design" by Robert Frost (1874-1963) and
"Apparently with no surprise" by Emily Dickinson

Frost's poem "Design" could not be included because of excessive permission costs. You can read the poem online: http://www.poets.org/viewmedia.php/prmMID/15718

Apparently with no surprise

> Apparently with no surprise
> To any happy flower,
> The frost beheads it at its play
> In accidental power.
>
> The blond assassin passes on,
> The sun proceeds unmoved
> To measure off another day
> For an approving God.

> Emily Dickinson (1830-1886)

The Dark Side of Nature
Student author: Nicky Newton

"Design," by Robert Frost, and "Apparently with no surprise," by Emily Dickinson, tackle the same subject: death in nature and the presence of God in those deaths. The poets, however, have differing approaches to the topic. Frost is accepting of the presence of death, but questions the existences of God in nature's design. He suggests an alternative "great designer" in the form of the Devil, and even goes so far as to question the existence of any design at all. This contrasts with Dickenson, who while acknowledging the existence of God in the death of a flower, is not accepting of such brutality from a supposedly benign force; she sarcastically questions God's motives, but not his existence. Both explore the darker side of nature: Frost from an observational, almost playfully philosophical point of view, and Dickenson from a bitterly rebellious standpoint.

"Design," by Robert Frost, is about the existence of a universal architect, as evidenced by the role of design in nature, and the part that death plays in that design. The poem explores the theme that all things white do not necessarily represent purity and innocence, and that if nature's great design is proof of the existence of a universal architect, this position could be held by the Devil equally as plausibly as by God. The question of there being any design at all is also explored. These themes are made clear by the lines; "Assorted characters of death and blight"(4), "ingredients of a witches' broth" (6), "What but design of darkness to appall/If design govern in a thing so small"(13/14).

Frost uses many elements of style to get his meaning across. The structure of this fourteen line poem is a mixture of the two sonnet styles – Petrarchan and Shakespearean – with its use of octet followed by sestet, and the use of a couplet to finish. The rhyme scheme is also a variation on that of the Shakespearean sonnet, being abba, abba, bcbc, cc. The use of the word "design" has multiple meanings: the spider has designs on the moth, but "design" also represents the more important idea of the existence of a great creator as the designer and architect of the universe. This play on words sets the mood right from the beginning, questioning the very idea of such a force. Irony is present with the word "right" (5) inferring a good start to the day, but this could also refer to the "rite" of the killing. The suggestions by lines four and five is that of collusion between the "characters" of the drama, like cheap thugs conspiring together in crime. Also ironic is the symbolic use of the "heal-all" as the flower in which the action takes place: it implies trickery not only on the part of the spider, but on the part of the great creator. The reader gets the impression that who or whatever this force is may not be the benign and benevolent patriarch we all envisage. The image of death is enhanced with the phrase "rigid satin cloth" (3), bringing to mind the interior of a coffin. The tone of the poem is one of observation of the proceedings; this is nature's way, it is accepted. It is not a bitter poem, but more ironically philosophical; the use of more euphonious language captures this mood.

To summarize, the poem suggests that if there is a universal architect apparent through nature's design, this force could just as easily be the Devil as God. This idea is explored through the observation of the ritual trapping and killing of a white moth by a spider, as the moth seeks the safety of a like-colored flower; that the moth is unusually white and thus camouflaged by the flower, makes this a premeditated event. Added to the question of whose design is it anyway is the last line of the poem, is the last line of the poem which suggests that in fact there is no design. This infers that neither God nor the Devil exists in this particular natural event; if that is the case, perhaps everything that occurs in the universe is by chance. In any event, Frost does not question the existence of death in nature, only the motive behind it: good or evil? In this respect, he differs from Emily Dickinson, who in "Apparently with no surprise" is unquestioning of the existence of God, but raises certain issues as to his intent.

Dickinson's poem, like Frost's, is about death in nature; unlike Frost's, it deals with the theme that all aspects of life, encompassing even brutal death, are as God intended them. This theme is supported by these lines: "The frost beheads it at it play/In accidental power" (3/4), "The sun proceeds unmoved" (6), and "an approving God" (8); the beheaded flower is accepted as a usual occurrence. The "blond assassin" – or the frost – was created by God, and its actions are portrayed as approved by God.

The poet's meaning is highlighted through the use of tone, irony, personification and harsh-sounding language. Dickinson's belief that so brutal and seemingly mindless an act could be condoned by God is evident from the title, with the use of the word "apparently". The irony is that the frost is white, the color of innocence and purity, yet is still capable of "assassinating" a "happy flower". Also ironic is that this event causes no surprise to anyone or anything else (except the poet), let alone the flower. Dickenson use personification to humanize the death of the flower, as well as painting the villain as the "blond assassin". The flower's death is symbolic of all deaths, including man's; that God would be approving of our own deaths raises serious questions as to his supposed all-loving intent. The poem is short (two four-line stanzas), bitter and appalled in tone, with more cacophonous language than Frost's. In sum, Dickenson finds it hard to accept death in nature as part of God's benevolent wisdom; that it created hardly a blip on nature's oscilloscope as "The sun proceeds unmoved" (7) is appalling to her. It is not God's existence being questioned in this poem, as in Frost's, but his motives.

Both poems deal with death in nature, but with differing approaches. Nature can be cold and unfeeling and does what is necessary to keep the world turning, but where does ultimate responsibility lie? Frost seems to assume that if the force is evil it must therefore be the Devil; he also questions whether there is any design at all underlying natural events. On the other hand, Dickinson assigns blame directly to God. Dickinson's conclusion, that God is capable of evil, is the most insidious. Frost's style is detached, while Dickinson's is one of offense taken and close involvement. The diversity of their approaches in exploring the same theme seems to heighten the impact of the subject.

Poems to convert haters into lovers of poetry
(option no. 10)

Poems: "Modern Love" by Douglas Dunn (b. 1942)
"Intimates" by D. H. Lawrence
"To a Mistress Dying" by William Davenant
"What I Heard at the Discount Store" by David Budbill

Douglas Dunn's poem "Modern Love" can be read online:
http://writersalmanac.publicradio.org/index.php?date=2011/07/14

Your can hear him reading his poems using this link
http://www.poetryarchive.org/poetryarchive/singlePoet.do?poetId=10984
The text of this poem could not be included because the permissions cost was extremely high.

Pheasant Hunting: Converting Haters into Lovers of Poetry
Student author: Martin Spence

"Poetry has been regarded as something central to existence, something having unique value to the fully realized life, something that we are better off for having and without which we are spiritually impoverished."(Perrine 3). Hawkins tells us that since "early history man has conveyed his deepest and most treasured thoughts in the form of verse . . . [enabling us] to share events, thoughts, or feelings that we may have experienced for ourselves, yet have not managed to express in words"(Hawkins 2). If poetry provides its readers with an enriched and broadened awareness, then what discourages the uninitiated reader from embracing one of literature's most appealing forms?

Popular misconceptions that poetry is didactic, bombastic and/or esoteric frequently prevent potential poetry lovers from exploring a world unlimited in its depth and breadth if sights, sounds and feelings. Many readers believe that poetry has little to do with real life or that it holds no relevance for them. Many are put off by the many allusions and references to classical literature, Greek and Roman legends and myths, and various philosophical and religious doctrines. My purpose here is to illustrate that one need not rely solely on an extensive background in world literature in order to experience the tremendous enjoyment poetry offers.

Wallace Stevens has stated that "Poetry is a pheasant disappearing in the brush." Below, with Stevens in mind, the reader is extended four written invitations to flush out the pheasant and, by so doing, to enjoy the elegance of multi-colored flight and to experience the excitement of the hunt.

Our first selection is a poem about love. As noted by Hawkins, from ancient to modern times, love has inspired poets to write about its many joys, sorrows, sacrifices and rewards. The Scottish poet Douglas Dunn's "Modern Love" does not depict the torrid or saccharine love scene, which often discourages new readers of poetry; instead, it relates a very domestic scene with which many readers may identify. Dunn's lovers are real and deeply and securely in love. The poem's tone reflects the calmness and security of the lovers, and the quiet image of "The tree shak[ing] out its shadows to the grass" adds to the relaxed atmosphere. One feels the security, warmth and relaxation of the scene and even anticipates the warm coziness of a purring pet. The creation of this tone or mood well illustrates the power of poetry to convey feelings.

The next selection, "Intimates," by D.H. Lawrence, presents another view of the love relationship. Lawrence's poem, however, does not impart a warm, affectionate atmosphere; instead, we witness insecurity, vanity and desertion. The reader is left in a state of wonder. We ponder the relationship between the lovers and question the characters of the lovers themselves. We can only guess at the true nature of the relationship between the poem's two "intimates": Are they lovers or strangers? The unanswered questions raised in poetry stimulate the reader's imagination and it is this stimulation, which magnifies the enjoyment of poetry.

Intimates

Don't you care for my love? She said bitterly.
I handed her the mirror, and said:
Please address these questions to the proper person!
Please make all requests to headquarters!
In all matters of emotional importance
Please approach the supreme authority direct—
So I handed her the mirror.
And she would have broken it over my head,
but she caught sight of her own reflection
and that held her spellbound for two seconds
While I fled.

D. H. Lawrence (1885-1930)

Sir William Davenant's poem, "To a Mistress Dying," is a good example of the timelessness and universal applicability of certain topics. Written in the 17th century, the poem contrasts the hope of the romantic with the dogma of the philosopher. The question of what awaits us after death – an afterlife or nothingness – is a question all of us are compelled to ask. Many find such contemplation unpleasant. Poetry, however, often transmutes unpleasant aspects of our existence into pleasurable experiences.

To a Mistress Dying

Lover: Your beauty, ripe and calm and fresh
As eastern summers are,
Must now, forsaking time and flesh,
Add light to some small star.

Philosopher: While she yet lives, were stars decay'd,
Their light by hers relief might find;
But Death will lead her to a shade
Where Love is cold, and Beauty blind.

Lover: Lovers, whose priests all poets are,
Think every mistress, when she dies
Is changed at least into a star:
And who dares doubt the poets wise?

Philosopher: But ask not bodies doom'd to die
To what abode they go;
Since Knowledge is but Sorrow's spy,
It is not safe to know.

Sir William Davenant (1606-1668)

In our final selection, the American poet David Budbil conveys vivid and emotional experience. The poem speaks to many of today's social issues: child abuse, working mothers, the educational system and class structure. These issues affect all of us in some way and it is this relevance which illustrates the pertinence poetry holds for each of us.

What I heard at the Discount Department Store

Don't touch that. And stop your whining too.
Stop it. I mean it. You know I do.
If you don't stop, I'll give you fucking something
to cry about right here
and don't you think I won't either.
So she did. She slapped him across the face.
And you could hear the snap of flesh against the flesh
halfway across the store. Then he wasn't whining anymore.
Instead, he wept. His little body heaved and shivered and wept.
He was seven or eight. She was maybe thirty.
Above her left breast, the pin said: Nurse's Aide.
Now they walk hand in hand down the aisle
between the tables piled with tennis shoes
and underpants and plastic bags of socks.
I told you I would. You knew I would.
You can't get away with shit like that with me,
you know you can't.
You're not in school anymore.
You're with your mother now.
You can get away with fucking murder there,
but you can't get away with shit like that with me.
Stop that crying now I say
or I'll give you another little something
like I did before.
Stop that now. You'd better stop.
That's better. That's a whole lot better.
You know you can't do that with me.
You're with your mother now.

David Budbill (b. 1940)

The above offerings were selected to illustrate both the timely and timeless nature of poetry, to emphasize its relevance to each of us, to stimulate the imagination and to entertain. Although it is impossible to eliminate completely one's subjectivity when compiling such a collection, it is hoped that the selected poems will hold some relevance to all readers on some level. It is the initial spark of relevance for the reader that we seek with the hope that it will be fanned into a flame to illuminate the way to an enhanced understanding of the life experience through poetry.

Connecting poems with novels (option no. 11)

Poem: "The Fish" by Elizabeth Bishop
Novel: *The Old Man and the Sea* by Ernest Hemingway

The text of the poem follows, and Hemingway's novel is available at most public libraries.

The Fish

I caught a tremendous fish
and held him beside the boat
half out of water, with my hook
fast in a corner of his mouth.
He didn't fight.
He hadn't fought at all .
He hung a grunting weight,
battered and venerable
and homely. Here and there
his brown skin hung in strips
like ancient wallpaper,
and its pattern of darker brown
was like wallpaper:
shapes like full-blown roses
stained and lost through age.
He was speckled with barnacles,
fine rosettes of lime,
and infested
with tiny white sea-lice,
and underneath two or three
rags of green weed hung down.
While his gills were breathing in
the terrible oxygen
-- the frightening gills,
fresh and crisp with blood,
that can cut so badly--
I thought of the coarse white flesh
packed in like feathers,
the big bones and the little bones,
the dramatic reds and blacks
of his slimy entrails,
and the pink swim-bladder
like a big peony.
I looked into his eyes
which were far larger than mine
but shallower, and yellowed,
the irises backed and packed
with tarnished tinfoil

seen through the lenses
of old scratched isinglass.
They shifted a little, but not
to return my stare.
--It was more like the tipping
of an object toward the light.
I admired his sullen face,
the mechanism of his jaw,
and then I saw
that from his lower lip
--if you could call it a lip--
grim, wet, and weaponlike,
hung five old pieces of fish-line,
or four and a wire leader
with the swivel still attached,
with all their five big hooks
grown firmly in his mouth.
A green line, frayed at the end
where he broke it, two heavier lines,
and a fine black thread
still crimped from the strain and snap
when it broke and he got away.
Like medals with their ribbons
frayed and wavering,
a five-haired beard of wisdom
trailing from his aching jaw.
I stared and stared
and victory filled up
the little rented boat,
from tile pool of bilge
where oil had spread a rainbow
around the rusted engine
to the bailer rusted orange,
the sun-cracked thwarts,
the oarlocks on their strings,
the gunnels -- until everything
was rainbow, rainbow, rainbow!
And I let the fish go.

Elizabeth Bishop (1911-1979)

Big Fish Stories: Similar Themes in Bishop's "The Fish" and Hemingway's *The Old Man and the Sea*

Student author: Carolyn Nash

The shared subject, that is, catching a magnificent fish in the waters off the coast of Key West, sets the stage for comparing the two works -- a poem, "The Fish," by Elizabeth Bishop, and a novella, *The Old Man and the Sea* (OMS) by Ernest Hemingway. On the one hand, "The Fish" is a simply elegant and forthrightly laudatory poem written by Bishop in 1940, igniting her public recognition. On the other hand, OMS is a thoughtfully forgiving and respectfully spare short novel written at the close of Hemingway's creative life, culminating an illustrative career. Both works are about gaining wisdom: In "The Fish" wisdom is gained by perceiving the fish's victory; in OMS, it is gained by observing the marlin in defeat. The authors' positions are similar in that they describe how human beings can receive wisdom and courage by being in the presence of beings (here fish) that have these traits.

The authors describe the characters of the fish. Hemingway writes, "Never have I had such a strong fish nor one who acted so strangely. Perhaps he is too wise to jump" (53). Bishop writes about the fish with respect for the valiant warrior and erstwhile survivor:

> That from his lower lip,
> hung five old pieces of fish line
> Like medals with their ribbons
> frayed and wavering, a five-haired beard
> of wisdom trailing from his aching jaw.

Hemingway further describes qualities in the fish that he admires, that is, he describes the marlin as noble even in death, picked clean of flesh by sharks, ". . . white naked line on his [marlin's] backbone and the dark mass of the head with the projecting bill and all nakedness in between" (133). Hemingway writes that even stripped, the marlin has backbone, that is, he symbolically has strength of character. He also has kept his head, or again symbolically, his calm resolve. Finally he died with his weapon drawn, that spear on his snout; here, symbolically, he went down fighting to the end. Bishop describes the heroism of the fish by its appearance in life:

> He hung a grunting weight,
> battered and venerable
> and homely (l. 7)
> and I admired his sullen face,
> the mechanism of his jaw, (l. 82)

The authors also describe the characters of the protagonists, that is, Bishop's "I" and Hemingway's Santiago – two fishermen. Hemingway's Santiago talks to himself, saying, "You were born to be a fisherman as the fish was born to be a fish" (116). It's as simple as that. This pecking order has been established, according to Santiago, because, "But, thank God, they are not as intelligent as we who kill them; although they are more noble and more able." Bishop might agree—examine the choice of the word, "shallower" (l. 36) to describe the fish's eye (the mirror to the soul) and speculate that the author refers to a lesser depth of intellect. But Bishop is awed by and grateful for the lessons that the fish has for her:

> I stared and stared
> and victory filled up
> the little rented boat,
> . . . until everything
> was rainbow, rainbow, rainbow!

Both authors have described fish of formidable stature which fact accounts for the fishermen's conflict when these heroic creatures are their victims. Bishop's "I" regrets catching the fish and lets it go. Hemingway's Santiago sorely regrets killing the marlin and as the fiasco of his bringing the fish to shore as nothing but a skeleton develops, he says, "I wish it were a dream and that I had never hooked him. I'm sorry about it, fish . . . I shouldn't have gone out so far, fish, neither for you nor for me. I'm sorry fish" (121). Santiago is disturbed by the marlin's miserable fate because he has respected the wily combatant. Because he has personified the marlin and because he has identified with him, he is filled with the sense of tragic loss, "I ruined us both" (127). More than once Santiago has referred to the fish as "brother," further indicating the depth of his attachment. Does Santiago now consider whether he is in fact more intelligent, or only better armed?

Both authors provide their protagonists with the experience of an epiphany at the end of the story; these insights reveal the characters' new wisdom. Bishop's "I" sees rainbows, concretely in the oil-slicked bilge water, and figuratively by virtue of her illumination at discovering wisdom and victory in the presence of the fish. She rewards these virtues by giving the fish its freedom. As for Santiago, the ordeal has left him spent. Just as he has identified with the living marlin during the three-day long chase, he now identifies with him in death. Santiago is an old man and he is tired. The reader is led to believe that Santiago will follow the fish in death and that this passage will be eased because of his understanding of the lessons of the marlin. But one day Santiago will go out too far or make a fatal error just as the fish did in grabbing Santiago's bait. Or less romantically, maybe Santiago will just die in his sleep.

Both authors write with respect about wise fish who have outsmarted most fishermen for a long time. Bishop has rewarded her fish. Hemingway has written a story about the survival of the fittest, that is, nature without compassion—animal nature. The narratives are linked by their similar situations and each author has created a preferred ending. Both authors know how to tell a whale of a story.

Connecting poems with movies (option no.11)

Comparison of a poetic film with a cinematic poem can illuminate the special connection between film and poetry. Because of their rich texture and style, some movies have close affinity with carefully crafted poems. Tracing similarity of theme and style between poems and movies can also be an enjoyable and informative exercise.

Is Your Enemy Human?
Similar answers of *Hiroshima Mon Amour* and "Vergissmeinnicht"
Sample essay by the author of this book

Let us consider Keith Douglas's poem "Vergissmeinnicht" (meaning "Forget me not") and Alain Resnais' film *Hiroshima Mon Amour* for this comparison. The poem (text in Chapter One) bears an uncanny resemblance to the film with regard to our usual attitude toward our enemies as opposed to how we ought to view them. The relevant details from *Hiroshima Mon Amour* should be juxtaposed with the poem by Keith Douglas.

The movie's relevant plot details

This highly acclaimed film is a story of two unnamed persons – a French woman (about 30) and a Japanese architect (about 40). The setting for this story is Hiroshima a few years after it was atom bombed. The woman has been in Hiroshima for some time but meets the Japanese man just one day before her return to France. They are instantly drawn to each other and possessed by mutual attraction.

With the hands of the clock moving inexorable on, as if in conspiracy against the two lovers (the dialogue refers repeatedly to the short time they are left with), we share the pain of their tragic pasts. Hers is a personal tragedy: Her German lover was killed on the eve of their elopement, and she had to suffer the agony of having her lover die in her arms. In Marguerite Duras' beautifully written script, the German lover in his dying moments "consoles her, almost apologies for having to make her suffer, for having to die" (Duras 87). In the poem, the German soldier must have found consolation and support in his beloved Steffi's words that she wrote on her picture for him. Those words became the poem's title that means "forget me not." In a way, the German soldier also dies in his beloved's "arms," cradled in his lover's photograph. Yet another similarity between the poem and the movie is the fact that the protagonists hail from two embattled countries – England and Germany in one case and Japan and France in the other.

One of the many themes of *Hiroshima Mon Amour*, is that we have to learn to acknowledge the full humanity of 'the enemy' if we are to prevent tragedies of war." This theme also describe the most important feeling in Keith Douglas's poem "Vergissmeinnicht." The French woman in the movie had followed literally the noble concept, "Love your enemy," by loving a German soldier of the occupying army. Her very human but idealistic behavior in a very imperfect environment, led to the brutal murder of her lover and her humiliation, shame, torture, and incarceration that were to leave life-long scars on her psyche. Something similar happens in the poem: The speaker, apparently a soldier in the victorious army, returns to the scene of the last battle. There he finds a dead German soldier's body "sprawling in the sun." Next to the body is the "dishonored picture of his girl" Steffi (line 10) with "Vergissmeinnicht" (meaning forget me not) written on it.

The gloating, victorious soldier's sensibility receives a jolt as he realizes that the dead man was not just a warrior – an enemy; he was also a lover, a many-dimensional human being. Forgetting his earlier impression of the dead man as the enemy, who had "hit my tank with one [gun] like the entry of a demon" (lines 7-8), the speaker now joins in the mourning by the bereaved beloved as he empathizes with her (lines 17-24).

The similarities between the poem and the movie are not confined to their subject and theme. They share some stylistic features as well. For one thing, they use the documentary style of authentication of their subjects. The film shows historical footage (newsreel clips) of the Hiroshima bombing; the poem structures itself around the photograph of Steffi – the dead German soldier's girlfriend. In both works there is a remarkable desire to authenticate the artistic expression by grounding it in objective reality. Both works, moreover, portray the horror of violent death with stark realism. The shots of devastation in the film are matched by the poem's description of the dead soldier:

> But she would weep to see to-day
> how on his skin the swart flies move
> the dust upon the paper eye
> and the burst stomach like a cave.

Both works of art, thirdly, rely on symbolism to condense and intensify the dominant emotions. Of the many instances of symbolism in the movie, one is that of the plants forcing their way out of the earth to affirm life over death, or, in Marguerite Duras' words from the script, to celebrate "life's obstinancy." For impact, the poem also relies on symbolism: The dead soldier's gun lies unscathed on the battlefield while the soldier's decomposing body is sprawling next to it. This juxtaposition is symbolic of the hopefully temporary ascendancy of implements of destruction and violence over the fragility of human beings. The dramatic change in the soldier-speaker's sensibility is an affirmation of innate human ties that compel us to reach out across the battle lines with compassion. We should remember that love plays a crucial role in both of these poems, as the titles of both of these works indicate. The poem's thematic emphasis is thus not unlike that of *Hiroshima Mon Amour.*

In Understanding Movies, Louis Giannetti says that some filmmakers are like those poets who write sonnets (a highly demanding 14-line poem). They choose this "rigid form precisely because of the technical challenge it presents. Much of the enjoyment we derive from reading a sonnet results from the tension between the content and the form. . . . When technique and subject matter are perfectly fused in this way, our aesthetic pleasure is heightened. The same principle can be applied to framing in film" (Giannetti 44). Giannetti's comment goes to the heart of this comparison between the movie and the poem.

Even though the poet and the filmmaker compared in this essay might have composed without any knowledge of each other's work, the similarities in their subject, theme, and style are unmistakable. Undoubtedly, there are many poems, plays stories, and novels whose themes and style bear a striking resemblance to those of certain movies. Of all these possibilities, the movie-poem connection lends itself readily to interesting discussion. In his theory of diologics, the Russian author Mikhail Bakhtin speaks of great artistic creations as if they were a part of the dialogue across the ages. *Hiroshima Mon Amour* and "Vergissmeinnicht" – one cinematic and the other a literary creation – which have been the subject of this essay, illustrate that dialogue in analogous creations.

Interpretation through character analysis
(option no. 12)

Poem: "The Love Song of J. Alfred Prufrock" by T. S. Eliot

T. S. Eliot's poem "The Love Song of J. Alfred Prufrock" has already been included earlier in this chapter. Joseph Nugent, the student author of this essay, is now a professor of English.

Prudence, Prurience, and Other Things That Begin With Pru
Student author: Joseph Nugent

In "The Love Song of J. Alfred Prufrock," T. S. Eliot takes as his task nothing less than the description of the malaise underlying the demoralisation of twentieth century man. The microcosm he chooses in which to describe his theme is modern middle class society. Calling upon the indecision and vacillation of the aptly named Prufrock (the great middle class virtue is prudence, and it is, ironically, the apparent cause of Prufrock's problems; he is, what is perhaps even more important, a prude) Eliot tells us that if life is to be worthwhile, to be fulfilling, each man must break from the societal constraints, and from the self-fettered chains of inhibition which consign so many of us to the half-life that is our fate in a world where high ideals, not acted upon, disintegrate in the banality of mere existence. This theme is explored in a stream of consciousness journey through, simultaneously, the mind of Prufrock and through the doubting streets which will lead to the social gathering which he both longs for and dreads, and to, just perhaps, love.

The mood of doubt and self-doubt which pervade this poem (is he alone, with the reader, or with part of his sub-conscious?), of postponed pain, and of ennui, is set in the very first lines:

> Let us go then you and I,
> When the evening is spread out against the sky
> Like a patient etherized upon a table.

An underlying anxiety begins to creep into the poem, into our hero, and into the reader through the very air of yellow fog that permeates the "half-deserted streets." Overall hangs some great question which, in the first of many water related images, threatens to "overwhelm" him.

But time presses. "And indeed there will be time" stated and re-stated in a rondo which at once summons up images of the useless repetition of his life, and of the tension he now feels as the meeting approaches, begins the body of the poem, and suggests the endless irresolute circle from which he cannot seem to escape. There is yet time for further procrastination. There is yet time to change his mind. There is yet time to "descend the stair" – back to the depths of a past life which, in a remarkable image at once both banal and stirring, he has measured out "with coffee spoons." Turning again to the ever approaching soiree, we see Prufrock gentle, meek, obsequious even. He does not despise even those who would, he fears, "pin him wriggling on the wall." Indeed he longs to be among them. He has been besotted by their ways, their braceleted arms "downed," he has observed," with light brown hair."

The images here are clearly erotic, and he wonders, as do we, if the "perfume from a dress" has distracted him. Have we here a hint that the attraction drawing him into this fearful place is essentially sexual? This section of the poem ends, as does each subsequent section, on a high note of anxiety and crisis.

> And should I then presume?
> And how should I begin?

As if after great pain, the tension is now dramatically lowered, and a new tone of melancholy is introduced. This central section consists of only five lines divided into a three and a two line segment. In the first, Prufrock manages to tear his mind from the immediate fears and display for us his more sensitive and more somber side. He is a man of compassion; he has come to understand – he alone, he thinks – that we share in a common humanity. But dare he share this insight? Dare he tell the others? No. He cannot summon up the courage. Indeed he cannot bear to recall the feeling he has felt for these "lonely men in shirt-sleeves, leaning out of windows." The image and the empathy disintegrate and die in Eliot's ellipsis. . . .

In an abrupt change of mood which quite shocks the reader, Prufrock, confronting his weakness and thrown into self-loathing cries out

> I should have been a pair of ragged claws
> Scuttling across the floor of silent seas.

This central image of what should be his redemption on two levels - one, his ability to identify with his fellow humans, and two, his ability to relate this to the others, thus ending his awful alienation - now collapses in these singular two lines in which he consigns himself to the status of a frightened crab scurrying along the sea-bed. The reader is here brought to the depths of the ocean and begins to associate this place with the depths of Prufrock's sub-conscious, where lie his deepest inhibitions. But this moment of crisis, too, passes with Eliot's stanza break.

Part three journeys through a series of conflicting emotions, illustrated by contrasting images reflecting Prufrock's heightened agitation. Retrieving, for the moment, his composure, he languishes in the broad vowel sounds of an afternoon "smoothed by long fingers, Asleep. . . tired. . . or. . . [and here a doubt begins again to appear] "malingers." Questioning, in this word, his own motivation, he is again cast into an agony of vacillation. He had failed not only to confront these pretentious, superficial women "who come and go, talking of Michelangelo," in reality; he had even failed to confront the crisis as performed in the dress rehearsal of his mind's eye.

In search of consolation he now begins to see himself, grandiosely, in a role, or series of roles, with Biblical allusions: as a penitential ascetic, as a prophet, and even as the Baptist. Thinking on John's fate now turns his mind to that one great certainty death. Here in a wonderful blending of images, Herodias' "platter" carries our thoughts from Herod's feast to the upcoming party where Death masquerades as a butler, taking Prufrock's coat and snickering along, no doubt, with the other guests.

In the contrast of the great and the small, the Biblical allusions and the theme of death continue to interweave with the cups and the tea, as Eliot pursues the mock-heroic and our hero, a comical Mitty reincarnated as Lazarus, comes back to tell them all. Would that impress? Probably not. Indeed it underlines the alienation. For it was Lazarus (the one of Luke, 16) who lived by the crumbs of the rich man's table. And when Lazarus and Abraham look from the above of the afterlife down on those who formerly sat at that table (the rich man's table or the society table - we can take our pick) Abraham tells them that "between us and you there is a great gulf fixed" (Luke 16,26). No. The gap is too great. The fear of rebuttal is too much. Of what use his lofty ideals, his profound thoughts, of what use this summoning up of heroic bravery, if but one should dismissively respond

> That is not what I meant at all.
> That is not it, at all?

The final part of this poem continues the movement from grandiose ideals to banal trivialities. Though the "no!" with which it opens is hardly resounding, the reader is relieved at this apparent end to indecision. But despite the irony in Prufrock's misunderstanding of the character of Hamlet, the reader feels, in a significant easing of tension, that Prufrock can at least take comfort in Shakespeare's stage metaphor for life. Coming further down from the lofty heights through which his mind had earlier rambled, he returns to the prosaic questions that define his little life – trouser turn-ups and hair partings. For though he has, like Ulysses, heard the mermaids sing to each other, he now tells us in a line – emphasized by Eliot in having it stand alone – of poignant resignation at the final understanding of his, and our, awful isolation, that

> I do not think that they will sing to me.

The last six lines return, as if to bid even the fantasy farewell, to the ocean, the scene of his unrealized dreams. The dream-like quality of the stanzas seems to be echoed in the sonorous, fluid assonance and alliteration of the chambers of the sea "when the wind blows the water white and black," and where lie "sea girls wreathed with seaweed."

This is where the dreams must remain because, as the journey has shown, they are too delicate, too tender, for the real world. "Till human voices wake us" returns us to the first lines, to the operating table, and to the question with which we began. Who is this "you and I?" Let us turn to Eliot's epilogue for clues. In this excerpt from "The Inferno" we are told that these words ate uttered only with the knowledge that the hearer will never return from those depths. Relating this to our poem we can see Eliot telling us that Prufrock's malaise is also ours.

But this poem is, above all, about a struggle, a split. Maybe Prufrock is here struggling with, and speaking to, himself, to another aspect of his character, to, perhaps, his alter ego; maybe he is speaking to that part of himself which lies deep down in his sub-conscious; maybe that "you" that is always with him is that part that contains the urges, the sexual and primeval urges which try time and again to come to the surface, but are time and again dragged down by timidity and by the weight of respectability. Can the real, the whole, Mr. Prufrock ever surface? Can this frock-coated Ulysses ever complete his voyage? Or will these fundamental urges remain in the depths of the ocean, in the depths of his personal purgatory, in the depths of his sub-conscious? Probably. For it is too late.

"I do not think that they will sing to me."

Poems that connect life's mysteries with the magic of art
(option no. 14)

Poems: "The Wild Swans at Coole" by William Butler Yeats
and "Ode to a Nightingale" by John Keats

Keats's "Ode to a Nightingale" has already been included earlier in this chapter.

The Wild Swans at Coole

The trees are in their autumn beauty,
The woodland paths are dry,
Under the October twilight the water
Mirrors a still sky;
Upon the brimming water among the stones   5
Are nine-and-fifty swans.

The nineteenth autumn has come upon me
Since I first made my count;
I saw, before I had well finished,
All suddenly mount   10
And scatter wheeling in great broken rings
Upon their clamorous wings.

I have looked upon those brilliant creatures,
And now my heart is sore.
All's changed since I, hearing at twilight,   15
The first time on this shore,
The bell-beat of their wings above my head,
Trod with a lighter tread.

Unwearied still, lover by lover,
They paddle in the cold   20
Companionable streams or climb the air;
Their hearts have not grown old;
Passion or conquest, wander where they will,
Attend upon them still.

But now they drift on the still water,   25
Mysterious, beautiful;
Among what rushes will they build,
By what lake's edge or pool
Delight men's eyes when I awake some day
To find they have flown away?   30

William Butler Yeats (1865-1939)

Kristen Schneider took advantage of the bonus option to use the stylistic elements of simile, metaphor, analogy, semicolon, and colon in her own writing to expand her range of expression.

Artistic Spans: Linking Ephemeral Human Existence with Nature's Permanence Through Art

Student author: Kristen Schneider

The poem "Ode to a Nightingale" expresses an intense response of someone listening to the beautiful, nocturnal song of a nightingale. The bird's music, softly pouring from the depths of a lush summer woodland, takes hold of and sends the speaker into a rich, melancholy rhapsody. The speaker longs to be free of his human pains and woes, to be one with the beauty he perceives. It is this bittersweet yearning of the heart which is also experienced by the speaker in "Wild Swans at Coole." However, here the response is to the majestic beauty of "nine-and-fifty swans." Both poets, with their own distinctive styles, poignantly express a deep feeling about life: nature, symbolized by the wild birds, continuously manifests beauty and balance in contrast to the fickleness and weary woes of human life.[2] The two worlds, harmonious nature and painful human existence, may be bridged when the poet's imagination is allowed to express itself through art.

The nightingale in Keats's poem represents nature; nature is delightful, divine, harmonious.

> That thou, light-winged Dryad of the trees,
> In some melodious plot
> Of beechen green, and shadows numberless,
> Singest of summer in full-throated ease.

Depicted as a wood nymph, the "immortal Bird" sings a "high requiem," surrounded by the heavenly splendor of summer flora:

> White hawthorn, and the pastoral eglantine;
> Fast fading violets covered up in leaves;
> And mid-May's eldest child,
> The coming musk-rose, full of dewy wine,
> The murmurous haunt of flies on summer eves.

That it is nighttime gives the poem a greater sense of the magical, mysterious aspects of the nightingale and nature itself. The wild swans in Yeats's poem are pictured in the magic of an autumn day draped in the silken veil of twilight. Swans, "those brilliant creatures," evoke images of serenity and poise; they are powerful and romantic. The birds in both poems are fitting symbols of nature. They seem closer to the mystical, the divine, by virtue of their wings and by their exquisite, ethereal spirits.

---

[2] Use of the colon. The colon in this sentence is used to introduce an explanatory independent clause which is preceded by an independent clause.

Both Yeats and Keats respond to the beauty of the wild birds with a combination of longing and regret. Human existence, unlike nature, is fraught with suffering. Keats's nightingale has never known

> The weariness, the fever, and the fret
> Here, where men sit and hear each other groan;
> Where palsy shakes a few, sad, last gray hairs,
> Where youth grows pale, and specter-thin, and dies;
> Where but to think is to be full of sorrow
> And leaden-eyed despairs,
> Where Beauty cannot keep her lustrous eyes,
> Or new Love pine at them beyond to-morrow.

Beauty and love are very important to the poet. We know this because they are capitalized. Yet these concepts appear to be out of reach to humans, except for a few brief moments. Yeats also senses the dull weariness and worry which burden human life. As he gazes upon nature in her tranquil golden mantle,[3] he feels the heaviness that has descended into his step since he first saw the swans almost two decades earlier. "And now my heart is sore,/All's changed since I, . . . Trod with a lighter tread . . ." The swans have not changed; they remain untouched by old age, despair, hopelessness, and even death.[4]

> Their hearts have not grown old;
> Passion or conquest, wander where they will,
> Attend upon them still.

Across the apparent chasm between human existence and nature, Keats and Yeats build their own bridge.[5] That bridge is their self-expression through poetry — their art — which makes it possible for them to be one with nature. As the poet James Dickey put it: "Poetry makes possible the deepest kind of personal possession of the world":

> Away! Away! for I will fly to thee,
> Not charioted by Bacchus and his pards,
> But on the viewless wings of Poesy.

Here Keats states clearly how he reaches the nightingale through poetry. Yeats reveals his own bridge without straightforwardly stating its existence. He comes, perhaps every year, to "count" the swans. He does not just count the swans; he reflects deeply, meditatively, wondering what will become of them if he "wakes up" from his sweet yet melancholy reverie. Yeats' imagination, also on the "wings of Poesy," is allowed to flee to the world of beauty and balance.

---

[3] Use of personification. Nature is given attributes of a lady.

[4] Use of the semicolon. The semicolon in this sentence is used between two independent clauses. The second   clause is non-explanatory.

[5] Use of analogy. This is an analogy which starts with the metaphor "build their own bridge." The image of a bridge spanning the two worlds of art and humanity surfaces many times in this paper. It is present even in the paper's title.

Although both poets use vivid imagery, the way each poet transports us to the realm of imagination and sensitive perception is quite different. The imagery in "Nightingale" is extremely rich and detailed. Magic unfolds in one cup of wine (itself a metaphor of summer's intoxicating loveliness):

> Tasting of Flora and the country green,
> Dance, and Provencal song, and sunburnt mirth!

In these lines Keats uses many figures of speech which all together have the effect of dazzling our senses, making us a part of this dreamscape of the imagination. The poet alludes to Greek mythology and to the warmth of Provence in southern France. We are swept far away to distant times, distant lands. He personifies the emotion of mirth, giving it flesh which can be sunburned, calling to mind country folk with smiling faces. We hear the romantic music of troubadours in "Provencal song." The wine then gurgles and bubbles inches from our faces:

> O for a <u>b</u>eaker full of the warm South,
> Full of the true, the <u>b</u>lushful Hippocrene,
> With <u>b</u>eaded <u>bubb</u>les winking at the <u>b</u>rim.

The elaborate, detailed imagery of "Nightingale" is like exquisitely jeweled, intricately designed attire befitting royalty. In Yeats' poem, the beauty of the imagery is like the graceful simplicity and serenity captured in the saffron robes of a Tibetan monk. Yeats makes less use of figures of speech such as metaphors, allusion, and personification. His choice of diction is simple, pure, and direct.

> The trees are in their autumn beauty,
> The woodland paths are dry,
> Under the October twilight the water
> Mirrors a still sky;
> Upon the brimming water among the stones
> Are nine-and-fifty swans.

The autumn twilight is reflected in the lake among the "stones" and "swans." Then, in all their magnificence, the swans

> All suddenly mount
> And scatter wheeling in great broken rings
> Upon their clamorous wings.

We are breathlessly taken into the air by this powerful image, evoked by the contrast of the quiet evening and the sudden, violent movement of the swans. The "bell-beat of their wings" is heard and we watch them "paddle in the cold/Companionable streams or climb the air."

> But now they drift on the still water,
> Mysterious, beautiful.

These images appropriately represent nature because just as the swans are sometimes still and sometimes violent and noisy, so is nature sometimes benevolent and sometimes destructive. Balance implies opposing forces which are in harmony with each other.

Both Yeats and Keats end their poems with a paradoxical question. Yeats asks where the swans will be when he wakes up one day "To find they have flown away." Up until this question we are led to believe that it is the human speaker of these poems who changes, grows old and dies, while the swans continue to "wander where they will." The question of the swans' disappearing into nature gives us a jolt; is life a dream? Keats's poem also ends in questioning:

> Was it a vision, or a waking dream?
> Fled is that music: Do I wake or sleep?

Was the nightingale's song only in Keats' imagination or just a moment of extraordinary perception? Where is that place that allows us to be one with nature or beauty? In the imagination? In dreams? In our hearts? In our souls? Or can we only truly be one with nature in death? The questions in both poems force us to wake up from musings in the realm of the imagination, yet still we are in a state of wonder.

After reading the poems, perhaps we realize that we may become united with the ethereal spirit of the wild birds through perfect self-expression or art. Both poets have succeeded in building mystical, magical bridges which permit passage to worlds of profound beauty. The constant flux of opposing elements in the poems – night and day, shadow and light, life and death, ecstasy and sorrow, age and youth, silence and sound – are all lovingly woven together to create poems which convey the sensitivity, intensity, and complexity with which John Keats and William Butler Yeats experienced life's beauty and pain.

Connecting a great poem from the past with a significant event of today
(option no. 15)

Poem: "Dover Beach" by Matthew Arnold (1822-1888)
Essay writer: Herb Caen (1916-1997)

Journalist Herb Caen reminisces about Matthew Arnold's famous nineteenth-century poem "Dover Beach," connecting it to the 1960s' major events. The text of Matthew Arnold's poem is in Chapter Six.

Dover Beach West[6]

IN THE WORDS of Robert Louis Stevenson, "it was a clear cold night of stars." Seeking to improve on perfection, and succeeding, somebody very big had pasted a full moon in the center of the sky. In less able hands, the effect might have been garish, but, as is usual with the truly great designers, it worked. The sea slapped restlessly at the shore, the wind etched a perfect rippling pattern on the sand . . . and that most satisfying of poems, "Dover Beach," came irresistibly to mind.

---

[6] *San Francisco Chronicle*, "Sunday Punch" page 1, June of 1992 (first published on June 16, 1968)

LAST WEEKEND at Stinson Beach. Or rather, in the hushed seclusion of Seadrift, where the Piels talk only to the Barretts and the Barretts talk only to God knows. Somehow, in the tragedy that was then at the full, it was necessary to get away from the city, away from the phone calls and ubiquitous intrusive television – gray of screen and mood – and away from the endless conversations made incoherent by grief and bewilderment. There was deep soul-searching, and some not so deep. And as you walked barefoot in the surf, your thoughts kept going back to the young man who had romped in the Oregon surf not so many days earlier. . . .

QUIET AND peaceful night, "where the sea meets the moon-blanched land" ("Listen! you hear the grating roar of pebbles which the waves draw back, and fling, at their return, up the high strand . . ."). Sand dollars and driftwood, campfires dotting the darkness, clusters of lights at the point, and far off in the Southern curving distance, the pale glow of the Sunset District as it spills into the ocean. Even here, the city cannot be forgotten. In the morning, you walk to the hilltops, amid the poppies and the foxglove, and around a bend, the towers of San Francisco would be visible again, pulling at your thoughts.

OF COURSE there is no escape, even there by rushing brook in a shaded glen where the ferns grow thick. The voices of the city, and how torn and even hysterical they were in the days of the aftermath: "There must be a return to law and order . . . It's the Supreme Court's fault . . . The students . . . Hippies . . . We have lost our sense of values . . . person. You call me a violent person again and I'll kill you . . . Burn all the guns . . . The ghettoes . . . Split the State! . . . What can I do, what can one person do, TELL me . . . I know this country is not sick, but . . . It all started with Vietnam . . . Burn the TV sets . . . "

EVEN SURROUNDED by the serene redwoods, you could hear the frantic tides ("Sophocles long ago heard it on the Aegean, and it brought into his mind the turbid ebb and flow of human misery"). Questions without answers, and all this thrashing about "as on a darkling plain." The students are "wrong" to demonstrate, but when they do, great men, who professed so vehemently that all was well, suddenly stop and listen – de Gaulle, Tito, even Grayson Kirk, admitting to a startled world that yes, yes, something really must be done, perhaps there is a point to all this protest. Suddenly Westmore land no longer sees the light at the end of the tunnel, and were the protesters right there, too? Could it be possible that the ordinary mortal, with access only to newspaper reports, knows more about what has been happening in Vietnam than all the chiefs and all their Top Secret documents? Thomas Sorensen admits as much in his new book on American propaganda, "The Word War." The correspondents in Vietnam were trying to report the truth, while the bureaucrats were doing what they do best – systematically feeding misinformation up through the channels.

EVEN OVER THERE amid the tall trees and the leaf-filtered light, walking a timeless silence, you hear the "confused alarms of struggle and flight." A chipmunk on its haunches and blue butterfly hovering, but the voices of the city reverberate down the corridors of eucalyptus: "We are not a violent people . . . the Black Panthers . . . It was million-to-one shot . . . There is no substitute for victory! . . . Why are you not horrified by the brutality of the Viet Cong when WE only attack military targets . . ." (Ah, love, let us be true to one another!).

"FOR THE WORLD, which seems to lie before us like a land of dreams, so various, so beautiful, so new, hath really neither joy, nor love, nor light, nor certitude, nor help for pain." Now you have come to the end of the National Seashore, and you look down at the shining sea, tipping upward to infinity and amid the cry of the birds, you hear the words of Lord Russell: "for we are all exiles on an inhospitable shore."

Herb Caen (1916-1977)

Writing on poems with significant historical and political themes
(option no. 17)

Poems: "First Writing Since" by Suheir Hammad
"The History of the Airplane" by Lawrence Ferlinghetti

Student author Jennifer Hammer writes on these two poems about the aftermath of the September 11, 2001 attack on the United States.

You can watch Suheir Hammad read "First Writing Since" that describes her reaction to the September 11 attacks on Youtube: http://www.youtube.com/watch?v=r7bxgaqNzKE.

First Writing Since

1. there have been no words.
i have not written one word.
no poetry in the ashes south of canal street.
no prose in the refrigerated trucks driving debris and dna.
not one word.

today is a week, and seven is of heavens, gods, science.
evident out my kitchen window is an abstract reality.
sky where once was steel.
smoke where once was flesh.

fire in the city air and i feared for my sister's life in a way never
before. and then, and now, i fear for the rest of us.

first, please god, let it be a mistake, the pilot's heart failed, the
plane's engine died.
then please god, let it be a nightmare, wake me now.
please god, after the second plane, please, don't let it be anyone
who looks like my brothers.

i do not know how bad a life has to break in order to kill.
i have never been so hungry that i willed hunger
i have never been so angry as to want to control a gun over a pen.
not really.
even as a woman, as a palestinian, as a broken human being.
never this broken.

more than ever, i believe there is no difference.
the most privileged nation, most americans do not know the difference
between indians, afghanis, syrians, muslims, sikhs, hindus.
more than ever, there is no difference.

2. thank you korea for kimchi and bibim bob, and corn tea and the
genteel smiles of the wait staff at wonjo the smiles never revealing

the heat of the food or how tired they must be working long midtown
shifts. thank you korea, for the belly craving that brought me into
the city late the night before and diverted my daily train ride into
the world trade center.

there are plenty of thank yous in ny right now. thank you for my
lazy procrastinating late ass. thank you to the germs that had me
call in sick. thank you, my attitude, you had me fired the week
before. thank you for the train that never came, the rude nyer who
stole my cab going downtown. thank you for the sense my mama gave me
to run. thank you for my legs, my eyes, my life.

3.   the dead are called lost and their families hold up shaky
printouts in front of us through screens smoked up.

we are looking for iris, mother of three. please call with any
information. we are searching for priti, last seen on the 103rd
floor. she was talking to her husband on the phone and the line
went. please help us find george, also known as a! ! del. his family is
waiting for him with his favorite meal. i am looking for my son, who
was delivering coffee. i am looking for my sister girl, she started
her job on monday.

i am looking for peace. i am looking for mercy. i am looking for
evidence of compassion. any evidence of life. i am looking for
life.

4.   ricardo on the radio said in his accent thick as yuca, "i will
feel so much better when the first bombs drop over there. and my
friends feel the same way."

on my block, a woman was crying in a car parked and stranded in hurt.
i offered comfort, extended a hand she did not see before she said,
"we"re gonna burn them so bad, i swear, so bad." my hand went to my
head and my head went to the numbers within it of the dead iraqi
children, the dead in nicaragua. the dead in rwanda who had to vie
with fake sport wrestling for america's attention.

yet when people sent emails saying, this was bound to happen, lets
! ! not forget u.s. transgressions, for half a second i felt resentful.
hold up with that, cause i live here, these are my friends and fam,
and it could have been me in those buildings, and we"re not bad
people, do not support america's bullying. can i just have a half
second to feel bad?

if i can find through this exhaust people who were left behind to
mourn and to resist mass murder, i might be alright.

thank you to the woman who saw me brinking my cool and blinking back
tears. she opened her arms before she asked "do you want a hug?" a
big white woman, and her embrace was the kind only people with the

warmth of flesh can offer. i wasn't about to say no to any comfort.
"my brother's in the navy," i said. "and we"re arabs". "wow, you
got double trouble." word.

5.   one more person ask me if i knew the hijackers.
one more motherfucker ask me what navy my brother is in.
one more person assume no arabs or muslims were killed.one more person
assume they know me, or that i represent a people.
or that a people represent an evil. or that evil is as simple as a
flag and words on a page.

we did not vilify all white men when mcveigh bombed oklahoma.
america did not give out his family's addresses or where he went to
church. or blame the bible or pat robertson.

and when the networks air footage of palestinians dancing in the
street, there is no apology that hungry children are bribed with
sweets that turn their teeth brown. that correspondents edit images.
that archives are there to facilitate lazy and inaccurate
journalism.

and when we talk about holy books and hooded men and death, why do we
never mention the kkk?

if there are any people on earth who understand how new york is
feeling right now, they are in the west bank and the gaza strip.

1.   today it is ten days. last night bush waged war on a man once
openly funded by the
cia. i do not know who is responsible. read too many books, know
too many people to believe what i am told. i don't give a fuck about
bin laden. his vision of the world does not include me or those i
love. and petittions have been going around for years trying to get
the u.s. sponsored taliban out of power. shit is complicated, and i
don't know what to think.

but i know for sure who will pay.

in the world, it will be women, mostly colored and poor. women will
have to bury children, and support themselves through grief. "either
you are with us, or with the terrorists" - meaning keep your people
under control and your resistance censored. meaning we got the loot
and the nukes.

in america, it will be those amongst us who refuse blanket attacks on
the shivering. those of us who work toward social justice, in
support of civil liberties, in opposition to hateful foreign
policies.

i have never felt less american and more new yorker, particularly
brooklyn, than these past days. the stars and stripes on all these

cars and apartment windows represent the dead as citizens first, not family members, not lovers.

i feel like my skin is real thin, and that my eyes are only going to get darker. the future holds little light.

my baby brother is a man now, and on alert, and praying five times a day that the orders he will take in a few days time are righteous and will not weigh his soul down from the afterlife he deserves.

both my brothers - my heart stops when i try to pray - not a beat to disturb my fear. one a rock god, the other a sergeant, and both palestinian, practicing muslim, gentle men. both born in brooklyn and their faces are of the archetypal arab man, all eyelashes and nose and beautiful color and stubborn hair.

what will their lives be like now?

over there is over here.

2.   all day, across the river, the smell of burning rubber and limbs floats through. the sirens have stopped now. the advertisers are back on the air. the rescue workers are traumatized. the skyline is brought back to human size. no longer taunting the gods with its height.

i have not cried at all while writing this. i cried when i saw those buildings collapse on themselves like a broken heart. i have never owned pain that needs to spread like that. and i cry daily that my brothers return to our mother safe and whole.

there is no poetry in this. there are causes and effects. there are symbols and ideologies. mad conspiracy here, and information we will never know. there is death here, and there are promises of more.

there is life here. anyone reading this is breathing, maybe hurting, but breathing for sure. and if there is any light to come, it will shine from the eyes of those who look for peace and justice after the rubble and rhetoric are cleared and the phoenix has risen.

affirm life.
affirm life.
we got to carry each other now.
you are either with life, or against it.
affirm life.

Suheir Hammad (b. 1973)

The History of the Airplane

And the Wright brothers said they thought they had invented
something that could make peace on earth when their wonderful
flying machine took off at Kitty Hawk into the kingdom of birds
but the parliament of birds was freaked out by this man-made bird
and fled to heaven

And then the famous Spirit of Saint Louis took off eastward and
flew across the Big Pond with Lindy at the controls in his leather
helmet and goggles hoping to sight the doves of peace but he did not
even though he circled Versailles

And then the famous Flying Clipper took off in the opposite
direction and flew across the terrific Pacific but the pacific doves
were frighted by this strange amphibious bird and hid in the orient sky

And then the famous Flying Fortress took off bristling with guns
and testosterone to make the world safe for peace and capitalism
but the birds of peace were nowhere to be found before or after Hiroshima

And so then clever men built bigger and faster flying machines and
these great man-made birds with jet plumage flew higher than any
real birds and seemed about to fly into the sun and melt their wings
and like Icarus crash to earth

And the Wright brothers were long forgotten in the high-flying
bombers that now began to visit their blessings on various Third
Worlds all the while claiming they were searching for doves of
peace

And they kept flying and flying until they flew right into the 21st
century and then one fine day a Third World struck back and
stormed the great planes and flew them straight into the beating
heart of Skyscraper America where there were no aviaries and no
parliaments of doves and in a blinding flash America became a part
of the scorched earth of the world

And a wind of ashes blows across the land
And for one long moment in eternity
There is chaos and despair

And buried loves and voices
Cries and whispers
Fill the air
Everywhere

Lawrence Ferlinghetti (b. 1919)

Emotional *versus* Intellectual Responses to 9-11
Student author: Jennifer Hammer

"First Writing Since" by Suheir Hammad was very moving, much more so than Ferlinghetti's poem. For one thing, it came from pure emotion and was much more personal. It also spanned the wider implications of 9/11 – regarding what happened, its effects on Hammad and her family (sister, brothers), the families of the dead, those who, through quirks of fate, were spared being in the World Trade Center buildings. She put herself in their shoes, she put their words in her mouth "Thank you, to the germs that had me call in sick." She also gave a scathing analysis of "the most privileged nation" that knows no difference between "Indians, Afghanis, Syrians, Muslims, Sikhs, and Hindus and touched on her rage that "we did not vilify all white men when McVeigh bombed Oklahoma" or "one more person assume they know me, or that I represent a people, or that a people represent an evil' or "when the networks air footage of Palestinians dancing in the street." She questions who is responsible and how she cannot know "how bad a life has to break in order to kill." She is sad and she is angry and she makes a heart-wrenching plea: "affirm life." Her poem is amazing in how much it covers and how it touches so many and from so many different directions.

"The History of the Airplane" by Lawrence Ferlinghetti is much more detached, shorter, linear, and cerebral. It's a "History of Aviation as a Destructive Force" juxtaposed with the fleeing of doves of peace. His tone is one of anger, but it's a general, analytic anger, not personal. He does not have to deal with the reactions of 9/11 toward himself and his family. (The ignorance of retaliation did not spill over to his ethnicity), he doesn't wrestle with trying to understand the motives of the hijackers, but rather sees it broadly as the Third World striking back and storming the great planes and flying them straight into the beating heart of Skyscraper America. He doesn't proffer any "what ifs." He focuses on the chaos and despair, but doesn't go much further.

I thought Hammad's poem was intense, eye-opening, and excellent.

Poems that handle emotional pain with aesthetic beauty
(option no. 18)

Poems: "Getting Through" by Deborah Pope
            "Getting Out" by Cleopatra Mathis
            "To Autumn" by John Keats

Getting Through

Like a car stuck in gear,
a chicken too stupid to tell
its head is gone,
or sound ratcheting on
long after the film   5
has jumped the reel,
or a phone
ringing and ringing
in the house they have all
moved away from,   10
through rooms where dust
is a deepening skin,
and the locks unneeded,
so I go on loving you,
my heart blundering on,   15
a muscle spilling out
what is no longer wanted
and my words hurtling past,
Like a train off its track
toward a boarded-up station,   20
closed for years,
like some last speaker
of a beautiful language
no one else can hear.

                    Deborah Pope

Getting Out

That year we hardly slept, waking like inmates
who beat the walls. Every night
another refusal, the silent work
of tightening the heart.
Exhausted, we gave up; escaped   5
to the apartment pool, swimming those laps
until the first light relieved us.
Days were different FM and full-blast
blues, hours of guitar "you gonna miss me
when I'm gone." Think how you tried   10
to pack up and go, for weeks stumbling
Over piles of clothing the unstrung tennis rackets.
Finally locked into blame, we paced
that short hall , heaving words like furniture.
I have the last unshredded pictures   15
of our matching eyes and hair. We've kept
to separate sides of the map,
still I'm startled by men who look like you.
And in the yearly letter, you're sure to say
you're happy now. Yet I think of the lawyer's bewilderment   20
when we cried, the last day. Taking bands
we walked apart, until our arms stretched
between us. We held on tight, and let go.

Cleopatra Mathis (b. 1947)

Closure in Deborah Pope's "Getting Through" and Cleopatra Mathis' "Getting Out"
Student author: Erin Kehoe

Relationships carry intense emotions, ones that can make us feel high, ones that can make us feel as if we are flailing blindly, so overwhelmed and consumed with love that we might burst. Conversely, when a relationship ends, we go through a different series of emotions, all just as intense, but with a sense of loss – of the partner, of self worth. The most important thing that one can get at the end of a relationship is closure. This feeling of mutual understanding is paramount to coming to terms with the situation and for emotional growth. Without closure, one can feel lost, destroyed. Two examples of closure, and lack thereof can be found in a poem by Deborah Pope and a poem by Cleopatra Mathis.

"Getting Through" by Deborah Pope is an intense poem about reeling blindly through a break up. Her poem runs on for 24 lines, creating an effect of denial, and of her love spilling out continuously even if there is no one to receive it. Her denial is clear by the way she writes strictly in similes, as if she doesn't want to face the reality of the situation and would prefer to hide from it. She makes only one attempt at showing herself:

> So I go on loving you,
> my heart blundering on,
> a muscle spilling out
> what is no longer wanted. (lines 15-18)

Even these lines show that she feels ridiculous for loving someone who is not coming back; she realizes that it is futile, but she cannot stop herself.

Pope's use of simile has a staggering effect and shows just how strongly she feels about her love. We are drawn in from the first line – "Like a car stuck in gear" – and our attention is held until the very end:

> like some last speaker
> of a beautiful language
> no one else can hear. (lines 22-24)

It is as if we are waiting to see that she will be all right. She vacillates between feeling stupid for loving so strongly and feeling like the tragic heroine of a love story, as if maybe her love will return if she suffers gracefully.

In sharp contrast to Pope's poem, Cleopatra Mathis' poem "Getting Out" is about the end of a marriage, but also about the acceptance of the situation. The subject is tracing the steps that led to the break up and laying them out matter-of-factly, as if to show that she has come to terms with the way things are. She still has strong feelings for her ex-husband, "still I'm startled by men who look like you" (line 18), but she accepts the reality that they could not stay together. She makes no claims that she docs not hurt deeply from this break up, but that she knows the relationship could not continue in the way it was going.

Where Pope writes in simile to express the present, Mathis uses similes to relay the past, as if she was a different person then. The similes are symbolic of disassociation with the situation at hand, like a form of escape. The subject no longer identifies with the person she used to be. Her similes are strong, intentional, and impressive: "heaving words like furniture" (line 14) shows the intensity of the relationship's demise; "waking like inmates/who beat the walls" (1-2) conjures up the desperate attempt of both the subject and her partner to end the painful relationship but finding no way to do it. This shows the frustration of loving someone, but no longer being in love with that person.

Another distinction between the two poems is the structure of the poets' stanzas. Where Pope's poem flows in one long, run-on sentence, Mathis' poem is broken up into three distinct stanzas, each telling a different part of the story. The first stanza is written with a tone of frustration. The subjects are trapped, tension is building, anticipation is high: "That year we hardly slept" (1), "the silent work/of tightening the heart" (3-4). The second stanza shows a kind of resignation to the fact that things must change. The subjects are clumsily falling into this new situation: "Think how you tried/ to pack up and go, for weeks stumbling" (10-11), and fighting the awful feeling that what they had tried so hard to create was actually dying by their own hands "Finally locked into blame" (13). The final stanza shifts to acceptance of their new situation. The subjects seem to find a kind of resolve with the reasons they had to part; they found closure. "We held on tight, and let go" (23). This acceptance shows maturity.

Closure is vital to one's ability to cope with loss. From these two examples, we can see the different outcomes when one does and does not receive closure at the end of a relationship and the effects it has on our emotional well-being.

Poetic Conclusions: The Art of Goodbye
Student author: Indigo Wilmann

Like Erin Kehoe, Indigo also chose to write on the theme of closure, but she focused on only one poem – "Getting Out" by Cleopatra Mathis. She also exercised the bonus option of using and footnoting some style and punctuation elements to widen her range of expression.

We are afforded very few guarantees in this life. Yet there is one that is served to us on a silver platter – the guarantee of change.[7] Even if decades pass and we find ourselves on the same job with the same spouse, even then, we still experience change. The very cells of our bodies are constantly changing. The earth shifts and the seasons change. Time ceaselessly ticks and our once supple skin begins to sag with age. Yes, change is our constant companion,[8] and as one phase gives way to the next, we learn to say goodbye. We say goodbye to the sun as it takes its nightly swim at dusk. We say goodbye to the love we never dreamed we could live without. We say goodbye to the children we birthed into this life and the parents we survive. We are always saying goodbye. And every once in a while, we read something that captures this human experience of change and goodbye so fully it is as if someone has stepped into our memories and stirred our grief.[9] Every once in a while, we come upon poetry.

The central themes of change and farewell form Cleopatra Mathis's poem "Getting Out." The first stanza begins with a simile – "waking like inmates who beat the walls" – (line 1) and continues in metaphor – "the silent work of tightening the heart" (lines 3- 4). When looked at together, an extended metaphor emerges. Mathis invokes subtle images of a graveyard shift that leaves the employees drained. She does this by stating, "we hardly slept" (line 1) and goes on to use the words "every night," (line 2) "work," (line 3) and "exhausted" (line 5). Finally in the last line of the first stanza she says, "the first light relieved us," (line 7) much as a worker is relieved at the change of shift. This metaphor immediately sets the tone of the relationship. She conveys through simile, metaphor, and figurative language that the evening hours, usually a time of intimacy for a couple, are exhausting work for this pair; they are relieved by the day.

---

[7] Explanatory dash

[8] Personification: "Change" is given a human attribute.

[9] 9. Simile: The words "as if" make this comparison a simile.

The image of inmates – of this relationship being like a prison – is returned to in the second stanza when the poet chooses the phrases "locked into blame" (line 13) and "paced that short hall" (lines 13- 14). The entire stanza is one of figurative language in which Mathis captures the turbulent endings of a relationship. From "full-blast blues" (line 8) and quoting the lyrics of the song that states "you gonna miss me when I'm gone," (lines 9-10) we know that the end is loud and everything about them has deteriorated into arguments; even their music is a shouting goodbye. And yet, the reality of how difficult it is to actually leave is also expressed with "Think how you tried to pack up and go, for weeks stumbling." The effective use of simile is shown again in "heaving words like furniture" and contributes to the understanding of their catastrophic ending.

A relationship cannot simply be judged by the way that it ends. To do so would invalidate the entire life of the relationship and only recognize its death. Mathis expresses her deep understanding of this fact when, at the start of the third and final stanza, the poem's tone takes a decided shift. In the first two stanzas we learn of their strife; in the last stanza we learn of their love. It begins "I have the last unshredded pictures of our matching eyes and hair" (lines 15-16). These lines reveal that there were elements to this relationship that were worth saving. Further, the line "our matching eyes and hair" (line 16) alludes to two people who became so close that they smothered each other, allowing their relationship to be an experience of confinement rather than freedom. It also reinforces the choice of the word "inmates" (line 1) at the beginning of the poem.

One can infer from the intensity of their closeness that now they must keep to "separate sides of the map" (line 17). Yet even that does not fully undermine the power of their bond as years later the woman is "startled by men who look like you" (line 18). Finally we know that their ending was not without love as the last four lines state:

> ...Yet I think of the lawyer's bewilderment
> when we cried, the last day. Taking hands
> we walked apart, until our arms stretched
> between us. We held on tight, and let go. (lines 20 - 23)

These lines illustrate the depth of the couple's connection and also illuminate their need to let go. The irony of the relationship is that by holding on too tightly, they began to walk apart and created a need to let go. But these last lines are much more than expository:[10] they are the universal experience of loving someone that you can no longer be with, and they give the poem its emotional power.

"Getting Out" is the passage to a bittersweet memory.[11] It is the poet's invitation to re-experience, through words and images, the heartbreak of yesterday, and the journey of change. The poem is the heart of a relationship simmered down into three stanzas and served with intimacy and truth. It is the conclusion, the end of the line, and the art of goodbye.

---

[10] Colon (used after an independent clause to explain something

[11] Metaphor (equates the poem with a passage to memory).

The final essay in this section is by Eithne Doorly. It is a reading of John Keats's famous poem "To Autumn." The text of this poem is in Chapter Six. This poem is also relevant to the topic of transmuting pain into aesthetic beauty (Option no. 18). Keats wrote the poem soon after his younger brother Tom's death. The poem is a celebration of life's cycle. For style variation in writing this essay, Eithne used the following optional elements of punctuation and style: semicolon, colon, explanatory dash, metaphor, simile, and analogy.

Tranquillity of Golden Autumn
Student author: Eithne Doorly

John Keats's poem "To Autumn" is a rich evocation of the sights, sounds, tastes and textures of that season. It leads us through the phases of the season from the heady ripeness of an Indian summer, through the busy harvest season, to the last days of autumn when nature resigns itself to the approaching sleep of winter. The passing of the season is mirrored in the passing of a day and becomes a reflection on the transience of life itself. However, the poem, while recognizing the inherent sorrow in the loss of youth and vigor, does not dwell on the irretrievable past but rather celebrates the unique beauty of each stage of life. It moves with a serenity that echoes, almost imperceptibly, the rhythms of nature itself, expressing the central theme that the meaning of life is found by accepting the endless cycle of nature and appreciating the time we are allotted by it. Keats weaves[12] his thematic design with careful arrangement of vivid imagery, evoking a different mood in each stanza, which he complements by employing the musical quality of language to great effect.

The first stanza opens by personifying the season and the sun as benevolent conspirators plotting to provide a bountiful harvest. The religious symbolism of "bless / with fruit the vines" introduces a sense of spirituality that references pagan and Christian religions. Keats piles image on top of image, using caesuras to break the lines into two images, reflecting the frenetic growth of early autumn. The words "swell," "plump," and "mossed" convey the textures of ripeness, and we can feel the warm sun on the droning bees. The bees symbolize the productivity of life at its prime; but the next line, "Until they think warm days will never cease," quickly reminds us that this time will pass. The last line of the stanza, "For summer hath o'er brimmed their clammy cells," indicates the necessity as well as the inevitability of the coming harvest.

In the second stanza, autumn is personified and apostrophized as a field worker. This is most appropriate since people play their most active roles in nature's garnering process during the harvest. Yet Keats' accentuates the peaceful aura by presenting set tableaux of inactivity: autumn sits "carelessly on a granary floor"; it sleeps in the cornfield and watches the cider press "with patient look." There is no hustle and bustle here, no sense of human interference with nature; it is as if the harvest happens because it is part of the natural order of things rather than a human design. This identification with nature reaches back into our earliest consciousness to a time when humanity was at one with nature

---

[12] Metaphor

and did not need to seek the meaning of life. The quality of patience, mentioned in the second-to-last line, is synonymous with this acceptance of nature and is developed when, past our prime, we begin to slow down and prepare for the onset of old age. The last line of the stanza –[13]"Thou watchest the last oozings hour by hour" – eases us into the last verse and the last days of the season before winter settles like a shroud over the land.[14]

The third stanza opens with a question, which expresses the shock of realization that we have grown old. But Keats uses apostrophe to sweep away any wistful desire for youth and "the songs of spring," reminding autumn that "thou hast thy music too." The stanza proceeds with images of a beautiful sunset and sundown chorus, which are formed into a requiem for the life that is passing from this world and being carried into the next.

> Then in a wailful choir the small gnats mourn
> Among the river sallows, borne aloft
> Or sinking as the light wind lives or dies.

There is a melancholy beauty here and a gracious acceptance of the inevitable. The last couplet, with its images of the red-breast and "gathering swallows twitter[ing] in the skies," symbolizes winter and impending death and departure, but they also serve to remind us that life continues:[15] the robin, with its red breast, is a potent symbol of life in winter and the swallows will return in the spring to begin the cycle of life anew.

Musical devices are used very effectively to heighten the mood of the poem. The phrases "winnowing wind" and "mists and mellow fruitfulness" are just two examples of alliteration used to soften and draw out the images. Assonance is also used to emphasize the mood;[16] the line "while barred clouds bloom the soft-dying day" uses a combination of alliteration and assonance to help recreate the mood of a peaceful sunset. Repetition is used in each stanza and each time it expresses a different mood. In the first stanza the flurry of images ends with "more, and still more," underlining the growth and vitality of the season, while the phrase "hours by hours" at the end of the second stanza slows the pace almost to a stop. In the third stanza the speaker echoes autumn's question, "Where are the songs of spring? Ay, where are they?" This repetition, combined with alliteration and consonance, produces a tone of yearning for things past.

"To Autumn" is an appeal to the spirit, through the senses, to realize that the meaning of life is inextricably bound to the ebb and flow of nature. The success of that appeal is a testament to Keats's own peace of mind when the poem was composed. He had accepted the harsh realities of life and extracted a poignant beauty from grief and loss. His younger brother Tom, whom Keats had tried to

---

[13] Explanatory dash

[14] Simile

[15] Colon (used between independent clauses when the second clause explains something from the preceding clause).

[16] Semicolon (used between independent clauses with no explanation involved).

nurse to health, had died of tuberculosis — a disease that was threatening his own life in the midst of rising financial difficulties. Keats's imagery in this poem is vivid but never harsh. Even the reaper's hook "spares the next swath and all its twined flowers"; implicit in this mood is the theme that if we cease to struggle against nature we will find peace and happiness. This is a romantic view of life and nature but not a false one; it takes threads of our common experience and weaves them into a tapestry of life,[17] presenting us with a total experience that addresses the very point of life itself.

Writing a research paper based on one or two poems
(option no. 19)

This option requires the use of at least two sources from literary criticism.

Poems: "These are the days when Birds come back"
by Emily Dickinson
"To Autumn" by John Keats

These are the days when Birds come back

These are the days when Birds come back—
A very few—a Bird or two—
To take a backward look.
These are the days when skies resume
The old—old sophistries of June—   5
A blue and gold mistake.
Oh fraud that cannot cheat the bee,
Almost thy plausibility
Induces my belief,
Till ranks of seeds their witness bear,   10
And softly through the altered air
Hurries a timid leaf.
Oh Sacrament of summer days,
Oh Last Communion in the Haze,   15
Permit a child to join.
Thy sacred emblems to partake,
They consecrated bread to take,
And thine immortal wine!
Emily Dickinson (1830-1886)

---

[17] Analogy that started with a metaphor

Scott Roland compares skeptical rationalism of Emily Dickinson with sensuous optimism of John Keats. Keats's poem is in Chapter Six.

Time, Sense, and Transcendence:
Dickinson and Keats on an Autumn Day

Student author: Scott Roland

From New England to Old England, autumn displays beauty and offers the fruit of summer's toil. It also signals the end of long, warm days and induces reflection before winter's chilling darkness. Emily Dickinson's "These are the days when Birds come back" and John Keats's "To Autumn" both explore the contradictions of this season with similar poetic skill, but with different emphasis, tone, and results.

Although Dickinson's poem is much shorter than Keats's, they share formal and structural similarities. Dickinson's poem is marked by the use of tercets (three-line units of verse), and Keats's poem consists of three stanzas. Dickinson joins pairs of tercets with common rhymes. "Look" and "mistake" (an approximate rhyme) denote the first stanza, "belief" and "leaf" the next two tercets, and "join" and "wine" the third pair of tercets. Thought and feeling move through these three stanzas from wonder to disappointment to faith. The rhyming words "partake" and "take" in the last tercet refer "back" to the beginning of the poem and its suspicions. Keats clearly separates his 11-line stanzas by skipping a line between them, and each stanza deals at length with a different subject. The first stanza describes the season's peak, the harvest follows in the second, and the third relates the season's departure. Keats employs a rhyme scheme in each stanza in which the final four lines repeat earlier occurring rhymes: ababcdedcce, ababcdecdde, ababcdecdde. Both poems therefore use sound to contribute a recurrent, cyclical element.

Both poems are marked by organized rhythm. "These are the days" follows an 8-8-6 syllabic, 4-4-3 foot pattern. However, the poem's division into six tercets creates reflective, suspenseful pauses. On the other hand, almost every line in "To Autumn" contains a pattern of 10 syllables and 5 feet that harmonizes the poem's many run-on lines into a flowing lyricism. The prevailing meter in both poems is iambic, but both poets introduce metrical variations to emphasize meaning. Dickinson inserts a rhetorical pause and stress in "the old – old sophistries of June" to convey familiarity with a perennial hope that is as unreliable as the weather. "Old" then becomes linked to the "blue and gold mistake" in the next line: autumn leaves are not as good as gold, but are about to fall away from the clear blue sky, and the reader is cued that conventional wisdom is about to be questioned. Line 12 begins with a dactylic foot in "Hurries a timid leaf" and rushes the reading on a sighing breath of air. Then, a hymn-like rhythm and rhyme scheme sustains the religious sentiment of the third stanza. Keats's insertion of dactylic, trochaic, anapestic, and spondaic feet motivates the rhythm of activities in the first two stanzas. "Season of mists" marks the introduction to Autumn, which is personified as "conspiring with him" (the sun). The phrase "To bend with apples the mossed-cottage trees" juxtaposes longevity with fertility, and "With a sweet kernel to set budding more" implies continuity. The depiction of the sleepy reaper who, in the second stanza "spares the next swath with all its twined flowers," creates an effect of elongated time and lingering beauty. But in the third stanza, "the soft-dying day" is the last variation; the rest of the poem proceeds in a regular meter toward its conclusion.

In both poems, the first two stanzas create a mood that leads to resolution in the third. Dickinson focuses on the uncertainty of the season. Flowers give way to "ranks of seeds" as the speaker senses the "altered air." The "plausibility" of an everlasting summer "almost . . . induces my belief" – a belief which will be expressed in the third stanza. Keats's first stanza illustrates a cornucopia loaded with "fruitfulness" and "ripeness" under a "maturing sun." Gourds "swell" near "plump" hazelnuts. The second stanza refers to the completion of the harvest. Autumn is "sitting careless on a granary floor," "drowsed with the fume of poppies," and "watching the oozings" of a cider press "hours by hours." This progression through the day from morning to lazy afternoon, as well as through the stages of the season, leads to the evening spell of the third stanza.

Birds and bees appear and play different roles in each poem. In the beginning of Dickinson's poem, the sighting of "a Bird or two" alerts the particular observer to "take a backward look" on the meaning of the season. Keats's poem closes with the "whistles" of robins and the distant "twitter in the skies" of swallows that affirm the presence of life even as darkness falls. In both poems, bees are given a last chance to enjoy the weather, but Dickinson's bee is more aware of a "fraud" while Keats's bees find more nectar for their "o'er-brimmed" hives. Thus, metaphorically, one poem emphasizes skeptical rationalism, the other sensuous optimism.

Spiritually, each poem leaves a different impression. The third stanza of Dickinson's poem recalls sacred choral music with "Oh Sacrament of summer days," with an appeal for a "child" of God to "partake" of "sacred emblems," "consecrated bread," and "immortal wine!" However, this allusion to the Last Supper, with its ritualization of death, is a hopeless "Last Communion in the Haze." Keats alludes to the mythical harvest goddess, Demeter, in the second stanza. Then in the third stanza, the "wailful choir" of gnats and the "bleat" of lambs recall Demeter's mourning of her daughter Persephone's absence, but these sounds are "borne aloft" and are received from a "hilly bourne." Spring will be reborn and there is no reference to a lifeless winter.

Finally, the two poems represent realistic and romantic views of not only autumn, but of life. The speaker in Dickinson's poem maintains distance when observing the signs of autumn. Emotional responses are intellectually tempered and then the certainty of religious belief is called into question, just as Dickinson "dared to reject Christianity and, in a church-centered village society, declined to attend church services" (Oates). Her theme has more to do with individual objectivity than with falling in with the religious "ranks" (line 10). Keats wrote his poem after a pleasant walk on a September day (Hilton 112) and each line immerses the reader in the atmosphere of the season. Man and nature combine through sensation, and a divine presence is pervasive. Together, the two poems present different aspects of a portion of time that invokes the meanings of contentment and disaffection in life, as well as the importance of being fully alive and perceptive in the moment regardless of the awareness of death.

POEMS ON SPECIFIC THEMES

Poems about Home, Immigration, Exile, and Barriers

Ellis Island

Beyond the red brick of Ellis Island
where the two Slovak children
who became my grandparents
waited the long days of quarantine,
after leaving the sickness,   5
the old Empires of Europe,
a Circle Line ship slips easily
on its way to the island
of the tall woman, green
as dreams of forests and meadows   10
waiting for those who' d worked
a thousand years
yet never owned their own.

Like millions or others,
I too come to this island,   15
nine decades the answerer
of dreams.

Yet only part of my blood loves that memory.
Another voice speaks
or native lands   20
within this nation.
Lands invaded
when the earth became owned.
Lands of those who followed
the changing Moon,   25
knowledge of the seasons
in their veins.

Joseph Bruchac (b. 1942)

The New Colossus

Not like the brazen giant of Greek fame,
With conquering limbs astride from land to land;
Here at our sea-washed, sunset gates shall stand
A mighty woman with a torch, whose flame
Is the imprisoned lightning, and her name   5
Mother of Exiles. From her beacon-hand
Glows world-wide welcome; her mild eyes command

The air-bridged harbor that twin cities frame.
"Keep ancient lands, your storied pomp!" cries she
With silent lips. "Give me your tired, your poor,   10
Your huddled masses yearning to breathe free,
The wretched refuse of your teeming shore.
Send these, the homeless, tempest-tost to me,
I lift my lamp beside the golden door!"

Emma Lazarus (1849-1887)

Questions on "Ellis Island" and "The New Colossus"

1.   Compare the tone and theme of Bruchac's poem with the American Emma Lazarus' famous poem "The New Colossus." The poem by Lazarus is engraved on a tablet fixed to the Statue of Liberty on Ellis Island. Bruchac's heritage is Slovakian mixed with Abenaki (Native American).

2.   Who are the people described by Bruchac in lines 11-13: "those who'd worked/a thousand years/yet never owned their own"?

3.   Which group of people, prominently featured in Bruchac's poem, were not embraced by the stirring words in the poem by Lazarus: "Give me your tired, your poor,/Your huddled masses yearning to breathe free,/The wretched refuse of your teeming shore"?

4.   Who are the people described in Bruchac's concluding lines?

5.   Comment on the effectiveness of Bruchac's giving his poem a 3-part structure? What does each part represent?

6.   In the poem by Lazarus, how appropriate is it to call the Lady Liberty the "Mother of Exiles"?

7.   Comment on the effectiveness of calling the flame of the Statue of Liberty's torch "the imprisoned lightning" in the poem by Lazarus.

8.   Relate the two poems to the theme of the American dream after you first define the dream.

9.   Explain the allusion to the "brazen giant of Greek fame" in line 1 of the poem by Lazarus. Compare and contrast it wih the "mighty woman with a torch" (line 4). How might the two images symbolize the Old World and the New World?

10. Identify the paradox in lines 9 and 10 of the poem by Lazarus. What is its function here?

11. Evaluate the poem by Lazarus as a sonnet that observes the classical conventions of rhyme scheme, introduction and development of the theme, and a resolution.

Harlem

What happens to a dream deferred?
Does it dry up
like a raisin in the sun?
Or fester like a sore –
And then run?
Does it stink like rotten meat?
Or crust and sugar over –
like a syrupy sweet?
Maybe it just sags
like a heavy load.
Or does it explode?
                    Langston Hughes (1902-1967)

Questions on "Harlem"

1. This poem is also titled "Dream Deferred." It inspired Lorraine Hansberry's play *A Raisin in the Sun.* Apply the poem's questions, images, and its explosive ending to characters, events, scenes, and themes in Hansberry's play. The play was discussed in Chapter Twelve.

2. The poem consists of five similes and a concluding metaphor. How effective is this style in communicating the poem's theme? Identify the theme.

3. For what possible effect did the poet italicize the last line?

La migra is the term used along the U.S.-Mexico border for the Border Patrol. "Agua dulce brota aqui', aqui', aqui'" means "sweet water gushes here, here, here."

La Migra

I
Let's play *La Migra*
I'll be the Border Patrol.
You be the Mexican maid.
I get the badge and sunglasses.
You can hide and run,
but you can't get away
because I have a jeep.
I can take you wherever
I want, but don't ask
questions because
I don't speak Spanish.
I can touch you wherever
I want but don't complain
too much because I've got
boots and kick – if I have to,

599

and I have handcuffs.
Oh, and a gun.
Get ready, get set, run.

II

Let's play *La Migra*
You be the Border Patrol.
I'll be the Mexican woman.
Your jeep has a flat,
and you have been spotted
by the sun.
All you have is heavy: hat,
glasses, badge, shoes, gun.
I know this desert,
where to rest,
where to drink.
Oh, I am not alone.
You hear us singing
and laughing with the wind,
Agua dulce brota aqui`,
aqui`, aqui`, but since you
can't speak Spanish,
you do not understand.
Get ready.

Pat Mora (b. 1942)

Questions on "La Migra"

1. Why does Mora describe this encounter between the two speakers as "a game"?
2. Which of the two speakers has a stronger claim to an enduring presence on the land? Support your answer with details from the poem.
3. How does the poet make the implements of power into a burden for the possessor?
4. In stanza one, the border patrol agent calls the female a "Mexican maid." However, in stanza two, she refers to herself as a "Mexican woman." How are these two different ways of identifying someone significant to the meaning of the poem?
5. The Mexican woman emphatically tells the border patrol agent that she is not alone. Who are her companions?
6. The poem's setting is an area that was part of Mexico until the U.S. invasion and conquest in 1847. Like millions of Mexicans who constantly cross the border in search of a better life, the Mexican woman in the poem may feel a strong emotional connection and claim to the land and tend to disregard the borders that were imposed on her people as a result of an expansionist war. How does the poet convey that attitude of the Mexican woman?
7. The following words from *A Passage to India*, a novel by E. M. Forster, read like a gloss on which line of the poem? How?

"The triumphant machine of civilization may suddenly hitch and be immobilized into a car of stone, and at such moments the destiny of the English [change to Americans] seems to resemble their predecessors', who also entered the country with intent to re-fashion it, but were in the end worked into it spattern and covered with its dust" (211).

Drum

Inside the dark human waters
of our mothers,
inside the blue drum of skin
that beat the slow song of our tribes
we knew the drifts of continents
and moving tides.

We are the people who left water
to enter a dry world.
We have survived soldiers and drought,
survived hunger
and living
inside the unmapped terrain
of loneliness.
That is why we have thirst.
It is why
when we love
we remember our lives in water,
that other lives fall through us
like fish swimming in an endless sea,
that we are walking another way
than time
to new life, backwards
to deliver ourselves to rain and river,
this water
that will become other water
this blood that will become other blood
and is the oldest place
the deepest world
the skin of water
that knows the drum before a hand meets it.

Linda Hogan (b. 1947)

Questions on "Drum"

1. In *The Heart as a Drum*: *Continuance and Resistance in American Indian Poetry*, Robin Riley Fast says that this poem's "two central images, water and drum, offer healing and survival, as they unite nature, spirit, and history." Use details from the poem to support Fast's assertion.
2. What specific resources, mentioned in the poem, make the Native Americans' survival possible?

3. History has always been integral to Native American Linda Hogan's writings. Identify one or two allusions in this poem to comment on their function and effectiveness.

4. Can this poem be considered an attempt at myth making? In almost all myths of creation, sound and water (the poem's two key elements) play a central role. The Bible has the voice of God travelling above the primeval ocean to decree the creation of land. Dancing in a ring of fire, the Hindu god Shiva holds a drum to symbolize the sound of creation. Can the poet's myth making be seen as a means to empower the first inhabitants of this continent? How?

5. Read Linda Hogan's poem "The New Apartment, Minneapolis" online: http://www.democraticunderground.com/discuss/duboard.php?az=view_all&address=105x692441 2. Then read an article on the poem by Holly Huffstutler:

http://www.helium.com/items/1423728-analysis-of-the-new-apartment-minneapolis-linda-hogan-analysis or

For an in-depth, scholarly look at Hogan's work, read online Chapter 5 of Robin Fast's book *The Heart as a Drum: Continuance and Resistance in American Indian Poetry (1999)*.. Here is a very long link via Google books to free access to Chapter 5, titled "To Make That Spiritual Realm More Manifest":

http://books.google.com/books/umichpress?id=-Cj8UcyeR4gC&pg=PA125&source=gbs_toc_r&cad=1#v=onepage&q&f=false.

Exile

I left my home behind me
but my past clings to my fingers
so that every word I write bears
the mark like a cancelled postage stamp
of my birthplace.
There was no angel to warn me
of the dangers of looking back.
Like Lot's wife, I would trade
my living blood for one last look
at the house where each window held
a face framed as in a family album.
and the plaza lined with palms
where my friends and I strolled in our pink
and yellow and white Sunday dresses, dreaming
of husbands, houses, and orchards where
our children would play in the leisurely summer
of our future. Glad would I spill
my remaining years like salt upon the ground,
to gaze again on the fishermen of the bay
dragging their catch in nets glittering

like pirate gold, to the shore.
Nothing remains of that world, I hear,
but the skeletons of houses, all colors
bled from the fabric of those
who stayed behind
inhabiting the dead cities
like the shadows of Hiroshima.

Judith Ortiz Cofer (b. 1952)

Questions on "Exile"

1. Explain the allusion to Lot's wife (line 8) and use of the word "salt" (line 18). How does this allusion add to the intensity of the poem's emotional appeal?

2. Comment on the effectiveness of the allusion to Hiroshima in the poem's last line.

3. What feeling dominates the poem – nostalgia, regret, or longing to return? Support your answer with details from the poem?

4. Being at home in several cultures and simultaneously being alienated from them is the response of a "cultural chameleon." Would you put Puerto Rican-American poet Cofer in that category?

5. Point out some similarities of views between Cofer's poem and Edward Said's following words from his "Reflections on Exile": "Exile is strangely compelling to think about but terrible to experience. It is the unhealable rift forced between a human being and a native place, between the self and its true home: its essential sadness can never be surmounted."

Mending Wall

Something there is that doesn't love a wall,
That sends the frozen-ground-swell under it,
And spills the upper boulders in the sun;
And makes gaps even two can pass abreast.
The work of hunters is another thing: 5
I have come after them and made repair
Where they have left not one stone on a stone,
But they would have the rabbit out of hiding,
To please the yelping dogs. The gaps I mean,
No one has seen them made or heard them made,   10
But at spring mending-time we find them there.
I let my neighbor know beyond the hill;
And on a day we meet to walk the line
And set the wall between us once again.
We keep the wall between us as we go.   15
To each the boulders that have fallen to each.
And some are loaves and some so nearly balls
We have to use a spell to make them balance:
"Stay where you are until our backs are turned!"

603

We wear our fingers rough with handling them. 20
Oh, just another kind of outdoor game,
One on a side. It comes to little more:
There where it is we do not need the wall:
He is all pine and I am apple orchard.
My apple trees will never get across   25
And eat the cones under his pines, I tell him.
He only says, "Good fences make good neighbors."
Spring is the mischief in me, and I wonder
If I could put a notion in his head:
"*Why* do they make good neighbors? Isn't it   30
Where there are cows? But here there are no cows.
Before I built a wall I'd ask to know
What I was walling in or walling out,
And to whom I was like to give offense.
Something there is that doesn't love a wall,   35
That wants it down." I could say "Elves" to him,
But it's not elves exactly, and I'd rather
He said it for himself. I see him there,
Bringing a stone grasped firmly by the top
In each hand, like an old-stone savage armed.   40
He moves in darkness as it seems to me,
Not of woods only and the shade of trees.
He will not go behind his father's saying,
And he likes having thought of it so well
He says again, "Good fences make good neighbors."   45

Robert Frost (1874-1963)

Questions on "Mending Wall"

1. This poem by Frost offers two perspectives on the necessity of fences – the speaker's and that of the neighbor. Briefly describe those two points of view. Whose view does the poet seem to favor? How? Do you agree with the speaker's neighbor that "Good fences make good neighbors"?

2. Identify the only word that is italicized in the poem. What is its function?

3. What role does Nature play in the poem? Does Nature seem to support the speaker or the neighbor, or does it appear neutral?

4. Apply this poem's theme to any of the current issues and trends, such as borders between countries, privacy, ownership, gated communities, etc. In *Reflections on Exile*, Edward Said pointed out this problem with borders: "Borders and barriers, which enclose us within the safety of familiar territory, can also become prisons, and are often defended beyond reason or necessity." How can we enrich our understanding of the poem with the help of Said's words? If interested, you can read Said's consciousness-altering essay by using this link:
www.dartmouth.edu/~germ43/pdfs/said_reflections.pdf.

Love Poems

The River-Merchant's Wife: A Letter

While my hair was still cut straight across my forehead
I played about the front gate, pulling flowers.
You came by on bamboo stilts, playing horse,
You walked about my seat, playing with blue plums,
And we went on living in the village of Chokan: 5
Two small people, without dislike or suspicion.

At fourteen I married My Lord you.
I never laughed, being bashful.
Lowering my head, I looked at the wall.
Called to, a thousand times, I never looked back.   10

At fifteen I stopped scowling,
I desired my dust to be mingled with yours
Forever and forever and forever.
Why should I climb the lookout?

At sixteen you departed,   15
You went into far Ku-to-yen, by the river of swirling eddies,
And you have been gone five months.
The monkeys make sorrowful noise overhead.

You dragged your feet when you went out.
By the gate now, the moss is grown, the different mosses,   20
Too deep to clear them away!
The leaves fall early this autumn, in wind.
The paired butterflies are already yellow with August
Over the grass in the West garden;
They hurt me. I grow older.   25
If you are coming down through the narrows of the river Kiang,
Please let me know beforehand,
And I will come out to meet you
As far as Cho-fu-sa.

Li-Po (701-762)
(translated by Ezra Pound)

Questions on "The River-Merchant's Wife"

1. This poem by Li-Po has been considered the ultimate love poem. What elements justify its reputation?

2. Compare the poem's style (including tone) and theme with the same elements in Pablo Neruda's poem "Here I Love You."

My Mistress' Eyes

My mistress' eyes are nothing like the sun;
Coral is far more red than her lips' red;
If snow be white, why then her breasts are dun;
If hairs be wires, black wires grow on her head.
I have seen roses damasked, red and white,   5
But no such roses see I in her cheeks;
And in some perfumes is there more delight
Than in the breath that from my mistress reeks.
I love to hear her speak, yet well I know
That music hath far more pleasing sound;   10
I grant I never saw a goddess go, –
My mistress, when she walks, treads on the ground.
And yet, by heaven, I think my love as rare
As any she belied with false compare.

William Shakespeare (1564-1616)

Questions on "My Mistress' Eyes"

1. In Shakespeare's poem, what is different from conventional love poems? Comment specifically on the exaggerated qualities that are associated with the beloved in traditional love poems. What qualities does the speaker in Shakespeare's poem attribute to his beloved to make it a unique love poem?

2. If you were the mistress of Shakespeare's poem, would you feel complimented or offended by the speaker's comparisons? Please note that in Shakespeare's time, the word *reek* simply meant *issue forth*. It did not suggest bad odor.

3. In his book *The Psychology of Imagination*, the French author Jean-Paul Sartre has stated that beautiful women often lead lonely lives. Men often put them on a pedestal. From that idealized, lofty position, such women are expected to conform to impossible standards, and thus the fulfillment of their normal human needs is compromised. Compare the perspective of Shakespeare's speaker with that of Sartre.

4. One complaint often heard in problematic love relations is that of unrealistic expectations on both sides. It is often phrased like this: "Love me for what I am, not for what you want me to become." The powerful myth of Pygmalion and Galatea often influences, consciously or unconsciously, most

romances. Explain that myth. You read the short story "Pygmalion" by John Updike in Chapter Two. Does that myth seem to exert any influence on the relationship between the speaker and his beloved? The word *mistress* had many meanings in Shakespeare's time. It could be used interchangeably with *beloved*.

5. Is Shakespeare's treatment of love more effective or less so in comparison with conventional poems on the topic?

6. Comment on the structure of Shakespearean sonnet. How is it different from the older Petrarchan model? What might have made Shakespeare reject the older model and introduce his own? In which form of the sonnet is the resolution part more challenging? How?

To His Coy Mistress

Had we but world enough, and time,
This coyness, lady, were no crime.
We would sit down, and think which way
To walk, and pass our long love's day.
Thou by the Indian Ganges' side
Shouldst rubies find; I by the tide
Of Humber would complain. I would
Love you ten years before the Flood,
And you should, if you please, refuse
Till the conversion of the Jews.
My vegetable love should grow
Vaster than empires, and more slow;
An hundred years should go to praise
Thine eyes, and on thy forehead gaze;
Two hundred to adore each breast,
But thirty thousand to the rest;
An age at least to every part,
And the last age should show your heart.
For, lady, you deserve this state,
Nor would I love at lower rate.

But at my back I always hear
Time's winge`d chariot hurrying near;
And yonder all before us lie
Deserts of vast eternity.
Thy beauty shall no more be found,
Nor, in thy marble vault, shall sound
My echoing song; then worms shall try
That long-preserved virginity,
And your quaint honor turn to dust,
And into ashes all my lust:
The grave's a fine and private place,

But none, I think, do there embrace.

Now therefore, while the youthful hue
Sits on thy skin like morning dew,
And while thy willing soul transpires
At every pore with instant fires,
Now let us sport us while we may,
And now, like amorous birds of prey,
Rather at once our time devour
Than languish in his slow-chapped power.
Let us roll all our strength and all
Our sweetness up into one ball,
And tear our pleasures with rough strife
Thorough the iron gates of life.
Thus, though we cannot make our sun
Stand still, yet we will make him run.

Andrew Marvell (1621-1678)

Questions on "To His Coy Mistress"

1. Is this poem by Marvell a poem about love or about lust? The word "love" is used in line 20, and the word "lust" in line 30. Support your answer with relevant details from the poem.

2. This poem has been regarded as the famous exemplar of the *carpe diem* (seize the day) theme. What details in the poem support that view?

3. The poem is structured like an argument in three stanzas, slowly starting with the supposition "Had we," quickly turning to the urgency of galloping time "But at my back," and concluding with the intimate details of love making "Now therefore." Sum up the three stanzas in a sentence each to gauge the validity of the speaker's argument. The old word "mistress" in the title simply means "sweetheart" today.

4. Give a few examples of hyperbole (exaggeration) from stanza 1. Is the speaker's tone tender or sarcastic?

5. From the speaker's description of the woman, she is acting coy (stanza 1) but her body language shows (to the speaker at least) that she is burning with passion (last stanza). Consider the situation from both perspectives: the woman would like to preserve her virginity until he marries her; the man thinks it hypocritical of her to play what he may consider cruel games.

6. Is there any demonstration of love's tenderness to counterbalance the almost vulgar statement by the male speaker, who literally tells his sweetheart that she is saving her virginity for the worms (lines 27-28)? Cite, if you can, any demonstration of tenderness of emotion on the male speaker's part.

7. Demonstrate how the images of stanza 1 suggest infinite time, distance, and physical separation between the lovers not as a source of longing but rather as a caricature of romantic love.

8. Demonstrate how the images of the last stanza, contrasting with the first stanza, embody fulfillment of fierce passion in defiance of the "slow-chapped power" of time.

9. This poem is famous for dramatizing the swift passage of time – "But at my back I always hear/Time's winge`d chariot hurrying near." Briefly comment on the effectiveness of image and rhythm in this rendition of time.

One Word Is Too Often Profaned

One word is too often profaned
Or me to profane it,
One feeling too falsely disdain'd
For thee to disdain it.
One hope is too like despair
For prudence to smother,
And pity from thee more dear
Than that from another.

I can give not what men call love;
But wilt thou accept not
The worship the heart lifts above
And the Heavens reject not:
The desire of the moth for the star,
Of the night for the morrow,
The devotion to something afar
From the sphere of our sorrow?

Percy Bysshe Shelley (1792-1822)

Questions on "One Word Is Too Often Profaned"

1. What is that one word that is too often profaned, according to the poem's title?

2. Can this poem be called a love poem in view of the speaker's words that he "can give not what men call love"?

3. Comment on the effect of the use of religious diction in the poem.

4. Does the speaker associate the object of his desire with happiness or sorrow?

La Belle Dame sans Merci
A Ballad

O, what can ail thee, knight-at-arms,
Alone and palely loitering?
The sedge has withered from the lake,
And no birds sing.

O, what can ail thee, knight-at-arms,   5
So haggard and so woe-begone?
The squirrel's granary is full,

And the harvest's done.

I see a lily on thy brow,
With anguish moist and fever dew;   10
And on thy cheeks a fading rose
Fast withereth too.

I met a lady in the meads,
Full beautiful – a faery's child,
Her hair was long, her foot was light,   15
And her eyes were wild.

I made a garland for her head,
And bracelets too, and fragrant zone;
She looked at me as she did love,
And made sweet moan.   20

I set her on my pacing steed,
And nothing else saw all day long;
For sidelong would she bend, and sing
A faery's song.

She found me roots of relish sweet,   25
And honey wild, and manna dew,
And sure in language strange she said –
"I love thee true."

She took me to her elfin grot,
And there she wept and signed full sore, 30
And there I shut her wild wild eyes
With kisses four.

And there she lulle`d me asleep
And there I dreamed – Ah! Woe betide!
The latest dream I ever dreamed   35
On the cold hill side.

I saw pale kings and princes too,
Pale warriors, death-pale were they all;
They cried – "La Belle Dame sans Merci
Hath thee in thrall!"   40

I saw their starved lips in the gloam
With horrid warning gape`d wide,
And I awoke and found me here
On the cold hill's side.

And this is why I sojourn here   45
Alone and palely loitering,
Though the sedge has withered from the lake,
And no birds sing.

       John Keats (1795-1821)

Questions on "La Belle Dame sans Merci"

Before answering the following questions, read an interpretation of this poem by using this link:
http://academic.brooklyn.cuny.edu/english/melani/cs6/belle.html

1. What makes Keats's "La Belle Dame" a unique love poem?

2. There are two speakers in the poem. Identify them with lines that are supposed to be spoken by them. Keats does not use quotation marks to separate the two speakers. Could there be a thematic reason for this stylistic feature?

3. Would you classify the poem's protagonist as a silly romanticist who rejects all precautions to pursue his seemingly senseless love, or do you regard him as someone blessed with a superior vision of what true love is? Support your answer with relevant evidence from the poem.

4. Write an interpretation of the speaker's dream. In spite of the warnings that he gets from the "kings, princes, and warriors" in his dream, the protagonist is undeterred in his quest to pursue the lady. What do the warners represent, and why do they have no effect on the protagonist?

5. Comment on the importance of the word "sojourn" at the end of the poem.

6. Discuss the beautiful lady without pity (the meaning of the poem's title) as representative of fate. The fate here is humanized as a being that is playing a fixed role allotted to it by a higher power. Personified as a woman, she has the foreknowledge of the outcome of her relationship with the knight-protagonist. She is not happy about that knowledge – hence her tears – but she has no control over the direction. Is it possible that the protagonist perceives all of this elusive knowledge that other people are unable to do? Or do you see him as blind to the peril of giving in to the spell of a playful collector and discarder of men? Support your answer with relevant details from the poem.

7. Typical of a ballad, the poem uses very simple words, a single event, gives very little information about the characters (a device to enhance our sense of mystery about them), and is non-judgmental. Comment on the appropriateness of diction: "faery," "elfin grot," squirrel's granary," "roots of relish sweet," "honey wild," and "manna dew." "Manna," in particular, connects the lady with the supernatural because manna was food that dropped from heaven.

8. Point out the use of incremental repetition, a device that is typical of story telling in ballads.

9. Discuss the poem's setting in terms of landscape and time of year. What does it symbolize? How much time seems to have elapsed between the protagonist's desertion by the lady and the time when he is met by the questioning passerby?

10. Is the poem's movement linear or cyclical? Make a connection between this movement and any of the poem's themes.

11. Discuss the poem as a dramatization of the ideal *versus* the real worlds.

Touched by an Angel

We, unaccustomed to courage
Exiles from delight
live coiled in shells of loneliness
until love leaves its high holy temple

and comes into our sight   5
to liberate us into life.

Love arrives
and in its train come ecstasies
old memories of pleasure
ancient histories of pain.   10

Yes if we are bold,
love strikes away the chains of fear
from our souls.
We are weaned from our timidity.
In the flush of love's light   15
we dare be brave.
And suddenly we see
that love costs all we are
and will ever be.
Yet it is only love   20
That will set us free.

Maya Angelou (b. 1928)

Questions on "Touched by an Angel"

1. Explain the paradox that concludes this poem by the African-American poet. How effective is it in communicating the poem's theme? Include a definition of paradox.

2. If love is a life-giving "Angel," could the inability to love be considered an angel of death. A related concept here is that of the Russian author Feodor Dostoevski, who equated the inability to love with being in hell.

3. In this poem, love is seen as an agent of liberation. Pursuing that thought process, can we say that being loveless is a form of imprisonment?

Here I Love You

Here I love you.
In the dark pines the wind disentangles itself.
The moon glows like phosphorus on the vagrant waters.
Days, all one kind, go chasing each other.

The snow unfurls in dancing figures.   5
A silver gull slips down from the west.
Sometimes a sail. High, high stars.

Oh the black cross of a ship.

Alone.
Sometimes I get up early and even my soul is wet.   10
Far away the sea sounds and resounds.
This is a port.
Here I love you.

Here I love you and the horizon hides you in vain.
I love you still among these cold things.   15
Sometimes my kisses go on those heavy vessels
that cross the sea towards no arrival.
I see myself forgotten like those old anchors.
The piers sadden when the afternoon moors there.
My life grows tired, hungry to no purpose.   20
I love what I do not have. You are so far.
My loathing wrestles with the slow twilights.
But night comes and starts to sing to me.

The moon turns its clockwork dream.
The biggest stars look at me with your eyes.   25
And as I love you, the pines in the wind
want to sing your name with their leaves of wire.

Pablo Neruda (1904-1973)
(translated by W. S. Merwin)

Questions on "Here I Love You"

1. Neruda is famous for the use of rich images to communicate strong feelings. Identify a few images in this poem and comment on their effectiveness.
2. Is Nature a companion or an adversary of the speaker-lover in Neruda's poem? How?
3. Between Li-Po and Neruda, which of the two poems has a restrained expression of love? To what cultural reasons do you attribute that restraint in tone?

If I die

If I die, survive me with such great force
that you waken the furies of the pallid and the cold,
from south to south lift your indelible eyes,
from sun to sun dream your singing mouth.
I don't want your laughter or your steps to waver,
I don't want my heritage of joy to die.
Don't call up my person. I am absent.
Live in my absence as if in a house.
Absence is a house so vast
that inside you will pass through its walls
and hang pictures on the air.

Absence is a house so transparent
that I, lifeless, will see you, living,
and if you suffer, my love, I will die again

Pablo Neruda (1904-1973)
(translated by W. S. Merwin)

Questions on "If I Die"

1. This poem is unique in that it urges the bereaved beloved against prolonged suffering that might kill the deceased lover's "heritage of joy." Usually lovers contemplate and may even secretly desire their surviving beloved's pain of separation as a proof of their love. Discuss how this poem is different from the conventional treatment of love.

2. Almost half of the poem is devoted to describing absence, but it is an absence infused by the cheering presence of the deceased lover. Which lines contribute to that effect?

3. Comment on the impact of the poem's last line.

4. This poem is a sonnet. Is it Shakespearean or Petrarchan in its form? Does the absence of rhyme diminish its rhythmic and musical quality?

Say I Love You

Say I love you . . .
So I may grow beautiful
Say I love you . . . that my fingers may turn
Into gold and my forehead become a lantern
Say I love you that my transformation may be complete
        and I become
A wheatstalk or palm tree
Say it now, do not hesitate
Some loves bear no postponement
Say I love you that my saintliness increase and
        my poetry of
Love become a holy book
I would change the calendar should you wish it
Erase seasons, add extra seasons
The old ear defunct in my hands
I would establish the kingdom of women.

Say I love you that my poems might become
Fluid and my writings divine.
Were you my lover I might
Invade the sun with horses and ships.
Don't be shy . . . this is my only chance
To become a god . . . or a prophet

Nizar Qabbani (b. 1923)

614

Questions on "Say I Love You"

1. Comment on the effect of the use of religious imagery in the poem.

2. What would be the transformative effect on the speaker if his beloved reciprocates his love?

3. Why does the speaker want to "invade the sun with horses and ships"?

Poems about Power, Decline, Mortality, and Eternity

Ozymandias

I met a traveler from an antique land
Who said: Two vast and trunkless legs of stone
Stand in the desert . . . Near them, on the sand,
Half sunk, a shattered visage lies, whose frown,
And wrinkled lip, and sneer of cold command,   5
Tell that its sculptor well those passions read
Which yet survive, stamped on these lifeless things,
The hand that mocked them, and the heart that fed;
And on the pedestal these words appear:
"My name is Ozymandias, king of kings;   10
Look on my works, ye Mighty, and despair!"
Nothing beside remains. Round the decay
Of that colossal wreck, boundless and bare
The lone and level sands stretch far away.

Percy Bysshe Shelley (1792-1822)

Questions on "Ozymandias"

1. The poem's title is an allusion. Relate it to the poem's contents. Who in Shelley's time had the Pharaoh-like attributes described in the poem? How does the poet's use of this allusion become a source of compression of meaning and intensification? Ezra Pound defined literature as "language charged with meaning to the utmost possible degree." Does that definition fit Shelley's poem?

2. The poem offers multiple perspectives. How many different points of view can you identify? What are those perspectives?

3. Discuss the effectiveness of Shelley's use of alliteration in the poem's last two lines. Comment also on the poem's shortest sentence: "Nothing besides remains." Could this be considered an example of understatement? What is being stated here? The sonnet form that Shelley uses in this poem is known for a demanding structure and use of rhyme. Is it a classical or Shakespearean sonnet? Write

a structural analysis of this poem by relating its form to conent. This poetic form was discussed at the beginning of this chapter.

Buffalo Bill

Buffalo Bill's
defunct
       who used to
       ride a watersmooth-silver
                  stallion
and break onetwothreefourfive pigeonsjustlikethat
                        Jesus
he was a handsome man
                and what I want to know is
how do you like your blue-eyed boy
Mister Death

                             e. e. cummings (1894-1962)

Questions on "Buffalo Bill"

1. Point out a similarity in the themes of "Buffalo Bill" and Shelley's sonnet "Ozymandias."
2. Compare and contrast Shelley's Ozymandias (a powerful and tyrannical pharaoh in ancient Egypt) with Buffalo Bill.
3. Analyze the contrasting tones the two poets have used to treat the topic of mortality.
4. Comment on the effectiveness of cummings' playful style in treating a serious subject. What elements of his style stand out?

Sailing to Byzantium

That is no country for old men. The young
In one another's arms, birds in the trees
– Those dying generations – at their song,
The salmon-falls, the mackerel-crowded seas,
Fish, flesh, or fowl, commend all summer long   5
Whatever is begotten, born, and dies.
Caught in that sensual music all neglect
Monuments of unaging intellect.

An aged man is but a paltry thing,
A tattered coat upon a stick, unless   10
Soul clap its hands and sing, and louder sing
For every tatter in its mortal dress,
Nor is there singing school but studying
Monuments of its own magnificence;

And therefore I have sailed the seas and come   15
To the holy city of Byzantium.

O sages standing in God's holy fire
As in the gold mosaic of a wall,
Come from the holy fire, perne in a gyre,
And be the singing-masters of my soul.   20
Consume my heart away; sick with desire
And fastened to a dying animal
It knows not what it is; and gather me
Into the artifice of eternity.

Once out of nature I shall never take   25
My bodily form from any natural thing,
But such a form as Grecian goldsmiths make
Of hammered gold and gold enameling
To keep a drowsy Emperor awake;
Or set upon a golden bough to sing   30
To lords and ladies of Byzantium
Of what is past, or passing, or to come.

William Butler Yeats (1865-1939)

Questions on "Sailing to Byzantium"

Before answering the following questions, read the poem's interpretation, using this link:
http://www.enotes.com/sailing-byzantium-criticism/sailing-byzantium-william-butler-yeats.

1. The speaker in Yeats's poem shows conflicting feelings. In the opening stanza, he ostensibly tries to reject the vital and vibrant world of "fish, flesh, or fowl" because his advanced age makes him irrelevant to that world. However, while reluctantly accepting this fact about his irrelevance in a youth-oriented culture, he shows that somehow he cannot drive this realm of the senses completely out of his mind. Which lines demonstrate his inability to completely disconnect with the physical, natural world and lose himself totally in the world of the spirit?

2. What does Byzantium represent in this poem?

3. Point out the paradox in this phrase: "Monuments of unageing intellect."

4. Phillip Roth's novel *The Dying Animal* was inspired by words from this poem. Make some thematic connections between the novel and Yeats's poem. You may want to look up Carolyn Nash's essay "Big Fish Stories" comparing Hemingway's novel *The Old Man and the Sea* with Elizabeth Bishop's poem "The Fish" earlier in this chapter.

5. The recent movie *Elegy*, starring Ben Kingsley and Penelope Cruz, was based on Phillip Roth's above-mentioned novel *The Dying Animal*. Connect Yeats's poem with the novel and/or the movie. An earlier essay in this chapter, "Is Your Enemy Human?" points out similarity of themes between the movie *Hiroshima Mon Amour* and the poem "Vergissmeinnicht."

6. Another popular recent movie *No Country for Old Men* gets its title from the opening lines of Yeats's poem. Do you see any relation between the movie's substance and Yeats's poem? Give supporting details for your answer.

7. Discuss the effectiveness of Yeats's use of imagery and symbolism in this poem. Analyze specifically his use of the spiraling gyre and the golden bird symbols and water and fire imagery.

8. Is the poem a celebration or reluctant acceptance of the mutual dependence of art and nature, physical and spiritual, temporal and eternal, youth and old age? Give supporting details from the poem.

9. Comment on the effectiveness of Yeats's use of the above-mentioned series of contrasts to structure his poem.

10. Discuss the poem as a dramatization of tension between art and life. Does the speaker embrace or reject Nature with its cycle of life and death? Why does he wish to be gathered into "the artifice of eternity"? Support your answer with details from the poem.

11. What stylistic device is Yeats using in the phrase "dying generations" (line 3)? Is it appropriate to convey his feelings?

12. The speaker apologizes to the sages for his heart that is "sick with desire/And fastened to a dying animal." What is the desire that he is stricken with and is unable to overcome?

13. This poem is often compared with John Keats's "Ode on a Grecian Urn." Read Keats's poem online and point out some notable thematic similarities and striking differences between the two poems. Is Yeats's "artifice of eternity" similar to "Cold Pastoral" in Keats's poem?

14. Do the speakers in the aforementioned two poems by Yeats and Keats want the same thing? Do they make a clear choice between being an art work and thus outside the decay-bound cycle of nature? Or do they seem to prefer, overtly or secretly, the ability to live a full life within the limits of mortality? As always, support your answer with relevant details from the poems.

15. In Yeats's poem, art seems to be eternal. Is art also eternal in Keats's poem? Notice Keats's opening lines that call the Grecian urn (the work of art) "foster-child of silence and slow time." Has the time just slowed down, not stopped, even for the urn?

16. Comment on a possible thematic reason for the care and adoration with which the two poets write about art – Keats's description of the still-life dynamic scenes on the Grecian urn and Yeats describing the "gold mosaic" and immortal creations by "Grecian goldsmiths."

POETRY IN TRANSLATION

We can make a case for poetry in translation as a means to bring different cultures and people together. However, since the cultural context of some international poets may be challenging, the informal journaling approach that is covered in Chapter Six may give us easier access to them. Of the poets included here, Omar Khayyam was an eleventh-century Persian poet-mathematician, who is best-known for his four-line poems called "Rubaiyat." Rumi was a thirteenth-century Persian poet who also founded the Sufi order known as the Whirling Derveshes. Bahadar Shah Zafar was the last Moghul emperor of India, who also wrote outstanding poetry in Urdu. Mirza Asadullah Khan Ghalib (nineteenth century) is regarded as the pre-eminent Indian poet who perfected the ghazal form. Faiz Ahmed Faiz was one of the greatest twentieth-century poets from the sub-continent of Indo-Pakistan. His translator, the American poet Naomi Lazard, says that Faiz is one of the few poets "whose stance and influence have altered the consciousness of the world" (Lazard xi). The third author, Rabindranath Tagore, one of India's foremost twentieth-century literary figures, has the distinction of having received the Nobel prize for literature. Enjoying the same prestige as Tagore in the subcontinent of India and Pakistan, Mohammad Iqbal is a philosopher who uses poetry as his medium of expression. The next selection is by Waseem Barelvi of India, considered to be one of the greatest living poets writing in the Urdu language.

Interpretations of these translated poems are by the author of this book. Some readings are informal like journal entries; others are like formal essays.

Ah, Fill the Cup

(translated from Persian by Edward Fitzgerald)

Ah, fill the Cup: – What boots it to repeat
How Time is slipping underneath our Feet.
Unborn Tomorrow, and dead yesterday,
Why fret about them if To-day be sweet?

Omar Khayyam (1048-1131); Fitzgerald 42

Interpretation

Even our moments of happiness are often contaminated with past sorrows and future apprehensions. It is on this painful aspect of human consciousness that the eleventh-century Persian poet Omar Khayyam offers his advice in this quatrain. We all know that time is constantly slipping away. Why worry about the inevitable? Why not focus on the passing moment and fill it with joy?

Perplext No More

Perplext no more with human or divine
Tomorrow's tangle to the winds resign,
And lose your fingers in the tresses of

The cypres-slender minister of wine. (Fitzgerald 91)

Khayyam, If You Are Drunk

The text of this quatrain is in Chapter Eleven.

Interpretation

On the surface, the first of these two quatrains may seem like a recommendation for irresponsible hedonism. However, the poem's real concern is with simply wanting to live the passing moments fully without being plagued by the tangled issues of human nature and the nature of divinity.

Taking the theme of seizing the micro-moments of time and making the best of them, Khayyam goes a step further in the second quatrain, which was also included in Chapter Eleven in the context of noting similarities between Camus' novel *The Stranger* and this quatrain. Khayyam invites us to transform the nothingness of life into something positive with the help of will power. Elements of existentialist thought that emphasize human encounter with nothingness have existed a long time before this philosophy was expounded systematically in the twentieth century. Omar Khayyam's quatrain is an interesting example of that thinking, of transforming nothingness into something of value.

The Chickpea

A chickpea leaps almost over the rim of
the pot
where it's being boiled.

"Why are you doing this to me?"
The cook knocks it down with the ladle.

Don't you try to jump out.
You think I'm torturing you,
I'm giving you flavor,
so you can mix with spices and rice
and be the lovely vitality of a human
being. . .

Jalaluddin Rumi (1207-1273)
(translated by Coleman Barks)

Interpretation

Through the ages, poets and thinkers have wrestled with the problem of pain and suffering in life. Rumi's short poem addresses that topic in a serio-comic way. People who complain about suffering are like the chickpea trying to find a way out of pain prematurely. One needs to see beyond immediate discomfort to realize that there may be a design that is not readily understood by us and that pain may be a necessary stage in the maturation process. Hamlet's famous words are relevant here: "There is a divinity that shapes our ends/Rough hew them how we will." Similarly, John Keats dismissed the notion that the world is a "vale of tears." He preferred to call it the "vale of soul-making."

My Heart Feels Dislocated in These Ruins: Some background information on the poet and the Ghazal form

A little background information about the poet-King and about the poetic form – the ghazal – that he used would help in understanding the emotion this poem is trying to communicate. Bahadur Shah Zafar (1775-1862) was the last Moghul Emperor of India. In 1857, after the war in which both Hindus and Muslims fought against the occupying British forces, he was arrested, his sons murdered, their severed heads hung on the Bloody Gate. He was exiled to Calcutta, then to Rangoon, where he died.

The celebrated poetic form, known as the ghazal, usually consists of four or more pairs of verses and a word that acts as a refrain. The verses are not necessarily couplets because every third line may be rhyme-free. The meter, however, is consistently uniform to maintain a strong rhythmic effect. In a ghazal, it is not just the last syllable that has to rhyme with its counterpart in the preceding line. The second-from-last syllable also has to rhyme with its counterpart in the line before. A good example is the following opening couplet from a ghazal by the Kashmiri American poet Agha Shahid Ali:

Where are you now? Who lies beneath your spell tonight?
Whom else from rapture's road will you expel tonight?

In these lines, it is not just the end words "tonight" that rhyme. The preceding syllables "spell" and "expel" also rhyme. The word "tonight" serves as a refrain throughout the ghazal. These stringent requirements make the ghazal one of the most demanding forms of poetry. It is stricter than the sonnet in this respect. Another feature unique to the ghazal is that each pair of lines is a self-contained thought, almost like a complete poem; there may or may not be any logical connection between one pair of verse and another, but often there is an emotional connection and uniformity of mood.

Traditionally, the topics treated in the ghazal range from unrequited love, the beloved's cruel indifference, brevity of life, melancholy perfumed with the scent of memories, vagaries of fortune, fatalism tinged with rebellion against fate, and similar concerns. In the Sufi ghazal tradition, God is seen as the ultimate beloved, and adoring the human object of love and longing is like worshipping God. In terms of style, which is often marked by hyperbole, imagery and symbol drawn from Nature abound, such as stars, the moon, the sun, the universe, flowers, song birds, etc.

Since the ghazal is a demanding form to practice and appreciate, it would be helpful to research the ghazal form and find a ghazal composed in English that observes its requirements. In response to the growing popularity of the ghazal, in the year 2000, Agha Shahid Ali compiled and edited the world's first anthology of English-language ghazals, *Ravishing DisUnities: Real Ghazals in English*. Consult that book or research online to select a ghazal to write an interpretation and assessment of its poetic achievement. Besides Agha Shahid Ali, of the many major poets who have written ghazals, some are the following:

- Robert Bly: *The Night Abraham Called to the Stars* and *My Sentence Was a Thousand Years of Joy*
- John Hollander: "Ghazal on Ghazals"
- Maxine Kumin: "On the Table"
- Marilyn Krysl: "Ghazals for the Turn of the Century"
- Adrienne Rich: "Ghazals: Homage to Ghalib"
- Spencer Reece: "Florida Ghazals"
- Phyllis Webb: *Water and Light: Ghazals and Anti Ghazals*

My translation of Zafar's poem is in free verse. The music, of course, is lost. At the same time, however, if one tries to use rhyme, the original poem's literal meaning may be compromised. Perhaps this is what Robert Frost meant when he said that poetry evaporates in translation. He was referring to the music and rhythm of strict forms of poetry like the ghazal and the sonnet. His words are not a disincentive to translation because the wealth of feelings and ideas from unfamiliar cultures can still be captured and nourished in translation.

My Heart Feels Dislocated
(Zafar's ghazal translated in the form of free verse)

My heart feels dislocated in these ruins.
Who has ever felt at home in this passing world?
Tell these yearnings to find a home elsewhere.
Where is space for them in this ravaged heart?
Of the long life of four days
Two were spent on longing and two on waiting.
How unfortunate is Zafar that for his burial
He couldn't find even two yards near the beloved!

Bahadur Shah Zafar (1775-1862)
(translated by Abdul Jabbar)

In its original form, not captured in this free verse translation, Zafar's poem follows a fixed rhyme scheme aaba, cada. To hear the rhyme, meter, and music of this ghazal in its original Urdu form, go to Youtube.com and enter "Bahadur Shah Zafar's ghazal "lagta nahiN hai jee mera." Also read the original poem in transliteration to appreciate its musical quality and to hear its refrain (not present in this free-verse translation). Use this link: http://www.urdupoetry.com/zafar04.html.

Interpretation

With the esthetic beauty of its verbal magic, rhythmic balance of its lines, use of verbal irony, and effective hyperbole, Zafar beautifies his lament over the cruel brevity of life and unfulfilled longings. This poem exemplifies well the belief that when adorned with artistic beauty, pain and suffering take on an esthetically pleasing shape. This transformation of inescapable pain into esthetic beauty may be the reason why well-crafted tragic creations continue to be regarded as the highest form of art.

Perhaps the greatest source of appeal of such poems is that they capture with perfection what most of us often feel but do not have the ability to communicate, even to ourselves. The eighteenth-century English poet Alexander Pope captured well poetry's power to articulate "what oft was thought but never so well expressed." In John Keats's famous words from his poem "The Fall of Hyperion," even mad people have dreams, but it takes a true poet to express them coherently:

> Poesy alone can tell her dreams, --
> With the fine spell of words alone can save
> Imagination from the sable chain
> And dumb [means wordless] enchantment.   (lines 8-12)

Notably effective in Zafar's poem is his use of verbal irony that consists of saying the opposite of what is expected and really intended. The words "long life of four days" are an example of irony because they do not constitute a long life. On the deeper level, the implication is that even those four days (hyperbole for a short life) might have been acceptable had they brought real fulfillment rather than being wasted on two days of longing – another striking use of hyperbole in the phrase "two days" – and another two days of waiting. As one looks back at one's life, even a fairly long life seems all too brief, indeed just like four days. The theme of the swift passage of time is not new, but the power of Zafar's captivating poetic expression is.

Suppressed Longings (aah ko chahiye)

Suppressed longings take a lifetime to have effect.
Life is too short for the long wait to make you mine.
Love demands patience but desire can't wait.
What hue of pain shall my heart wear until the agony ends?
I believe that you will not ignore me .
But I will be dust before you know my love.
What, Asad, can cure the sadness of Being except death?
Life, like a candle, is destined to burn and melt through the night.

Mirza Asadullah Khan Ghalib (19th century)
(translated in free verse from Urdu by Abdul Jabbar)

To have a feel for the music of words in this famous ghazal, you should first read the following transliteration of the poem in Urdu. The rhyme scheme is aaba cada.

> aah ko chahiye ik umr asar hone` tek
> kon jeeta hai teri zulf ke ser hone` tek
>
> aashqi sabr talab aur tamanna beitaab
> dil ka kia rung karooN khoone jigar hone` tek
>
> humne mana ke taghafal na karoge laikin
> khak ho jaiN ge hum tumko khabar hone tek.

gham-e hasti ka asad kis se ho juz marg ilaj
shama her rung maiN jalti hai sehar hone` tek.

The next step will be listening to one of the world's famous singers Jagjit Singh singing it. This link will take you there: http://www.youtube.com/watch?v=OgTYmFUd6s8

Interpretation

Like most ghazal writers, Ghalib did not title his poem, but it is clearly about the difficulty of waiting for love's reciprocity. As in ghazals, each pair of lines forms an independent unit in terms of meanings. Even the topic can change from pair to pair. However, there is an underlying unity that is achieved both through the words' associated meanings as well as tone that creates the desired mood. The speaker in this poem is acutely aware of the brevity of life, which makes every hour of waiting for his beloved's desired response unbearably painful The poem in this chapter that can help us understand this concept of *carpe diem* (seize the day) is Andrew Marvell's poem "To His Coy Mistress." The following lines, in particular, capture this feeling:

> Had we but world enough, and time,
> This coyness, lady, were no crime. . . .
> But at my back I always hear
> Time's winged chariot hurrying near.

Just like the speaker in Marvell's poem, Ghalib's speaker feels acutely the swift passage of time. He realizes that he needs to be patient, but his ardent desire makes patience impossible. He trusts the beloved's promise to reciprocate but is unhappy with the long wait that he must suffer through.

Like most ghazals, this poem also uses hyperbole when the speaker says that unfulfilled desire is ravishing his heart. The same stylistic element is present also when he says that he will be dust before the beloved knows his love. In the poem's concluding lines, Ghalib uses a startling simile in comparing the speaker's life and life in general to a candle that has no choice but to continue burning through the night. This comparison creates a feeling of warmth and light and gives the poem somewhat of a positive note to relieve the overbearing sadness of existence that in the speaker's view only death can end. It must be noted that almost all ghazals are suffused with sadness, but at the same time the beauty of verbal magic and music of the poem distracts the mind from sadness to the spell of art. It is like the tragic plays in which painful feelings co-exist with artistic elegance to bring about the cathartic effect associated with tragedy.

Another possible interpretation of this complex poem could be that the speaker's longings are not even communicated to the beloved. It seems like a truly hopeless love. It does not go beyond the speaker's painful awareness that his love, if expressed, will remain unrequited. To understand such complex literary works, we can draw on the precious resource of analogues. In this case, besides the above-noted comparison with Marvell, there are two more helpful examples. The first is this opening line of a poem by Ghalib himself: "I have thousands of desires, each one of them a potential killer." The second, more helpful analogue is in the form of the following words from the English Romantic poet William Blake's poem "The Sick Rose":

O Rose, thou art sick!
The invisible worm
That flies in the night,
In the howling storm,
Has found out thy bed
Of crimson joy,
And his dark secret love
Does thy life destroy.

Blake's "howling storm" is the secret, suppressed longing of the speaker in Ghalib's poem. And Blake's "bed of crimson joy" is the sweet unrest of Ghalib's longed for but unrealized fulfillment. In both cases, the "invisible worm" leads to strangled desires.

Walk Alone

If they answer not to thy call,
Walk Alone.
If they tremble and cower mutely
Facing the Wall,
O thou of evil luck,
Open thy mind and speak out alone.
If, when crossing the wilderness,
They turn away and desert you,
O thou of evil luck,
Trample the thorns under thy tread,
And along the blood-strewn path,
Walk alone.
If, when the night is troubled
With storm,
They do not hold up the light,
O thou of evil luck,
With the thunder flame of pain,
Ignite thine own heart,
And let it burn alone.

Rabindranath Tagore (1861-1941); Wolpert 252

Interpretation

Tagore's poem was written many years before Faiz's "Blackout." However, we can imagine the person addressed in Tagore's poem to be someone like the speaker in Faiz's poem – an idealist in a state of isolation. There are times when one finds oneself alone. In that unfortunate situation that no one desires, a person should not cower before the might of the wrongdoer. The situation requires courage, sacrifice, determination, and willingness to suffer for the sake of a worthy ideal. If there is no other light left in the world, in that state of total blackout, one can still fall back upon one's own heart that, metaphorically, can burn like a candle and light the way.

These two poems by Faiz and Tagore bring to mind Margaret Mead's inspirational words:

> Never doubt that a small group of thoughtful, committed citizens
> can change the world. Indeed, it's the only thing that ever does.

This prose translation by Ralph Russell leaves out the meter and rhyme of Iqbal's original poem.

Life

Life is more than the calculation of gain and loss.
Life sometimes means going on living
and sometimes means giving up one's life.
Life is not to be measured in todays and tomorrows.
It is eternal, ever moving, ever young.
If you number yourself amongst the living,
create your own world.
Life is the secret of Adam,
the essence of God's creative command.

Muhammad Iqbal (1877-1938); Russell 178.

Interpretation

Iqbal once said that poets not only write words that live but words to live by. Poems like this have made him a source of inspiration for all readers. This brief section from his famous poem "Khizar e Rah" ("The Guide of the Way") contains his view of life. The message is for people to create their own lives rather than attribute their condition to outside forces. In creating each day of life, the individual is imitating the divine act of creation. The implication is that we can count ourselves fully alive only in those moments when we are pursuing a worthy ideal with full vigor and devotion. A mere tally of yesterdays and todays does not constitute the stream of true life, which is eternal, for ever flowing, and for ever young.

The true meaning of the poem's third line is not giving up life in the literal sense. It rather means occasionally having to submit to the vagaries of life without getting disheartened. In the poem's second-from-last line, instead of "Adam," the meaning closer to the original would be "the secret of being human" that every living being is challenged to unravel.

Nationalism

If there is rivalry between the nations of the world, this *vataniyat* [nationalism]
is the cause of it.
If the object of trade is conquest, this is the cause of it.
If politics is devoid of sincerity, this is the cause of it.
If the home of the weak is destroyed, this is the cause of it.
It is that divides God's creation [humankind] into nations.
It is this that severs the root of the community of Islam.

Muhammad Iqbal (1877-1938); Russell 181

Interpretation

After the First World War, at a time when the world was fast splintering into warring nation states, Iqbal's message was for the people to espouse inclusive globalism rather than exclusive nationalism. Surely, he was far ahead of his time, for only recently have we come to regard the planet earth as a global village with a network of mutually interdependent people. Iqbal found the self-indulgent, chauvinistic nationalism and its narrow confines responsible for numerous ills that plague and divide the world, some of which are listed in this excerpt from his longer poem.

The Artist

These cheeks of yours
like decayed tombs.
These cheeks of yours
kissed by calamities.
Had they remained youthful,
the pages of the book of life
would have lost thousands of legends.

Waseem Barelvi (b. 1940)
(translated by Abdul Jabbar)

Interpretation

Poets have contemplated the role of the artist through the ages. Waseem Barelvi's treatment of that topic is unique. Blessed with the gift of empathy to an unusual degree, artists feel the pain of others as if it were their own pain. This gift, however, comes at a high price. In Barelvi's poem, the face of the artist, "kissed by calamities," reflects the anguish of humanity. Just as a candle burns and melts in order to give light, the poet undergoes self-immolation to give forth the light of love and beauty. The gift of compassion that the artist is endowed with does not come without pain and sacrifice. The end result is a huge benefit to humanity in the form of thousands of legends that the artist is able to create and cultivate with his life blood. Carrying the heavy burden of sensitivity is not a recipe for staying youthful. Premature aging is more like the fate of the artist.

The elusive last lines are the heart of Barelvi's poem. When faced with hard-to-explicate lines, we have the resource of literary analogues available – something that was used in Chapter Eleven to explicate some of Camus' difficult lines from his novel *The Stranger*. Analogical interpretation consists of comparing the subject lines to other literary works that have dealt with similar themes. The validity of this method is upheld by the famous psychologist Carl Jung's view that all artists draw their inspiration, images, and symbols from a common source that he calls the collective unconscious.

Using analogical reasoning, what helps us understand Barelvi's depiction of the artist is a poem by the English Romantic poet John Keats. In his words from "The Fall of Hyperion," truly great poets "feel the giant agony of the world." The lofty position in the temple of poetry is reserved only for those poets "to whom the miseries of the world/Are misery, and will not let them rest." The true poet "is a sage;/A humanist, physician to all men." In the poem, Moneta, the high priestess in the temple of poetry, who guides the aspiring poet, reveals how her loss is humanity's gain: "My power, which to me is still a curse,/Shall be to thee a wonder." Another relevant voice is that of Percy Shelley, who, like Keats, was a major Romantic poet and Keats's contemporary. In Shelley's words from his famous essay "A Defence of Poetry," a poet "is a nightingale, who sits in darkness and sings to cheer its own solitude with sweet sounds; his auditors are as men entranced by the melody of an unseen musician, who feel that they are moved and softened, yet know not whence or why."

Similarly Barelvi's artist burns his youth and vigor to create the warmth and glow of legends for humanity's benefit. In the process, the artist loses surface beauty but gains the beauty of the face as a book, on which are recorded the experiences and ravages of time. In this way, the face of the artist in itself becomes a complex work of art. Artists falsify the common saying that if you laugh, the world will laugh with you; if you weep, you will weep alone. Barelvi's poem reassures us that as long as art lives, no one will weep alone because the reach of the compassionate artist, transcending all barriers, embraces all. The uniqueness of Barelvi's poem is its austere beauty. In just seven lines of a total of 23 words (seven lines and 31 words in English translation), the poet has crafted a memorable short poem with a big theme.

After reading these informal journal entries on international poems, you may wish to explore outstanding poems from unfamiliar cultures. Literature is, after all, a means to expand our knowledge of the world.

Blackout

Ever since the lights went dark,
I have been seeking in the dust
my eyes that I have lost I know not where.
You who know me, show me the way to myself.

It is as if, wave by wave,
a river of fatal poison has entered my veins.
Tangled in memory and longing, my love,
I know not in which wave my heart is drowning.

Be patient. From another world a lightning flash,
working miracles like Moses, may restore my eyes.
Emerging from the bowl of darkness, it may give me back
the night-expelling shine of my diamond eyes.

Wait a moment. The river of my heart,
cleansed of its poison
may find a new harbor.

Then, with my new vision, new eyes, new heart,
once again will I write about beauty and love.   September 1965

Faiz Ahmed Faiz (1911-1984)

(translated by Abdul Jabbar)

Interpretation

This may be considered a unique anti-war poem. The poet was a Pakistani citizen living in the city of Lahore when it was bombed by India in 1965. However, in the entire poem, he does not take the usual patriotic position of criticizing the invader, even though he himself could have perished in one of the air raids.

The poem's title "Blackout" apparently refers to the requirement of extinguishing all lights in the city under attack in order to protect the people. However, more important is the implied meaning. The poem is really about the mental blackout, in which the light of reason and brotherhood is extinguished.

The war drives the poem's speaker to self-analysis, which leads him to believe that war is an indication of his personal failure as a human being and as an artist. In the lines that point to his hatred-filled veins, the speaker represents the mass of humanity. He regards the ugly specter of war as a collective failure of humanity and no cause for finger pointing. As a poet who would only like to compose poems of "beauty and love," he suddenly finds himself without an occupation because he sees no beauty and no love in his environment. His forced silence means suspension of his favorite activity. However, he is hopeful that this suspension will some day end miraculously when he will regain his lost vision and his heart, cleansed of its poison, will find a new harbor.

Moving from an informal reading to an essay

In view of the special nature of this pro-peace poem and its timely and timeless message, I have expanded the preceding informal interpretation into the following full-length essay.

Faiz Ahmed Faiz and the Cure for Blindness
by the author of this book

In addition to being a renowned poet, Faiz Ahmed Faiz was also a diagnostician and a healer. He put his finger on what ails humanity and how it could heal itself. His poetry is full of invaluable remedies. Even though "Blackout" reads like a nightmare, it also contains a cure for the mental blackout that leads to endless warfare. The date of this poem's composition, appended at its end, is September 1965. This date is the only clue that the poem is referring to the war between India and Pakistan that broke out at that time. One meaning of the poem's title "Blackout," the literal one, is that during an air raid, city lights are extinguished to make it difficult for the enemy to find targets.

However, the second and more important meaning of the poem's title points to the blackout that either leaves the mind paralyzed or pushes it toward destruction. During this state of mental and spiritual blackout, human beings cannot see their way. They feel lost. After knowing the facts surrounding this poem's composition, readers wait and look for the poet's condemnation of the invading enemy's aggression. During any conflict, it is human nature to resort to finger pointing. The air raid that is the subject of this poem was such that could have resulted in the poet's own death. However, people looking for the usual comfort of blaming "the enemy" will be disappointed because, in the entire poem,

Faiz has abstained from choosing the easy way out. He has presented a truly unique and revolutionary point of view.

Every individual is responsible for the death and destruction of war. The poet includes himself among the purveyors of violence and communicates the poem's message in the form of self-castigation. As an example of individual responsibility, if every soldier lays down his arms and refuses to fight, there can be no war. This poem gives us a jolt of awareness of our personal responsibility in nurturing hate in the world. It also points to our duty of transforming hate into love and human sympathy. Conventions of literary criticism require that we do not equate a poem's speaker with the poet. However, there are some poems in which keeping the two separate is difficult and unnecessary. The speaker of this poem could be a soldier who, during a brief respite during war, is forced to contemplate his conduct and responsibility. A point to remember in this context is that the poet himself had served in the army as a colonel. The speaker of this poem could also be a poet who is lamenting the ineffectiveness of his art in achieving the desired change in human consciousness – someone who, despite being surrounded by the ugliness of war, tries to spread love and beauty. Or he could be mourning the fact that he spent his creative energies on offering the world beautiful poems about love and beauty and neglected an artist's prime duty of creating peace in the world. Thus the poem's speaker could be a soldier, a poet, or any thinker. Whatever identity we may give him, the speaker is so lost and disoriented under the weight of his actions and failure to make a difference that it seems impossible for him to recognize his true self:

> Ever since the lights went dark, I have been seeking in the dust
> my eyes that I have lost I know not where.
> You who know me, tell me how to recognize myself.
> Emerging from the bowl of darkness, it may give me back
> the night-expelling shine of my diamond eyes.

Entering the speaker's consciousness, the poet does not take long to diagnose the cause of this blindness:

> It is as if, wave by wave,
> a river of fatal poison has entered my veins.
> Carrying your memory and deep longing for you, my love,
> I know not in which wave my heart is drowning.

Hatred that fills the speaker's veins is the plague that has infected humanity through the ages and which causes human beings to fall short of realizing their full humanity. Parallel thoughts of other thinkers and poets help us understand Faiz's poem better: Gandhi's famous proclamation is relevant here: "Be the change that you want to see in the world." Gandhi's compatriot, friend, and rival, Muhammad Ali Jinnah, the founder of Pakistan, also stresses individual responsibility: "If we want to make the world a secure, clean, and happy place, our reform work has to start with the individual. It is the same message that many Faiz-inspired poets after him have offered. An example is Nausha Asrar:

> The only requirement is to keep moving forward;
> the obstacles will always be there.

> To change anything, one has to first change oneself.
>
> (translated by Abdul Jabbar)

The miseducation of centuries can be cured only by a miracle, in search of which Faiz's poem struggles to move forward:

> Be patient. From another world a lightning flash,
> working miracles like Moses, may restore my eyes.

In Chapter Eleven, we discussed analogues as a means to understanding a complex literary work. We have used that strategy in referring to Gandhi and Asrar in search of reaching the essence of Faiz's poem. Works of several other prominent, Faiz-inspired authors are relevant as well. Iqbal Azeem's verse comes close to capturing the essence of Faiz's thought:

> Those whose hearts have lost their vision
> How can they see anything with their eyes?

The last part of Faiz's poem is suffused with the same yearning that the poet Khushbir Singh Shad has also expressed:

> We chose this self-inflicted burning under the pitiless heat of the sun.
> We could have chosen the comfort of an oasis.

"Blackout" also offers us a glimpse of Faiz's mentor Muhammad Iqbal. Addressing Sufis in his poem "To the Sufi," Iqbal had said:

> Your world is one of miracles
> Mine is that of collisions.

The difference between Iqbal and Faiz is that in this poem, Faiz has united Sufis with poets and also the miracles with collisions. Faiz's poem starts with a conflict and ends with a miracle. It contains Rumi and the Sufis' doctrine of annihilation of the inferior self in order to reach spiritual heights. What makes this poem unique is that even though the poet himself was at risk of being killed during the blackout described in the poem, he chose to shun jingoistic verse, offering instead a probing self-analysis and a way to human exaltation through self-negation.

According to this poem, the miracle of healing can occur only when two conditions are met – a new heart and new eyes:

> Wait a moment. The river of my heart,
> cleansed of its poison
> may find a new harbor.
> Then, with my new vision, new eyes, new heart,
> once again will I write about beauty and love.

Only after crossing the river of poison and hate and armed with a new heart and new eyes can one feel that the world can be a beautiful place. The poet can then use his ability to add to the world's beauty by returning to his favorite topic of love and beauty. As we have seen, despite its bleak title, this poem is filled with a throbbing desire for light – the light of reason, love, and beauty.

To experience the full meaning of "Blackout," we need to contrast it with Faiz's poem "Sinkiang" that I have translated from Urdu into English. It embodies this great poet's beautiful dream of peace. It is a dream whose fulfillment can transform this world from hell into heaven. That state of being is possible only if, armed with a new heart and a new vision, we move beyond the mental blackout and blindness. While "Blackout" is a very serious poem whose lines, unadorned with rhyme, struggle to move under the crushing weight of its meaning, "Sinkiang" is fast-moving, stirring, and filled with joy. Its ecstatic proclamation is something that the world has been dying to hear:

Sinkiang

No drums of war now; no horsemen
departing to the valley of death.
No wars breaking out; no more
Quenching of burning blood
with nocturnal tears.
No night-long, anxious heartbeats
No fear perching like an ominous bird
No blood-drenched tyranny of animals of prey.
Wars are over for ever.
Bring wine and glasses.
No more shedding of tears and blood.
Let's dance like the morning breeze
And have a ghazal, scented with colorful henna.

Faiz Ahmed Faiz (1911-1984)
(translated by Abdul Jabbar)

Transition from the nightmare of "Blackout" to the joyous celebration of "Sinkiang" is, indeed, possible if we have the sense to use Faiz's recipe proffered in his uniquely revolutionary poetry.

Naomi Lazard, the Faiz scholar who translated his poetry, has rightly assessed the achievement of Faiz: "This century has given us a few great poets whose stance and influence have altered the consciousness of the world" (Lazard xi). She places Faiz among them.

In view of the nature of the two poems discussed in this essay, it would be appropriate to end with the poet's own words from his Lenin Peace Prize acceptance speech:

> I believe that humanity . . . will, after all, be successful; . . . at long last, instead
> of wars, hatred and cruelty, the foundation will rest on the message of Hafiz, an
> old Persian poet: 'Every foundation you see is defective, except the foundation
> of love, which is faultless'."[18]

---

[18] Faiz's Lenin Peace Prize acceptance speech of 1962 is a great piece of humanist literature. It appears as a brief preface to his collection *Dast-i-tah-i-Sang* (*Hand under the Rock*).

632

More Poems in Translation

The next group of poems in translation have no interpretations. You are encouraged to create your own informal or formal responses. You may use the journal format if you like. For help consult any one of the numerous journal entries in Chapter Six. The chapter's concluding section "Poems for Further Reading" also has some translated poems, such as those by Pablo Neruda and Mahmoud Darwish.

Stream of Life

The same
stream of life
that runs through
my veins
runs through
the world
and dances in
rhythmic measure.

It is the same life
that shoots in joy
through the dust
of the earth
into numberless
blades of grass
and breaks into
tumultuous waves
of leaves and
flowers.

It is the same life
that is rocked in
the ocean cradle
of birth
and death
in ebb
and flow.

My limbs are
made glorious
by the touch
of this world
of life.

And my pride
is from
the life throb
of ages dancing
in my blood
at this moment.　　Rabindranath Tagore (1861-1941

Morning Star

To my neighbors, the sun and moon, I would bid goodbye,
No more do I like to play the herald of the morning light.
The habitat of the starry sky is not the place for me,
I would rather live on earth, lowly though she be.
The sky where I abide is an inane place,
The shredded twilight shrouds my corpse at every break of day.
I take my birth every night, every day I die,
I have to drink the bowl of death when early morn arrives.
I do not like my rank and statue, nor the alloted task,
It is better to be plunged in dark than living by fits and starts.
I wouldn't be a star at all if I could but help,
I wish I were a sparkling pearl reared in the river bed.
Troubled by the angry waves, I would leap ashore,
And become a glittering pendant round a beauteous throat.

Only as a splendid ornament the pearl shows its grace
Ah! To deck the regal coronet of some empress great!
A piece of stone, blessed by luck, become a diamond non-pareil,
And in Solomon's signet-ring occupies an honored place.
But things of pomp and pelf are bound to perish soon or late,
Rare and precious pearls too are subject to decay.
We should live such a life which is not afeared of death,
To live beneath the shade of death is a humiliating act.
If there is an end to everything that the world adores,
Why not then change to dew and slide down the velvet rose?
Failing that I would settle on some scent-sprinkled brow,
Or live amidst the sparkling sighs of some deep oppressed soul.
Or, turned to a fear, sit suspended on the eyes
Of a sensitive wife, stirred with simmering sighs.

The wife whose husband is setting out for the battlefield,
Fully dressed in armour, goaded by patriotic zeal,
Whose face reflects the colours of alternating hope and fear,
Whose silence is more eloquent than speech, loud and clear.
Whose submission to her husband gives her courage and peace,
Whose modesty urges her not to weep, but speak.
Whose rosy colour has all but gone for fear of separation,
Whose beauty gets an added glow from inward agitation.
I'll spill out from her eyes despite her self-control,
As the cup abrim with wine is bound to overflow.
Mixing myself in the dust I'll gain immortal life,
And show how much of fire a passionate tear may hide.

Muhammad Iqbal (1877-1938)
(translated by K.C. Kanda)

The next poem by Iqbal makes extensive use of religious and historical allusions that you may want to look up in order to fully enjoy the poem.

The Story of Adam[19]

What a story I have to tell, to anyone who will listen,
Of how I travelled in foreign lands!
I forgot the story of the First Covenant.
In the garden of heaven,
When I drank the fiery cup of awareness I felt uneasy.
I have always searched for the truth about the world,
Showing the celestial heights of my thought.
Such was my fickle temperament
That in no place under the sky could I settle for good.
At times I cleared the Ka'bah of stone idols,
But at times put statues in the same sanctuary;
At times, to savour talk, I went to Mount Sinai,
And hid the eternal light in the folds of my sleeve;
By my own people I was hung on the cross;
I travelled to the skies, leaving earth behind.
For years I hid in the Cave of Hira;
I served the world its last cup of wine;
Arriving in India, I sang the Divine Song;
I took a fancy to the land of Greece;
When India did not heed my call,
I went to live in China and Japan;
I saw the world composed of atoms,
Contrary to what the men of faith taught.
By stirring up the conflict between reason and faith,
I soaked in blood hundreds of lands.
When I failed to probe the reality of the stars,
I spent nights on end wrapped in thought.
The sword of the Church could not frighten me;
I taught the proposition of the revolving earth.
I donned the lens of far-seeing reason,
And told the world the secret of gravity.
I captured rays and the restless lightning,
Making this earth the envy of paradise.
But although my reason held the world captive to my ring,
Yet I remained ignorant of the secret of existence.
When at last my eyes, worshippers of appearance, were opened,
I found it already lodged in the mansion of my heart!

Muhammad Iqbal (1877-1938)(translated by Mustansir Mir)

---

[19] *Tulip in the Desert, selected poems of Muhammad Iqbal.* Ed. and trans. Mustansir Mir. Kingston, Canada: McGill-Queen's University Press, 2008.

New Shrine

To tell the truth, O Brahmin, if you don't mind,

The idols in your idol house have outlived their use.

From your idols you learned only malice for your people,

From his god, the preacher learned only the tumult of war.

Fed up at last I gave up both the temple and the mosque,

Rejected the preacher's sermons and your false legends.

You think there's a god in a stone image,

To me, homeland's every speck of dust is a god.

Come, let's undo the barriers of estrangement for once,

Reunite the separated and erase the mark of otherness.

My heart has been a wilderness for too long.

Come, let's build a new shrine in this land,

Our sacred shrine should be the loftiest of all.

Let us raise its pinnacle to the hem of the skies.

We will give such a love potion to worshippers all

That every morning they will sing sweet songs.

In songs of the holy ones power and peace live together.

Only love can bring deliverance to dwellers of this earth.

Muhammad Iqbal (1877-1938)
(translated by Abdul Jabbar)

A Child's Prayer

A prayer rises from my lips like a wish.

Beseeching you, Almighty, to make my life a lamp.

May my presence dispel the world's darkness.

May I be the source of light everywhere.

May my breath beautify my country

The way a flower beautifies a garden.

May my life be in the form of a moth

In love with the lamp of knowledge.

May my life's goal be helping the poor

And loving the afflicted and the weak.

O my Creator, save me from evil deeds.

Make me tread the path that leads to virtue.

Muhammad Iqbal (1877-1938)
(translated by Abdul Jabbar)

Prayer

Let's also raise our hands in prayer
We who've forgotten the ritual of praying.
We who remember no god, nor idol
Other than the tenderness of love.
Let's pray that the Beauty of life
May infuse the sweetness of tomorrow
Into the bitterness of today.
Those who are too weak to bear
The crushing weight of time.
Make days and nights light on them.
For those denied even the promise of a hopeful dawn
Bless their nights with light.
For those with no path to follow
Show their eyes a new way.
Those who follow a creed of lies and deceit
Give them the courage to deny and question.
The heads that await the sword of cruelty
Give them the strength to shake off the murderer's hand.
In the hidden secret of love is the life flame
It cries out for acknowledgement to satisfy the soul.
The world of truth which rankles in the heart like a thorn
If confessed will end the torment.

> Faiz Ahmed Faiz (1911-1984)
> (translated by Abdul Jabbar)

An excerpt from "The Subject of Poetry"

The crowds of people in these glittering cities
Why do they live with only one hope, that of dying?
These beautiful fields that can barely contain their youthful vigor
Why only hunger grows in them?

These mysterious unyielding walls on all sides
Have witnessed the snuffing out of a thousand youthful flames.
At every step are slaughterhouses of those dreams
Whose reflections have illumined thousands of minds.

> Faiz Ahmed Faiz (1911-1984)
> (translated by Abdul Jabbar)

POEMS FOR FURTHER READING

To Toussaint L'Ouverture

Toussaint, the most unhappy man of men!
Whether the whistling rustic tend his plow
Within thy hearing, or thy head be now
Pillowed in some deep dungeon's earless den –
O miserable chieftain! Where and when
Wilt thou find patience? Yet die not; do thou
Wear rather in thy bonds a cheerful brow;
Though fallen thyself, never to rise again,
Live, and take comfort. Thou hast left behind
Powers that will work for thee: air, earth, and skies;
There's not a breathing of the common wind
That will forget thee; thou hast great allies;
Thy friends are exultations, agonies,
And love, and man's unconquerable mind.

William Wordsworth (1770-1850)

Three poems by George Gordon, Lord Byron (1788-1824)
She Walks in Beauty

I

She walks in Beauty, like the night
    Of cloudless climes and starry skies;
And all that's best of dark and bright
    Meet in her aspect and her eyes:
Thus mellowed to that tender light
    Which Heaven to gaudy day denies.

II

One shade the more, one ray the less,
    Had half impaired the nameless grace
Which waves in every raven tress,
    Or softly lightens o'er her face;
Where thoughts serenely sweet express,
    How pure, how dear their dwelling place.

III

And on that cheek, and o'er that brow,
    So soft, so calm, yet eloquent,
The smiles that win, the tints that glow,
    But tell of days in goodness spent,

A mind at peace with all below,
A heart whose love is innocent!

Sonnet on Chillon

Eternal Spirit of the chainless Mind!
Brightest in dungeons, Liberty! Thou art,
For there thy habitation is the heart –
The heart which love of thee alone can bind;
And when thy sons to fetters are consigned –
To fetters, and the damp vault's dayless gloom,
Their country conquers with their martyrdom,
And Freedom's fame finds wings on evry wind.
Chillon! Thy prison is a holy place,
And thy sad floor an altar – for 'twas trod,
Until his very steps have left a trace
Worn, as if thy cold pavement were a sod,
By Bonnivard! – May none those marks efface!
For they appeal from tyranny to God.

Childe Harold's Pilgrimage from Canto IV

178

There is a pleasure in the pathless woods,
There is a rapture on the lonely shore,
There is society, where none intrudes,
By the deep Sea, and Music in its roar:
I love not Man the less, but Nature more,
From these our interviews, in which I steal
From all I may be, or have been before,
To mingle with the Universe, and feel
What I can ne'er express – yet can not all conceal.

179

Roll on, thou deep and dark blue Ocean – roll!
Ten thousand fleets sweep over thee in vain;
Man marks the earth with ruin – his control
Stops with the shore; -- upon the watery plain
The wrecks are all they deed, nor doth remain
A shadow of man's ravage, save his own,
When, for a moment, like a drop of rain,
He sinks into thy depths with bubbling groan –
Without a grave – unknelled, uncoffined, and unknown.

184

And I have loved thee, Ocean! And my joy
Of youthful sports was on they breast to be
Borne, like they bubbles, onward: from a boy
I wantoned with thy breakers – they to me

Were a delight; and if the freshening sea
Made them a terror – 'twas a pleasing fear,
For I was as it were a Child of thee,
And trusted to thy billows far and near,
And laid my hand upon thy mane – as I do here.

Ulysses

It little profits that an idle king,
By this still hearth, among these barren crags,
Matched with an agèd wife, I mete and dole
Unequal laws unto a savage race,
That hoard, and sleep, and feed, and know not me.
I cannot rest from travel: I will drink
Life to the lees: all times I have enjoyed
Greatly, have suffered greatly, both with those
That loved me, and alone; on shore, and when
Through scudding drifts the rainy Hyades
Vexed the dim sea: I am become a name;
For always roaming with a hungry heart
Much have I seen and known; cities of men
And manners, climates, councils, governments,
Myself not least, but honoured of them all;
And drunk delight of battle with my peers,
Far on the ringing plains of windy Troy.
I am a part of all that I have met;
Yet all experience is an arch wherethrough
Gleams that untravelled world, whose margin fades
For ever and for ever when I move.
How dull it is to pause, to make an end,
To rust unburnished, not to shine in use!
As though to breathe were life. Life piled on life
Were all too little, and of one to me
Little remains: but every hour is saved
From that eternal silence, something more,
A bringer of new things; and vile it were
For some three suns to store and hoard myself,
And this grey spirit yearning in desire
To follow knowledge like a sinking star,
Beyond the utmost bound of human thought.
This my son, mine own Telemachus,
To whom I leave the sceptre and the isle—
Well-loved of me, discerning to fulfil
This labour, by slow prudence to make mild
A rugged people, and through soft degrees
Subdue them to the useful and the good.
Most blameless is he, centred in the sphere

Of common duties, decent not to fail
In offices of tenderness, and pay
Meet adoration to my household gods,
When I am gone. He works his work, I mine.
There lies the port; the vessel puffs her sail:
There gloom the dark broad seas. My mariners,
Souls that have toiled, and wrought, and thought with me—
That ever with a frolic welcome took
The thunder and the sunshine, and opposed
Free hearts, free foreheads—you and I are old;
Old age hath yet his honour and his toil;
Death closes all: but something ere the end,
Some work of noble note, may yet be done,
Not unbecoming men that strove with Gods.
The lights begin to twinkle from the rocks:
The long day wanes: the slow moon climbs: the deep
Moans round with many voices. Come, my friends,
'Tis not too late to seek a newer world.
Push off, and sitting well in order smite
The sounding furrows; for my purpose holds
To sail beyond the sunset, and the baths
Of all the western stars, until I die.
It may be that the gulfs will wash us down:
It may be we shall touch the Happy Isles,
And see the great Achilles, whom we knew
Though much is taken, much abides; and though
We are not now that strength which in old days
Moved earth and heaven; that which we are, we are;
One equal temper of heroic hearts,
Made weak by time and fate, but strong in will
To strive, to seek, to find, and not to yield.

Alfred, Lord Tennyson (1809-1892)

Tithonus

The woods decay, the woods decay and fall,
The vapours weep their burthen to the ground,
Man comes and tills the field and lies beneath,
And after many a summer dies the swan.
Me only cruel immortality
Consumes: I wither slowly in thine arms,
Here at the quiet limit of the world,
A white-haired shadow roaming like a dream
The ever-silent spaces of the East,
Far-folded mists, and gleaming halls of morn.
Alas! for this gray shadow, once a man -
So glorious in his beauty and thy choice,

Who madest him thy chosen, that he seemed
To his great heart none other than a God!
I asked thee, "Give me immortality."
Then didst thou grant mine asking with a smile,
Like wealthy men who care not how they give.
But thy strong Hours indignant worked their wills,
And beat me down and marred and wasted me,
And though they could not end me, left me maimed
To dwell in presence of immortal youth,
Immortal age beside immortal youth,
And all I was, in ashes. Can thy love,
Thy beauty, make amends, though even now,
Close over us, the silver star, thy guide,
Shines in those tremulous eyes that fill with tears
To hear me? Let me go: take back thy gift:
Why should a man desire in any way
To vary from the kindly race of men,
Or pass beyond the goal of ordinance
Where all should pause, as is most meet for all?
A soft air fans the cloud apart; there comes
A glimpse of that dark world where I was born.
Once more the old mysterious glimmer steals
From thy pure brows, and from thy shoulders pure,
And bosom beating with a heart renewed.
Thy cheek begins to redden through the gloom,
Thy sweet eyes brighten slowly close to mine,
Ere yet they blind the stars, and the wild team
Which love thee, yearning for thy yoke, arise,
And shake the darkness from their loosened manes,
And beat the twilight into flakes of fire.
Lo! ever thus thou growest beautiful
In silence, then before thine answer given
Departest, and thy tears are on my cheek.
Why wilt thou ever scare me with thy tears,
And make me tremble lest a saying learnt,
In days far-off, on that dark earth, be true?
"The Gods themselves cannot recall their gifts."

Ay me! ay me! with what another heart
In days far-off, and with what other eyes
I used to watch -if I be he that watched -
The lucid outline forming round thee; saw
The dim curls kindle into sunny rings;
Changed with thy mystic change, and felt my blood
Glow with the glow that slowly crimsoned all
Thy presence and thy portals, while I lay,
Mouth, forehead, eyelids, growing dewy-warm

With kisses balmier than half-opening buds
Of April, and could hear the lips that kissed
Whispering I knew not what of wild and sweet,
Like that strange song I heard Apollo sing,
While Ilion like a mist rose into towers.

Yet hold me not for ever in thine East:
How can my nature longer mix with thine?
Coldly thy rosy shadows bathe me, cold
Are all thy lights, and cold my wrinkled feet
Upon thy glimmering thresholds, when the steam
Floats up from those dim fields about the homes
Of happy men that have the power to die,
And grassy barrows of the happier dead.
Release me, and restore me to the ground;
Thou seest all things, thou wilt see my grave:
Thou wilt renew thy beauty morn by morn;
I earth in earth forget these empty courts,
And thee returning on thy silver wheels.

Alfred, Lord Tennyson (1809-1892)

My Last Duchess

That's my last Duchess painted on the wall,
Looking as if she were alive. I call
That piece a wonder, now: Frà Pandolf's hands
Worked busily a day, and there she stands.
Will 't please you sit and look at her? I said
'Frà Pandolf' by design, for never read
Strangers like you that pictured countenance,
The depth and passion of its earnest glance,
But to myself they turned (since none puts by
The curtain I have drawn for you, but I)
And seemed as they would ask me, if they durst,
How such a glance came there; so, not the first
Are you to turn and ask thus. Sir, 't was not
Her husband's presence only, called that spot
Of joy into the Duchess' cheek: perhaps
Frà Pandolf chanced to say, 'Her mantle laps
Over my lady's wrist too much,' or 'Paint
Must never hope to reproduce the faint
Half-flush that dies along her throat:' such stuff
Was courtesy, she thought, and cause enough
For calling up that spot of joy. She had
A heart -- how shall I say? -- too soon made glad,
Too easily impressed; she liked whate'er
She looked on, and her looks went everywhere.

Sir, 't was all one! My favour at her breast,
The dropping of the daylight in the West,
The bough of cherries some officious fool
Broke in the orchard for her, the white mule
She rode with round the terrace -- all and each
Would draw from her alike the approving speech,
Or blush, at least. She thanked men, -- good! but thanked
Somehow -- I know not how -- as if she ranked
My gift of a nine-hundred-years-old name
With anybody's gift. Who'd stoop to blame
This sort of trifling? Even had you skill
In speech -- (which I have not) -- to make your will
Quite clear to such an one, and say, 'Just this
Or that in you disgusts me; here you miss,
Or there exceed the mark' -- and if she let
Herself be lessoned so, nor plainly set
Her wits to yours, forsooth, and made excuse,
--e'en then would be some stooping; and I choose
Never to stoop. Oh, sir, she smiled, no doubt,
Whene'er I passed her; but who passed without
Much the same smile? This grew; I gave commands;
Then all smiles stopped together. There she stands
As if alive. Will 't please you rise? We'll meet
The company below then. I repeat,
The Count your master's known munificence
Is ample warrant that no just pretence
Of mine for dowry will be disallowed;
Though his fair daughter's self, as I avowed
At starting, is my object. Nay, we'll go
Together down, sir. Notice Neptune, though,
Taming a sea-horse, thought a rarity,
Which Claus of Innsbruck cast in bronze for me!

Robert Browning (1812-1889)

The Buried Life

LIGHT flows our war of mocking words, and yet
Behold, with tears mine eyes are wet!
I feel a nameless sadness o'er me roll.
Yes, yes, we know that we can jest,
We know, we know that we can smile!
But there 's a something in this breast,
To which thy light words bring no rest,
And thy gay smiles no anodyne;
Give me thy hand, and hush awhile,
And turn those limpid eyes on mine,
And let me read there, love! thy inmost soul.

Alas! is even love too weak
To unlock the heart, and let it speak?
Are even lovers powerless to reveal
I knew the mass of men conceal'd
Their thoughts, for fear that if reveal'd
They would by other men be met
With blank indifference, or with blame reprov'd;
I knew they liv'd and mov'd
Trick'd in disguises, alien to the rest
Of men, and alien to themselves—and yet
The same heart beats in every human breast!

But we, my love!—doth a like spell benumb
Our hearts, our voices?—must we too be dumb?
Ah! well for us, if even we,
Even for a moment, can get free
Our heart, and have our lips unchain'd;
For that which seals them hath been deep-ordain'd!

Fate, which foresaw
How frivolous a baby man would be—
By what distractions he would be possess'd,
How he would pour himself in every strife,
And well-nigh change his own identity—
That it might keep from his capricious play
His genuine self, and force him to obey
Even in his own despite his being's law,
Bade through the deep recesses of our breast
The unregarded river of our life
Pursue with indiscernible flow its way
And that we should not see
The buried stream, and seem to be
Eddying at large in blind uncertainty,
Though driving on with it eternally.

But often, in the world's most crowded streets,
But often, in the din of strife,
There rises an unspeakable desire
After the knowledge of our buried life;
A thirst to spend our fire and restless force
In tracking out our true, original course;
A longing to inquire
Into the mystery of this heart which beats
So wild, so deep in us—to know
Whence our lives come and where they go.

And many a man in his own breast then delves
But deep enough, alas! none ever mines.

And we have been on many thousand lines,
And we have shown, on each, spirit and power;
But hardly have we, for one little hour,
Been on our own line, have we been ourselves—
Hardly had skill to utter one of all
The nameless feelings that course through our breast,
But they course on for ever unexpress'd.
And long we try in vain to speak and act
Our hidden self, and what we say and do
Is eloquent, is well—but 't is not true!
And then we will no more be rack'd
With inward striving, and demand
Of all the thousand nothings of the hour
Their stupefying power;
Ah yes, and they benumb us at our call!
Yet still, from time to time, vague and forlorn,
From the soul's subterranean depth upborne
As from an infinitely distant land,
Come airs, and floating echoes, and convey
A melancholy into all our day.

Only—but this is rare—
When a beloved hand is laid in ours,
When, jaded with the rush and glare
Of the interminable hours,
Our eyes can in another's eyes read clear,
When our world-deafen'd ear
Is by the tones of a lov'd voice caress'd—
A bolt is shot back somewhere in our breast,
And a lost pulse of feeling stirs again.
The eye sinks inward, and the heart lies plain,
And what we mean, we say, and what we would, we know.
A man becomes aware of his life's flow,
And hears its winding murmur, and he sees
The meadows where it glides, the sun, the breeze.

And there arrives a lull in the hot race
Wherein he doth for ever chase
The flying and elusive shadow, rest.
An air of coolness plays upon his face,
And an unwonted calm pervades his breast.
And then he thinks he knows
The hills where his life rose,
And the sea where it goes.

Matthew Arnold (1822-1888)

Memorial Verses

Goethe in Weimar sleeps, and Greece,
Long since, saw Byron's struggle cease.
But one such death remain'd to come;
The last poetic voice is dumb—
We stand to-day by Wordsworth's tomb.

When Byron's eyes were shut in death,
We bow'd our head and held our breath.
He taught us little; but our soul
Had felt him like the thunder's roll.
With shivering heart the strife we saw
Of passion with eternal law;
And yet with reverential awe
We watch'd the fount of fiery life
Which served for that Titanic strife.

When Goethe's death was told, we said:
Sunk, then, is Europe's sagest head.
Physician of the iron age,
Goethe has done his pilgrimage.
He took the suffering human race,
He read each wound, each weakness clear;
And struck his finger on the place,
And said: Thou ailest here, and here!

He look'd on Europe's dying hour
Of fitful dream and feverish power;
His eye plunged down the weltering strife,
The turmoil of expiring life—
He said: The end is everywhere,
Art still has truth, take refuge there!
And he was happy, if to know
Causes of things, and far below
His feet to see the lurid flow
Of terror, and insane distress,
And headlong fate, be happiness.

And Wordsworth!—Ah, pale ghosts, rejoice!
For never has such soothing voice
Been to your shadowy world convey'd,
Since erst, at morn, some wandering shade
Heard the clear song of Orpheus come
Through Hades, and the mournful gloom.
Wordsworth has gone from us—and ye,
Ah, may ye feel his voice as we!
He too upon a wintry clime
Had fallen—on this iron time

647

Of doubts, disputes, distractions, fears.
He found us when the age had bound
Our souls in its benumbing round;
He spoke, and loosed our heart in tears.
He laid us as we lay at birth
On the cool flowery lap of earth,

Smiles broke from us and we had ease;
The hills were round us, and the breeze
Went o'er the sun-lit fields again;
Our foreheads felt the wind and rain.
Our youth return'd; for there was shed
On spirits that had long been dead,
Spirits dried up and closely furl'd,
The freshness of the early world.

Ah! since dark days still bring to light
Man's prudence and man's fiery might,
Time may restore us in his course
Goethe's sage mind and Byron's force;
But where will Europe's latter hour
Again find Wordsworth's healing power?
Others will teach us how to dare,
And against fear our breast to steel;
Others will strengthen us to bear—
But who, ah! who, will make us feel?
The cloud of mortal destiny,
Others will front it fearlessly—
But who, like him, will put it by?
Keep fresh the grass upon his grave,
O Rotha, with thy living wave!
Sing him thy best! for few or none
Hears thy voice right, now he is gone.

Matthew Arnold (1822-1888)

The Second Coming

Turning and turning in the widening gyre
The falcon cannot hear the falconer;
Things fall apart; the centre cannot hold;
Mere anarchy is loosed upon the world,
The blood-dimmed tide is loosed, and everywhere
The ceremony of innocence is drowned;
The best lack all conviction, while the worst
Are full of passionate intensity.

Surely some revelation is at hand;
Surely the Second Coming is at hand.
The Second Coming! Hardly are those words out

648

When a vast image out of Spiritus Mundi
Troubles my sight: a waste of desert sand;
A shape with lion body and the head of a man,
A gaze blank and pitiless as the sun,
Is moving its slow thighs, while all about it
Wind shadows of the indignant desert birds.

The darkness drops again but now I know
That twenty centuries of stony sleep
Were vexed to nightmare by a rocking cradle,
And what rough beast, its hour come round at last,
Slouches towards Bethlehem to be born?

William Butler Yeats (1865-1939)

Let America Be America Again

Let America be America again.
Let it be the dream it used to be.
Let it be the pioneer on the plain
Seeking a home where he himself is free.

(America never was America to me.)

Let America be the dream the dreamers dreamed—
Let it be that great strong land of love
Where never kings connive nor tyrants scheme
That any man be crushed by one above.

(It never was America to me.)

O, let my land be a land where Liberty
Is crowned with no false patriotic wreath,
But opportunity is real, and life is free,
Equality is in the air we breathe.

(There's never been equality for me,
Nor freedom in this "homeland of the free.")

Say, who are you that mumbles in the dark?
And who are you that draws your veil across the stars?

I am the poor white, fooled and pushed apart,
I am the Negro bearing slavery's scars.
I am the red man driven from the land,
I am the immigrant clutching the hope I seek—
And finding only the same old stupid plan
Of dog eat dog, of mighty crush the weak.

I am the young man, full of strength and hope,
Tangled in that ancient endless chain
Of profit, power, gain, of grab the land!

649

Of grab the gold! Of grab the ways of satisfying need!
Of work the men! Of take the pay!
Of owning everything for one's own greed!

I am the farmer, bondsman to the soil.
I am the worker sold to the machine.
I am the Negro, servant to you all.
I am the people, humble, hungry, mean—
Hungry yet today despite the dream.
Beaten yet today—O, Pioneers!
I am the man who never got ahead,
The poorest worker bartered through the years.

Yet I'm the one who dreamt our basic dream
In the Old World while still a serf of kings,
Who dreamt a dream so strong, so brave, so true,
That even yet its mighty daring sings
In every brick and stone, in every furrow turned
That's made America the land it has become.
O, I'm the man who sailed those early seas
In search of what I meant to be my home—
For I'm the one who left dark Ireland's shore,
And Poland's plain, and England's grassy lea,
And torn from Black Africa's strand I came
To build a "homeland of the free."

The free?

Who said the free? Not me?
Surely not me? The millions on relief today?
The millions shot down when we strike?
The millions who have nothing for our pay?
For all the dreams we've dreamed
And all the songs we've sung
And all the hopes we've held
And all the flags we've hung,
The millions who have nothing for our pay—
Except the dream that's almost dead today.

O, let America be America again—
The land that never has been yet—
And yet must be—the land where every man is free.
The land that's mine—the poor man's, Indian's, Negro's, ME—
Who made America,
Whose sweat and blood, whose faith and pain,
Whose hand at the foundry, whose plow in the rain,
Must bring back our mighty dream again.

Sure, call me any ugly name you choose—
The steel of freedom does not stain.

From those who live like leeches on the people's lives,
We must take back our land again,
America!

O, yes,
I say it plain,
America never was America to me,
And yet I swear this oath—
America will be!

Out of the rack and ruin of our gangster death,
The rape and rot of graft, and stealth, and lies,
We, the people, must redeem
The land, the mines, the plants, the rivers.
The mountains and the endless plain—
All, all the stretch of these great green states—
And make America again!

Langston Hughes (1902-1967)

You can hear Marguerite Guzman Bouvard, author of The Invisible Wounds of War: Coming Home from Iraq and Afghanistan, *reading her poem, "Specialist Noah Charles Pierce" and get background information on the subject of suicides in the U.S. military using this link:*
http://www.democracynow.org/2012/8/21/the_invisible_wounds_of_war_number

Specialist Noah Charles Pierce

In the Dungeon of my Skin

In Suez they thought I was Egyptian
In Manitoba they wonder if I'm native-born
In India they said derisively:
Indian Christian! Goan! Anglo-Indian!
In the Bronx, wayside vendors spoke to me
in the guttural music of Cervantes and Borges.
A long time ago, in my native place
on coral shores beside the Pirates' Main
they said, "You surely must be Spanish."
In a country famous for its indiscriminate racial copulation
ethnic nomenclature was the order of the day
and "Spanish"
was a mantle that gathered in its folds
all who bore or seemed to bear some trace,
however faint, of European ancestry.
It labelled you a cut above
the blacks and Hindus, low men on the totem pole;
rendered you a more pleasing place in the racial mosaic.

Now though the landscape of my being
negates the burnished faces of my youth
while molten rhythms
forged from the heart of Africa and India
elude me now
and I have cast from consciousness
satiric folk-songs spawned from the tortured metres of our
bastard English tongue
have clipped the bonds of cultures and boundaries
and made myself a universal woman
yet this poor frame, no castle
proves itself no fortress, but a dungeon from which
there can be no release.

Madeline Coopsammy (b. 1939)

Uluhaimalama

We have gathered
With manacled hands;
We have gathered
With shackled feet;
We have gathered
In the dust of forget
Seeking the vein
Which will not collapse
We have bolted
The gunner's fence
Given sacrament
On bloodstained walls.
We have linked souls
End to end
Against the razor's slice.
We have kissed brothers
In frigid cells
Pressing our mouths
Against their ice-hard pain.
We have feasted well
On the stones of this land:
We have gathered
In dark places
And put down roots.

We have covered the Earth
Bold flowers for her crown
We have climbed
The high wire of treason —
We will not fall.

(O Moon, lift the brittle white dust,
The red augury of tears;
Call forth the sea,
Enchant its blue heart;
Form this place holy,
And holy again.)

Mahealani Kamauu (b. 1947)

How to Watch Your Brother Die

1 When the call comes, be calm.
2 Say to your wife, "My brother is dying. I have to fly
   to California."
3 Try not to be too shocked that he already looks like

653

simile

a cadaver.

4 Say to the young man sitting by your brother's side,
"I'm his brother."

5 Try not to be shocked when the young man says,
"I'm his lover. Thanks for coming."

6 Listen to the doctor with a steel face on.

7 Sign the necessary forms.

8 Tell the doctor you will take care of everything.

9 Wonder why doctors are so remote.

10 Watch the lover's eyes as they stare into
your brother's eyes as they stare into
space.

11 Wonder what they see there.

12 Remember the time he was jealous and
opened your eyebrow with a sharp stick.

13 Forgive him out loud
even if he can't
understand you.

14 Realize the scar will be
all that's left of him.

15 Over coffee in the hospital cafeteria
say to the lover, "You're an extremely good-looking
young man."
Hear him say,

16 "I never thought I was good enough looking to
deserve your brother."

17 Watch the tears well up in his eyes. Say,
"I'm sorry. I don't know what it means to be
the lover of another man."
Hear him say,

18 "It's just like a wife, only the commitment is
deeper because the odds against you are so much
greater."

19 Say nothing, but
take his hand like a brother's.

20 Drive to Mexico for unproven drugs that might
help him live longer.

21 Explain what they are to the border guard.

22 Fill with rage when he informs you,
"You can't bring those across."

23 Begin to grow loud.

24 Feel the lover's hand on your arm
restraining you. See in the guard's eye

25 how much a man can hate another man.

holding (sense of touch)

another eye

26 Say to the lover, "How can you stand it?"
Hear him say, "You get used to it."
27 Think of one of your children getting used to
another man's hatred.

society's indifference / views about the gay community

28 Call your wife, on the telephone. Tell her,
"He hasn't much time.
29 I'll be home soon." Before you hang up say,
"How could anyone's committment be deeper than
a husband and wife?" Hear her say,
30 "Please. I don't want to know the details."

When he slips into an irrevocable coma,
31 hold his lover in your arms while he sobs,
no longer strong. Wonder how much longer
you will be able to be strong.
32
33 Feel how it feels to hold a man in your arms
whose arms are used to holding men.
34 Offer God anything to bring your brother back.
35 Know you have nothing God could possibly want.
36 Curse God, but do not
abandon Him.

holding
sympathize, comfort, support

Stare at the face of the funeral director
37 when he tells you he will not
embalm the body for fear of
contamination. Let him see in your eyes
38 how much a man can hate another man.

eyes
turnover of power
— minor someone's emotion or feelings
The eyes hold more impact or reveal truths about us than what we say

39 Stand beside a casket covered in flowers,
white flowers. Say,
40 "Thank you for coming," to each of the several hundred
men
who file past in tears, some of them
holding hands. Know that your brother's life
41
was not what you imagined. Overhear two
42
mourners say, "I wonder who'll be next?" and
"I don't care anymore,
as long as it isn't you."

peace, purity / cleanliness

unity (?)
come together to be strong
holding again

Arrange to take an early flight home. 43
His lover will drive you to the airport. 44
When your flight is announced say, 45
awkwardly, "If I can do anything, please
let me know." Do not flinch when he says, 46
"Forgive yourself for not wanting to know him
after he told you. He did."
Stop and let it soak in. Say, 47
"He forgave me, or he knew himself?"

he was completely unaware of his brother's lifestyle and he's now seeing his brothers' whole life; friends, considered lover, family, flash before his eyes.

I think there are eye / sight references because the author is trying to suggest we should learn to observe and just see / open our eyes to realities or social issues

they don't conform to society's conventional heterosexuality. Therefore instigates fear, people are afraid of what they don't know

Like in the case of HIV, there is no knowledge / studies yet at the time so they squirm / stigma is prevalent back then.

be more understanding / have the initiative to learn / accept people for who they are

48 "Both," the lover will say, not knowing what else
to do. Hold him like a brother while he
49 kisses you on the cheek. Think that
50 you haven't been kissed by a man since
your father died. Think,
51 "This is no moment not to be strong."

52 Fly first class and drink Scotch. Stroke
your split eyebrow with a finger and
53 think of your brother alive. Smile
at the memory and think
how your children will feel in your arms,
warm and friendly and without challenge.

Michael Lassell (b. 1947)

Escapism?

"Smile at the memory" thinking that your kids won't experience that

Black Cat Blues

I showed up for jury duty—
turns out the one on trial was me.

Paid me for my time & still
I couldn't make bail.

Judge that showed up
was my ex-wife.

Now that was some
hard time.

She sentenced me
to remarry.

I chose firing squad instead.
Wouldn't you know it—

Plenty of volunteers
to take the first shot

But no one wanted to spring
for the bullets.

Governor commuted my sentence to life
in a cell more comfortable

Than this here skin
I been living in.

Kevin Young (b. 1970)

The Prison Cell

It is possible...
It is possible at least sometimes...
It is possible especially now
To ride a horse

Inside a prison cell
And run away...

It is possible for prison walls
To disappear,
For the cell to become a distant land
Without frontiers:

What did you do with the walls?
I gave them back to the rocks.
And what did you do with the ceiling?
I turned it into a saddle.
And your chain?
I turned it into a pencil.

The prison guard got angry.
He put an end to the dialogue.
He said he didn't care for poetry
And bolted the door of my cell.

He came back to see me
In the morning.
He shouted at me:

Where did all this water come from?
I brought it from the Nile.
And the trees?
From the orchards of Damascus.
And the music?
From my heartbeat.

The prison guard got mad.
He put an end to my dialogue.
He said he didn't like my poetry,
And bolted the door of my cell.

But he returned in the evening:

Where did this moon come from?
From the nights of Baghdad.
And the wine?
From the vineyards of Algiers.
And this freedom?
From the chain you tied me with last night.

The prison guard grew so sad...
He begged me to give him back
His freedom.

Mahmoud Darwish (1941-2008)
(Translated by Ben Bennani)

Tailgate in the Twilight Zone

Who is that
in my rear view mirror
riding my bumper on the highway
pushing me
with the brute force
of unsympathetic impatience
when I am an old man
and my reflexes are slower?

Oh
I recognize him.
It's me
in my youth
chomping at the bit
grinding my teeth
in a big hurry
to get where I am now.

Good luck boy.
I'd take it easy if I were you.
This trip is quicker than you think.
The ride ends
sooner than you want.
No point
talking to you though.
You're going too fast to listen.
You wouldn't believe me anyway.
I better just pull over
so you can catch up to me
at the
end
of the road.

Gary Becker (b. 1947)

Pro-Peace Poems and Songs

Poet Laureate Richard Blanco, a Cuban-American born in Madrid and raised and educated in Miami, became the first Hispanic and first openly gay man to read the inaugural poem, on January 21, 2013, for President Barack Obama's second term.

Start this part of the chapter by reading Richard Blanco's poem "One Today" online. One way to get a deeper understanding of this poem is by comparing and contrasting its major themes with those of Langston Hughes' famous poem "Let America Be America Again (pages 649-651). You may use the following comments by this book's author before writing your own interpretation.

An overarching theme in both poems concerns truth and reconciliation in search of peace. Both poets celebrate the struggles, resilience, achievements, and optimism of America's "common man." They map the immense promise of America and weave its many cultural strands into a desired mosaic. Blanco's poem opens with words that suggest at least one manifestation of national unity at the physical level:

> "One sun rose on us today, kindled over our shores,
>
> peeking over the Smokies, greeting the faces
>
> of the Great Lakes, spreading a simple truth
>
> across the Great Plains, then charging across the Rockies."

Celebrating people's daily duties and "the rhythm of traffic lights," the poem affirms the importance of each individual activity: "All of us as vital as the one light we move through." Blanco shuns facile optimism by showing Americans struggling and working hard to provide opportunities for their children: ". . . ring up groceries as my mother did/ for twenty years, so I could write this poem." About his father's hard work, he speaks of "hands . . . as worn as my father's cutting sugarcane/so my brother and I could have books and shoes."

Langston Hughes' poem also details the common man's struggles. In comparison with Blanco, Hughes has a stronger strain of despairing moments because his poem covers a much broader sweep of America's history. His words are especially poignant when he writes about those groups who were not embraced by the American dream and empathizes with the American youth whose idealistic longings collide with America's crass materialism and greed:

> "I am the poor white, fooled and pushed apart,/I am the Negro bearing slavery's scars./I am the red man driven from the land,/I am the immigrant clutching the hope I seek—/And finding only the same old stupid plan/Of dog eat dog, of mighty crush the weak./I am the young man, full of strength and hope,/ Tangled in that ancient endless chain/ Of profit, power, gain, of grab the land! . . . ./ Of owning everything for one's own greed! /. . . . I am the man who never got ahead,/ The poorest worker bartered through the years."

Like Hughes, Blanco ponders the somber side of America's as yet unfulfilled promise. He introduces a painful loss in the following lines:

"... the impossible vocabulary of sorrow that won't explain
the empty desks of twenty children marked absent/today, and forever."

The poem does not tell us why those twenty students are absent "forever," but we may be able to surmise that their circumstances might have robbed them of the joys and opportunities of childhood. Blanco also mentions people's state of exhaustion from labor: "One sky, toward which we sometimes lift our eyes tired from work." It seems that Blanco may also be holding back stronger criticism of his nation because the poem was meant to celebrate a unique moment in the country's history: For the first time an African-American was being sworn in as President. That moment injected revolutionary hope in the country's history.

Ultimately, both poems are an affirmation of optimism about America's future. Blanco affirms the joy of America's daily symphony of many voices: "Hear it/ through the day's gorgeous din of honking cabs,/buses launching down avenues, the symphony/of footsteps, guitars, and screeching subways,/the unexpected song bird on your clothes line." Even the sky "yields to our resilience." The poem begins with dawn and ends with dusk. Chronicling one historic day in the nation's history, the poem concludes with lines brimming with breathless excitement of hope that the people of America are about to discover, name, and map a "new constellation."

After a vivid rendition of the exciting idea, despairing reality, and hopeful potential of the American dream, Hughes also ends his poem on a strident, optimistic note:

"O, let America be America again—
The land that never has been –
And yet must be—the land where every man is free."

Masters of War (song)

Come you masters of war
You that build all the guns
You that build the death planes
You that build the big bombs
You that hide behind walls
You that hide behind desks
I just want you to know
I can see through your masks

You that never done nothin'
But build to destroy
You play with my world
Like it's your little toy
You put a gun in my hand

And you hide from my eyes
And you turn and run farther
When the fast bullets fly

Like Judas of old
You lie and deceive
A world war can be won
You want me to believe
But I see through your eyes
And I see through your brain
Like I see through the water
That runs down my drain

You fasten the triggers
For the others to fire
Then you set back and watch
When the death count gets higher
You hide in your mansion
As young people's blood
Flows out of their bodies
And is buried in the mud

You've thrown the worst fear
That can ever be hurled
Fear to bring children
Into the world
For threatening my baby
Unborn and unnamed
You ain't worth the blood
That runs in your veins

How much do I know
To talk out of turn
You might say that I'm young
You might say I'm unlearned
But there's one thing I know
Though I'm younger than you
Even Jesus would never
Forgive what you do

Let me ask you one question
Is your money that good
Will it buy you forgiveness
Do you think that it could
I think you will find
When your death takes its toll
All the money you made
Will never buy back your soul

And I hope that you die
And your death'll come soon
I will follow your casket
In the pale afternoon
And I'll watch while you're lowered
Down to your deathbed
And I'll stand o'er your grave
'Til I'm sure that you're dead.

Bob Dylan (b. 1941)

Lives in the Balance (song)

I've been waiting for something to happen
For a week or a month or a year
With the blood in the ink of the headlines
And the sound of the crowd in my ear
You might ask what it takes to remember
When you know that you've seen it before
Where a government lies to a people
And a country is drifting to war

And there's a shadow on the faces
Of the men who send the guns
To the wars that are fought in places
Where their business interest runs

On the radio talk shows and the TV
You hear one thing again and again
How the USA stands for freedom
And we come to the aid of a friend
But who are the ones that we call our friends—
These governments killing their own?
Or the people who finally can't take any more
And they pick up a gun or a brick or a stone
There are lives in the balance
There are people under fire
There are children at the cannons
And there is blood on the wire

There's a shadow on the faces
Of the men who fan the flames
Of the wars that are fought in places
Where we can't even say the names

They sell us the President the same way
They sell us our clothes and our cars
They sell us everything from youth to religion
The same time they sell us our wars
I want to know who the men in the shadows are

I want to hear somebody asking them why
They can be counted on to tell us who our enemies are
But they're never the ones to fight or to die
And there are lives in the balance
There are people under fire
There are children at the cannons
And there is blood on the wire

Jackson Browne (b.1948)

Imagine (Song)

Imagine there's no heaven
It's easy if you try
No hell below us
Above us only sky
Imagine all the people living for today

Imagine there's no countries
It isn't hard to do
Nothing to kill or die for
And no religion too
Imagine all the people living life in peace

You, you may say
I'm a dreamer, but I'm not the only one
I hope some day you'll join us
And the world will be as one

Imagine no possessions
I wonder if you can
No need for greed or hunger
A brotherhood of man
Imagine all the people sharing all the world

You, you may say
I'm a dreamer, but I'm not the only one
I hope some day you'll join us
And the world will live as one

John Lennon (1940-1980)

Idle No More: Poem to the World

A poem from the Idle No More, One Million Strong Movement, an indigenous Canadian movement to celebrate the revolution in protecting mother earth, the air, water and our rights as human beings. Published on Jan 2, 2013. You can find readings of the poem on YouTube.

I sit quietly waiting
Looking to the skies for answers
I get down on my knees and start praying

What has happened to my world
The sacred drums why cannot I hear you
The truth buried in lies is getting oh so old

I seek counsel it only helps for so long
The pain the apathy does anyone care anymore
Then I hear in the distance a new song

A song of prayer of peace and kinship
At first it is a mild murmur off in the distance
Then comes this great big blast of friendship

The time is ripe the time is now
Here is the revolution that shows us how
This great big giant . . . POW WOW!

Here we are folks December twenty-first
We now know what the end of the Mayan cycle means
The earth its creatures and the people now come first

It is the end of the world as we know
Very different than the fear we were told
It is the end of oppression and the time to grow

We are all one family on Mother Earth
It is time we stand up dust our selves off
   and do the task ahead of us
To live in Peace Friendship and Harmony
   on Planet Earth
   the place that gave us birth

Daniel Leo Richard

Poems Online

There are many poetry classics, such as the following, that could not be included in this book to keep the cost affordable. However, you can enjoy reading them online. "Fra Lippo Lippi" by Robert Browning, "A Daily Joy to be Alive " and "Roots" by Jimmy Santiago Baca, "Mother to Son" and "Island" by Langston Hughes. The links are in Chapter Thirteen-related material on my website.

Exercises to Test Your Mastery of Chapter Thirteen

1. Select for analysis and interpretation a poem to demonstrate how literature deals with human suffering to offer consolation and healing. In this chapter, the poems with that potential on which students have written are "Getting Through" by Deborah Pope, "Getting Out" by Cleopatra Mathis, and "To Autumn" by John Keats.

2. In *The Discovery of Poetry*, Frances Mayes writes: "Art reveals a culture's values, pressures, breakdowns, new directions. Contemporary poems are comments on our time; poems from other times and places give us glimpses into other lives" (Mayes 4). Select a poem from another time and a poem from the present to illustrate any one of the points mentioned in Mayes' words cited above.

3. Using my sample essay on Keats's "Ode to a Nightingale" as your guide, write an essay on major themes from a poem of your choice.

4. Using my essay on e. e. cummings' "the greedy the people" as a sample, write an essay on a few notable elements of style in a poem of your choice.

5. Write a character analysis of Prufrock from T. S. Eliot's poem "The Love Song of J. Alfred Prufrock" by comparing/contrasting him with the speaker in Keats's "Ode to a Nightingale." Focus on the two characters' values and attitudes toward life, death, human society, and suffering. Which of the two characters shows optimism? Support your answer with details from the two poems.

6. This chapter's essay titled "Complex Poems and Conflicting Interpretations" stated some of the poem's prominent themes in T.S. Eliot's "The Love Song of J. Alfred Prufrock." Give supporting details for each of those themes.

7. Do you agree with the view that Prufrock's stream of consciousness is littered with insecurities?

8. "The Love Song of Prufrock" is famous for its use of the style known as the stream of consciousness. Explain the meaning of this term. Give examples.

9. At the beginning of this chapter, I cited Virginia Woolf's reasons for the difficulty of some modern poetry under the heading "Reasons for the Difficulty of Some Modern Poetry." Analyze a difficult modern poem to illustrate Virginia Woolf's points in specific terms. If the poem that you choose uses the stream-of-consciousness technique, explain and discuss how it functions in the poem.

10. Of all the definitions of poetry included at the beginning of this chapter under "Some Definitions of Poetry," which definition do you find most appealing? Apply that definition to a poem of your choice.

11. Percy Shelley said that "Poets are the unacknowledged legislators of the world." What, in your view, is he emphasizing? Do you agree with him?

12. Compare and/or contrast the major male and female characters in Manto's short story "Odor" (Chapter Six) and their counterparts in Keats's poem "La Belle Dame sans Merci," meaning the beautiful lady without pity (this chapter).

13. "Bright Star," directed by Jane Campion, is a movie that celebrates the famous English Romantic poet John Keats's life and his love for Fanny Brawne. In his review, David Gritten offers this critique: "Together with her gifted cinematographer Craig Fraser, Campion also sets the mood through silent imagery. His camera remains largely static; every shot is lit and framed with a care and precision

665

that does justice to, and even correlates to Keats's poetry." Demonstrate how some of the scenes and silent images of the movie relate to scenes and images in any of Keats's poems.

14. Discuss Keats's sonnet "Bright Star" in the context of the themes and concepts of mortality and eternity. Compare this poem with Keats's "Ode on a Grecian Urn" that you can read online.

15. Make a comparison between Keats's "Bright Star" and Iqbal's poem "Morning Star" to point out their thematic similarities and differences.

16. Of all the love poems that you have read in this chapter – those by William Shakespeare ("My mistress' eyes"), Andrew Marvell, Li-Po, John Keats ("La Belle Dame sans Merci" and "Bright Star)," T. S. Eliot, Pablo Neruda, Maya Angelou, Douglas Dunn, Percy Shelley ("One word is too often profaned"), Nizar Qabbani, and Amjad Islam Amjad (whose "A Love Poem" is on my website), which one do you find most appealing? Describe what makes your selected poem stand out? For an optional part to this question, read Thomas Hardy's "Neutral Tones" on the internet and compare its neutrality of tone about love with the typically passionate love poems.

17. Compare/contrast the themes and styles of Robert Hayden's sonnet "Winter Sundays" (included and discussed in this chapter) with Judith Wright's poem "Portrait" that you can read online or in a book.

18. This chapter has listed 19 essay topics under "Options for Writing." Without repeating any of the items mentioned in the immediately preceding questions in this exercise, write an essay on any one of the 19 topics.

19. Write on a poem by a non-Western international poet to write on its substance and to show how it brings you closer to an unfamiliar culture. What is the poem's cultural and/or historical significance? Write on a poem that has not been discussed in this chapter, or offer an interpretation that is different from the one given in the chapter.

20. What makes Faiz's poem "Blackout" unique as an anti-war poem?

21. Discuss Iqbal's poem "Nationalism" as a cure for chauvinistic, close-minded nationalism. Point out some similarities between this poem and Edward Said's essay "Reflections on Exile" that you read in Chapter Nine. Here is the link to Said's essay:

www.dartmouth.edu/~germ43/pdfs/said_reflections.pdf
Another relevant must-read essay is Albert Camus' "Letters to a German Friend" that he wrote clandestinely during the Nazis' occupation of France in the Second World War.

22. .Compare Waseem Barelvi's poem "The Artist" with another poem, a story, or an essay on that topic to discuss their similarities and differences. Barelvi's poem is about the role of the artist.

23. Robert Frost said that "poetry is what evaporates from all translations." What features of poetry are likely to be lost in translation? Give examples from the international poets whose translated poems you have read in this chapter. What features of translated poems are not lost in translation? Include a comment on the importance and relevance of translating outstanding literary works.

24. Summarize a movie about your favorite poet and relate the movie content to some of the subject poet's works. *The Faber Book of Movie Verse*, edited by Philip French and Ken Waschin, lists several films based on the lives of poets: *Tom and Viv* about T. S. Eliot; Ken Russell's *Gothic* that shows Shelley, Byron, and others having orgies; *The Bad Lord Byron* and *Lady Caroline Lamb* about Byron; *Beautiful Dreamers* with Rip Torn as Walt Whitman; *Orlando* about Swift, Pope, and Addison; *Total*

Eclipse about Verlaine and Rimbaud (with Leonardo Di Caprio); *The Cage* about Ezra Pound; *The Barretts of Wimpole Street* about Robert and Elizabeth Browning; and *Stevie* about Stevie Smith (with Glenda Jackson). There is also a series called "Poems in Movies." You may also check it on the internet.

25. Internet assignment: Type "poem with analysis" in Google search. Here you will find many poems analyzed as well as advice on poetry analysis. Select a poem that you like. Summarize the main points from its analysis. Add your own interpretation.

26. Internet assignment: Go to the website PoemHunter.com. You will find classical, modern, and today's poems listed by poets and by topics. Select a poem that appeals to you and analyze it for its theme and style. Membership for this website is free.

An important internet/library assignment to expand your choices of poems and to take advantage of the wealth of poetry available to us.

Select a poem from the following list and write a critical evaluation of the position it takes on an important historical, social, romantic, existential, or political topic. If you like, you can make it into a research paper. (Suggested length: 500 to 750 words for longer poems; 250 words for shorter poems). If you choose very short poems, you can write on more than one with a similar or contrasting theme. Brief explanatory words are included, where needed.

27. "Lost Sister" from *Picture Bride* by Cathy Song
28. "Refugee Ship" from *The Americas Review* (formerly *Revista Chicano-Riquena*), by Lorna Dee Cervantes
29. "Ancestor" from *Immigrants in Our Own Land* by Jimmy Santiago Baca
30. "Hometown" from *Breaking Silence* by Luis Cabalquinto
31. "Going Home" taken from *Between Two Rivers: Selected Poems* by Maurice Kenny
32. Six very short poems (some less than 6 lines long) by Langston Hughes from *Collected Poems of Langston Hughes*
    "Dream Variations," "Island," "Mother to Son," "Cross," "Negro," and "The Negro Speaks of Rivers" (history, resilience, and dreams of African Americans)
33. "Character of the Happy Warrior" by William Wordsworth
34. "To Toussaint L'Ouverture" by William Wordsworth (a sonnet; a stirring tribute to the eighteenth-century Haitian revolutionary leader of slave revolt). This poem is included in this chapter.
35. "Composed upon Westminster Bridge" by William Wordsworth (a sonnet)
36. "Work Without Hope" by Samuel Coleridge (a sonnet)
37. "She Walks in Beauty" by Lord Byron (an 18-line poem; a tribute to the beloved). This poem is in this chapter.
38. "Sonnet on Chillon" by Lord Byron (honoring the memory of Francois Bonivard, the sixteenth-century lone survivor of a martyred family in Geneva; he was imprisoned in the castle of Chillon.). This poem is included in this chapter.

39. "There is a pleasure in the pathless woods" by Lord Byron (a 9-line stanza No. 178 – a celebration of the poet's communion with Nature – from his poem *Childe Harold's Pilgrimage, Canto IV)*. The poem is in this chapter.

40. "Roll on, thou deep and dark blue Ocean – roll" (another 9-line stanza No. 179 from the same poem, celebrating the might of the ocean). An interesting assignment would be comparing this poem by Byron with Gerard Manley Hopkins' sonnet "God's Grandeur," focusing on the two poet's attitude toward Nature. Hopkins' poem is included toward the end of Chapter Four. Byron's poem is in this chapter.

41. "One words if too often profaned for me to profane it" by Percy Shelley (a 16-line unique love poem, included in this chapter).

42. "When I have fears that I may cease to be" by John Keats (a sonnet; meditation on love, fame, and death).

43. "Ode on a Grecian Urn" by John Keats (a dramatic presentation of contrast between time-bound passionate human life and timeless but cold world of art). This poem contrasts well with "When I have fears" sonnet, mentioned in No. 42 above.

44. "Ulysses" by Lord Alfred Tennyson (celebration of life's ceaseless voyage, included in this chapter).

45. "Tithonus" by Tennyson (Limits of mortality are good for humans). The poem is in this chapter.

46. "The Poet" by Tennyson

47. "Crossing the Bar" by Tennyson

48. "My Last Duchess" by Robert Browning (dramatic portraits of the vibrant duchess and her cruel husband). The poem is in this chapter.

49. "Prospice" by Robert Browning

50. "Epilogue: At the midnight in the silence" by Robert Browning

51. "The Buried Life" by Matthew Arnold on the theme that the ultimate source of strength and peace is within us. The poem is in this chapter.

52. "Growing Old" by Matthew Arnold

53. "The Story of Adam" by Muhammad Iqbal. This short poem (included in this chapter) traces major schools of religion, science, and philosophy to show the essential unity of humanity in its collective struggle for peace and tranquility.

54. Using my sample essay "Is Your Enemy Human: Similar answers of 'Hiroshima Mon Amour' and 'Vergissmeinnicht'," demonstrate similarities of themes and, if possible, of style between another poem and a movie. Add supporting details.

55. In *Understanding Movies*, Louis Giannetti says that some filmmakers are like those poets who write sonnets (a highly demanding 14-line poem). They choose this "rigid form precisely because of the technical challenge it presents. Much of the enjoyment we derive from reading a sonnet results from the tension between the content and the form . . . . When technique and subject matter are perfectly fused in this way, our aesthetic pleasure is heightened. The same principle can be applied to framing in film" (Giannetti 44).

    Compare any tightly structured poem (like a sonnet) with a similarly wrought film to elucidate the point made by Giannetti in the preceding quotation.

CHAPTER FOURTEEN

FILM

Movies have become an important part of popular culture. Supplementing the role of literature, they give us new ideas, bring us entertainment and aesthetic pleasure, and serve a therapeutic function by stirring strong emotions as well as providing an outlet for them. An especially useful aspect of the study of film as an aid to literature is the clarity with which it can help us understand literary style. The cinematographic devices in film are much more deliberate than stylistic elements in literature. By looking at film cinematography (style), we can see the presence of at least some conscious design in literary style. Leo Braudy's words from *The World in a Frame* help us understand this point:

"When we are faced with a film, we should . . . assume everything has meaning because everything is the result of a choice – to write, cast, stage, act, shoot, edit, or score in a particular way – all dictated by formal necessities that in another art could seem disjunctive and fragmentary" (Braudy 9).

Enhanced awareness of the function of lighting, color, camera angles, close-ups, long shots, music, etc., in movies can bring us greater appreciation and understanding of similar and parallel functions of the elements of style in literature (discussed in Chapter Four).

This chapter will thus add film as a source to deepen your appreciation of literature. It will also suggest numerous film-based writing and discussion topics. Since literature is the primary focus of this book, the films chosen for discussion in this chapter are adaptations of well-known literary works or have screenplays of considerable literary merit. They can be easily rented in the form of DVDs or watched online. This narrowing of focus to literary films is necessary also because the study of film, in itself, is a vast and complex subject.

Movies can be enjoyed as cinematic art, and, at the same time, they can serve as a means of access to great books. We have no difficulty in perceiving the influence of literature on film, especially in the case of film adaptations of literary works. However, we seldom acknowledge the book-reviving influence of movies in instances where nearly forgotten literary classics regain popularity as a result of their film adaptations. Some examples are *Emma, Sense and Sensibility, Pride and Prejudice* (based on Jane Austen's novels); *The Hours*, a modern interpretation of *Mrs. Dalloway* set against a reconstruction of Virginia Wolfe's final days; *The Wings of the Dove* (based on a Henry James novel); numerous film versions of *Hamlet*; Stephen Frears' adaptation of Choderlos de Laclos' eighteenth-century classic, *Dangerous Liaisons*; and many B.B.C. productions of literary works. Lately some writers have become better known through film adaptations of their books. Patricia Highsmith, for example, has earned her well-deserved fame because her novel, *The Talented Mr. Ripley*, was made into a movie, directed by Anthony Minghella.

Even though literary classics and their cinematic renditions are two different media, the principles of literary interpretation that have been presented throughout this book apply also to film analysis. In fact, film shares with literature the elements of theme, characters, and plot, covered in the first three chapters of this book. Even many elements of style, such as setting, point of view, atmosphere, imagery, dialogue, symbolism, allusion, understatement, irony, paradox, etc., are common to both media. Further strengthening the close connection between these two media is the fact that good movies create in the viewers a desire to go back to the literary source. Many times we are compelled to go back to the filmed literary work to see why the director's reading differs from our own. This kind of open-minded curiosity enhances our comprehension. A good film, moreover, allows us to benefit from the film director's extended involvement with the literary work. Like literature, film can also serve as a means to raise and answer some of the enduring questions and embody important themes. In a reading and writing course, therefore, combining the two media can lead to interesting topics and to a deeper appreciation of these potentially symbiotic forms.

Film Interpretation

The requirements of film and literary interpretation are quite similar. Since there is a tendency to regard movies as mere entertainment, it is all the more important for film appreciation to stress the same skills that are needed in literary interpretation:

1. An ability to understand the thought content is the first requirement. We demonstrate this capability through theme formulation by interpreting significant events, statements, occurrences, drawing a cause-and-effect connection between them, and by analyzing the values, hopes, fears, and aspirations of major characters.

2. The second skill needed in film interpretation is an ability to appreciate the stylistic accomplishments, which in film terminology are called cinematography and technical elements, including special effects. As in literature, some of the stylistic/technical aspects of film are intricately connected with themes, while other elements serve any number of the following ends: creating and sustaining a desired mood, building up emotion, startling the viewer into a new awareness (often with the use of special visual and sound effects), revealing a motive, developing a character, a motif, a sensation, a clue, etc.

Because of the complementary nature of the two media, this chapter will give you an opportunity to review some of the important points from previous chapters, such as your understanding of style in literature, and sharpen the skills needed to enjoy and interpret complex movies.

Technical and Stylistic Elements in Film

To access emotions and ideas in a movie, you can use the same advice that was given to discover and formulate themes in literary works in Chapter One. The purpose of this part of the chapter is to introduce you to something that has not been covered so far: technical and stylistic elements – also called cinematography – in film. The following glossary of technical terms will help you acquire an appreciation of this challenging part of film art while also helping to review, with sharper understanding, the elements of setting, imagery, symbolism, irony, etc., which were also covered in the chapter on style. As you will see, in film these elements serve important cinematographic functions.

In spite of the obvious similarities of stylistic features between film and literature, we need to be aware that movies give literary devices a cinematic form. Approximate equivalents can be found in literature for various camera angles, lenses and filters for image manipulation, many forms of nonverbal expression, use of light and color, and numerous varieties of shots (close-up, long shot, etc.). To appreciate film art, you may wish to supplement your knowledge of literary style with those terms that are distinctly cinematic.

A glossary or a dictionary of cinematic terms is a good companion to study the motion picture's technical elements. One good source of information is *The Glossary of Film Terms* compiled by John Mercer. Both Louis Giannetti's *Understanding Movies* and Thomas and Vivian Sobchack's *An Introduction to Film* also have glossaries of cinematic terms. You will notice that film style and literary style are quite similar, as the following explanations of various elements will demonstrate.

Definitions and examples of the following elements of film style are given on my website:

1. Setting
2. Dialogue and soliloquy
3. Stream of consciousness, flashback, and flash forward
4. Montage
5. Camera
a. The long shot in film and the omniscient, cosmic perspective in literature
b. The close-up in film and minute detail in literature
6. Composition
7. Camera angles in film serving as tone and point of view
8. Music
9. Imagery
10. Symbolism
11. Irony

TOPICS FOR WRITING AND DISCUSSION

Having learned from Chapter Seven how to write on themes from literary works, you should have no difficulty writing on prominent themes from movies. As in fiction, important topics that surface in a movie's narrative are often developed into themes. Tracing and proving such developments is an interesting exercise in critical thinking, which also enhances interpretive skills. An essay on film appreciation may be organized the same way you organized your essays on themes and stylistic elements in literary works, remembering that you always have the freedom to vary organizational strategies to suit your style.

Topic Suggestions

In addition to writing on themes, movies offer other interesting topics, some of which are listed and explained below. Most of the suggested topics and sample essays are on new tasks that have not been covered in previous chapters. Because of space limitations and prior coverage, not all assignment topics are accompanied by a sample essay.

I. **Writing on dominant ideas and emotions in a movie**: This option may include a plot summary, the movie's general subject, and interrelated, complementary themes.

II. **Interpreting a complex movie**: The sample essay on Alain Resnais' *Hiroshima Mon Amour* exemplifies the completion of this assignment.

III. **Writing a plot summary** with emphasis on the movie's subject and characters.

IV. **Focusing on just one prominent topic from the movie**. After identifying and exemplifying the topic, you should try to uncover the director's feelings on that topic, thus leading to the movie's theme. The sample essay on Stephen Frears' *Dangerous Liaisons* is in response to this topic.

V. **Comparing the film adaptation with the literary work** on which it is based to do any or all of the following:

1. Showing the changes made by the filmmaker and pointing out the artistic merit of those changes.

2. Adding depth to the viewer's understanding of the movie by citing important passages from the book which the film could not fully accommodate.

3. Pointing out those subtleties in the book that the film was incapable of conveying.

VI. **Character-related topics**: These will be the same as in literary works demonstrated in earlier chapters, specifically in Chapter Two (on Characters).

VII. **Plot-related topics**: These will also be the same as in literary works shown in the preceding chapters, specifically in Chapter Three.

VIII. **Style-related topics**: a movie's technical elements/cinematography. Analyzing a movie's technical elements to demonstrate their effectiveness in communicating themes and expressing characters' feelings. The sample essay on Satyajit Ray's *Charulata* and a review of Sam Mendes' *American Beauty* exemplify this option.

IX. **Film as a catalyst for reform: Writing on a movie that concerns a pressing racial, cultural, or social issue.** Among numerous relevant movies, a few are *American History X* (directed by Tony Kaye),

House of Sand and Fog (directed by Vadim Perelman), *The Color of Fear* (directed by Lee Mun Wah), *Crash* (directed by Paul Haggis), and *Pieces of April* (written and directed by Peter Hedges). The student Allan Fisher's essay, titled"Colliding American Cultures" shows one possible way to complete this assignment.

X.   **Film-literature connection: similarities and differences**. The sample essay on thematic similarities between Resnais' movie *Hiroshima Mon* Amour and Keith Douglas's poem 'Vergissmeinnicht" in Chapter Thirteen (on poetry)) shows one possible way to complete this assignment.

XI.   **Film as a means to know an unfamiliar culture**.

XII.   **The complete movie review/critique**: This comprehensive assignment covers theme, characters, plot, and the movie's technical aspects. Detailed guidelines for writing this review precede the sample review on Steven Spielberg's *Schindler's List* on my website.

Topics relating to themes, characters, plot, and style in literature have already been covered in Chapters One, Two, Three, and Four respectively. You can use that same knowledge, enhanced significantly by this chapter's opening section on "Technical and Stylistic Elements in Film," to generate meaningful discussions of the film-related topics listed above. Since you know the steps and have already seen their implementation in numerous interpretation and analysis samples, only new information is included in this chapter.

SAMPLE ESSAYS AND EXERCISES

My website has sample essays on many of the above-mentioned topics along with Exercises to Test Your Mastery of Chapter Fourteen. www.professorjabbar.com

List of Sample essays and exercises

Sample essay on Alain Resnais' *Hiroshima Mon Amour*
Sample essay on Stephen Frears' *Dangerous Liaisons*
Sample essay on Satyajit Ray's *Charulata*
Sample review and essay on Sam Mendes' *American Beauty*
Sample essay on Paul Haggis' *Crash*
Sample review of Steven Spielberg's *Schindler's List*
Sample essay on similarities of themes in Alain Resnais' movie *Hiroshima Mon Amour* and Keith Douglas's poem "Vergissmeinnicht"

List of movies discussed or mentioned in this chapter: In alphabetical order

American History X, Bartleby, Bonnie and Clyde, Charulata, Citizen Kane, The Color of Fear, Crash, Dangerous Liaisons, Doctor Zhivago, Easy Rider, Elegy, Emma, Gandhi, The Great Gatsby, Hamlet, Hiroshima Mon Amour, The Hours, La Soufriere, La Strada, Lackawanna Blues, The Last Picture Show, The Last Temptation of Christ, Lawrence of Arabia, The Misfits, An Occurrence at Owl Creek Bridge, Pieces of April, Pride and Prejudice, Rashomon, The Return of the Native, Schindler's List, Sense and Sensibility, Shall We Dance, The Talented Mr. Ripley, Tom and Viv

CHAPTER FIFTEEN

PLAYFUL RESPONSES TO SERIOUS WORKS: LITERATURE FOR LAUGHTER

Playful interaction, even with classics of tragedy, can create laughter as well as an increased awareness of their substance while making you less fearful of the classics. This chapter continues what was introduced in a limited way as a source of humor in chapters on the novel and drama. It should be noted that when studying literary works that are not primarily comic, the appropriate time to introduce humorous responses to them is after their serious aspects have been fully covered. Besides humorous responses to serious literature, some comic works are also included in this chapter.

Putting this chapter at the end of the book rather than earlier, I am reminded of the humorist Jack Handey bemoaning the difficulty of finding books on humor in a bookstore because the humor section is as far removed from the entrance as possible and located in an obscure section. Here is his comic advice:

"It is a good idea to make a lot of noise when you approach the Humor section, to avoid surprising people engaged in a sex act. More prostitutes are arrested in Humor sections than in any other part of the bookstore" (Handey, NY Times, Sept. 12, 2008).

Use of Humor in the Study of Serious Classics

Judicious use of humor can introduce the element of entertainment that is often missing in the study of serious classics. For example, we can humorously ponder the serious topic of the decline of language by replacing some of the key words in Hamlet's famous soliloquy "To be, or not to be" with clichés and trite expressions. Here is, in Shakespeare's language, Hamlet's anguished awareness of a thinking person's dilemma in a corrupt world:

> To be, or not to be: that is the question:
> Whether 'tis nobler in the mind to suffer
> The slings and arrows of outrageous fortune,
> Or to take arms against a sea of troubles,
> And by opposing end them? To die: to sleep;
> No more; and, by a sleep to say we end
> The heart-ache and the thousand natural shocks
> That flesh is heir to, 'tis a consummation

Devoutly to be wish'd. To die, to sleep;

To sleep: perchance to dream: ay, there's the rub;

For in that sleep of death what dreams may come

When we have shuffled off this mortal coil,

Must give us pause.   (III, i, 62-74)

Here is how the thoughts of Hamlet may sound in clichés, banalities, and limited vocabulary, resulting in a comic effect that characterizes parodies:

Wow! Here is a big mess.

And I don't have a clue

Who to hit for an answer.

Should I do myself in and croak quietly

Or go for it? I mean the fight.

Like I said I don't have no clue

Ya know what I mean.

I ain't afraid of kicking the bucket.

What gives me the creeps is something else.

It's life hereafter, you know.

Like what will I do there at the end of the day

If He asks, "Stupid kid, why did you do yourself in?

Ya know what I mean.

Piggybacking on that idea,

I don't want to throw out the baby with the bath water.

I have been to college and did good in philosophy

But this hassle has me stumped. That's the bottom line.

Your parody could proceed along these lines. The purpose is to make the reader laugh. The point of this parody is to show how profound thoughts can become trivialized without appropriate language.

Use of the following prompt could yield some interesting results in completing this humorous exercise that will also ensure a deep engagement with the important topic of language and literature.

After reading my above parody, attempt a similar rendition of a different passage from "Hamlet" or a famous passage from any other work. Include the text that you choose to parody.

Humor in Tragic Plays

Shakespeare liked to mix tragedy and comedy in his plays, unlike classical Greek plays that were either pure comedies or pure tragedies. As a result even his tragic plays are full of humorous scenes. For example, almost every scene with Hamlet in it has some humor in the form of sarcasm, double entendre (use of words with double meanings), wit, puns, exaggeration, understatement, parody, and similar humor-making devices. Shakespeare's use of the device of parody to ridicule legal jargon was discussed in Chapter Three in the context of the three classical unities practiced in classical drama. You may want to go back to that chapter and entertain yourself with Hamlet's excoriation of the legalese in V, i, 99-113.

Hamlet's very first words in the play are like a puzzle. When the newly crowned King Claudius addresses him with "But now, my cousin Hamlet, and my son," Hamlet's *aside* (words that he shares with the audience but not with the King) is a pun: "A little more than kin, and less than kind!" (I, ii, 66). Hamlet is letting the audience know that he is not just a distant cousin. Because of Claudius' marrying Hamlet's mother, the relation has become very close. At the same time, Hamlet denies that he is the kind of person that Claudius is.

Later, in the same scene, when the King asks, "How is it that the clouds still hang on you," implying that Hamlet is mourning the death of his father too long, Hamlet responds with another pun: "Not so, my lord. I am too much in the sun," thus sarcastically expressing his discomfort with the courtly pomp and festivities so soon after the death of his father, King Hamlet.

Another memorable phrase is "Thrift, Horatio" when his friend Horatio expresses his surprise at the speed with which Claudius married Hamlet's mother Queen Gertrude after her husband's death in dubious circumstances. Hamlet, sarcastically, tells Horatio that this combining of marriage with funeral was intended to economize:

> Thrift, thrift, Horatio. The funeral baked meat
> Did coldly furnish forth the marriage tables (I, ii, 180-181).

Numerous such statements provoke laughter throughout the play. We should not forget to enjoy Hamlet's irrepressible sense of humor even in the worst of circumstances.

Like Shakespeare, even though not to the same extent, Eugene O'Neill also has humorous moments in his tragic plays. For example, in *Long Day's Journey into Night*, in a state of drunkenness, Jamie has a fall. Here is a very humorous description of his fall just before a very serious scene that followed. Jamie reports his fall to his brother Edmund that will make anyone laugh: "The front steps tried to trample on me. Took advantage of fog to waylay me" (O'Neill 158).

Ridiculing Trendy Speech Patterns

Whereas I took a stab at the comically absurd struggle of trite language to express great ideas, Sheila, in the excerpt below, pokes fun at the endemic use of the words "like" and "cool" in modern lingo. After reading the following piece "Like Cool," you should write in the same vein humorously to mimic those linguistic trends that you find humorous – overuse of "You know," for example. Sheila doesn't but you can make use of "at the end of the day" – a phrase we hear all the time. Sheila's brief composition is not literature, but it gives you ammunition to use when writing parodies of literary works.

Like, Cool

Editor – Omigod, I am like, so glad that, ya know, like, you guys are so cool at the chronicle, ya know? Because, like, you did these like vignette-type things, oh, stories, about really cool people on spring break (*People*, March 24). Wow, ya know? And like, these really cool people were, ya know, like doing really cool things like driving really fast, ya know, and drinking tons of beer, and being really sexy, ya know?

But, like, I have a thought, ya know, like a question. Like, why did that one guy, like, want to go to the Tenderloin to like, help people? Ya know, because that's just like not at all cool or sexy, ya know. Can I just say, ya know, it was like, what's wrong with this picture anyway, ya know? He totally just like did not at all like fit in. That sucked, ya know.

SHEILA MOMANEY
Berkeley
(*San Francisco Chronicle*, page A 24, 3-25-93)

Parody of Serious Poetry

Poetry lends itself eminently to parody. Anthony Hecht's "Dover Bitch" parodies Mathew Arnold's famous poem "Dover Beach" (that you read in Chapter Six), and William Carlos William (1883-1963) has been a favorite of parodists. English satirist John Hamilton Reynolds (1794-1852) has parodied the weighty, nature-based philosophy of his fellow countryman, poet William Wordsworth (1770-1850). Wordsworth's philosophy is contained in poems like "Peter Bell" and in these famous concluding lines of his ode "Intimations of Immortality from Recollections of Early Childhood":

> Thanks to the human heart by which we live
> Thanks to its tenderness, its joys and fears,
> To me the meanest flower that blows can give
> Thoughts that do often lie too deep for tears.

Here is Reynold's parody of Wordsworth's above-quoted lines:

"It has been my aim and my achievement to deduce moral thunder from buttercups, daisies, celandines, and (as a poet, scarcely inferior to myself, hath it) 'such small deer.' Out of sparrow's eggs I have hatched great truths, and with sextons' barrows have I wheeled into human hearts, piles of the weightiest philosophy."

Using Reynold's preceding example, you can write a parody of any poet.

Writing a Comic Letter about a Serious Work

A scenario full of comic possibilities is imagining yourself representing an organization that is seeking to popularize a classic. You may write a letter to a famous author or to his/her estate, asking for authorization to make changes in their masterpiece so that it becomes appealing to contemporary readers. It is another humorous approach to serious literature and will ensure a thorough understanding of the classic and entertainment for you and your reader.

You can satirizes the condescending attitude that tries to "improve" the classics for the sake of popularity. This practice is evident in some film adaptations that introduce arbitrary changes in the original story. You may write your imaginary letter to the great American author Henry David Thoreau (1817-62), advising him to jazz up his classic *Walden* with some romantic interludes and battle scenes. Suggest to him that he should change his book to a murder mystery.

Advise Thoreau to quicken the pace of his narrative and lay off the weighty philosophical ideas because the modern reader reads for fun, not to go to sleep. After suggesting big changes that will completely alter the nature of the book, you can use verbal irony, an element of style that has been a perennial source of humor. You can say that with the *minor* changes suggested, Thoreau's book will pick up in sales. The italicized word *minor* is ironic because the revisions that Thoreau is being asked to make will involve a complete rewriting of his classic.

In your comic letter you are encouraged you to use any humor-making devices, such as irony, sarcasm, understatement, hyperbole (exaggeration), paradox, etc., to make the reader laugh. When using the listed or similar stylistic elements for humorous effects, remember that the term "satire" refers to a literary work while verbal irony, sarcasm, hyperbole, understatement, etc., are the means to write a satire. For further help with elements of style, turn to Chapter Four, which covers style.

Using the above-noted instructions, the student Erin Kehoe has written a highly entertaining essay, "Befriending the Stranger." Her focus is Albert Camus' famous novel *The Stranger*. She wrote in response to the following prompt:

Write a letter to a famous author or his/her estate, asking them to authorize changes that would make the work more appealing and a sensational crowd-pleaser.

You will find the following piece by student author Erin Kehoe humorous and entertaining only if you are familiar with Albert Camus' famous novel "The Stranger." This novel has been discussed in great detail in Chapter Eleven. If you did not have a chance to read my chapter or Camus' novel, you can access the novel's plot summary online.

Erin Kehoe satirizes the hunger for sensationalism and trends that trivialize the classics. The paragraph on portrayal of the novel's Arab character shows effective use of verbal irony to ridicule anti-Arab racism and silly stereotyping. Sarcasm is the tool with which Erin demolishes gross generalizations as in the paragraph about the French people's "questionable" morals. "The Stranger" fuels the comic satire of this piece. The letter is addressed to the late Camus' daughter, who supposedly has the authority to allow the suggested changes that Erin, using verbal irony, calls "minor." Obviously the changes are anything but minor. If implemented, they will change the entire spirit and point of the novel. An example would be the silly suggestion toward the end of the essay to make Meursault cry on the priest's shoulder, sobbing and clutching at his robes.

679

Befriending *The Stranger*
Student author: Erin Kehoe

Dear Miss Camus,

I am writing to you on behalf of the Novel Selection Team of our "Book of the Century Club" to let you know that we would be thrilled to have your father's work, *The Stranger*, as our book of the month for July. We found your father's book to be absolutely charming, and we have no doubt that it will be warmly received by the American audience. We do have a few minor requests, however, but we feel strongly that they will pose no obstacles for you whatsoever. We have been informed that you and your family have exclusive rights to revisions and addenda, and we'd like to humbly ask for your consent to slightly modify your father's great work. If you would kindly take the time to consider these revisions, we feel confident that our loyal fans will love this novel as much as we did.

One major setback in attracting an audience such as ours is the realization that the main character's mother is in a retirement home! This is taboo here in the United States! Regardless of the fact that many elderly family members end up in these homes, no one wants to either believe it or think about it, lest they experience some sort of guilt or resentment towards the rest of the family. We also fear that this information will upset our elderly readers. Can you put Meursault's mother back in their house; perhaps with a caretaker? She can still die, but we feel it would be much more comforting to know that she died peacefully at home. You will have to alter one other minor detail to support this change, Meursault's profession, but this shouldn't be too difficult. Are we ever really clear on what he does for a living anyway?

Contrary to what most people think, men *do* cry. Your father must have been a proud man, projecting his emotionally unavailable nature onto the main character in his book, leaving Meursault looking like some kind of monster for not mourning his mother's death. We have three words for you. Emotion! Emotion! Emotion! We feel strongly that in order for Meursault to be a lovable character, something paramount to a great novel, he must be emotional, even overly so, and properly pay respect to the passing of the woman who gave birth to him. Every great novel that we've endorsed through our program has had a male character to whom our target audience, mainly women, could relate to and even connect with. One sure sign of a success with our members is a deluge of tears. They sure do love those tear-jerkers!

Also, Miss Camus, are you aware of how health conscious our viewers are? We beg you to please make Meursault a non-smoker, thereby eliminating any mixed messages we might be sending our loyal audience. And perhaps consider limiting the amount of alcohol he consumes as well. Our club leaders are firm believers in one glass a day with dinner and suggest this regimen to our viewers as a standard of health conducive to longevity.

We wanted to tell you that we liked your father's characters very much, with the exception of a few minor details. May we offer some suggestions to make them more likable? As far as Marie is concerned, we love that she is so jovial, so vibrant, so carefree! But, we feel that might be part of the problem. As far as we can see, Meursault isn't exactly giving her anything to be smiling about all the time. To us, this makes her seem like she's a bit, well, simple. Maybe Meursault can crack a few jokes here and there, or even give her a quick kiss on the cheek every once in a while, just to show his response to her having a great time. Also, if you could perhaps make Marie Meursault's long-term girlfriend, this might avoid some criticism from our Christian readers. Gratuitous sex is frowned upon by our audience who much prefer for the characters to be in love. In addition, premarital sex is a slight issue here in the U.S., but we feel that our audience, upon realizing that your father was French, will understand that morals are different, if not questionable, in your part of the world.

Another character that could use a little polishing is Salamano. We find him to be a little gross, to be perfectly blunt. We see you doing your father a great service by making Salamano's dog cuter, perhaps an adorable little pomeranian? Also, please leave out any talk of "scabs," either on Salamano or his dog. And for heaven's sake, please omit the part about him beating his dog! The folks at PETA will have a fit, and we can't afford to lose our dog-loving crowd, either.

Speaking of beatings, we find it deeply troubling that such a character as Raymond would be applauded as he is by your father. As a woman, I'm sure you can understand how the character's behavior is offensive and appalling, and would never be accepted by our readers. We question the reasons why Meursault would even consider befriending someone like Raymond in the first place, but since it is vital to the rest of the events in the story, we ask that you perhaps just leave out the part about him beating up the Moorish girl and merely make him yell at her. I guarantee that this will make our audience much happier.

One last character that we are a little confused about is the robot lady. What purpose does she serve, exactly? She should just be omitted entirely.

Considering how long ago this novel was written, how apropos that the enemy is an Arab! We were delighted at the way your father was able to stay current over all of these years and provide us with a tangible antagonist today. The Arabs in the story really exemplify what we think of Arabs today: as violent, revenge-thirsty animals who carry weapons and attack for no reason at all.[1] We think that their violent nature should be the motive for Meursault killing one of them. Seeing the way that they behave, we think that Meursault's actions should be out of self-defense, instead of whatever reason it was that he did it (we're still unclear – something about the sun?). We feel that the story will flow much better from this point on with this minor change.

As far as Meursault's trial is concerned, we found it to be quite boring. From the point where he gets arrested to the day of his sentencing, we found ourselves yawning and losing interest in the novel completely. Perhaps you could liven it up a little bit. Give Meursault some dialogue; heat up the arguments of the lawyers. This will surely capture the interest of the readers far more than what is currently there.

Finally, one last suggestion is that we would like to see Meursault ask forgiveness from the Lord in the final chapter. We found the scene with the priest a little harsh, and we think that it would be more pleasing if he hugged the priest, maybe cried on his shoulder a little bit, or even sobbed and clutched at his robes. How moving that would be! Also, maybe clean up the dialogue a bit. We fear that our audience would not understand the complexity of the discussion between Meursault and the priest.

And hooray to justice! We loved that Meursault was served justice for killing a man, even if that man was a terrorist. We feel that the greatest books of our time serve as a lesson to all of us in our daily lives and your father's novel certainly falls into that category.

---

1. The writer is using verbal irony here to ridicule negative stereotyping of Arabs in our media.

Miss Camus, we feel that with these minor changes, your father's novel will skyrocket to the top of the bestsellers charts in no time and become the success that it was meant to be. We'd like to thank you on behalf of our club and let you know how honored we would be to have the improved version of Albert Camus' *The Stranger* on our book list.

Sincerely,

Dinah Faire
Novel Selection Team, Book of the Century Club

Creating a Missing Scene for Comic Effects

Like all other exercises in this Chapter, the point is to make the reader laugh while ensuring a thorough understanding of the classic. You may try your hand at any of the following:

1. Create a scene that is implied but not created in a literary work. Use humorous dialogue of 15 to 20 lines of poetry, prose, or a mixture of the two. An example would be imagining the scene from *Hamlet* in which Claudius might have proposed marriage to Gertrude soon after murdering her husband. In creating this missing scene with dialogue, give Claudius and Gertrude words and actions that suit their personalities as perceived by you. (Your perception may be comic or serio-comic.)

2. Using yet another option, create an imaginary humor-filled scene of about 20 lines in any serious literary work. This comic device has unlimited possibilities. Let us use *Hamlet* as an example. You could write up a scene in which Rosencrantz and Guildenstern plead in vain with the King of England that some mistake has been made in the death warrant (that was meant for Hamlet but wrongly bears their names). Envision their telling the English King that they are loyal servants of Claudius, King of Denmark, and deserve reward, not death. Hamlet finds out that they are betraying his deep friendship with them for the sake of pleasing the criminal King Claudius. They are escorting him to England, where he is to be executed by the English King in compliance with Claudius' orders contained in a letter that Rosencrantz and Guildenstern are carrying with them. Becoming suspicious, Hamlet searches their belongings, finds the letter, and puts their names in the place of his own.

    The punishment that they receive at the end is often called poetic justice, a literary convention whereby the good get rewarded and the evil punished. The end of Rosencrantz and Guildenstern would be considered poetic justice only if you believe that they were complicit in planning Hamlet's death. If you feel they were not aware of the contents of Claudius's letter to the King of England that they are carrying, then their end would be more like situational irony: what happens is the opposite of what the two characters were expecting. In that case, it will be tragic, not humorous

3. For uproarious laughter, create a missing scene in 15 to 20 lines of poetry or prose (or a mixture of the two). If we were to use Shakespeare's play *Measure for Measure* to demonstrate this comic device, here is how it will work. It is only implied in the play that Angelo has sex with Mariana while thinking all the time that he is having sex with Isabella. Your job here is to make the implied explicit. In writing up this scene in Shakespearean language or your own (or a mixture of the two), comedy

will result from disparity between the imagined and the real: Angelo thinks he is making love to Isabella – a chaste woman with whose beauty he is smitten and obsessed.

Creating this scene has the potential of great comedy, especially in the dialogue between Angelo and Mariana, whose pre-arranged trysting place is purposely so dark for secrecy that the two can hardly see each other's face. Mariana is impersonating Isabella with the latter's consent. Isabella agrees to this substitution trick to bring the estranged Angelo back to his doting Mariana and, in the process, save her brother from an undeserved death sentence. Abusing his position of power as the acting Duke in the real Duke's absence, Angelo had offered to pardon Isabella's jailed brother only if she had sex with him. She had no such interest in him. The dialogue that you create should capture all the necessary nuances in order to be effective.

Writing a Comic Character Sketch:
Potential for an irreverent research paper

Another highly amusing exercise would be taking on the persona of a famous character from a literary work or a movie. This assignment could be completed in the form of a short personal essay, using the first person pronoun "I." You may begin by stating the purpose for which the author created you, the real values that you represent, and how you have been understood and misunderstood by readers and viewers. You may make fun of selected critics' overly serious and harshly opinionated treatment of your character. If you like, you can make it a research paper by including quotations from selected critics. Targeting relatively self-righteous and dogmatic critics will give you a chance to enjoy ridiculing their narrow-mindedness while illuminating the character at the same time.

Example

I am Hamlet. I am tired of listening to the critics talk about me *ad infinitim* as if they understood anything about my dilemma, my motives, and my reason for being. Let me set the record straight. . . . Ernest Jones, in his book *Hamlet and Oedipus* mouths off this nonsense: [Put in a suitable quotation here.] Follow it up by dismantling its conclusions as absurd. Include quotations from at least two other critics – if you are making it into a research paper – to similarly ridicule the critics' comically pompous claims of profundity. This potentially great humorous essay could proceed along these lines for your and your reader's entertainment. Perhaps, as a result of this exercise, you will not be fearful of research papers any more.

Humorous Comparative Character Analysis

Another enjoyable exercise would be comparing two suitable characters from two different works for entertainment. For instance, a comparison of Gertrude from *Hamlet* with the anti-hero female character in Gaius Petronius's short story "The Widow of Ephesus" would comically capture clichéd misogyny. Both women have comically short mourning periods after their husbands die. Both allow themselves to

683

be seduced into new amorous ties too soon after they become widows. Read "The Widow of Ephesus" online *via* Google: http://www.pitt.edu/~dash/widow.html#ephesus.

There are several ways to complete this exercise:

- Parallel lines from the two works depicting the two women's conduct could be spiced up with creative, comic exaggeration, irony, paradox, and other humorous devices.

- The two widows could be presented as having a dialogue about their respective experiences, their defiance of conventional morality, and their refusal to submit to a prolonged period of mourning.

Comic Treatment of a Serious Topic in an Essay
"On Being Crazy" by W.E.B. Du Bois

"On Being Crazy" by the African-American sociologist, historian, civil rights activist and author, W. E. B. Du Bois, is a humorous treatment of the serious topic of racism. The essay uses dialogue effectively to dramatize racist views. Du Bois also fully exploits the comedy-making devices of deliberate misunderstanding, irony, understatement, and reduction to absurdity through exaggeration. After reading this essay and its analysis in Chapter Nine, use Du Bois's essay as a sample to create your own comic treatment of a serious topic.

Two More Humorous Essays

Two more highly entertaining essays are "Courtship Through the Ages" by James Thurber and "Love Is a Fallacy" by Max Shulman (1919-1988). Thurber treats male-female relationships and roles comically, whereas Shulman's essay is a hilarious crash course on fallacies that violate logic, such as begging the question, false analogy, post hoc, etc.

After reading Shulman's essay from a book, make a list of all the fallacies that he presents in the essay humorously and write their definitions with an example of each fallacy. You may use Shulman's exact words for definitions, but create your own examples.

After reading James Thurber's following essay "Courtship Through the Ages," comment on the humor-making devices (exaggeration, humorous dichotomy between what happens and what was expected, and similar elements) that he has used effectively.

Courtship Through the Ages

Surely nothing in the astonishing scheme of life can have nonplussed Nature so much as the fact that none of the females of any of species she created really cared very much for the male, as such. For the past ten million years Nature has been busily inventing ways to make the male attractive to the female, but the whole business of courtship, from the marine annelids up to man, still lumbers heavily along, like a complicated musical comedy. I have been reading the sad and absorbing story of the Encyclopedia

Britannica. In this volume you can learn about cricket, cotton, costume designing, crocodiles, crown jewels, and Coleridge, but none of this subject is so interesting as the Courtship of animals, which recounts the sorrowful lengths to which all males must go to arouse the interest of a lady.

We all know, I think, that Nature gave man whiskers and a mustache with the quaint idea in mind that these would prove attractive to the female. We all know that, far from attracting her, whiskers and mustaches only made her nervous and gloomy, so that man had to go in for somersaults, tilting with lances, and performing feats of parlor magic to win her attention; he also had to bring her candy, flowers, and the furs of animals. It is common knowledge that in spite of all these "love displays" the male is constantly being turned down, insulted, or thrown out of the house. It is rather comforting, then, to discover that the peacock, for all his gorgeous plumage, does not have a particularly easy time in courtship; none of the males in the world do. The first peahen, it turned out, was only faintly stirred by her suitor's beautiful train. She would often go quietly to sleep while he was whisking it around. The Britannica tells us that the peacock actually had to learn a certain little trick to wake her up and revive her interest: he had to learn to vibrate his quills so as to make a rustling sound. In ancient times man himself, observing the ways of the peacock, probably tried vibrating his whiskers to make a rustling sound; if so, it didn't get him anywhere. He had to go in for something else; so, among other things, he went in for gifts. It is not unlikely that he got this idea from certain flies and birds who were making no headway at all with rustling sounds.

One of the flies of the family Empidae, who had tried everything, finally hit on something pretty special. He contrived to make a glistening transparent balloon which was even larger than himself. Into this he would put sweetmeats and tidbits and he would carry the whole elaborate envelope through the air to the lady of his choice. This amused her for a time, but she finally got bored with it. She demanded silly little colorful presents, something that you couldn't eat but that would look nice around the house. So the male Empis had to go around gathering flower petals and pieces of bright paper to put into his balloon. On a courtship flight a male Empis cuts quite a figure now, but he can hardly be said to be happy. He never knows how soon the female will demand heavier presents, such as Roman coins and gold collar buttons. It seems probable that one day the courtship of the Empidae will fall down, as man's occasionally does, of its own weight.

The bowerbird is another creature that spends so much time courting the female that he never gets any work done. If all the male bowerbirds became nervous wrecks within the next ten or fifteen years, it would not surprise me. The female bowerbird insists that a playground be built for her with a specially constructed bower at the entrance. This bower is much more elaborate than an ordinary nest and is harder to build; it costs a lot more, too. The female will not come to the playground until the male has filled it up with a great many gifts: silvery leaves, red leaves, rose petals, shells, beads, berries, bones, dice, buttons, cigar bands, Christmas seals, and the Lord knows what else. When the female finally condescends to visit the playground, she is in a coy and silly mood and has to be chased in and out of the bower and up and down the playground before she will quit giggling and stand still long enough even to shake hands. The male bird is, of course, pretty well done in before the chase starts, because he has worn himself out hunting for eyeglass lenses and begonia blossoms. I imagine that many a bowerbird, after chasing a female for two or three hours, says the hell with it and goes home to bed. Next day, of course, he telephones someone else and the same trying ritual is gone through with again. A male bowerbird is as exhausted as a night-club habitue before he is out of his twenties.

The male fiddler crab has a somewhat easier time, but it can hardly be said that he is sitting pretty. He has one enormously large and powerful claw, usually brilliantly colored, and you might suppose that all he had to do was reach out and grab some passing cutie. The very earliest fiddler crab may have tried this, but, if so, they got slapped for their pains. A female fiddler crab will not tolerate any caveman stuff; she never has and she doesn't intend to start now. To attract a female, a fiddler crab has to stand on tiptoe and brandish his claw in the air. If any female crab in the neighborhood is interested--and you'd be surprised how many are not--she comes over and engages him in light badinage, for which he is not in the mood. As many as a hundred females may pass the time of day with him and go on about their business. By nightfall of an average courting day, a fiddler crab who has been standing on tiptoe for eight or ten hours waving a heavy claw in the air is in pretty sad shape. As in the case of the male of all species, however, he gets out of bed next morning, dashes some water on his face, and tries again.

The next time you encounter a male web-spinning spider, stop and reflect that he is too busy worrying about his love life to have any desire to bite you. Male web-spinning spiders have a tougher life than any other males in the animal kingdom. This is because the female web-spinning spiders have very poor eyesight. If a male lands on a female's web, she kills him before he has time to lay down his cane and gloves, mistaking him for a fly or a bumblebee who has tumbled into her trap. Before the species figured out what to do about this, millions of males were murdered by ladies they called on. It is the nature of spiders to perform a little dance in front of the female, but before a male spinner could get near enough for the female to see who he was and what he was up to, she would lash out at him with a flat-iron or a pair of garden shears. One night, nobody knows when, a very bright male spinner lay awake worrying about calling on a lady who had been killing suitors right and left. It came to him that this business of dancing as a love display wasn't getting anybody anywhere accepts the grave. He decided to go in for web- twitching, or strand-vibrating. The next day he tried it on one of the nearsighted girls. Instead of dropping in on her suddenly, he stayed outside the web and began monkeying with one of its strands. He twitched it up and down and in and out with such a lilting rhythm that the female was charmed. The serenade worked beautifully; the female let him live. The Britannica's spider-watcher, however, report that this system is not always successful. Once in a while, even now, a female will fire three bullets into a suitor or run him through with a kitchen knife. She keeps threatening him from the moment he strikes the first low notes on the outside strings, but usually by the time he has got up to the high notes played around the center of the web, he is going to town and she spares his life.

Even the butterfly, as handsome a fellow ash is, can't always win a mate merely by fluttering around and showing off. Many butterflies have to have scent scales on their wings. Hepialus carries a powder puff in a perfumed pouch. He throws perfume at the ladies when they pass. The male tree cricket, Oecanthus, goes Hepialus one better by carrying a tiny bottle of wine with him and giving drinks to such doxies as he has designs on. One of the male snails throws darts to entertain the girls. So it goes, through the long list of animals, from the bristle worm and his rudimentary dance steps to man and his gift of diamonds and sapphires. The golden-eye drake raises a jet of water with his feet as he flies over a lakes Hepialus has his power puff, Oecanthus his wine bottle, man his etchings. It is a bright and melancholy story, the age-old desire of the male for the female, the age-old desire of the female to be amused and entertained. Of all the creatures on earth, the only males who could be figured as putting any irony into their courtship are the grebes and certain other diving birds. Every now and then, with a mighty "Whoosh!" he pops out suddenly a few feet from his girl friend, splashing water all over her. She seems to be persuaded that this is a purely loving display, but I like to think that the grebe always has a faint hope of drowning her or scaring her to death.

I will close this investigation into the mournful burdens of the male with Britannica's story about a certain Argus pheasant. It appears that the Argus displays himself in front of a female who stands perfectly still without moving a feather.... The male Argus the Britannica tells about was confined in a cage with a female of another species, a female who kept moving around, emptying ashtrays and fussing with lampshades all the time the male was showing off his talents. Finally, in disgust, he stalked away and began displaying in front of his water trough. He reminds me of a certain male (Homo sapiens) of my acquaintance who one night after dinner asked his wife to put down her detective magazine so that he could read a poem of which he was very fond. She sat quietly enough until he was well into the middle of the thing, intoning with great ardor and intensity. Then suddenly there came a sharp, disconcerting slap! It turned out that all during the male's display, the female had been intent on a circling mosquito and had finally trapped it between the palms of her hands. The male in this case did not stalk away and display in front of a water trough; he went over to Tim's and had a flock of drinks and recited the poem to the fellas. I am sure they all told bitter stories of their own about how their displays had been interrupted by females. I am also sure that they all ended up saying "Honey, Honey, Bless Your Heart."

James Thurber (1894-1961)

Humorous Short Stories

The Chapter's two short stories seem to have been written as much to entertain as to instruct. The stories are given first, followed by an analysis of their humor-making devices in the hope that you can create your own comic narrative to entertain the reader.

The Morning After the Night Before
by Khushwant Singh (b. 1915)

Read this story online by using this link: www.books.google.com/books?isbn=8175300442

Analysis of Singh's humorous devices

The thrust of Khushwant Singh's "The Morning After the Night Before" is a comic and forgiving rendition of the foibles of drunkenness. Other topics covered are harmless, comic hypocrisy, showing off, exaggeration ("I bit my lips till they bled and burst"), comic descriptions almost bordering on caricature (especially of the narrator's wife), comic stereotypes – "dancing [with the opposite sex] was not suited to the Indian temperament – "amorous escapade" in a dream sequence, and a pleasantly surprising ending. Masterly use of these stylistic elements, no less than the story's content, contribute to its appeal.

The Open Window

by H. H. Munro (Saki) (1870-1916)

Read this story on your own from a book or online.:

Analysis of Munro's humor-making devices

This story is a celebration of the 15-year old girl Vera's fertile imagination. The object of her practical joke is Frampton Nuttel, a hypochondriac, who is seeking nerve cure in the countryside. While he is waiting to meet Vera's aunt (Mrs. Sappleton), the young girl quickly perceives the threat of boredom from the stranger. Grasping the details about Mr. Nuttel's being a total stranger to everyone in Vera's family, Vera starts concocting a tale about Mrs. Sappleton's husband and two young brothers, who, she tells the stranger, went on a hunting trip through the open French window three years ago but never returned. Vera tells the visitor that Mrs. Sappleton continues to hope that all three of them will return some day through the open window. Vera tells the stranger that she herself feels that way. When Mrs. Sappleton meets this uninvited guest, she reinforces Vera's report by talking about the open window and her expectation that the three men may return any time. Mr. Nuttel feels sorry for his hostess without realizing that it is he who is being set up for a shocking surprise by the young girl. As the three men appear at the open window, Mr. Nuttel flees, unable to handle the stressful mystery. When the husband asks, "Who was that who bolted out as we came up," the wife tells him what she knows: "A most extraordinary man . . . could only talk about his illnesses, and dashed off without a word of good-bye or apology when you arrived. One would think he had seen a ghost." The word "ghost" here has a double meaning because for Mr. Nuttel what he saw was, indeed, a ghost.

Seizing upon the opportunity to fabricate another story instantly, Vera explains to the confused family that the stranger had "a horror of dogs," and seeing the spaniel with the three men triggered the phobic reaction. She goes on to embellish her tale with more creative lies: Mr. Nuttel was "once hunted into a cemetery somewhere on the banks of the Ganges by a pack of pariah dogs, and had to spend the night in a newly dug grave with the creatures snarling . . . just above him . . . . Enough to make any one lose their nerve."

Humor-making devices that drive this story are irony (the stranger goes to the countryside seeking nerve cure only to have his nerves rudely rattled), elaborate set-up using foreshadowing to create suspense (Vera's masterly invention about the reason for the open window), double meaning words (as in the word "ghost"), and double-meaning settings (the appearance of Mrs. Sappleton's husband and brothers means one thing to her and to Vera but has a totally different meaning for the visiting stranger). It is proof of a well-crafted story that the author has planted credible links to the surprise ending.

Comic Poetry

Of the various forms of poetry, the limerick is one of the easiest to create and is used strictly in humorous verse. It consists of only five lines. Each of the first, second, and fifth lines has three accents; these lines rhyme with one another; lines three and four have two accents and rhyme with each other. "A monkey sprang down from a tree" and "Two brothers devised what a sight" are both limericks by American author Laurence Perrine (1915-1995). They will make you laugh and, hopefully inspire you to write a limerick of your own.

> Two brothers devised what a sight
> Seemed a bicycle crossed with a kite.
> They predicted – rash pair
> It would fly through the air!
> And what do you know? They were Wright

"Two brothers" achieves its comical effect with the help of a pun. The punning word is "Wright." It echoes the missing word "right." The allusion is to the Wright brothers' invention of the airplane. In its rudimentary form, a plane must have looked like "a bicycle crossed with a kite" – a comic description. Even in this most basic form of poetic humor, the poet makes use of the device of verbal irony by calling the Wright Brothers a "rash pair!" In verbal irony, one says the opposite of what is meant. The inventors of the airplane were anything but rash in predicting the success of their experiment at flying.

Perrine's other limerick "A monkey" is also comic but with a serious critique of human nature. Here is the poem in its entirety.

> A monkey sprang down from a tree
> And angrily cursed Charles D.
> "I hold with the Bible
> He cried. "It's a libel
> That man is descended from me!

The monkey is outraged at the Darwinian attempt to suggest a link between monkeys and humans. Dismissing the theory of evolution as a libel, the monkey in this poem favors the Biblical view of creation. This little, humorous poem can trigger a lively, entertaining debate on evolution *versus* creationism. Its implied condemnation of the inherent streak of evil in human nature and the monkeys' freedom from the taint of deliberate violence also invites a response.

Humor and Wit in Today's Serious Literature

Proving that humor and poetry are not mutually exclusive, Kevin Young's poem "Black Cat Blues" from his 2008 volume of poems *Dear Darkness* shows the contrapuntal and thereby meaning-enhancing coexistence of playful wit and serious ideas. The poem's opening lines evoke humor with the help of situational irony:

> I showed up for jury duty –
> Turns out the one on trial was me.

By definition, in this form of irony, what happens is the opposite of what was expected. Ordinarily, when we show up for jury duty, we are expecting to be the jurors, not the accused. Thus humor in this case is caused by the disparity between our expectation and reality.

The poem's conclusion makes its big point with small, witty, barbed words: The accused speaker has his sentence commuted to "life in a cell" that he finds "more comfortable/Than this here skin I been living in."

Whether we call it gallows humor or sardonic wit, the exuberance of language is there to enjoy as much as it is important to ponder the poem's painful, parting words. The impact of the conclusion is enhanced by the fact that the speaker is black, who finds the prison cell more comfortable than the prison of his skin he has been living in. This combination of serious content, starkly simple style, and lively wit make it a striking poem.

An Invitation

There is no shortage of great comic literary works. In this Chapter, we have looked at a few examples, such as "On Being Crazy" and "Courtship through the Ages," (essays); "The Open Window" and "Morning of the Night Before" (stories); and the two limericks (poetry). However, an equally important part of this chapter explores the potential for playful interaction with serious literature:

- parody of Wordsworth's serious Nature-based poetry,
- parody of cliché-filled, inadequate vocabulary to carry the weight of great ideas, demonstrated in my parody of a part of Hamlet's soliloquy, "To be or not to be."
- inventive playfulness in creating a missing scene in a serious work, such as Shakespeare's *Hamlet* or *Measure for Measure*
- writing a letter to an author, asking him/her to change the serious content of the original masterpiece by introducing sensational content to enhance the work's popular appeal.

To make it easier for you to appreciate and create humor, here are some of the humor-making devices that we have discussed in this chapter: comic exaggeration (also called hyperbole), comic stereotyping, deliberate misunderstanding, double-meaning words, irony, paradox, puns, reduction to absurdity, and humorous suspense.

As you try your hand at the exercises that follow, you will discover that even serious literature and everyday life experiences have the potential to create laughter. You have seen examples of almost all the humor-making devices listed above. Use of double-meaning words and creating intentional misunderstanding for humor are frequently used in everyday speech. For example, if you want to describe your intentions to shirk work, you could say it in Henry Bergson's words, "I don't like working between meals." While I have you laughing, I think it is a good time for me to take your leave.

Exercises to Test Your Mastery of Chapter Fifteen

1. Using as a sample my parody of Hamlet's "To be or not to be" attempt your own comic rendition of a speech. The purpose of this exercise is to effectively and humorously demonstrate how great ideas cannot be expressed without adequate vocabulary and style. It is also to show how profound thoughts can become trivialized without appropriate language. Choose a different passage from *Hamlet* or a famous passage from any other classic. Include the original text that you choose for this exercise. The length of your composition will depend on the passage that you parody.

2. Read Sheila Momaney's letter "Like, Cool" for inspiration to create a humorous paragraph ridiculing the trendy use of expressions like "you know," "like," and "cool" to cover up deficient vocabulary. Be sure to include "at the end of the day" – a phrase that has become endemic these days.

3. Using the guidelines provided in this chapter to create a missing scene with comic effects, try your hand at humor-making. Use any literary work, and clearly identify the missing scene that you are trying to create. Since the author left out the scene that you are imagining, we know the contents of this scene only by inference and assumption. The purpose is to make the reader laugh without seriously compromising the integrity of the selected work. Some stretching of credibility is permissible for humorous effects. (Suggested length: 150 to 250 words)

4. Use this chapter's advice on humorous comparative character analysis, given in the context of comparing Gertrude with the widow of Ephesus, to create comic interaction between any two literary characters. (Suggested length: 250 to 500 words).

5. Write a humorous letter of 250 to 500 words to a well-known author, requesting him/her to authorize changes in the story to cater to popular taste. Use the student Erin Kehoe's letter in the chapter as a sample.

6. Using this chapter's sample "I Am Hamlet" under "Writing a Comic Character Sketch," write a similar comic self-analysis of a famous character.

7. W. E. B. Du Bois' essay "On Being Crazy" is a humorous treatment of the serious topic of racism. The essay is included in Chapter Nine and re-introduced in this chapter. It uses dialogue effectively to dramatize racist views. Du Bois also fully exploits the comedy-making devices of verbal irony, deliberate misunderstanding, understatement, and reduction to absurdity through exaggeration. Use these and/or similar stylistic devices to address a serious topic humorously. For help with questions relating to style, turn to Chapter Four.

8. Try your hand at composing a parody of a poem of your choice. Use this chapter's sample parody of William Wordsworth by Reynolds under "Parody of Serious Poetry." William Carlos Williams' poem "This Is Just to Say" has been a favorite of parodists. You can find the poem on the internet (Google.com). Try also to find a parody of the poem.

9. Using the chapter's two limericks by Laurence Perrine for inspiration, compose a limerick of your own. Remember that the form of a limerick restricts the poem's length to five lines and requires a specific rhyme scheme. Read the chapter's advice for further help in writing this easiest and most humorous of poetic forms.

10. Identify, analyze, and evaluate at least two comic devices that the chapter's discussion of Khushwant Singh's short story "The Morning After the Night Before" leaves out.

11. Besides irony, suspense, double meaning words, and a surprise ending, discussed in the chapter's analysis of the author Saki's short story, what other comic device can you identify and analyze in that story?

12. Read a few limericks by Edward Lear and Conrad Aiken in *A Seizure of Limericks.* You can get the book from a library or find a few of their poems online. Write to celebrate their humor-making qualities.

13. Identify and explain some of the outstanding humor-creating devices used by James Thurber in his essay "Courtship Through the Ages" in this chapter.

14. What methods does Thurber use to prevent the reader's mistaking his fanciful and comic fabrications of data for facts?

15. According to Thurber, which of the male species in the animal kingdom has the toughest time? Why?

16. From Thurber's essay, which one of the examples of courtship rituals do you find most comic? Why?

APPENDIX

Information on Research and Citation

Not only for writing papers but also for literary study, use of reference and research material is crucial. Most of you have been relying more and more on the rich offerings in electronic resources. That trend is likely to become stronger as more databases and websites get created to serve our needs. All internet resources continue to undergo changes, and many of them are not reliable. The first responsibility, therefore, that you have is being vigilant about online resources. There are many books like Diana Hacker's *Rules for Writers* that contain detailed information about gathering and documenting research material. You may use the latest editions of books like that for reference whenever you have a question. In this appendix I am going to give you some basic information on this topic.

1. Books

Books are easiest to locate both in libraries and in electronic form. You can access them *via* author, title, or subject. However, much of the information in books is at least a year old because it takes time for a book to go through the printing process. For subjects like literature, it is not much of a problem because the content of books of literary criticism remains valid for a long time. If you are looking for current information, however, you will need to read essays and articles in academic journals, magazines, and newspapers.

2. Periodicals and Indexes

The term "periodicals" refers to publications that appear periodically – daily, weekly, monthly, quarterly, annually, etc. Since there are dozens of journals to choose from, to find a desired article, you will need to consult a periodical index – often available in libraries in both print and electronic formats. Some periodical indexes, such as *Readers' Guide to Periodical Literature*, provide information on articles from popular periodicals. Other indexes are more specialized, such as *Humanities Index* and *Social Sciences Index*. Some indexes only list titles of articles with dates; others also give summaries of articles. Some indexes even offer full texts of the listed articles. Search processes for books and periodicals are the same: by author, title, or subject.

For literature and film, an indispensable resource is *Essay and General Literature Index* (also available in print format). It is a convenient digital guide to some 86,000 essays from nearly 7,000 anthologies and collections and covers the entire range of the social sciences and humanities, including literary works, art history, drama, and film.

A companion is *Essay and General Literature Index Retrospective: 1900-1984*. It is a resource to 8 decades of literature, unlocking information in thousands of collections and anthologies, citing nearly 250,000 essays in works going back to 1900.

3. Audio Visual Resources

Every library has a media center with holdings in audio and video formats, such as audio lectures, video lectures, documentaries, film adaptations of literary works, feature films, etc. A quick glance at the catalogue will give you an idea as to the availability of relevant material. Use of audio-visual resources is necessary to watch film adaptations of plays, since plays are essentially written for viewing. Poetry also comes alive when we hear it recited. Many authors have made videos to accompany their books. Maynard Mack's video lectures on the Elizabethan World and *Hamlet*, mentioned in Chapter Twelve, are one of the many examples. The video on elements of tragedy, produced by Films for the Humanities and Sciences production and also mentioned in Chapter Twelve, greatly facilitates understanding of tragic drama. That video blends well with A. C. Bradley's chapter on "The Substance of Shakespearean Tragedy," included in Chapter Twelve.

In addition to the standard formats of audiovisual material such as CDs, DVDs, VHS tapes, etc., streaming videos over the internet are sometimes available. As an example, most of the documentaries produced by Films for the Humanities and Sciences are now available via streaming for a subscription fee.

4. Internet Resources

Of all means of information and knowledge, the internet is the most used avenue. Search engines and websites are there in abundance. Some sites are free; others allow only fee-based access. The internet is a wonderful, revolutionary means in providing public access to knowledge and information. Their main drawback is that there is no quality control; so you have to be vigilant in evaluating all internet channels that you use. Anyone can operate a website, and all sorts of data – tested and untested, valid and invalid – get posted on the internet.

Evaluating websites and using them judiciously

Just as you can have an idea about a book by looking at its cover, table of contents, and sampling of the author's style, you can judge a website from the quality of its home page, the level of analytic and critical thinking shown in its postings, and its adherence to the principle of balanced presentation. You can usually trust university sites, government sites (national and international) and some nonprofit sites (.edu, .gov, .org). Fortunately, there are agencies that evaluate websites on a regular basis. For the purposes of literary studies, the following are among those considered respectable:

- Gale Literature Resource Center: it has an impressive range and quality of literary criticism. The immensely helpful "Explicator" series on all forms of literary works – the pride of literary criticism in paper format – has been adopted by Gale.
- Gale Literature Resource Center also has Gale Virtual Reference Library, MLA International Bibliography, and LitFinder:
  www.gale.cenage.com/LitSolutions/lit_resources/lrc/-

- The Questia Online Library offers full-text literary criticism – essays, books, journals, and articles. http:// www.questia.com/PM
- JSTOR: an electronic archive of the most important journals in academia, it is the best source of high-quality articles. http://www.jstor.org
- Ethnic Newswatch allows you to choose authors and material by ethnic groups.
- Bartleby offers complete literary works. http://www.bartleby.com
- University of California at Berkeley Library has developed a short but excellent tutorial at http://www.lib.berkeley.edu/TeachingLib/Guides/Internet/Evaluate.html

Project Gutenberg offers texts of literary selections, accompanied by audios and videos. You can download over 30000 free e-books to read on your PC. www.gutenberg.org

Of these sites, only Bartleby and Project Gutenberg are free; the rest allow access with subscription. Most college and public libraries subscribe to these and many more sites. Using the barcode on your library card, you can access these sites from a remote source.

Search Engines and Sites

For high-quality literary criticism, Gale Literature Resource Center and JSTOR (for journal articles) are among the best resources. For general comprehensive research, Yahoo and Google continue to be among the leading search engines. Google, in particular, continues to add new depths and dimensions to its offerings. Google Books (http://www.books.google.com) gives you access to information about books. Some entries come with excerpts from books; some allow you to search the entire book for keywords; some are available in their entirety. Its "Advanced Search" feature enables seekers to refine their searches.

Google Scholar (http://scholar.google.com) indexes academic and professional journal articles. Only a small selection of articles are available in full text for free but you may always take the citation to a librarian who will try to acquire it via another database or through Interlibrary Loan.

Here are a few examples of Google's vast scope. The discussion level is quite basic, but the material presented is easy to read, and it is a good start.

From Google.com, if you type "Glaspell Trifles" in Google search, you will find the following list:

1. Glaspell "Trifles" summary
2. Glaspell "Trifles" analysis
3. "   "   full text
4. "   "   Wikipedia
5. "   "   characters
6. "   "   symbolism
7. "   "   themes
8. Glaspell "Trifles" Study Guide

Similarly, if you type "poem with analysis" in Google search, you will find many poems analyzed as well as advice on poetry analysis. To get access to discussions about novels, type "novels with analysis" in Google search. Here you can study "Novel Analysis Questions" and "How to Analyze a Novel." Typing "Plays with analysis" in Google search will yield similar results.

5. Genre-specific sites

In addition to the Google search feature described above that applies to all literary genres, there are numerous websites relating to various literary forms.

Novels, short stories, plays, and poetry

For help with novels, go to this website: www.novelguide.com/novelanalysis.html

Clicking on the above link will open up a list of novels. You may choose "Novel Analysis" of any of the numerous listed novels. You will get information on the following items:

- Summary
- Character Profiles
- Metaphor Analysis
- Theme Analysis
- Top Ten Quotes
- Biography

Novelguide covers criticism not only of novels but also of plays and short stories. Once again, the information is basic, but it is a good beginning.

Besides Google and Novelguide that cover all literary genres, there are sites specific to each. Some of them are listed below. Most of them are available in both electronic and print formats. Please remember that that these sites start up and shut down often. A simple Google search for "literary resources on the web" can help locate the latest ones.

- Short Story Index: indexes some 4300 stories from more than 200 collections and 50 periodicals each year.
- Play Index (1998-2002): annotated entries on nearly 4100 individual plays. Earlier editions from 1949 through 1997 are also available.
- Drama Criticism Published by Gale. Each volume of this resource covers four to eight significant dramatists or plays. 90-95% of critical essays are full text.
- Poetry Index – Read Online – The Literature Page
  www.literaturepage.com/category/poems.html -
- Famous Poetry/Online www.poetry-online.org
- Verse: Poetry anthologies and thousands of poems. www.bartleby.com/verse/
- Poetry: www.poets.org/poems
- poemhunter.com will give you access to poems and their discussion.
- Princeton Arabic Poetry Project. www.princeton.edu/~arabic/poetry/
- Poetry in the Yahoo Directory: http://dir.yahoo.com/Arts/humanities/literature/Poetry/
- Online companion to the *Anthology of Modern American* Poetry, with features on poets, including criticism, bibliographies, and commentary.
  dir.yahoo.com/Arts/humanities/literature/Poetry/
- The Columbia Granger's World of Poetry *<www.columbiagrangers.org/ ->*
- Literary Reference Center for poetry
- Fiction/*Novel Index - www.readbookonline.net/fictionNovel/ -*
- http://www.amazon.com/Literary-Criticism-on-the-Novel/lm/383IKT2Q5BXN2

- Literary Criticism: Novels Research Guide – UCF Libraries... Book and periodical sources of *criticism* for single authors, as well as general studies (*criticism* of the American *novel* by period), *library.ucf.edu/reference/Guides/NovelCriticism.asp* –

Sites and sources relevant to literature in general

- Book Review www.NPR.org>
- *Book Review Digest* with excerpts from more than 8000 books and reviews annually, covering 109 publications
- Book Review Site www.booklistonline.com
- Book Index with reviews
- *Biography Index*
- *Bibliographic Index*
- Magill on Literature Plus

6. Still extremely valuable conventional sources in paper format

A visit to the reference section of any college or public library would reveal the wealth of its resources. Just a few of them are listed below.

1. *Oxford English Dictionary*
2. *Literature Criticism* (published by Gale)
3. *Nineteenth-Century Literature Criticism*
4. *Twentieth-Century Literature Criticism*
5. *Short Story Criticism*
6. *Shakespearean Criticism*
7. *World Literature Criticism*
8. *Dictionary of Literary Biography*
9. *Twentieth-Century American Literature Series*
10. *Critical Survey of Short Fiction* (Magill)
11. *The Concise Oxford Dictionary of Literary Terms,* ed. Chris Baldich
12. *A Dictionary of Literary Terms,* ed. J. A. Cuddon
13. *The Reader's Companion to World Literature*
14. *Brewer's Dictionary of Phrase and Fable*
15. *Biographical Dictionary and Synopsis of Books by C. D. Warner*
16. *Miriam Webster's Dictionary of Allusions*
17. *The Facts on File Dictionary of Cultural and Historical Allusions*

Literary Encyclopedia Series

- *The Concise Encylopedia of Modern World Literature,* ed. Geoffrey Grigson
- *Casssell's Encyclopaedia of World Literature*
- *Benet's Reader's Encylopedia*
- *Encyclopedia of the Novel,* ed. Paul Schellinger
- *Cyclopedia of Literary Characters* (Magill Series)

MLA International Bibliography

It provides a listing and subject index for books and articles on modern languages, literature, folklore, and linguistics. It annually indexes over 66,000 books and articles.

Documentation and Citations

Advice on correct forms of documentation and citation, including electronic sources, can be found on Google. If you type MLA in Google search, you will have instant access to MLA citation format, works cited format, and related items. Another website EasyBib provides access to all three major styles – MLA, APA, and Chicago citation style. www.easybib.com. Sometimes you will find conflicting information on websites. In such cases, only trust university websites or MLA's own website. Whenever in doubt, consult the latest edition in book form at a library.

7. Perils of Plagiarism

Use of someone else's words (more than three at a stretch) without acknowledging the source constitutes plagiarism. Some articles that you read on the internet may have already used someone else's ideas without acknowledgement. If you quote from such sources, the integrity of your ideas may be compromised. Since anyone can contribute to a site such as Wikipedia, the quality of its articles is uneven, and the information given is sometimes is inaccurate. Use it as a starting point to gather general information about a subject, literary work, or author. Don't use it as a research reference in your essays. Be on guard against succumbing to the temptation of websites, such as cheat.com that offer already written papers on almost any topic. Your professors are very well aware of those sites. The need for caution against direct or indirect plagiarism can never be overemphasized.

WORKS CITED

For information on the literary works included in this book, see the acknowledgement pages at the end of the book.

Adler, Mortimer. "How to Mark a Book." *From Reading, Writing.* Eds. Jo Ray McCuen and Anthony Winkler. New York: Harcourt, 1988.

Alexie, Sherman. "The Only Traffic Signal on the Reservation Doesn't Flash Red Anymore." *The Lone Ranger and Tonto Fistfight in Heaven.* New York: Atlantic Monthly Press, 1993.

Aligarh Muslim University Alumni Association Sir Syed Day 2011 International Mushaira. Indian Community Center, Milpitas, California. October 15, 2011.

al-Faraj, Ghalib Hamzah Abu. "Violets." *Assassination of Light: Modern Saudi Short Stories.* Collected and tr. Ava Molnar Heinrichsdorff and Abu Bakr Bagader. Boulder, CO: Three Continents Press, 1990.

al-Quddus, Abd. "A Fairy Tale." *Arabic and Middle Eastern Literatures, Vol. 1, No. 2.* Cambridge, MA: Carfax Publishing Ltd., July 1998.

An-Nasir, Ibrahim. "Homecoming." *Assassination of Light: Modern Saudi Short Stories.* Collected and tr. Ava Molnar Heinrichsdorff and Abu Bakr Bagader. Boulder, CO: Three Continents Press, 1990.

A Reader's Companion to the Short Story in English. Eds. Erin Fallon, R.C. Feddersen, et al. Westport, CT: Greenwood Press, 2001.

Aristotle. *The Poetics*, Ch. X. Cited in Clifford Leach. *Tragedy.* London: Methuen, 1969.

Asad, Muhammad, *The Message of THE QURAN.* Gibraltar: Dar al-Andalus Ltd., 1980.

Asrar, Nausha. Aligarh Muslim University Mushaira, October 15, 2011

Austen, Jane. *Pride and Prejudice.* New York: Penguin, 1972.

Barnet, Sylvan, Morton Berman, and William Burto, eds. *Aspects of the Drama.* Boston: Little, Brown, and Co., 1962.

Beardsley, Monroe. "Style and Good Style." *Contemporary Essays on Style.* Eds. Glen A. Love and Michael Payne. Glenview, Illinois: Scott, Foresman and Co., 1969.

Bennet, James. *Prose Style.* San Francisco: Chandler Publishing Co., 1971.

Bergson, Henri. *Laughter.* Cited in *Comedy: Plays, Theory, and Criticism.* Ed. Marvin Felheim. New York: Harcourt, 1962.

Berkoff, Steven. *I Am Hamlet.* New York: Grove Weidenfeld, 1989.

Bewley, Marius. "Scott Fitzgerald's Criticism of America." *F. Scott Fitzgerald: A Collection of Critical Essays.* Mizener, Arthur, ed. New Jersey: Prentice Hall Inc., 1963.

Borges, Jorge Luis. "Tlon, Uqbar, Orbis Tertius." *Ficciones.* Trans. Alastair Reid. New York: Alfred Knopf, 1962.

Blake, William. "London." *Blake.* New York: Dell, 1960.

Bradley, A. C. *Shakespearean Tragedy.* New York: Fawcett Publications, 1965.

Braudy, Leo. *The World in a Frame: What We See in Films.* Garden City, New York: Anchor Press/Doubleday, 1977.

Bree, Germaine. *Camus.* New Jersey: Rutgers University Press, 1964.

Brown, G. E. *George Bernard Shaw.* New York: Arco Publishing Co., 1971.

Bruccoli, Matthew, ed. *The Great Gatsby* by F. Scott Fitzgerald. New York: Scribner's, 1992.

Bulosan, Carlos. *America Is in the Heart.* Seattle: University of Washington Press, 1996.

Burke, Edmund. "The Impeachment of Warren Hastings."
www.ourcivilisation.com/smartboard/shop/burkee/extracts/chap12.htm

Butcher, S. H. *Aristotle's Theory of Poetry and Fine Art.* New York: Dover Publications, 1951.

Callahan, John F. *The Illusions of a Nation: Myth and History in the Novels of F.Scott Fitzgerald.* Urbana, Illinois: University of Illinois Press, 1972.

Camus, Albert. "The Guest." *Exile and the Kingdom.* Trans. Justin O'Brien. New York: Vintage, 1957.

Camus, Albert. *Lyrical and Critical Essays.* New York: Alfred Knopf, 1968

Capote, Truman. Cited in Donald Hall, ed. *The Modern Stylists.* New York: The Free Press, 1968.

Caputi, Anthony. Ed. *Modern Drama.* New York: Norton, 1966

Churchill, Caryl. *Seven Jewish Children—A Play for Gaza*
http://www.guardian.co.uk/stage/2009/feb/26/caryl-churchill-seven-jewish-children-play-gaza

Clarke, John Henrik."The Boy Who Painted Christ Black: A Short Story." *Opportunity: A Journal of Negro Life, Vol. 18, No. 9,* September, 1940.

Clinton, Bill. *San Francisco Chronicle.* June 7, 1994.

Cofer, Judith Ortiz. "Exile." *Crossing into America: The New Literature of Immigration.* Eds. Louis Mendoza and S. Shankar. New York: The New Press, 2003.

Cruickshank, John. *Albert Camus and the Literature of Revolt.* London: Oxford University Press, 1960.

Day-Lewis, C. *Poetry for You: A Book for Boys and Girls on the Enjoyment of Poetry.* New York: Oxford Univ. Press, 1947.

Dick, Bernard. *Anatomy of Film.* New York: St. Martin's Press, 1978.

Dillard, Annie. "Solar Eclipse." *Reading Critically, Writing Well.* Eds. Rise Axelrod, Charles Cooper, and Allison Warriner. New York: Bedford/St. Martin's, 2001.

Doctorow, E. L. "Review," *San Francisco Chronicle.* September 21, 1980

Dunn, Douglas. "Modern Love." *Selected Poems 1964-1983.* Faber and Faber.

Duvall, John N., ed. *The Cambridge Companion to American Fiction After 1945.* Cambridge, UK: Cambridge University Press, 2012.

Dyson, A.E. "The Great Gatsby: Thirty-Six Years After." *F. Scott Fitzgerald: A Collection of Critical Essays.* Mizener, Arthur, ed. New Jersey: Prentice Hall Inc., 1963.

Eastman, Richard M. *A Guide to the Novel.* Scranton, PA: Chandler Publishing Co., 1965.

Eastman, Richard. *Style.* Third Edition. New York: Oxford University Press, 1984.

Eggers, Dave. *What's the What.* New York: Vintage, 2007.

Elbow, Peter. "Comment and Rebuttal." *College Composition and Communication* 30 (April 1969): 594.

Eliot, T. S. Ed. *Literary Essays of Ezra Pound.* New York: New Directions, 1954.

Faiz. The Lenin Peace Prize acceptance speech:
http://www.dawn.com/2011/02/17/faiz-ahmed-faiz-life-and-poetry.html

Faiz. "Sinkiang." Translated by Abdul Jabbar, the author of this book.

Fallon, Erin, R.C. Feddersen et al. *A Reader's Companion to the Short Story in English.* Westport, CT: Greenwood Press, 2001.

Faulkner, William. "A Rose for Emily." *Collected Stories of William Faulkner.* New York: Random, 1958.

Felheim, Marvin. Ed. *Comedy: Plays, Theory, and Criticism.* New York: Harcourt, 1962.

Fitzgerald, Edward. Trans. *Rubaiyat of Omar Khayyam.* New York: Doubleday, n.d..

Fitzgerald, F. Scott. *The Great Gatsby.* New York: Modern Library, 1934.

Fitzgerald, F. Scott. *The Great Gatsby.* New York: Simon and Schuster, 1995.

Flemming, Leslie A. *Another Lonely Voice: The Urdu Short Stories of Saadat Manto.* Berkeley: South Asian Studies, University of California, 1979) 69-70.

Forster, E. M. *A Passage to India.* New York: Harcourt, Brace and World, 1924.

Forster, E. M. *Aspects of the Novel.* New York: Harcourt, Brace and World, 1954.

Frye, Northrop. *Anatomy of Criticism.* Princeton, New Jersey: Princeton University Press, 1973.

Frye, Northrop. "Comic Myth in Shakespeare." *Discussions of Shakespeare's Romantic Comedy.* Ed. Herbert Weil, Jr. Boston: Heath, 1966.

Gaines, Ernest. "The Sky Is Gray." *Bloodline.* New York: Vintage, 1997.

Gallagher, Tess. *A Concert of Tenses: Essays on Poetry.* Ann Arbor: Univ. of Michigan Press, 1986.

Gefvert, Constance J. *The Confident Writer.* New York: Norton, 1985.

Giannetti, Louis. *Understanding Movies.* Englewood Cliffs, New Jersey: Prentice-Hall, 1982.

Gibran, Kahlil. *The Prophet.* New York: Alfred Knopf, 1966.

Gittings, Robert. *John Keats.* London: Heinemann, 1968.

Graff, Gerald. *Professing Literature*: *An Institutional History.* Chicago: The Univ. of Chicago Press, 1987.

The Great Hamlets, Programs 1 and 2. Two videos. Films for the Humanities and Sciences.

Greenberg, Joanne. "Hunting Season." *Readings for Writers.* Eds. J. R. McCuen and Anthony Winkler. New York: Harcourt Brace Jovanovich, 1988.

Greenblatt, Stephen. *Will in the World: How Shakespeare Became Shakespeare.* New York: Norton, 2004.

Gritten, David. Review of the movie "Bright Star." http://www.telegraph.co.uk/culture/film/cannes-film-festival/5329970/Cannes.2009-film-charts-John-Keats-romance-with-FannyBrawnein.Luton.html

Guerard, Albert J. "Introduction to the Issue 'Perspectives on the novel'," *Daedalus*, 92 (Spring 1963), 201-202

Hall, Donald. *The Modern Stylists.* New York: The Free Press, 1968.

Hall, Donald. *Writing Well.* Boston: Little, Brown & Co. 1973.

Hamilton, Edith. *The Greek Way to Western Civilization.* New York: Norton, 1983

Hampton, Christopher. *Les Liaisons Dangereuses*, a play by Christopher Hampton, from the novel by Cholerlos de Laelos. Boston: Faber and Faber, 1985

Hansberry, Lorraine. *A Raisin in the Sun.* New York: New American Library, 1988. (All quotations are taken from this publication.)

Hardy, Thomas. *The Return of the Native.* Boston: Houghton Mifflin Co., 1967.

Harrington, John. *Film and/as Literature.* Englewood Cliffs, New Jersey: Prentice-Hall, 1977.

Hawkins, Robert. *Preface to Poetry.* New York: Basic Books, 1965.

Hemingway, Ernest. *Death in the Afternoon.* New York: Scribner's, 1932.

Hemingway, Ernest. "A Clean, Well-Lighted Place." *Winner Take Nothing.* New York: Charles Scribner's Sons, 1961

Henkle, Roger. *Reading the Novel: An Introduction to the Techniques of Interpreting Fiction.* New York: Harper and Row, 1977.

Highet, Gilbert. "Diogenes and Alexander." *From Reading, Writing.* Eds. Anthony Winkler and Jo Ray McCuen. New York: Harcourt Brace Jovanovich, 1988.

Hilton, Timothy. *Keats and His World.* New York: Viking Press, 1971.

Hinchliffe, Arnold P. *Harold Pinter.* New York: Twayne Publishers, Inc., 1967

Hinden, Michael. *Long Day's Journey Into Night: Native Eloquence.* Boston: Twayne Publishers, 1990.

Hurwitt, Robert. "Solis' 'Gibraltar' Drills the Depths of Love and Loss." *San Francisco Chronicle* 11 July 2005: C-1, 2.

Hurwitt, Robert. "Playwright Defined a Nation's Conscience." *San Francisco Chronicle* 12 Feb. 2005: A-12

Ionesco, Eugene. "The Chairs." *New York Times* 1 June 1958.

Ionesco, Eugene. *Notes and Counter Notes: Writings on the Theater.* Trans. from French by Donald Watson. New York: Grove Press, 1964.

Iqbal, Muhammad. Zarbe Kaleem. Lahore, Pakistan: Shaikh Ghulam Ali and Sons, 1977

Ispahani, Mahnaz. "Saadat Hasan Manto," *Grand Street,* Vol. 7, No. 4 (Summer, 1988).

http://www.jstor.org/stable/25007150.

Jackson, Esther. *The Broken World of Tennessee Williams*. Madison: The University of Wisconsin Press, 1966.

Jaffe, Rona. "Rima the Bird Girl." *Images of Women in Literature*. Ed. Mary Anne Ferguson. Boston: Houghton Mifflin Co., 1977.

Jinnah, Muhammad Ali. "What the Quaid-e-Azam Said," Pakistan Times USA, Nov. 10, 2011.

Johnson, Samuel. "Biography.*" Rambler No. 60.*

Joseph, Bertram. *Conscience and the King: A Study of Hamlet*. London: Chatto and Windus, 1953.

Journal of South Asian Literature (special volume on Manto), Vol. XX, Summer, Fall, 1985, No. 2

Journal of Thought. College of Education. Texas Tech University. 15:2

Joyce, James. "Araby." *Dubliners.* New York: Viking, 1947.

Keats, John. "Bright Star," *Complete Poems and Selected Letters*, ed. Clarence Thorpe (New York: The Odyssey Press, 1935)

Kennison, Katrina and Lorrie Moore, eds. *The Best American Short Stories 2004.* (The Best American Series). Boston: Houghton Mifflin Harcourt, Oct 14, 2004.

Kirby, David. "If Poetry Seems Remote, Move Closer." *San Francisco Sunday Examiner* and Chronicle 14 May 2000.

Knight, G. Wilson. *The Wheel of Fire*. Oxford, UK: Routledge, 2001.

Kochakian, Mary Jo. "The Love Burnout Dilemma." *San Francisco Chronicle* 3 October 1988.

Kronenberger, Louis "Some Prefatory Words on Comedy," *The Thread of Laughter*. New York: Knopf, 1952.

Krutch, Joseph Wood, "The Tragic Fallacy." *The Modern Temper: A Study and a Confession*. Harcourt, Brace and Co., 1929.

Lahr, John. Ed. *Grove Press Modern Drama*. New York: Grove Press, 1975.

Lanham, Richard A. *Style, An Anti-textbook*. New Haven: Yale University Press, 1974.

Langer, Susanne. "The Great Dramatic Forms: The Complete Rhythm.*" Comedy: Plays, Theory, and Criticism*. Ed. Marvin Felheim. New York: Harcourt, 1962.

La Salle, Mick. "In Misfits Arthur Miller reveals his life with Marilyn." *San Francisco Chronicle,* 18 February 2005.

Lawrence, D. H. *Women in Love.* New York: Penguin Books, 1980.

Lazard, Naomi. *The True Subject: Selected Poems of Faiz Ahmed Faiz*. Translated by Naomi Lazard. Bilingual Edition. Princeton University Press, 1988.

Leach, Clifford. *Tragedy*. London: Methuen and Co., 1969.

Leonard, David and Peter McGuire. *Readings in Technical Writing.* New York: Macmillan, 1983.

Long Day's Journey Into Night (Modern Critical Interpretations series). Ed. Harold Bloom. New York: Chelsea House, 1987.

Love, Glen A. and Michael Payne. *Contemporary Essays on Style*. Glenview, Illinois: Scott, Foresman, and Co., 1969.

Lucas, F. L. *Tragedy*. New York Collier Books, 1965.

Lucas, F. L. "What is Style." From *Reading, Writing*. Eds. Anthony Winkler and Jo Ray McCuen. New York: Harcourt Brace Jovanovich, 1988.

Mahfouz, Naguib. "Child's Paradise." *God's World.* Tr. Akeb Abadir & Roger Allen. Minneapolis, MN: Bibliotheca Islamica, Inc., 1988.

Mannes, Marya. *But Will It Sell?* Philadelphia, PA: Lippincott, 1964.

Manto, Saadat Hasan. "Bu" ("Odor"), tr. Hamid Jalal. *A Treasury of Modern Asian Stories*. Eds. Daniel Milton and William Clifford. New York: New American Library, 1961.

Manto, Saadat Hasan. "Odor," *The Best of Manto*. Ed. and tr. from Urdu by Jai Ratan. Lahore, Pakistan: Vanguard, 1990.

Manto, Saadat Hasan. *Bitter Fruit*: *The Very Best of Saadat Hasan Manto*. Ed. and trans. by Khalid Hasan. New York: Penguin Books, 2008.

Marill, Rene. *The Revolt of Today's Authors*. Paris: Correa, 1949.

Marquez, Gabriel Garcia. "One of These Days." *Gabriel Garcia Marquez, Collected Stories*. NY: Harper Collins, 1984.

Mast, Gerald. *A Short History of the Movies*. Third edition. Indianapolis: Bobbs-Merrill Educational Publishing, 1981.

May, Charles E. "It's the language, not the subject, of fiction that matters." *San Francisco Chronicle* 8 September, 2006.

Mayes, Frances. *The Discovery of Poetry*. New York: Harcourt Brace Jovanovich, 1987.

McCullers, Carson. "The Sojourner," *The Ballad of the Sad Café*. Boston: Houghton, 1955.

Miller, Arthur. "Tragedy and the Common Man." *Death of a Salesman, Text and Criticism*. Ed. Gerard Weale. New York: Viking, 1967.

Morford, Mark. "Notes and Errata." *San Francisco Chronicle* 14 October 2005.

Muller, Gilbert H. *The McGraw-Hill Reader*. New York: McGraw Hill, 1991.

Munro, H. H. (Saki). "The Open Window." *The Short Stories of Saki*. New York: Viking, 1930.

Natwar-Singh, K. Ed. *E. M. Forster: A Tribute*. New Delhi, India: Rupa and Co., 2002.

Nagarajan, S. Ed. *Shakespeare's Measure for Measure*. New York: New American Library, 1964.

Neruda, Pablo. *The Poetry of Pablo Neruda*. Ed. Ilan Stavans. New York: Farrar, Straus and Giroux, 2003.

Nicoll, Allardyce. *The Theory of Drama*. New York: Benjamin Blom 1966.

O. Henry (William Sidney Porter). "Gifts of the Magi." *Collected Stories of O. Henry*. Ed. P. Horowitz. NY: Crown Publishers, Avenel Books, 1979.

Oates, Joyce Carol. "Introduction." *The Essential Dickinson*. 21 November 1998. http://www.storm.usfca.edu/~southerr/essdickinson.html # introduction.

O'Donnell, Norbert F. "The Conflict of Wills in Shaw's Tragicomedy." *Modern Drama*. 4. Feb. 1962.

O'Neill, Eugene. "Desire Under the Elms." *The New York Tribune* 13 February1921. Also cited in *Modern Drama*. Ed. Anthony Caputi. New York: Norton 1966: 447-449.

O'Neill, Eugene. *Long Day's Journey Into Night. New Haven: Yale University Press, 1989.*

Ortega, Julio. "Las Papas." *Global Cultures: A Transnational Short Fiction Reader*. Ed. Young-Bruehl, trans. Regina Harrison. Middletown, CT: Wesleyan University Press, 1994.

Pedersen, Lise. "Shakespeare's *Taming of the Shrew* vs. Shaw's *Pygmalion*: Male Chauvinism vs. Women's Lib?"

Perrine, Laurence and Thomas Arp. *Sound and Sense: An Introduction to Poetry*. New York: Harcourt Brace Jovanovich, 1992.

Plath, Sylvia. "Mirror."*The Collected Poems of Sylvia Plath*. New York: HarperCollins, 1960.

Pritchett, V.S. Cited in *San Francisco Chronicle*. 20 April 20 1989.

Prose, Francine. *Reading Like A Writer: A Guide for People Who Love Books And For Those Who Want to Write Them*. New York: Harper Collins, 2006.

Qabbani, Nizar, "Say I Love You." *On Entering the Sea: The Erotic and Other Poetry of Nizar Qabbani."* Tr. Lena Jayyusi & Sharif Elmusa. NY: Interlink Books, 1996, p. 126.

Read, Herbert. *English Prose Style*. Boston: Beacon Press/Pantheon Books, 1963.

Rifaat, Alifa. "Bahiyya's Eyes" *Distant View of a Minaret and Other Stories*. London: Heinemann, 1987.

Roa Bastos, Augusto. "The Vacant Lot." *Contemporary Latin American Short Stories*. Ed. Pat McNees. NY: Ballantine Books, 1996.

Russell, Bertrand. "A Free Man's Worship," *Mysticism and Logic*. Cited in Richard M. Weaver. *A Rhetoric and Handbook*. New York: Holt, Rinehart and Winston, 1967.

Russell, Ralph. *The Pursuit of Urdu Literature*. London and New Jersey: Zed Books Ltd. 1992.

Sakda, Paradon. "Black Night at Miawaddy." *Short Story International: Tales of the World's Great Contemporary Writers* (unabridged).

San Francisco Chronicle Book Review. "Best Books of 2004." Review of William Trevor's collection of stories *A Bit on the Side*. New York: Viking, 2004.

Scharbach, J. Alexander and Carl Markgraf. "Voice as Self-Discovery." *Making the Point.* New York: Crowell, 1975.

Schlegel, Augustus W. *A Course of Lectures on Dramatic Art and Literature.* London: Henry G. Bohn, 1846.

Scholes, Robert, Nancy Comley et al. *Elements of Literature.* New York: Oxford University Press, 1982.

Seaman, Barbara. "The Scoop on Sleep." *Modern Maturity*. July-August, 1996: 67.

Sethi, Ali. "The Seer of Pakistan: The Stories of Saadat Hasan Manto," *The New Yorker*, August 30, 2012.

Sewall, Richard. *The Vision of Tragedy.* New Haven: Yale University Press, 1959.

Shad, Khushbir Singh. Aligarh Muslim University Mushaira, October 15, 2011

Shakespeare,William. *The Tragedy of Hamlet.* Ed. Edward Hubler. New York: Penguin Books/Signet, 1987. All quotations from Hamlet are taken from this edition.

Shakespeare, William. *King Lear.* All quotations from King Lear are taken from the Oxford University Press edn., 1959.

Shakespeare, William. *Macbeth.* All quotations from Macbeth are taken from Shakespeare: *Complete Plays and Poems.* Houghton Mifflin Co., 1942.

Shaughnessy, Mina. *Errors and Expectations.* New York: Oxford University Press, 1977.

Shaw, George Bernard. *Complete Plays with Prefaces.* New York: Dodd, Mead, and Co., 1962.

Shaw, George Bernard. "Epistle Dedicatory." *Man and Superman.* London: Longmans, Green and Co., 1968.

Shaw, George Bernard. *Pygmalion: A Romance in Five Acts.* Ed. Dan H. Laurence. New York: Penguin, 1987.

Shelley, Mary. *Frankenstein.* England: Penguin Books, 1818.

Singh, Kushwant. "The Rape" in *Tales from Modern India.* Ed. K. Natwar-Singh. NY: MacMillan, 1966.

Skagg, Calvin. Ed. *The American Short Story*, Vol. 2. New York: Dell, 1980

Skloot, Floyd. "A Glimpse into the genius behind the written word." *San Francisco Chronicle* 15 September 2000.

Smith, Zadie. "Love Actually." *The Guardian*, 1 November 2003.
    http://www.guardian.co.uk/books/2003/nov/01/classics.zadiesmith

Sobchack, Thomas and Vivian. *An Introduction to Film.* Boston: Little, Brown and Co., 1980.

Sophocles, *Oedipus the King.* In *Sophocles, with an English Translation. Vol. 1.* Tr. F. Storr. London: William Heinemann, 1912. (The Loeb Classical Library).

Stein, Ruthe. "Tops at Toronto." "Datebook." *San Francisco Chronicle*. 21 September 2008.

Stone, Wilfred. *The Cave and the Mountain: A Study of E.M. Forster.* Palo Alto: Stanford University Press, 1966.

Styan, J.L. *The Dark Comedy.* Cambridge: Cambridge University Press, 1962.

Tan, Amy. *The Joy Luck Club.* New York: Random, 1989.

Tanner, Tony. Ed. *Pride and Prejudice* by Jane Austen. New York: Penguin,1985.

Terkel, Studs. "Make New Sounds: Studs Terkel Interviews Lorraine Hansberry." *American Theatre.* November 1984.

Toomer, Jean "Fern." *Cane.* New York: Liveright, 1975.

Trimbe, John R. *Writing with Style: Conversations on the Art of Writing.* Englewood Cliffs, New Jersey: Prentice-Hall, 1975.

Tulip in the Desert, selected poems of Muhammad Iqbal. Ed. and trans. Mustansir Mir. Kingston, Canada: McGill-Queen's University Press, 2008.

Updike, John "Pygmalion." *Sudden Fiction* : American Short Stories. Eds. Robert Shapard and James Thomas. Layton, Utah: Gibbs M. Smith, Inc., 1986.

Warren, Austin. "Novels of E.M. Forster." *American Review*. May 1937: 247-248.

Weil, Herbert Jr. Ed. *Discussions of Shakespeare's Romantic Comedy*. Boston: D.C. Heath, 1966.

Weintraub, Rodelle. Ed. *Fabian Feminist: Bernard Shaw and Women*. University Park: Pennsylvania State University Press, 1977.

Wellek, Rene. *Style in Language*. Ed. Thomas A. Sebeok. Cambridge, Mass. : M.I.T. Press, 1971.

Wilder, Thornton. "Some Thoughts on Playwriting." Cited in *Aspects of the Drama*. Eds. Sylvan Barnet, Morton Berman, and William Burto. Boston: Little, Brown, and Co., 1962.

Williams, Joseph M. *Ten Lessons in Clarity and Grace*. Glenview, Illinois: Scott, Foresman, and Co., 1989.

Williams, Tennessee. *Sweet Bird of Youth*. New York: New Directions, 2008.

Wilson, John Dover. *What Happens in Hamlet*. 3rd edition. Cambridge, UK: Cambridge University Press, 1951.

Winkler, Anthony C. and Jo Ray McCuen. Eds. *From Reading, Writing*. New York: Harcourt Brace Jovanovich, 1988.

Wood, James. *How Fiction Works*. New York: Farrar, Straus and Giroux, 2008.

Wolpert, Stanley. *India*. Berkeley, CA: University of California Press, 2005.

Woolf, Virginia. *The Common Reader*. New York: Harcourt, Brace and Company, 1948.

INDEX

Note: Page numbers that start with capital E or A-refer to articles from *San Francisco Chronicle*. They are included in the chapters as parenthetical citation. For some of the dates, you may need to look up *San Francisco Chronicle* archives. The word (website) after an entry means that you can find the item on my website <www.professorjabbar.com>

"Homecoming" by Dilman Dila from , © 2008 Dilman Dila.

"Violets" by Ghalib Hamzah Abu al-Faraj from Assassination of Light: Modern Saudi Short Stories, by Ava M. Heinrichsdorff & Abubaker Bagader, eds., © 1990 Three Continents Press.

"Courtship Through The Ages" by James Thurber from My World and Welcome to It, © 1970 Rosemary A. Thurber C/O Barbara Hogenson Agency.

"On Being Crazy" by W.E.B. DuBois from .

"The Myth of Sisyphus" from The Myth of Sisyphus: And Other Essays, by Albert Camus, © 1991 Vintage Books, a division of Random House, Inc..

"August 8, 1945" by Albert Camus from Between Hell and Reason: Essays from the Resistance Newspaper Combat, 1944-1947, by Translated by Alexandre de Gramont; Contributed by Elisabeth Young-Bruehl, © 1991 Wesleyan University Press.

"Black Cat Blues" by Kevin Young from Dear Darkness, © 2008 Random House, Inc..

"The Second Coming" by William Butler Yeats from Collected Poems (Collector's Library).

"To Toussaint L'Ouverture" by William Wordsworth from William Wordsworth - The Major Works: including The Prelude (Oxford World's Classics), by Stephen Gill, ed., © 2008 Oxford University Press.

"The Lotus Eaters" by Lord Alfred Tennyson from .

"Tithonus" by Lord Alfred Tennyson from .

"Ulysses" by Lord Alfred Tennyson from .

"Stream of Life" by Rabindranath Tagore from , © .

"Not Waving but Drowning" from Collected Poems of Stevie Smith, by Stevie Smith, © 1972 New Directions Publishing Corporation.

"One Word is Too Often Profaned" from The Complete Poems of Percy Bysshe Shelley (Modern Library), by Percy Bysshe Shelley.

(cont'd)

"A Fairy Tale" by Ihsan Abd al-Quddus from Arabic and Middle Eastern Literatures, © 1998 Carfax Publishing Company.

"Selection" from America is in the Heart: A Personal History, by Carlos Bulosan.

"Walden Pond As Best-Seller" from The San Francisco Chronicle, by Angus Stocking, © 1990 San Francisco Chronicle.

"Going from Bard to Worse" from The San Francisco Chronicle, by Prince Charles, © 1989 San Francisco Chronicle.

Excerpt from Reading and Writing with Multicultural Literature, by Abdul Jabbar, © Abdul Jabbar.

"Mirror" from The Collected Poems of Sylvia Plath, by Sylvia Plath, © 1960 HarperCollins Publishers.

"The Man From Kabul" from The Housewarming and Other Stories, by Rabindranath Tagore.

"Vergissmeinnicht" from The Complete Poems: Third Edition, by Keith Douglas, © 2000 Farrar, Straus & Giroux, Inc.

"Entire text" from The Other Side of the Hedge, by E.M. Forster.

"Pygmalion" from The Atlantic Monthly, by John Updike, © 1981 Atlantic Monthly Co..

"Naming of Parts" from New Statesman and Nation, by Henry Reed, © 1942 New Statesman Ltd..

"Meeting at Night" from The Oxford Book of English Verse, by Robert Browning.

"God's Grandeur" from Gerard Manley Hopkins: The Major Works, by Gerard M. Hopkins, © 1986 Oxford University Press.

"To Autumn" from The Poetical Works of John Keats, by John Keats.

"Discovery of the New World" from Ponca War Dances, by Carter Revard, © 1980 Cottonwood Arts Foundation
Point Riders Press.

"Those Winter Sundays" by Robert Hayden from Collected Poems of Robert Hayden, © 1966 W. W. Norton & Co., Inc..

"Dover Beach" by Matthew Arnold from New Poems.

"Khayyam, If You are Drunk (Quatrain)" from Rubaiyat of Omar Khayyam, by Omar Khayyam.

"The Substance of Shakespearean Tragedy" from Shakespearean Tragedy, by A.C. Bradley.

"Act III, Scene ii, Lines 1-38" from Hamlet, by William Shakespeare.

"Solis' "Gibraltar" Drills the Depths of Love and Loss" from The San Francisco Chronicle, by Robert Hurwitt, © 2005 San Francisco Chronicle.

"Ode to a Nightingale" from The Poetical Works of John Keats, by John Keats.

"The Love Song of J. Alfred Prufrock" from Prufrock and Other Observations, by T.S. Eliot.

"The Greedy The People" from Complete Poems, 1904-1962, by E.E. Cummings, © 1994 Liveright Publishing Corporation.

"Bright Star" from The Poetical Works of John Keats, by John Keats.

"London" from Favorite Works of William Blake, by William Blake.

"Insect Collection" from We, the Dangerous: New Selected Poems, by Janice Mirikitani, © 1995 Celestial Arts Publishing.

"Ars Poetica" from Collected Poems 1917 to 1982, by Archibald MacLeish, © 1985 Houghton Mifflin Harcourt Publishing Company.

"Ars Poetica" from Carnival Evening: New and Selected Poems 1968-1998, by Linda Pastan, © 1999 W. W. Norton & Co., Inc..

"Intimates" from Complete Poems, by D.H. Lawrence, © 1994 Penguin Putnam, Inc..

"To a Mistress Dying" from The Oxford Book of English Verse: 1250–1900, by Sir William Davenant.

"What I Heard at a Discount Department Store" from Judevine, by David Budbill, © 1999 Chelsea Green Publishing.

"The Fish" from Complete Poems of Elizabeth Bishop, by Elizabeth Bishop, © 1969 Farrar, Straus & Giroux, Inc..

"Excerpt" from The Wild Swans at Coole, by William Butler Yeats.

CPSIA information can be obtained
at www.ICGtesting.com
Printed in the USA
FSHW021612200119
55128FS